FACULTY REQUEST

SCC
70.00

Collin College Library
SPRING CREEK CAMPUS
Plano, Texas 75074

OECD Factbook 2010

ECONOMIC, ENVIRONMENTAL AND SOCIAL STATISTICS

WITHDRAWN

D1364889

OECD

FOREWORD

The world economy is slowly emerging from the most serious crisis of our lifetime. It is also, arguably, the first truly "global" crisis. A crisis, that has affected to different degrees all countries and regions in the world. It has reminded us of how interconnected our economies and societies have become, and of how quickly disequilibria in one country can spread to others. Strategic policy making in such a dynamic, globalised and interconnected world requires appropriate tools for decision makers to analyse, respond and manage regional, national and global challenges.

In this context, comparative statistics can offer an indispensible support for policy analysis, agenda setting and policy action. Cross-country comparisons and best policy practices on a sound empirical basis are among the critical comparative advantages of the OECD. This *OECD Factbook,* in its sixth edition, contains comparable statistics on long-term trends of key economic, social and environmental phenomena. It provides a synthetic description of the key characteristics of the world in which we are living. The *OECD Factbook* has established itself as *the* flagship statistical publication and it is designed to be a source and empirical base for strategic policy making.

OECD work on comparative statistics and their role as a basic tool for policy making is evolving rapidly. There are two main drivers of change:

First, the crisis has led to a debate about the best way to measure progress in our societies, and the well-being of the people beyond the gauges of output. The OECD has pioneered work in this field and will continue to provide leadership in its implementation. Our 3rd OECD World Forum on Statistics, Knowledge and Policies, hosted by the Korean Government and held in Busan on 27-30 October 2009, gathered high-profile political, academic and business leaders, testifying their commitment to this agenda. This work will lead to a stream of new statistical reports and indicators in the years ahead.

Second, one of the most visible consequences of the crisis has been the change in the architecture of global governance and the related co-operation and joint action of advanced and emerging economies. The role of the G20 Summits as the future format of global economic governance at Leaders' level is a major manifestation of this change, but not the only one. We need different fora for the dialogue between industrialised, emerging and developing economies. The OECD is increasingly engaging key global players in its analytic and policy work, and is taking steps to include these countries in its databases. This issue of the *OECD Factbook* provides information on the major emerging economies of Brazil, China, India, Indonesia and South Africa. Moreover, the OECD is working toward its enlargement: Chile has signed its accession agreement in January, and Estonia, Israel, Slovenia and the Russian Federation are engaged in discussions to follow suit. Data for these five accession countries are also included in this issue of the *OECD Factbook.*

Angel Gurría
Secretary-General

PREFACE

The *OECD Factbook* is the most comprehensive statistical publication of the Organisation. It is a tool to evaluate the long-term trends in economic, environmental and social developments in OECD countries using solid and comparable indicators. It draws on the full range of statistics available within the Organisation, including data from three agencies affiliated to the OECD – the *International Energy Agency (IEA)*, the *Nuclear Energy Agency (NEA)* and the *European Conference of Ministers of Transport (ECMT)*.

The OECD Factbook is written in a non-technical language and aims to:

- provide a wide range of users with a one-stop resource for comparative, country-based economic, social and environmental data;
- help users to assess the position and performance of individual countries in a wide range of domains;
- encourage readers to go deeper in the goldmine of OECD statistics by linking to sources and further readings;
- highlight measurement issues and areas where the comparability of statistics across countries still needs improvement.

The tables and charts included in the *OECD Factbook* are available on-line at *www.sourceoecd.org/factbook*. The on-line version also contains longer time series and more metadata than the paper version. The data included in the *OECD Factbook* are also used to produce the "Country Statistical Profiles" available at *www.oecd.org*. Finally, data contained in the *OECD Factbook* can be visualised dynamically on the OECD Statistics Portal (*www.oecd.org/statistics*), using eXplorer, the software developed by the National Center for Visual Analytics.

This year, the *OECD Factbook* includes many more data and indicators for countries that are in the process of accession to the OECD (Chile, Estonia, Israel, the Russian Federation and Slovenia), as well as for some key emerging economies with which the OECD has developed an enhanced partnership (Brazil, China, India, Indonesia, and South Africa).

The Focus chapter in this year's edition deals with the economic and financial crisis. It presents a broad range of indicators on its causes, consequences and policy responses.

The *OECD Factbook* reflects the work of statisticians throughout the Organisation and was developed in co-operation with the Directorate for Public Affairs and Communications. The report also benefitted greatly from the concerted efforts of statisticians from all OECD and non-member countries who have worked, over many years, to develop the wide range of statistics shown here.

Marco Mira D'Ercole edited the report and co-ordinated the production of this year's edition of the *OECD Factbook*. Vincent Finat-Duclos, Michela Gamba, Ingrid Herrbach, Frédéric Parrot and Katia Sarrazin had overall responsibility for technical work on the manuscript.

Martine Durand
Chief Statistician and Director of the OECD Statistics Directorate

TABLE OF CONTENTS

OECD FACTBOOK 2010 – © OECD 2010

Environment

Education

Public finance

Quality of life

Special focus:
The crisis and beyond

READER'S GUIDE

Main Features:

- Tables and charts are preceded by short texts that explain how the statistics are defined (**Definition**) and that identify any problems there may be in comparing the performance of one country with another (**Comparability**). To avoid misunderstandings, the tables and charts must be read in conjunction with the texts that accompany them.

- Tables and charts are also available as Excel files (see below). In their electronic version, tables may feature longer time series; when appropriate, footnotes may provide additional information.

- While media comment on statistics usually focuses on the short term – what has happened to employment, prices, GDP and so on in the last few months – the *OECD Factbook* takes a longer view; the text and charts mostly describe developments during the fourteen year period from 1995 to 2008. This long-term perspective provides a good basis for comparing the successes and failures of policies in raising living standards and social conditions in countries.

- To facilitate cross-country comparisons, many indicators in the *OECD Factbook* have been standardised by relating them to each country's gross domestic product (GDP). In cases where GDP needs to be converted to a common currency, purchasing power parities (PPPs) have been used rather than exchange rates. When PPPs are used, differences in GDP levels across countries reflect only differences in the volume of goods and services, *i.e.* differences in price levels are eliminated.

Conventions

Unless otherwise specified:

- *OECD total* refers to all the OECD countries listed in a table or chart; when the indicator is a ratio or a mean, *OECD total* is the weighted average of country values.

- *OECD average* refers to the unweighted, arithmetic average of the listed OECD countries.

- For each country, the average value in different periods only takes into account the years for which data are available. The *average annual growth rate* of an indicator over a period of time is the geometric average of the growth rates of that indicator across the period (*i.e.* the annual compound growth rate).

- Each table and chart specifies the period covered. The mention, *XXXX or latest available year* (where XXXX is a year or a period) means that data for later years are not taken into account.

Signs, abbreviations and acronyms

..	Missing value, not applicable or not available	**DAC**	Development Assistance Committee
0	Less than half of the unit precision level of the observation	**ILO**	International Labor Organisation
–	Absolute zero	**IMF**	International Monetary Fund
|	Break in series	**ITF**	International Transport Forum
		ITU	International Telecommunications Union
USD	US dollars	**NAFTA**	North American Free Trade Agreement
		UN	United Nations
		UNCTAD	United Nations Conference on Trade and Development
		UNECE	United Nations Economic Commission for Europe
		UNODC	United Nations Office on Drugs and Crime
		UNWTO	World Tourism Organisation
		WTO	World Trade Organisation

For most of the charts, the OECD Factbook uses ISO codes for countries

AFRIC	Africa	**FIN**	Finland	**NMAS**	Non-OECD Asia
ASME	Middle East	**FRA**	France	**NOC**	Non-OECD
AUS	Australia	**G7M**	Major Seven	**NOR**	Norway
AUT	Austria	**GBR**	United Kingdom	**NZL**	New Zealand
BEL	Belgium	**GRC**	Greece	**OECD**	OECD total or OECD average
BRA	Brazil	**HUN**	Hungary	**POL**	Poland
CAN	Canada	**IDN**	Indonesia	**PRT**	Portugal
CHE	Switzerland	**IND**	India	**RUS**	Russian Federation
CHL	Chile	**IRL**	Ireland	**SVK**	Slovak Republic
CHN	China	**ISL**	Iceland	**SVN**	Slovenia
CZE	Czech Republic	**ISR**	Israel	**SWE**	Sweden
DAC	DAC total	**ITA**	Italy	**TALIS**	TALIS average
DEU	Germany	**JPN**	Japan	**TUR**	Turkey
DNK	Denmark	**KOR**	Korea	**USA**	United States
EA16	Euro area	**LUX**	Luxembourg	**XBL**	Belgium-Luxembourg
ESP	Spain	**MEX**	Mexico	**ZAF**	South Africa
EST	Estonia	**NLD**	Netherlands		
EU27	European Union (total or average)	**NMAM**	Non-OECD America		

Statistics for Israel

The statistical data for Israel are supplied by and under the responsibility of the relevant Israeli authorities. The use of such data by the OECD is without prejudice to the status of the Golan Heights, East Jerusalem and Israeli settlements in the West Bank under the terms of international law.

StatLinks

This publication includes OECD's unique *StatLink* service, which enables users to download Excel® versions of tables and charts. *StatLink* are provided at the bottom of each table and chart. *StatLink* behave like internet addresses: simply type the *StatLink* in your internet browser to obtain the corresponding data in Excel® format.

For more information about OECD's *StatLink*, please visit: *www.oecd.org/statistics/statlink*

Accessing OECD publications

- OECD publications cited in the *OECD Factbook* are available through OECDiLibrary (*www.oecdilibrary.org*), the OECD electronic library.
- All the OECD working papers can be downloaded from OECDiLibrary.
- All OECD databases mentioned in the book can also be accessed through OECDiLibrary.
- In addition, print editions of all OECD books can be purchased via the OECD online bookshop (*www.oecdbookshop.org*).

Glossary of Statistical Terms

The online *OECD Glossary of Statistical Terms* (available at *www.oecd.org/statistics/glossary*) is the perfect companion for the *OECD Factbook*. It contains almost 7 000 definitions of statistical terms, acronyms and concepts in an easy to use format. These definitions are primarily drawn from existing international statistical guidelines and recommendations that have been prepared over the last few decades by organisations such as the United Nations, ILO, OECD, Eurostat, IMF and national statistical institutes.

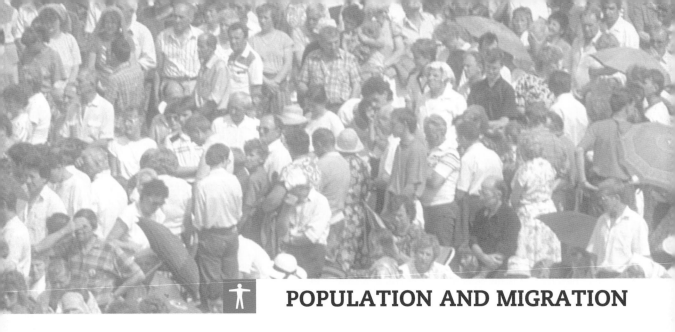

POPULATION AND MIGRATION

TOTAL POPULATION

The size and growth of a country's population are both causes and effects of economic and social developments. The pace of population growth has slowed in all OECD countries.

Definition

Data refer to the resident population. For countries with overseas colonies, protectorates or other territorial possessions, their populations are generally excluded. Growth rates are the annual changes in the population resulting from births, deaths and net migration during the year.

The total fertility rate is the total number of children that would be born to each woman if she were to live to the end of her child-bearing years and give birth to children in agreement with the prevailing age-specific fertility rates.

Comparability

For most OECD countries, population data are based on regular, ten-yearly censuses, with estimates for intercensal years derived from administrative data. In several European countries, population estimates are based entirely on administrative records. Population data are fairly comparable.

For some countries the population figures shown here differ from those used for calculating GDP and other economic statistics on a per capita basis, although differences are normally small.

Population projections are taken from national sources where these are available, but for some countries they are based on UN or Eurostat projections; the projection for the world comes from UN. All population projections require assumptions about future trends in life expectancy, fertility rates and migration. Often, a range of projections is produced using different assumptions about these future trends. The estimates shown here correspond to the median or central variant.

Sources
- For OECD member countries: National Sources, United Nations and Eurostat.
- For Brazil, China, India, Indonesia, Russian Federation and South Africa: UN World population prospects, 1950-2050 (the 2006 revision), United Nations, New York.
- Fertility rates: OECD (2009), *Society at a Glance: OECD Social Indicators – 2009 Edition*, OECD, Paris, (See *www.oecd.org/els/social/indicators/SAG*).

Further information
Analytical publications
- Bagnoli, P., T. Goeschl and E. Kovacs (2008), *People and Biodiversity Policies: Impacts, Issues and Strategies for Policy Action*, OECD, Paris.
- OECD (2009), *OECD Employment Outlook*, OECD, Paris.

Statistical publications
- Maddison, A. (2003), *The World Economy: Historical Perspectives*, OECD, Paris, also available on CD-ROM, *www.theworldeconomy.org*.
- OECD (2009), *Society at a Glance: OECD Social Indicators – 2009 Edition*, OECD, Paris, (See *www.oecd.org/els/social/indicators/SAG*).

Methodological publications
- d'Addio, A. C. and M. Mira d'Ercole (2005), *Trends and Determinants of Fertility Rates: The Role of Policies*, OECD Social Employment and Migration Working Papers, No. 27, OECD, Paris.
- OECD (2009), *Labour Force Statistics*, OECD, Paris.

Online databases
- *Employment Statistics*.
- *OECD Family database*, (See *www.oecd.org/els/social/family/database*).
- *World Bank – World Development Indicators*.

Web sites
- World Population Prospects: The 2008 Revision Population Database, *http://esa.un.org/unpp*.

Overview

In 2007, OECD countries accounted for 18% of the world's population of 6.7 billion. China accounted for 20% and India for 17%. Within OECD, the United States accounted for 25% of the OECD total, followed by Japan (11%), Mexico (9%), Germany (7%) and Turkey (6%).

In the three years to 2007, growth rates above the OECD population average (0.7% per year) were recorded in Iceland, Mexico and Turkey (high birth rate countries) and in Australia, Canada, Luxembourg, Ireland, New Zealand, Norway, Spain and United States (high net immigration). In Hungary and Poland, populations declined due to a combination of low birth rates and net emigration. Growth rates were very low, although still positive, in Japan and the Slovak Republic. The population of OECD countries is expected to grow by less than 0.3 per cent per year until 2050.

Total fertility rates in OECD countries have declined dramatically over the past few decades, falling on average from 2.7 in 1970 to 1.6 children per woman of childbearing age in the 2000s. In all OECD countries, fertility rates declined for young women and increased at older ages. A modest recovery in total fertility rates started in 2002, to an average level of 1.7 in 2008. In 2008, the total fertility rate was below its replacement level of 2.1 in all OECD countries except New Zealand, Iceland, Ireland, Mexico, Turkey and the United States.

Population levels
Thousands

	1996	1997	1998	1999	2000	2001	2002	2003	2004	2005	2006	2007	2020	2050
Australia	18 311	18 518	18 711	18 926	19 153	19 413	19 651	19 895	20 127	20 395	20 698	21 015	23 663	28 081
Austria	7 959	7 968	7 977	7 992	8 012	8 043	8 084	8 118	8 175	8 233	8 282	8 315	8 651	8 986
Belgium	10 157	10 181	10 203	10 226	10 251	10 287	10 333	10 376	10 421	10 479	10 548	10 626	10 801	10 897
Canada	29 611	29 907	30 157	30 404	30 689	31 021	31 373	31 676	31 995	32 312	32 649	32 976	36 344	41 896
Czech Republic	10 315	10 304	10 295	10 283	10 273	10 224	10 201	10 202	10 207	10 234	10 267	10 323	10 287	9 457
Denmark	5 262	5 284	5 301	5 319	5 337	5 355	5 374	5 387	5 401	5 416	5 435	5 457	5 582	5 621
Finland	5 125	5 140	5 153	5 165	5 176	5 188	5 201	5 213	5 228	5 246	5 266	5 289	5 538	5 747
France	58 026	58 207	58 398	58 673	59 049	59 454	59 863	60 264	60 643	60 996	61 353	61 707	65 102	69 993
Germany	81 915	82 035	82 047	82 100	82 212	82 350	82 488	82 534	82 516	82 469	82 376	82 247	82 635	74 422
Greece	10 709	10 777	10 835	10 883	10 917	10 950	10 988	11 024	11 062	11 104	11 149	11 193	11 426	10 605
Hungary	10 311	10 290	10 267	10 238	10 211	10 188	10 159	10 130	10 107	10 087	10 071	10 050	9 856	8 718
Iceland	269	271	274	277	281	285	288	289	293	296	304	311	327	355
Ireland	3 626	3 664	3 703	3 742	3 790	3 847	3 917	3 980	4 045	4 134	4 240	4 339	4 774	5 482
Italy	56 856	56 886	56 902	56 912	56 937	56 972	57 151	57 597	58 167	58 597	58 931	59 336	59 001	55 710
Japan	125 864	126 166	126 486	126 686	126 926	127 291	127 435	127 619	127 687	127 768	127 770	127 771	122 735	95 152
Korea	45 525	45 954	46 287	46 617	47 008	47 357	47 622	47 859	48 039	48 138	48 297	48 456	49 326	42 343
Luxembourg	414	419	425	430	436	442	446	452	458	465	473	480	523	644
Mexico	93 130	94 478	95 790	97 115	98 439	99 716	100 909	102 000	103 002	103 947	104 874	105 791	115 762	121 856
Netherlands	15 531	15 611	15 707	15 812	15 926	16 046	16 149	16 225	16 282	16 320	16 346	16 382	16 762	16 789
New Zealand	3 732	3 781	3 815	3 835	3 858	3 881	3 949	4 027	4 088	4 134	4 185	4 228	4 565	5 046
Norway	4 381	4 405	4 431	4 462	4 491	4 514	4 538	4 565	4 592	4 623	4 661	4 709	5 061	5 854
Poland	38 289	38 292	38 284	38 270	38 258	38 248	38 232	38 195	38 180	38 161	38 132	38 116	37 038	33 576
Portugal	10 058	10 091	10 129	10 172	10 226	10 293	10 368	10 441	10 502	10 549	10 584	10 608	10 501	9 332
Slovak Republic	5 374	5 383	5 391	5 395	5 401	5 380	5 379	5 379	5 383	5 387	5 391	5 398	5 417	4 880
Spain	39 479	39 583	39 722	39 927	40 264	40 721	41 314	42 005	42 692	43 398	44 068	44 874	45 568	42 703
Sweden	8 841	8 846	8 851	8 858	8 872	8 896	8 925	8 958	8 994	9 030	9 081	9 148	9 658	10 490
Switzerland	7 072	7 089	7 110	7 144	7 184	7 230	7 285	7 339	7 390	7 437	7 484	7 550	7 993	8 067
Turkey	62 911	64 063	65 214	66 338	67 393	68 367	69 304	70 231	71 151	72 065	72 971	73 875	84 301	96 498
United Kingdom	58 164	58 314	58 475	58 684	58 886	59 114	59 324	59 557	59 846	60 238	60 587	60 975	66 754	76 959
United States	269 394	272 647	275 854	279 040	282 158	284 915	287 502	289 986	292 806	295 583	298 442	301 280	341 387	439 010
EU27 total	477 367	478 051	478 674	479 562	480 808	482 159	483 825	485 841	487 988	490 103	492 076	494 269	500 487	484 603
OECD total	1 096 611	1 104 556	1 112 194	1 119 926	1 128 050	1 136 184	1 144 135	1 151 981	1 159 853	1 167 527	1 175 228	1 183 167	1 249 678	1 318 459
Brazil	164 157	166 650	169 162	171 675	174 175	176 659	179 123	181 537	183 864	186 075	188 158	190 120	209 051	218 512
Chile	14 631	14 840	15 039	15 231	15 419	15 602	15 780	15 955	16 127	16 297	16 467	16 636	18 639	20 657
China	1 223 083	1 234 764	1 245 993	1 256 729	1 266 954	1 276 684	1 285 984	1 294 940	1 303 667	1 312 253	1 320 724	1 329 090	1 431 155	1 417 045
Estonia	1 418	1 402	1 389	1 379	1 370	1 363	1 357	1 353	1 349	1 347	1 345	1 343	1 333	1 233
India	935 960	954 298	972 746	991 287	1 009 914	1 028 610	1 045 547	1 062 388	1 079 117	1 095 722	1 112 186	1 128 521	1 326 155	..
Indonesia	194 264	197 014	199 760	202 513	205 280	208 064	210 858	213 656	216 443	219 210	221 954	224 670	254 218	288 110
Israel	5 534	5 683	5 821	5 954	6 084	6 211	6 334	6 454	6 573	6 692	6 811	6 932	8 307	10 649
Russian Federation	148 284	148 003	147 648	147 205	146 670	146 042	145 339	144 598	143 864	143 170	142 530	141 941	135 406	116 097
Slovenia	1 972	1 976	1 979	1 982	1 985	1 988	1 991	1 994	1 997	2 001	2 005	2 010	2 053	1 954
South Africa	42 167	42 890	43 562	44 215	44 872	45 536	46 197	46 849	47 477	48 073	48 639	49 173	52 671	56 802
World	5 801 566	5 883 317	5 964 309	6 044 563	6 124 124	6 202 980	6 281 210	6 359 055	6 436 827	6 514 751	6 592 901	6 671 227	7 667 090	9 191 287

StatLink http://dx.doi.org/10.1787/823560113307

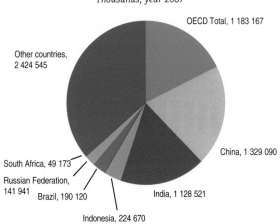

World population
Thousands, year 2007

OECD Total, 1 183 167

Other countries, 2 424 545

South Africa, 49 173
Russian Federation, 141 941
Brazil, 190 120

Indonesia, 224 670

India, 1 128 521

China, 1 329 090

StatLink http://dx.doi.org/10.1787/817451835814

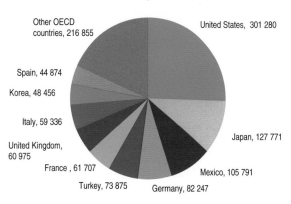

OECD population
Thousands, year 2007

Other OECD countries, 216 855

Spain, 44 874

Korea, 48 456

Italy, 59 336

United Kingdom, 60 975

France , 61 707

Turkey, 73 875

United States, 301 280

Japan, 127 771

Mexico, 105 791

Germany, 82 247

StatLink http://dx.doi.org/10.1787/817532305520

Population growth rates
Annual growth in percentage

	1994	1995	1996	1997	1998	1999	2000	2001	2002	2003	2004	2005	2006	2007
Australia	1.06	1.22	1.32	1.13	1.05	1.15	1.20	1.36	1.23	1.24	1.17	1.33	1.49	1.53
Austria	0.39	0.15	0.14	0.11	0.11	0.19	0.24	0.39	0.51	0.42	0.70	0.72	0.59	0.40
Belgium	0.31	0.21	0.20	0.24	0.21	0.23	0.24	0.34	0.45	0.42	0.43	0.55	0.66	0.74
Canada	1.11	1.05	1.05	1.00	0.84	0.82	0.94	1.08	1.13	0.97	1.01	0.99	1.04	1.00
Czech Republic	0.05	-0.05	-0.15	-0.11	-0.08	-0.12	-0.10	-0.47	-0.23	0.01	0.05	0.27	0.32	0.55
Denmark	0.30	0.44	0.64	0.43	0.32	0.34	0.34	0.33	0.36	0.24	0.26	0.27	0.34	0.42
Finland	0.43	0.38	0.33	0.30	0.27	0.23	0.21	0.23	0.24	0.24	0.29	0.34	0.38	0.43
France	0.33	0.32	0.31	0.31	0.33	0.47	0.64	0.69	0.69	0.67	0.63	0.58	0.58	0.58
Germany	0.35	0.29	0.29	0.15	0.02	0.06	0.14	0.17	0.17	0.06	-0.02	-0.06	-0.11	-0.16
Greece	0.84	0.77	0.70	0.63	0.54	0.44	0.32	0.30	0.34	0.33	0.35	0.38	0.40	0.40
Hungary	-0.14	-0.14	-0.17	-0.20	-0.23	-0.28	-0.26	-0.23	-0.28	-0.29	-0.22	-0.20	-0.16	-0.21
Iceland	0.84	0.52	0.58	0.74	1.06	1.24	1.43	1.39	0.88	0.60	1.15	1.12	2.86	2.32
Ireland	0.33	0.43	0.69	1.05	1.06	1.04	1.28	1.52	1.82	1.60	1.64	2.19	2.56	2.34
Italy	0.02	0.00	0.03	0.05	0.03	0.02	0.04	0.06	0.31	0.78	0.99	0.74	0.57	0.69
Japan	0.26	0.24	0.23	0.24	0.25	0.16	0.19	0.29	0.11	0.14	0.05	0.06	0.00	0.00
Korea	1.01	1.01	0.96	0.94	0.72	0.71	0.84	0.74	0.56	0.50	0.38	0.21	0.33	0.33
Luxembourg	1.37	1.42	1.37	1.26	1.25	1.36	1.35	1.20	1.05	1.22	1.43	1.54	1.61	1.56
Mexico	1.71	1.62	1.53	1.45	1.39	1.38	1.36	1.30	1.20	1.08	0.98	0.92	0.89	0.87
Netherlands	0.60	0.50	0.46	0.52	0.62	0.67	0.72	0.76	0.64	0.47	0.35	0.23	0.16	0.22
New Zealand	1.34	1.47	1.60	1.32	0.89	0.53	0.59	0.59	1.75	1.99	1.50	1.14	1.23	1.04
Norway	0.57	0.52	0.51	0.54	0.60	0.69	0.65	0.51	0.54	0.59	0.59	0.68	0.81	1.04
Poland	0.08	0.06	0.04	0.01	-0.02	-0.04	-0.03	-0.03	-0.04	-0.10	-0.04	-0.05	-0.08	-0.04
Portugal	0.22	0.26	0.27	0.33	0.38	0.42	0.53	0.66	0.73	0.70	0.58	0.45	0.33	0.23
Slovak Republic	0.43	0.30	0.19	0.18	0.14	0.08	0.10	-0.39	-0.02	0.00	0.07	0.09	0.07	0.12
Spain	0.27	0.23	0.23	0.26	0.35	0.52	0.84	1.14	1.46	1.67	1.64	1.65	1.54	1.83
Sweden	0.71	0.53	0.16	0.06	0.06	0.08	0.16	0.27	0.33	0.37	0.39	0.40	0.56	0.74
Switzerland	0.80	0.67	0.44	0.24	0.30	0.48	0.56	0.63	0.76	0.74	0.69	0.64	0.63	0.88
Turkey	1.89	1.86	1.85	1.83	1.80	1.72	1.59	1.45	1.37	1.34	1.31	1.28	1.26	1.24
United Kingdom	0.26	0.28	0.24	0.26	0.28	0.36	0.34	0.39	0.36	0.39	0.48	0.66	0.58	0.64
United States	1.23	1.20	1.17	1.21	1.18	1.15	1.12	0.98	0.91	0.86	0.97	0.95	0.97	0.95
EU27 total	0.21	0.18	0.16	0.14	0.13	0.19	0.26	0.28	0.35	0.42	0.44	0.43	0.40	0.45
OECD total	0.79	0.76	0.74	0.72	0.69	0.70	0.73	0.72	0.70	0.69	0.68	0.66	0.66	0.68
Brazil	1.53	1.52	1.52	1.52	1.51	1.49	1.46	1.43	1.39	1.35	1.28	1.20	1.12	1.04
Chile	1.76	1.65	1.53	1.43	1.34	1.28	1.23	1.19	1.14	1.11	1.08	1.06	1.04	1.03
China	1.08	1.04	1.00	0.96	0.91	0.86	0.81	0.77	0.73	0.70	0.67	0.66	0.65	0.63
Estonia	-2.05	-1.80	-1.46	-1.16	-0.90	-0.73	-0.64	-0.55	-0.42	-0.32	-0.24	-0.20	-0.16	-0.13
India	2.03	2.01	1.98	1.96	1.93	1.91	1.88	1.85	1.65	1.61	1.57	1.54	1.50	1.47
Indonesia	1.50	1.47	1.44	1.42	1.39	1.38	1.37	1.36	1.34	1.33	1.30	1.28	1.25	1.22
Israel	3.69	3.35	2.98	2.68	2.44	2.28	2.18	2.09	1.98	1.89	1.84	1.81	1.79	1.77
Russian Federation	-0.05	-0.10	-0.14	-0.19	-0.24	-0.30	-0.36	-0.43	-0.48	-0.51	-0.51	-0.48	-0.45	-0.41
Slovenia	0.39	0.33	0.27	0.22	0.18	0.16	0.15	0.15	0.14	0.15	0.16	0.19	0.21	0.24
South Africa	2.38	2.16	1.92	1.71	1.57	1.50	1.49	1.48	1.45	1.41	1.34	1.26	1.18	1.10
World	1.51	1.48	1.44	1.41	1.38	1.35	1.32	1.29	1.26	1.24	1.22	1.21	1.20	1.19

StatLink ᕦᕤ *http://dx.doi.org/10.1787/823587486160*

Population growth rates
Average annual growth in percentage

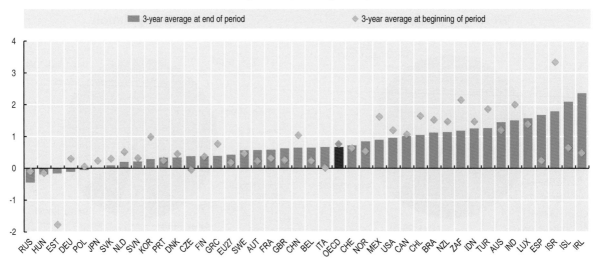

StatLink ᕦᕤ *http://dx.doi.org/10.1787/817541454352*

OECD FACTBOOK 2010 – © OECD 2010

Total fertility rates
Number of children born to women aged 15 to 49

	1970	1996	1997	1998	1999	2000	2001	2002	2003	2004	2005	2006	2007	2008
Australia	2.86	1.80	1.78	1.76	1.76	1.76	1.73	1.76	1.75	1.76	1.79	1.82	1.93	..
Austria	2.29	1.45	1.39	1.37	1.34	1.36	1.33	1.39	1.38	1.42	1.41	1.41	1.38	1.41
Belgium	2.25	1.59	1.61	1.60	1.62	1.72	1.76	1.65	1.72	1.76	1.77	1.80	1.81	1.82
Canada	2.33	1.62	1.58	1.54	1.51	1.49	1.51	1.50	1.53	1.53	1.54	1.59	1.66	..
Czech Republic	1.91	1.19	1.17	1.16	1.13	1.14	1.15	1.17	1.18	1.23	1.28	1.33	1.44	1.50
Denmark	1.95	1.75	1.75	1.72	1.74	1.77	1.75	1.72	1.76	1.78	1.80	1.85	1.85	1.89
Finland	1.83	1.76	1.75	1.71	1.73	1.73	1.73	1.72	1.76	1.80	1.80	1.84	1.83	1.85
France	2.48	1.73	1.73	1.76	1.79	1.87	1.88	1.86	1.87	1.90	1.92	1.98	1.96	2.00
Germany	2.03	1.32	1.37	1.36	1.36	1.38	1.35	1.34	1.34	1.36	1.34	1.33	1.37	1.38
Greece	2.39	1.30	1.31	1.29	1.28	1.27	1.26	1.27	1.29	1.31	1.34	1.41	1.42	1.51
Hungary	1.97	1.46	1.38	1.33	1.29	1.33	1.31	1.31	1.28	1.28	1.32	1.35	1.32	1.35
Iceland	2.81	2.12	2.04	2.05	1.99	2.08	1.95	1.93	1.99	2.03	2.05	2.07	2.09	2.14
Ireland	3.87	1.89	1.94	1.95	1.91	1.90	1.96	1.98	1.98	1.95	1.88	1.90	2.03	2.10
Italy	2.43	1.22	1.23	1.21	1.23	1.26	1.25	1.27	1.29	1.33	1.32	1.35	1.38	1.41
Japan	2.13	1.43	1.39	1.38	1.34	1.36	1.33	1.32	1.29	1.29	1.26	1.32	1.34	1.37
Korea	4.53	1.57	1.52	1.45	1.41	1.47	1.30	1.17	1.18	1.15	1.08	1.12	1.25	1.19
Luxembourg	1.98	1.76	1.71	1.67	1.71	1.78	1.66	1.63	1.62	1.66	1.62	1.64	1.61	1.60
Mexico	6.77	2.84	2.74	2.71	2.73	2.77	2.60	2.46	2.34	2.25	2.20	2.17	2.13	2.10
Netherlands	2.57	1.53	1.56	1.63	1.65	1.72	1.71	1.73	1.75	1.73	1.71	1.72	1.72	1.77
New Zealand	3.17	1.96	1.96	1.89	1.97	1.98	1.97	1.89	1.93	1.98	1.97	2.01	2.17	2.18
Norway	2.50	1.89	1.86	1.81	1.85	1.85	1.78	1.75	1.80	1.83	1.84	1.90	1.90	1.96
Poland	2.20	1.53	1.47	1.41	1.37	1.37	1.32	1.25	1.22	1.23	1.24	1.27	1.31	1.39
Portugal	2.83	1.44	1.47	1.48	1.51	1.56	1.46	1.47	1.44	1.40	1.41	1.36	1.33	1.37
Slovak Republic	2.40	1.47	1.43	1.37	1.33	1.29	1.20	1.19	1.20	1.24	1.25	1.24	1.25	1.32
Spain	2.90	1.16	1.18	1.16	1.19	1.23	1.24	1.26	1.31	1.33	1.35	1.38	1.40	1.46
Sweden	1.94	1.61	1.53	1.51	1.50	1.55	1.57	1.65	1.72	1.75	1.77	1.85	1.88	1.91
Switzerland	2.10	1.50	1.48	1.47	1.48	1.50	1.38	1.39	1.39	1.42	1.42	1.44	1.46	1.48
Turkey	5.00	2.69	2.63	2.56	2.48	2.27	2.25	2.24	2.22	2.23	2.20	2.17	2.15	2.14
United Kingdom	2.43	1.73	1.72	1.71	1.68	1.64	1.63	1.64	1.71	1.77	1.79	1.84	1.90	1.96
United States	2.48	1.98	1.97	2.00	2.01	2.06	2.03	2.01	2.04	2.05	2.05	2.10	2.12	..
OECD average	2.71	1.68	1.65	1.63	1.63	1.65	1.61	1.60	1.61	1.62	1.62	1.65	1.68	1.71
Brazil	..	2.48	2.45	2.43	2.41	2.39	2.34	2.27	2.20	2.13	2.06	1.99	1.93	1.86
Chile	3.95	2.28	2.21	2.17	2.12	2.08	2.04	2.00	1.99	1.98	1.97	1.96	..	..
China	5.78	1.91	1.90	1.90	1.89	1.89	1.89	1.88	1.88	1.85	1.81	1.78	..	..
Estonia	..	1.37	1.32	1.28	1.32	1.39	1.34	1.37	1.37	1.47	1.50	1.55	1.64	1.66
India	5.77	3.35	3.30	3.22	3.15	3.07	3.00	2.92	2.92	2.68	2.61	2.54	..	..
Israel	..	2.94	2.93	2.98	2.94	2.95	2.89	2.89	2.95	2.90	2.84	2.88	2.90	2.96
Russian Federation	..	1.27	1.22	1.23	1.16	1.19	1.22	1.29	1.32	1.34	1.29	1.30	..	..
Slovenia	2.21	1.28	1.25	1.23	1.21	1.26	1.21	1.21	1.20	1.25	1.26	1.31	1.31	..
South Africa	5.65	3.04	3.00	2.97	2.93	2.90	2.86	2.84	2.82	2.80	2.78	2.73	..	..

StatLink http://dx.doi.org/10.1787/823625874732

Total fertility rates
Number of children born to women aged 15 to 49

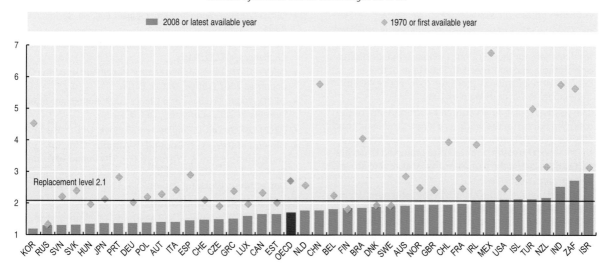

■ 2008 or latest available year ◆ 1970 or first available year

StatLink http://dx.doi.org/10.1787/817542708333

DEPENDENT POPULATION

Demographic trends in OECD countries have implied a sharp increase in the share of the dependent population (*i.e.* the sum of the elderly and youth population) in the total, and this increase is expected to continue in the future. These trends have a number of implications for government and private spending on pensions, health care and education and, more generally, for economic growth and welfare.

Definition

Population is defined as the resident population, *i.e.* all persons, regardless of citizenship, who have a permanent place of residence in the country. Population projections by age and gender are taken from national sources where these are available; for other countries they are based on Eurostat and UN projections.

The elderly population refers to people aged 65 and over and the youth population to people aged less than 15. The share of dependent population is calculated as the sum of the elderly and youth population expressed as a ratio of the total population.

Comparability

All population projections require assumptions about future trends in life expectancy, fertility rates and migration, and these assumptions may differ across countries. Often, a range of projections is produced The estimates shown here correspond to the median or central variant of these projections.

Sources

- OECD (2009), *Labour Force Statistics*, OECD, Paris.
- Eurostat, United Nations, national sources and OECD estimates.

Further information

Analytical publications

- Burniaux, J.-M., R. Duval and F. Jaumotte (2004), *Coping with Ageing*, OECD Economics Department Working Papers, No. 371, OECD, Paris.
- OECD (2001), *Ageing and Transport Mobility Needs and Safety Issues*, OECD, Paris.
- OECD (2003), *Ageing, Housing and Urban Development*, OECD, Paris.
- OECD (2006), *Ageing and Employment Policies*, series, OECD, Paris.
- OECD (2007), *Ageing and the Public Service: Human Resource Challenges*, OECD, Paris.
- OECD (2007), *Pensions at a Glance: Public Policies across OECD Countries 2007 Edition*, OECD, Paris.
- OECD (2009), *Pensions at a Glance 2009: Retirement-Income Systems in OECD Countries*, OECD, Paris.
- OECD (2009), *OECD Employment Outlook*, OECD, Paris.
- Oliveira Martins J., F. Gonand, P. Antolin, C. de la Maisonneuve and K.-Y. Yoo (2005), *The Impact of Ageing on Demand, Factor Markets and Growth*, OECD Economics Department Working Papers, No. 420, OECD, Paris.

Methodological publications

- OECD (1997), "Sources and Methods – Labour and Wage Statistics", *Main Economic Indicators: April Volume 1997 Issue 4*, OECD, Paris.

Online databases

- *Employment Statistics*.

Overview

The share of dependent population reflects the combined effect of fertility rates and longer life expectancy. In the year 2005, this share was higher in emerging countries (ranging between 38% in India and 34% in Brazil and Indonesia) than in most OECD countries (at 33% on average).

By 2050, the share of dependent population is projected to increase sharply in all OECD countries, to an average level of 41.6% for the OECD as a whole, while declining only in India and South Africa. The share of the dependent population is projected to be above 45% in Italy, Japan, Korea and Spain by 2050.

The youth population accounted for around 30% of the total population for the world as a whole, and for around 20% for the OECD area. Because of lower fertility rates, the share of the youth population is projected to decline to less than 20% at the world level by 2050, and to around 15% for the OECD area.

In 2005, the share of the elderly in the total population ranged between less than 4% in South Africa, India, Indonesia and Mexico, and above 18% in Greece, Germany, Japan and Italy. By 2050, this share is projected to be below 10% only in South Africa, and to exceed one third of the total in Italy, Japan, Korea and Spain.

Share of the dependent population
As a percentage of the total population

	Youth population (aged less than 15)							Elderly population (aged 65 and over)						
	2000	2005	2010	2020	2030	2040	2050	2000	2005	2010	2020	2030	2040	2050
Australia	20.7	19.7	18.4	17.0	16.2	15.5	15.1	12.4	12.9	14.3	18.3	22.2	24.5	25.7
Austria	17.0	16.0	14.9	14.4	14.3	13.8	13.6	15.4	16.3	17.4	19.3	23.4	26.4	27.4
Belgium	17.6	17.1	16.3	15.7	15.4	14.8	14.7	16.8	17.2	17.6	20.7	24.9	27.4	27.7
Canada	19.2	17.6	16.2	15.3	14.7	13.8	13.6	12.6	13.1	14.1	18.2	23.1	25.0	26.3
Czech Republic	16.4	14.8	13.6	13.7	12.7	12.2	12.4	13.8	14.1	15.4	20.1	22.7	26.5	31.2
Denmark	18.5	18.8	17.9	16.3	16.8	16.9	16.5	14.8	15.1	16.8	20.9	24.1	26.2	25.4
Finland	18.2	17.4	16.5	16.6	16.1	15.5	15.6	14.9	15.9	17.3	22.8	26.2	27.0	27.6
France	18.8	18.4	18.3	17.5	16.7	16.5	16.3	16.1	16.4	16.7	20.3	23.4	25.6	26.2
Germany	15.6	14.3	13.6	13.0	12.7	12.0	11.9	16.4	18.9	20.4	22.7	27.8	31.1	31.5
Greece	15.3	14.4	14.2	14.0	12.6	12.1	12.3	16.6	18.3	18.9	21.3	24.8	29.4	32.5
Hungary	16.8	15.5	14.8	15.1	14.4	13.7	13.9	15.1	15.7	16.7	20.1	21.5	23.9	26.9
Iceland	23.3	22.1	20.8	19.7	19.0	18.2	18.1	11.6	11.7	12.4	15.5	19.2	20.9	21.5
Ireland	21.8	20.6	21.0	19.7	16.8	16.1	16.0	11.2	11.1	11.9	14.9	18.5	22.4	26.3
Italy	14.3	14.1	14.0	13.1	12.1	12.4	12.7	18.3	19.6	20.5	23.3	27.3	32.2	33.6
Japan	14.6	13.8	13.0	10.8	9.7	9.3	8.6	17.4	20.2	23.1	29.2	31.8	36.5	39.6
Korea	21.1	19.2	16.2	12.4	11.4	10.3	8.9	7.2	9.1	11.0	15.6	24.3	32.5	38.2
Luxembourg	18.9	18.5	17.8	17.0	17.3	16.9	16.6	14.1	14.1	14.6	16.6	20.0	22.3	22.1
Mexico	34.1	31.3	28.1	23.2	20.8	18.5	16.8	4.7	5.2	5.9	8.1	11.8	16.7	21.2
Netherlands	18.6	18.4	17.5	15.9	16.1	16.2	16.0	13.6	14.2	15.5	19.8	23.4	25.0	23.5
New Zealand	22.8	21.5	20.3	18.1	16.9	16.3	15.6	11.8	12.0	13.3	17.1	21.9	25.2	26.2
Norway	20.0	19.6	18.7	17.5	17.5	16.9	16.4	15.2	14.7	15.1	18.0	20.6	22.9	23.2
Poland	19.4	16.5	14.7	14.5	14.1	12.8	13.0	12.2	13.2	13.5	18.5	22.7	25.0	29.6
Portugal	16.1	15.6	15.5	14.0	12.7	12.9	13.1	16.2	17.1	17.5	20.1	23.9	28.2	31.6
Slovak Republic	19.5	16.8	14.8	16.4	13.4	12.6	13.2	11.4	11.7	12.8	17.3	21.6	25.0	30.1
Spain	14.8	14.5	14.9	14.1	11.6	11.3	11.4	16.8	16.7	17.4	20.0	25.1	31.6	35.7
Sweden	18.4	17.4	16.4	17.2	17.1	16.4	16.6	17.3	17.3	18.5	21.2	22.8	24.0	23.6
Switzerland	17.4	16.1	15.0	14.0	13.6	13.0	12.7	15.3	15.9	17.2	20.2	24.2	27.0	27.9
Turkey	30.0	28.4	26.6	23.2	21.1	19.1	17.7	5.4	5.9	6.3	7.8	10.4	14.2	17.6
United Kingdom	19.0	17.9	17.4	17.8	16.9	16.3	16.3	15.8	16.0	16.5	19.0	21.9	23.7	24.1
United States	21.4	20.7	20.1	20.0	19.5	19.3	19.3	12.4	12.4	13.0	16.1	19.3	20.0	20.2
EU27 total	17.1	16.0	15.4	14.9	14.1	13.7	13.8	15.7	16.7	17.5	20.6	24.4	27.7	29.3
OECD total	20.4	19.3	18.4	17.2	16.4	15.9	15.8	13.0	13.8	14.8	18.0	21.5	24.2	25.8
Brazil	29.6	27.5	25.5	20.1	17.0	15.3	14.7	5.5	6.2	6.9	9.6	13.7	17.7	22.5
Chile	27.8	24.9	22.3	20.2	18.6	17.2	16.5	7.3	8.1	9.2	12.1	16.8	20.2	22.1
China	25.7	22.0	19.9	18.7	16.9	15.3	15.3	6.8	7.6	8.2	11.7	15.9	21.8	23.3
Estonia	18.1	15.2	15.4	18.3	16.9	15.3	16.8	15.1	16.7	17.1	18.6	20.7	22.0	24.2
India	35.0	33.1	30.8	26.7	22.8	19.7	18.2	4.3	4.6	4.9	6.3	8.4	10.7	13.7
Indonesia	30.3	28.4	26.7	22.9	20.0	18.8	17.4	4.9	5.5	6.1	7.5	10.7	14.7	18.6
Israel	28.3	27.9	27.6	24.9	22.1	20.6	18.7	9.9	10.1	10.2	12.8	14.7	16.8	19.2
Russian Federation	18.2	15.1	15.0	16.7	15.2	14.7	16.2	12.4	13.8	12.9	15.4	19.4	20.5	23.4
Slovenia	15.9	14.2	13.8	14.5	13.5	13.1	14.3	14.0	15.5	16.4	20.3	24.6	27.5	30.2
South Africa	33.6	31.7	30.3	28.6	26.2	24.3	22.5	3.7	4.1	4.6	6.3	7.9	8.5	9.8
World	30.3	28.4	26.9	25.0	22.7	20.7	19.6	6.8	7.3	7.6	9.3	11.7	14.2	16.2

StatLink ⟶ http://dx.doi.org/10.1787/823628673425

Share of the dependent population
As a percentage of the total population

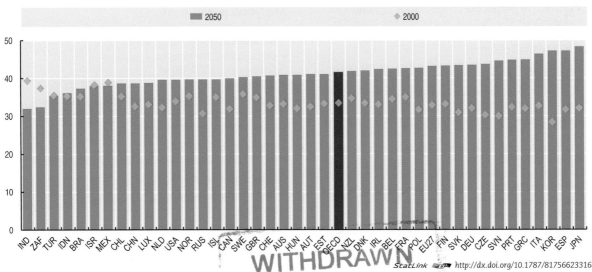

StatLink ⟶ http://dx.doi.org/10.1787/817566233168

POPULATION BY REGION

Population is unevenly distributed among regions within countries. Differences in climatic and environmental conditions discourage human settlement in some areas and favour concentration of the population around a few urban centres. This pattern is reinforced by the higher economic opportunities and wider availability of services stemming from urbanisation itself.

Definition

The number of inhabitants of a given region, *i.e.* its total population, can be measured as either its average annual population or as the population at a specific date during the year considered. The average population during a calendar year is generally calculated as the arithmetic mean of the population on 1 January of two consecutive years, although some countries estimate it on a date close to 1 July.

The index of geographic concentration offers a picture of the spatial distribution of the population. It compares the share of population and land area over all regions in a given country, and it takes into account both within- and between-country differences in the size of all regions. This index lies between 0 (no concentration) and 100 (maximum concentration) and is suitable for international comparisons.

Comparability

The main problem with economic analysis at the sub-national level is the unit of analysis, *i.e.* the region. The word "region" can mean very different things both within and among countries, with significant differences in area and population.

The smallest OECD region (Melilla, Spain) has an area of 13 square kilometres whereas the largest region (Northwest Territories and Nunavut, Canada) has an area of over 3 million square kilometres. Similarly, the population across OECD regions ranges from about 400 inhabitants in Balance ACT (Australia) to more than 47 million in Kanto (Japan).

To address this issue, the OECD has classified regions within each country based on two territorial levels. The higher level (Territorial Level 2) consists of 578 large regions and the lower level (Territorial Level 3) is composed of 1 793 small regions, including the accession and enhanced enlargement countries. This classification (which, for European Union countries, is largely consistent with the Eurostat NUTS classification) facilitates comparability of regions at the same territorial level.

All the data shown here refer to small regions with the exception of Brazil, Chile, China, India, Russian Federation and South Africa.

In addition, the OECD has established a typology according to which regions have been classified as predominantly urban, predominantly rural and intermediate, based on the percentage of regional population living in rural communities.

Overview

The concentration of population is highest in Australia, Canada, Iceland, the United States, Mexico and Chile where 10% of regions account for no less than 45% of their population. In contrast, the territorial distribution is more balanced in the Slovak Republic, Poland, Denmark, the Czech Republic and Belgium.

The index of geographic concentration is highest in Canada, Australia, Iceland and Israel; and lowest in the Slovak Republic, Slovenia, the Czech Republic, Hungary and Belgium.

Paris, in France, is the region with the highest population density, recording more than 20 000 inhabitants per km², while Pohia Eesti, in Estonia, has only 121 inhabitants per km².

Almost half of the OECD population (46%) lives in predominantly urban regions, which accounted for less than 6% of the total area. Concentration in urban regions is over 60% in the Netherlands, Belgium and United Kingdom. Predominantly rural regions account for almost one fourth of total population (24%) and extend on an area of 80% of the total. In Ireland, Finland, Sweden and Norway the share of national population in rural regions is more than twice than the OECD average.

Sources

• OECD (2009), *OECD Regions at a Glance 2009*, OECD, Paris.

Further information

Analytical publications

• OECD (2006), *OECD Territorial Reviews – Competitive Cities in the Global Economy*, OECD, Paris.
• OECD (2006), *The New Rural Paradigm: Policies and Governance*, OECD, Paris.
• OECD (2008), *OECD Territorial Reviews*, OECD, Paris.
• Spiezia, V. (2003), "Measuring Regional Economies", OECD Statistics Brief, No. 6, October, OECD, Paris, *www.oecd.org/std/statisticsbrief*.

Statistical publications

• OECD (2009), *Labour Force Statistics*, OECD, Paris.

Online databases

• *OECD Regional Database*.

Web sites

• OECD eXplorer, *www.oecd.org/gov/regionaldevelopment*.
• Territorial grids, *www.oecd.org/gov/regional/statisticsindicators*.

Share of national population in the ten per cent of regions with the largest population, small regions
Percentage

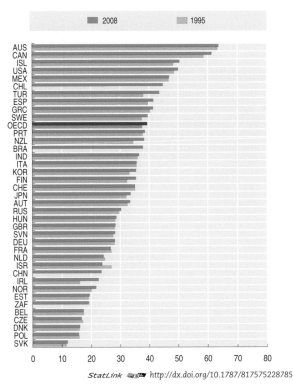

StatLink http://dx.doi.org/10.1787/817575228785

Regions with the highest population density in each country, small regions
Inhabitants per km², 2008

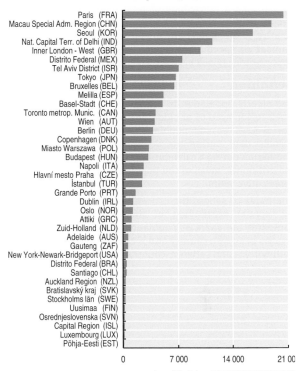

StatLink http://dx.doi.org/10.1787/817588537262

Distribution of the national population into urban, intermediate and rural regions, small regions
Percentage, 2008

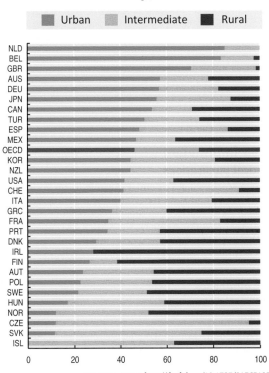

StatLink http://dx.doi.org/10.1787/817651371158

Index of geographic concentration of population, small regions

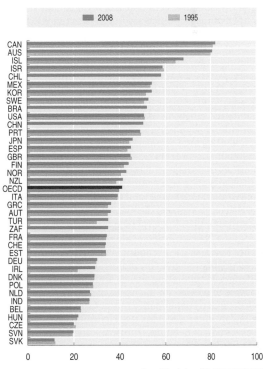

StatLink http://dx.doi.org/10.1787/817723667414

ELDERLY POPULATION BY REGION

In all OECD countries, populations aged 65 years and over have dramatically increased over the last 30 years, both in size and as a percentage of total population. As elderly people tend to be concentrated in few areas within each country, a small number of regions will have to face a number of specific social and economic challenges and opportunities raised by ageing population.

Definition

The elderly population is the number of inhabitants of a given region aged 65 or older. The population can be either the average annual population or the population at a specific date during the year considered. The average population during a calendar year is generally calculated as the arithmetic mean of the population on 1 January of two consecutive years.

The index of geographic concentration offers a picture of the spatial distribution of the elderly population. It compares the share of population and land area over all regions in a given country and is constructed to account for both within- and between-country differences in the size of

all regions. It lies between 0 (no concentration) and 100 (maximum concentration) and is suitable for international comparisons.

The elderly dependency rate is defined as the ratio between the elderly population and the working age (15-64 years) population.

Comparability

As for the other regional statistics, the comparability of elderly population data is affected by differences in the definition of the regions and the different geography of rural and urban communities (see Population by region), both within and among countries.

Overview

The elderly population tends to be concentrated in few areas within each country. About 35% of elderly people within the OECD live in only 10% of regions. This share has not changed significantly in the past ten years with the exception of Ireland, due to the increase of this share in the region of Dublin.

According to the geographic concentration index, Canada, Australia and Iceland are the countries with the highest concentration of elderly population. A high geographic concentration of the elderly can facilitate the provision of services. The concentration of the elderly population in a given region may be a function of its total population – the higher its total population, the more its elderly people – or of regional disparities in the age structure – same population but more elderly people. A comparison of the concentration indexes of total and elderly population shows that, on average, the elderly population is less concentrated than the total population.

Besides the concentration of elderly people, the balance between the economically active and the retired population gives an indication of a region's challenges in generating wealth and sufficient resources to provide for the needs of elderly people. In 2008, the elderly dependency rate across OECD regions was higher in rural regions than in urban ones, with the exception of Belgium, Hungary, Italy, Poland and the Czech Republic.

Sources
* OECD (2009), *OECD Regions at a Glance 2009*, OECD, Paris.

Further information
Analytical publications
* Oliveira Martins J., F. Gonand, P. Antolin, C. de la Maisonneuve and K.-Y. Yoo (2005), *The Impact of Ageing on Demand, Factor Markets and Growth*, OECD Economics Department Working Papers, No. 420, OECD, Paris.
* Spiezia, V. (2003), "Measuring Regional Economies", OECD Statistics Brief, No. 6, October, OECD, Paris, *www.oecd.org/std/statisticsbrief*.

Online databases
* *OECD Regional Database*.

Web sites
* OECD eXplorer, *www.oecd.org/gov/regionaldevelopment*.
* Territorial grids, *www.oecd.org/gov/regional/statisticsindicators*.

Elderly dependency rate in urban and rural regions, small regions
Percentage, 2008

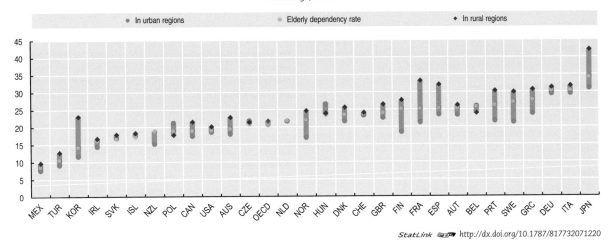

StatLink http://dx.doi.org/10.1787/817732071220

Share of elderly population in the ten per cent of small regions with the largest elderly population
Percentage

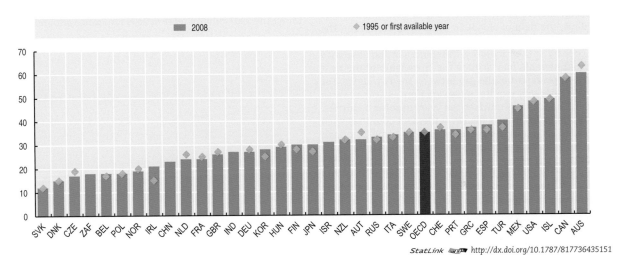

StatLink http://dx.doi.org/10.1787/817736435151

Index of geographic concentration of the elderly and total population, small regions
Year 2008

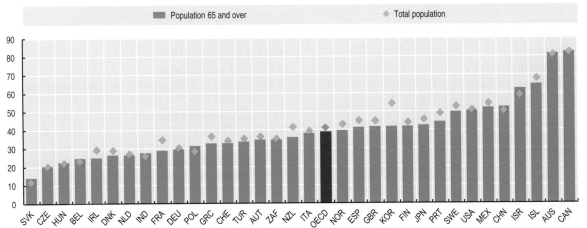

StatLink http://dx.doi.org/10.1787/817741046441

IMMIGRANT POPULATION

National views on the appropriate definition of the immigrant population vary from country to country. Despite this, it is possible to provide an internationally comparable picture of the size of the immigrant population, based either on nationality or country-of-birth criteria.

Definition

Nationality and place of birth are the two criteria most commonly used to define the "immigrant" population. The foreign-born population covers all persons who have ever migrated from their country of birth to their current country of residence. The foreign population consists of persons who still have the nationality of their home country. It may include persons born in the host country.

Comparability

The difference across countries between the size of the foreign-born population and that of the foreign population depends on the rules governing the acquisition of citizenship in each country. In some countries, children born in the country automatically acquire the citizenship of their country of birth (jus soli, the right of soil) while in other countries, they retain the nationality of their parents (jus sanguinis, the right of blood). In others yet, they retain the nationality of their parents at birth but receive that of the host country at their majority. Differences in the ease with which immigrants may acquire the citizenship of the host country explain part of the gap between the two series. For example, residency requirements vary from as little as three years in Canada to as much as ten years in some countries. The naturalisation rate is high in settlement countries such as Australia, Canada, New Zealand and in some European countries including Belgium, Sweden and the Netherlands. In general, the foreign-born criterion gives substantially higher percentages for the immigrant population than the definition based on nationality. This is because many foreign-born persons acquire the nationality of the host country and no longer appear as foreign nationals. The place of birth, however, does not change, except when there are changes in country borders.

The data shown for the year 2000 come from a special census data collection covering almost all OECD countries. The foreign-born population data shown here include persons born abroad as nationals of their current country of residence. The prevalence of such persons among the foreign-born can be significant in some countries, in particular France and Portugal (repatriations from former colonies).

For a number of countries, reliable data on the foreign-born population are available only at the time of a population census. To make up for this deficiency, the OECD has developed estimates for a certain number of countries, applying two methods, the choice of which depends on the auxiliary information available (see *www.oecd.org/els/ migration/foreignborn*).

For the foreign-born population, the data shown in the table under the 2000 column refer to 1999 for France; 2001 for Greece, Italy, the Slovak Republic, Spain; 2002 for Poland; the data under the 2007 column refer to 2003 for Germany and 2005 for Mexico. For the foreign population, the data shown in the table under the 2000 column refer to 1999 for France; 2001 for Australia, Canada, Greece; 2002 for Poland; those under the 2007 column refer to 2005 for France and Ireland.

Overview

The foreign-born population has increased in the past decade in all countries for which data are available. It is especially high in Australia, Canada, Luxembourg, New Zealand and Switzerland. Other countries, such as Spain, the Slovak Republic and Ireland, still do not report a high share of foreign-born population but have seen a spectacular increase in recent years. By contrast, the foreign population tends to increase more slowly, because inflows of foreign nationals tend to be counterbalanced by persons acquiring the nationality of the host country.

Sources

- OECD (2009), *International Migration Outlook: SOPEMI 2009*, OECD, Paris.

Further information

Analytical publications

- OECD (2008), *A Profile of Immigrant Populations in the 21st Century: Data from OECD Countries*, OECD, Paris.

Methodological publications

- Lemaître, G. and C. Thoreau (2006), *Estimating the foreign-born population on a current basis*, OECD, Paris.
- OECD (2005), "Counting immigrants and expatriates in OECD countries – a new perspective", *Trends in International Migration: SOPEMI – 2004 Edition*, OECD, Paris.

Online databases

- *Database on Immigrants in OECD Countries (DIOC)*.
- *OECD International Migration Statistics*.

Foreign-born and foreign populations

	As a percentage of total population										As a percentage of all foreign-born
	Foreign-born population					Foreign population					Foreign-born nationals
	1995	2000	2005	2006	2007	1995	2000	2005	2006	2007	2000
Australia	23.0	23.0	23.8	24.1	25.0	..	7.4	..	7.7	..	68.4
Austria	..	10.5	13.5	14.1	14.2	8.5	8.8	9.7	9.9	10.1	40.9
Belgium	9.7	10.3	12.1	12.5	13.0	9.0	8.4	8.6	8.8	9.1	40.8
Canada	17.2	18.1	19.5	19.8	20.1	..	5.3	..	6.0	..	72.6
Czech Republic	..	4.2	5.1	5.5	6.2	1.5	1.9	2.7	3.1	3.8	79.8
Denmark	4.8	5.8	6.5	6.6	6.9	4.2	4.8	5.0	5.1	5.5	40.3
Finland	2.0	2.6	3.4	3.6	3.8	1.3	1.8	2.2	2.3	2.5	41.6
France	..	7.4	8.1	8.3	8.5	..	..	5.6	..	..	53.1
Germany	11.5	12.5	..	..	..	8.8	8.9	8.2	8.2	8.2	..
Greece	..	..	..	..	..	..	2.9	5.2	5.3	5.7	41.5
Hungary	2.8	2.9	3.3	3.4	3.8	1.4	1.1	1.5	1.6	1.7	71.1
Ireland	..	8.7	12.7	14.4	15.7	2.7	3.3	6.3	..	..	45.2
Italy	..	..	..	..	..	1.7	2.4	4.6	5.0	5.8	47.5
Japan	..	..	..	..	..	1.1	1.3	1.6	1.6	1.7	..
Korea	..	..	..	..	..	0.2	0.4	1.1	1.4	1.7	..
Luxembourg	30.9	33.2	33.8	34.8	36.2	33.4	37.3	40.4	41.6	43.2	13.0
Mexico	0.4	0.5	0.4	..	..	..	..	..	..	..	..
Netherlands	9.1	10.1	10.6	10.6	10.7	4.7	4.2	4.2	4.2	4.2	65.0
New Zealand	..	17.2	20.5	21.2	21.6	..	..	..	..	..	..
Norway	5.5	6.8	8.2	8.7	9.5	3.8	4.0	4.8	5.1	5.7	47.6
Poland	..	..	..	..	..	..	..	..	0.1	0.2	96.1
Portugal	5.4	5.1	6.3	6.1	6.1	1.7	2.1	4.1	4.1	4.2	66.3
Slovak Republic	..	..	4.6	5.6	6.8	0.4	0.5	0.5	0.6	0.8	84.2
Spain	..	4.9	11.1	11.9	13.4	..	3.4	9.5	10.3	11.6	30.9
Sweden	10.5	11.3	12.4	12.9	13.4	6.0	5.4	5.3	5.4	5.7	62.5
Switzerland	21.4	21.9	23.8	24.1	24.9	18.9	19.3	20.3	20.3	20.8	29.3
Turkey	..	1.9	..	..	..	..	..	..	..	..	79.2
United Kingdom	6.9	7.9	9.7	10.1	10.2	3.4	4.0	5.2	5.8	6.5	..
United States	9.3	11.0	12.9	13.0	13.6	6.0	6.6	..	7.4	..	46.4
Brazil	..	0.4	..	..	..	..	0.4	0.4	0.4	0.4	25.4
Chile	..	..	..	..	..	..	1.2	..	..	..	..
Estonia	..	18.4	..	..	..	..	6.9	..	..	..	38.1
Russian Federation	..	8.3	..	..	..	..	1.0	..	..	..	..
Slovenia	..	10.8	11.1	11.3	..	2.4	2.1	..	..	..	..

StatLink http://dx.doi.org/10.1787/823651035743

Foreign-born population

As a percentage of total population, 2007 or latest available year

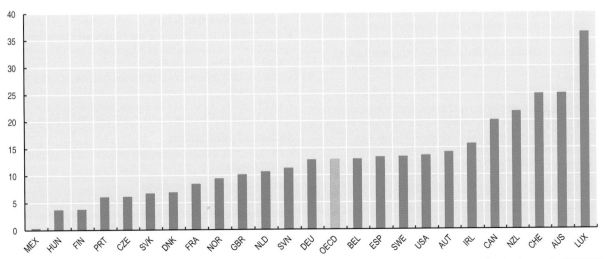

StatLink http://dx.doi.org/10.1787/817748232510

TRENDS IN MIGRATION

Migration movements include not only entries of persons of foreign nationality, on which public attention tends to be focused, but also include movements of nationals and of emigrants. Net migration summarises the overall effect of these movements. Migration currently represents, in almost all OECD countries, the main source of increases in population.

Definition

Net migration is defined as the total number of immigrant nationals and foreigners minus the total of emigrant foreigners and nationals. Arrivals and departures for purposes such as tourism and business travel are not included in the statistics.

The net migration rate is expressed per 1 000 inhabitants. The three-year averages referred to concern the years 2006 to 2008 (end of period); and 1995 to 1997 (beginning of period).

Comparability

The main sources of information on migration vary across countries. This may pose problems for the comparability of available data on inflows and outflows of migrants. However, since the comparability problems generally relate to the extent to which short-term movements are covered, taking the difference between arrivals and departures tends to eliminate the movements that are the main source of non-comparability.

Despite this feature, net migration data should be interpreted with care, because unauthorised movements are not taken into account in the inflows and these unauthorised movements are significant in some OECD countries. In addition, the data on outflows are of uneven quality, with departures being only partially recorded in many countries or having to be estimated in others.

The net migration rate is used to describe the contribution of international migration to population increase, the other component being natural increase, defined as the difference between the number of births and the number of deaths in a given year.

Sources
- OECD (2009), *Labour Force Statistics*, OECD, Paris.

Further information
Analytical publications
- OECD (2001), *Migration Policies and EU Enlargement: The Case of Central and Eastern Europe*, OECD, Paris.
- OECD (2003), *Migration and the Labour Market in Asia: Recent Trends and Policies – 2002 Edition*, OECD, Paris.
- OECD (2004), *Migration for Employment: Bilateral Agreements at a Crossroads*, OECD, Paris.
- OECD (2004), *Trade and Migration: Building Bridges for Global Labour Mobility*, OECD, Paris.
- OECD (2006), *Local Economic and Employment Development (LEED) – From Immigration to Integration: Local Solutions to a Global Challenge*, OECD, Paris.
- OECD (2009), *International Migration Outlook: SOPEMI 2009*, OECD, Paris.
- OECD (2008), *A Profile of Immigrant Populations in the 21st Century: Data from OECD Countries*, OECD, Paris.

Statistical publications
- OECD (2007), *OECD Employment Outlook – 2007 Edition*, OECD, Paris.

Methodological publications
- Dumont, J.-C. and G. Lemaître (2005), *Counting Immigrants and Expatriates in OECD Countries: A New Perspective*, OECD Social Employment and Migration Working Papers, No. 25, OECD, Paris.

Online databases
- *OECD International Migration Database.*

Overview

Estonia, Poland, the Netherlands, Japan and Turkey are the only countries among those shown here that recorded negative or zero net migration in the three years to 2008. Ireland, Iceland, Luxembourg and Spain top the league showing net migration rates above 10 per thousand in recent years. The former emigration countries (Ireland, Italy, Portugal and Spain) figure prominently among those countries experiencing high net migration, a trend which is likely to continue in the future.

In most countries, net migration rates are higher than the levels recorded in the mid 1990s, with the increase being especially large in several Nordic countries, in countries in southern and continental Europe as well as in Australia. With the retirement of baby-boomers in the near future and the entry of smaller youth cohorts in the labour market, labour supply needs may well require a further rise in net migration in the future.

There are nonetheless a number of countries where net migration rates are currently lower than was the case five to ten years ago. These include Israel, New Zealand, the Russian Federation, Greece, Germany, Turkey and the Netherlands.

Net migration rate
Per 1 000 inhabitants

	1995	1996	1997	1998	1999	2000	2001	2002	2003	2004	2005	2006	2007	2008
Australia	5.9	5.3	3.9	4.8	5.5	5.8	7.0	5.6	5.5	5.3	6.7	8.8	10.3	..
Austria	0.3	0.5	0.2	1.1	2.5	2.2	4.1	4.1	4.9	6.2	5.4	2.9	4.2	4.1
Belgium	2.7	2.4	1.9	2.1	2.7	2.5	3.4	4.0	3.9	4.2	4.5	4.8	..	..
Canada	5.5	5.6	5.2	3.9	5.2	6.5	8.1	7.0	6.7	6.6	7.0	6.9	7.3	..
Czech Republic	1.0	1.0	1.2	0.9	0.9	0.6	-0.8	1.2	2.5	1.8	3.5	3.4	8.1	6.9
Denmark	5.5	3.2	2.3	2.1	1.7	1.7	2.2	1.7	1.1	0.9	1.2	1.8	4.2	5.3
Finland	0.6	0.6	0.8	0.6	0.6	0.4	1.2	1.0	1.2	1.3	1.7	1.9	2.5	2.6
France	0.7	0.6	0.7	0.8	1.0	1.2	1.4	1.6	1.7	1.7	1.6	1.5	1.1	1.2
Germany	4.9	3.4	1.1	0.6	2.5	2.0	3.3	2.7	1.7	1.0	1.0	0.3	0.5	..
Greece	7.3	6.6	5.7	5.1	4.1	2.7	3.5	3.5	3.3	3.7	3.5	3.6	3.6	..
Hungary	1.7	1.7	1.7	1.7	1.7	1.7	1.0	0.4	1.6	1.8	1.7	1.9	1.4	..
Iceland	-2.6	-2.6	0.3	3.2	4.0	6.1	3.4	-1.0	-0.5	1.8	13.0	17.3	16.5	3.6
Ireland	1.6	4.6	5.1	4.5	6.4	8.4	10.0	8.4	7.8	11.6	15.9	..	..	..
Italy	1.6	2.6	2.2	1.6	1.8	3.1	2.2	6.1	10.6	9.6	5.2	6.4	..	..
Japan	-0.4	-0.1	0.1	0.3	-0.1	0.3	-0.4	0.5	-0.3	-0.4	-	-	-0.4	..
Luxembourg	11.2	8.9	9.0	9.6	10.9	8.2	2.5	5.8	12.0	9.6	13.1	11.4	12.5	15.8
Netherlands	0.9	1.1	1.8	2.7	2.6	3.4	3.2	1.5	-	-1.0	-1.7	-1.9	-0.4	1.6
New Zealand	7.7	6.6	2.0	-1.7	-2.3	-2.9	2.5	9.7	8.7	3.7	1.7	3.6	1.4	0.9
Norway	1.4	1.4	2.5	3.2	4.3	2.0	1.8	3.7	2.4	2.8	3.9	5.1	8.5	9.0
Poland	-0.5	-0.3	-0.3	-0.3	-0.4	-0.5	-0.4	-0.5	-0.4	-0.2	-0.3	-0.9	-0.5	-0.4
Portugal	2.2	2.6	2.9	3.2	3.7	4.6	6.3	6.8	6.1	4.5	3.6	..	..	..
Slovak Republic	0.5	0.4	0.3	0.2	0.3	0.3	0.2	0.2	0.3	0.5	0.6	0.7	1.3	1.3
Spain	0.9	1.3	1.6	3.1	4.9	8.9	10.1	15.7	14.5	14.7	15.0	14.2	16.0	..
Sweden	1.2	0.7	0.7	1.2	1.6	2.8	3.3	3.5	3.2	2.8	3.0	5.6	5.9	6.1
Switzerland	2.1	-0.8	-1.0	0.2	2.3	2.8	5.8	6.7	5.9	5.4	4.8	5.2	9.9	12.8
Turkey	1.6	1.6	1.6	1.5	1.5	-	-	-	-	-	-	..	..	..
United States	4.4	4.6	4.8	4.2	4.4	4.6	3.8	3.7	3.0	3.1	3.3	3.2	2.9	2.9
Chile	0.8	..	..	..	..	0.4	..	..	..	..	0.4	..	..	..
Estonia	-5.7	-4.0	-1.8	-0.8	-0.4	-0.7	-1.4	-1.1	-1.6	-1.4	-2.4	-2.5	-0.5	-0.6
Israel	11.9	10.4	9.2	8.2	11.9	9.8	6.2	3.3	1.6	2.0	2.4	2.4	2.1	1.8
Russian Federation	4.4	3.5	3.5	2.9	1.8	2.5	1.9	1.6	0.6	0.7	0.9	1.1	1.8	1.8
Slovenia	1.3	3.3	1.2	-1.1	1.2	1.3	1.5	0.9	1.7	1.0	3.2	3.1	7.1	9.2

StatLink http://dx.doi.org/10.1787/823677044676

Net migration rate
Per 1 000 inhabitants, annual average

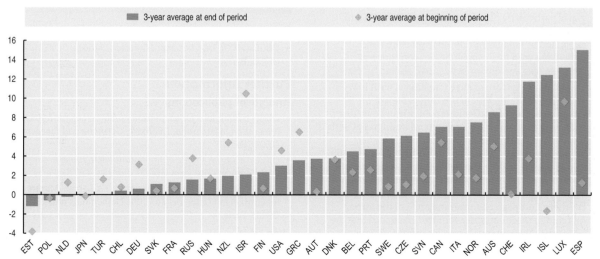

StatLink http://dx.doi.org/10.1787/817761100575

MIGRATION AND EMPLOYMENT

In most OECD countries, employment rates for immigrants are lower than for native-born persons. However, the situation is more diverse if one disaggregates employment rates by educational attainment.

Definition

The employment rate is calculated as the share of employed persons aged 15-64 in the total population (active and inactive persons) of the same age. In accordance with ILO definitions, employed persons are those who worked at least one hour or who had a job but were absent from work during the reference week. The educational classification shown is based on the International Standard Classification of Education (ISCED) categories. Generally speaking, "low" corresponds to less than upper secondary education; "intermediate" to upper secondary education; and "high" to tertiary education. Tertiary education includes high-level vocational education feeding into technical or semi-professional occupations.

Comparability

Data for European countries are from the *European Union Labour Force Survey*. Data for the United States and Canada are from the *Current Population Survey* (March supplement) and the 2006 Census, respectively. Even if employment levels can at times be affected by changes in survey design (this occurred in France in 2004) and by survey implementation problems (*e.g.* non-response), data on employment rates are generally consistent over time. However, comparability of education levels between immigrants and the native-born population and across countries is only approximate. The educational qualifications of other countries may not fit exactly into national educational categories because the duration of study or the programme content for what appear to be equivalent qualifications may not be the same. Likewise, the reduction of the ISCED classification into three categories may result in some loss of information regarding the duration of study, the programme orientation, etc. For example, high educational qualifications can include programmes of durations varying from two years (in the case of short, university-level technical programmes) to seven years or more (in the case of PhDs).

Overview

Labour market outcomes of immigrants and natives vary significantly across OECD countries, and differences by educational attainment are even larger. In all OECD countries, the employment rate increases with educational level. While people with tertiary education find work more easily and are less exposed to unemployment, access to tertiary education does not necessarily guarantee equal employment rates for immigrants and native-born persons. In all OECD countries, employment rates are higher for native-born persons with high educational qualification than for foreign-born persons with the same qualification. The gap is particularly high for countries such as Poland, Germany and Austria. This difference can be partly explained by language proficiency problems and difficulties with the recognition or acceptance of competences and diplomas acquired abroad.

The situation is more diverse for persons with low educational attainment. In the United States, Luxembourg and some southern European countries such as Greece and Italy, foreign-born immigrants with low educational qualifications have much higher employment rates than their native-born counterparts. The reverse is true for the Netherlands, Denmark and Sweden. This higher employment rate of the foreign-born population with low educational attainment in southern European countries may reflect the strong demand in these countries for low-skilled jobs that are no longer taken up by the smaller cohorts of young native-born workers.

Sources

- OECD (2009), *International Migration Outlook: SOPEMI 2009*, OECD, Paris.

Further information

Analytical publications

- OECD (2007), *Jobs for Immigrants (Vol. 1): Labour Market Integration in Australia, Denmark, Germany and Sweden*, OECD, Paris.
- OECD (2008), *A Profile of Immigrant Populations in the 21st Century: Data from OECD Countries*, OECD, Paris.
- OECD (2008), *Jobs for Immigrants Vol. 2: Labour Market Integration in France, Belgium, the Netherlands and Portugal*, OECD, Paris.

Web sites

- OECD International Migration Statistics, *www.oecd.org/els/migration/statistics*.

Employment rates of native-born and foreign-born population by educational attainment

As a percentage of total population, 2007

	Native-born				Foreign-born			
	Low education	Intermediate education	High education	Total	Low education	Intermediate education	High education	Total
Austria	49.8	76.6	89.2	72.8	54.6	69.7	75.1	65.0
Belgium	41.4	66.9	85.0	63.5	35.4	55.8	72.6	50.9
Canada	50.6	75.5	82.7	73.0	51.6	68.9	77.4	70.5
Czech Republic	23.7	72.6	84.1	66.1	40.5	72.4	82.0	67.3
Denmark	65.0	82.6	88.6	78.8	53.7	69.1	76.2	62.5
Finland	46.4	74.2	85.5	70.5	40.9	72.8	75.6	63.5
France	46.6	69.8	81.3	65.3	50.1	64.3	68.0	58.5
Germany	43.2	74.2	87.9	70.9	49.4	67.7	72.3	61.0
Greece	48.7	61.7	82.6	60.9	66.0	65.8	70.6	66.6
Hungary	27.2	64.7	80.1	57.2	38.8	67.3	76.7	64.5
Ireland	48.9	73.7	87.4	68.2	49.6	75.9	80.6	72.9
Italy	45.1	67.5	77.9	58.0	59.7	71.0	74.5	65.9
Luxembourg	39.3	61.6	81.8	59.2	64.0	66.2	84.7	71.1
Netherlands	61.8	81.1	88.0	77.0	49.3	65.8	77.3	62.4
Norway	57.8	81.7	89.6	77.2	51.5	72.6	86.7	69.9
Poland	24.9	61.1	82.9	57.1	68.8	29.3	66.0	36.8
Portugal	65.5	63.9	83.9	67.3	..	71.8	86.0	73.1
Slovak Republic	14.6	69.0	83.0	60.7	..	69.8	..	66.0
Spain	55.1	66.6	83.4	64.5	63.9	74.3	78.1	70.3
Sweden	54.9	82.5	89.5	76.2	46.9	68.4	77.6	63.1
Switzerland	55.4	81.3	92.6	80.4	64.8	75.0	82.1	73.7
Turkey	41.5	50.0	72.9	45.8	41.3	55.8	66.3	48.7
United States	35.1	71.6	84.2	69.8	61.5	72.2	79.9	71.2
OECD average	45.3	70.9	84.5	67.0	52.5	67.0	76.7	64.2
Estonia	32.7	74.6	87.6	68.6	41.8	73.6	83.1	74.5
Israel	27.6	56.0	83.0	56.3	40.0	63.3	79.9	66.7
Slovenia	41.6	70.7	87.8	67.8	54.8	72.7	81.8	68.0

StatLink http://dx.doi.org/10.1787/823685188133

Gap in employment rate between native-born and foreign-born population by educational level

Percentage points, 2007 or latest available year

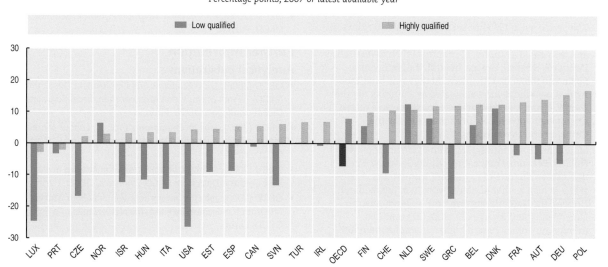

StatLink http://dx.doi.org/10.1787/817830358176

MIGRATION AND UNEMPLOYMENT

Immigrant workers are more affected by unemployment in traditional European immigration countries. Conversely, in North America, Australia and, to a lesser extent, Southern Europe, the unemployment rate depends less on the place of birth. Some groups, such as young immigrants, women or older immigrants have greater difficulties in finding jobs.

Definition

The unemployment rate is the share of the unemployed in the total labour force (employed and unemployed persons). In accordance with the ILO standards, unemployed persons consist of those persons who report that they are without work during the reference week, that they are available for work and that they have taken active steps to find work during the four weeks preceding the interview.

Comparability

Data for the European countries are from the *European Union Labour Force Survey*. Data for Australia are taken from the *National Labour Force Survey*; those for Canada from the *Survey of Labour and Income Dynamics* and the 2006 Census; and those for the United States from the *Current Population Survey* (March supplement). Even if unemployment levels can at times be affected by changes in the survey design (this occurred in France in 2004) and by survey implementation problems (*e.g.* non-response), data on unemployment rates are generally consistent over time.

Overview

In 2007, unemployment rates decreased both for foreign- and native-born populations in most OECD countries but immigrants in most European OECD countries remained much more affected by unemployment than the native population. In Belgium, Finland, Germany and France, the unemployment rate of immigrants was above 13%. The unemployment rate was more than twice the level observed for the native-born population in Switzerland, Austria, Belgium, the Netherlands, Denmark, Sweden, Norway and Finland. In other countries, especially in settlement countries (Australia, Canada, the United States) and in recent immigration countries (Greece, Portugal), the unemployment rate does not vary much by birth status.

The period since 1995 has seen some sizable declines in the unemployment rates of the foreign-born (both men and women) in a number of countries, such as Australia, Denmark, Sweden, Greece, Ireland, the Netherlands, Spain and the United Kingdom. At the same time, labour market conditions have stagnated in a number of other countries and have had adverse consequences on the unemployment rates for immigrants in Austria, Germany and Luxembourg.

More than 15% of immigrant women are unemployed in Finland, Belgium, France, Greece and Germany. The unemployment rate of immigrant women is at least twice as high as that of native women in Switzerland, Norway, the Netherlands, Belgium, Finland, Austria, Luxembourg and Sweden. In all OECD countries, immigrant women have a higher unemployment rate than native women, but this difference does not always increase with the level of qualifications.

Sources

- OECD (2009), *International Migration Outlook: SOPEMI 2009*, OECD, Paris.

Further information

Analytical publications

- OECD (2006), *Local Economic and Employment Development (LEED) – From Immigration to Integration: Local Solutions to a Global Challenge*, OECD, Paris.
- OECD (2007), *Jobs for Immigrants (Vol. 1): Labour Market Integration in Australia, Denmark, Germany and Sweden*, OECD, Paris.
- OECD (2008), *A Profile of Immigrant Populations in the 21st Century: Data from OECD Countries*, OECD, Paris.
- OECD (2008), *Jobs for Immigrants Vol. 2: Labour Market Integration in France, Belgium, the Netherlands and Portugal*, OECD, Paris.

Web sites

- OECD International Migration Statistics, *www.oecd.org/els/migration/statistics*.

Unemployment rates of foreign- and native-born populations

As a percentage of total labour force

	Men						Women						Total	
	Native-born			Foreign-born			Native-born			Foreign-born			Native-born	Foreign-born
	1995	2000	2007	1995	2000	2007	1995	2000	2007	1995	2000	2007	2007	2007
Australia	8.4	6.6	3.4	10.6	6.5	4.1	7.7	5.8	4.2	9.6	7.0	5.1	4.2	4.2
Austria	3.6	4.3	3.1	6.6	8.7	8.4	4.6	4.2	4.1	7.3	7.2	9.7	3.5	9.0
Belgium	6.3	4.2	5.6	16.9	14.7	15.8	11.2	7.4	7.5	23.8	17.5	17.2	6.4	16.4
Canada	8.6	5.7	..	10.4	6.1	..	9.8	6.2	..	13.3	8.7	..	..	..
Czech Republic	..	..	4.2	..	..	7.6	..	..	6.7	..	..	10.8	5.3	9.0
Denmark	6.4	3.4	3.0	20.5	9.5	8.6	8.4	4.3	3.9	20.7	9.6	7.9	3.4	8.2
Finland	17.7	10.3	6.5	..	..	12.0	16.1	12.0	7.0	..	..	17.4	6.7	14.5
France	9.1	7.7	7.2	16.6	14.5	11.9	13.6	11.3	7.7	19.0	19.7	15.1	7.4	13.4
Germany	..	6.9	7.7	..	12.9	14.9	..	8.0	8.1	..	12.1	13.5	7.8	14.3
Greece	6.1	7.4	5.3	14.0	9.5	4.9	13.7	16.6	12.8	20.8	21.1	14.3	8.4	8.7
Hungary	..	7.3	7.2	..	..	2.6	..	5.8	7.7	..	..	6.1	7.5	4.3
Ireland	12.0	4.4	4.7	16.8	..	6.0	11.9	4.2	4.1	15.4	..	5.7	4.4	5.9
Italy	9.3	8.4	4.9	..	6.5	5.3	16.3	14.9	7.6	23.5	21.2	11.4	6.0	7.9
Luxembourg	..	..	3.0	..	..	4.3	..	..	4.4	..	..	5.1	3.6	4.6
Netherlands	4.9	1.8	2.7	19.5	5.4	7.5	7.7	3.0	3.6	19.8	7.6	7.7	3.1	7.6
Norway	..	3.4	2.3	..	6.8	6.1	..	3.2	2.3	..	..	4.0	2.3	5.1
Poland	..	..	9.1	..	..	..	..	..	10.4	..	..	..	8.4	9.4
Portugal	6.6	3.1	7.0	..	3.9	7.3	7.8	4.9	10.0	..	5.4	12.1	..	9.6
Slovak Republic	..	..	9.9	..	..	..	..	..	12.8	..	..	..	11.2	..
Spain	18.0	9.5	6.0	24.4	12.4	8.4	30.5	20.5	10.5	30.5	20.7	12.6	7.9	10.3
Sweden	7.9	5.1	5.1	24.8	12.3	11.7	6.6	4.2	5.5	18.5	10.8	12.6	5.3	12.1
Switzerland	..	..	2.0	..	..	5.8	..	..	3.2	..	..	8.8	2.6	7.1
United Kingdom	9.9	5.9	5.3	14.2	9.6	7.0	6.7	4.6	4.4	10.9	7.8	8.4	4.9	7.6
United States	6.2	4.5	5.4	7.9	4.5	4.8	5.3	4.2	4.3	8.2	5.5	4.0	4.9	4.5
OECD average	8.8	5.8	5.2	15.6	9.0	7.9	11.1	7.7	6.6	17.2	12.1	9.9	5.7	8.8
Estonia	..	..	5.3	..	13.4	..	..	11.8	3.9	..	11.1	..	4.6	5.7
Israel	5.8	8.8	7.4	5.2	7.8	5.4	9.0	9.4	8.8	7.9	8.9	6.6	8.0	6.0
Slovenia	..	..	4.1	..	10.0	4.0	..	7.1	5.8	..	7.9	7.8	4.9	5.7

StatLink http://dx.doi.org/10.1787/823715202068

Foreign-born unemployment rate relative to native-born unemployment rate

Ratio, 2007 or latest available year

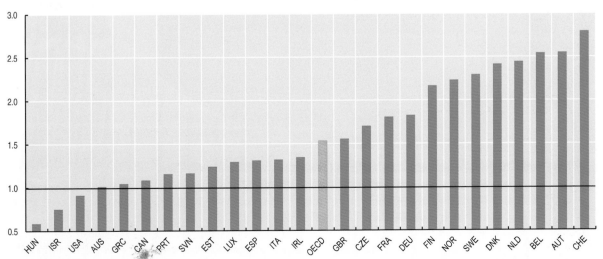

StatLink http://dx.doi.org/10.1787/818012473347

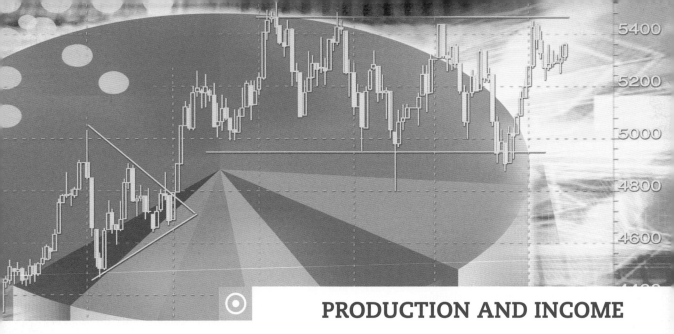

PRODUCTION AND INCOME

SIZE OF GDP

Gross domestic product (GDP) is the standard measure of the value of the goods and services produced by a country during a period. Per capita GDP is a broad indicator of economic living standards.

Each country calculates GDP in its own currency. In order to compare countries, these estimates have to be converted into a common currency. Often, the conversion is made using exchange rates, but these give a misleading comparison of the volumes of goods and services produced. Comparisons of GDP between countries are best made using purchasing power parities (PPPs) to convert each country's GDP into a common currency. PPPs are currency converters that equalise the purchasing power of the different currencies (see also Rates of conversion).

Definition

What does gross domestic product mean? "Gross" signifies that no deduction has been made for the depreciation of machinery, buildings and other capital products used in production. "Domestic" means that it refers to production by the resident institutional units of each country. As many products are used to produce other products, GDP measures production in terms of value added.

GDP can be measured in three different ways: as output less intermediate consumption (i.e. value added) plus taxes on products (such as VAT) less subsidies on products; as income earned from production, obtained by summing employee compensation, the gross operating surplus of enterprises and government, the gross mixed income of unincorporated enterprises and net taxes on production and imports (VAT, payroll tax, import duties, etc, less subsidies); or as final expenditure on the goods and services produced, obtained by summing final consumption expenditures, gross fixed capital formation, changes in inventories and exports less imports.

Comparability

All OECD countries follow the 1993 System of National Accounts, implying that data are highly comparable across countries. Because of a relatively large number of frontier workers, data on GDP per capita for Luxembourg and, to a lesser extent, Switzerland, are to some extent overstated compared with other countries. GDP data for Australia and New Zealand refer to fiscal years.

For some countries, data for the latest year have been estimated by the OECD. For several countries, historical data have also been estimated by the OECD (by linking the new and old series when countries revise their methodologies but only supply revised data for recent years).

Relatively minor differences in the measured per capita GDP can result in a different country order that may not be statistically or economically significant.

Sources
- OECD (2010), *National Accounts of OECD Countries*, OECD, Paris.
- For Brazil, China, India, Indonesia and South Africa: IMF (2009), *World Economic Outlook (WEO)*, IMF, Washington, DC.

Further information
Analytical publications
- OECD (2003), *The Sources of Economic Growth in OECD Countries*, OECD, Paris.
- OECD (2008), *OECD Economic Outlook, June No. 83 – Vol. 2008/1*, OECD, Paris.

Statistical publications
- Maddison, A. (2003), *The World Economy: Historical Perspectives*, OECD, Paris, also available on CD-ROM, *www.theworldeconomy.org*.
- OECD, African Development Bank (2008), *African Economic Outlook 2007/2008*, OECD, Paris, also available on CD-ROM, *www.sourceoecd.org/9789264045514*.
- OECD (2008), *OECD Latin American Economic Outlook 2009*, OECD, Paris, also available on CD-ROM, *www.sourceoecd.org/9789264038264*.
- OECD (2009), *National Accounts at a Glance 2009*, OECD, Paris, also available on CD-ROM, *www.sourceoecd.org/9789264067219*.

Methodological publications
- OECD (2000), *OECD Glossaries, System of National Accounts, 1993 – Glossary*, OECD, Paris.
- UN, OECD, IMF, Eurostat (eds.) (1993), *System of National Accounts 1993*, United Nations, Geneva, *http://unstats.un.org/unsd/sna1993*.

Online databases
- *OECD National Accounts Statistics.*
- *OECD Economic Outlook Statistics.*

Web sites
- OECD Economic Outlook – Sources and Methods, *www.oecd.org/eco/sources-and-methods*.

Overview

Among OECD countries, the United States has, by far, the largest GDP, followed by Japan and, by some distance, the four largest EU members – Germany, the United Kingdom, France and Italy. The next four OECD countries are Mexico, Spain, Korea and Canada. China's GDP is a little over half of that of the US, while those of India and the Russian Federation are equivalent to 23% and 16%.

Per capita GDP for the OECD as a whole was 33 700 US dollars in 2008. Six OECD countries had per capita GDP in excess of 40 000 US dollars – Luxembourg, Norway, United States, Switzerland, Ireland and the Netherlands. About half of all OECD countries had per capita GDP between 30 000 and 45 000 US dollars, while 10 countries had per capita GDP below 30 000 US dollars, with Turkey, Mexico and Poland at the bottom of the distribution.

Gross domestic product
Billion US dollars, current prices and PPPs

	1995	1996	1997	1998	1999	2000	2001	2002	2003	2004	2005	2006	2007	2008
Australia	391.9	411.7	436.9	463.8	497.4	525.4	552.1	584.9	622.3	655.6	696.8	742.9	795.7	831.2
Austria	186.8	193.5	198.5	208.0	215.9	230.5	231.6	244.3	252.3	266.3	274.8	292.0	305.8	315.6
Belgium	227.6	231.5	242.6	248.4	259.0	283.1	292.9	310.0	313.7	324.4	336.6	351.8	368.2	377.9
Canada	666.2	690.0	731.9	770.5	825.0	874.1	909.8	937.8	989.3	1 049.1	1 132.0	1 202.2	1 267.9	1 300.2
Czech Republic	132.4	140.7	142.5	143.7	147.2	154.0	165.4	172.1	183.5	197.0	208.4	224.1	247.7	256.9
Denmark	120.3	126.6	133.5	138.6	143.3	153.9	157.7	165.3	164.0	174.5	179.9	191.3	198.3	202.2
Finland	95.9	98.8	107.9	116.7	122.3	132.9	138.2	143.3	144.2	156.0	160.7	171.6	186.9	190.8
France	1 201.5	1 240.6	1 301.1	1 368.7	1 425.2	1 534.9	1 629.9	1 711.2	1 699.6	1 766.5	1 869.4	1 953.4	2 071.8	2 121.7
Germany	1 836.8	1 888.2	1 934.7	1 989.2	2 063.8	2 133.0	2 211.6	2 275.4	2 357.0	2 466.4	2 586.5	2 710.2	2 853.2	2 909.7
Greece	156.1	162.5	172.9	178.8	185.4	201.0	218.3	237.3	250.2	267.2	273.6	293.8	311.1	324.7
Hungary	93.3	97.2	103.7	111.0	115.3	123.7	138.2	149.9	156.0	164.7	171.0	180.5	188.7	198.1
Iceland	6.2	6.5	7.1	7.6	7.9	8.1	8.7	8.9	8.9	9.9	10.4	10.6	11.3	11.8
Ireland	64.5	70.9	79.6	89.0	97.2	109.0	117.8	129.8	137.7	148.2	160.4	175.3	193.4	184.4
Italy	1 200.1	1 239.7	1 284.7	1 350.2	1 377.2	1 457.6	1 545.9	1 532.0	1 563.1	1 594.7	1 649.4	1 739.8	1 840.1	1 871.7
Japan	2 826.9	2 960.0	3 059.8	3 031.0	3 071.1	3 250.3	3 330.1	3 417.2	3 509.9	3 708.5	3 872.8	4 080.4	4 297.5	4 358.3
Korea	601.6	656.1	698.7	658.2	731.2	809.4	860.7	936.0	965.8	1 039.1	1 096.7	1 191.1	1 287.7	1 344.4
Luxembourg	15.9	16.7	17.1	18.4	21.1	23.4	23.8	25.7	27.4	29.8	31.8	36.5	39.6	41.4
Mexico	686.6	735.8	799.6	849.3	894.1	987.1	1 009.2	1 047.7	1 109.1	1 186.3	1 293.9	1 403.3	1 493.0	1 545.3
Netherlands	333.2	351.5	376.1	400.1	425.8	468.3	494.0	515.8	514.2	540.4	572.9	607.4	648.5	675.1
New Zealand	63.8	66.5	69.8	71.3	76.4	80.3	84.7	89.2	93.3	99.0	102.8	109.1	115.2	116.4
Norway	102.8	114.1	123.2	121.5	133.0	162.3	167.4	168.2	174.8	194.0	218.7	242.6	253.2	280.0
Poland	286.4	310.9	339.7	362.5	382.6	404.3	418.9	442.1	457.7	496.8	526.1	561.1	621.7	659.2
Portugal	131.1	137.0	145.7	153.7	163.9	174.7	183.2	191.3	196.2	201.3	217.9	229.3	240.2	247.3
Slovak Republic	44.6	48.5	52.4	55.6	56.1	59.3	64.9	69.7	73.1	78.8	87.1	96.8	109.4	119.7
Spain	629.8	659.5	700.5	750.4	791.5	858.5	920.1	994.3	1 039.4	1 108.0	1 188.1	1 306.1	1 412.1	1 434.2
Sweden	193.0	200.1	207.2	214.7	228.5	246.3	248.8	258.9	269.3	288.3	291.7	311.7	336.5	340.5
Switzerland	188.5	194.1	202.6	210.4	215.2	228.0	233.9	245.2	246.3	257.4	266.1	288.7	318.5	329.9
Turkey	425.8	465.7	510.9	535.4	517.7	589.3	561.1	572.1	587.7	688.5	781.2	873.7	938.7	991.7
United Kingdom	1 144.0	1 217.9	1 307.5	1 362.8	1 423.0	1 535.4	1 630.5	1 713.7	1 777.5	2 065.1	1 902.2	1 971.3	2 131.5	2 186.0
United States	7 359.3	7 783.9	8 278.9	8 741.0	9 301.0	9 898.8	10 233.9	10 590.2	11 089.2	11 812.3	12 579.7	13 336.2	14 010.8	14 369.4
EU27 total	8 348.3	8 696.0	9 112.2	9 529.6	9 920.3	10 579.4	11 155.6	11 631.9	11 954.6	12 588.4	13 207.4	14 003.4	14 870.1	15 283.6
OECD total	21 413.0	22 516.7	23 767.2	24 720.7	25 914.3	27 696.7	28 783.4	29 879.6	30 972.8	32 871.3	34 809.0	36 978.4	39 094.1	40 135.5
Brazil	1 027.3	1 069.4	1 125.0	1 138.2	1 157.8	1 233.8	1 278.3	1 333.5	1 377.8	1 494.7	1 584.6	1 701.2	1 849.1	1 984.5
Chile	107.3	117.4	127.3	132.9	133.8	142.8	151.1	157.1	166.8	182.0	198.4	214.1	230.5	243.0
China	1 833.4	2 055.1	2 285.8	2 491.9	2 720.8	3 013.2	3 337.3	3 700.1	4 157.8	4 697.9	5 314.4	6 124.4	7 119.4	7 926.5
Estonia	9.1	9.8	11.2	11.7	12.1	13.5	14.6	16.3	18.1	19.9	22.3	24.8	27.7	27.7
India	1 039.6	1 139.5	1 213.1	1 300.2	1 410.6	1 523.1	1 618.0	1 719.2	1 876.5	2 096.1	2 357.8	2 673.6	3 007.9	3 297.8
Indonesia	442.3	486.0	517.8	454.9	465.2	500.7	530.7	563.6	603.2	650.2	705.2	768.2	839.8	909.7
Israel	93.0	100.1	104.6	110.3	130.9	147.8	151.2	154.6	149.0	160.9	162.1	177.1	192.4	204.0
Russian Federation	832.7	818.1	843.0	806.9	870.7	998.3	1 074.5	1 167.9	1 339.3	1 476.3	1 698.0	1 883.2	2 096.7	2 262.7
Slovenia	25.8	27.3	29.3	30.9	32.9	34.8	36.5	39.3	40.8	44.3	47.0	49.9	53.6	56.3
South Africa	234.4	249.1	260.3	264.6	274.8	292.4	307.2	323.6	340.9	366.5	398.8	433.7	468.8	493.5

StatLink ᵐˢᵖ http://dx.doi.org/10.1787/823716683245

Gross domestic product
Billion US dollars, current prices and PPPs, 2008

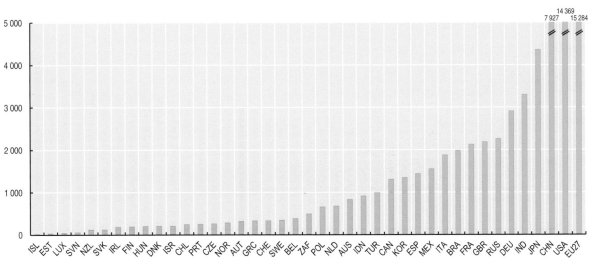

StatLink ᵐˢᵖ http://dx.doi.org/10.1787/818023134435

SIZE OF GDP

GDP per capita
US dollars, current prices and PPPs

	1995	1996	1997	1998	1999	2000	2001	2002	2003	2004	2005	2006	2007	2008
Australia	21 541	22 353	23 479	24 657	26 128	27 266	28 277	29 610	31 137	32 416	33 963	35 679	37 616	38 637
Austria	23 502	24 317	24 913	26 076	27 011	28 773	28 804	30 231	31 077	32 592	33 409	35 312	36 839	37 858
Belgium	22 450	22 797	23 827	24 348	25 333	27 628	28 493	30 014	30 238	31 146	32 141	33 365	34 665	35 288
Canada	22 737	23 301	24 472	25 549	27 135	28 482	29 330	29 893	31 233	32 790	35 033	36 821	38 448	38 975
Czech Republic	12 813	13 644	13 829	13 962	14 312	14 994	16 176	16 872	17 990	19 300	20 366	21 827	23 995	24 631
Denmark	22 993	24 052	25 259	26 139	26 926	28 826	29 442	30 756	30 424	32 296	33 196	35 183	36 326	36 808
Finland	18 773	19 281	20 986	22 650	23 686	25 671	26 635	27 560	27 661	29 851	30 644	32 587	35 346	35 918
France	20 222	20 807	21 747	22 794	23 628	25 276	26 649	27 777	27 396	28 269	29 692	30 819	32 495	33 090
Germany	22 493	23 056	23 579	24 250	25 142	25 952	26 859	27 587	28 563	29 895	31 366	32 905	34 683	35 432
Greece	14 679	15 177	16 043	16 506	17 032	18 412	19 932	21 598	22 699	24 155	24 641	26 356	27 793	28 896
Hungary	9 032	9 425	10 073	10 811	11 260	12 114	13 562	14 755	15 403	16 299	16 952	17 920	18 763	19 732
Iceland	23 220	24 164	26 095	27 825	28 632	28 844	30 449	31 084	30 764	33 692	35 025	34 958	36 325	36 964
Ireland	17 908	19 554	21 746	23 996	25 909	28 680	30 515	33 047	34 512	36 518	38 675	41 218	44 381	41 493
Italy	21 112	21 802	22 583	23 726	24 196	25 597	27 132	26 804	27 134	27 411	28 144	29 517	30 990	31 253
Japan	22 512	23 519	24 254	23 966	24 245	25 608	26 156	26 805	27 487	29 021	30 312	31 935	33 635	34 132
Korea	13 342	14 411	15 205	14 220	15 685	17 219	18 174	19 656	20 181	21 630	22 783	24 661	26 574	27 658
Luxembourg	38 842	40 095	40 712	43 083	48 857	53 383	53 917	57 546	60 703	64 967	68 313	77 141	82 456	84 713
Mexico	7 536	7 951	8 515	8 918	9 261	10 046	10 136	10 398	10 887	11 532	12 462	13 397	14 128	14 501
Netherlands	21 552	22 641	24 096	25 479	26 933	29 409	30 793	31 943	31 699	33 203	35 111	37 173	39 594	41 063
New Zealand	17 143	17 625	18 322	18 601	19 819	20 706	21 514	22 224	22 865	23 995	24 626	25 831	27 020	27 036
Norway	23 597	26 042	27 962	27 414	29 800	36 130	37 098	37 052	38 294	42 250	47 319	52 041	53 802	58 717
Poland	7 483	8 120	8 871	9 468	9 996	10 568	10 952	11 563	11 983	13 012	13 786	14 715	16 312	17 294
Portugal	13 071	13 619	14 438	15 173	16 113	17 089	17 803	18 447	18 789	19 168	20 656	21 662	22 638	23 283
Slovak Republic	8 308	9 025	9 739	10 316	10 399	10 973	12 063	12 957	13 587	14 646	16 163	17 956	20 270	22 141
Spain	15 989	16 704	17 696	18 891	19 824	21 323	22 595	24 067	24 745	25 953	27 377	29 638	31 469	31 455
Sweden	21 867	22 632	23 418	24 263	25 801	27 761	27 968	29 004	30 059	32 060	32 298	34 328	36 785	36 790
Switzerland	26 622	27 319	28 487	29 501	30 028	31 622	32 109	33 391	33 262	34 531	35 478	38 201	41 800	42 783
Turkey	7 126	7 676	8 296	8 571	8 171	9 171	8 615	8 667	8 789	10 164	11 391	12 585	13 362	13 952
United Kingdom	19 716	20 939	22 422	23 305	24 249	26 074	27 583	28 888	29 845	31 785	32 724	34 085	34 957	35 631
United States	27 606	28 860	30 330	31 653	33 298	35 051	35 871	36 765	38 143	40 267	42 494	44 630	46 434	47 186
EU27 total	17 440	18 137	18 975	19 818	20 592	21 904	23 035	23 956	24 517	25 700	26 839	28 341	29 954	30 651
OECD total	19 680	20 547	21 536	22 252	23 170	24 581	25 361	26 144	26 913	28 371	29 846	31 501	33 077	33 732
Brazil	6 466	6 629	6 869	6 846	6 861	7 204	7 354	7 560	7 698	8 231	8 603	9 168	9 854	10 466
Chile	7 455	8 045	8 601	8 859	8 804	9 275	9 707	9 979	10 479	11 308	12 194	13 031	13 888	14 495
China	1 514	1 679	1 849	1 997	2 163	2 377	2 615	2 880	3 217	3 614	4 064	4 659	5 389	5 970
Estonia	6 280	6 894	7 959	8 420	8 752	9 863	10 695	11 967	13 368	14 756	16 531	18 462	20 620	20 648
India	1 086	1 168	1 221	1 285	1 370	1 455	1 520	1 588	1 706	1 875	2 078	2 321	2 573	2 780
Indonesia	2 265	2 450	2 572	2 226	2 243	2 441	2 552	2 674	2 825	3 005	3 207	3 449	3 722	3 980
Israel	16 764	17 602	17 947	18 470	21 365	23 503	23 489	23 535	22 271	23 630	23 390	25 106	26 801	27 902
Russian Federation	5 612	5 522	5 700	5 464	5 914	6 810	7 361	8 038	9 265	10 265	11 864	13 217	..	..
Slovenia	12 966	13 737	14 741	15 581	16 593	17 471	18 346	19 702	20 446	22 197	23 494	24 837	26 557	27 865
South Africa	5 715	5 957	6 111	6 111	6 253	6 567	6 821	7 106	7 409	7 887	8 504	9 151	9 797	10 136

StatLink http://dx.doi.org/10.1787/823716823112

GDP per capita
US dollars, current prices and PPPs, 2008

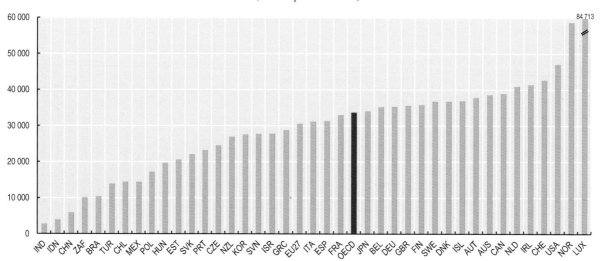

StatLink http://dx.doi.org/10.1787/818057245736

Volume index of GDP per capita

OECD = 100 in 2000, at 2000 price levels and PPPs

	1995	1996	1997	1998	1999	2000	2001	2002	2003	2004	2005	2006	2007	2008
Australia	97.1	99.6	103.0	107.2	110.2	110.9	113.6	115.9	119.1	121.0	122.9	125.1	127.7	128.4
Austria	101.8	104.0	106.1	109.8	113.2	117.1	117.2	118.6	119.0	121.2	123.4	127.0	131.0	133.1
Belgium	98.7	99.9	103.4	105.1	108.7	112.4	112.9	113.9	114.3	117.5	118.9	121.4	124.1	124.4
Canada	99.1	99.7	102.9	106.2	111.1	115.9	116.7	118.7	119.8	122.3	124.8	127.0	128.9	128.0
Czech Republic	56.3	58.7	58.3	57.9	58.8	61.0	62.8	64.1	66.4	69.4	73.6	78.3	82.7	83.8
Denmark	104.0	106.3	109.2	111.2	113.6	117.3	117.7	117.8	118.0	120.4	123.0	126.7	128.3	126.4
Finland	83.6	86.5	91.5	96.1	99.6	104.4	107.0	108.4	110.1	113.9	116.6	121.9	126.5	127.2
France	91.5	92.2	93.9	96.9	99.6	102.8	104.0	104.3	104.7	106.5	107.7	109.4	111.3	111.1
Germany	96.2	96.9	98.4	100.5	102.4	105.6	106.7	106.5	106.2	107.5	108.4	112.0	114.9	116.5
Greece	64.9	66.0	67.9	69.9	71.9	74.9	77.8	80.2	84.7	88.3	90.0	93.6	97.4	99.0
Hungary	40.2	40.7	42.5	44.8	46.9	49.3	51.4	53.9	56.3	59.2	61.4	63.9	64.7	65.2
Iceland	97.2	101.3	105.5	111.0	114.1	117.3	120.3	119.4	121.5	129.4	137.6	139.6	144.0	142.2
Ireland	77.8	83.5	92.2	98.7	108.0	116.7	121.5	127.1	130.6	134.3	139.5	143.3	148.4	141.1
Italy	94.9	96.0	97.7	99.0	100.5	104.1	106.0	106.1	105.3	105.8	105.7	107.3	108.2	106.1
Japan	100.3	102.8	104.2	101.8	101.5	104.2	104.1	104.2	105.5	108.3	110.4	112.7	115.4	114.6
Korea	58.9	62.5	64.8	59.9	65.1	70.1	72.3	77.0	78.8	82.1	85.2	89.3	93.6	95.4
Luxembourg	172.6	172.8	180.7	190.0	203.1	217.2	221.1	227.8	228.5	235.2	244.2	253.8	266.0	261.4
Mexico	33.8	35.0	36.8	38.1	39.0	40.9	40.3	40.1	40.3	41.5	42.4	44.2	45.3	45.5
Netherlands	101.1	104.1	107.9	111.5	115.9	119.6	121.0	120.3	120.2	122.5	124.7	128.7	133.0	135.2
New Zealand	76.9	78.5	79.1	79.0	82.7	84.2	86.0	88.5	90.8	93.1	94.7	95.4	97.4	95.4
Norway	126.4	132.2	138.5	141.4	143.3	147.0	149.2	150.6	151.2	156.2	159.4	161.6	165.1	166.4
Poland	33.0	35.1	37.5	39.4	41.2	43.0	43.5	44.2	45.9	48.4	50.2	53.3	57.0	59.8
Portugal	58.0	60.0	62.3	65.0	67.3	69.5	70.5	70.5	69.4	70.1	70.4	71.1	72.3	72.2
Slovak Republic	38.1	40.6	42.3	44.1	44.1	44.6	46.4	48.5	50.8	53.4	56.9	61.6	68.1	72.2
Spain	72.5	74.1	76.8	79.9	83.3	86.7	88.9	90.9	91.3	92.7	94.5	96.8	98.5	97.7
Sweden	96.3	97.6	99.9	103.7	108.4	112.9	113.8	116.2	118.0	122.4	125.9	130.5	132.8	131.0
Switzerland	118.4	118.7	121.0	123.9	124.9	128.6	128.8	128.3	127.0	129.4	131.9	135.7	139.5	140.3
Turkey	32.8	34.5	36.6	37.2	35.4	37.3	34.7	36.4	37.8	40.8	43.7	46.1	47.7	47.6
United Kingdom	90.9	93.3	96.2	99.3	102.4	106.1	108.3	110.2	112.8	115.6	117.3	120.0	122.2	122.2
United States	122.1	125.3	129.4	133.5	138.4	142.6	142.7	143.9	146.2	150.0	153.2	155.9	157.7	156.9
EU27 total	78.0	79.3	81.3	83.6	86.0	89.1	90.6	91.5	92.4	94.2	95.7	98.3	100.7	101.0
OECD total	87.6	89.7	92.3	94.1	96.7	100.0	100.6	101.6	102.9	105.4	107.6	110.2	112.4	112.4
Chile	32.9	34.9	36.7	37.4	36.6	37.7	38.6	39.0	40.1	42.0	43.9	45.4	47.1	48.1
Estonia	27.5	29.5	33.5	36.0	36.3	40.1	43.3	46.9	50.7	54.5	59.8	65.9	70.8	68.4
Israel	84.9	87.4	87.7	89.3	89.9	95.6	93.4	90.9	90.6	93.5	96.5	99.8	103.2	105.4
Russian Federation	25.3	24.4	24.8	23.5	25.1	27.7	29.2	30.8	33.2	35.7	38.2	41.3	..	..
Slovenia	57.4	59.5	62.5	64.8	68.3	71.1	73.0	75.8	77.9	81.2	84.7	89.3	94.8	98.0

StatLink http://dx.doi.org/10.1787/823725156646

Growth of GDP per capita in volume terms

Annual growth in percentage

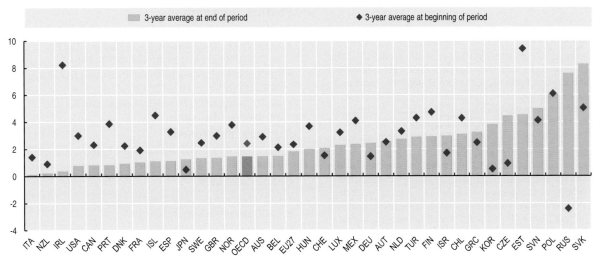

StatLink http://dx.doi.org/10.1787/818072647305

EVOLUTION OF GDP

Measuring GDP growth is self-evidently important but GDP can grow simply via inflation. Abstracting from price changes to create real GDP provides a sounder basis for assessing growth in economic production.

Definition

In order to calculate the growth rate of GDP free of the direct effects of inflation, data at fixed, or constant, prices should be used. Price relativities change over time, and the 1993 *System of National Accounts* recommends that the fixed prices used should be representative of the periods for which the growth rates are calculated. This means that new fixed prices should be introduced frequently, typically every year. The growth rates of GDP between successive periods are linked together to form chain volume indices. All OECD countries derive their "volume" estimates in this way, except for Mexico who only revises its fixed weights every ten years. Such practices tend to lead to biased growth rates, usually upward. For the definition of GDP, please refer to the definition under Size of GDP.

The growth rates for OECD total are averages of the growth rates of individual countries, weighted by the relative size of each country's GDP in US dollars. Conversion to US dollars is done using purchasing power parities.

Comparability

The GDP statistics used to compute these growth rates have been compiled according to the 1993 *System of National Accounts*. GDP estimates at current prices are generally regarded as highly comparable across countries. However, there is more variability in how countries calculate their volume estimates of GDP, particularly in respect of services, government consumption and some types of capital expenditures, although this doesn't necessarily imply lower comparability in estimated GDP growth rates.

Three-year averages refer to the years 2006 to 2008 (end of period); and 1995 to 1997 (beginning of period).

Real GDP growth
Annual growth in percentage

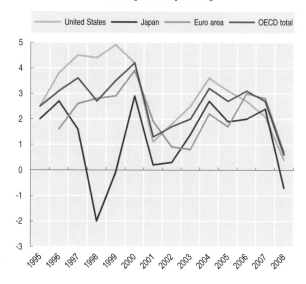

StatLink http://dx.doi.org/10.1787/818081345127

Sources

- OECD (2010), *National Accounts of OECD Countries*, OECD, Paris, *www.sourceOECD.org/nationalaccounts*.
- For non-member countries: national sources.

Further information

Analytical publications

- OECD (2006), *Development Centre Studies – The Rise of China and India: What's in it for Africa?*, OECD, Paris.
- OECD (2008), *Economic Policy Reforms: Going for Growth 2008*, OECD, Paris.
- OECD (2008), *OECD Economic Outlook, June No. 83 – Vol. 2008/1*, OECD, Paris.

Statistical publications

- OECD (2009), *National Accounts at a Glance 2009*, OECD, Paris.

Online databases

- OECD National Accounts Statistics.
- OECD Economic Outlook Statistics.

Web sites

- OECD Economic Outlook – Sources and Methods, *www.oecd.org/eco/sources-and-methods*.

Overview

Annual GDP growth for OECD total averaged 3.1% in the three years to 2008. Over this period, GDP growth rates of the Russian Federation, the Slovak Republic, India and China substantially outperformed the OECD average, with an annual growth rate of 7% or more. At the other end of the scale, Italy, Portugal, Japan, New Zealand and Denmark recorded average GDP growth rates of 1.4% or less over the period 2006-2008.

For most countries, the GDP growth rates recorded in the late 2000s (before the onset of the global recession of late 2008) were below those recorded in the three years to 1997. This was especially the case for Portugal, Norway, Ireland, Turkey, Korea and Estonia. Conversely, higher GDP growth rates were experienced by Switzerland, Brazil, India and by the Slovak and Czech Republics.

Real GDP growth

Annual growth in percentage

	1995	1996	1997	1998	1999	2000	2001	2002	2003	2004	2005	2006	2007	2008
Australia	4.1	3.9	4.5	5.2	4.0	1.9	3.8	3.2	4.0	2.8	3.0	3.3	3.7	2.3
Austria	2.5	2.2	2.1	3.6	3.3	3.7	0.5	1.6	0.8	2.5	2.5	3.5	3.5	2.0
Belgium	2.4	1.4	3.7	1.9	3.5	3.7	0.8	1.4	0.8	3.2	1.8	2.8	2.9	1.0
Canada	2.8	1.6	4.2	4.1	5.5	5.2	1.8	2.9	1.9	3.1	3.0	2.9	2.5	0.4
Czech Republic	5.9	4.0	-0.7	-0.8	1.3	3.6	2.5	1.9	3.6	4.5	6.3	6.8	6.1	2.5
Denmark	3.1	2.8	3.2	2.2	2.6	3.5	0.7	0.5	0.4	2.3	2.4	3.4	1.7	-0.9
Finland	3.9	3.7	6.2	5.2	3.9	5.1	2.7	1.6	1.8	3.7	2.8	4.9	4.2	1.0
France	2.1	1.1	2.2	3.5	3.3	3.9	1.9	1.0	1.1	2.5	1.9	2.2	2.3	0.4
Germany	1.9	1.0	1.8	2.0	2.0	3.2	1.2	0.0	-0.2	1.2	0.8	3.2	2.5	1.3
Greece	2.1	2.4	3.6	3.4	3.4	4.5	4.2	3.4	5.9	4.6	2.2	4.5	4.5	2.0
Hungary	1.5	1.0	4.3	5.2	4.2	4.9	4.1	4.4	4.3	4.9	3.5	4.0	1.0	0.6
Iceland	0.1	4.8	4.9	6.3	4.1	4.3	3.9	0.1	2.4	7.7	7.5	4.3	5.6	1.3
Ireland	9.6	8.1	11.5	8.4	10.7	9.4	5.7	6.5	4.4	4.6	6.2	5.4	6.0	-3.0
Italy	2.8	1.1	1.9	1.4	1.5	3.7	1.8	0.5	0.0	1.5	0.7	2.0	1.6	-1.0
Japan	2.0	2.7	1.6	-2.0	-0.1	2.9	0.2	0.3	1.4	2.7	1.9	2.0	2.4	-0.7
Korea	9.2	7.0	4.7	-6.9	9.5	8.5	4.0	7.2	2.8	4.6	4.0	5.2	5.1	2.2
Luxembourg	1.4	1.5	5.9	6.5	8.4	8.4	2.5	4.1	1.5	4.4	5.4	5.6	6.5	0.0
Mexico	-6.2	5.2	6.8	5.0	3.8	6.6	0.0	0.8	1.4	4.0	3.3	5.0	3.4	1.3
Netherlands	3.1	3.4	4.3	3.9	4.7	3.9	1.9	0.1	0.3	2.2	2.0	3.4	3.6	2.0
New Zealand	4.2	3.5	1.7	0.5	5.3	2.4	3.6	4.9	4.3	3.8	3.0	1.8	3.1	-1.1
Norway	4.2	5.1	5.4	2.7	2.0	3.3	2.0	1.5	1.0	3.9	2.7	2.3	3.1	2.1
Poland	7.0	6.2	7.1	5.0	4.5	4.3	1.2	1.4	3.9	5.3	3.6	6.2	6.8	5.0
Portugal	4.3	3.6	4.2	4.9	3.8	3.9	2.0	0.8	-0.8	1.5	0.9	1.4	1.9	0.0
Slovak Republic	5.8	6.9	4.4	4.4	0.0	1.4	3.5	4.6	4.8	5.0	6.7	8.5	10.6	6.2
Spain	2.8	2.4	3.9	4.5	4.7	5.0	3.6	2.7	3.1	3.3	3.6	4.0	3.6	0.9
Sweden	4.0	1.5	2.5	3.8	4.6	4.4	1.1	2.4	1.9	4.1	3.3	4.2	2.5	-0.2
Switzerland	0.4	0.6	2.1	2.6	1.3	3.6	1.2	0.4	-0.2	2.5	2.6	3.6	3.6	1.8
Turkey	7.2	7.0	7.5	3.1	-3.4	6.8	-5.7	6.2	5.3	9.4	8.4	6.9	4.7	0.9
United Kingdom	3.1	2.9	3.3	3.6	3.5	3.9	2.5	2.1	2.8	3.0	2.2	2.9	2.6	0.6
United States	2.5	3.8	4.5	4.4	4.9	4.2	1.1	1.8	2.5	3.6	3.1	2.7	2.1	0.4
Euro area	..	1.6	2.6	2.8	2.9	3.9	1.9	0.9	0.8	2.2	1.7	3.0	2.8	0.7
EU27 total	..	1.8	2.7	3.0	3.0	3.9	2.0	1.2	1.3	2.5	2.0	3.2	2.9	0.8
OECD total	2.5	3.1	3.6	2.7	3.5	4.2	1.3	1.7	2.0	3.2	2.7	3.1	2.7	0.6
Brazil	4.2	2.1	3.4	0.0	0.3	4.3	1.3	2.7	1.1	5.7	3.2	4.0	5.7	5.1
Chile	..	7.4	6.6	3.3	-0.7	4.5	3.3	2.2	4.0	6.0	5.6	4.6	4.7	3.2
China	10.9	10.0	9.3	7.8	7.6	8.4	8.3	9.1	10.0	10.1	10.4	11.6	13.0	9.0
Estonia	..	5.7	11.7	6.7	-0.3	10.0	7.5	7.9	7.6	7.2	9.4	10.0	7.2	-3.6
India	7.4	7.6	4.6	6.0	6.9	5.7	3.9	4.6	6.9	7.9	9.2	9.8	9.4	7.3
Indonesia	8.2	7.8	4.7	-13.1	0.8	5.4	3.6	4.5	4.8	5.0	5.7	5.5	6.3	6.1
Israel	..	5.6	2.9	4.3	3.3	9.2	0.0	-0.7	1.5	5.0	5.1	5.3	5.2	4.0
Russian Federation	..	-3.6	1.4	-5.3	6.4	10.0	5.1	4.7	7.3	7.2	6.4	7.7	8.1	5.6
Slovenia	..	3.6	4.9	3.6	5.4	4.4	2.8	4.0	2.8	4.3	4.5	5.8	6.8	3.5
South Africa	3.1	4.3	2.6	0.5	2.4	4.2	2.7	3.7	3.1	4.9	5.0	5.3	5.1	3.1

StatLink http://dx.doi.org/10.1787/823740485502

Real GDP growth

Average annual growth in percentage

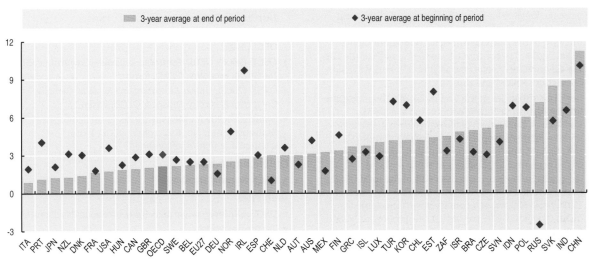

Legend: 3-year average at end of period; 3-year average at beginning of period

StatLink http://dx.doi.org/10.1787/818085232057

GDP BY REGION

Disparities in economic performance across OECD countries are often smaller than those prevailing among regions of the same country. Further, these regional disparities have persisted over time, even when economic disparities among countries were falling.

Definition

Regional inequalities in economic performance are here measured by regional GDP per capita. GDP per capita is calculated by dividing the GDP of a region by the population (number of inhabitants) living there, and is measured according to the definitions of the 1993 *System of National Accounts*.

The Gini index is one summary measure of regional disparities within each country. It looks not only at the regions with the highest and the lowest GDP per capita but at differences among all regions. The index ranges between 0 and 1: the higher its value, the larger the disparities. Regional disparities tend to be underestimated when the size of regions is large. This may be the case for those countries, where GDP figures are only available for Territorial Level 2 regions (see Population by region).

Comparability

As for the other regional statistics, comparability is affected by differences in the meaning of the word "region". The word "region" can mean very different things both within and among countries, with significant differences in terms of area and population. To address this issue, the OECD has classified regions within each member country based on two levels: territorial level 2 (TL2, large regions) and territorial level 3 (TL3, small regions). All the data shown here refer to small regions with the exception of Australia, Brazil, Canada, China, India, Mexico, Russian Federation, South Africa and the United States.

Part of the observed differences in GDP per capita within a country are due to commuting, which tends to increase GDP per capita in those regions where people are employed and reduce the GDP per capita of those regions where commuters reside.

"2006 or latest available year" refers to 2006 in all countries except Japan (2005); New Zealand (2003); Russian Federation (2005) and Turkey (2001). "1995-2006 or latest available period" refers to data from 1995 to 2006 in all countries except Italy (2000-06), Mexico (1995-2004); Poland (2000-05); and the United States (1997-2005).

Overview

Regional disparities in the economic performance within countries are often substantial. For example, the GDP per capita in Inner London-West (United Kingdom) is more than four times higher than the national average, while that of the Isle of Anglesey is only half the national average. Large differences are also found in the Russian Federation, Brazil, United States, Turkey and Poland. Regional inequalities within countries remain large also when using a measure of regional productivity (for example GDP per worker).

Regional disparities in GDP per capita result from different patterns of economic growth within countries. In recent years, the 10% most dynamic OECD regions were responsible for more than one third of the total increase in the OECD GDP. In Greece, almost all the increase in the national GDP is accounted for by the Attiki region. The contribution to GDP growth of the 10% fastest growing regions was around 60% in the Russian Federation, Poland and Hungary.

Regional disparities in the Gini index of GDP per capita are the highest in Turkey, Mexico and the Slovak Republic. A comparison between regional disparities and the share of people living in regions with low GDP per capita (below the national median) gives a measure of the economic implications of these regional inequalities. In 2006, more than 40% of the total OECD population lived in regions with low GDP per capita. In Turkey and Mexico, two countries with the same Gini index of regional GDP per capita, this proportion varied from 35% in Turkey to almost 60% in Mexico.

Sources
• *OECD Regional Database*.
• OECD (2009), *OECD Regions at a Glance 2009*, OECD, Paris.

Further information
Analytical publications
• OECD (2009), *Regions Matter: Economic Recovery, Innovation and Sustainable Growth*, OECD, Paris.
• OECD (2009), *How Regions Grow: Trends and Analysis*, OECD, Paris.
• OECD (2003), *Geographic Concentration and Territorial Disparity in OECD Countries*, OECD, Paris.
• OECD (2005), *Local Governance and the Drivers of Growth*, OECD, Paris.
• OECD (2006), *OECD Territorial Reviews – Competitive Cities in the Global Economy*, OECD, Paris.
• OECD (2007), *Higher Education and Regions: Globally Competitive, Locally Engaged*, OECD, Paris.
• Spiezia, V. (2003), "Measuring Regional Economies", OECD Statistics Brief, No. 6, October, OECD, Paris, *www.oecd.org/std/statisticsbrief*.

Online databases
• *OECD Regional Database*.

Web sites
• OECD eXplorer, *www.oecd.org/gov/regionaldevelopment*.
• Territorial grids, *www.oecd.org/gov/regional/statisticsindicators*.

Range in regional GDP per capita, small regions

As a percentage of national GDP per capita, 2006 or latest available year

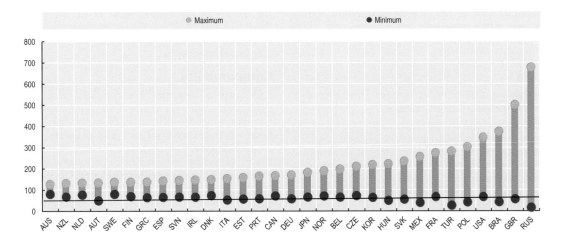

StatLink http://dx.doi.org/10.1787/818135428215

Share of GDP increase of each country due to the ten per cent of most dynamic regions, small regions

Percentage, 1995-2006 or latest available period

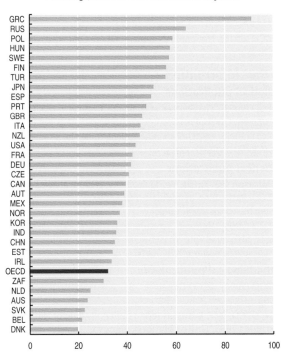

StatLink http://dx.doi.org/10.1787/818145715674

Gini index of regional GDP per capita and share of the population in regions with low GDP per capita, small regions

2006 or latest available year

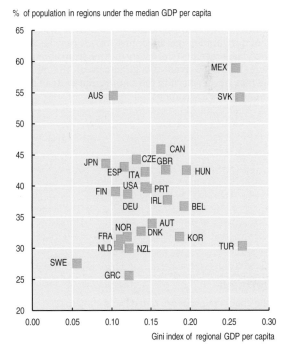

StatLink http://dx.doi.org/10.1787/818166553241

NATIONAL INCOME PER CAPITA

While per capita gross domestic product is the indicator most commonly used to compare living standards across countries, two other measures are preferred by many analysts. These are per capita gross national income (GNI) and net national income (NNI).

Definition

GNI is defined as GDP plus net receipts from abroad of wages and salaries and property income.

Wages and salaries from abroad are those that are earned by residents, *i.e.* by persons who essentially live and consume inside the economic territory of a country but work abroad (this happens in border areas on a regular basis) or by persons that live and work abroad for only short periods (seasonal workers). Guest-workers and other migrant workers who live abroad for one year or more are considered to be resident in the country where they are working. Such persons may send part of their earnings to relatives at home; these remittances, however, are treated as transfers between resident and non-resident households rather than net receipts from abroad of wages and salaries.

Property income from abroad includes interest, dividends and all or part of the retained earnings of foreign enterprises owned fully or in part by residents. In most countries, net receipts of property income account for most of the difference between GDP and GNI. Note that retained earnings of foreign enterprises owned by residents may not actually return to the residents concerned as, in some countries, there are restrictions on the repatriation of profits. Receipt of retained earnings is an imputation; since there is no actual transaction, an outflow of the same amount is recorded as a financial transaction (a reinvestment of earnings abroad). Countries with large stocks of outward foreign direct investment may be shown as having large receipts of property income from abroad and therefore high GNI even though much of the property income may never return to the country, but instead add to the foreign direct investment.

Depreciation, which is deducted from GNI to obtain NNI, is the decline in the market value of fixed capital assets – dwellings, buildings, machinery, transport equipment such as physical infrastructure, software, etc. – through wear and tear and obsolescence.

Comparability

Both income measures are compiled according to the definitions of the 1993 *System of National Accounts*. There are, however, practical difficulties in measuring international flows of wages and salaries and property income and depreciation. Because of these difficulties, GDP per capita is the most widely used indicator of income despite being theoretically inferior to either GNI or NNI.

Note that data for Australian and New Zealand refer to fiscal years.

Sources

- OECD (2010), *National Accounts of OECD Countries*, OECD, Paris.

Further information

Analytical publications

- OECD (2003), *The Sources of Economic Growth in OECD Countries*, OECD, Paris.
- OECD (2008), *OECD Economic Outlook, June No. 83 – Vol. 2008/1*, OECD, Paris.

Statistical publications

- Maddison (2003), *The World Economy: Historical Perspectives*, OECD, Paris, also available on CD-ROM, *www.theworldeconomy.org*.
- OECD (2009), *National Accounts at a Glance 2009*, OECD, Paris, also available on CD-ROM, *www.sourceoecd.org/9789264067219*.

Methodological publications

- OECD (2000), *OECD Glossaries, System of National Accounts, 1993 – Glossary*, OECD, Paris.
- UN, OECD, IMF, Eurostat (eds.) (1993), *System of National Accounts 1993*, United Nations, Geneva, *http://unstats.un.org/unsd/sna1993*.

Online databases

- *OECD National Accounts Statistics*.
- *OECD Economic Outlook Statistics*.

Web sites

- OECD Economic Outlook – Sources and Methods, *www.oecd.org/eco/sources-and-methods*.

Overview

In the chart, countries are ranked according to GNI, which is usually around 15-19% higher than NNI. The country rankings are not greatly affected by the choice of income measure. The only countries that would be more than one place lower in the ranking if NNI were used instead of GNI are Australia, Denmark, Iceland and Switzerland; the only countries that would be more than one place higher in the ranking if NNI were used are Ireland and the United Kingdom.

Gross national income per capita
US dollars, current prices and PPPs

	1995	1996	1997	1998	1999	2000	2001	2002	2003	2004	2005	2006	2007	2008
Australia	20 729	21 569	22 743	23 909	25 389	26 525	27 521	28 770	30 255	31 212	32 640	34 113	35 938	36 897
Austria	23 135	24 161	24 623	25 723	26 529	28 285	28 187	29 854	30 775	32 347	33 083	34 920	36 100	37 256
Belgium	22 808	23 220	24 295	24 777	25 826	28 260	28 951	30 417	30 704	31 484	32 350	33 656	34 997	35 523
Canada	21 936	22 512	23 704	24 700	26 217	27 740	28 500	29 145	30 497	32 121	34 377	36 451	37 963	38 593
Czech Republic	12 787	13 455	13 613	13 702	13 975	14 655	15 633	16 103	17 215	18 240	19 452	20 743	22 316	22 875
Denmark	22 747	23 744	24 902	25 844	26 699	28 216	29 027	30 393	30 238	32 444	33 659	35 839	36 699	37 323
Finland	18 173	18 775	20 607	22 127	23 373	25 493	26 584	27 643	27 478	30 063	30 813	32 907	35 329	35 837
France	20 260	20 915	21 890	22 966	23 990	25 623	26 965	27 853	27 568	28 493	29 884	31 120	32 840	33 309
Germany	22 326	22 935	23 408	23 999	24 873	25 709	26 592	27 246	28 364	30 182	31 738	33 602	35 390	36 017
Greece	15 044	15 504	16 393	16 859	17 160	18 462	20 058	21 655	22 570	23 977	24 224	25 787	26 981	27 947
Hungary	8 738	9 073	9 551	10 241	10 651	11 560	12 917	14 009	14 705	15 462	16 027	16 882	17 429	18 407
Iceland	22 570	23 609	25 501	27 225	28 071	28 046	29 492	31 033	30 282	32 323	33 674	32 309	33 035	22 515
Ireland	16 161	17 749	19 423	21 279	22 304	24 717	25 795	27 422	29 501	31 273	33 164	35 873	37 997	35 581
Italy	20 787	21 526	22 437	23 563	24 091	25 406	26 953	26 594	26 912	27 253	28 056	29 467	30 795	30 774
Japan	22 586	23 774	24 572	24 296	24 557	25 935	26 593	27 252	27 965	29 581	31 027	32 843	34 759	35 258
Korea	13 286	14 344	15 111	13 978	15 491	17 131	18 132	19 668	20 198	21 694	22 762	24 699	26 623	27 839
Luxembourg	35 969	37 325	39 182	39 633	43 897	46 516	47 893	47 726	47 060	56 760	58 668	58 806	65 342	63 978
Mexico	7 196	7 628	8 256	8 695	9 028	9 811	9 926	10 216	10 696	11 376	12 260	13 193	13 936	14 305
Netherlands	21 872	22 844	24 417	25 215	27 226	30 044	31 026	32 236	32 059	34 092	35 280	38 173	40 165	39 983
New Zealand	16 042	16 318	17 168	17 705	18 625	19 355	20 291	21 028	21 668	22 494	22 897	23 968	24 982	24 997
Norway	23 310	25 746	27 669	27 105	29 550	35 643	37 131	37 166	38 532	42 331	47 646	52 079	54 189	59 253
Poland	7 375	8 065	8 805	9 403	9 940	10 530	10 925	11 524	11 867	12 653	13 523	14 342	15 727	16 900
Portugal	13 045	13 545	14 264	14 954	15 843	16 668	17 278	18 065	18 537	18 865	20 255	20 886	21 801	22 346
Slovak Republic	8 345	9 091	9 753	10 324	10 340	10 912	12 061	12 909	12 911	14 056	15 706	17 402	19 734	21 545
Spain	15 895	16 546	17 535	18 705	19 638	21 143	22 230	23 703	24 458	25 608	26 991	29 145	30 743	30 648
Sweden	21 355	22 127	22 907	23 919	25 546	27 523	27 696	28 905	30 330	31 990	32 249	34 903	37 674	37 780
Switzerland	27 376	28 190	29 916	31 110	31 961	33 946	33 588	34 469	35 774	36 994	38 822	41 107	42 338	39 735
United Kingdom	19 561	20 799	22 358	23 527	24 141	26 026	27 747	29 315	30 251	32 240	33 272	34 298	35 432	36 259
United States	27 520	28 881	30 467	32 024	33 652	35 659	36 415	37 012	38 322	40 605	43 091	45 610	46 867	47 320
EU27 total	17 329	18 044	18 895	19 737	20 501	21 810	22 923	23 825	24 424	25 717	26 845	28 375	29 920	30 511
OECD total	19 554	20 479	21 522	22 290	23 197	24 683	25 440	26 144	26 924	28 469	30 024	31 815	33 216	33 748
Chile	..	7 822	8 370	8 686	8 566	8 950	9 382	9 583	9 847	10 381	11 115	11 396	12 311	13 299
Estonia	6 283	6 923	7 753	8 319	8 632	9 541	10 259	11 475	12 676	14 046	15 902	17 487	19 174	19 402
Israel	16 301	17 035	17 290	17 787	20 461	21 935	22 433	22 579	21 360	22 850	23 149	24 974	26 726	27 448
Russian Federation	5 550	5 443	5 577	5 225	5 680	6 634	7 259	7 884	8 984	10 043	11 569	12 811	..	..
Slovenia	13 081	13 834	14 792	15 621	16 647	17 482	18 385	19 593	20 288	21 940	23 295	24 543	26 007	27 222

StatLink http://dx.doi.org/10.1787/823762510007

Gross and net national income per capita
US dollars, current prices and PPPs, 2008 or latest available year

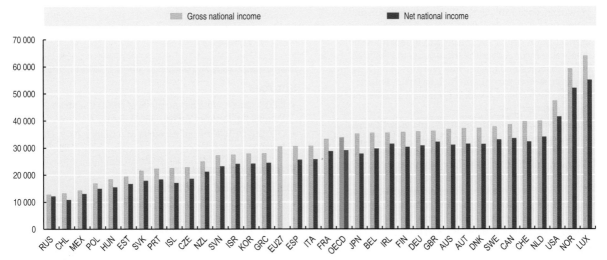

StatLink http://dx.doi.org/10.1787/818176348655

HOUSEHOLD DISPOSABLE INCOME

Household disposable income, as a concept, is closer to the concept of income generally used in economics and is an important indicator of well-being and living standards. Ignoring changes in net worth that arise from capital transfers or holding gains, household disposable income can be seen as the maximum amount that households can afford to spend on consumption goods or services without having to reduce their financial or non-financial assets or to increase their liabilities.

Definition

Household disposable income is the sum of household final consumption expenditure and savings (minus the change in net equity of households in pension funds). It also corresponds to the sum of wages and salaries, mixed income, net property income, net current transfers and social benefits other than social transfers in kind, less taxes on income and wealth and social security contributions paid by employees, the self-employed and the unemployed.

The figures shown here for the household sector include the disposable income of non-profit institutions serving households (NPISH). The price deflator used to obtain real values is consistent with that used to deflate the final consumption expenditure of households and NPISH.

Comparability

Household disposable income is compiled according to the definitions of the 1993 *System of National Accounts*. There are, however, practical difficulties in measuring some income components, such as remittances.

Overview

Over the period 2006-2008, household disposable income in real terms increased by around 2.5% per year among the OECD countries considered here. Household disposable income fell in real terms in Hungary, while it expanded by less than 0.5% in Italy and Germany. Its growth exceeded 10% in the Russian Federation and Estonia.

In most OECD countries, the growth of real household disposable income over the three years to 2008 was below that recorded in the three years to 1997. There are, however, several exceptions such as Japan, France, Austria, Switzerland, Sweden, Canada, Australia and the Czech Republic.

Among the major seven countries, the growth of real household disposable income fell sharply in the United Kingdom, and more moderately in the United States, Germany and Italy. In 2008, for all countries except Canada, Germany, Portugal, and the United Kingdom, growth rates in household disposable income fell compared to 2007. With a few notable exceptions, such as Hungary, growth rates in non OECD countries and former transition economies tended to be higher than in other OECD countries.

Sources

- OECD (2009), *National Accounts of OECD Countries 2009, Volume IIa, Detailed Tables*, OECD, Paris.
- OECD (2010), *National Accounts at a Glance 2009*, OECD, Paris.

Further information
Methodological publications

- OECD (2007), *Understanding National Accounts*, OECD, Paris.
- OECD (2000), *OECD Glossaries, System of National Accounts, 1993 – Glossary*, OECD, Paris.
- UN, OECD, IMF, Eurostat (eds.) (1993), *System of National Accounts 1993*, United Nations, Geneva.

Household disposal income
Annual growth in percentage

	1995	1996	1997	1998	1999	2000	2001	2002	2003	2004	2005	2006	2007	2008
Australia	4.1	2.3	1.1	4.0	4.2	4.1	1.3	0.1	4.9	5.6	4.5	4.6	..	..
Austria	..	-0.1	-1.6	2.4	3.8	1.9	0.0	1.2	1.9	2.4	2.6	3.0	1.7	1.7
Belgium	..	-0.6	0.6	2.1	2.4	1.8	3.1	-0.4	-0.3	-0.2	0.1	2.9	1.8	1.2
Canada	1.8	0.1	2.2	2.8	2.9	4.8	2.8	1.8	2.1	3.8	2.5	5.7	3.4	4.3
Czech Republic	..	3.7	2.2	-2.6	2.1	1.0	0.9	2.8	5.3	0.8	5.3	6.8	6.6	3.3
Denmark	..	1.4	0.2	2.9	-2.9	0.5	3.7	1.4	2.1	2.9	2.0	2.9	0.2	-0.3
Finland	7.4	0.0	5.0	2.7	4.5	0.4	3.4	2.3	5.7	4.1	1.3	2.5	3.3	2.0
France	3.1	0.6	1.5	3.4	3.1	3.4	3.4	3.7	0.6	2.4	1.4	2.5	3.1	0.6
Germany	..	1.1	0.3	1.2	2.2	1.9	2.1	-0.4	0.5	0.2	0.6	1.0	-0.2	0.6
Greece	..	..	..	..	..	..	3.2	3.6	5.0	4.4	3.4	5.1	..	..
Hungary	..	-2.4	-0.2	3.3	1.3	3.1	6.0	8.1	5.8	5.5	2.2	2.7	-1.8	-2.9
Ireland	..	..	..	..	..	..	..	..	1.9	6.8	3.5	4.4	4.2	1.6
Italy	0.3	1.8	0.0	-1.1	1.0	0.3	3.0	1.1	0.1	0.6	0.5	0.7	0.7	-0.4
Japan	..	..	0.3	-0.1	-0.5	-0.9	-2.1	1.3	-0.7	1.7	1.7	1.3	0.8	..
Korea	..	..	..	..	..	..	0.9	3.4	4.9	4.7	2.3	2.6	2.7	0.8
Netherlands	2.7	2.8	4.1	3.4	2.3	2.2	5.5	-0.6	-2.4	0.7	-0.3	0.6	4.4	0.2
New Zealand	4.0	5.1	0.8	1.7	2.8	3.0	..	..	..	..	..	..	..	..
Norway	2.9	3.8	3.7	5.7	2.5	3.8	0.0	8.0	4.4	3.6	7.6	-6.3	5.4	..
Poland	..	5.3	7.1	5.5	3.5	1.7	3.8	-0.9	1.3	3.6	1.4	4.4	4.6	..
Portugal	..	1.6	2.4	4.9	5.0	4.2	2.5	1.0	0.0	1.6	0.8	0.5	-0.2	2.1
Slovak Republic	..	13.7	4.6	4.7	-1.3	2.0	3.0	5.1	-0.6	3.9	6.2	3.7	9.3	5.3
Spain	..	..	..	..	..	..	3.0	3.1	3.2	3.1	4.1	3.2	2.9	2.3
Sweden	..	-0.9	-0.4	2.0	2.6	4.6	6.2	3.6	1.4	1.3	1.2	3.3	3.6	3.6
Switzerland	..	-1.3	1.3	2.8	2.7	3.7	2.7	-1.2	-0.7	2.1	2.6	3.0	3.7	..
United Kingdom	..	3.0	4.1	2.0	2.5	4.0	4.4	1.8	3.1	0.4	2.2	0.2	-0.1	1.8
United States	2.7	2.8	3.3	6.0	3.1	4.8	2.5	3.6	2.9	3.0	1.4	3.9	1.9	0.8
Euro area	..	..	..	..	..	2.2	2.9	1.4	0.8	1.5	1.3	1.8	1.6	0.9
EU27 total	..	..	..	..	..	2.5	3.3	1.6	1.6	1.4	1.7	1.7	1.6	1.5
Chile	..	..	3.8	4.9	-0.9	3.5	3.2	2.2	3.4	7.8	7.7	7.0	7.1	..
Estonia	..	9.7	9.5	2.3	-1.8	9.1	6.4	8.6	5.6	5.5	10.5	12.1	11.7	..
Russian Federation	..	..	..	..	..	..	..	..	7.9	9.8	11.3	12.0	..	..
Slovenia	..	..	..	..	..	..	4.7	3.3	0.5	4.0	4.9	3.1	4.6	..

StatLink http://dx.doi.org/10.1787/823771515813

Household disposal income
Average annual growth in percentage

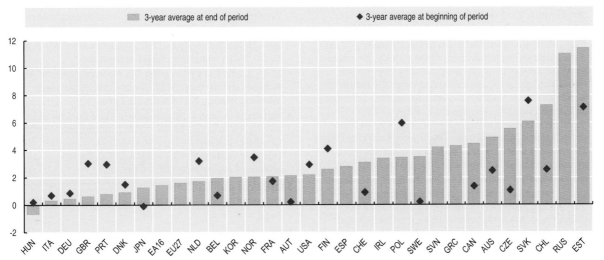

StatLink http://dx.doi.org/10.1787/818188300134

HOUSEHOLD SAVINGS

Household savings are the main domestic source of funds to finance capital investment, which is a major driver of long-term economic growth.

Definition

In the national accounts, household savings are estimated by subtracting household consumption expenditure from household disposable income plus the change in net equity of households in pension funds (since this component is also a determinant of household disposable income but with an opposite sign).

Household disposable income consists essentially of income from employment and from the operation of unincorporated enterprises, plus receipts of interests, dividends and social benefits minus payments of income taxes, interest and social security contributions. Note that enterprise income includes imputed rents paid by owner-occupiers of dwellings.

Household consumption expenditure consists mainly of cash outlays for consumer goods and services. It also includes the imputed expenditures that owner occupiers pay, as occupiers, to themselves as owners of their dwellings and the production of goods such as agricultural products for own-final use.

Household saving rates may be measured on either a net or a gross basis. The net saving rates shown here are measured after deducting consumption of fixed capital (depreciation), in respect of assets used in enterprises operated by households and in respect of owner-occupied dwellings. This consumption of fixes capital is deducted from both savings and the disposable income of households.

Overview

Household saving rates differ significantly across countries. In 2008 or the most recent available year, these saving rates ranged between values above 10% of household disposable income in Belgium, France, Germany, Sweden, Switzerland, the Russian Federation and Slovenia and negative values in Denmark, Finland, Greece, Norway, Portugal, United Kingdom and Estonia.

These differences are partly due to institutional differences between countries. These include the extent to which old-age pensions are funded by government rather than through personal savings, and the extent to which governments provide insurance against sickness and unemployment. The age composition of the population is also relevant, as the elderly tend to run down financial assets acquired during their working life. This implies that a country with a high share of retired persons will usually have a low household saving rate.

Over the last 10-15 years covered in the table, household saving rates have increased in Austria, Germany and Sweden and remained stable in Belgium, France and Switzerland. A downward trend over the same period has occurred in Canada, Italy, Japan, Korea, Poland and the United States.

Households include households plus non-profit institutions serving households. The household saving rate is calculated as the ratio of household savings to household disposable income (plus the change in net equity of households in pension funds).

Comparability

Because savings are a residual between two large aggregates (household disposable income and household consumption expenditure), both of which are subject to estimation errors, measures of household savings are also subject to large errors and to revisions over time.

Data for Australia and New Zealand refer to fiscal years. Three-year averages refer to the years 2006 to 2008 (end of period); and 1995 to 1997 (beginning of period).

Sources
* OECD (2010), *National Accounts of OECD Countries*, OECD, Paris.

Further information
Analytical publications
* Cotis, J.-P., J. Coppel and L. de Mello (2004), *Is the US Prone to Over-consumption?*, paper presented at The Macroeconomics of Fiscal Policy, Federal Reserve, Bank of Boston Economic Conference, Cape Cod, 14-16 June, *www.oecd.org/eco/speeches*.
* Harvey, R. (2004), *Comparison of Household Saving Ratios: Euro Area/United States/Japan*, OECD Statistics Brief, No. 8, June, OECD, Paris, *www.oecd.org/std/statisticsbrief*.
* Kohl, R. and P. O'Brien (1998), *The Macroeconomics of Ageing, Pensions and Savings*, OECD Economics Department Working Papers, No. 200, OECD, Paris.
* de Serres, A. and F. Pelgrin (2003), "The Decline of Private Saving Rates in the 1990s in OECD Countries: How Much Can Be Explained by Non-wealth Determinants?", *OECD Economic Studies*, No. 36, 2003/1, OECD, Paris, *www.oecd.org/oecdeconomicstudies*.

Statistical publications
* OECD (2010), *National Accounts at a Glance 2009*, OECD, Paris.

Web sites
* OECD Economic Outlook – Sources and Methods, *www.oecd.org/eco/sources-and-methods*.

Household net saving rates

As a percentage of household disposable income

	1995	1996	1997	1998	1999	2000	2001	2002	2003	2004	2005	2006	2007	2008
Australia	6.4	6.2	2.9	1.9	1.8	2.2	0.6	-2.7	-3.2	-2.1	-0.2	0.8	..	..
Austria	11.8	9.3	7.7	8.5	9.8	9.2	8.1	8.0	9.2	9.4	9.7	10.9	11.4	12.0
Belgium	16.4	14.3	13.2	12.7	13.1	12.3	13.7	12.9	12.2	10.8	10.0	10.9	11.2	11.5
Canada	9.4	7.2	5.0	4.9	4.1	4.8	5.3	3.5	2.7	3.2	2.2	3.6	2.6	3.8
Czech Republic	10.0	6.1	6.0	4.1	3.4	3.3	2.2	3.0	2.4	0.5	3.2	4.8	6.3	5.8
Denmark	1.3	0.9	-1.6	0.0	-3.3	-1.9	3.7	4.1	4.1	0.7	-1.5	0.4	-1.0	-0.3
Finland	3.9	0.4	2.0	0.6	2.1	-0.1	0.2	0.6	1.4	2.5	0.7	-1.4	-1.2	-1.0
France	12.7	11.7	12.6	12.2	11.9	11.8	12.5	13.7	12.5	12.4	11.4	11.4	12.0	11.6
Germany	11.0	10.5	10.1	10.1	9.5	9.2	9.4	9.9	10.3	10.4	10.5	10.5	10.8	11.2
Greece	..	..	..	..	..	-6.0	-7.5	-8.0	-7.3	-7.2	-8.0	-7.3	..	..
Hungary	14.4	15.6	14.2	13.5	9.9	8.9	8.5	6.4	4.3	6.8	6.1	7.5	4.6	3.0
Ireland	..	..	..	..	..	..	..	5.4	5.4	8.3	5.6	3.8	2.7	4.1
Italy	17.0	17.9	15.1	11.4	10.2	8.4	10.5	11.2	10.3	10.2	9.9	9.1	8.2	8.6
Japan	..	11.5	11.0	11.8	10.3	8.9	5.2	5.1	3.9	3.6	3.8	3.6	3.8	..
Korea	..	..	..	..	..	9.3	5.2	0.4	5.2	9.2	7.2	5.2	2.9	2.8
Netherlands	14.0	12.4	13.0	12.0	8.9	6.7	9.5	8.4	7.5	7.3	6.3	6.0	8.1	6.8
New Zealand	-3.6	-2.6	-4.6	-4.2	-5.3	-3.8	..	..	..	..	..	..	..	..
Norway	4.8	2.6	3.0	5.7	4.7	4.3	3.1	8.2	8.9	7.2	10.1	0.1	-1.2	..
Poland	14.6	11.7	11.7	12.1	11.1	10.3	12.3	8.3	7.8	8.0	7.1	6.8	7.4	..
Portugal	6.9	5.5	4.3	4.0	3.3	3.8	4.6	4.1	4.0	3.1	2.5	1.1	-1.1	-0.9
Slovak Republic	5.2	8.9	9.4	7.7	6.3	6.1	3.9	3.5	1.2	0.5	1.2	0.5	2.5	1.8
Spain	..	..	..	..	..	5.9	5.6	5.6	6.0	4.9	4.7	4.2	3.6	6.1
Sweden	9.5	7.3	4.9	4.0	3.6	4.8	9.3	9.1	9.0	7.7	6.8	7.8	9.1	12.1
Switzerland	12.7	10.9	10.7	10.7	10.8	11.7	11.9	10.7	9.4	9.0	10.1	11.4	12.7	..
United Kingdom	6.9	5.9	5.9	3.5	0.9	0.1	1.5	-0.1	0.4	-1.7	-1.3	-2.9	-4.3	-4.5
United States	5.7	5.1	4.7	5.4	3.2	3.0	2.8	3.7	3.8	3.4	1.5	2.5	1.7	2.7
Euro area	..	..	..	..	9.3	8.4	9.2	9.7	9.4	9.3	8.6	8.2	8.3	8.9
EU27 total	..	..	..	..	7.4	6.6	7.5	7.4	7.3	6.6	6.4	5.8	5.5	5.8
Chile	..	7.2	5.6	6.5	7.3	6.5	7.0	6.8	6.4	7.2	7.1	7.7	7.7	..
Estonia	4.2	2.0	-0.1	-2.8	-5.4	-3.0	-4.0	-6.5	-8.4	-11.7	-10.4	-9.6	-5.2	..
Russian Federation	..	..	..	..	..	..	..	12.8	13.2	11.8	12.0	12.6	..	..
Slovenia	..	..	..	..	..	7.0	9.0	9.9	7.6	9.2	11.1	11.2	10.5	..

StatLink http://dx.doi.org/10.1787/823876227135

Household net saving rates

As a percentage of household disposable income

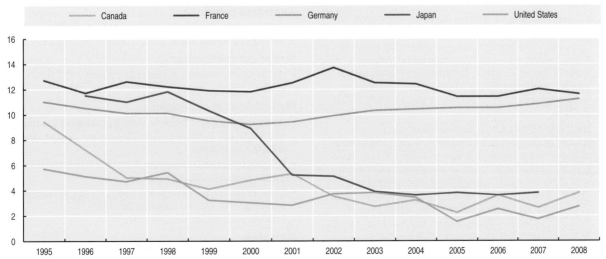

StatLink http://dx.doi.org/10.1787/818204663301

INVESTMENT RATES

The share of total GDP that is devoted to investment in fixed assets is an important determinant of future economic growth. However, not all types of investment contribute to future GDP growth in the same way, and future GDP growth may also depend on expenditures that are conventionally considered as consumption (*e.g.* education, health).

Definition

The total of gross fixed capital formation (investment or GFCF) is here shown as a share of GDP. GFCF reflects the acquisition, less disposal, of fixed assets, *i.e.* products that are expected to be used in production for several years. Acquisitions include both purchases of assets (new or second-hand) and the construction of assets by producers for their own use. Disposals include sales of assets for scrap as well as sales of used assets in a working condition to other producers. New Zealand, Mexico and some Central European countries import substantial quantities of used assets, which are included in GFCF.

Fixed assets consist of machinery and equipment; dwellings and other buildings; roads, bridges, airfields and dams; orchards and tree plantations; improvements to land such as fencing, levelling and draining; draught animals and other animals that are kept for the milk and wool that they produce; computer software and databases; entertainment, literary or artistic originals, and expenditures on mineral exploration. What all these things have in common is that they contribute to future production. This may not be obvious in the case of dwellings but, in the national accounts, flats and houses are considered to produce services that are consumed by owners or tenants over the life of the building.

In calculating shares, GFCF and GDP are both valued at current market prices. Three-year averages refer to the years 2006 to 2008 (end of period); and 1995 to 1997 (beginning of period).

Comparability

When the *System of National Accounts* was revised in 1993, the scope of GFCF was widened to include mineral exploration, computer software and entertainment, as well as literary and artistic originals. Comparability of these items has improved in recent years but the coverage of the various items differs across countries. This applies particularly in the case of own-account production of software.

Data for Australia and New Zealand refer to fiscal years.

Overview

The total investment rate, for the period 2006-2008 averaged 21% for the OECD as a whole. Among OECD countries, investment rates are substantially higher in Spain, Iceland, Korea and Australia and significantly lower in United Kingdom, Germany, the United States, Sweden, and Luxembourg. These investment rates exceed 30% of GDP in Estonia and India, and 40% of GDP in China.

For the OECD as a whole, total investment rates are broadly unchanged compared to 1995-1997. Investment rates fell by 4 percentage points or more in Korea, Japan and the Slovak Republic where investment rates remain well above the OECD average as well as in Israel and Chile (where investment rates are comparatively lower). Total investment rates are now much higher than in 1995-1997 in Iceland, Spain, Ireland and Australia. Part of this rise may reflect an unsustainable boom in housing construction.

Sources

- OECD (2010), *National Accounts of OECD Countries*, OECD, Paris.
- For Russian Federation and South Africa: OECD (2010), *Main Economic Indicators*, OECD, Paris.
- For China: National Bureau of Statistics.
- For Brazil: National sources and OECD (2010), *Main Economic Indicators*, OECD, Paris.

Further information

Analytical publications

- OECD (2008), *OECD Economic Outlook, June No. 83 – Vol. 2008/1*, OECD, Paris.

Statistical publications

- OECD (2009), *National Accounts at a Glance 2009*, OECD, Paris.

Methodological publications

- Ahmad, N. (2004), "Towards More Harmonised Estimates of Investment in Software", *OECD Economic Studies*, No. 37, 2003/2, OECD, Paris.
- OECD (2000), *OECD Glossaries, System of National Accounts, 1993 – Glossary*, OECD, Paris.
- UN, OECD, IMF, Eurostat (eds.) (1993), *System of National Accounts 1993*, United Nations, Geneva, *http://unstats.un.org/unsd/sna1993*.

Web sites

- OECD Economic Outlook – Sources and Methods, *www.oecd.org/eco/sources-and-methods*.

Gross fixed capital formation

As a percentage of GDP

	1995	1996	1997	1998	1999	2000	2001	2002	2003	2004	2005	2006	2007	2008
Australia	22.9	22.9	24.0	24.2	24.8	22.0	22.9	24.8	25.4	25.8	27.0	27.2	28.3	29.4
Austria	23.6	24.1	23.9	24.0	23.5	24.0	23.3	21.7	22.4	22.0	21.7	21.6	21.8	21.8
Belgium	19.9	20.1	20.5	20.6	20.7	21.1	20.8	19.1	18.8	19.8	20.7	21.0	21.7	22.6
Canada	17.6	17.9	19.8	19.9	19.8	19.2	19.6	19.5	19.6	20.3	21.3	22.4	22.6	22.7
Czech Republic	31.5	32.1	29.9	28.2	27.0	28.0	28.0	27.5	26.7	25.8	24.9	24.7	25.2	23.9
Denmark	18.4	18.6	19.6	20.4	19.8	20.2	19.8	19.6	19.3	19.3	19.5	21.7	22.3	20.9
Finland	16.6	17.1	18.3	19.0	19.0	19.4	19.5	18.0	18.1	18.2	18.9	19.3	20.4	20.6
France	18.1	17.9	17.5	17.9	18.8	19.5	19.5	18.8	18.8	19.3	20.0	20.7	21.6	21.9
Germany	21.9	21.3	21.0	21.1	21.3	21.5	20.0	18.3	17.9	17.5	17.4	18.2	18.8	19.0
Greece	17.0	17.8	18.1	19.4	20.8	21.6	21.6	22.5	23.3	22.2	20.6	21.5	21.4	19.4
Hungary	20.6	21.2	21.3	22.3	23.0	23.4	23.0	23.1	22.3	22.5	23.0	21.7	21.2	20.9
Iceland	15.7	18.9	19.7	24.0	21.8	22.9	21.5	18.2	20.0	23.5	28.4	34.0	28.2	24.2
Ireland	17.3	18.9	20.1	21.6	23.1	23.1	22.4	21.6	22.4	24.4	26.6	26.9	26.0	21.7
Italy	19.1	18.9	18.9	19.3	19.6	20.3	20.3	20.9	20.4	20.5	20.7	21.1	21.2	20.9
Japan	28.0	28.3	27.7	25.9	25.5	25.2	24.7	23.3	22.8	22.7	23.3	23.3	23.4	23.1
Korea	36.0	36.1	34.3	29.2	28.6	30.0	28.8	28.6	29.3	29.2	28.9	28.7	28.5	29.3
Luxembourg	19.9	20.1	21.7	21.8	23.5	20.8	22.6	22.6	22.2	21.5	20.5	19.1	19.9	19.3
Mexico	16.2	17.9	19.5	20.9	21.2	21.4	20.0	19.3	18.9	19.7	20.3	20.9	21.4	22.2
Netherlands	20.8	21.6	21.9	22.2	22.9	21.9	21.1	20.0	19.5	18.8	18.9	19.7	20.0	20.4
New Zealand	22.1	22.0	21.1	20.1	20.9	20.4	20.8	21.4	22.6	23.7	24.1	23.5	23.3	22.1
Norway	19.8	20.2	22.0	25.0	21.9	18.4	18.1	17.9	17.3	18.0	18.8	19.6	21.3	20.8
Poland	17.7	19.8	22.4	24.1	24.4	23.7	20.7	18.7	18.2	18.1	18.2	19.7	21.6	22.1
Portugal	22.5	23.0	25.2	26.5	26.8	27.1	26.5	25.0	22.9	22.6	22.2	21.7	21.8	21.7
Slovak Republic	24.8	31.8	33.9	35.8	29.5	25.8	28.5	27.4	24.8	24.0	26.6	26.5	26.2	24.9
Spain	21.5	21.4	21.8	23.0	24.6	25.8	26.0	26.3	27.2	28.0	29.4	30.6	30.7	28.8
Sweden	15.7	15.9	15.5	16.3	17.0	17.6	17.5	16.8	16.3	16.4	17.4	18.2	19.0	19.5
Switzerland	23.3	22.1	21.6	22.2	22.2	22.7	21.9	21.3	20.5	20.8	21.2	21.3	21.5	21.3
Turkey	22.2	23.3	24.6	22.9	18.9	20.4	15.9	16.7	17.0	20.3	21.0	22.3	21.4	19.9
United Kingdom	16.6	16.7	16.7	17.7	17.4	17.1	16.8	16.8	16.4	16.7	16.7	17.1	17.8	16.8
United States	17.7	18.1	18.5	19.1	19.7	20.0	19.4	18.2	18.2	18.8	19.5	19.7	18.9	17.9
EU27 total	19.7	19.6	19.5	20.1	20.4	20.6	20.2	19.6	19.5	19.6	20.0	20.7	21.3	21.1
OECD total	20.5	20.8	21.0	21.0	21.2	21.4	20.7	20.0	19.8	20.2	20.7	21.1	21.1	20.6
Brazil	18.3	16.9	17.4	17.0	15.7	16.8	17.0	16.4	15.3	16.1	15.9	16.4	17.4	18.7
Chile	25.1	26.4	26.9	25.8	20.4	20.2	21.0	20.5	20.1	19.3	21.2	19.0	19.9	24.0
China	33.0	32.4	31.8	33.0	33.6	34.3	34.6	36.3	39.2	40.6	41.0	40.7	40.1	41.1
Estonia	26.9	26.4	28.1	30.4	24.6	25.7	26.4	29.7	31.6	30.9	32.1	34.9	34.5	29.3
India	..	..	23.3	22.7	23.2	22.9	23.3	23.8	24.4	27.5	30.4	32.1	34.0	34.5
Indonesia	25.6	26.7	25.5	22.9	18.1	19.9	19.7	19.4	19.5	22.4	23.6	24.1	25.0	27.6
Israel	23.9	23.8	22.6	20.7	20.2	18.7	17.8	17.3	16.6	16.4	16.5	17.2	18.7	18.0
Russian Federation	20.6	20.2	17.9	15.9	14.5	16.6	18.7	17.8	18.2	18.1	17.5	18.2	20.7	21.5
Slovenia	21.8	22.5	23.8	24.9	26.6	26.1	24.7	23.1	24.0	24.9	25.5	26.5	27.7	28.9
South Africa	15.9	16.3	16.5	17.1	15.5	15.1	15.0	15.0	15.9	16.2	17.1	18.8	21.1	23.2

StatLink 🔗 http://dx.doi.org/10.1787/824150721364

Gross fixed capital formation

As a percentage of GDP

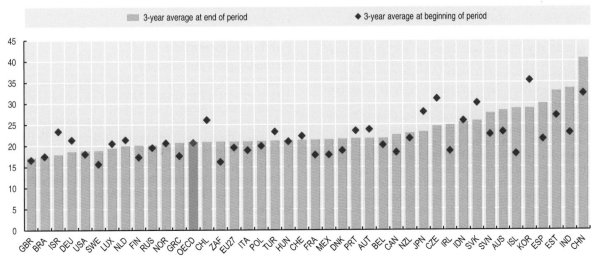

StatLink 🔗 http://dx.doi.org/10.1787/818238325032

LABOUR PRODUCTIVITY LEVELS

Productivity is a measure of the efficiency with which available resources are used in production. Labour productivity, together with use of labour resources, is one of the main determinants of living standards.

Definition

Labour productivity is measured as GDP per hour worked. The estimates shown here are based on OECD Annual National Accounts data on GDP at current prices, converted to a common currency using OECD Purchasing Power Parities (PPPs) for 2008.

Differences in GDP per capita levels vis-à-vis the United States can be decomposed into differences in labour productivity levels and differences in the extent of labour utilisation, measured as the number of hours worked per capita.

Comparability

Comparisons of productivity and income levels across countries first require comparable data on output. All OECD countries have implemented the 1993 *System of National Accounts*. However, there are differences such as the measurement of software investment that can affect the comparability of GDP across countries, although these differences are usually small. Second, in a number of countries, employment data are derived from labour force surveys that may not be entirely consistent with national account concepts; this reduces the comparability of labour utilisation across countries. Third, the measure of labour inputs also requires hours worked data, which are derived either from labour force surveys or from business surveys. Several OECD countries estimate hours worked from a combination of these sources or integrate these sources in a system of labour accounts, which is comparable to the national accounts. The OECD Productivity database uses consistent estimates of employment and hours worked. Nonetheless, the cross-country comparability of hours worked remains limited, generating a margin of uncertainty in estimates of productivity levels.

A final problem relates to the conversion of output from national currency into a common unit. Market exchange rates cannot be used directly, as they are volatile and reflect a range of factors. The preferred alternative is to use Purchasing Power Parities (PPPs), which measure the prices of the same basket of consumption goods in different countries.

Overview

In 2008, labour productivity ranged from over 70 USD in Norway and Luxembourg to less than 20 USD in Chile and Mexico. Gaps in GDP per capita relative to the United States ranged from around 70% in Mexico, Turkey and Chile and 20% or less in Australia, Canada and several European countries. In Norway and Luxembourg, GDP per capita levels were higher than in the US. Much of the differences in GDP per capita reflect differences in labour productivity, with gaps relative to the United States ranging between 60% or more in Chile, Mexico, Poland and Estonia, to 5% or less in France, Belgium, Ireland and the Netherlands, with Norway and Luxembourg recording higher labour productivity than in the US.

Cross-country differences in labour utilisation were significantly smaller than in the case of GDP per capita and per hour. In Belgium and France, lower labour utilisation accounted for 87% (i.e. 26 points out of the 30 points gap in GDP per capita) and 92% (i.e. 23 points out of 25 points gap in GDP per capita), respectively, of the gap in living standard relative to the US, while in Turkey the contribution of lower labour utilisation was only 20%. In 2008, several non-EU countries (Canada, Iceland, Japan, Korea, New Zealand and Switzerland) recorded higher levels of labour utilisation than in the United States, contributing to narrow their gap in GDP per capita. Cross-country differences in labour utilisation reflect high unemployment and low participation rates of the working age population, on the one hand, and lower working hours among employed people, on the other hand.

Sources
- *OECD National Accounts Statistics.*
- *OECD Productivity Database.*

Further information
Methodological publications
- OECD (2001), *Measuring Productivity – OECD Manual Measurement of Aggregate and Industry-level Productivity Growth*, OECD, Paris.
- OECD (2004), "Clocking In (and Out): Several Facets of Working Time", *OECD Employment Outlook: 2004 Edition*, Chapter 1, see also Annex I.A1, OECD, Paris.
- Pilat, D. and P. Schreyer (2004), "The OECD Productivity Database – An Overview", *International Productivity Monitor*, No. 8, Spring, CSLS, Ottawa, pp. 59-65.

Web sites
- OECD Compendium of Productivity Indicators, *www.oecd.org/statistics/productivity/compendium.*
- OECD Productivity, *www.oecd.org/statistics/productivity/.*

GDP per hour worked

US dollars, current prices and PPPs, 2008

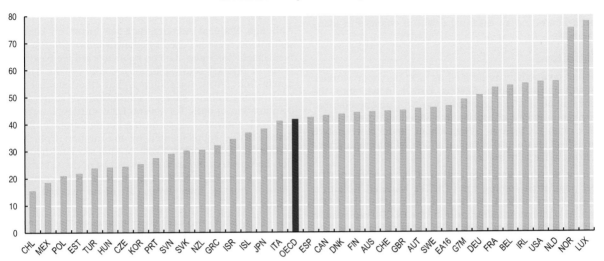

StatLink ᵍᵍ▤ http://dx.doi.org/10.1787/818246855568

Levels of GDP per capita and labour productivity

Percentage point differences with respect to the United States, 2008

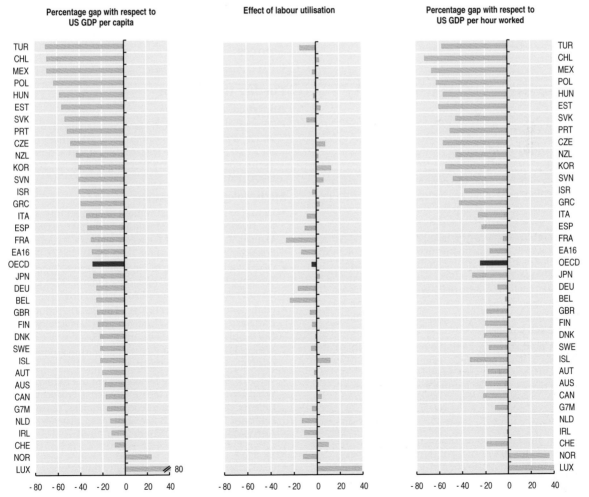

Percentage gap with respect to US GDP per capita

Effect of labour utilisation

Percentage gap with respect to US GDP per hour worked

StatLink ᵍᵍ▤ http://dx.doi.org/10.1787/818248323450

LABOUR PRODUCTIVITY GROWTH

Labour productivity growth is a key dimension of economic performance and an essential driver of changes in living standards.

Definition

Labour productivity is defined as GDP per hour worked. Growth in per capita GDP is broken down into the contribution of labour productivity growth, on one side, and changes in labour utilisation (measured as hours worked per capita), on the other. High labour productivity growth can reflect greater use of capital and/or falling employment of low-productivity workers.

The indicators shown here are based on measures of GDP and population coming from OECD's National Accounts. Actual hours worked are derived from either the OECD Annual National Accounts or from the OECD Employment Outlook. Hours worked reflect regular hours worked by full-time and part-time workers, paid and unpaid overtime, hours worked in additional jobs and time not worked because of public holidays, annual paid leaves, strikes and labour disputes, bad weather, economic conditions and other reasons.

For zone aggregates, GDP estimates have been converted to constant US dollars using 2000 constant Purchasing Power Parities (PPPs).

Comparability

Although National Account data are based on common definitions, methods used by countries may differ in some respects. In particular, data on hours worked are based on a range of primary sources. In most countries, the data are drawn from labour force surveys, but other countries rely upon establishment surveys, administrative sources or a combination of both. For several EU countries, hours data are OECD estimates based on the Spring European Labour Force Survey, supplemented by information from other sources on hours not worked. Annual working hours for non-European countries are provided by national statistical offices. In general, these data are most suited for comparing changes rather than levels of hours worked across countries.

The estimates shown here are not adjusted for differences in the business cycle; cyclically adjusted estimates might show different patterns.

Sources

- *OECD Productivity Database.*

Further information
Analytical publications

- Ahmad, N., F. Lequiller, P. Marianna, D. Pilat, P. Schreyer and A. Wölfl (2003), *Comparing Labour Productivity Growth in the OECD Area: The Role of Measurement*, OECD Science, Technology and Industry Working Papers, No. 2003/14, OECD, Paris.

Methodological publications

- OECD (2001), "The Measurement of Productivity: What Do the Numbers Mean?", *Measuring Productivity – OECD Manual Measurement of Aggregate and Industry-level Productivity Growth*, Chapter 3, pp. 29-61, OECD, Paris.
- OECD (2004), "Clocking In (and Out): Several Facets of Working Time", *OECD Employment Outlook: 2004 Edition*, Chapter 1, see also Annex I.A1, OECD, Paris.
- Pilat, D. and P. Schreyer (2004), "The OECD Productivity Database – An Overview", *International Productivity Monitor*, No. 8, Spring, CSLS, Ottawa, pp. 59-65.
- Schreyer, P. and D. Pilat (2001), "Measuring Productivity", *OECD Economic Studies*, OECD, Paris.
- Van Ark, B. (2004), "The Measurement of Productivity: What Do the Numbers Mean?", *Fostering Productivity – Patterns, Determinants and Policy Implications*, G. Gelauff, L. Klomp, S. Raes and T. Roelandt (eds.), Elsevier, Amsterdam; Boston, Chapter 3, pp. 29-61.

Web sites

- OECD Compendium of Productivity Indicators, *www.oecd.org/statistics/productivity/compendium*.
- OECD Productivity, *www.oecd.org/statistics/productivity/*.

Overview

Labour productivity growth varies considerably among countries. Over the period 1995-2000, labour productivity growth ranged between 4.8% and 6.2% in Ireland, Korea, Poland and the Slovak Republic, while it was below 1.0% in Italy and Spain.

In several OECD countries, labour productivity accelerated in the second half of the 1990s but slowed in the first half of the new millennium. The Czech Republic was the only country experiencing a strong increase in labour productivity growth in 2001-2008 compared to the period 1995-2000. Over the same period, labour productivity growth fell in Ireland, Poland and Portugal.

Labour productivity growth is a major determinant of changes in living standards, as measured by GDP per capita. For the OECD area as a whole, labour productivity growth accounted for the entire rise in GDP per capita, while labour utilisation declined marginally. In Portugal, France, Germany, the United States, Japan, the United Kingdom, Sweden, Ireland, Iceland and Korea labour productivity growth accounted for 90% or more of the rise in GDP per capita. In most of these countries, rates of labour utilisation in the years 2001-2008 fell in absolute terms.

Growth in GDP per hour worked

Average annual growth in percentage

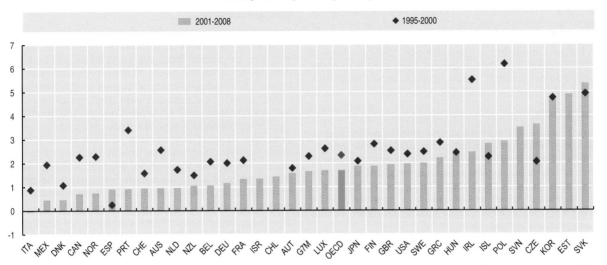

StatLink ▱▱ http://dx.doi.org/10.1787/818262068028

Contribution of labour productivity and labour utilisation to GDP per capita

Percentage change 2001-2008, annual rate

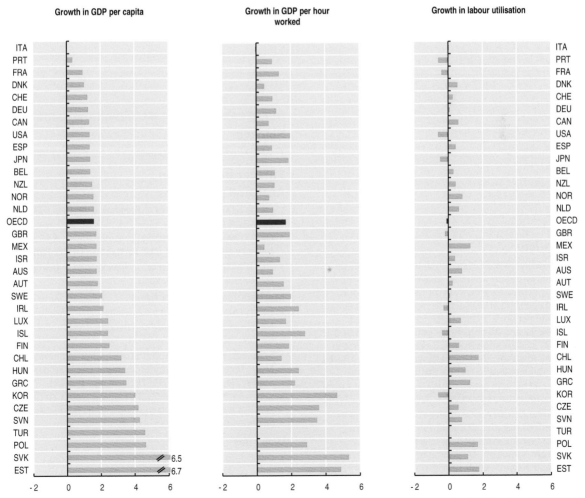

StatLink ▱▱ http://dx.doi.org/10.1787/818276564572

PRODUCTIVITY AND GROWTH ACCOUNTING

Economic growth can be increased either by raising the labour and capital inputs used in production, or by greater overall efficiency in how these inputs are used together, *i.e.* higher multi-factor productivity (MFP). Growth accounting involves breaking down GDP growth into the contribution of labour inputs, capital inputs and MFP growth.

Definition

Growth accounting explains output growth by the rates of change of labour and capital inputs and by MFP growth, computed as a residual. In these calculations, the growth rates of labour and capital inputs are weighted with their respective share in total costs. Thus, for example, the contribution of labour to GDP growth is measured as the speed with which labour input grows, multiplied by the share of labour in total costs.

In the tables and graphs, the contribution of capital to GDP growth is broken down into ICT capital (ICT capital includes hardware, communication and software) and non-ICT capital (transport equipment and non residential construction; products of agriculture, metal products and machinery other than hardware and communication equipment; and other products of non-residential gross fixed capital formation).

Comparability

The appropriate measure for capital input with the growth accounting framework is the flow of productive services that can be drawn from the cumulative stock of past investments in capital assets. These services are estimated by the OECD using the rate of change of the "productive capital stock". This measure takes into account wear and tear and retirements, *i.e.*, reductions in the productive capacity of the fixed assets. The price of capital services for each type of asset is measured as their rental price. In principle, the latter could be directly observed if markets existed for capital services. In practice, however, rental prices have to be imputed for most assets, using the implicit rent that capital goods' owners "pay" themselves (or "user costs of capital").

The measure of total hours worked is an incomplete measure of labour input because it does not account for changes in the skill composition of workers over time, such as those due to higher educational attainment, and work experience. Adjustment for such attributes would provide a more accurate indication of the contribution of labour to production. In the absence of these adjustments, as is the case in the series shown here, more rapid output growth due to a rise in skills of the labour force are captured by the MFP residual, rather than being attributed to labour. This should be kept in mind when interpreting rates of MFP growth.

Overview

From 1985 to 2008, GDP growth in most OECD countries was for a large part driven by growth in capital and MFP. In many countries, growth in capital accounted for around one third of GDP growth from 1985 to 2008. Over the same period, ICT capital services represented between 0.2 and 0.6 percentage points of growth in GDP. The GDP-contribution from ICT capital was largest in Sweden, Australia, the United Kingdom and the United States and smallest in France, Austria and Ireland.

In contrast, growth in labour input was important for a few countries over 1985-2008, notably Ireland, Australia, and Canada. However, Germany, Finland and Japan experienced negative GDP contributions of labour inputs. Over the same period, MFP growth was a significant source of GDP growth in Ireland, Finland, Japan and Belgium, while its contribution was very small in Italy, Spain and Canada.

Sources
- OECD Productivity Database.

Further information
Analytical publications
- OECD (2003), *The Sources of Economic Growth in OECD Countries*, OECD, Paris.
- OECD (2004), *Understanding Economic Growth A Macro-level, Industry-level, and Firm-level Perspective*, OECD, Paris.
- OECD (2007), *OECD Science, Technology and Industry Scoreboard 2007*, OECD, Paris.

Methodological publications
- OECD (2001), *Measuring Productivity – OECD Manual Measurement of Aggregate and Industry-level Productivity Growth*, OECD, Paris.
- Schreyer, P. (2004), "Capital Stocks, Capital Services and Multi-factor Productivity Measures", *OECD Economic Studies No. 37, 2003/2*, OECD, Paris, pp. 163-184.
- Schreyer, P., P.-E. Bignon and J. Dupont (2003), *OECD Capital Services Estimates*, OECD Statistics Working Papers, No. 2003/6, OECD, Paris.

Web sites
- OECD Compendium of Productivity Indicators, *www.oecd.org/statistics/productivity/compendium*.
- OECD Productivity, *www.oecd.org/statistics/productivity/*.

Contributions to GDP growth

Average annual growth in percentage, 1985-2008 (or closest comparable period)

	Labour input	ICT capital	Non-ICT capital	Multi-factor productivity	GDP growth
Australia	1.27	0.55	0.55	0.94	3.31
Austria	0.60	0.21	0.18	1.22	2.20
Belgium	0.22	0.46	0.28	1.30	2.26
Canada	1.19	0.44	0.66	0.37	2.65
Denmark	0.29	0.42	0.35	0.64	1.70
Finland	−0.22	0.36	0.29	2.04	2.45
France	0.03	0.24	0.31	1.16	1.75
Germany	−0.16	0.29	0.31	1.07	1.50
Ireland	1.68	0.21	0.62	3.33	5.84
Italy	0.35	0.35	0.71	0.22	1.63
Japan	−0.34	0.40	0.45	1.60	2.10
Netherlands	0.85	0.45	0.39	1.07	2.77
New Zealand	0.87	0.51	0.46	0.66	2.50
Portugal	0.32	0.36	0.48	1.26	2.42
Spain	0.67	0.25	0.54	0.30	1.76
Sweden	0.17	0.56	0.35	1.24	2.32
Switzerland	0.22	0.40	0.37	0.54	1.53
United Kingdom	0.45	0.55	0.40	1.27	2.67
United States	0.94	0.54	0.32	1.09	2.89

StatLink http://dx.doi.org/10.1787/824238771241

Contributions to GDP growth

Average annual growth in percentage, 1985-2008 (or closest comparable period)

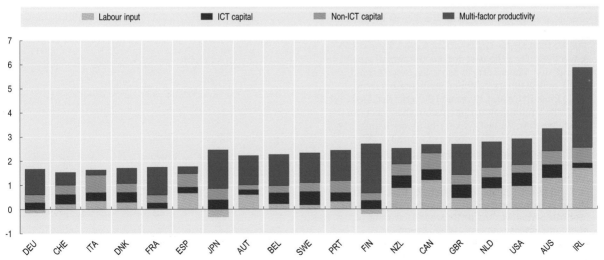

StatLink http://dx.doi.org/10.1787/818276737521

UNIT LABOUR COSTS

Unit labour costs are a key determinant of the competitiveness of the productive system of a country in both domestic and foreign markets. Unit labour costs reflect the combined evolution of compensation of employees per unit of labour input and of labour productivity, and can be an indicator of inflationary pressure on producer prices.

Definition

Unit labour costs measure the average cost of labour per unit of output produced. They are calculated as the ratios of total labour costs to real output. Equivalently, they may be expressed as the ratio of total labour costs per hours worked by employee (or per employee, if hours data is not available) to output per total hours worked (or per person employed if hours data is not available).

Data are taken from the *OECD System of Unit Labour Cost and Related Indicators*, which provides annual and quarterly information for OECD countries as well as for selected non-members countries. Labour productivity estimates are produced as a by-product of calculating unit labour cost. Data are presented as annual growth rates in unit labour costs for the economy as a whole; they refer to 34 countries (30 OECD member countries and 4 non-member countries) and 4 geographical regions in the period between 1998 and 2008.

Comparability

These indicators are compiled according to a specific methodology to ensure comparability across countries. The primary data source for these indicators is the OECD National Accounts database, where data are compiled on a similar basis across countries according to the 1993 *System of National Accounts*. Due to the high level of comparability, cross country comparisons of developments in the annual growth of unit labour costs can be made with a strong degree of confidence.

Overview

Unit labour costs in the total economy increased at an annual average rate of 2.3% for the OECD area as a whole over the decade since 1998. Annual average growth rates in unit labour costs ranged from negative values in Japan and Brazil to the values exceeding 6% in Estonia, Hungary and Mexico, and above 30% in Turkey.

Annual average growth in unit labour costs for other geographical regions, i.e. G7, Euro area and EU27, were smaller than for the OECD total at 1.2%, 1.5% and 2.0%, respectively. Over the past decade, the annual growth rates of unit labour costs in Australia, New Zealand, Spain, and Denmark exhibited an increasing trend, while those in Iceland, Korea and Slovenia declined over time. The annual growth rates in unit labour costs for the Czech Republic, Hungary, Korea, the Slovak Republic and Sweden displayed a high degree of volatility.

During this ten-year period, ten countries (Austria, the Czech Republic, Finland, France, Germany, Korea, Japan, Poland, the Slovak Republic and Sweden) displayed stronger growth in labour productivity than in unit labour cost. Subdued growth in labour compensation over this period was mainly related to low rates of inflation in these countries. When looking at geographical regions, stronger growth in labour productivity than in unit labour cost was recorded by the G7 countries. This reflected higher growth of labour productivity than in unit labour costs in Japan, France and Germany, and similar growth rates for labour productivity and unit labour costs in Canada, the United Kingdom and the United States. Italy was the only G7 country who experienced lower growth of labour productivity than in unit labour costs over the period.

Sources
• *OECD Main Economic Indicators*.

Further information
Analytical publications
• *OECD Compendium of Productivity Indicators*.

Statistical publications
• OECD (2010), *Main Economic Indicators*, OECD, Paris.

Unit labour costs, total economy

Annual growth in percentage

	1995	1996	1997	1998	1999	2000	2001	2002	2003	2004	2005	2006	2007	2008
Australia	2.7	1.7	0.6	-0.4	1.4	3.2	0.9	2.2	1.9	4.3	3.9	3.7	..	..
Austria	-2.8	0.3	-1.6	-0.2	0.3	-0.1	1.0	0.3	1.1	-0.6	1.2	0.6	0.8	2.3
Belgium	-0.1	1.0	0.6	1.3	1.6	0.4	3.7	2.2	0.5	0.2	1.5	1.8	2.9	3.7
Canada	0.4	1.5	1.5	1.2	-0.4	2.0	2.2	1.0	2.5	2.2	2.4	3.6	..	..
Czech Republic	12.5	13.8	10.7	7.6	2.4	2.1	6.5	5.8	4.7	1.0	-0.8	0.1	2.8	4.6
Denmark	1.4	3.0	1.2	3.8	1.6	0.2	4.4	3.7	2.2	1.1	2.8	2.5	4.1	6.8
Finland	2.0	0.2	-1.0	1.4	0.6	0.4	3.3	1.6	2.0	0.4	2.4	-0.4	1.1	6.1
France	0.6	1.2	-0.1	-0.4	0.7	1.6	2.3	2.9	1.9	0.9	1.8	2.1	1.6	2.5
Germany	1.8	0.1	-1.0	0.1	0.6	0.3	0.4	0.3	0.7	-0.9	-0.9	-1.6	-0.3	2.1
Greece	13.2	6.7	10.0	4.3	4.2	1.5	0.1	9.6	2.1	-1.5	2.4	2.2	..	..
Hungary	18.3	17.4	16.2	9.6	4.1	12.1	11.0	8.8	6.6	8.3	3.2	0.8	5.6	4.2
Iceland	4.6	4.3	2.5	9.1	6.7	4.4	6.1	8.5	1.6	2.1	3.5	..	..	..
Ireland	-0.9	-0.3	0.0	4.8	1.6	4.0	3.2	0.7	4.0	3.3	5.4	3.8	2.6	..
Italy	1.4	4.8	3.0	-1.9	1.8	-0.4	3.3	3.4	4.4	1.5	3.1	1.8	1.8	3.8
Japan	-0.5	-2.0	0.5	0.4	-2.7	-2.4	-1.3	-3.8	-3.1	-3.1	-2.1	-0.6	-1.1	..
Korea	8.9	8.0	1.2	4.0	-6.0	-0.5	5.5	1.2	5.3	1.3	2.4	0.2	0.7	1.5
Luxembourg	1.4	2.9	0.6	-0.9	1.0	3.4	5.7	2.3	1.5	1.6	1.9	0.9	1.5	7.0
Mexico	21.4	21.5	21.8	17.1	17.6	11.1	10.6	6.8	6.1	2.0	3.2	2.5	..	..
Netherlands	0.5	1.2	1.1	2.7	2.0	3.1	4.7	4.5	2.3	0.3	-0.3	0.7	2.0	2.6
New Zealand	1.2	2.6	1.9	1.5	-2.6	0.6	3.0	2.0	4.1	4.2	4.9	4.9	..	..
Norway	1.6	1.7	2.5	7.3	4.3	2.0	4.3	3.5	1.6	1.5	3.2	7.3	7.3	6.4
Poland	27.8	22.5	17.3	13.5	3.9	5.4	3.2	-1.0	-2.8	-1.9	0.7	-0.8	2.7	6.9
Portugal	0.8	4.3	4.5	4.2	3.3	4.5	3.3	3.4	3.3	0.8	3.5	1.1	..	..
Slovak Republic	14.3	7.5	9.1	5.5	4.2	11.0	1.0	4.0	5.4	4.0	5.1	0.3	1.0	4.4
Spain	2.4	2.9	2.0	2.1	2.0	2.7	3.1	3.0	3.2	2.5	3.5	3.2	3.5	4.3
Sweden	-0.4	4.6	0.7	0.4	-1.1	4.5	5.4	0.7	0.9	-1.2	0.4	-0.7	4.5	2.6
Switzerland	2.1	0.0	-0.4	-0.7	1.2	1.0	4.7	2.1	0.4	-2.3	1.1	1.6	..	..
Turkey	60.8	87.3	88.8	73.1	82.4	33.1	49.9	30.0	21.2	9.5	-1.0	4.0	..	..
United Kingdom	1.7	1.3	2.4	3.6	2.2	2.9	3.7	2.5	3.0	2.2	2.9	2.2	1.5	2.6
United States	1.4	0.6	1.1	2.2	1.6	4.1	2.3	0.8	2.1	1.3	2.2	3.0	2.8	..
Euro area	1.1	1.7	-1.4	-0.1	1.8	1.0	2.1	2.3	2.0	0.7	1.2	1.0	1.4	3.1
EU27 total	..	3.1	2.1	1.8	1.5	2.5	3.3	2.6	2.5	0.9	2.0	1.2	1.9	3.3
Major seven	1.0	0.5	0.9	1.2	0.6	1.9	1.6	0.4	1.3	0.4	1.3	1.8	1.6	..
OECD total	3.0	3.8	3.9	3.8	3.1	3.0	3.4	1.7	2.1	0.8	1.5	1.8	1.8	..
Brazil	..	-29.2	-11.2	-2.7	1.9	-1.5	0.4	0.2	2.1	-6.7	2.2	-0.6	..	..
Estonia	..	19.4	9.2	5.3	3.3	2.7	2.3	2.9	5.4	3.8	3.0	8.9	20.3	16.6
Slovenia	..	7.8	5.4	5.0	5.2	6.5	8.7	5.6	4.4	3.7	0.9	0.9	2.6	8.1
South Africa	10.1	7.6	7.5	8.8	5.7	4.7	4.4	5.8	6.5	3.9	4.1	5.1	6.2	..

StatLink ᵐˢᴸ http://dx.doi.org/10.1787/824253208267

Unit labour costs and labour productivity, total economy

Average annual growth in percentage, 1998-2008 or latest available period

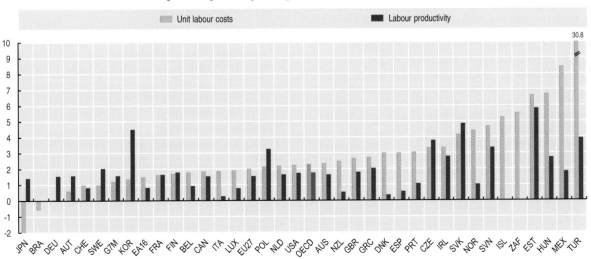

StatLink ᵐˢᴸ http://dx.doi.org/10.1787/818288570372

VALUE ADDED BY ACTIVITY

The structure of total value added has changed considerably over recent decades. The share of agriculture is now relatively small in almost all OECD countries. The share of industry has also fallen while services now account for well over 60% of total gross value added in most OECD countries.

Definition

Gross value added is defined as output minus intermediate consumption. This also equals the sum of employee compensation, gross operating surplus of government and corporations, gross mixed income of unincorporated enterprises and other taxes less other subsidies on production. The shares of each sector are calculated by dividing the value added in each sector by total value added. Total value added is less than GDP because it excludes value-added tax (VAT) and other product taxes.

Agriculture consists of agriculture; hunting and forestry; and fishing. Industry consists of mining and quarrying; manufacturing; production and distribution of electricity, gas and water; and construction. Services consists of retail and wholesale trade; transport and communications; real estate, finance, insurance and business services; education, health and other personal services; public administration; and defence.

Comparability

All OECD countries follow the international 1993 *System of National Accounts*. This assures good comparability between countries in terms of definitions of value added and sectoral coverage. It should be recognised, however, that part of the decline in the share of industry and of the rise in that of services reflects the outsourcing of service activities that were previously carried out internally within industrial enterprises. For example, if cleaning and security services were earlier provided by employees of a manufacturing enterprise, their salaries would have formed part of value added of industry; if these services are now purchased from specialised producers, the salaries of these employees will now be included in the value added of "other business services".

Data for Australia and New Zealand refer to fiscal years.

Overview

The share of agriculture in total value added has been declining throughout the period in almost all countries. By 2008, agriculture made a significant contribution to total value added only in Iceland (fishing), Hungary and Turkey. Shares in industry have also been falling (or, in some counties, remained stable) throughout the period. Manufacturing is the most important industrial activity in all countries except Norway, where oil and gas production is more important.

Service activities account for around 60% of total gross value added for the OECD countries as a whole. The share of services is very high in Belgium, France, Greece, Luxembourg, the United Kingdom and the United States and rather low in the Czech Republic, Korea, Norway and the Slovak Republic. In most countries, the largest part of service value added is "goods-related", and consists of trade, transport and business services purchased by industry. A high share of service value added does not necessarily imply that a country has become a service economy. In fact, production, transport and distribution of goods remain the predominant activities in most OECD countries in terms of both employment and value added.

Sources

• OECD (2010), *National Accounts of OECD Countries*, OECD, Paris.

Further information

Analytical publications

• Lal, K. (2003), *Measurement of Output, Value Added, GDP in Canada and the United States*, OECD Statistics Working Papers, No. 2003/4, OECD, Paris.
• OECD (1996), *Services: Measuring Real Annual Value Added*, OECD, Paris.
• OECD (2002), *Measuring the Non-Observed Economy: A Handbook*, OECD, Paris.

Statistical publications

• OECD (2010), *National Accounts at a Glance 2009*, OECD, Paris.

Online databases

• STAN: OECD Structural Analysis Statistics – online database.

Web sites

• OECD National Accounts, *www.oecd.org/std/national-accounts*.
• OECD National Accounts Archive, *www.oecd.org/std/national-accounts/papers*.

Value added in agriculture, industry and services

As a percentage of total value added

	Share of value added in agriculture				Share of value added in industry				Share of value added in services			
	1990	2000	2005	2008	1990	2000	2005	2008	1990	2000	2005	2008
Australia	3.6	4.0	3.1	..	30.1	26.1	28.0	..	66.3	69.9	68.9	..
Austria	3.7	2.0	1.6	1.7	32.2	30.8	29.5	30.7	64.1	67.2	68.9	67.6
Belgium	2.1	1.4	0.8	0.7	31.5	27.0	24.1	23.1	66.6	71.6	75.1	76.2
Canada	2.9	2.3	..	..	31.3	33.2	..	..	65.8	64.5	..	..
Czech Republic	8.7	3.9	3.0	2.5	43.2	38.1	37.9	37.6	47.1	58.0	59.1	59.9
Denmark	4.0	2.6	1.4	1.2	25.6	26.8	25.5	25.6	70.4	70.6	73.1	73.2
Finland	6.3	3.5	3.0	3.0	33.3	33.7	31.4	31.6	60.3	62.8	65.7	65.3
France	4.2	2.8	2.3	2.0	27.1	22.9	20.7	20.4	68.7	74.3	77.0	77.6
Germany	1.5	1.3	0.9	0.9	37.3	30.3	29.1	29.8	61.2	68.5	70.0	69.3
Greece	9.0	6.6	4.9	3.7	25.2	21.0	19.6	19.0	63.4	72.5	75.5	77.3
Hungary	..	5.4	4.2	4.3	..	31.8	30.2	29.1	..	62.8	65.6	66.6
Iceland	11.2	8.6	5.8	..	30.3	26.1	23.7	..	58.6	65.3	70.5	..
Ireland	8.9	3.5	1.9	..	35.0	41.1	35.0	..	55.9	55.5	63.1	..
Italy	3.5	2.8	2.2	2.0	32.1	28.4	26.9	27.0	64.4	68.8	70.9	71.0
Japan	2.5	1.7	1.5	..	38.6	31.1	29.1	..	59.1	67.2	69.4	..
Korea	8.5	4.6	3.3	..	38.8	38.4	38.0	..	52.0	57.0	58.7	..
Luxembourg	1.5	0.7	0.4	0.3	29.4	18.4	16.6	15.4	69.5	81.0	82.9	84.3
Mexico	8.1	4.2	3.3	..	36.4	35.8	34.1	..	61.0	61.5	62.5	..
Netherlands	4.4	2.6	2.1	1.8	29.4	24.9	24.2	25.5	66.2	72.4	73.7	72.8
New Zealand	6.7	8.6	..	..	26.7	24.5	..	..	66.6	66.9	..	..
Norway	3.4	2.1	1.5	1.2	34.0	42.0	42.9	46.2	62.6	56.0	55.6	52.6
Poland	..	5.0	4.5	3.7	..	31.7	30.7	32.0	..	63.3	64.8	64.2
Portugal	9.1	3.8	2.8	2.3	28.1	27.6	24.5	23.9	63.5	68.6	72.6	73.8
Slovak Republic	..	4.5	3.7	3.1	..	36.2	36.5	38.0	..	59.3	59.8	58.9
Spain	5.5	4.4	3.2	2.6	33.0	29.2	29.7	28.4	61.5	66.4	67.1	69.0
Sweden	3.6	2.0	1.1	1.6	30.6	28.6	27.7	28.0	65.9	69.4	71.2	70.5
Switzerland	2.9	1.6	1.3	1.2	31.9	27.3	27.2	28.2	65.1	71.1	71.6	70.7
Turkey	13.4	10.8	10.6	8.5	38.6	30.0	28.0	27.1	47.2	59.2	61.3	64.4
United Kingdom	1.8	1.0	0.7	0.9	34.1	27.3	23.5	23.6	64.1	71.7	75.9	75.2
United States	2.1	1.2	1.3	..	28.0	24.2	22.3	..	69.9	74.6	76.4	..
EU27 total	..	2.4	1.9	1.8	..	27.9	26.2	26.5	..	69.7	71.9	71.7
OECD total	..	2.0	..	..	..	27.8	..	..	..	70.3	..	..
Brazil	..	5.6	5.7	5.9	..	27.7	29.3	27.3	..	66.7	65.0	66.7
Chile	..	5.3	4.4	3.9	..	34.0	42.0	43.8	..	61.1	53.5	52.3
China	27.1	15.1	12.2	11.3	41.3	45.9	47.7	48.6	31.5	39.0	40.1	40.1
Estonia	..	4.8	3.5	2.9	..	27.5	28.6	29.1	..	67.6	67.9	68.0
India	..	24.0	19.1	17.4	..	25.9	28.6	29.2	..	50.1	52.3	53.4
Indonesia	..	15.6	13.1	14.4	..	45.9	46.5	48.1	..	38.5	40.3	37.5
Israel	..	1.7	2.0	..	..	25.3	21.9	..	..	72.9	76.1	..
Russian Federation	..	6.7	5.4	4.9	..	37.9	38.2	36.1	..	55.4	56.4	59.0
Slovenia	..	3.3	2.7	2.4	..	35.8	34.1	33.9	..	60.9	63.2	63.8

StatLink http://dx.doi.org/10.1787/824276856832

Value added in services

As a percentage of total value added

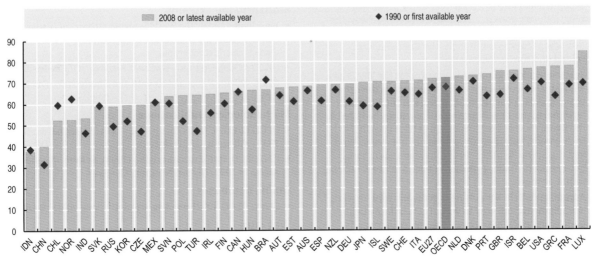

StatLink http://dx.doi.org/10.1787/818305304618

EVOLUTION OF VALUE ADDED BY ACTIVITY

GDP growth has not been evenly spread across economic activities. Some economic activities have grown faster than others and some have declined in importance. A convenient way to show how the patterns of economic growth have changed is to distinguish between agriculture, industry and services.

Definition

Gross value added is defined as output minus intermediate consumption. It also equals the sum of employee compensation, net operating surplus, net mixed income, depreciation of capital assets and other taxes less other subsidies on production. The growth rates shown here refer to volume estimates of gross value added.

Agriculture consists of agriculture; hunting and forestry; and fishing. Industry consists of mining and quarrying; manufacturing; production and distribution of electricity, gas and water; and construction. Services consists of retail and wholesale trade; transport and communications; real estate, finance, insurance and business services; education, health and other personal services; public administration; and defence.

The graphs show annual growth rates in years 2006 to 2008 (end of period); and in 1995 to 1997 (beginning of period).

Comparability

All OECD countries follow the 1993 System of National Accounts. This assures good comparability between countries as regards the definitions and coverage. It is important to recognise, however, that part of the decline of industry and the rise of service activities reflects the outsourcing of service activities that were previously carried out internally within industrial enterprises; because of this, the trends shown here overstate real changes in these activities. For example, if cleaning and security services were earlier provided by employees of a manufacturing enterprise, their salaries would have formed part of value added by industry; if these services are now purchased from specialised producers, the salaries of these employees will form part of the value added of the service sector.

Data for Australia and New Zealand refer to fiscal years.

Overview

In the three years to 2008, the volume of agricultural value added in OECD countries increased at an annual rate of around 3%, almost identical to the growth rate recorded in the three years to 1997. Agricultural production declined in eight countries, especially in Luxembourg, the Czech Republic and Ireland, while it increased by 5% or more in the Slovak Republic, Sweden and Switzerland.

Real value added in industry for the OECD as a whole expanded at a rate of 2% per year in the three years to 2008. Industry grew in all countries except Norway, the United Kingdom and Greece, with the pace of growth exceeding 8% per year in India, the Czech Republic, Poland and the Slovak Republic.

Real value added in the service sector for the OECD as a whole increased at a rate of 2.6% per year in the three years to 2008, a pace significantly lower than the one recorded in the 1995-97 period. All countries included in the figure recorded expansions in service activity, with such growth exceeding 6% per year in Ireland, Iceland and the Slovak Republic. In the Russian Federation, Indonesia and India, growth in service activity was close to 10% or more.

Annual growth in agriculture is generally very uneven, with changes from year to year of 10% or more being quite common, while growth rates in industry and services have tended to be more stable.

Sources
• OECD (2010), National Accounts of OECD Countries, OECD, Paris.

Further information
Analytical publications
• OECD (2008), OECD Economic Outlook, June No. 83 – Vol. 2008/1, OECD, Paris.

Statistical publications
• Maddison (2003), The World Economy: Historical Perspectives, OECD, Paris, also available on CD-ROM, www.theworldeconomy.org.
• OECD (2009), Quarterly National Accounts, OECD, Paris.
• OECD (2010), National Accounts at a Glance 2009, OECD, Paris.

Methodological publications
• OECD (2000), OECD Glossaries, System of National Accounts, 1993 – Glossary, OECD, Paris.
• UN, OECD, IMF, Eurostat (eds.) (1993), System of National Accounts 1993, United Nations, Geneva.

Online databases
• STAN: OECD Structural Analysis Statistics – online database.

Web sites
• OECD National Accounts, www.oecd.org/std/national-accounts.

Real value added in agriculture
Annual growth in percentage

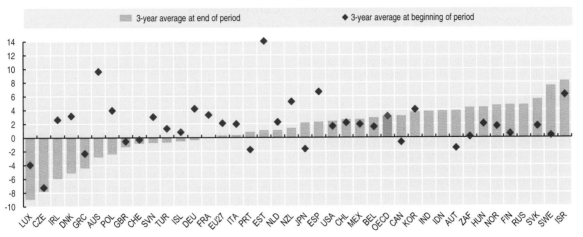

StatLink ⟶ http://dx.doi.org/10.1787/818312622321

Real value added in industry
Annual growth in percentage

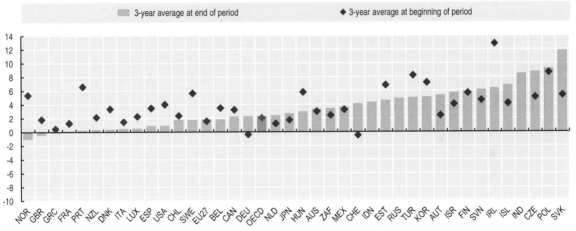

StatLink ⟶ http://dx.doi.org/10.1787/818346743466

Real value added in services
Annual growth in percentage

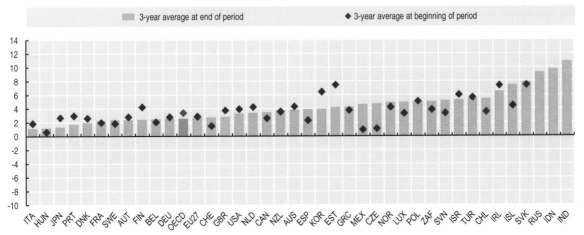

StatLink ⟶ http://dx.doi.org/10.1787/818382306804

SMALL AND MEDIUM-SIZED ENTERPRISES

Small firms, and especially recent start-ups, can be very dynamic and innovative. A few very high-performance new and small firms can make an important contribution to employment creation and economic growth. Although the majority of small firms have more modest economic impacts individually, together they make an important difference.

Definition

An enterprise is a legal entity possessing the right to conduct business on its own; for example to enter into contracts, own property, incur liabilities and establish bank accounts. It may consist of one or more establishments situated in a geographically separate area. In this section, small enterprises refer to those with less than 20 persons engaged. Data on the number of small enterprises and the number of employees working in them refer to the manufacturing sector.

Employees includes all persons covered by a contractual arrangement, working in the enterprise and receiving compensation for their work. They include salaried managers, students who have a formal commitment whereby they contribute to the unit's process of production in return for remuneration and/or education services, and employees engaged under a contract designed to encourage the recruitment of unemployed persons. They also include persons on sick leave, paid leave or vacation, while excluding working proprietors, active business partners, unpaid family workers and home-workers, irrespective of whether or not they are on the payroll.

Comparability

Most countries present information using the enterprise as the statistical unit. Japan, Korea, and Mexico are exceptions, as data refer to establishments. As most enterprises correspond to a single establishment, these differences do not significantly distort comparisons. An area where considerable differences do arise concerns the coverage of data on enterprises/establishments. In many countries, this information is based on business registers, economic censuses or surveys that may have a size cut off. All countries have thresholds of one sort or another, often depending on tax legislation and legal provisions reducing administrative burdens on small enterprises. For Ireland, only enterprises with 3 or more persons engaged are reflected, while the data for Japan and Korea do not include establishments with fewer than 4 and 5 persons engaged respectively. Also, it is typically difficult, if not impossible, to cover enterprises operating in the underground economy. These differences, however, do not prevent meaningful comparisons across countries.

Employment data for Australia and Switzerland refer to the total number of persons engaged rather than to the number of employees. Data refer to 2006 in the case of Australia, Korea, Norway, Turkey and the United Kingdom, to 2001 for Switzerland, 2003 for Mexico, 2004 for the United States and 2005 for Iceland.

Note that because data do not follow the same enterprise over time, they do not show the contribution that small enterprises make to economic and employment growth as they move from the start-up phase to some optimal size.

Overview

The contribution of small enterprises varies considerably across countries. In most economies, the share of enterprises with less than 20 persons engaged exceeds 70%, ranging between 67% in Ireland and above 95% in Greece. Small enterprises account for a smaller share of the total number of employees, ranging between around 11% in the United States and the Czech Republic and more than 35% in Greece.

Some larger economies are characterised by a lower proportion of small enterprises, partly reflecting the greater scope for growth in larger markets (due to the existence of a greater pool of workers and larger demand) but also due to a statistical phenomenon (*i.e.* when an enterprise opens a new establishment in the same economy within which it is registered, it will move from being a small to a large enterprise).

Sources

- OECD (2010), *SMEs, Entrepreneurship and Innovation*, OECD, Paris.
- *Structural and Demographic Business Statistics, OECD database*.

Further information

Analytical publications

- OECD (2009), *The Impact of the Global Crisis on SME and Entrepreneurship Financing and Policy Responses*, OECD, Paris.
- OECD (2008), *Enhancing the Role of SMEs in Global Value Chains*, OECD, Paris.
- OECD (2008), *Removing Barriers to SME Access to International Markets*, OECD, Paris.

Statistical publications

- OECD, Eurostat (2009), *Measuring Entrepreneurship – a collection of indicators, OECD-Eurostat Entrepreneurship Indicators Programme*, OECD, Paris.
- OECD (2010), *Structural and Demographic Business Statistics 2009*, OECD, Paris.

Methodological publications

- OECD, Eurostat (2008), *Eurostat-OECD Manual on Business Demography Statistics*, OECD, Paris.

Number of employees and number of enterprises in manufacturing

Breakdown by size-class of enterprise, 2007 or latest available year

Number of persons engaged	As a percentage of total number of employees in manufacturing							As a percentage of total number of enterprises in manufacturing					
	Less than 20	20 or more	Less than 10	10-19	20-49	50-249	250 or more	Less than 20	20 or more	Less than 10	10-19	20-49	50-249	250 or more
Australia	28.9	71.1	19.3	9.6	13.9	..	..	94.2	5.8	88.5	5.7	3.8	..	..
Austria	14.2	85.8	7.3	6.9	11.3	27.0	47.5	85.2	14.8	73.8	11.4	7.9	5.3	1.6
Belgium	13.5	86.5	7.0	6.5	13.2	25.9	47.5	89.0	11.0	81.4	7.6	6.4	3.7	0.9
Czech Republic	11.4	88.6	5.7	5.7	10.6	29.8	48.3	94.1	5.9	90.5	3.6	3.0	2.3	0.6
Denmark	12.3	87.7	5.8	6.5	12.0	28.4	47.4	83.4	16.6	72.8	10.7	8.9	6.3	1.4
Finland	13.2	86.8	7.4	5.9	10.1	24.8	51.9	90.1	9.9	83.2	7.0	5.2	3.8	1.0
France	17.9	82.1	10.7	7.3	12.1	22.2	47.8	91.3	8.7	84.1	7.2	5.1	2.8	0.8
Germany	13.0	87.0	5.0	8.0	7.5	25.3	54.3	81.7	18.3	60.5	21.3	7.8	8.4	2.1
Greece	35.3	64.7	30.4	4.9	12.1	25.6	27.1	97.8	2.3	96.5	1.2	1.3	0.8	0.2
Hungary	16.5	83.5	9.8	6.7	11.6	26.4	45.4	91.4	8.6	85.3	6.2	4.7	3.1	0.8
Iceland	..	..	..	..	..	..	..	88.9	11.1	80.2	8.7	6.7	3.8	0.7
Ireland	11.3	88.7	5.0	6.2	12.9	30.1	45.8	67.0	33.0	46.8	20.2	17.7	12.1	3.2
Italy	30.8	69.2	15.1	15.7	18.2	24.7	26.3	92.9	7.1	82.7	10.3	4.8	2.0	0.3
Japan	19.2	80.8	8.6	10.7	17.6	31.0	32.2	69.6	30.4	45.4	24.2	18.4	10.2	1.8
Korea	25.8	74.2	11.3	14.5	20.9	..	..	76.1	23.9	49.5	26.6	16.5	..	..
Luxembourg	8.9	91.1	4.3	4.6	7.6	23.1	60.5	78.8	21.2	66.5	12.3	9.3	8.9	3.0
Mexico	13.7	86.3	9.4	4.3	7.3	21.6	57.3	92.8	7.2	89.7	3.1	2.2	1.8	0.7
Netherlands	20.5	79.5	10.7	9.8	15.9	29.4	34.2	86.2	13.8	76.8	9.4	8.1	4.7	1.1
New Zealand	21.9	78.1	11.6	10.3	14.8	..	..	90.9	9.1	82.1	8.8	5.7	..	..
Norway	18.4	81.7	9.9	8.5	14.5	28.3	38.9	89.2	10.8	81.0	8.2	6.3	3.8	0.8
Poland	14.5	85.5	10.8	3.7	9.4	30.7	45.4	91.7	8.3	88.3	3.4	3.9	3.5	0.9
Portugal	31.7	68.3	19.7	12.0	19.4	30.1	18.9	91.7	8.3	84.0	7.7	5.4	2.6	0.3
Slovak Republic	9.5	90.5	4.5	5.0	8.1	26.1	56.3	75.0	25.0	51.1	23.9	9.9	11.4	3.7
Spain	25.8	74.2	14.0	11.8	20.6	25.3	28.3	89.1	10.9	79.1	10.0	7.5	2.9	0.5
Sweden	14.4	85.6	8.2	6.1	10.3	23.7	51.6	92.6	7.4	87.3	5.3	3.9	2.7	0.7
Switzerland	22.7	77.3	14.9	7.8	13.0	29.2	35.1	87.8	12.2	79.1	8.7	6.7	4.5	0.9
Turkey	21.4	78.6	..	..	17.3	25.9	35.4	93.6	6.4	..	..	4.2	1.9	0.4
United Kingdom	16.6	83.4	9.5	7.1	11.8	26.7	44.9	85.9	14.2	75.0	10.9	7.8	5.2	1.2
United States	11.1	88.9	5.7	5.4	..	..	..	76.7	23.3	62.6	14.2	..	..	..
Estonia	17.3	82.7	9.1	8.2	16.8	38.4	27.6	77.5	22.5	64.4	13.1	12.6	8.6	1.3
Slovenia	14.8	85.2	9.3	5.5	9.0	28.4	47.8	92.1	8.0	86.7	5.3	3.8	3.3	0.9

StatLink 📊 http://dx.doi.org/10.1787/824283220655

Manufacturing enterprises with less than 20 persons engaged

As a percentage of total number of employees or total number of enterprises, 2007 or latest available year

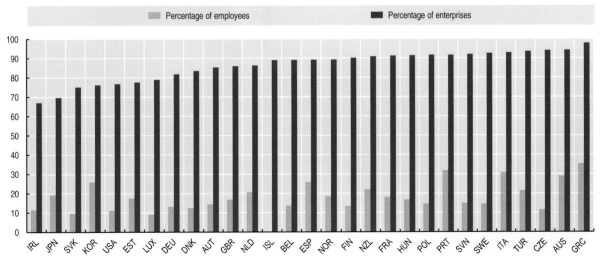

StatLink 📊 http://dx.doi.org/10.1787/818387841621

GLOBALISATION

TRADE

FDI AND MULTINATIONAL ENTERPRISES

SHARE OF INTERNATIONAL TRADE IN GDP

International trade is a principal channel of economic integration. International trade tends to be more important for countries that are small in terms of geographic size or population and surrounded by neighbouring countries with open trade regimes than for countries that are large, relatively self-sufficient, or geographically isolated and penalised by high transport costs. Other factors that help explain differences in the importance of international trade across countries are history, culture, trade policy, the structure of the economy (especially the weight of non-tradable services in GDP), re-exports and the presence of multinational firms (which leads to much intra-firm trade).

Definition

The importance of international trade in different countries is measured here by the share of trade in goods and services in GDP. The rates shown correspond to the average of imports and exports of both goods and services at current prices as a percentage of GDP. Goods consist of merchandise imports and exports. Services cover transport, travel, communications, construction, IT, financial, other business, personal and government services, as well as royalties and license fees.

The data are taken from OECD national accounts statistics compiled according to the 1993 *System of National Accounts*.

Comparability

The ratios shown in this table are compiled using common standards and definitions.

The trade-to-GDP ratio is often called the "trade openness ratio". However, the term openness may be somewhat misleading as a low ratio for a country does not necessarily imply high tariff or non-tariff obstacles to foreign trade, but may be due to a range of other factors mentioned above.

The trade-to-GDP ratios shown here differ from those published by WTO, IMF and OECD trade indicators, which refer to the sum of imports and exports (rather than the average).

Data for Australia and New Zealand refer to fiscal years.

Overview

In 2008, the trade-to-GDP ratio for OECD countries was 29%, while the rate for the EU27 was 41%. For the reasons noted above, there were large differences in these ratios across countries. The ratios exceeded 50% for small countries – Austria, Belgium, the Czech Republic, Denmark, Hungary, Ireland, Korea, Luxembourg, the Netherlands, the Slovak Republic, Sweden, and Switzerland – but were under 20% for the two largest OECD countries – Japan and the United States.

Between 1998 and 2008, trade-to-GDP ratios for the OECD as a whole increased by 8 percentage points. Substantial increases in trade-to-GDP ratios were recorded for Luxembourg, Hungary, the Czech Republic, and the Slovak Republic. Both Canada and Ireland saw falls in their trade-to-GDP ratios over this period, with the decline being especially large for Canada (-6%).

Sources
- OECD (2010), *National Accounts of OECD Countries*, OECD, Paris.

Further information
Statistical publications
- OECD (2009), *International Trade by Commodity Statistics*, OECD, Paris.
- OECD (2010), *Main Economic Indicators*, OECD, Paris.
- OECD (2009), *Monthly Statistics of International Trade*, OECD, Paris.
- OECD (2008), *Statistics on International Trade in Services*, OECD, Paris.
- OECD (2010), *National Accounts at a Glance 2009*, OECD, Paris.

Methodological publications
- Lindner, A., *et al.* (2001), "Trade in Goods and Services: Statistical Trends and Measurement Challenges", OECD Statistics Brief, No 1, October, OECD, Paris, *www.oecd.org/std/statisticsbrief*.
- UN, EC, IMF, OECD, UNCTAD and the WTO (2002), *Manual on Statistics of International Trade in Services*, United Nations, New York.

Web sites
- OECD International Trade Statistics, *www.oecd.org/std/its*.

International trade in goods and services

As a percentage of GDP

	1995	1996	1997	1998	1999	2000	2001	2002	2003	2004	2005	2006	2007	2008
Australia	19.4	19.3	20.3	19.9	20.9	22.5	21.1	20.4	18.8	19.9	21.0	21.2	21.6	24.5
Austria	35.3	36.3	39.7	40.8	41.7	45.5	47.4	46.7	46.8	50.0	52.2	54.4	56.8	56.5
Belgium	63.5	64.1	68.0	67.9	68.0	76.8	76.1	74.1	71.7	74.2	78.2	80.4	81.5	85.3
Canada	35.7	36.4	38.5	40.4	41.4	42.7	40.7	39.4	36.2	36.3	35.9	34.9	33.9	34.3
Czech Republic	52.9	51.8	54.7	54.8	56.0	64.9	66.6	61.3	62.9	70.1	70.6	74.7	77.6	74.8
Denmark	35.5	35.4	36.9	37.2	38.2	43.5	43.9	44.3	42.2	42.9	46.5	50.5	51.2	53.7
Finland	32.6	33.4	34.7	34.0	33.7	38.7	36.7	35.7	35.1	36.5	39.6	42.7	43.2	45.0
France	22.2	22.4	24.3	25.0	25.1	28.1	27.5	26.3	25.1	25.7	26.5	27.4	27.4	27.7
Germany	23.7	24.4	26.8	28.0	29.0	33.2	33.8	33.4	33.7	35.9	38.5	42.5	43.4	44.1
Greece	21.8	22.1	24.0	24.6	27.4	31.6	30.6	27.8	26.1	27.2	27.0	27.9	28.3	28.3
Hungary	44.8	47.9	53.9	61.3	64.7	74.9	71.6	63.8	63.1	64.5	66.9	77.5	79.7	81.7
Iceland	33.7	36.0	36.0	36.9	35.9	37.2	39.3	36.7	35.8	36.9	37.8	41.1	40.2	45.9
Ireland	70.4	71.5	73.1	81.1	82.4	91.6	92.4	85.5	75.8	76.5	75.9	74.9	75.8	78.3
Italy	23.8	22.4	23.3	23.6	23.5	26.6	26.4	25.2	24.3	25.0	26.0	28.1	29.1	29.1
Japan	8.5	9.6	10.3	10.0	9.5	10.3	10.2	10.7	11.2	12.3	13.6	15.5	16.8	17.4
Korea	27.8	28.0	30.9	37.6	33.8	37.1	34.6	32.4	34.2	38.8	37.9	39.0	41.2	53.5
Luxembourg	95.8	101.0	112.2	119.3	124.6	139.5	137.8	130.9	125.1	140.2	143.0	153.2	160.5	156.5
Mexico	26.5	28.3	27.7	28.9	28.8	29.1	26.1	25.3	26.1	27.5	27.9	28.7	29.1	29.4
Netherlands	56.5	57.0	60.5	60.2	60.9	67.3	64.4	60.9	59.9	62.7	65.4	69.0	70.5	72.6
New Zealand	28.6	27.8	27.9	29.3	31.0	34.7	33.9	31.5	28.9	29.3	28.9	29.8	29.4	32.8
Norway	34.9	36.3	37.3	36.7	35.7	38.0	37.3	34.4	33.8	35.3	36.4	37.4	37.8	38.4
Poland	22.1	23.0	25.4	28.4	27.1	30.3	28.9	30.4	34.7	38.7	37.5	41.3	42.2	42.0
Portugal	31.8	31.7	32.6	33.4	33.0	35.2	33.9	32.1	31.3	32.3	33.0	35.1	36.5	37.7
Slovak Republic	56.7	58.7	61.2	64.6	63.4	71.7	76.8	74.8	76.8	75.9	78.6	86.4	87.2	84.2
Spain	22.4	23.4	25.9	26.8	27.6	30.6	29.8	28.4	27.5	27.9	28.3	29.5	30.3	29.5
Sweden	36.4	35.3	38.4	39.8	39.9	43.4	43.2	41.2	40.4	42.2	44.9	47.4	48.8	50.5
Switzerland	33.4	34.1	37.5	38.2	39.3	43.6	43.5	41.1	40.8	42.9	45.6	48.4	51.1	50.8
Turkey	17.5	19.5	21.8	20.8	19.4	21.6	25.4	24.4	23.5	24.9	23.6	25.1	24.9	26.1
United Kingdom	28.3	29.3	28.3	26.9	26.9	28.6	28.3	27.4	26.6	26.6	28.1	30.1	28.2	30.4
United States	11.6	11.8	12.1	11.8	12.0	13.0	11.9	11.5	11.7	12.6	13.2	13.9	14.4	15.2
EU27 total	28.8	29.1	30.9	31.5	32.0	35.8	35.6	34.5	33.9	35.2	36.9	39.9	39.9	41.0
OECD total	19.1	19.8	20.7	21.0	20.8	22.2	21.7	21.5	22.1	23.6	24.7	26.4	27.5	28.9
Chile	28.1	28.1	28.1	27.9	28.4	30.6	32.5	32.8	34.5	36.2	37.1	38.2	40.3	43.1
Estonia	71.9	67.4	77.2	79.6	72.9	86.4	81.1	74.6	72.9	76.6	81.0	86.0	78.4	77.7
Israel	32.7	31.9	31.8	31.3	35.5	37.2	34.1	36.4	36.9	41.3	42.7	42.6	43.3	40.8
Russian Federation	27.6	24.0	23.6	27.9	34.7	34.0	30.6	29.8	29.5	28.3	28.3	27.4	26.0	26.5
Slovenia	50.9	50.7	52.1	52.2	49.7	55.7	55.9	54.6	54.1	58.7	62.3	66.8	70.4	69.2

StatLink http://dx.doi.org/10.1787/824333188522

International trade to GDP ratios

Difference between 2008 and 1998 ratios in percentage points

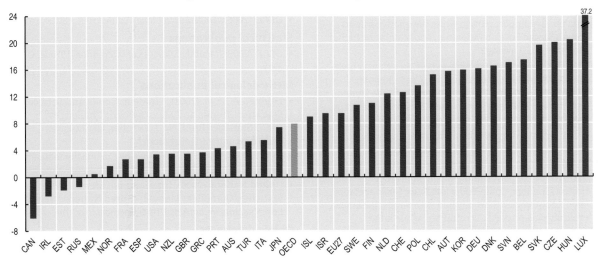

StatLink http://dx.doi.org/10.1787/818408344514

INTERNATIONAL TRADE IN GOODS

Since its creation, the OECD has sought to promote international trade, considering it an effective way of enhancing economic growth and raising living standards. Member countries benefit from increased trade as do OECD's trade partners in the rest of the world.

Definition

According to United Nations guidelines, international merchandise trade statistics record all goods which add to or subtract from the stock of material resources of a country by entering (as imports) or leaving (as exports) its economic territory. Goods being transported through a country or temporarily admitted or withdrawn (except for goods for inward or outward processing) are not included in the merchandise trade statistics.

Comparability

All OECD countries use the United Nations guidelines so far as their data sources allow. There are some, generally minor, differences across countries in the coverage of certain types of transactions such as postal trade, imports and exports of military equipment under defence agreements, sea products traded by domestic vessels on the high seas and goods entering or leaving bonded customs areas.

Exports are usually valued free on board (f.o.b.), with the exception of the United States which values exports free alongside ship (f.a.s.), which is lower than f.o.b. by the cost of loading the goods on board. Imports are valued by most countries at cost, insurance and freight (c.i.f.) i.e. the cost of the goods plus the costs of insurance and freight to bring the goods to the borders of the importing country. Canada, however, reports imports at f.o.b. values. The trade balances shown in the table are, therefore, not strictly comparable because imports are not valued in the same way by all countries.

The introduction by the European Union of the single market in 1993 resulted in some loss of accuracy for intra-EU trade because custom documents were no longer available to record all imports and exports. Note that while the OECD data mostly follow the UN recommendations, trade statistics reported by Eurostat follow Community definitions, and are not strictly comparable with those reported here.

OECD total includes Mexico from 1990, Hungary and Poland from 1992, the Czech Republic from 1993, Korea from 1994 and the Slovak Republic from 1997 onwards.

Overview

Over the ten-year period from 1998 to 2008, relative import growth (i.e. import growth in a single country divided by growth for all OECD countries) was low in Ireland, the United Kingdom and Canada while it was particularly high in the Slovak Republic, Korea, the Czech Republic and Poland. China and India continued to show high relative import growth while the relative import growth for the Russian Federation and Brazil were higher than the OECD average.

Over the same period, relative export growth was high for the Slovak Republic, Poland, the Czech Republic, Turkey and Hungary. The United Kingdom, the United States, Ireland, France, Japan and Canada were among the countries with below average growth rates.

China recorded higher growth in imports as well as exports than any country in this comparison.

The United States trade deficit has been large throughout the period and growing in most years. The United Kingdom, Spain, India and France also recorded large trade deficits. Germany had, on average, the largest trade surplus of all OECD countries, while large surpluses were also recorded by the Russian Federation and China.

Sources

- OECD (2009), *International Trade by Commodity Statistics*, OECD, Paris.
- UN Commodity Trade Statistics Database.

Further information

Analytical publications

- OECD (2005), *Trade and Structural Adjustment: Embracing Globalisation*, OECD, Paris.
- OECD (2006), *The Development Dimension – Aid for Trade: Making it Effective*, OECD, Paris.
- OECD (2006), *Trade Based Money Laundering*, OECD, Paris.

Statistical publications

- OECD (2009), *Monthly Statistics of International Trade*, OECD, Paris.

Methodological publications

- Lindner, A., et al. (2001), "Trade in Goods and Services: Statistical Trends and Measurement Challenges", OECD Statistics Brief, No 1, October, OECD, Paris, *www.oecd.org/std/statisticsbrief*.
- OECD (2004), *International Trade by Commodity Statistics – Definitions*, OECD, Paris.
- United Nations (2004), International Merchandise Trade Statistics: Compilers Manual, United Nations, New York, *http://unstats.un.org/unsd/trade/methodology.htm*.

Online databases

- *ITCS International Trade by Commodity Statistics*.
- *Monthly International Trade*.

Trade balance: exports of goods minus imports of goods
Billion US dollars

	1995	1996	1997	1998	1999	2000	2001	2002	2003	2004	2005	2006	2007	2008
Australia	-4.4	-1.2	1.0	-5.0	-9.5	-4.0	2.4	-4.5	-14.6	-17.3	-13.2	-9.3	-16.9	-4.7
Austria	-8.5	-10.1	-6.9	-6.2	-6.2	-5.2	-4.4	-0.1	-2.3	-0.4	-2.2	-0.2	0.5	-2.6
Belgium	15.4	11.4	12.3	14.4	14.3	13.5	11.6	17.7	20.7	21.1	13.8	15.4	17.3	6.5
Canada	16.5	19.2	18.1	13.3	23.2	37.6	39.4	30.2	31.8	43.1	45.7	38.2	39.9	47.4
Czech Republic	-3.9	-5.8	-4.4	-2.2	-2.0	-3.2	-3.1	-2.2	-2.5	0.5	1.7	1.7	4.1	2.3
Denmark	4.7	5.7	3.7	1.7	4.7	5.2	5.8	6.4	8.4	8.0	8.3	6.3	3.6	5.0
Finland	10.9	9.7	10.0	10.8	10.2	11.7	10.7	11.0	10.9	10.1	6.8	7.8	8.3	4.7
France	10.6	6.2	16.8	14.7	9.5	-8.5	-4.4	1.1	-4.5	-20.5	-41.6	-50.9	-71.8	-100.6
Germany	59.6	68.3	67.1	72.3	69.3	54.8	85.7	125.6	146.8	193.6	198.0	199.7	269.5	261.9
Greece	-15.0	-15.7	-15.8	-19.4	-18.8	-18.8	-17.9	-21.8	-31.2	-37.6	-37.4	-42.8	-52.6	-63.8
Hungary	-2.6	-3.1	-2.1	-2.7	-3.0	-4.0	-3.2	-3.3	-4.7	-4.8	-3.6	-2.9	-0.1	-0.6
Iceland	-	-0.1	-0.2	-0.6	-0.5	-0.7	-0.3	-	-0.4	-0.8	-1.9	-2.5	-1.9	-0.8
Ireland	11.5	12.4	14.4	19.9	24.0	25.6	26.4	36.0	38.7	42.0	39.7	32.2	35.3	42.8
Italy	27.2	43.9	29.9	26.5	14.7	1.8	8.1	7.7	2.0	-1.9	-17.0	-25.4	-11.6	-13.6
Japan	107.1	61.8	82.2	107.5	107.2	99.6	54.0	79.1	88.5	110.5	79.1	67.7	92.1	18.9
Korea	-10.4	-19.6	-8.5	39.0	23.9	11.8	9.3	10.4	15.0	29.4	23.2	16.1	14.6	-13.3
Luxembourg	..	..	..	..	-2.8	-2.8	-2.9	-2.9	-3.7	-4.6	-4.9	-5.5	-6.1	-7.8
Mexico	6.8	6.2	0.5	-8.0	-5.7	-5.8	-7.6	-8.7	-5.6	-8.8	-7.6	-6.1	-11.2	-17.3
Netherlands	19.6	16.5	15.5	10.9	2.7	5.4	5.6	11.9	18.3	32.8	36.9	38.7	55.6	48.1
New Zealand	-0.7	-0.6	-0.8	-0.6	-2.4	-1.2	..	-1.2	-2.0	-2.8	-4.5	-4.0	-3.9	-3.8
Norway	9.0	14.0	12.8	2.9	11.3	25.5	26.0	24.7	29.0	33.7	48.3	57.9	56.1	83.1
Poland	-6.1	-12.7	-16.5	-18.8	-18.5	-17.3	-14.2	-14.1	-14.4	-14.4	-12.2	-16.1	-25.4	-38.6
Portugal	-10.2	-10.6	-11.1	-12.8	-15.3	-15.6	-15.4	-14.2	-15.3	-19.2	-23.1	-23.3	-26.9	-34.2
Slovak Republic	..	..	-2.1	-2.4	-1.1	-0.9	-2.1	-2.2	-0.7	-1.9	-2.4	-3.1	-2.1	-2.4
Spain	-23.0	-21.0	-18.2	-25.8	-36.4	-39.5	-38.8	-40.0	-53.4	-76.5	-96.8	-115.9	-137.5	-139.5
Sweden	15.8	18.9	18.3	16.4	16.3	14.2	12.8	15.9	18.2	22.8	18.9	20.3	16.2	16.5
Switzerland	1.5	1.5	0.2	-1.2	0.4	-2.0	-2.1	4.2	4.2	6.8	4.4	6.5	10.9	17.2
Turkey	-14.1	-20.4	-22.3	-19.0	-14.1	-26.7	-10.1	-15.5	-22.1	-34.4	-43.3	-54.0	-62.8	-70.0
United Kingdom	-25.9	-28.7	-26.3	-46.9	-53.2	-56.6	-65.4	-78.8	-85.8	-119.9	-131.4	-150.1	-184.7	-176.6
United States	-187.9	-194.8	-210.5	-263.9	-366.4	-477.7	-449.1	-509.1	-581.4	-707.4	-828.0	-882.0	-854.6	-864.9
EU27 total	103.7	114.8	118.3	82.0	37.0	-15.9	28.9	77.3	68.4	45.4	-23.8	-95.1	-117.8	-270.1
OECD total	3.7	-48.7	-43.0	-85.1	-224.0	-383.7	-343.0	-336.1	-411.7	-518.9	-741.3	-885.8	-844.8	-1 000.6
Brazil	-7.2	-9.0	-12.1	-9.7	-3.7	-3.8	-0.2	10.7	23.4	31.4	42.1	46.5	40.0	24.7
Chile	1.0	-1.4	-1.4	-2.2	1.7	1.6	2.6	2.0	2.7	8.5	8.7	21.2	23.0	10.9
China	16.7	12.2	40.4	43.6	29.2	24.1	22.5	30.4	25.5	32.1	102.0	177.5	261.8	298.1
Estonia	-0.7	-1.1	-1.5	-1.5	-1.1	-1.2	-1.2	-1.5	-2.3	-2.5	-2.5	-4.6	-4.9	-3.6
India	-4.9	-5.6	-6.6	-9.2	-13.0	-6.1	-7.6	-8.6	-14.2	-28.4	-46.3	-57.0	-72.7	-133.9
Indonesia	4.8	6.9	11.8	21.5	24.7	28.6	25.4	25.9	28.5	21.5	28.0	39.7	39.6	7.8
Israel	-9.3	-9.4	-6.5	-4.2	-5.2	-4.3	-4.2	-3.6	-2.4	-2.3	-2.3	-1.0	-2.5	-3.8
Russian Federation	..	27.6	19.7	28.6	42.6	69.2	58.0	60.5	76.3	106.0	142.7	163.4	152.5	200.9
Slovenia	-1.2	-1.1	-1.0	-1.1	-1.5	-1.4	-0.9	-0.6	-1.1	-1.7	-1.7	-2.0	-2.9	-4.7
South Africa	..	..	..	..	..	-0.5	3.7	-3.1	-2.9	-2.9	-7.3	-8.0	-15.9	-15.8	-13.6

StatLink ⟞⟞⟝ http://dx.doi.org/10.1787/824347818584

Trade balance: exports of goods minus imports of goods
Billion US dollars, average 2006-2008

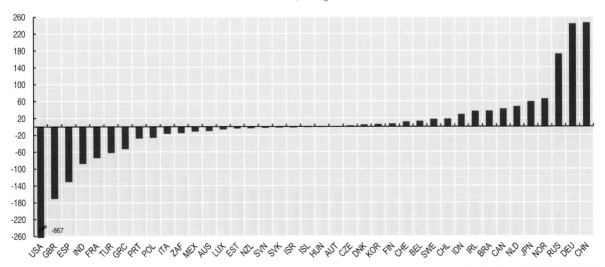

StatLink ⟞⟞⟝ http://dx.doi.org/10.1787/818412306552

Imports of goods

Billion US dollars

	1995	1996	1997	1998	1999	2000	2001	2002	2003	2004	2005	2006	2007	2008
Australia	57.4	61.4	61.8	60.8	65.5	67.8	60.9	69.5	84.8	103.8	119.0	132.7	157.8	191.6
Austria	66.3	67.1	63.6	67.1	68.7	67.4	69.0	71.4	91.5	111.3	120.0	134.3	156.1	175.4
Belgium	152.3	159.4	158.3	164.9	164.6	171.7	178.7	198.1	234.8	285.4	320.2	353.7	413.6	470.7
Canada	164.5	171.0	197.1	201.3	215.6	240.0	221.6	222.4	240.2	273.8	314.4	350.0	380.4	408.3
Czech Republic	20.8	27.4	27.2	30.5	28.8	32.2	36.5	40.7	51.2	66.7	76.5	93.4	116.8	140.3
Denmark	45.6	45.0	44.5	46.2	44.3	44.4	44.3	49.3	56.2	66.8	75.0	85.3	98.0	110.8
Finland	29.5	30.9	31.0	32.4	31.6	34.1	32.2	33.6	41.6	50.7	58.5	69.4	81.8	92.2
France	273.5	277.7	266.6	285.8	292.8	304.0	293.9	303.8	362.5	434.2	476.0	529.9	611.1	695.5
Germany	464.3	444.4	445.3	471.6	473.5	495.4	486.3	490.1	601.8	718.2	779.8	922.2	1 059.3	1 204.2
Greece	25.9	27.0	27.0	30.3	29.5	29.8	28.2	32.5	44.9	52.8	54.9	63.7	76.1	89.3
Hungary	15.5	16.2	21.2	25.7	28.0	32.1	33.7	37.6	47.7	60.2	65.9	77.0	94.7	108.8
Iceland	1.8	2.0	2.0	2.5	2.5	2.6	2.3	2.3	2.8	3.6	5.0	6.0	6.7	6.2
Ireland	32.3	35.8	39.2	44.4	46.5	50.7	51.1	52.3	54.2	62.3	70.3	76.6	86.7	84.1
Italy	204.0	208.2	208.1	215.6	220.3	238.1	236.1	246.6	297.4	355.3	384.8	442.6	511.9	553.2
Japan	336.1	349.2	338.8	280.6	309.9	379.7	348.6	337.6	383.5	455.2	515.9	579.1	622.2	762.5
Korea	137.9	144.1	144.6	93.3	119.8	160.5	141.1	152.1	178.8	224.5	261.2	309.4	356.8	435.3
Luxembourg	..	..	..	..	10.6	10.6	11.2	11.5	13.6	16.8	17.6	19.6	22.3	25.4
Mexico	72.5	89.5	109.8	125.3	142.0	171.1	165.1	168.7	170.5	196.8	221.8	256.1	283.2	308.6
Netherlands	157.7	162.5	158.3	156.8	167.9	174.7	169.9	163.4	209.0	257.7	283.2	331.5	421.3	437.5
New Zealand	13.9	14.7	14.5	12.5	14.3	13.9	13.3	15.0	18.6	23.2	26.2	26.4	30.9	34.4
Norway	33.0	35.6	35.8	37.5	34.2	34.4	33.0	34.9	39.9	48.5	55.5	64.3	80.3	94.5
Poland	28.9	37.1	42.3	47.0	45.9	48.8	50.2	55.1	68.0	88.2	101.5	125.6	164.2	210.5
Portugal	33.6	35.2	35.1	37.0	39.8	39.9	39.5	40.0	47.1	54.9	61.2	66.7	78.2	90.1
Slovak Republic	..	..	11.7	13.1	11.1	12.7	14.7	16.6	22.6	29.5	34.2	44.8	60.2	72.6
Spain	116.5	123.6	124.4	137.2	147.9	152.9	155.0	165.9	209.7	259.3	289.6	330.0	391.2	418.7
Sweden	61.6	64.0	63.2	68.6	68.5	73.1	63.5	67.1	84.2	100.5	111.4	127.1	152.8	167.3
Switzerland	80.2	78.2	75.9	80.1	79.9	82.5	84.2	83.7	96.4	110.0	126.6	141.4	161.2	183.6
Turkey	35.7	43.6	48.6	45.9	40.7	54.5	41.4	51.3	69.3	97.5	116.8	139.6	170.1	202.0
United Kingdom	268.2	287.6	307.5	320.3	323.8	339.4	338.0	359.4	393.5	468.1	515.8	598.4	624.7	636.0
United States	770.8	817.6	898.0	944.4	1 059.2	1 258.1	1 180.1	1 202.3	1 305.1	1 525.3	1 732.3	1 919.0	2 017.1	2 164.8
EU27 total	..	..	..	..	..	2 402.9	2 386.6	2 496.5	3 011.1	3 642.1	4 020.4	4 645.4	5 420.3	6 033.3
OECD total	3 700.2	3 856.2	4 001.4	4 078.5	4 327.7	4 817.1	4 623.4	4 774.9	5 521.5	6 601.0	7 391.0	8 415.7	9 487.5	10 574.2
Brazil	53.7	56.7	65.1	60.8	51.7	55.9	55.6	47.2	48.3	62.8	73.6	91.3	120.6	173.2
Chile	14.9	16.8	18.1	17.1	13.9	16.6	16.1	15.4	17.4	22.4	29.9	34.7	42.7	58.2
China	132.1	138.8	142.4	140.2	165.7	225.1	243.6	295.2	412.8	561.2	660.0	791.5	956.0	1 132.6
Estonia	2.5	3.2	4.4	4.8	4.1	5.1	5.2	5.9	7.9	9.1	11.0	14.6	16.7	17.3
India	36.6	39.1	41.4	42.4	50.0	52.9	50.7	57.5	72.4	99.0	140.9	178.2	218.6	315.7
Indonesia	40.6	42.9	41.7	27.3	24.0	33.5	31.0	31.3	32.6	46.5	57.7	61.1	74.5	129.2
Israel	28.3	29.9	29.0	27.5	31.1	35.7	33.3	33.1	34.2	41.0	45.0	47.8	56.6	65.2
Russian Federation	..	61.1	67.6	43.7	30.3	33.9	41.9	46.2	57.3	75.6	98.7	137.8	199.7	267.1
Slovenia	9.5	9.4	9.4	10.1	10.1	10.1	10.1	10.9	13.9	17.6	19.6	23.0	29.4	34.0
South Africa	..	..	..	..	..	26.8	25.6	26.2	34.5	47.6	55.0	68.5	79.9	87.6

StatLink ᴍᴬᴾ http://dx.doi.org/10.1787/824364441318

Relative annual growth of imports of goods

Growth over the period 1998-2008, OECD total = 1.0

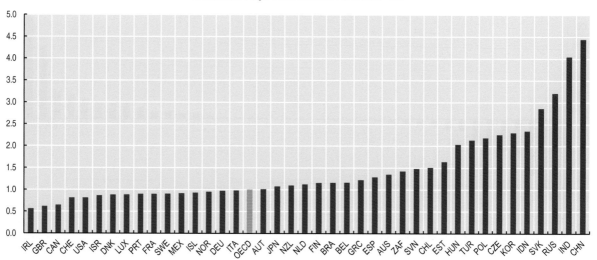

StatLink ᴍᴬᴾ http://dx.doi.org/10.1787/818430164256

Exports of goods
Billion US dollars

	1995	1996	1997	1998	1999	2000	2001	2002	2003	2004	2005	2006	2007	2008
Australia	53.0	60.2	62.8	55.8	56.0	63.8	63.3	65.0	70.2	86.4	106.0	123.3	140.9	186.9
Austria	57.8	57.1	56.7	60.9	62.4	62.3	64.7	71.3	89.2	110.8	117.7	134.2	156.6	172.8
Belgium	167.7	170.8	170.7	179.3	178.9	185.2	190.3	215.8	255.5	306.4	334.0	369.1	430.9	477.2
Canada	181.0	190.2	215.1	214.6	238.9	277.6	261.1	252.6	272.1	317.2	360.6	388.2	420.2	455.7
Czech Republic	16.8	21.7	22.7	28.3	26.8	29.1	33.4	38.5	48.7	65.8	78.2	95.1	120.9	142.6
Denmark	50.3	50.7	48.2	47.9	49.0	49.6	50.1	55.7	64.6	74.7	83.3	91.6	101.6	115.8
Finland	40.4	40.6	41.0	43.2	41.8	45.8	42.8	44.7	52.5	60.9	65.2	77.3	90.1	96.9
France	284.1	283.9	283.4	300.5	302.3	295.6	289.6	304.9	358.1	413.7	434.4	479.0	539.4	594.9
Germany	523.9	512.7	512.4	543.8	542.8	550.2	572.0	615.6	748.5	911.8	977.1	1 122.0	1 328.8	1 466.1
Greece	11.0	11.3	11.2	10.9	10.7	11.0	10.3	10.8	13.7	15.2	17.5	20.9	23.5	25.5
Hungary	12.9	13.1	19.1	23.0	25.0	28.1	30.5	34.3	43.0	55.5	62.3	74.1	94.6	108.2
Iceland	1.8	1.9	1.9	1.9	2.0	1.9	2.0	2.2	2.4	2.8	3.1	3.5	4.8	5.4
Ireland	43.8	48.2	53.6	64.2	70.5	76.3	77.4	88.3	92.9	104.3	110.0	108.8	122.0	126.9
Italy	231.3	252.1	238.0	242.1	235.1	239.9	244.3	254.2	299.5	353.5	373.0	417.2	500.2	539.6
Japan	443.3	410.9	421.0	388.1	417.1	479.2	402.6	416.7	472.0	565.7	594.9	646.7	714.3	781.4
Korea	127.5	124.5	136.2	132.3	143.7	172.3	150.4	162.5	193.8	253.8	284.4	325.5	371.5	422.0
Luxembourg	..	..	..	..	7.8	7.9	8.3	8.6	10.0	12.2	12.7	14.2	16.2	17.7
Mexico	79.3	95.7	110.2	117.3	136.3	165.3	157.5	160.8	164.9	188.0	214.2	250.0	272.0	291.3
Netherlands	177.4	179.0	173.8	167.6	170.5	180.1	175.5	175.3	227.3	290.5	320.1	370.2	476.8	485.6
New Zealand	13.3	14.2	13.7	11.9	11.9	12.7	13.3	13.8	16.5	20.3	21.7	22.4	26.9	30.6
Norway	42.0	49.6	48.5	40.4	45.5	59.9	59.0	59.6	67.9	82.5	103.8	122.2	136.4	177.6
Poland	22.9	24.4	25.7	28.2	27.4	31.6	36.1	41.0	53.5	73.8	89.4	109.6	138.8	171.9
Portugal	23.4	24.6	24.0	24.2	24.5	24.4	24.1	25.8	31.8	35.7	38.1	43.4	51.3	55.9
Slovak Republic	..	..	9.6	10.7	10.1	11.8	12.6	14.5	22.0	27.9	31.9	41.7	58.0	70.2
Spain	93.5	102.6	106.2	111.4	111.5	113.3	116.1	125.9	156.3	182.7	192.8	214.1	253.8	279.2
Sweden	77.4	82.9	81.5	85.0	84.8	87.4	76.3	82.9	102.4	123.2	130.3	147.4	169.1	183.9
Switzerland	81.6	79.7	76.2	78.9	80.3	80.5	82.1	87.9	100.7	116.8	130.9	147.9	172.1	200.8
Turkey	21.6	23.2	26.2	27.0	26.6	27.8	31.3	35.8	47.3	63.1	73.5	85.5	107.3	132.0
United Kingdom	242.2	258.9	281.2	273.4	270.7	282.9	272.6	280.6	307.7	349.0	384.4	448.4	440.0	459.3
United States	583.0	622.8	687.5	680.4	692.8	780.3	731.0	693.2	723.7	817.9	904.3	1 037.0	1 162.5	1 299.9
EU27 total	..	..	..	..	..	2 349.1	2 366.1	2 533.8	3 034.3	3 641.0	3 939.3	4 479.3	5 239.4	5 763.2
OECD total	3 703.9	3 807.5	3 958.4	3 993.4	4 103.7	4 433.5	4 280.5	4 438.7	5 108.9	6 082.4	6 649.8	7 530.1	8 641.5	9 573.6
Brazil	46.5	47.7	53.0	51.1	48.0	55.1	58.3	60.4	73.2	96.7	118.5	137.8	160.6	197.9
Chile	15.9	15.4	16.7	14.8	15.6	18.2	18.7	17.4	20.1	30.9	38.6	55.9	65.7	69.1
China	148.8	151.0	182.8	183.8	194.9	249.2	266.1	325.6	438.2	593.3	762.0	968.9	1 217.8	1 430.7
Estonia	1.8	2.1	2.9	3.2	3.0	3.8	4.0	4.3	5.6	6.5	8.2	10.0	11.7	13.7
India	31.7	33.5	34.8	33.2	36.9	42.4	43.9	50.1	59.3	75.9	100.4	121.2	145.9	181.9
Indonesia	45.4	49.8	53.4	48.8	48.7	62.1	56.3	57.2	61.1	71.6	85.7	100.8	114.1	137.0
Israel	19.0	20.5	22.5	23.3	25.8	31.4	29.1	29.5	31.8	38.6	42.8	46.8	54.1	61.3
Russian Federation	..	88.7	87.4	72.3	72.9	103.1	99.9	106.7	133.7	181.6	241.5	301.2	352.3	468.0
Slovenia	8.3	8.3	8.4	9.1	8.5	8.7	9.3	10.4	12.8	15.9	17.9	21.0	26.5	29.3
South Africa	..	..	..	..	..	26.3	26.0	23.1	31.6	40.3	47.0	52.6	64.0	74.0

StatLink ◀▨◨◀ http://dx.doi.org/10.1787/824370122572

Relative annual growth of exports of goods
Growth over the period 1998-2008, OECD total = 1.0

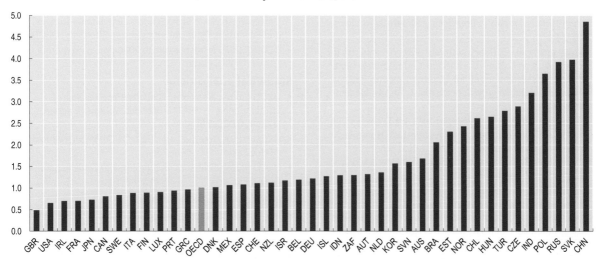

StatLink ◀▨◨◀ http://dx.doi.org/10.1787/818444001112

INTERNATIONAL TRADE IN SERVICES

International trade in services is growing in importance both among OECD countries and with the rest of the world. Traditional services – transport, insurance on merchandise trade, and travel – account for about half of total international trade in services, but trade in newer types of services, particularly those that can be conducted via the Internet, is growing rapidly.

Definition

International trade in services is defined according to the 5th edition of the *IMF Balance of Payments Manual* (BPM5). Services include transport (both freight and passengers), travel (mainly expenditure on goods and services by tourists and business travellers), communications services (postal, telephone, satellite, etc.), construction services, insurance and financial services, computer and information services, royalties and license fees, other business services (merchanting, operational leasing, technical and professional services, etc.), cultural and recreational services (rents for films, fees for actors and other performers, but excluding purchases of films, recorded music, books, etc.) and government services not included in the list above.

Comparability

BPM5 was issued in 1993 and countries began to implement it in the next two or three years. Prior to that, services were defined according to BPM4. All OECD countries now report international trade in services broadly according to the BPM5 framework, and BPM4 is of interest principally for some historic series that have not been revised. The main difference between them is that BPM5 makes a clear distinction between transactions in services and payments of income. In BPM4, labour and non-financial property incomes were included with services. Countries have tried to preserve continuity by revising earlier figures in line with BPM5 but this has not always been possible.

Overview

Between 1998 and 2008, growth of service imports among OECD countries was highest in Greece. This growth was also well above average in Poland, Ireland and Hungary. Imports of services grew relatively slowly in Japan.

In the same period, the growth rate of service exports for Ireland was well above the average and relatively high growth was also recorded for Luxembourg and Finland. Rather low relative growth occurred in Turkey, Mexico and Italy.

Averaged over the three years to 2008, trade in services was relatively balanced for most countries. However, large surpluses were recorded for United States and United Kingdom, and substantial deficits occurred in Germany and Japan.

For the OECD as a whole, the fastest growing categories of services in the period 2002-2008, both for imports and for exports, were financial services and computer and information services. The slowest growing categories were government services, among exports; and travel services, among imports.

Sources

- OECD (2010), *Main Economic Indicators*, OECD, Paris.
- OECD (2009), *Statistics on International Trade in Services*, OECD, Paris.

Further information

Analytical publications

- OECD (2004), *Promoting Trade in Services: Experience of the Baltic States*, OECD, Paris.
- OECD (2005), *Trade and Structural Adjustment: Embracing Globalisation*, OECD, Paris.
- OECD (2006), *Export Credit Financing Systems in OECD Member Countries and Non-Member Economies*, OECD, Paris.
- OECD (2006), *OECD Trade Policy Studies – Liberalisation and Universal Access to Basic Services: Telecommunications, Water and Sanitation, Financial Services, and Electricity*, OECD, Paris.
- OECD (2007), *Infrastructure to 2030 (Vol.2): Preparing the Future*, OECD, Paris.

Statistical publications

- OECD (2002), *Measuring Globalisation: The Role of Multinationals in OECD Economies, Volume II: Services 2001 Edition*, OECD, Paris.
- OECD (2009), *International Trade by Commodity Statistics*, OECD, Paris.
- OECD (2009), *Statistics on International Trade in Services*, OECD, Paris.

Methodological publications

- IMF (1993), *Balance of Payments Manual*, 5th edition, IMF, Washington, DC.

Web sites

- OECD International Trade in Services, *www.oecd.org/std/trade-services*.

Services trade balance: exports of services minus imports of services

Billion US dollars

	1995	1996	1997	1998	1999	2000	2001	2002	2003	2004	2005	2006	2007	2008
Australia	-0.9	0.2	0.2	-0.9	0.1	0.9	0.7	1.2	1.8	0.5	0.5	0.9	0.6	-3.1
Austria	5.0	4.7	4.0	5.1	6.2	6.6	6.4	7.1	8.7	10.1	11.9	12.1	15.2	19.2
Belgium	-0.1	0.2	1.3	0.8	1.4	2.1	1.8	1.8	1.7	3.6	5.0	6.2	5.5	3.9
Canada	-7.4	-6.7	-6.4	-4.3	-4.5	-3.9	-5.0	-4.6	-8.2	-8.5	-9.9	-12.3	-17.7	-21.1
Czech Republic	1.8	1.9	1.8	1.9	1.2	1.4	1.5	0.7	0.5	0.6	1.5	2.1	2.4	4.8
Denmark	0.7	1.3	0.1	-0.3	2.0	2.4	3.4	2.0	3.5	3.3	6.2	7.1	7.9	10.0
Finland	-2.2	-1.7	-1.6	-1.1	-1.1	-1.4	-0.2	0.6	-0.7	0.6	-0.7	-1.1	1.0	2.7
France	14.3	15.1	16.7	17.3	18.6	19.8	17.8	17.1	15.8	16.5	16.6	16.8	20.5	21.1
Germany	-53.4	-51.7	-48.1	-51.6	-57.9	-55.0	-54.1	-43.2	-50.7	-51.1	-46.7	-34.1	-37.3	-40.9
Greece	..	..	7.2	7.0	7.6	8.2	7.9	9.7	13.0	19.2	19.5	19.3	22.7	25.1
Hungary	0.6	1.5	1.7	1.7	1.3	0.8	1.1	-	-1.2	0.1	1.4	1.6	1.4	1.3
Iceland	-	-	-	-	-0.1	-0.1	-	-	-0.1	-0.2	-0.5	-0.7	-0.7	-0.3
Ireland	-6.3	-7.7	-9.0	-9.9	-10.8	-12.8	-11.9	-13.0	-12.5	-12.7	-11.6	-8.5	-1.7	-7.2
Italy	6.3	7.2	7.8	4.9	1.2	1.1	-	-2.9	-2.7	1.5	-0.7	-1.6	-9.7	-10.7
Japan	-57.3	-62.3	-54.1	-49.3	-54.0	-47.6	-43.7	-42.0	-35.5	-39.0	-27.9	-20.1	-23.2	-22.0
Korea	-3.0	-6.2	-3.2	1.0	-0.7	-2.8	-3.9	-8.2	-7.4	-8.0	-13.7	-19.0	-19.8	-16.7
Luxembourg	3.2	3.5	4.0	4.2	5.4	6.8	6.4	8.1	9.9	13.0	16.3	20.8	27.4	29.5
Mexico	0.7	0.4	-0.7	-0.9	-1.8	-2.3	-3.6	-4.0	-4.6	-4.6	-4.7	-5.7	-6.3	-7.1
Netherlands	1.1	2.0	3.3	2.5	2.6	-2.1	-2.5	-1.0	-0.7	4.3	6.8	9.4	12.1	13.0
New Zealand	-0.2	-0.2	-0.6	-0.7	-0.2	-0.1	0.1	0.6	1.1	1.0	0.4	0.2	0.2	-0.7
Norway	0.5	1.4	1.4	0.7	1.0	2.7	2.6	1.6	1.1	1.0	0.7	1.5	2.1	1.1
Poland	3.5	3.4	3.2	4.2	1.4	1.4	0.8	0.8	0.5	0.1	0.7	0.7	4.8	5.0
Portugal	..	1.4	1.5	1.9	2.0	2.0	2.6	3.1	4.0	5.0	4.8	6.2	8.8	9.5
Slovak Republic	0.7	0.2	0.2	0.2	0.2	0.4	0.5	0.5	0.2	0.3	0.3	0.8	0.5	-0.7
Spain	17.4	19.0	18.2	19.7	20.5	19.4	20.6	21.1	26.2	26.9	27.7	27.8	31.3	38.1
Sweden	-0.4	-0.9	-1.3	-1.6	-1.3	-1.5	-0.6	-0.8	2.0	5.8	7.8	10.0	16.3	17.6
Switzerland	14.3	14.0	14.9	15.9	16.7	17.9	17.3	18.0	21.5	24.4	26.9	31.3	37.7	46.0
Turkey	9.6	6.7	10.9	13.5	7.5	11.4	9.1	7.9	10.5	12.8	15.3	13.7	13.3	17.5
United Kingdom	17.6	22.3	27.5	24.8	25.2	22.9	24.4	29.1	36.9	52.1	46.9	63.6	89.4	100.9
United States	77.8	86.9	90.2	82.1	82.7	74.9	64.4	61.2	54.0	61.8	75.6	86.9	129.6	144.3
Euro area	..	..	5.0	0.7	-8.9	-8.1	-2.5	16.0	25.4	39.6	48.1	52.2	66.1	59.4
OECD total	..	..	95.1	90.5	74.7	77.3	70.8	83.8	98.0	151.3	193.3	259.6	343.5	396.1
Brazil	-7.5	-8.1	-9.3	-9.0	-7.0	-7.2	-7.8	-5.0	-4.9	-4.7	-8.3	-9.7	-13.2	-16.7
Chile	-0.3	-	-0.1	-0.5	-0.7	-0.7	-0.8	-0.7	-0.6	-0.7	-0.6	-0.6	-1.0	-0.6
China	-6.1	-2.0	-3.4	-2.8	-5.3	-5.6	-5.9	-6.8	-8.6	-9.7	-9.4	-9.0	-8.0	-11.8
Estonia	0.4	0.5	0.6	0.6	0.6	0.6	0.6	0.6	0.8	1.1	1.0	1.0	1.3	1.8
India	0.2	0.3	1.3	2.1	2.2	3.4	2.9	4.4	6.4	13.0	20.0	29.4	39.3	46.9
Indonesia	-8.1	-8.5	-9.7	-7.6	-7.8	-10.4	-10.4	-10.4	-12.1	-8.8	-9.1	-9.9	-11.8	-12.7
Israel	-0.4	-0.6	0.2	0.8	2.1	3.5	1.0	1.3	2.5	3.2	3.7	4.5	3.5	4.2
Russian Federation	-9.6	-5.4	-5.9	-4.1	-4.3	-6.7	-9.1	-9.9	-10.9	-12.7	-13.8	-13.6	-19.6	-25.1
Slovenia	0.6	0.6	0.6	0.5	0.4	0.4	0.5	0.6	0.6	0.9	1.1	1.2	1.4	2.4
South Africa	-1.4	-0.7	-0.6	-0.3	-0.5	-0.8	-0.4	-0.5	0.3	-0.6	-1.0	-2.3	-3.0	-4.4

StatLink ⌐ᵐᴵˢ http://dx.doi.org/10.1787/824373103577

Services trade balance: exports of services minus imports of services

Billion US dollars, average 2006-2008

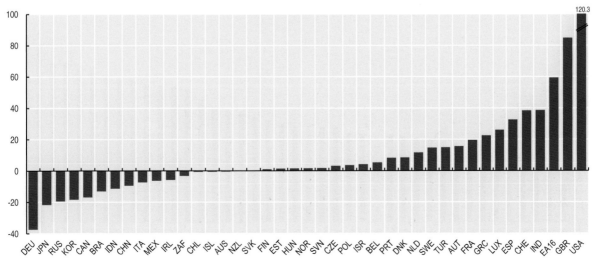

StatLink ⌐ᵐᴵˢ http://dx.doi.org/10.1787/818457315474

Imports of services
Billion US dollars

	1995	1996	1997	1998	1999	2000	2001	2002	2003	2004	2005	2006	2007	2008
Australia	17.4	18.9	19.2	18.0	18.8	18.9	17.3	18.3	21.8	27.9	30.4	32.2	39.7	47.5
Austria	19.3	19.9	17.9	18.1	17.3	16.5	17.6	18.8	23.8	27.8	30.6	33.6	39.1	42.8
Belgium	29.7	29.0	27.8	30.0	31.2	32.3	33.6	35.9	42.9	49.1	51.1	53.3	69.0	82.1
Canada	33.5	35.9	38.0	38.1	40.6	44.1	43.8	45.0	52.3	58.7	65.7	72.8	82.5	87.1
Czech Republic	4.9	6.3	5.4	5.7	5.9	5.4	5.6	6.4	7.3	9.0	10.2	11.8	14.4	17.3
Denmark	13.2	13.9	14.2	15.6	18.4	22.1	23.5	25.1	27.9	33.3	37.3	45.1	53.9	62.2
Finland	9.6	8.8	8.2	7.8	7.6	9.1	9.4	9.8	12.1	14.6	17.7	18.6	22.3	29.2
France	64.5	66.8	64.2	67.5	63.1	60.8	62.4	68.7	82.9	98.4	105.7	111.8	129.2	142.1
Germany	133.4	135.3	130.7	135.6	141.9	138.2	142.7	145.5	173.8	196.9	210.2	224.0	259.2	285.7
Greece	..	..	4.1	4.5	9.7	11.5	11.6	9.6	11.2	14.0	14.7	16.4	20.2	24.8
Hungary	3.6	3.5	4.1	4.2	4.4	4.8	5.6	6.8	9.2	10.2	11.5	12.1	15.8	18.7
Iceland	0.6	0.7	0.8	1.0	1.0	1.2	1.1	1.1	1.5	1.8	2.5	2.6	3.0	2.4
Ireland	11.3	13.4	15.2	23.9	27.7	32.8	37.5	42.8	54.5	65.4	71.5	80.2	94.7	107.8
Italy	51.1	53.4	54.2	59.1	55.7	55.6	57.8	63.0	74.3	83.3	90.0	100.4	121.7	129.8
Japan	122.8	130.0	123.4	111.7	114.9	116.8	108.2	107.8	108.8	133.7	134.0	134.5	149.3	163.3
Korea	25.8	29.6	29.5	24.5	27.2	33.4	32.9	36.6	40.4	49.9	58.8	68.9	83.1	92.7
Luxembourg	7.5	8.5	8.7	9.9	11.5	13.2	13.3	12.4	15.5	21.0	24.6	29.9	38.0	41.3
Mexico	9.0	10.2	11.8	12.4	13.5	16.0	16.2	16.7	17.1	18.6	20.8	22.0	23.8	25.1
Netherlands	44.8	45.3	45.8	47.2	49.5	51.4	53.8	57.0	63.9	69.5	73.3	75.3	84.2	92.2
New Zealand	4.7	4.9	4.8	4.4	4.5	4.5	4.3	4.8	5.7	7.2	8.3	7.9	9.2	9.7
Norway	13.1	13.4	14.3	14.8	15.4	15.0	15.8	17.8	20.6	24.3	29.2	31.7	38.9	44.2
Poland	7.1	6.3	5.7	6.6	7.0	9.0	9.0	9.2	10.6	13.4	15.5	19.9	24.2	30.6
Portugal	..	6.5	6.2	6.9	7.3	7.1	6.8	7.2	8.3	9.8	10.4	12.2	14.4	16.7
Slovak Republic	1.8	2.0	2.1	2.3	1.8	1.8	2.0	2.3	3.1	3.5	4.1	4.7	6.5	9.1
Spain	22.9	25.5	25.6	28.6	32.0	33.2	35.2	38.8	48.0	59.2	67.1	78.6	96.4	104.5
Sweden	16.8	18.4	19.7	21.3	23.2	24.6	24.2	24.8	28.7	33.2	35.3	39.6	48.2	54.5
Switzerland	12.1	12.7	11.2	12.3	13.1	12.8	12.3	12.9	14.8	19.5	22.8	23.5	28.0	31.9
Turkey	5.3	6.4	8.3	9.7	8.9	8.1	6.1	6.1	7.4	10.1	11.4	11.7	15.3	17.3
United Kingdom	66.9	74.3	79.8	89.9	98.6	101.1	101.6	112.0	130.3	154.8	169.7	183.5	212.0	212.0
United States	141.4	152.6	165.9	180.7	199.2	223.7	221.8	231.1	250.4	291.2	313.5	349.0	375.2	405.3
Euro area	..	..	241.4	262.8	274.2	276.5	285.5	294.5	347.2	412.8	455.6	501.6	607.1	686.1
OECD total	..	..	901.7	953.0	1 008.7	1 051.9	1 061.6	1 116.3	1 283.7	1 505.4	1 630.1	1 776.0	2 043.6	2 257.7
Brazil	13.6	12.7	15.3	16.7	14.2	16.7	17.1	14.5	15.4	17.3	24.4	29.1	37.2	47.1
Chile	3.7	3.6	4.0	4.4	4.6	4.8	5.0	5.1	5.7	6.8	7.8	8.5	9.9	11.4
China	25.2	22.6	28.0	26.7	31.6	36.0	39.3	46.5	55.3	72.1	83.8	101.0	130.0	158.9
Estonia	0.5	0.6	0.7	0.9	0.9	0.9	1.0	1.1	1.4	1.7	2.2	2.5	3.1	3.4
India	6.7	7.1	7.8	9.6	12.3	13.3	14.5	15.0	17.5	25.2	32.6	40.3	47.7	56.2
Indonesia	13.5	15.1	16.6	12.1	12.4	15.6	15.9	17.0	17.4	20.9	22.0	21.4	24.3	28.0
Israel	8.3	8.9	9.0	9.3	10.3	11.9	11.8	10.9	11.2	12.8	13.7	14.7	17.6	19.9
Russian Federation	20.2	18.7	20.0	16.5	13.4	16.2	20.6	23.5	27.1	33.3	38.7	44.7	59.1	76.4
Slovenia	1.4	1.5	1.4	1.5	1.5	1.4	1.5	1.7	2.2	2.6	2.8	3.3	4.3	5.0
South Africa	6.0	5.7	6.0	5.7	5.8	5.8	5.2	5.5	8.0	10.3	12.2	14.3	16.6	17.0

StatLink ᴹˢᴸ http://dx.doi.org/10.1787/824476760308

Relative annual growth of imports of services
Growth over the period 1998-2008, OECD total = 1.0

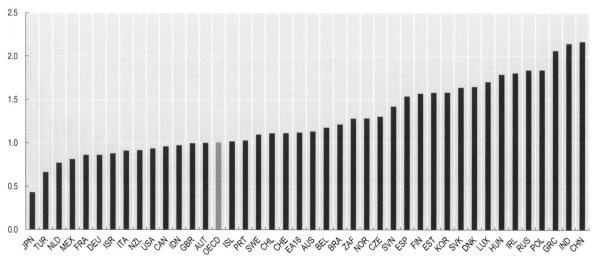

StatLink ᴹˢᴸ http://dx.doi.org/10.1787/818472382102

Exports of services
Billion US dollars

	1995	1996	1997	1998	1999	2000	2001	2002	2003	2004	2005	2006	2007	2008
Australia	16.5	19.1	19.3	17.2	18.9	19.9	18.1	19.6	23.6	28.5	31.0	33.1	40.3	44.3
Austria	24.3	24.6	21.9	23.2	23.5	23.1	24.0	25.9	32.5	37.9	42.4	45.6	54.3	62.0
Belgium	29.6	29.3	29.1	30.8	32.6	34.3	35.4	37.7	44.6	52.7	56.1	59.5	74.4	86.1
Canada	26.1	29.2	31.6	33.9	36.1	40.2	38.8	40.4	44.1	50.3	55.8	60.5	64.8	66.0
Czech Republic	6.7	8.2	7.2	7.6	7.1	6.9	7.1	7.1	7.8	9.6	11.8	13.9	16.8	22.1
Denmark	13.9	15.1	14.3	15.3	20.4	24.5	26.9	27.1	31.4	36.6	43.5	52.2	61.8	72.2
Finland	7.4	7.1	6.7	6.7	6.5	7.7	9.2	10.4	11.5	15.2	17.0	17.5	23.3	31.9
France	78.9	81.9	80.9	84.8	81.7	80.6	80.2	85.8	98.7	114.8	122.3	128.6	149.8	163.2
Germany	79.9	83.6	82.6	84.0	84.0	83.2	88.6	102.3	123.1	145.8	163.5	189.9	221.9	244.8
Greece	..	..	11.2	11.5	17.4	19.6	19.5	19.2	24.2	33.2	34.3	35.6	42.9	49.8
Hungary	4.3	5.0	5.7	5.9	5.6	5.6	6.6	6.9	8.0	10.3	12.9	13.7	17.3	20.0
Iceland	0.7	0.8	0.8	1.0	0.9	1.0	1.1	1.1	1.4	1.6	2.0	1.9	2.3	2.1
Ireland	5.0	5.7	6.2	14.1	16.9	20.0	25.6	29.8	42.0	52.7	59.9	71.6	93.0	100.6
Italy	57.5	60.6	62.0	64.0	58.9	56.7	57.9	60.1	71.6	84.7	89.4	98.8	111.9	119.1
Japan	65.5	67.7	69.3	62.4	60.9	69.2	64.5	65.7	73.3	94.7	106.1	114.4	126.2	141.3
Korea	22.8	23.4	26.3	25.6	26.5	30.5	29.1	28.4	33.0	41.9	45.1	49.9	63.3	76.0
Luxembourg	10.7	12.0	12.7	14.2	16.9	20.0	19.8	20.5	25.4	33.9	40.9	50.7	65.4	70.8
Mexico	9.7	10.6	11.1	11.5	11.7	13.7	12.7	12.7	12.5	14.0	16.1	16.2	17.5	18.0
Netherlands	45.9	47.2	49.0	49.7	52.1	49.3	51.3	56.0	63.2	73.7	80.1	84.7	96.4	105.2
New Zealand	4.5	4.7	4.2	3.8	4.3	4.4	4.4	5.4	6.8	8.2	8.7	8.1	9.4	8.9
Norway	13.7	14.8	15.7	15.5	16.4	17.8	18.4	19.4	21.7	25.2	29.9	33.2	40.4	44.8
Poland	10.7	9.7	8.9	10.8	8.4	10.4	9.8	10.0	11.2	13.5	16.3	20.6	28.9	35.6
Portugal	..	7.9	7.7	8.8	9.3	9.0	9.4	10.3	12.3	14.7	15.2	18.4	23.2	26.2
Slovak Republic	2.5	2.2	2.3	2.4	2.1	2.2	2.5	2.8	3.3	3.7	4.4	5.4	7.0	8.5
Spain	40.3	44.5	43.9	48.4	52.5	52.6	55.8	59.9	74.2	86.2	94.8	106.4	127.6	142.6
Sweden	16.4	17.5	18.4	19.7	21.7	22.7	23.0	23.3	30.7	38.9	43.1	49.7	64.5	72.1
Switzerland	26.4	26.7	26.2	28.2	29.7	30.7	29.6	30.9	36.3	43.9	49.7	54.8	65.7	77.9
Turkey	14.9	13.1	19.2	23.2	16.4	19.5	15.2	14.0	18.0	22.9	26.8	25.4	28.6	34.8
United Kingdom	84.5	96.5	107.4	114.7	123.8	124.0	126.4	141.0	167.2	206.9	216.7	247.1	301.4	312.9
United States	219.2	239.5	256.1	262.8	281.9	298.6	292.3	292.3	304.3	353.1	389.1	435.9	504.8	549.6
Euro area	..	..	246.4	263.5	265.3	268.3	283.0	310.5	372.6	452.5	503.7	553.8	673.2	745.5
OECD total	..	..	996.8	1 043.4	1 083.4	1 129.1	1 132.4	1 200.1	1 381.8	1 656.7	1 823.4	2 035.7	2 386.4	2 652.9
Brazil	6.1	4.7	6.0	7.6	7.2	9.5	9.3	9.6	10.4	12.6	16.0	19.5	24.0	30.5
Chile	3.3	3.6	3.9	4.0	3.9	4.1	4.1	4.4	5.1	6.0	7.1	7.8	8.8	10.8
China	19.1	20.6	24.6	23.9	26.2	30.4	33.3	39.7	46.7	62.4	74.4	92.0	122.0	147.1
Estonia	0.9	1.1	1.3	1.5	1.5	1.5	1.6	1.7	2.2	2.8	3.2	3.5	4.4	5.2
India	6.9	7.5	9.1	11.7	14.5	16.7	17.3	19.5	23.9	38.3	52.6	69.7	86.9	103.1
Indonesia	5.5	6.6	6.9	4.5	4.6	5.2	5.5	6.7	5.3	12.0	12.9	11.5	12.5	15.2
Israel	8.0	8.3	9.2	10.1	12.3	15.4	12.9	12.2	13.7	16.0	17.4	19.2	21.1	24.1
Russian Federation	10.6	13.3	14.1	12.4	9.1	9.6	11.4	13.6	16.2	20.6	25.0	31.1	39.4	51.3
Slovenia	2.0	2.1	2.0	2.0	1.9	1.9	1.9	2.3	2.8	3.5	4.0	4.5	5.7	7.4
South Africa	4.6	5.1	5.4	5.4	5.2	5.0	4.8	5.0	8.3	9.7	11.2	12.0	13.6	12.6

StatLink http://dx.doi.org/10.1787/824477670776

Relative annual growth of exports of services
Growth over the period 1998-2008, OECD total = 1.0

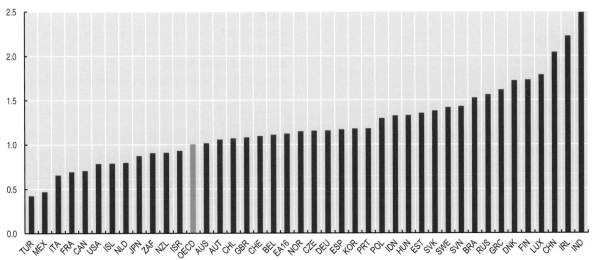

StatLink http://dx.doi.org/10.1787/81537802643

TRADING PARTNERS

The pattern of OECD merchandise trade – where imports come from and where exports go to – has undergone significant shifts over the last decade. These shifts have occurred in response to changes in the distribution of global income and to globalisation – in particular, the outsourcing of manufacturing from OECD countries to the rest of the world.

Definition

The data shown here refer to total OECD imports and exports and show merchandise trade both within the OECD area and with countries in the rest of the world. The definitions of merchandise imports and exports are explained under "Trade in goods".

NAFTA is the North American Free Trade Area and consists of Canada, Mexico and the United States. OECD Asia and Oceania includes Australia and New Zealand as well as Japan and Korea. Non-OECD America covers the Caribbean, South America and Central America, except Mexico. Non-OECD Asia covers Central Asia, China, the Indian sub continent and South East. Middle East covers the Gulf Arabian Countries, Iran, Israel, Jordan, Lebanon, the occupied Palestinian territory and the Syrian Arab Republic.

Comparability

OECD countries follow common definitions and procedures in compiling their merchandise trade statistics. These statistics are therefore comparable and of good quality. The removal of customs frontiers following the creation of a common market in Europe required EU countries to adopt a system of recording trade flows through sample surveys of exporters and importers. This led to some fall in the reliability of merchandise trade statistics for trade between the EU countries. Statistics on trade between EU countries and non-EU countries, however, were not affected.

Sources
- OECD (2009), *International Trade by Commodity Statistics*, OECD, Paris.

Further information
Analytical publications
- OECD, IOM and the World Bank (eds.) (2004), *Trade and Migration: Building Bridges for Global Labour Mobility*, OECD, Paris.
- OECD (2004), *Agriculture, Trade and the Environment: The Dairy Sector*, OECD, Paris.
- OECD (2004), *Trade and Competitiveness in Argentina, Brazil and Chile Not as Easy as A-B-C*, OECD, Paris.
- OECD (2005), *OECD Trade Policy Studies – Environmental Requirements and Market Access*, OECD, Paris.
- OECD (2005), *Trade and Structural Adjustment: Embracing Globalisation*, OECD, Paris.
- OECD (2006), *The Development Dimension – Aid for Trade: Making it Effective*, OECD, Paris.

Statistical publications
- OECD (2009), *Monthly Statistics of International Trade*, OECD, Paris.
- OECD (2009), *Statistics on International Trade in Services*, OECD, Paris.

Methodological publications
- UN, EC, IMF, OECD, UNCTAD and the WTO (2002), *Manual on Statistics of International Trade in Services*, United Nations, New York.

Online databases
- *ITCS International Trade by Commodity Statistics*.
- *Monthly International Trade*.

Web sites
- OECD International Trade Statistics, *www.oecd.org/std/its*.

Overview

Since 1988, there has been a steady decline in the share of OECD imports and exports among OECD countries. In 1988, imports from OECD countries accounted for 80% of total OECD imports. By 2008 this share had fallen to 65%. For exports, the fall in intra-OECD trade was less marked – down from 81% in 1988 to 74% in 2008.

OECD imports from Non-OECD Asia have risen from 7% to 18% of the total over the period, while exports to these countries have increased from 7.5% to 11%. A large change occurred in trade between OECD and China. In 1988 China supplied a little over 1% of total OECD imports but by 2008 this share had risen to 10%. China's importance as a destination for OECD countries has increased less sharply, rising from 1% in 1988 to 4% in 2008.

Partner countries and regions of OECD merchandise trade

	Imports As a percentage of total OECD merchandise imports				Exports As a percentage of total OECD merchandise exports				Merchandise trade As a percentage of total OECD merchandise trade			
	1990	2000	2005	2008	1990	2000	2005	2008	1990	2000	2005	2008
OECD total	**77.8**	**73.0**	**67.2**	**65.5**	**80.5**	**79.0**	**75.4**	**74.1**	**79.1**	**75.8**	**71.3**	**69.6**
Major seven	52.1	47.5	40.2	37.3	51.8	51.0	46.1	43.0	52.0	49.2	43.0	40.0
NAFTA	16.7	21.7	16.0	14.9	18.4	26.1	21.5	18.5	17.5	23.8	18.6	16.6
Canada	4.5	5.6	4.6	4.2	4.1	4.8	4.0	3.6	4.3	5.3	4.3	3.9
Mexico	1.5	3.3	2.7	2.6	1.5	3.0	2.3	2.2	1.5	3.2	2.5	2.4
United States	10.7	12.8	8.7	8.0	12.8	18.3	15.1	12.7	11.7	15.4	11.7	10.3
OECD Asia Oceania	10.0	9.4	7.5	6.1	7.3	6.5	5.4	5.1	8.7	8.0	6.6	5.6
Japan	7.1	6.3	4.6	3.3	4.1	3.4	2.5	2.2	5.6	4.9	3.7	2.8
Korea	1.7	2.0	1.8	1.7	1.8	1.8	1.7	1.7	1.7	1.9	1.8	1.7
OECD Europe	51.3	42.0	43.5	44.5	55.0	46.4	48.5	50.5	53.1	44.0	46.1	47.3
Austria	1.3	1.0	1.2	1.3	1.6	1.4	1.5	1.6	1.4	1.2	1.3	1.4
Belgium-Luxembourg	3.9	2.6	2.6	3.2	4.5	3.2	3.2	3.8	4.2	2.8	3.4	3.5
France	6.9	5.1	4.9	4.2	8.1	6.0	6.2	5.3	7.4	5.5	5.5	4.7
Germany	12.4	9.2	10.2	10.2	10.6	8.8	9.0	9.4	11.6	9.0	9.7	9.8
Italy	5.2	3.7	3.1	3.5	5.1	3.7	3.5	3.7	5.2	3.7	3.3	3.6
Netherlands	4.5	3.5	3.8	4.1	4.8	3.9	3.7	4.2	4.6	3.7	3.8	4.1
Spain	1.8	1.9	2.1	2.2	2.7	2.8	3.4	3.2	2.2	2.4	2.7	2.7
Sweden	1.9	1.5	1.5	1.4	1.8	1.4	1.4	1.5	1.9	1.5	1.5	1.5
Switzerland	2.1	1.4	1.1	1.5	2.6	1.7	1.4	1.9	2.4	1.6	1.4	1.7
United Kingdom	5.3	4.9	4.0	3.6	7.0	6.1	5.7	5.6	6.1	5.4	4.8	4.6
Non-OECD	**20.7**	**26.0**	**31.3**	**33.6**	**17.6**	**20.1**	**22.7**	**25.0**	**19.2**	**23.1**	**27.3**	**29.5**
Africa	3.4	2.4	3.5	4.2	2.8	1.9	2.6	3.0	3.1	2.2	3.1	3.6
South Africa	0.4	0.5	0.5	0.6	0.4	0.4	0.5	0.5	0.4	0.4	0.5	0.5
America	3.3	3.0	3.4	3.5	2.3	3.0	2.6	3.3	2.8	3.0	3.0	3.4
South America	2.7	2.2	2.7	2.9	1.4	1.9	1.6	2.2	2.1	2.1	2.2	2.6
Brazil	1.0	0.8	1.0	1.0	0.5	0.8	0.7	1.0	0.8	0.8	0.8	1.0
Chile	0.3	0.3	0.4	0.4	0.2	0.2	0.2	0.3	0.2	0.2	0.3	0.3
Asia	8.7	14.6	17.2	17.6	7.8	10.9	11.7	11.0	8.3	12.8	14.6	14.5
China	1.8	5.5	9.3	10.1	0.9	2.2	4.0	4.0	1.3	3.9	6.8	7.2
India	0.5	0.6	0.7	0.8	0.5	0.5	0.8	1.0	0.5	0.5	0.8	0.9
Chinese Taipei	1.9	2.1	1.3	..	1.5	2.0	1.5	..	1.7	2.0	1.4	..
Europe	1.8	2.4	3.7	4.6	2.1	1.9	3.4	4.9	1.9	2.2	3.6	4.8
Estonia	..	0.1	0.1	0.1	..	0.1	0.1	0.1	..	0.1	0.1	0.1
Russian Federation	0.1	1.4	2.1	2.7	0.1	0.6	1.2	2.0	0.1	1.0	1.7	2.4
Slovenia	..	0.1	0.2	0.2	..	0.2	0.2	0.3	..	0.2	0.2	0.2
Middle East	3.5	3.5	3.9	4.2	2.6	2.2	2.8	3.1	3.0	2.9	3.4	3.7
Israel	0.4	0.5	0.4	0.4	0.4	0.6	0.5	0.4	0.4	0.6	0.5	0.4

StatLink http://dx.doi.org/10.1787/824503768206

Partner countries and regions of OECD merchandise trade
As a percentage of total OECD merchandise trade

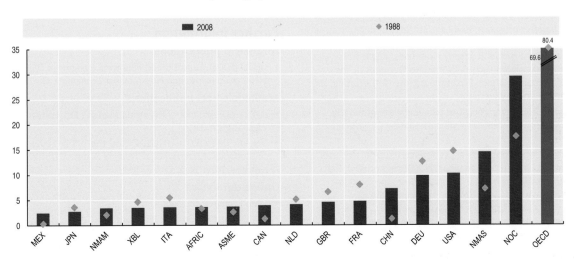

StatLink http://dx.doi.org/10.1787/818556324750

BALANCE OF PAYMENTS

The current account balance is the difference between current receipts from abroad and current payments to abroad. When the current account is positive, the country can use the surplus to repay foreign debts, to acquire foreign assets or to lend to the rest of the world. When the current account balance is negative, the deficit will be financed by borrowing from abroad or by liquidating foreign assets acquired in earlier periods.

Definition

Current account transactions consist of exports and imports of goods; exports and imports of services such as travel, international freight and passenger transport, insurance and financial services; income flows consisting of wages and salaries, dividends, interest and other investment income (*i.e.* property income in *System of National Accounts*); and current transfers such as government transfers (*i.e.* international cooperation), worker's remittances or other transfers such as gifts, inheritances and prizes won from lotteries.

Note that investment income includes retained earnings (*i.e.* profits not distributed as dividends to the direct investor) of foreign subsidiaries or branches. In general, earnings of direct investment enterprises are treated as if they were remitted abroad to the direct investor, with the part that is actually retained in the country where the direct investment enterprises are located shown as direct investment income-reinvested earnings (debit) in the current account and (with the opposite sign) as inward direct investment in the financial account.

Comparability

The data are taken from balance of payments statistics compiled according to the International Monetary Fund (IMF) *Balance of Payments Manual* (BPM5). The IMF closely monitors balance of payments statistics reported by its member countries through regular meetings of balance of payments compilers. As a result, there is relatively good comparability across countries.

Because all earnings of direct investment enterprises are treated as though they are remitted to the direct investor even though a large part may in practice be retained by the direct investment enterprise in the countries where they are located, the existence of direct investment enterprises in an economy will tend to reduce its current account balance.

Note also that portfolio income balance plays a role of growing importance for current account balances.

Overview

Current account balances as a percentage of GDP have been negative throughout the period since 1990 in Australia, Mexico, New Zealand, Spain, the United Kingdom and the United States; this is partly due to the way in which earnings of direct investment enterprises are treated. The portfolio investment balance, as well as the balance on goods, had a significant impact on trends in current account balances up to the recent crisis that affected the world economy. Countries which have recorded current account surpluses throughout the period include Japan, Luxembourg, the Netherlands, Norway and Switzerland.

Since 1990, current account balances have generally moved from deficit to surplus in Austria, Canada and Germany.

Current account balances, as a percentage of GDP and averaged over the three years to 2008, recorded deficits of 5% of GDP or more in Iceland (where the average deficit reached 30%), Greece, Portugal, Spain, New Zealand, Hungary, the Slovak Republic, Turkey, the United States and Australia. Surpluses in excess of 5% were recorded by Norway, Switzerland, Sweden, Luxembourg, the Netherlands, and Germany.

Sources
- OECD (2010), *Main Economic Indicators*, OECD, Paris.

Further information
Analytical publications
- OECD (2006), *Export Credit Financing Systems in OECD Member Countries and Non-Member Economies*, OECD, Paris.

Methodological publications
- IMF (1993), *Balance of Payments Manual*, 5th edition, IMF, Washington, DC.
- UN, EC, IMF, OECD, UNCTAD and the WTO (2002), *Manual on Statistics of International Trade in Services*, United Nations, New York.

Online databases
- *Main Economic Indicators*.
- *OECD Economic Outlook Statistics*.

Web sites
- OECD Economic Outlook – Sources and Methods, *www.oecd.org/eco/sources-and-methods*.

Current account balance

As a percentage of GDP

	1995	1996	1997	1998	1999	2000	2001	2002	2003	2004	2005	2006	2007	2008
Australia	-5.0	-3.6	-2.8	-4.7	-5.1	-3.6	-1.9	-3.7	-5.2	-5.9	-5.5	-5.1	-6.1	-4.4
Austria	-2.9	-2.9	-2.5	-1.7	-1.7	-0.7	-0.8	2.7	1.7	2.2	2.2	2.8	3.6	3.2
Belgium	5.4	5.0	5.5	5.2	5.1	4.0	3.4	4.6	4.1	3.5	2.6	2.0	2.2	-2.5
Canada	-0.8	0.5	-1.3	-1.2	0.3	2.7	2.3	1.7	1.2	2.3	1.9	1.4	1.0	0.5
Czech Republic	-2.5	-6.6	-6.2	-2.0	-2.4	-4.8	-5.3	-5.5	-6.3	-5.2	-1.3	-2.6	-3.2	-3.1
Denmark	0.7	1.4	0.4	-0.9	1.9	1.6	2.6	2.9	3.5	2.3	4.3	3.0	1.5	2.2
Finland	4.1	4.0	5.6	5.6	6.2	8.1	8.6	8.8	5.2	6.6	3.6	4.5	4.2	3.0
France	0.7	1.3	2.7	2.6	3.1	1.6	1.9	1.4	0.8	0.6	-0.4	-0.5	-1.0	-2.3
Germany	-1.2	-0.6	-0.5	-0.7	-1.3	-1.7	0.0	2.1	1.9	4.7	5.1	6.5	7.9	6.7
Greece	..	..	-3.9	-2.7	-3.8	-7.8	-7.3	-6.8	-6.6	-5.9	-7.4	-11.3	-14.5	-14.5
Hungary	-3.3	-3.8	-4.3	-6.9	-7.7	-8.5	-6.0	-6.9	-8.0	-8.3	-7.2	-7.4	-6.8	-7.1
Iceland	0.7	-1.8	-1.8	-6.7	-6.8	-10.1	-4.3	1.5	-4.8	-9.8	-16.2	-25.7	-20.1	-44.2
Ireland	2.6	2.8	2.3	0.8	0.2	-0.4	-0.7	-0.9	0.0	-0.6	-3.5	-3.5	-5.3	-5.3
Italy	2.2	3.1	2.8	1.9	0.7	-0.5	-0.1	-0.8	-1.3	-0.9	-1.7	-2.6	-2.4	-3.4
Japan	2.1	1.4	2.3	3.1	2.6	2.6	2.1	2.9	3.2	3.7	3.6	3.9	4.8	3.2
Korea	-1.6	-4.0	-1.5	11.2	5.3	2.3	1.6	0.9	1.9	3.9	1.8	0.6	0.6	-0.7
Luxembourg	12.1	11.2	10.4	9.2	8.4	13.2	8.8	10.5	8.1	11.9	11.0	10.3	9.7	5.4
Mexico	-0.5	-0.7	-1.7	-3.5	-2.7	-2.9	-2.6	-2.0	-1.0	-0.7	-0.5	-0.5	-0.8	-1.5
Netherlands	6.1	5.1	6.5	3.2	3.8	1.9	2.4	2.5	5.5	7.5	7.3	9.3	8.7	4.8
New Zealand	-5.0	-5.7	-6.3	-3.9	-6.2	-5.2	-2.7	-3.8	-4.1	-6.2	-8.3	-8.5	-8.0	-8.8
Norway	3.5	6.8	6.3	0.0	5.6	15.0	16.1	12.5	12.3	12.7	16.3	17.3	14.1	18.5
Poland	-1.7	-0.9	-2.7	-4.0	-6.9	-6.0	-3.1	-2.8	-2.5	-4.0	-1.2	-2.8	-4.8	-5.1
Portugal	..	-4.2	-5.9	-7.0	-8.5	-10.2	-9.9	-8.1	-6.1	-7.6	-9.5	-10.0	-9.4	-12.1
Slovak Republic	2.6	-9.3	-8.5	-8.9	-4.8	-3.4	-8.3	-7.9	-5.9	-7.8	-8.5	-7.9	-5.3	-6.5
Spain	-0.3	-0.2	-0.1	-1.2	-2.9	-4.0	-3.9	-3.3	-3.5	-5.3	-7.4	-9.0	-10.0	-9.6
Sweden	3.3	3.5	4.1	3.8	4.1	3.8	3.8	4.0	7.2	6.7	7.0	8.5	8.8	9.8
Switzerland	6.5	7.0	9.3	9.2	10.8	12.1	8.2	8.8	13.3	13.4	14.0	15.2	10.0	2.4
Turkey	-1.0	-1.0	-1.0	0.7	-0.4	-3.7	1.9	-0.3	-2.5	-3.7	-4.6	-6.0	-5.9	-5.7
United Kingdom	-1.2	-0.8	-0.1	-0.4	-2.4	-2.6	-2.1	-1.7	-1.6	-2.1	-2.6	-3.3	-2.7	-1.6
United States	-1.5	-1.6	-1.7	-2.5	-3.2	-4.2	-3.9	-4.3	-4.7	-5.3	-6.0	-6.0	-5.2	-4.9
OECD total	..	..	0.2	-0.1	-0.7	-1.3	-1.1	-1.1	-1.0	-0.9	-1.5	-1.6	-1.3	-1.6
Brazil	-1.8	-2.2	-2.7	-3.0	-2.2	-2.0	-1.8	-0.6	0.3	0.8	0.9	0.8	0.1	-1.4
Chile	-2.1	-4.1	-4.4	-4.9	0.1	-1.2	-1.6	-0.9	-1.1	2.2	1.2	4.9	4.4	-2.0
China	0.1	0.4	1.6	1.3	0.8	0.7	0.5	1.0	1.1	1.5	3.0	4.1	5.2	5.4
Estonia	-4.2	-8.4	-11.1	-8.6	-4.3	-5.4	-5.2	-10.6	-11.3	-11.3	-10.0	-16.9	-17.8	-9.4
India	-0.5	-0.5	-0.3	-0.5	-0.2	-0.3	0.1	0.4	0.5	0.0	-0.4	-0.4	-0.4	-1.1
Indonesia	-1.5	-1.6	-0.9	0.9	1.2	1.6	1.3	1.4	1.3	0.2	0.0	1.4	1.2	0.0
Israel	-5.0	-4.9	-3.0	-0.9	-1.8	-1.8	-1.6	-1.1	0.5	1.7	3.1	5.0	2.8	1.0
Russian Federation	2.2	2.8	0.0	0.1	12.6	18.0	11.1	8.5	8.2	10.1	11.1	9.6	5.9	6.1
Slovenia	-0.3	0.2	0.3	-0.6	-3.2	-2.7	0.2	1.0	-0.8	-2.6	-1.7	-2.5	-4.8	-6.2
South Africa	-1.1	-0.7	-0.9	-0.8	-0.2	-0.1	0.1	0.3	-0.6	-3.8	-1.9	-2.4	-4.4	-4.3

StatLink http://dx.doi.org/10.1787/824532532285

Current account balance

As a percentage of GDP

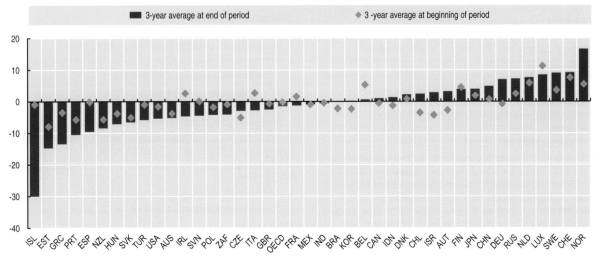

StatLink http://dx.doi.org/10.1787/818557825873

FDI FLOWS AND STOCKS

Foreign direct investment (FDI) is a key element in international economic integration. FDI creates direct, stable and long-lasting links between economies. It encourages the transfer of technology and know-how between countries, and allows the host economy to promote its products more widely in international markets. Finally, FDI is an additional source of funding for investment and, under the right policy environment, it can be an important vehicle for enterprise development.

Definition

FDI is defined as investment by a resident entity in one economy that reflects the objective of obtaining a lasting interest in an enterprise resident in another economy. The lasting interest implies the existence of a long-term relationship between the direct investor and the enterprise and a significant degree of influence by the direct investor on the management of the enterprise. The ownership of at least 10% of the voting power, representing the influence by the investor, is the basic criterion used. Hence, control by the foreign investor (ownership of more than 50% of the voting power) is not required.

Inward stocks are all direct investments held by non-residents in the reporting economy; outward stocks are the investments of the reporting economy held abroad.

The table on FDI stocks also shows their distribution according to broad sectors of the industry, namely manufacturing and services.

Negative flows generally indicate disinvestments or the impact of substantial reimbursements of inter-company loans.

Comparability

FDI stocks should be valued at market prices. However, departing from international standards, most OECD countries report the data using enterprise's book values. These may differ substantially from market values; rules for estimating them also vary between countries.

Despite recent improvements, there are also methodological differences between countries as regards inward and outward FDI flows.

OECD totals refer to countries for which data are available. Data for 2007 and 2008 are provisional.

Overview

Quarterly statistics show that OECD FDI flows collapsed in first half of 2009, following the recession which started in 2008. In the first half of 2009 inflows dropped by 50% and outflows by 40% from the last quarter of 2008. These decline followed the one recorded in 2008, when FDI inflows fell by 35% and outflows by 19%.

These falls are much sharper than those recorded on 2001, following the investment boom of the late 1990s. At that time, FDI into the OECD area continued to decline until 2004, when inflows picked up timidly by 8% and outflows more significantly by 41%. The global environment for FDI further improved in 2006, thanks to strong macro-economic growth, stock prices and corporate profitability. In this period, multinational enterprises based in emerging economies were active to acquire enterprises in the OECD area. Large amounts of investments by financial investors such as private equity companies were also recorded in 2006. Direct investment into OECD grew further by 31% in 2007 reaching USD 1 583 billion.

At end-2007, inward FDI stocks of OECD countries stood at USD 11 trillion and outward investments at USD 13 trillion. The stocks of both inward and outward FDI for the United States and the United Kingdom are the highest in the OECD area. Outside the OECD area, China remains the foremost destinations of FDI at end-2007 while its outward investment is limited.

Sources

- OECD (2006), *Reviews of Foreign Direct Investment*, OECD, Paris.
- OECD (2008), *OECD Reviews of Innovation Policy: China*, OECD, Paris.

Further information

Statistical publications

- OECD (2002), *Measuring Globalisation: The Role of Multinationals in OECD Economies*, OECD, Paris.
- OECD (2005), *Measuring Globalisation: OECD Economic Globalisation Indicators*, OECD, Paris.

Methodological publications

- IMF, OECD (1999), *Report on the Survey of Implementation of Methodological Standards for Direct Investment*.
- OECD (1996), *OECD Benchmark Definition of Foreign Direct Investment*, Third edition, OECD, Paris.
- OECD (2001), *Non-Tariff Measures in the ICT Sector: A Survey*, OECD, Paris.
- OECD (2005), *Measuring Globalisation: OECD Handbook on Economic Globalisation Indicators*, OECD, Paris.

Web sites

- OECD International Investment, *www.oecd.org/daf/investment*.

Outward and inward FDI stocks
Million US dollars

	Outward direct investment stocks							Inward direct investment stocks						
	1990	1995	2000	2004	2005	2006	2007	1990	1995	2000	2004	2005	2006	2007
Australia	30 495	53 009	85 385	203 776	175 541	225 393	289 669	73 615	104 074	111 138	263 390	213 530	260 803	341 837
Austria	4 747	11 832	24 820	69 806	71 807	105 697	156 043	11 097	21 363	31 165	70 714	82 551	111 072	163 404
Canada	84 813	118 106	237 647	372 652	388 317	450 287	521 653	112 850	123 182	212 723	315 247	341 630	376 404	497 204
Czech Republic	..	345	738	3 759	3 610	5 017	8 556	..	7 350	21 647	57 246	60 662	79 838	112 396
Denmark	..	24 703	73 112	126 311	129 283	148 326	179 787	..	23 801	73 585	116 489	116 443	134 463	157 801
Finland	11 227	14 993	52 109	85 023	81 860	96 208	115 813	5 132	8 465	24 272	57 379	54 802	70 569	92 148
France	110 121	204 430	445 087	845 451	868 469	1 044 456	1 291 546	84 931	191 433	259 773	641 807	628 017	762 151	950 297
Germany	130 760	233 107	486 750	814 671	830 650	1 012 236	1 248 883	74 067	104 367	462 529	719 261	647 936	800 237	1 001 709
Greece	..	..	5 852	13 791	13 602	19 560	31 650	..	..	14 113	28 482	29 189	41 317	53 221
Hungary	..	278	1 279	6 022	7 810	12 561	17 595	569	11 304	22 856	62 624	61 970	82 115	100 328
Iceland	75	177	663	4 025	10 085	13 753	27 285	147	149	491	1 998	4 696	7 674	11 994
Ireland	..	..	27 925	106 692	104 152	120 728	145 862	..	..	127 088	207 647	163 530	156 491	193 451
Italy	60 195	106 319	180 274	280 481	293 475	378 931	520 087	60 009	65 347	121 169	220 720	224 079	294 878	364 839
Japan	201 440	238 452	278 441	370 544	386 581	449 567	542 614	9 850	33 508	50 322	96 984	100 899	107 634	132 851
Korea	..	..	..	32 166	38 683	49 187	74 777	..	..	..	87 766	104 879	119 143	121 956
Luxembourg	..	4 703	7 927	27 883	32 691	42 358	72 912	..	18 503	23 492	49 733	43 650	60 671	80 145
Mexico	..	..	..	21 673	29 641	36 447	44 703	22 424	41 130	97 170	202 885	223 830	243 121	267 807
Netherlands	106 896	172 675	305 459	587 252	615 727	757 870	876 920	68 729	116 051	243 730	477 218	451 234	513 301	724 076
New Zealand	..	7 676	6 065	13 957	11 584	12 825	15 066	..	25 728	28 070	52 640	52 230	63 055	70 941
Norway	10 889	22 521	34 022	80 950	92 923	120 425	143 025	12 404	19 836	30 261	79 413	76 322	95 662	121 593
Poland	..	539	1 018	3 354	6 279	14 319	19 371	109	7 843	34 233	86 633	90 741	125 601	175 863
Portugal	..	..	19 793	43 940	41 965	53 984	67 708	..	18 973	32 043	66 970	63 340	88 461	115 315
Slovak Republic	..	139	379	842	597	1 325	1 609	..	1 297	4 761	21 881	23 656	33 612	40 702
Spain	..	36 547	167 718	282 294	305 427	413 605	590 587	..	110 291	156 347	407 472	384 538	460 583	605 140
Sweden	50 720	73 143	123 260	214 736	208 777	265 546	327 297	12 636	31 089	93 998	196 305	171 818	227 330	289 957
Switzerland	66 087	142 481	232 176	400 590	431 980	559 970	657 911	34 245	57 064	86 810	197 679	170 156	264 952	337 536
Turkey	..	..	3 668	7 060	8 315	8 866	12 210	..	19 209	38 523	71 299	95 078	157 649
United Kingdom	229 307	304 865	897 845	1 247 190	1 198 637	1 454 903	1 841 206	203 905	199 772	438 631	701 913	840 652	1 139 154	1 263 781
United States	616 655	885 506	1 531 607	2 498 494	2 651 721	2 948 172	3 451 482	505 346	680 066	1 421 017	1 727 062	1 874 263	2 154 062	2 450 132
EU27 total	..	..	..	4 627 432	4 575 957	5 810 496	7 471 726	..	..	..	4 405 989	4 548 405	5 913 974	7 575 624
OECD total	1 714 426	2 656 546	5 231 017	8 765 384	9 040 191	10 822 522	13 293 826	1 292 065	2 021 985	4 242 644	7 254 082	7 372 545	8 969 431	10 996 072
of which: Manufacturing	36%	37%	27%	22%	24%	24%	..	37%	37%	30%	27%	25%	25%	..
Services	53%	57%	68%	73%	72%	72%	..	50%	57%	67%	69%	70%	69%	..
Brazil	..	..	..	69 196	79 259	113 925	136 103	..	..	..	161 259	195 562	236 186	328 455
Chile	..	..	11 154	17 413	21 359	26 596	32 695	..	..	45 753	60 541	74 196	80 297	99 488
China	..	..	..	52 704	64 493	90 630	115 960	..	..	..	368 970	471 549	614 383	703 667
Estonia	..	..	259	1 419	1 940	3 596	6 174	..	..	2 645	10 059	11 290	12 727	16 815
India	..	..	2 609	10 072	12 832	27 036	44 080	..	..	20 278	44 669	50 614	70 870	105 429
Indonesia	..	..	..	-102	-1 762	1 042	353	..	..	..	15 858	41 187	54 534	59 125
Israel	..	2 867	9 091	18 493	23 010	38 741	48 466	365	5 741	22 556	31 471	35 691	48 137	55 699
Russian Federation	..	2 420	20 141	107 291	146 679	216 488	370 161	..	345	32 204	122 295	180 228	265 873	491 232
Slovenia	..	490	768	3 025	3 290	4 547	7 197	..	1 763	2 893	7 590	7 236	8 985	14 048
South Africa	15 010	23 301	32 325	39 083	37 706	50 826	65 878	9 210	15 014	43 451	64 451	78 986	87 765	110 415

StatLink ᴹᔕ᠍᠍᠍ http://dx.doi.org/10.1787/824532554644

FDI stocks
As a percentage of GDP, 2007 or latest available year

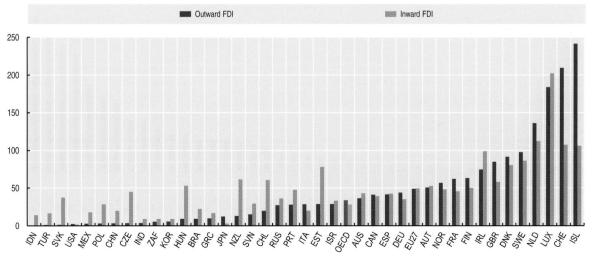

StatLink ᴹᔕ᠍᠍᠍ http://dx.doi.org/10.1787/818560207840

Inflows of foreign direct investment
Million US dollars

	1995	1996	1997	1998	1999	2000	2001	2002	2003	2004	2005	2006	2007	2008
Australia	11 963	6 111	7 633	6 003	3 268	13 950	8 297	16 996	7 975	37 334	-31 999	27 883	44 326	46 565
Austria	1 904	4 429	2 656	4 534	2 975	8 842	5 921	357	7 151	3 892	10 777	7 938	29 592	13 525
Belgium	..	..	..	..	..	..	..	16 265	33 508	43 583	34 351	58 926	110 795	59 564
Canada	9 255	9 633	11 522	22 803	24 747	66 796	27 670	22 146	7 486	-445	25 693	59 765	108 404	44 689
Czech Republic	2 562	1 428	1 301	3 716	6 326	4 980	5 645	8 483	2 109	4 975	11 654	5 465	10 446	10 704
Denmark	4 180	768	2 799	7 726	16 748	33 803	11 525	6 646	2 612	-10 721	12 892	2 709	11 851	10 708
Finland	1 063	1 109	2 116	12 141	4 610	8 836	3 732	8 053	3 322	2 828	4 747	7 656	12 353	-4 192
France	23 679	21 960	23 171	30 984	46 546	43 258	50 485	49 079	42 538	32 585	84 887	71 882	103 886	96 990
Germany	12 025	6 573	12 243	24 597	56 077	198 313	26 419	53 571	32 398	-10 195	47 411	57 175	56 415	24 891
Greece	1 198	1 196	1 089	72	561	1 108	1 589	50	1 276	2 103	606	5 366	1 918	5 083
Hungary	5 102	3 300	4 171	3 337	3 313	2 763	3 936	2 994	2 137	4 508	7 711	7 536	6 096	6 552
Iceland	9	83	148	148	67	170	173	91	328	654	3 075	3 992	3 062	-379
Ireland	1 442	2 616	2 710	8 856	18 211	25 784	9 653	29 350	22 803	-10 614	-31 670	-5 545	30 597	-12 278
Italy	4 816	3 535	4 962	4 280	6 911	13 377	14 873	14 558	16 430	16 824	19 959	39 261	40 209	16 999
Japan	41	228	3 224	3 193	12 743	8 318	6 244	9 239	6 324	7 819	2 778	-6 503	22 548	24 418
Korea	1 776	2 325	2 844	5 412	9 333	9 283	3 528	2 392	3 526	9 246	6 309	3 586	1 579	2 200
Luxembourg	..	..	..	..	..	..	..	115 242	89 287	78 687	116 107	125 251	186 260	80 373
Mexico	9 679	10 087	14 165	8 612	13 844	18 028	29 802	23 722	16 475	23 659	21 922	19 316	27 278	21 950
Netherlands	12 307	16 660	11 137	36 925	41 206	63 866	51 937	25 060	21 063	4 602	47 763	7 454	118 398	-9 063
New Zealand	2 850	3 922	1 917	1 826	940	1 344	-113	1 658	2 450	2 547	1 472	7 760	2 494	1 975
Norway	2 409	3 207	3 982	3 935	6 792	7 095	2 122	791	3 472	2 544	5 414	6 413	4 435	-95
Poland	3 658	4 500	4 914	6 368	7 276	9 446	5 697	4 121	4 867	12 873	10 281	19 643	22 733	15 980
Portugal	660	1 344	2 362	3 005	1 157	6 637	6 232	1 801	7 155	1 936	3 927	10 908	3 056	3 525
Slovak Republic	241	396	231	707	429	2 383	1 584	4 144	2 161	3 033	2 427	4 700	3 269	3 410
Spain	6 285	6 821	6 388	11 798	18 744	39 582	28 347	39 249	25 844	24 775	25 005	26 903	68 842	65 412
Sweden	14 447	5 437	10 967	19 843	61 001	23 433	10 905	12 270	4 981	11 022	9 915	27 261	22 079	40 395
Switzerland	2 224	3 078	6 642	8 942	11 714	19 266	8 859	6 284	16 505	933	-949	30 854	49 261	17 407
Turkey	885	722	805	940	783	982	3 352	1 082	1 702	2 785	10 031	20 185	22 046	18 171
United Kingdom	19 968	24 441	33 245	74 349	87 973	118 824	52 650	24 052	16 846	56 000	175 973	148 850	183 412	95 968
United States	57 776	86 502	105 603	179 045	289 444	321 274	167 021	84 372	63 750	145 966	112 638	241 961	275 758	319 737
EU27 total	..	..	..	..	..	..	..	..	..	230 952	573 183	638 587	810 471	469 615
OECD total	225 299	246 334	301 456	524 242	896 253	1 292 729	632 802	584 118	468 481	505 739	751 107	1 044 551	1 583 400	1 021 184
Brazil	4 859	11 200	19 650	31 913	28 576	32 779	22 457	16 590	10 144	18 166	15 066	18 782	34 585	45 058
Chile	2 957	4 815	5 271	4 628	8 761	4 860	4 200	2 550	4 307	7 173	6 984	7 298	12 577	16 787
China	35 849	40 180	44 237	43 751	38 753	38 399	44 241	49 308	47 077	54 937	79 127	78 095	138 413	147 791
Estonia	201	150	266	581	305	387	542	285	919	966	2 941	1 787	2 737	1 969
India	2 144	2 426	3 577	2 635	2 169	3 584	5 472	5 626	4 323	5 771	7 606	20 336	25 127	41 169
Indonesia	4 346	6 194	4 677	-241	-1 866	-4 550	-2 977	145	-597	1 896	8 336	4 914	6 928	8 340
Israel	1 350	1 397	1 634	1 737	3 763	5 919	4 179	1 910	4 087	2 529	4 270	14 762	9 961	10 544
Russian Federation	2 065	2 579	4 865	2 761	3 309	2 714	2 748	3 377	7 958	15 444	12 886	29 701	55 073	73 053
Slovenia	150	173	335	216	107	136	503	1 660	302	831	540	649	1 483	1 808
South Africa	1 248	816	3 811	550	1 503	969	7 270	1 480	783	701	6 522	-184	5 737	9 632

StatLink ⌐⌐⌐■ http://dx.doi.org/10.1787/824545340160

Inflows of foreign direct investment
Billion US dollars

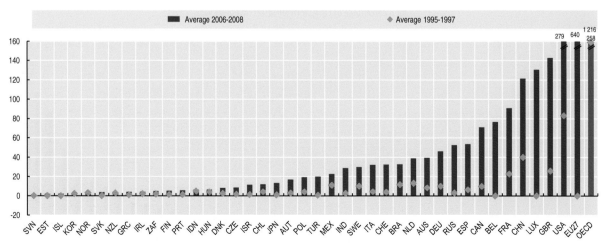

StatLink ⌐⌐⌐■ http://dx.doi.org/10.1787/818627720265

Outflows of foreign direct investment
Million US dollars

	1995	1996	1997	1998	1999	2000	2001	2002	2003	2004	2005	2006	2007	2008
Australia	3 282	7 088	6 428	3 345	-421	3 158	11 962	7 852	16 205	10 257	-37 984	23 419	16 804	35 780
Austria	1 131	1 935	1 988	2 745	3 301	5 741	3 138	5 812	7 143	8 305	11 138	13 678	33 387	28 159
Belgium	..	..	..	..	..	..	..	12 288	38 359	34 038	32 640	50 713	93 919	68 146
Canada	11 462	13 094	23 059	34 349	17 250	44 678	36 037	26 761	22 935	43 341	27 540	44 404	59 631	77 626
Czech Republic	37	153	25	127	90	43	165	206	207	1 014	-19	1 469	1 621	1 895
Denmark	3 063	2 519	4 207	4 477	17 006	26 533	13 364	5 708	1 139	-10 371	16 194	8 447	20 523	27 299
Finland	1 497	3 597	5 292	18 642	6 616	24 035	8 372	7 378	-2 282	-1 080	4 220	4 808	7 656	1 626
France	15 758	30 419	35 581	48 613	126 859	177 482	86 783	50 486	53 197	56 762	114 964	110 737	169 105	199 963
Germany	39 052	50 806	41 794	88 837	108 692	56 567	39 691	18 963	5 827	20 559	75 848	127 287	179 572	156 160
Greece	..	..	..	-276	552	2 137	616	655	413	1 030	1 450	4 169	5 339	2 646
Hungary	59	-4	462	278	250	620	368	278	1 644	1 119	2 179	3 876	3 742	1 637
Iceland	25	63	56	74	123	393	342	320	373	2 553	7 063	5 255	12 866	-8 100
Ireland	820	728	1 014	3 902	6 109	4 630	4 066	11 035	5 555	18 079	14 304	15 332	20 778	13 202
Italy	5 731	6 465	12 245	16 078	6 722	12 318	21 476	17 138	9 079	19 273	41 795	42 091	90 797	43 754
Japan	22 628	23 419	25 991	24 155	22 747	31 539	38 349	32 280	28 799	30 963	45 830	50 244	73 545	127 981
Korea	3 552	4 670	4 449	4 740	4 198	4 999	2 420	2 617	3 426	4 650	4 291	8 127	15 276	12 794
Luxembourg	..	..	..	..	..	..	..	125 770	99 863	84 083	124 542	110 781	250 865	103 931
Mexico	..	..	..	..	..	..	4 404	891	1 253	4 432	6 474	5 758	8 260	690
Netherlands	20 176	32 098	24 522	36 475	57 611	75 649	50 602	32 046	44 076	29 181	131 738	65 211	28 549	53 117
New Zealand	1 783	-1 240	-1 566	401	1 073	609	-1 082	372	879	-456	-1 520	501	3 234	100
Norway	2 855	6 098	5 290	2 542	5 834	9 510	807	5 760	6 065	5 317	21 970	21 321	15 589	28 074
Poland	42	53	45	316	31	17	-89	229	301	904	3 406	8 862	4 647	3 387
Portugal	685	729	2 092	4 029	3 191	8 134	6 263	-149	6 590	7 457	2 110	7 143	5 491	2 102
Slovak Republic	43	63	95	147	-377	29	65	11	247	-21	149	512	384	258
Spain	4 158	5 590	12 547	18 938	44 384	58 224	33 113	32 744	28 745	60 567	41 804	100 305	138 523	77 168
Sweden	11 214	5 025	12 648	24 379	21 929	40 970	7 348	10 598	21 131	21 124	26 215	23 553	37 812	40 189
Switzerland	12 214	16 150	17 748	18 769	33 264	44 698	18 326	8 212	15 443	26 282	50 994	75 860	49 677	86 255
Turkey	113	110	251	367	645	870	497	143	480	780	1 064	924	2 106	2 585
United Kingdom	43 560	34 056	61 620	122 861	201 437	233 488	58 885	50 347	62 439	91 083	80 818	86 285	275 521	110 407
United States	98 750	91 885	104 803	142 644	224 934	159 212	142 349	154 460	149 564	316 223	36 235	241 244	398 597	332 012
EU27 total	..	..	..	..	..	..	..	..	..	281 845	532 598	662 661	883 596	634 725
OECD total	315 418	343 381	410 570	651 061	1 046 374	1 244 645	689 263	621 210	629 093	887 450	887 452	1 262 315	2 023 813	1 630 842
Brazil	1 384	-467	1 042	2 721	1 690	2 282	-2 258	2 482	249	9 471	2 517	28 203	7 067	20 457
Chile	752	1 133	1 463	1 483	2 558	3 987	1 610	343	1 606	1 563	2 183	2 742	3 009	6 891
China	2 000	2 114	2 563	2 634	1 775	916	6 884	2 518	-152	1 805	11 306	21 160	16 995	53 471
Estonia	3	40	137	6	83	63	200	132	156	268	688	1 111	1 737	1 089
India	117	239	113	48	79	510	1 398	1 678	1 879	2 179	2 978	14 344	17 280	18 362
Indonesia	603	600	178	..	..	..	..	..	..	3 408	3 065	2 641	4 675	5 861
Israel	820	815	923	1 124	829	3 335	687	981	2 086	4 533	2 946	14 944	6 782	7 719
Russian Federation	605	922	3 185	1 270	2 208	3 177	2 533	3 966	9 727	13 782	12 768	23 151	45 916	52 629
Slovenia	-10	7	31	-6	48	65	133	151	476	550	629	905	1 574	1 465
South Africa	2 494	1 048	2 324	1 634	1 584	277	-3 515	-402	553	1 305	909	5 929	2 982	-2 305

StatLink http://dx.doi.org/10.1787/824555606076

Outflows of foreign direct investment
Billion US dollars

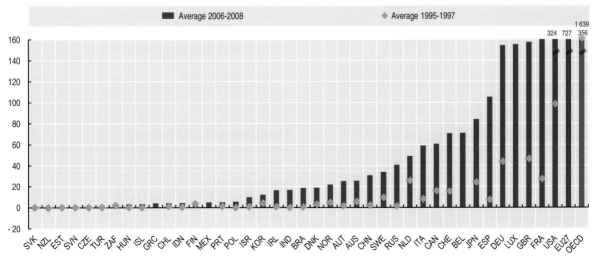

StatLink http://dx.doi.org/10.1787/818643108775

EMPLOYMENT IN FOREIGN AFFILIATES

Firms in OECD countries increasingly adopt global strategies and establish overseas sales, marketing, production and research units to cope with new competitive pressures. Indicators on the activity of affiliates under foreign control are thus an important complement to information on FDI when analysing the weight and economic contribution of such firms in host countries.

While data on the manufacturing sector have been available since the beginning of the 1980s, the OECD started collecting data on the activity of affiliates under foreign control in the service sector only in the second half of the 1990s; data are not yet available for all OECD countries.

Definition

An affiliate under foreign control is defined as one in which a single foreign investor holds more than 50% of the shares with voting rights. The notion of control allows all of a company's activities to be attributed to the controlling investor. This means that variables such as a company's turnover, staff or exports are all attributed to the controlling investor and the country from which he or she comes. Control may be direct or indirect.

Employment in foreign affiliates is shown as a percentage of total employment in each country.

Comparability

Data on employment of foreign affiliates in the manufacturing sector are available as times series for most OECD countries. Conversely, fewer countries are able to supply estimates of employment in service affiliates because collection of employment data on services began later.

For employment in manufacturing, there are breaks in the series for Austria (2001/2002), the Czech Republic (1999/2000), France (2001/2002), Germany (2001/2002), Hungary (2002/2003), Portugal (2002/2003) and the United States (1996/1997). These breaks reflect changes in data collection methods.

For employment in services, the main comparability problem is that financial institutions are excluded in the case of Belgium, Germany, Ireland, Netherlands, Portugal, Spain, Sweden, the United Kingdom and the United States. Breaks in series for France (2003), Germany (2002), Hungary (2003) and Portugal (2002) are due to changes in the data collection methods.

Overview

The shares of foreign affiliates in manufacturing employment show considerable variation across OECD countries, ranging from under 15% in Italy, Portugal, Switzerland, Turkey and the United States to 35% or more in the Czech Republic, Hungary, Luxembourg, the Slovak Republic and Ireland. Employment in service sector foreign affiliates is lower in all countries although, as noted above, data are affected in several countries by the exclusion of employment in banking and insurance services.

In the period from 2003 to 2006, the share of foreign-controlled manufacturing affiliates in total employment grew or remained stable in all countries for which data are available except France and Ireland, where their shares slightly fell, and in Sweden and the United States, where the shares have remained fairly stable. Particularly sharp increases were recorded by the Czech Republic, Poland and the United Kingdom.

Over the same period, the share of foreign-controlled service affiliates in total employment grew or remained stable in all countries for which data are available, except Belgium and Hungary. The biggest increases were recorded in the Czech Republic, the Netherlands, Poland and Sweden.

Sources

- OECD (2009), *OECD Science, Technology and Industry Scoreboard 2009*, OECD, Paris.

Further information

Analytical publications

- OECD (2010), *Measuring Globalisation: OECD Economic Globalisation Indicators*, OECD, Paris.

Statistical publications

- OECD (2007), *Measuring Globalisation: Activities of Multinationals – Volume I: Manufacturing, 2000-2004, 2007 Edition*, OECD, Paris.
- OECD (2008), *Measuring Globalisation: Activities of Multinationals, Volume II, 2008 Edition: Services, 2000-2004*, OECD, Paris.

Methodological publications

- OECD (2005), *Measuring Globalisation: OECD Handbook on Economic Globalisation Indicators*, OECD, Paris.

Online databases

- *Measuring Globalisation Statistics.*

Web sites

- OECD Measuring Globalisation, *www.oecd.org/sti/measuring-globalisation.*
- OECD Science, Technology and Industry, *www.oecd.org/sti.*

Employment in affiliates under foreign control

As percentage of total employment

	Share of employment in manufacturing							Share of employment in services						
	2001	2002	2003	2004	2005	2006	2007	2001	2002	2003	2004	2005	2006	2007
Austria	18.0 |	24.0	22.5	..	..	..	29.1	9.7	..	10.3	..	..	..	..
Belgium	..	32.3	34.5	32.8	33.1	34.8	..	..	17.2	16.2	15.3	14.2	10.8	..
Czech Republic	28.9	27.2	32.6	37.2	37.8	39.6	45.5	..	..	21.1	22.7	24.9	18.7	..
Denmark	14.1	14.4 |	..	19.3	20.8	21.2	22.6	..	..	..	..	..	..	..
Finland	17.2	..	..	..	17.3	17.8	19.2	11.9	..	14.5	15.9	16.1	..	..
France	30.8 |	26.4	26.8	26.2	26.4	26.3	26.1	5.6	5.2 |	10.0	10.5	11.3	11.3	..
Germany	5.8 |	14.8	15.5	15.7	15.8	16.5	..	2.9 |	7.2	6.1	6.3	6.7	6.4	..
Hungary	45.2	43.6 |	27.1	32.4	33.4	36.9	..	15.1	14.8 |	..	11.3	10.7	..	..
Ireland	49.2	48.4	46.7	48.0	49.3	47.8	46.0	28.4	28.5	27.3	27.5	31.6	26.7	..
Italy	10.8	13.1	12.5	12.4	12.5	10.1	..	5.1	5.4	5.7	6.1	6.7	6.9	..
Luxembourg	41.7	42.4	42.8	45.0	44.3	..	..	..	..	..	..	..	..	..
Netherlands	21.0	25.7	24.1	25.7	24.3	..	..	9.1	12.1	11.6	12.6	14.3	..	..
Norway	24.3	23.0	21.3	21.4	22.3	23.9	22.4	17.3	17.5	17.5	17.5	..	18.4	..
Poland	21.9	24.1	25.4	28.1	29.5	30.9	32.5	13.4	15.3	15.3	17.1	17.9	19.9	..
Portugal	9.5	8.9 |	12.8	12.6	13.1	13.3	..	4.7 |	..	7.4	7.0	7.3	8.4	..
Slovak Republic	..	..	34.9	41.4	44.3	43.8	..	..	..	..	23.5	23.9	21.6	..
Spain	16.4	15.9	15.4	15.6	15.6	16.0	16.1	..	8.7	10.0	9.5	9.7	8.5	..
Sweden	32.7	34.8	33.2	32.4	33.8	34.3	33.4	..	17.5	20.6	22.4	20.3	21.1	..
Switzerland	..	..	11.6	12.2	12.5	13.2	13.6	..	..	7.3	7.6	8.2	8.7	9.2
Turkey	7.0	..	..	..	..	..	..	..	..	..	..	..	..	..
United Kingdom	24.0	24.6	26.1	25.8	27.6	28.4	30.4	..	..	11.6	12.0	12.0	12.6	..
United States	11.1	11.3	11.4	11.1	11.3	11.3	..	..	4.5	..	..	..	..	..
Estonia	..	..	38.4	41.8	43.7	45.0	..	..	..	..	..	..	..	..
Israel	..	11.0	10.8	12.6	12.6	..	..	..	..	..	..	..	..	..
Slovenia	..	..	15.9	16.0	..	..	18.7	..	..	..	..	..	..	..

StatLink ᴹᔆ▬ http://dx.doi.org/10.1787/824582367013

Employment in manufacturing and services in affiliates under foreign control

As a percentage of total employment, 2007 or latest available year

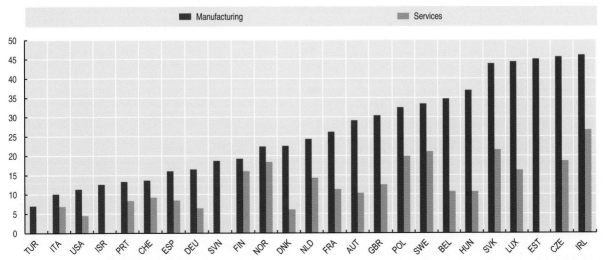

StatLink ᴹᔆ▬ http://dx.doi.org/10.1787/818660713260

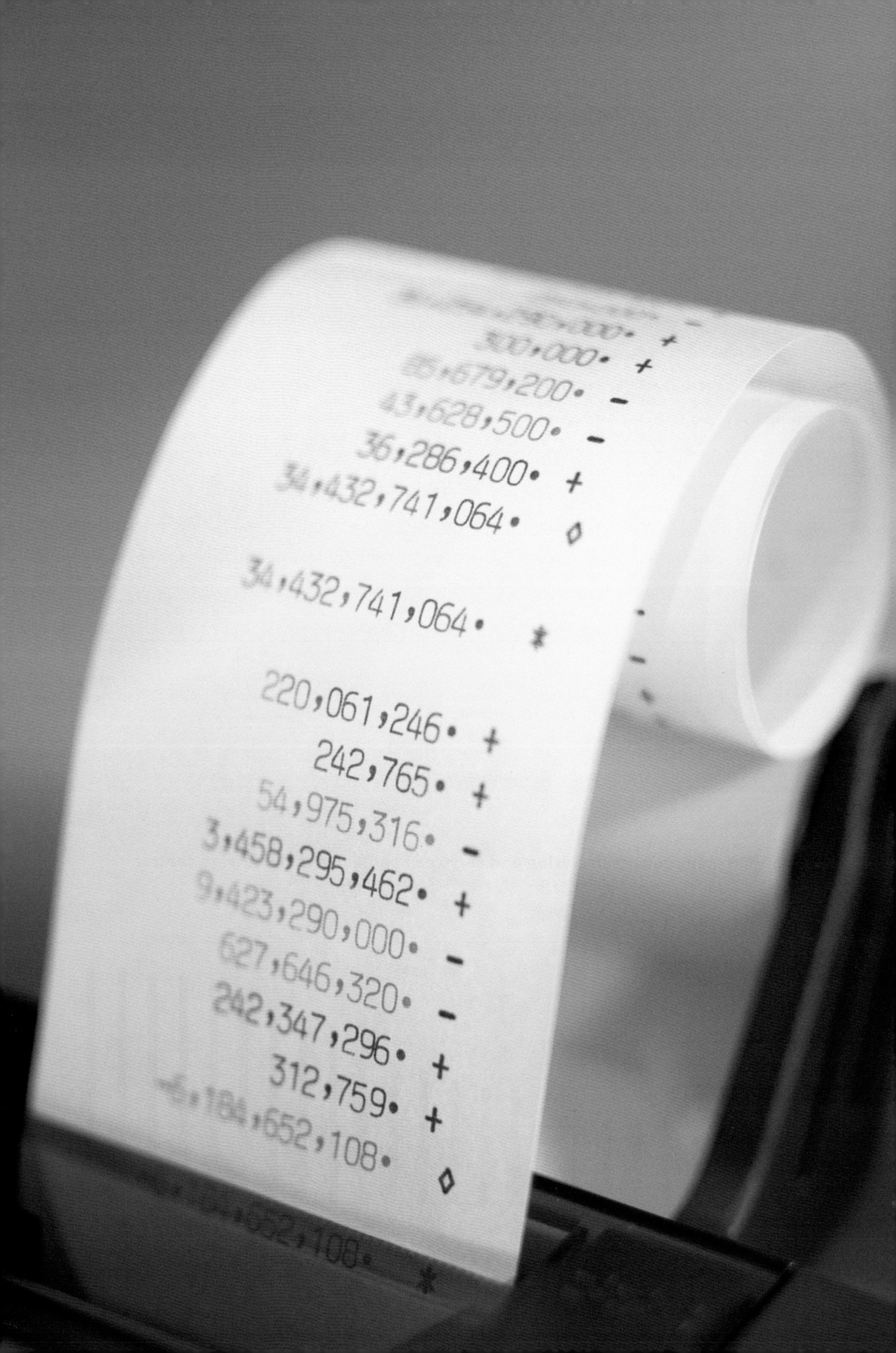
300,000• +
43,628,500• -
36,286,400• +
34,432,741,064• ◊
34,432,741,064• *
220,061,246• +
242,765• +
54,975,316• -
3,458,295,462• +
9,423,290,000• -
627,646,320• -
242,347,296• +
312,759• +
652,108• ◊

PRICES

PRICES, LABOUR COSTS AND INTEREST RATES

CONSUMER PRICE INDICES
PRODUCER PRICE INDICES
LABOUR COMPENSATION
LONG-TERM INTEREST RATES

PURCHASING POWER PARTIES AND EXCHANGE RATES

RATES OF CONVERSION
EFFECTIVE EXCHANGE RATES

CONSUMER PRICE INDICES

Consumer price indices have a long history in official statistics. They measure the erosion of living standards through price inflation and are probably one of the best known economic statistics used by the media and general public.

Definition

Consumer price indices (CPI) measure the change in the prices of a basket of goods and services that are typically purchased by specific groups of households. The CPI shown in these tables cover virtually all households except for "institutional" households – people in prisons and military barracks, for example – and, in some countries, households in the highest income group.

The CPI: all items excluding food and energy provides a measure of underlying inflation, which is less affected by short-term effects. The index for food covers food and non-alcoholic beverages but excludes purchases in restaurants. The index for energy covers all forms of energy, including fuels for motor vehicles, heating and other household uses.

Comparability

There are a number of differences in the ways that these indices are calculated. The most important ones concern the treatment of dwelling costs, the adjustments made for changes in the quality of goods and services, the frequency with which the basket weights are updated, and the index formulae used. In particular, country methodologies for the treatment of owner-occupied housing vary significantly. The European Harmonized Indices of Consumer Prices (HICP) exclude owner-occupied housing as do national CPIs for Belgium, France, Greece, Italy, Korea, Luxembourg, Poland, Portugal, Spain, Turkey, the United Kingdom and most of the countries outside the OECD area. For the United Kingdom, the national CPI is the same as the HICP. The European Union CPI refers to the HICP published by Eurostat and covers the 27 countries for the entire period of the time series. In addition, there are practical difficulties in measuring consumer prices in countries experiencing very high inflation – such as Hungary, Mexico and Turkey during the period considered here.

Overview

In the three years to 2008, annual inflation has been below 4.5% in all OECD countries except Hungary, Iceland and Turkey. The CPI for the OECD total has dropped from 5.5% in the three years to 1997 to 2.9% for the three years to 2008. Over the entire period covered by the table, inflation has been nil in Japan but substantial in Greece, Mexico, Turkey, as well as in the Czech Republic, Hungary, Poland and the Slovak Republic.

Annual inflation has been significantly higher outside the OECD area, with annual increases above 10% in the Russian Federation in the three years to 2008.

Since 1995, consumer prices for energy have recorded large swings, with spikes in 1996, 2000, 2005 and again since mid-2007. Across OECD countries, annual inflation for food has been increasing since 2005. When excluding these more volatile items, the underlying consumer price index (i.e. all items excluding food and energy) points to a progressive decline until 2003 and then stability at annual rates of around 2.0%. In the three years to 2008, the CPI excluding food and energy fell at an average rate of 0.2% per year in Japan, while increasing by around 8% per year in Turkey and Iceland.

Sources

- OECD (2010), *Main Economic Indicators*, OECD, Paris.

Further information

Analytical publications

- Brook, A.M. et al. (2004), *Oil Price Developments: Drivers, Economic Consequences and Policy Responses*, OECD Economics Department Working Papers, No. 412, OECD, Paris.
- OECD (2008), *OECD Economic Outlook, June No. 83 – Vol. 2008/1*, OECD, Paris.

Methodological publications

- ILO, IMF, OECD, Eurostat, World Bank (2004), *Consumer Price Index Manual: Theory and Practice*, ILO, Geneva.
- OECD (1999), *Main Economic Indicators: July Volume 1999 Issue 7*, OECD, Paris.
- OECD (2002), "Comparative Methodological Analysis: Consumer and Producer Price Indices", *Main Economic Indicators, Volume 2002, Supplement 2*, OECD, Paris.

Web sites

- OECD Main Economic Indicators, *www.oecd.org/std/mei*.

CPI: all items
Annual growth in percentage

	1995	1996	1997	1998	1999	2000	2001	2002	2003	2004	2005	2006	2007	2008
Australia	4.6	2.6	0.3	0.9	1.5	4.5	4.4	3.0	2.8	2.3	2.7	3.5	2.3	4.4
Austria	2.2	1.9	1.3	0.9	0.6	2.3	2.7	1.8	1.4	2.1	2.3	1.4	2.2	3.2
Belgium	1.5	2.1	1.6	0.9	1.1	2.5	2.5	1.6	1.6	2.1	2.8	1.8	1.8	4.5
Canada	2.1	1.6	1.6	1.0	1.7	2.7	2.5	2.3	2.8	1.9	2.2	2.0	2.1	2.4
Czech Republic	9.1	8.8	8.5	10.7	2.1	3.9	4.7	1.8	0.1	2.8	1.9	2.6	3.0	6.3
Denmark	2.1	2.1	2.2	1.8	2.5	2.9	2.4	2.4	2.1	1.2	1.8	1.9	1.7	3.4
Finland	0.8	0.6	1.2	1.4	1.2	3.0	2.6	1.6	0.9	0.2	0.6	1.6	2.5	4.1
France	1.8	2.0	1.2	0.6	0.5	1.7	1.6	1.9	2.1	2.1	1.7	1.7	1.5	2.8
Germany	1.7	1.4	1.9	0.9	0.6	1.5	2.0	1.4	1.0	1.7	1.6	1.6	2.3	2.6
Greece	8.9	8.2	5.5	4.8	2.6	3.2	3.4	3.6	3.6	2.9	3.6	3.2	2.9	4.2
Hungary	28.3	23.5	18.3	14.2	10.0	9.8	9.1	5.3	4.7	6.7	3.6	3.9	8.0	6.0
Iceland	1.7	2.3	1.8	1.7	3.2	5.1	6.4	5.2	2.1	3.2	4.0	6.7	5.1	12.7
Ireland	2.5	1.7	1.4	2.4	1.6	5.6	4.9	4.6	3.5	2.2	2.4	3.9	4.9	4.1
Italy	5.2	4.0	2.0	2.0	1.7	2.5	2.8	2.5	2.7	2.2	2.0	2.1	1.8	3.3
Japan	-0.1	0.1	1.8	0.7	-0.3	-0.7	-0.8	-0.9	-0.2	0.0	-0.3	0.2	0.1	1.4
Korea	4.5	4.9	4.4	7.5	0.8	2.3	4.1	2.7	3.6	3.6	2.8	2.2	2.5	4.7
Luxembourg	1.9	1.2	1.4	1.0	1.0	3.2	2.7	2.1	2.0	2.2	2.5	2.7	2.3	3.4
Mexico	35.0	34.4	20.6	15.9	16.6	9.5	6.4	5.0	4.5	4.7	4.0	3.6	4.0	5.1
Netherlands	1.9	2.0	2.2	2.0	2.2	2.4	4.2	3.3	2.1	1.2	1.7	1.2	1.6	2.5
New Zealand	3.8	2.3	1.2	1.3	-0.1	2.6	2.6	2.7	1.8	2.3	3.0	3.4	2.4	4.0
Norway	2.4	1.2	2.6	2.3	2.3	3.1	3.0	1.3	2.5	0.5	1.5	2.3	0.7	3.8
Poland	28.0	19.8	14.9	11.6	7.2	9.9	5.4	1.9	0.7	3.4	2.2	1.3	2.5	4.2
Portugal	4.2	3.1	2.3	2.8	2.3	2.9	4.4	3.6	3.3	2.4	2.3	3.1	2.5	2.6
Slovak Republic	9.8	5.8	6.1	6.7	10.6	12.0	7.3	3.1	8.6	7.5	2.7	4.5	2.8	4.6
Spain	4.7	3.6	2.0	1.8	2.3	3.4	3.6	3.1	3.0	3.0	3.4	3.5	2.8	4.1
Sweden	2.5	0.5	0.7	-0.3	0.5	0.9	2.4	2.2	1.9	0.4	0.5	1.4	2.2	3.4
Switzerland	1.8	0.8	0.5	0.0	0.8	1.6	1.0	0.6	0.6	0.8	1.2	1.1	0.7	2.4
Turkey	89.1	80.4	85.7	84.6	64.9	54.9	54.4	45.0	21.6	8.6	8.2	9.6	8.8	10.4
United Kingdom	2.7	2.5	1.8	1.6	1.3	0.8	1.2	1.3	1.4	1.3	2.0	2.3	2.3	3.6
United States	2.8	2.9	2.3	1.6	2.2	3.4	2.8	1.6	2.3	2.7	3.4	3.2	2.9	3.8
EU27 total	..	..	7.3	4.6	3.0	3.5	3.2	2.5	2.1	2.3	2.3	2.3	2.4	3.7
OECD total	6.1	5.7	4.8	4.2	3.6	4.0	3.7	2.8	2.4	2.4	2.6	2.6	2.5	3.7
Brazil	66.0	15.8	6.9	3.2	4.9	7.0	6.8	8.5	14.7	6.6	6.9	4.2	3.6	5.7
Chile	8.2	7.4	6.1	5.1	3.3	3.8	3.6	2.5	2.8	1.1	3.1	3.4	4.4	8.7
China	16.8	8.3	2.8	-0.8	-1.4	0.3	0.7	-0.7	1.1	3.8	1.8	1.6	4.8	5.9
Estonia	..	..	..	..	3.3	4.0	5.7	3.6	1.3	3.0	4.1	4.4	6.6	10.4
India	10.2	9.0	7.2	13.2	4.7	4.0	3.8	4.3	3.8	3.8	4.2	5.8	6.4	8.3
Indonesia	9.4	8.0	6.2	58.4	20.5	3.7	11.5	11.9	6.8	6.1	10.5	13.1	6.4	10.2
Israel	10.0	11.3	9.0	5.4	5.2	1.1	1.1	5.7	0.7	-0.4	1.3	2.1	0.5	4.6
Russian Federation	197.5	47.9	14.7	27.8	85.7	20.8	21.5	15.8	13.7	10.9	12.7	9.7	9.0	14.1
Slovenia	13.5	9.9	8.4	7.9	6.2	8.9	8.4	7.5	5.6	3.6	2.5	2.5	3.6	5.7
South Africa	8.7	7.4	8.6	6.9	5.2	5.3	5.7	9.5	5.7	-0.7	2.1	3.2	6.2	10.1

StatLink ᵐˢˡ http://dx.doi.org/10.1787/824636028278

CPI: all items
Annual growth in percentage

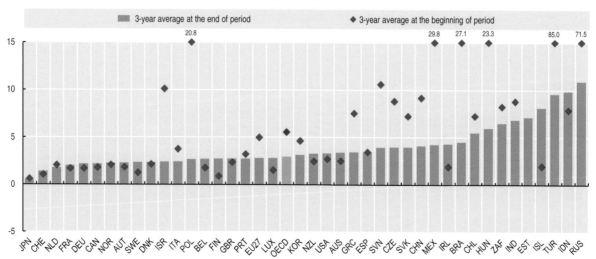

StatLink ᵐˢˡ http://dx.doi.org/10.1787/818665222251

CONSUMER PRICE INDICES

CPI: all items non food non energy
Annual growth in percentage

	1995	1996	1997	1998	1999	2000	2001	2002	2003	2004	2005	2006	2007	2008
Australia	4.7	2.6	-0.2	0.8	1.1	4.2	4.3	3.1	2.5	2.1	2.2	2.1	2.5	3.6
Austria	2.3	1.5	1.1	1.2	0.7	1.7	2.6	2.2	1.4	1.8	1.7	0.9	1.6	1.9
Belgium	1.8	1.8	1.3	1.3	1.3	1.5	2.2	2.1	1.7	1.7	1.9	0.8	1.6	1.8
Canada	2.2	1.5	1.6	1.5	1.4	1.5	2.1	2.8	2.4	1.3	1.2	1.5	2.0	1.0
Czech Republic	..	9.2	9.1	11.5	3.7	3.2	4.8	2.9	0.5	2.5	1.7	2.0	2.8	5.6
Denmark	1.9	1.5	1.7	1.9	2.2	0.7	2.2	2.5	2.4	1.4	1.3	1.3	1.4	2.1
Finland	2.9	0.3	1.1	1.6	1.2	2.6	2.6	1.5	0.6	-0.2	0.2	1.3	2.6	2.5
France	1.9	1.9	1.0	0.8	0.6	0.5	1.2	2.1	2.0	2.2	1.2	1.1	1.4	1.3
Germany	2.1	1.6	1.9	1.3	0.5	0.6	1.3	1.6	0.9	1.7	0.8	0.7	1.9	1.3
Greece	9.7	8.5	7.1	5.8	3.4	2.1	3.5	3.5	3.2	3.2	3.3	2.5	2.9	2.9
Hungary	26.4	24.6	17.4	14.2	11.5	8.6	8.9	6.1	5.3	6.4	3.3	2.2	5.6	3.4
Iceland	1.5	1.9	1.1	1.9	3.3	4.7	6.5	6.2	3.0	3.2	5.1	6.3	6.6	11.4
Ireland	2.6	1.5	1.3	2.4	1.4	5.3	5.3	4.9	3.8	2.1	2.0	3.9	5.3	3.2
Italy	5.1	4.1	2.5	2.4	1.9	2.1	2.6	2.6	2.5	2.2	1.9	1.7	1.7	2.3
Japan	0.5	0.5	1.7	0.9	-0.1	-0.6	-0.9	-0.7	-0.3	-0.4	-0.4	-0.4	-0.2	0.1
Korea	5.3	5.0	3.5	4.8	-0.2	1.8	3.5	3.1	3.2	2.4	2.1	2.0	2.5	3.6
Luxembourg	2.0	0.9	1.3	1.1	0.9	2.2	2.6	2.2	2.1	1.8	1.7	2.1	2.1	2.0
Mexico	33.1	32.1	20.8	16.0	16.7	9.9	6.5	5.0	3.7	3.6	3.3	3.2	3.2	4.1
Netherlands	2.3	2.0	1.7	2.1	2.4	1.6	3.5	3.4	2.0	1.5	1.1	0.4	1.5	1.8
New Zealand	4.4	2.4	0.9	1.1	-0.4	2.0	2.2	2.8	2.0	1.9	2.7	2.5	2.1	2.2
Norway	2.2	0.9	2.1	2.6	2.2	2.3	3.3	2.3	0.1	0.7	1.4	0.2	2.3	1.5
Poland	..	21.1	15.8	13.3	9.3	8.8	5.7	2.5	0.6	1.8	1.3	0.6	1.1	2.2
Portugal	4.9	3.5	2.7	2.8	2.8	2.8	3.7	4.3	3.3	2.5	2.4	2.7	2.3	1.8
Slovak Republic	..	6.4	6.9	7.6	9.1	8.5	6.3	1.6	7.7	6.7	2.7	3.1	3.0	3.8
Spain	4.5	3.5	2.6	2.6	2.5	2.9	3.5	2.8	2.9	2.4	2.5	2.8	2.5	2.3
Sweden	2.7	1.5	0.4	-0.5	0.3	0.4	2.0	2.1	1.4	0.2	0.1	0.8	2.5	2.1
Switzerland	1.9	0.8	0.3	0.3	0.8	0.4	1.0	0.9	0.5	0.6	0.7	0.7	0.7	1.4
Turkey	86.2	80.8	83.5	87.8	71.5	58.0	51.1	43.2	21.8	10.3	8.5	9.2	7.5	7.1
United Kingdom	3.3	2.2	1.9	1.5	0.7	0.1	1.1	1.5	1.3	1.1	1.5	1.3	1.7	1.6
United States	3.0	2.7	2.4	2.3	2.1	2.4	2.7	2.3	1.5	1.8	2.2	2.5	2.3	2.3
EU27 total	..	..	3.3	2.4	1.5	1.2	2.1	2.5	1.8	1.8	1.5	1.4	1.9	1.9
OECD total	6.1	5.4	4.8	4.6	3.8	3.4	3.4	3.1	2.0	1.8	1.8	1.9	2.1	2.2
Chile	..	..	..	..	..	3.1	3.3	2.7	1.6	1.2	2.4	3.0	2.4	5.2
Estonia	..	..	..	..	5.8	3.9	4.1	2.9	2.4	1.2	1.9	3.3	5.4	6.5
Israel	10.7	11.3	8.8	5.5	4.7	0.4	1.1	5.9	-0.3	-0.9	0.1	1.3	-0.2	2.5
Slovenia	..	..	..	..	..	7.3	8.1	6.3	3.9	1.7	1.4	2.8	3.7	

StatLink http://dx.doi.org/10.1787/824728567477

CPI: all items non food non energy
Annual growth in percentage

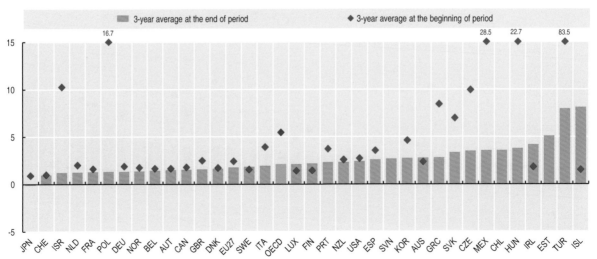

StatLink http://dx.doi.org/10.1787/818680216063

CPI: food and energy

Annual growth in percentage

	CPI: food							CPI: energy						
	2002	2003	2004	2005	2006	2007	2008	2002	2003	2004	2005	2006	2007	2008
Australia	3.7	3.7	2.0	2.0	9.4	1.8	4.3	0.6	5.1	6.6	10.2	9.7	1.2	12.7
Austria	1.4	1.8	1.9	2.1	1.8	4.2	6.3	−2.4	0.9	6.4	9.8	6.2	4.2	10.3
Belgium	2.3	2.0	1.2	1.8	2.5	3.9	6.1	−3.1	−0.1	6.6	11.5	7.5	0.2	19.9
Canada	2.5	1.4	1.8	2.3	2.3	2.6	3.9	−2.0	7.9	6.8	9.7	5.2	2.3	9.8
Czech Republic	−1.9	−2.2	3.4	−0.3	0.8	4.8	8.1	0.4	1.0	4.1	6.6	8.7	1.6	8.4
Denmark	2.2	1.4	−1.0	0.6	2.7	4.4	7.6	2.2	0.9	2.3	7.4	5.3	0.3	7.6
Finland	2.9	0.6	0.8	0.6	1.4	2.1	8.6	−0.9	4.8	3.8	6.8	5.9	1.8	13.5
France	2.7	2.3	0.5	0.1	1.7	1.5	5.1	−1.5	2.3	4.8	9.9	6.4	1.9	10.9
Germany	0.8	−0.1	−0.3	0.1	2.0	3.8	6.1	0.2	3.9	4.1	9.9	8.5	4.0	9.6
Greece	5.3	5.0	0.5	0.6	3.7	3.2	5.4	−0.2	4.0	5.8	14.1	9.0	2.0	13.4
Hungary	4.3	1.4	5.7	1.7	8.2	11.9	10.4	2.2	6.0	10.3	7.6	6.5	13.6	11.8
Iceland	4.2	−2.6	1.1	−2.6	8.0	−1.1	16.0	−2.1	2.0	7.5	6.1	8.0	1.7	21.7
Ireland	3.4	1.4	−0.2	−0.7	1.4	2.8	6.5	3.5	4.1	8.4	12.7	8.2	4.6	8.8
Italy	3.6	3.2	2.2	0.0	1.7	2.9	5.4	−2.7	3.2	2.3	8.7	8.1	1.0	10.3
Japan	−1.1	−0.2	1.1	−1.3	0.6	0.3	3.0	−2.4	0.1	1.7	3.7	5.8	1.6	9.0
Korea	4.8	4.6	8.0	2.6	0.5	2.5	5.0	−3.2	3.7	5.4	5.2	7.0	2.8	12.9
Luxembourg	3.9	1.9	1.8	1.6	2.4	3.4	5.4	−4.0	2.3	9.2	15.2	10.0	2.3	14.2
Mexico	3.8	5.6	7.3	5.5	3.6	6.5	8.1	8.1	9.4	7.7	6.2	7.3	3.8	6.2
Netherlands	3.3	1.1	−3.5	−1.3	1.7	1.0	5.6	2.4	4.6	5.5	11.9	7.6	3.7	4.5
New Zealand	2.9	−0.5	0.4	1.2	3.0	4.0	8.4	1.3	4.1	10.0	10.5	12.5	2.5	12.7
Norway	−1.7	3.4	1.8	1.6	1.4	2.7	4.2	−2.4	19.6	−2.6	2.4	17.8	−10.1	18.1
Poland	−0.7	−1.2	6.0	2.2	0.6	4.7	5.6	4.4	4.4	5.0	5.7	5.0	3.8	8.7
Portugal	2.0	2.6	1.1	−0.6	2.7	2.4	3.7	1.0	4.8	5.0	9.5	7.6	3.5	6.3
Slovak Republic	1.5	3.4	4.8	−1.4	1.4	4.0	7.7	12.1	19.8	14.3	7.8	12.4	0.9	4.0
Spain	5.0	4.1	3.9	3.2	4.1	3.7	5.9	−0.8	1.4	4.8	9.6	8.0	1.7	11.9
Sweden	3.2	0.3	−0.4	−0.7	0.8	2.0	6.9	1.0	10.7	3.3	5.9	7.1	0.3	10.6
Switzerland	2.3	1.3	0.5	−0.7	0.0	0.5	3.1	−5.0	1.2	4.6	10.4	7.1	1.8	12.8
Turkey	49.6	22.7	6.8	4.9	9.7	12.4	12.8	45.7	18.2	4.7	14.7	11.3	6.3	22.4
United Kingdom	0.8	1.2	0.7	1.5	2.5	4.5	9.1	−0.8	2.7	6.2	11.0	14.7	5.4	17.0
United States	1.3	2.1	3.8	1.9	1.8	4.2	6.4	−5.9	12.2	10.9	16.9	11.2	5.5	13.9
EU27 total	2.9	2.0	1.8	1.1	2.4	3.5	6.4	1.5	3.9	5.4	9.9	8.5	3.3	11.0
OECD total	2.9	2.3	2.7	1.4	2.2	3.7	6.1	−0.9	7.3	7.1	11.9	9.3	4.0	12.4
Brazil	9.7	20.4	4.0	3.1	0.0	6.8	13.1	..	..	..	..	..	..	..
Chile	2.0	3.3	−1.9	2.9	2.6	9.6	17.2	1.8	11.9	6.6	10.1	8.2	8.4	14.9
China	−0.6	3.4	9.8	2.8	2.4	12.4	14.4	..	..	..	..	..	..	..
Estonia	3.0	−1.7	4.2	3.5	5.0	9.3	14.2	6.6	2.4	8.2	13.5	8.2	7.8	23.2
Indonesia	10.8	1.1	5.9	10.3	14.9	11.0	17.0	..	..	..	..	..	..	..
Israel	2.8	2.8	−0.7	1.7	5.1	4.0	12.3	10.8	9.9	6.6	9.9	4.3	0.8	11.2
Russian Federation	12.3	11.2	10.4	13.7	9.6	9.0	20.9	..	..	..	..	..	..	..
Slovenia	7.5	4.6	0.5	−0.8	2.3	7.8	10.1	4.2	3.5	6.9	11.9	8.2	3.1	10.6
South Africa	17.4	8.2	1.4	1.7	6.0	10.0	15.5	..	..	..	..	..	..	..

StatLink ᴹᔆᴸ http://dx.doi.org/10.1787/824748118261

Consumer price index for OECD total

Annual growth in percentage

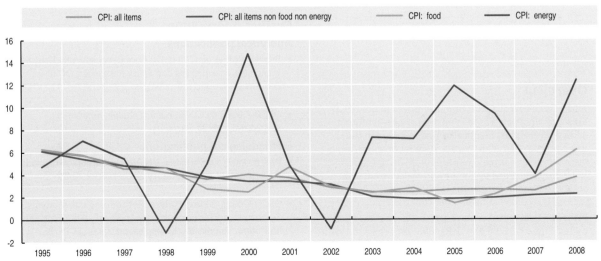

StatLink ᴹᔆᴸ http://dx.doi.org/10.1787/818705625663

PRODUCER PRICE INDICES

A variety of price indices may be used to measure inflation in an economy. These include consumer price indices (CPI), price indices relating to specific goods and/or services, GDP deflators and producer price indices (PPI). Whereas CPIs are designed to measure changes over time in average retail prices of a fixed basket of goods and services taken as representing the consumption habits of households, PPIs aim to provide measures of average movements of prices received by the producers of various commodities. They are often seen as advanced indicators of price changes throughout the economy, including changes in the prices of consumer goods and services.

Definition

Producer price indices (PPI) measure the rate of change in prices of products sold as they leave the producer. They exclude any taxes, transport and trade margins that the purchaser may have to pay. Manufacturing covers the production of semi-processed goods and other intermediate goods as well as final products such as consumer goods and capital equipment.

The indexes shown here are weighted averages of monthly price changes in the manufacturing sector. These indexes capture the production of products intended for the domestic market.

Comparability

The precise ways in which PPIs are defined and constructed depend on their intended use. In this context, national practices may differ and these differences may affect cross-country comparability. This is especially the case for aspects such as the weighting and aggregation systems, the treatment of quality differences, the sampling and collection of individual prices, the frequency with which the weights are updated, and in the index formulae used. Differences may also arise concerning the scope of the manufacturing sector and the statistical unit used for measurement. In some countries, for example, indices may reflect price changes in the output of the manufacturing sector as opposed to manufactured products.

While the PPI series for most countries refer to domestic sales of manufacturing goods, those for Australia, Canada, Chile, China, New Zealand, Switzerland, and the United States include prices applied for foreign sales (i.e. "total market").

Overview

In the three years to 2008, producer prices in the OECD area as a whole increased at an annual rate of around 4.5%, a level almost identical to that recorded in the three years to 1997. This average stability, however, hides large differences across countries with, on one side, huge drops recorded by Turkey and Mexico and, to a smaller extent, in the Czech and Slovak republics, and increases recorded in most other countries.

PPI inflation in recent years ranged between rates a little higher than 1% in the Slovak Republic and close to 15% in Iceland.

Sources
- OECD (2010), *Main Economic Indicators*, OECD, Paris.

Further information

Analytical publications
- Brook, A.M. et al. (2004), *Oil Price Developments: Drivers, Economic Consequences and Policy Responses*, OECD Economics Department Working Papers, No. 412, OECD, Paris.
- OECD (2008), *OECD Economic Outlook, June No. 83 – Vol. 2008/1*, OECD, Paris.

Methodological publications
- IMF, ILO, OECD, Eurostat, UN, World Bank (2004), Producer Price Index Manual: Theory and Practice, IMF, Washington, DC.
- OECD (2002), "Comparative Methodological Analysis: Consumer and Producer Price Indices", *Main Economic Indicators, Volume 2002, Supplement 2*, OECD, Paris.

Web sites
- OECD Main Economic Indicators, *www.oecd.org/std/mei*.

PPI: domestic manufacturing
Annual growth in percentage

	1995	1996	1997	1998	1999	2000	2001	2002	2003	2004	2005	2006	2007	2008
Australia	3.6	0.9	1.2	0.7	0.7	7.1	3.1	0.2	0.5	4.0	6.0	7.9	2.3	8.3
Austria	..	..	..	..	..	3.8	0.0	-1.4	0.3	2.2	3.7	1.7	3.4	3.4
Belgium	2.3	0.7	1.9	-1.5	0.0	9.8	-1.0	0.1	0.9	4.2	2.0	4.7	4.7	5.9
Canada	7.5	0.4	0.7	0.4	1.8	4.3	1.0	0.1	-1.4	3.2	1.5	2.4	1.6	4.3
Czech Republic	8.4	4.9	4.8	4.6	0.1	6.3	2.4	-1.3	-0.4	5.7	2.0	0.6	3.5	3.1
Denmark	3.1	1.4	1.6	-0.6	0.3	4.0	2.9	1.0	0.0	1.0	3.1	3.4	4.8	5.7
Finland	2.3	-1.1	0.3	-1.3	-0.8	5.7	-1.5	-2.0	-1.4	0.4	4.7	5.6	4.5	8.1
France	3.6	0.2	0.2	-1.3	-0.1	4.0	1.3	-0.6	0.8	2.8	3.0	3.3	3.0	5.3
Germany	2.1	0.1	0.6	-0.2	-0.3	3.1	1.3	0.2	0.6	1.7	2.4	2.3	2.3	3.1
Greece	9.5	6.0	3.8	2.9	2.4	5.9	3.4	2.1	2.1	3.8	6.4	7.9	3.5	9.7
Hungary	..	..	..	9.1	6.9	16.1	9.4	2.0	3.7	7.3	4.3	5.7	4.3	8.6
Iceland	..	..	..	..	..	..	..	..	..	..	..	17.5	1.8	31.0
Ireland	2.1	1.6	0.8	0.4	1.5	7.5	2.4	2.1	0.8	0.4	1.8	1.8	1.6	5.1
Italy	8.2	1.8	0.8	0.6	0.2	4.0	1.1	0.8	1.4	3.3	3.1	4.0	3.3	5.0
Japan	-1.1	-2.0	0.1	-1.8	-1.8	-0.4	-2.6	-2.4	-1.4	0.3	0.8	1.9	1.3	4.1
Korea	4.9	2.2	3.4	14.5	-3.3	2.9	-2.1	-1.5	1.8	7.5	6.8	0.2	0.8	11.9
Luxembourg	3.4	-4.4	3.0	2.7	-2.3	6.4	2.5	0.9	3.3	14.8	0.0	9.0	7.6	12.9
Mexico	48.1	33.9	17.3	14.8	15.1	8.9	4.1	3.2	6.6	8.6	4.5	6.0	5.0	8.6
Netherlands	2.6	1.5	2.2	-1.8	0.3	9.1	1.9	-0.6	1.3	3.6	4.6	4.2	5.2	7.3
New Zealand	0.0	-0.8	-1.3	0.9	1.0	7.0	4.8	0.3	-1.3	2.0	3.6	4.6	3.3	11.2
Norway	0.8	1.4	1.5	2.6	3.0	5.0	1.9	-0.4	1.4	3.1	3.5	3.0	4.4	7.8
Poland	..	..	..	..	..	7.9	0.6	-1.7	0.6	7.9	1.2	1.9	3.6	3.4
Portugal	5.0	5.8	3.0	-4.7	3.6	15.0	2.7	0.4	0.4	2.9	3.2	4.2	2.5	5.2
Slovak Republic	11.6	4.7	4.9	2.3	3.9	8.6	3.8	2.5	-0.1	2.5	1.3	1.5	0.2	2.0
Spain	6.9	1.7	1.3	-0.4	0.9	5.7	1.7	0.6	1.4	3.7	4.7	5.0	3.4	6.0
Sweden	7.5	-1.7	0.9	-0.2	0.4	3.9	3.1	0.6	-0.9	1.8	4.0	3.9	3.3	3.9
Switzerland	..	..	..	..	..	..	..	..	0.0	1.4	1.4	1.7	2.6	3.3
Turkey	81.0	70.4	80.6	66.7	57.2	56.1	66.7	48.3	23.8	11.0 |	9.6	9.3	5.6	11.8
United Kingdom	..	2.4	-1.4	-2.0	-0.2	1.9	-0.6	-0.3	1.1	2.2	4.0	3.1	3.0	9.5
United States	2.9	2.3	0.3	-1.1	1.7	4.1	0.8	-0.7	2.5	4.3	5.5	4.0	3.8	7.9
EU27 total	4.7	1.3	0.5	-0.6	0.1	4.3	1.2	0.1	1.0	2.9	3.3	3.5	3.2	5.5
OECD total	6.6	3.9	2.9	1.8	2.2	5.1	2.0	0.8	1.8	3.6	4.1	3.7	3.2	6.8
Chile	..	..	..	..	..	..	..	..	..	..	2.9	5.0	6.0	15.9
China	14.9	2.9	-0.3	-4.1	-2.4	2.8	-1.3	-2.3	2.4	6.1	4.9	3.0	3.1	6.9
Estonia	..	..	..	..	..	..	..	..	-0.6	3.4	2.3	4.8	10.1	7.6
Israel	..	8.6	6.3	4.2	7.1	3.6	-0.1	3.9	4.3	5.4	6.2	5.7	3.5	9.6
Slovenia	..	..	..	..	2.7	8.4	9.9	4.9	2.9	4.2	3.3	2.4	4.4	5.2
South Africa	10.0	8.0	7.2	3.8	5.3	7.6	7.1	13.3	4.6	2.0	3.7	6.4	9.8	15.2

StatLink http://dx.doi.org/10.1787/824763217211

PPI: domestic manufacturing
Annual growth in percentage

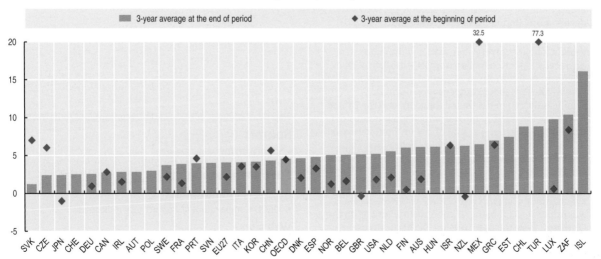

StatLink http://dx.doi.org/10.1787/818714771152

LABOUR COMPENSATION

Labour compensation per unit labour input shows the average compensation received by employees in the economy. This item is closely linked with other competitiveness indicators, *e.g.* unit labour costs, shown elsewhere in this publication.

Definition

Labour compensation per unit labour input is defined as total compensation of employees divided by total hours worked by employees in the case of Australia, Austria, Canada, Czech Republic, Denmark, Estonia, France, Germany, Greece, Hungary, Ireland, Italy, Korea, Mexico, Norway, Slovak Republic, Spain and Sweden. For all other countries, where data on actual hours worked by employees are not available, labour compensation per unit of labour input is defined as total compensation of employees divided by the number of employees.

The annual measures of labour compensation shown here provide one of the building blocks for international comparisons of competitiveness elaborated by the OECD.

Comparability

Compensation of employees is the sum of the gross wages and salaries and of employers' social security contributions. Data refer to the total economy.

Data on total compensation of employees, total hours worked by them and number of employees are based on annual national account data. This assures a fairly good degree of comparability across countries despite differences in the ways in which countries may implement international guidelines in this field.

Differences in the definition of labour inputs (*i.e.* hours worked in some countries, number of employees in others) affect the comparability of this series across countries.

Overview

Between 1998 and 2008, labour compensation per unit of labour input in the total economy increased in all OECD countries except Japan. The average annual growth of the labour compensation over this period ranged from -0.6% in Japan to over 35% in Turkey. About two-thirds of all OECD countries (19 countries) recorded annual growth rates in labour compensation per unit of labour of less than 5%. For the OECD area as a whole, the average annual growth hovered around 4%, with a decline from around 6% in 1998 to around 3% in 2007.

Amongst individual OECD countries, the annual growth rates of labour compensation declined the most drastically in Mexico (falling from 24% in 1998 to 5% in 2006) and in Turkey (from 74% to 10%). The annual growth rates of labour compensation decreased significantly also in the United Kingdom and the United States. On the other hand, the annual growth rates of labour compensation per unit of labour input increased in New Zealand and Spain. Hungary, Poland and Estonia experienced high variability in their annual growth rates of labour compensation over the period.

When looking at broader geographical regions, the average annual growth rate of EU27 was 3.6%, while it was limited to 2.8% in the G7 countries and to 2.3% in the Euro area. Over the past 10 years, the annual growth rates of the labour compensation for these three regions have been broadly stable.

Sources

• OECD (2010), *Main Economic Indicators*, OECD, Paris.

Further information
Analytical publications

• *OECD Compendium of Productivity Indicators.*

Web sites

• *Main Economic Indicators, www.oecd.org/std/mei.*
• OECD Productivity,
  www.oecd.org/statistics/productivity/.

Labour compensation per unit labour input, total economy
Annual growth in percentage

	1995	1996	1997	1998	1999	2000	2001	2002	2003	2004	2005	2006	2007	2008
Australia	4.3	5.5	3.6	3.1	3.1	3.9	5.0	3.1	4.3	4.4	4.7	4.5	..	..
Austria	4.6	1.0	0.0	2.1	2.3	2.0	1.1	2.3	1.4	1.3	3.4	3.5	3.1	2.9
Belgium	1.4	1.4	3.4	1.3	3.5	2.0	3.6	3.8	1.7	1.9	2.1	3.3	3.8	3.4
Canada	1.6	1.5	5.2	2.9	2.3	5.3	3.1	2.2	3.1	2.7	4.7	4.8	..	..
Czech Republic	..	16.9	8.5	8.2	5.9	6.2	13.7	9.1	9.1	4.7	4.0	5.9	6.7	6.1
Denmark	3.6	4.9	1.6	3.1	2.9	3.0	3.7	4.5	3.9	3.1	3.3	3.1	2.2	4.2
Finland	4.1	2.6	1.6	4.5	2.2	3.7	4.7	1.8	2.8	3.6	3.8	2.9	3.4	5.3
France	3.5	1.7	2.3	2.3	2.4	5.1	3.1	6.0	3.1	1.5	3.2	4.8	1.6	3.2
Germany	4.7	2.7	1.6	1.3	2.0	3.3	2.4	2.1	2.0	0.1	0.6	1.2	0.8	2.2
Greece	..	10.3	16.1	4.2	4.1	5.5	3.5	12.4	7.1	4.0	2.9	0.0	..	..
Hungary	..	21.1	19.8	13.9	4.1	15.8	17.5	12.7	11.1		6.5	7.0	4.9	6.8	6.4
Ireland	..	4.4	5.0	4.8	5.2	8.3	7.8	6.2	6.7	5.5	6.2	5.1	6.4	..
Italy	4.3	4.6	4.9	-2.5	2.1	2.2	4.1	2.9	2.9	2.8	3.7	2.1	2.2	3.4
Japan	1.6	0.6	1.5	-0.1	-1.1	0.4	-0.5	-1.6	-1.4	-1.3	-0.1	0.4	-0.4	..
Korea	14.7	12.9	6.5	8.4	0.1	2.4	8.1	7.4	10.0	5.4	6.9	4.3	6.6	6.1
Luxembourg	1.3	1.9	2.6	0.9	4.0	5.3	3.5	3.1	1.1	3.3	4.6	3.3	3.6	2.0
Mexico	..	20.8	20.5	23.7	16.7	19.7	12.1	3.0	9.6	3.7	1.9	5.3	..	..
Netherlands	1.2	1.7	2.8	4.6	4.2	5.1	5.3	5.3	3.8	3.7	1.7	2.2	3.7	3.5
New Zealand	1.6	2.9	3.7	-0.6	-0.6	3.3	4.3	3.9	4.6	4.9	3.3	4.3	4.7	..
Norway	4.6	4.7	5.2	7.1	5.5	6.1	7.6	5.4	4.8	2.8	4.2	5.7	5.5	5.4
Poland	34.0	27.0	21.5	16.3	11.3	12.2		5.2	2.3	1.6	1.9	1.7	1.8	4.9	7.5
Portugal	..	6.1	6.0	5.5	5.2	6.4	4.0	3.6	3.5	2.6	4.7	2.1	..	..
Slovak Republic	..	15.1	16.6	10.9	7.3	13.4	6.8	11.9	11.8	5.5	7.5	7.7	9.0	9.3
Spain	3.7	3.9	2.1	1.6	1.9	2.8	3.9	3.5	3.7	3.1	4.1	4.1	5.5	5.3
Sweden	2.4	6.3	4.6	2.6	0.8	8.5	5.7	4.5	4.3	2.4	3.4	2.3	3.9	0.9
Turkey	66.9	93.4	101.8	74.2	74.8		44.9	43.6	37.8	27.9	16.5	6.2	10.4		..	..
United Kingdom	3.6	3.4	4.1	6.8	4.7	5.4	4.9	3.7	4.7	4.1	3.8	4.6	3.7	3.3
United States	3.3	3.2	3.8	5.9	4.7	5.4	3.2	2.4	3.7	3.8	3.7	3.8	3.7	2.5
Euro area	3.3	2.8	0.2	0.8	2.7	2.6	2.6	2.6	2.3	2.2	2.0	2.3	2.6	3.1
EU27 total	..	4.8	4.3	3.3	3.2	4.6	4.2	4.1	3.8	2.6	3.4	3.4	3.2	3.7
Major seven	3.2	2.6	3.2	3.4	2.9	4.0	2.6	2.1	2.6	2.3	2.7	3.0	2.4	2.7
OECD total	..	6.0	6.4	6.0	5.1	5.6	4.4	3.4	3.8	2.9	3.0	3.4	2.9	..
Estonia	..	28.6	20.1	13.8	8.3	14.5	9.6	9.1	10.9	10.6	9.7	14.7	26.3	14.7
Slovenia	..	13.7	12.5	8.7	8.7	10.2	11.9	8.7	8.0	7.8	5.3	5.5	6.4	8.5

StatLink http://dx.doi.org/10.1787/824765740726

Labour compensation per unit labour input, total economy
Average annual growth in percentage, 1998-2008 or latest available period

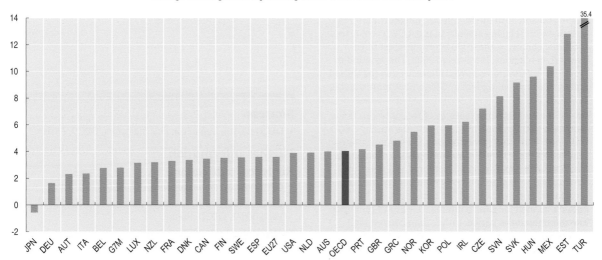

StatLink http://dx.doi.org/10.1787/818715472216

LONG-TERM INTEREST RATES

Long-term interest rates are one of the determinants of business investment. Low interest rates encourage investment in new equipment and high interest rates discourage it. Investment is, in turn, a major source of economic growth.

Definition

Long-term interest rates refer to government bonds with a residual maturity of about ten years. They are not the interest rates at which the loans were issued, but the interest rates implied by the prices at which these government bonds are traded on financial markets. For example if a bond was initially bought at a price of 100 with an interest rate of 9%, but it is now trading at a price 90, the interest rate shown here will be 10% ([9/90] x 100).

The long-term interest rates shown are, where possible, averages of daily rates. In all cases, they refer to bonds whose capital repayment is guaranteed by governments.

Long-term interest rates are mainly determined by three factors: the price that lenders charge for postponing consumption, the risk that the borrower may not repay the capital, and the fall in the real value of the capital that the lender expects to occur because of inflation during the lifetime of the loan. The interest rates shown here refer to government borrowing and the risk factor is very low. To an important extent the interest rates in this table are driven by the expected rates of inflation.

Comparability

Comparability of these data is considered to be high. There may be differences, however, in the size of these government bonds outstanding, and in the extent to which these rates are representatives of financial conditions in various countries.

Evolution of long-term interest rates
Percentage

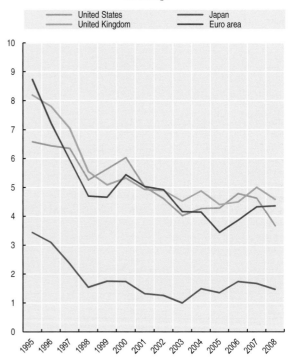

StatLink 🔗 http://dx.doi.org/10.1787/818846053831

Overview

Since 1995 and until the mid-2000s, long-term interest rates have been falling steadily in most OECD countries. For many countries, these long-term interest rates reached an historical low level in 2005. The rebound in long-term interest rates proved short-lived in the United States, the United Kingdom and Japan but more durable in the Euro area.

One of the most striking features of recent trends is the reduction in the variance of interest rates among OECD countries. The convergence of long-term interest rates mainly reflected the increasing integration of financial markets – one aspect of globalisation – and was particularly pronounced among members of the Euro area. Japan and Switzerland are exceptions to this pattern, as their long-term interest rates have remained low throughout the period, rather than converging towards the levels prevailing in most other OECD countries.

Sources
- OECD (2010), *Main Economic Indicators*, OECD, Paris.

Further information
Analytical publications
- OECD (2008), *Financial Market Trends*, series, OECD, Paris.
- OECD (2008), *OECD Economic Outlook, June No. 83 – Vol. 2008/1*, OECD, Paris.

Methodological publications
- OECD (1998), *Main Economic Indicators – Sources and Methods: Interest Rates and Share Price Indices*, OECD, Paris.

Long-term interest rates

Percentage

	1995	1996	1997	1998	1999	2000	2001	2002	2003	2004	2005	2006	2007	2008
Australia	9.21	8.21	6.95	5.49	6.01	6.31	5.62	5.84	5.37	5.59	5.34	5.59	6.00	5.82
Austria	7.13	6.32	5.68	4.71	4.68	5.56	5.08	4.97	4.15	4.15	3.39	3.80	4.30	4.26
Belgium	7.38	6.30	5.59	4.70	4.71	5.57	5.06	4.89	4.15	4.06	3.37	3.81	4.33	4.40
Canada	8.16	7.24	6.14	5.28	5.54	5.93	5.48	5.30	4.80	4.58	4.07	4.21	4.27	3.60
Czech Republic	..	..	..	..	..	..	6.31	4.88	4.12	4.82	3.54	3.80	4.30	4.63
Denmark	8.27	7.19	6.26	5.04	4.92	5.66	5.09	5.06	4.31	4.30	3.40	3.81	4.29	4.28
Finland	8.79	7.08	5.96	4.79	4.72	5.48	5.04	4.98	4.14	4.11	3.35	3.78	4.29	4.29
France	7.54	6.31	5.58	4.64	4.61	5.39	4.94	4.86	4.13	4.10	3.41	3.80	4.30	4.23
Germany	6.86	6.23	5.66	4.58	4.50	5.27	4.80	4.78	4.07	4.04	3.35	3.76	4.22	3.98
Greece	..	..	..	8.48	6.31	6.11	5.30	5.12	4.27	4.26	3.59	4.07	4.50	4.80
Iceland	9.65	9.24	8.71	7.66	8.47	11.20	10.36	7.96	6.65	7.49	7.73	9.33	9.85	11.07
Ireland	8.23	7.25	6.26	4.75	4.77	5.48	5.02	4.99	4.13	4.06	3.32	3.79	4.33	4.55
Italy	12.21	9.40	6.86	4.88	4.73	5.58	5.19	5.03	4.30	4.26	3.56	4.05	4.49	4.68
Japan	3.44	3.10	2.37	1.54	1.75	1.74	1.32	1.26	1.00	1.49	1.35	1.74	1.67	1.47
Korea	..	..	..	..	..	..	6.86	6.59	5.05	4.73	4.95	5.15	5.35	5.57
Luxembourg	7.23	6.30	5.60	4.73	4.67	5.52	4.86	4.68	3.32	2.84	2.41	3.30	..	..
Mexico	-	34.38	22.45	-	24.13	16.94	13.79	8.54	7.37	7.74	9.28	7.51	7.60	8.09
Netherlands	6.90	6.15	5.58	4.63	4.63	5.41	4.96	4.89	4.12	4.10	3.37	3.78	4.29	4.23
New Zealand	7.78	7.89	7.19	6.29	6.41	6.85	6.39	6.53	5.87	6.07	5.88	5.78	6.26	6.08
Norway	7.43	6.77	5.89	5.40	5.50	6.22	6.24	6.38	5.05	4.37	3.75	4.08	4.77	4.46
Poland	..	..	..	..	..	..	10.68	7.36	5.78	6.90	5.22	5.23	5.48	6.07
Portugal	11.47	8.56	6.36	4.88	4.78	5.60	5.16	5.01	4.18	4.14	3.44	3.91	4.42	4.52
Slovak Republic	..	..	..	..	..	..	8.04	6.94	4.99	5.03	3.52	4.41	4.49	4.72
Spain	11.27	8.74	6.40	4.83	4.73	5.53	5.12	4.96	4.13	4.10	3.39	3.78	4.31	4.36
Sweden	10.24	8.03	6.61	4.99	4.98	5.37	5.11	5.30	4.64	4.43	3.38	3.70	4.17	3.89
Switzerland	4.52	4.00	3.36	3.04	3.04	3.93	3.38	3.20	2.66	2.74	2.10	2.52	2.93	2.90
United Kingdom	8.20	7.81	7.05	5.55	5.09	5.33	4.93	4.90	4.53	4.88	4.41	4.50	5.01	4.59
United States	6.58	6.44	6.35	5.26	5.64	6.03	5.02	4.61	4.02	4.27	4.29	4.79	4.63	3.67
Euro area	8.73	7.23	5.96	4.70	4.66	5.44	5.03	4.92	4.16	4.14	3.44	3.86	4.33	4.36
Russian Federation	..	..	..	..	87.38	35.16	19.38	15.82	9.12	8.29	8.11	6.98	6.72	7.52
South Africa	16.11	15.48	14.70	15.12	14.90	13.79	11.41	11.50	9.62	9.53	8.07	7.94	7.99	9.10

StatLink http://dx.doi.org/10.1787/824804175268

Long-term interest rates

Percentage

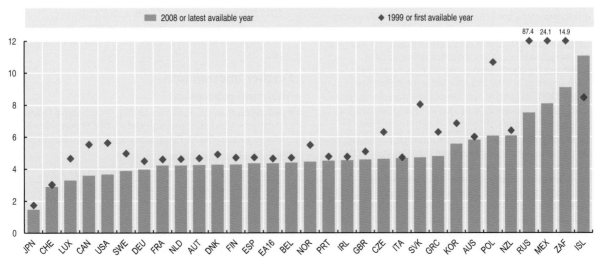

StatLink http://dx.doi.org/10.1787/818744665752

RATES OF CONVERSION

To compare a single country's real GDP over a period of years, it is necessary to remove any movements that are due to price changes. In the same way, in order to compare the real GDPs of a group of countries at a single point in time, it is necessary to remove any differences in their GDPs that are due to differences in their price levels. Price indices are used to remove the effects of price changes in a single country over time; purchasing power parities (PPPs) are used to remove the effects of the different levels of prices within a group of countries at a point in time.

Definition

PPPs are currency converters that equalise price levels between countries. The PPPs shown here have been calculated by comparing the prices in OECD countries of a common basket of about 2 500 goods and services. Countries are not required to price all the items in the common basket because some of the items may be hard to find in certain countries. However, the common basket has been drawn up in such a way that each country can find prices for a wide range of the goods and services that are representative of their markets.

The goods and services to be priced cover all those that enter into final expenditure – household consumption, government services, capital formation and net exports. Prices for the different items are weighted by their shares in total final expenditures to obtain the PPPs for GDP shown here.

Comparability

The PPPs shown here have been calculated jointly by the OECD and Eurostat using standard procedures. In consultation with their member countries, OECD and Eurostat keep their methodology under review and improvements are made regularly.

Overview

Over the period 1995-2008, there were significant differences between changes in PPPs and changes in market exchange rates. Even when the two indicators moved in the same direction, changes differed in their magnitude – as illustrated by the experience of Ireland and the Czech Republic.

Market exchange rates are sometimes used to convert the GDP in different currencies to a common currency. However, comparisons of GDP based on exchange rates do not reflect the real volumes of goods and services in the GDP of the countries being compared. For many of the low-income countries, for example, the differences between GDP converted using market exchange rates and GDP converted using PPPs are considerable. For Turkey and Mexico, the difference between GDP estimates for 2008 based on either PPPs or market exchange rate is over 35%. For India the difference is above 180%. In general, the use of market exchange rates understates the real GDP of low-income countries and overstates the real GDP of high-income countries.

Price level indices are the PPPs estimates for 2008 divided by market exchange rates for the same year, with the OECD set equal to 100. In general, there is a positive correlation between GDP levels and price levels. Denmark, Norway and Switzerland, three of the OECD countries with the highest per capita income, also recorded the highest price levels in 2008, exceeding the OECD level by 40% or more, while India had a price levels of around 35% of the OECD average.

Sources

- OECD (2008), *Purchasing Power Parities and Real Expenditures: 2005 Benchmark Year, 2007 Edition*, OECD, Paris.
- For Brazil, China, India, Indonesia and South Africa: IMF (2009), *World Economic Outlook (WEO)*, IMF, Washington, DC.

Further information
Analytical publications

- Schreyer, P. and F. Koechlin (2002), "Purchasing Power Parities – Measurement and Uses", OECD Statistics Brief, No. 3, March, OECD, Paris, *www.oecd.org/std/statisticsbrief*.

Statistical publications

- OECD (2009), *Main Economic Indicators*, OECD, Paris.
- OECD (2010), *National Accounts of OECD Countries*, OECD, Paris.

Web sites

- Joint World Bank-OECD Seminar on Purchasing Power Parities, 2001, *www.oecd.org/std/ppp/seminar2001*.
- OECD Purchasing Power Parities, *www.oecd.org/std/ppp*.

Purchasing power parities

National currency units per US dollar

	1995	1996	1997	1998	1999	2000	2001	2002	2003	2004	2005	2006	2007	2008
Australia	1.32	1.33	1.32	1.31	1.30	1.31	1.33	1.34	1.35	1.37	1.39	1.41	1.42	1.48
Austria	0.935	0.931	0.924	0.918	0.917	0.900	0.917	0.896	0.885	0.874	0.886	0.877	0.885	0.893
Belgium	0.912	0.913	0.912	0.925	0.921	0.891	0.886	0.865	0.879	0.896	0.900	0.905	0.910	0.912
Canada	1.22	1.21	1.21	1.19	1.19	1.23	1.22	1.23	1.23	1.23	1.21	1.21	1.21	1.23
Czech Republic	11.1	12.0	12.7	13.9	14.1	14.2	14.2	14.3	14.0	14.3	14.3	14.4	14.3	14.4
Denmark	8.48	8.45	8.43	8.39	8.47	8.41	8.47	8.30	8.54	8.40	8.59	8.53	8.53	8.59
Finland	1.00	1.00	1.00	1.00	1.00	0.99	1.01	1.00	1.01	0.98	0.98	0.97	0.96	0.97
France	0.994	0.989	0.974	0.967	0.960	0.939	0.919	0.905	0.938	0.940	0.923	0.925	0.915	0.919
Germany	1.006	0.994	0.990	0.988	0.975	0.967	0.955	0.942	0.918	0.896	0.867	0.858	0.851	0.858
Greece	0.574	0.605	0.630	0.662	0.681	0.678	0.671	0.660	0.689	0.695	0.714	0.716	0.728	0.736
Hungary	61.7	73.2	85.0	94.2	101.1	107.9	110.7	114.9	120.6	126.3	128.6	131.6	134.7	134.0
Iceland	73.1	75.0	74.5	77.2	79.7	84.3	88.9	91.3	94.5	94.2	99.1	109.8	115.1	125.1
Ireland	0.824	0.828	0.853	0.882	0.930	0.962	0.993	1.004	1.015	1.006	1.010	1.008	0.981	0.986
Italy	0.789	0.810	0.816	0.808	0.818	0.817	0.808	0.845	0.854	0.873	0.867	0.854	0.840	0.840
Japan	175	170	168	167	162	155	149	144	140	134	130	124	120	116
Korea	691	713	733	767	755	745	757	770	794	796	789	763	757	762
Luxembourg	0.950	0.948	0.958	0.948	0.941	0.940	0.948	0.934	0.942	0.923	0.953	0.937	0.947	0.951
Mexico	2.93	3.76	4.35	4.96	5.63	6.10	6.31	6.55	6.81	7.21	7.13	7.37	7.49	7.82
Netherlands	0.916	0.910	0.910	0.906	0.907	0.893	0.906	0.902	0.927	0.909	0.896	0.889	0.877	0.883
New Zealand	1.46	1.47	1.46	1.45	1.43	1.44	1.47	1.47	1.50	1.51	1.54	1.52	1.54	1.56
Norway	9.17	9.05	9.09	9.39	9.33	9.13	9.18	9.11	9.12	8.99	8.90	8.90	8.99	9.10
Poland	1.18	1.36	1.52	1.66	1.74	1.84	1.86	1.83	1.84	1.86	1.87	1.89	1.89	1.93
Portugal	0.649	0.661	0.672	0.693	0.697	0.700	0.706	0.708	0.706	0.716	0.684	0.678	0.679	0.673
Slovak Republic	0.433	0.444	0.455	0.470	0.501	0.526	0.522	0.528	0.555	0.572	0.566	0.569	0.563	0.562
Spain	0.710	0.719	0.719	0.719	0.733	0.734	0.740	0.733	0.753	0.759	0.765	0.754	0.745	0.759
Sweden	9.38	9.26	9.30	9.37	9.29	9.14	9.35	9.35	9.34	9.10	9.38	9.31	9.10	9.26
Switzerland	1.98	1.94	1.89	1.88	1.87	1.85	1.84	1.77	1.78	1.75	1.74	1.70	1.64	1.64
Turkey	0.025	0.043	0.076	0.131	0.202	0.283	0.428	0.613	0.774	0.812	0.831	0.868	0.898	0.958
United Kingdom	0.641	0.642	0.635	0.645	0.653	0.636	0.627	0.628	0.641	0.632	0.636	0.642	0.656	0.662
United States	1.00	1.00	1.00	1.00	1.00	1.00	1.00	1.00	1.00	1.00	1.00	1.00	1.00	1.00
Brazil	0.69	0.79	0.84	0.86	0.92	0.96	1.02	1.11	1.23	1.30	1.36	1.39	1.41	1.46
Chile	264	266	273	275	278	285	289	296	307	320	334	363	371	364
China	3.32	3.46	3.46	3.39	3.30	3.29	3.29	3.25	3.27	3.40	3.45	3.46	3.61	3.79
Estonia	4.76	5.79	6.27	6.71	6.95	7.12	7.46	7.47	7.53	7.60	7.85	8.34	8.83	9.08
India	11.0	11.3	12.2	13.1	13.4	13.6	13.8	14.0	14.2	14.5	14.7	14.8	15.1	15.9
Indonesia	1 136	1 211	1 340	2 322	2 612	2 775	3 102	3 233	3 338	3 531	3 934	4 347	4 703	5 446
Israel	3.11	3.36	3.57	3.79	3.50	3.44	3.42	3.46	3.63	3.53	3.72	3.67	3.56	3.56
Russian Federation	1.72	2.45	2.78	3.26	5.54	7.32	8.32	9.27	9.89	11.55	12.74	14.29	15.79	18.42
Slovenia	0.399	0.434	0.461	0.485	0.511	0.532	0.565	0.588	0.615	0.611	0.612	0.623	0.645	0.659
South Africa	2.34	2.48	2.64	2.81	2.96	3.15	3.32	3.61	3.70	3.81	3.87	4.02	4.26	4.63

StatLink http://dx.doi.org/10.1787/824816616030

Changes in exchange rates and purchasing power parities

Average annual growth in percentage, 1998-2008

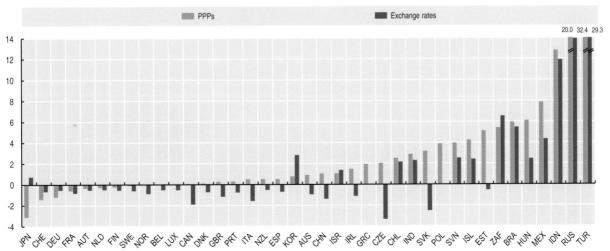

StatLink http://dx.doi.org/10.1787/818848163281

RATES OF CONVERSION

Exchange rates

National currency units per US dollar

	1995	1996	1997	1998	1999	2000	2001	2002	2003	2004	2005	2006	2007	2008
Australia	1.3490	1.2779	1.3474	1.5918	1.5500	1.7248	1.9334	1.8406	1.5419	1.3598	1.3095	1.3280	1.1951	1.1922
Austria	0.73265	0.76936	0.88691	0.89962	0.93863	1.08540	1.11751	1.06255	0.88603	0.80537	0.80412	0.79714	0.73064	0.68268
Belgium	0.73079	0.76752	0.88681	0.89982	0.93863	1.08540	1.11751	1.06255	0.88603	0.80537	0.80412	0.79714	0.73064	0.68268
Canada	1.3724	1.3635	1.3846	1.4835	1.4857	1.4851	1.5488	1.5693	1.4011	1.3010	1.2118	1.1344	1.0741	1.0670
Czech Republic	26.541	27.145	31.698	32.281	34.569	38.598	38.035	32.739	28.209	25.700	23.957	22.596	20.294	17.072
Denmark	5.6024	5.7987	6.6045	6.7008	6.9762	8.0831	8.3228	7.8947	6.5877	5.9911	5.9969	5.9468	5.4437	5.0981
Finland	0.73442	0.77258	0.87314	0.89881	0.93863	1.08540	1.11751	1.06255	0.88603	0.80537	0.80412	0.79714	0.73064	0.68268
France	0.76095	0.77986	0.88980	0.89938	0.93863	1.08540	1.11751	1.06255	0.88603	0.80537	0.80412	0.79714	0.73064	0.68268
Germany	0.73275	0.76938	0.88661	0.89970	0.93863	1.08540	1.11751	1.06255	0.88603	0.80537	0.80412	0.79714	0.73064	0.68268
Greece	0.67986	0.70642	0.80134	0.86729	0.89698	1.07234	1.11751	1.06255	0.88603	0.80537	0.80412	0.79714	0.73064	0.68268
Hungary	125.68	152.65	186.79	214.40	237.15	282.18	286.49	257.89	224.31	202.75	199.58	210.39	183.63	172.11
Iceland	64.692	66.500	70.904	70.958	72.335	78.616	97.425	91.662	76.709	70.192	62.982	70.180	64.055	87.948
Ireland	0.79198	0.79362	0.83757	0.89170	0.93863	1.08540	1.11751	1.06255	0.88603	0.80537	0.80412	0.79714	0.73064	0.68268
Italy	0.84127	0.79687	0.87958	0.89668	0.93863	1.08540	1.11751	1.06255	0.88603	0.80537	0.80412	0.79714	0.73064	0.68268
Japan	94.06	108.78	120.99	130.91	113.91	107.77	121.53	125.39	115.93	108.19	110.22	116.30	117.75	103.36
Korea	771.3	804.5	951.3	1 401.4	1 188.8	1 131.0	1 291.0	1 251.1	1 191.6	1 145.3	1 024.1	954.8	929.3	1 102.1
Luxembourg	0.73079	0.76752	0.88681	0.89982	0.93863	1.08540	1.11751	1.06255	0.88603	0.80537	0.80412	0.79714	0.73064	0.68268
Mexico	6.419	7.599	7.918	9.136	9.560	9.456	9.342	9.656	10.789	11.286	10.898	10.899	10.928	11.130
Netherlands	0.72863	0.76503	0.88545	0.90018	0.93863	1.08540	1.11751	1.06255	0.88603	0.80537	0.80412	0.79714	0.73064	0.68268
New Zealand	1.5239	1.4549	1.5124	1.8683	1.8896	2.2012	2.3788	2.1622	1.7221	1.5087	1.4203	1.5421	1.3607	1.4227
Norway	6.3352	6.4498	7.0734	7.5451	7.7992	8.8018	8.9917	7.9838	7.0802	6.7408	6.4425	6.4133	5.8617	5.6400
Poland	2.4250	2.6961	3.2793	3.4754	3.9671	4.3461	4.0939	4.0800	3.8891	3.6576	3.2355	3.1032	2.7680	2.4092
Portugal	0.75371	0.76937	0.87445	0.89835	0.93863	1.08540	1.11751	1.06255	0.88603	0.80537	0.80412	0.79714	0.73064	0.68268
Slovak Republic	0.9863	1.0175	1.1159	1.1695	1.3730	1.5281	1.6051	1.5046	1.2206	1.0707	1.0296	0.9858	0.8197	0.7091
Spain	0.74940	0.76125	0.87997	0.89788	0.93863	1.08540	1.11751	1.06255	0.88603	0.80537	0.80412	0.79714	0.73064	0.68268
Sweden	7.1333	6.7060	7.6349	7.9499	8.2624	9.1622	10.3291	9.7371	8.0863	7.3489	7.4731	7.3783	6.7588	6.5911
Switzerland	1.1825	1.2360	1.4513	1.4498	1.5022	1.6888	1.6876	1.5586	1.3467	1.2435	1.2452	1.2538	1.2004	1.0831
Turkey	0.0458	0.0814	0.1519	0.2607	0.4188	0.6252	1.2256	1.5072	1.5009	1.4255	1.3436	1.4285	1.3029	1.3015
United Kingdom	0.63367	0.64096	0.61084	0.60382	0.61806	0.66093	0.69466	0.66722	0.61247	0.54618	0.55000	0.54349	0.49977	0.54397
United States	1.000	1.000	1.000	1.000	1.000	1.000	1.000	1.000	1.000	1.000	1.000	1.000	1.000	1.000
Euro area	0.76452	0.78756	0.88180	0.89199	0.93863	1.08540	1.11751	1.06255	0.88603	0.80537	0.80412	0.79714	0.73064	0.68268
Brazil	0.9177	1.0051	1.0780	1.1605	1.8139	1.8294	2.3496	2.9204	3.0775	2.9251	2.4344	2.1753	1.9471	1.8338
Chile	396.77	412.27	419.30	460.29	508.78	539.59	634.94	688.94	691.40	609.53	559.77	530.28	522.46	522.46
China	8.3510	8.3140	8.2900	8.2790	8.2780	8.2790	8.2770	8.2770	8.2770	8.2770	8.1940	7.9730	7.6080	6.9490
Estonia	11.465	12.038	13.882	14.075	14.678	16.969	17.478	16.612	13.856	12.596	12.584	12.466	11.434	10.694
India	32.430	35.430	36.310	41.260	43.060	44.940	47.190	48.610	46.580	45.320	44.100	45.310	41.350	43.510
Indonesia	2 249	2 342	2 909	10 014	7 855	8 422	10 261	9 311	8 577	8 939	9 705	9 159	9 141	9 699
Israel	3.0113	3.1917	3.4494	3.8001	4.1397	4.0773	4.2057	4.7378	4.5541	4.4820	4.4877	4.4558	4.1081	3.5880
Russian Federation	4.559	5.121	5.785	9.705	24.620	28.129	29.169	31.349	30.692	28.814	28.284	27.191	25.581	24.853
Slovenia	0.49457	0.56486	0.66637	0.69326	0.75851	0.92913	1.01297	1.00254	0.86427	0.80279	0.80414	0.79715	0.73064	0.68268
South Africa	3.6270	4.2990	4.6080	5.5280	6.1090	6.9400	8.6090	10.5410	7.5650	6.4600	6.3590	6.7720	7.0450	8.2610

StatLink ⟨⟩ http://dx.doi.org/10.1787/825016135532

Differences in GDP when converted to US dollars using exchange rates and PPPs

PPP-based GDP minus exchange rate-based GDP as per cent of exchange rate-based GDP, 2008

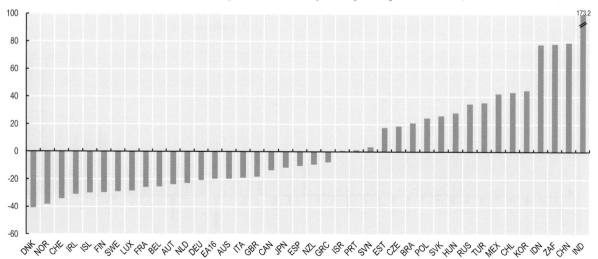

StatLink ⟨⟩ http://dx.doi.org/10.1787/818863132860

Indices of price levels
OECD = 100

	1995	1996	1997	1998	1999	2000	2001	2002	2003	2004	2005	2006	2007	2008
Australia	86	95	97	84	85	81	77	80	90	98	104	105	114	115
Austria	113	111	103	104	99	88	92	93	102	106	108	109	116	121
Belgium	110	110	102	105	100	88	89	90	102	109	110	112	119	123
Canada	78	82	86	82	81	88	88	87	90	92	98	105	107	106
Czech Republic	37	41	40	44	42	39	42	48	51	54	59	63	67	78
Denmark	134	134	126	128	123	111	114	117	133	137	140	142	149	155
Finland	120	120	113	114	108	98	101	105	117	118	119	121	125	131
France	115	117	108	110	104	92	92	94	108	114	113	115	119	124
Germany	121	119	110	112	105	95	96	98	106	109	106	106	111	116
Greece	74	79	78	78	77	67	67	69	80	84	87	89	95	99
Hungary	43	44	45	45	43	41	43	49	55	61	63	62	70	72
Iceland	100	104	104	111	112	114	102	110	126	131	154	155	171	131
Ireland	92	96	101	101	101	94	99	105	117	122	123	125	128	133
Italy	83	94	92	92	89	80	81	88	99	106	106	106	110	113
Japan	164	144	137	130	144	153	137	127	123	121	115	106	97	104
Korea	79	82	76	56	64	70	66	68	68	68	76	79	78	64
Luxembourg	115	114	107	108	102	92	95	97	109	112	116	116	124	128
Mexico	40	46	54	56	60	69	76	75	65	62	64	67	65	65
Netherlands	111	109	102	103	98	88	91	94	107	110	109	110	114	119
New Zealand	85	93	95	79	77	70	69	75	89	98	106	97	108	101
Norway	128	129	127	127	121	111	114	126	132	130	135	137	146	149
Poland	43	46	46	49	45	45	51	50	48	50	57	60	65	74
Portugal	76	79	76	79	75	69	71	74	82	87	83	84	89	91
Slovak Republic	39	40	40	41	37	37	36	39	47	52	54	57	65	73
Spain	84	87	81	82	79	72	74	77	87	92	93	93	97	103
Sweden	116	127	120	120	114	106	101	106	118	121	123	125	128	130
Switzerland	148	145	129	132	127	117	122	126	135	138	137	134	130	140
Turkey	47	48	49	51	49	48	39	45	53	56	61	60	66	68
United Kingdom	89	92	103	109	107	103	101	104	107	113	113	117	125	112
United States	88	92	99	102	102	107	112	111	102	98	98	99	95	92
EU27 total	97	99	96	98	94	85	86	89	98	102	102	103	108	111
OECD total	100	100	100	100	100	100	100	100	100	100	100	100	100	100
Brazil	66	72	77	76	52	56	48	42	41	43	55	63	69	73
Chile	59	59	64	61	56	56	51	48	45	51	58	68	68	64
China	35	38	41	42	40	42	44	44	40	40	41	43	45	50
Estonia	37	44	45	49	48	45	48	50	56	59	61	66	74	78
India	30	29	33	32	32	32	33	32	31	31	33	32	35	34
Indonesia	45	48	45	24	34	35	34	38	40	39	40	47	49	52
Israel	91	97	102	102	86	90	91	81	82	77	81	81	83	91
Russian Federation	33	44	47	34	23	28	32	33	33	39	44	52	59	68
Slovenia	71	71	68	71	68	61	62	65	73	74	75	77	84	89
South Africa	57	53	56	52	49	48	43	38	50	58	60	59	58	52

StatLink http://dx.doi.org/10.1787/825027465851

Indices of price levels
OECD = 100, year 2008

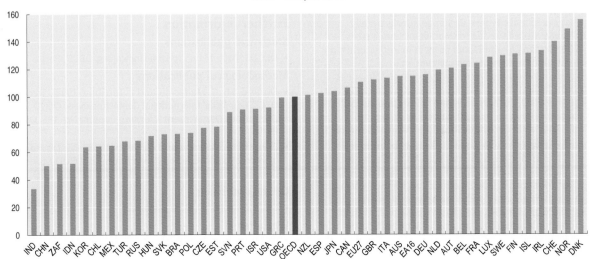

StatLink http://dx.doi.org/10.1787/818868164248

EFFECTIVE EXCHANGE RATES

Effective exchange rates are a summary measure of the changes in the exchange rates of a country vis-à-vis its trading partners. In addition to indices of nominal exchanges rates, which reflect only variations in market exchange rates, this section also shows two indicators of real effective exchange rates, namely changes in either consumer good prices or unit labour costs in manufacturing of a given country relative to those of its competitors. These indicators provide a broad interpretation of a country's price competitiveness. This competitiveness is, in turn, a major determinant of the success of different countries in raising productivity, fostering innovation and improving living standards.

Definition

The nominal effective exchange rate indices are calculated by comparing, for each country, the change in its own exchange rate against the US dollar to a weighted average of changes in its competitors' exchange rates, also against the US dollar. Changes in the competitor exchange rates are weighted using a matrix measuring the importance of bilateral trade flows in the current year.

The two indicators of real effective exchange rates shown here, relative consumer price indices and relative unit labour costs in manufacturing, take into account not only changes in market exchange rates but also variations in relative prices using, respectively, consumer prices and unit labour costs in manufacturing.

The change in a country's relative consumer prices between two years is obtained by comparing the change in the country's consumer price index converted into US dollars at market exchange rates to a weighted average of changes in its competitors' consumer price indices, also expressed in US dollars. The weighted average of competitors' prices is based on a matrix for the current year expressing the importance of bilateral trade. Changes in the index of relative unit labour costs in manufacturing are calculated in the same way.

A rise in the indices represents a deterioration in that country's competitiveness. Note that the indices only show changes in the international competitiveness of each country over time. Differences between countries in the levels of the indices have no significance.

Comparability

All three indices shown here are constructed using a common procedure that assures a high degree of comparability both across countries and over time.

Overview

Since 2000, Germany and Italy experienced higher nominal effective exchange rates, while the United States experienced a continuous depreciation in effective terms. Since 2007, nominal effective exchange rates depreciated significantly in the United Kingdom, while they appreciated in Japan.

Changes in real effective exchange rates generally followed those recorded for market exchange rates. When looking at unit labour costs in manufacturing, a significant improvement in international competitiveness was recorded by Japan and, to a less extent, by the United States, Germany and France. Since the year 2000, the exchange rate of Italy appreciated in real terms by more than 50%, while a similar appreciation in the United Kingdom was partly reversed.

Movements in relative consumer prices point to real effective appreciations in Italy but also, to a lesser extent in the United Kingdom and the United States, as well as to depreciations in Japan, Germany and France. Changes in relative consumer prices are however a poorer measure of countries' competitive positions, as their movements also reflect trends in the price of non-tradable goods.

Sources
- OECD (2008), *OECD Economic Outlook, June No. 83 – Vol. 2008/1*, OECD, Paris.

Further information
Statistical publications
- OECD (2010), *Main Economic Indicators*, OECD, Paris.

Methodological publications
- Durand, M., C. Madaschi and F. Terribile (1998), *Trends in OECD Countries' International Competitiveness*, OECD Economics Department Working Papers, No. 195, OECD, Paris.
- Durand, M., J. Simon and C. Webb (1992), *OECD's Indicators of International Trade and Competitiveness*, OECD Economics Department Working Papers, No. 120, OECD, Paris.

Online databases
- *OECD Economic Outlook Statistics*.

Web sites
- OECD Economic Outlook – Sources and Methods, *www.oecd.org/eco/sources-and-methods*.

Nominal effective exchange rates
Year 2005 = 100

	1995	1996	1997	1998	1999	2000	2001	2002	2003	2004	2005	2006	2007	2008
Australia	86.6	94.9	96.1	89.4	89.7	83.3	78.1	80.9	90.4	97.6	100.0	98.5	104.7	102.4
Austria	97.9	97.0	95.1	97.0	97.7	95.5	95.9	96.5	99.7	100.7	100.0	100.1	100.6	101.1
Belgium	98.4	96.8	92.9	95.2	94.9	91.2	92.3	93.9	98.8	100.5	100.0	100.1	101.4	103.6
Canada	85.2	86.8	87.0	82.9	82.7	83.5	81.0	79.7	88.1	93.5	100.0	106.6	111.5	111.2
Czech Republic	79.5	80.8	78.4	79.7	79.4	80.4	84.5	94.1	93.8	94.1	100.0	105.0	107.2	119.6
Denmark	97.4	96.5	94.2	96.6	96.0	92.1	93.8	95.1	99.6	100.9	100.0	99.9	101.1	103.3
Finland	93.0	90.7	88.7	91.3	93.9	89.7	91.6	93.5	98.9	100.8	100.0	99.8	101.4	104.0
France	96.4	96.7	94.1	96.4	95.7	92.2	93.1	94.6	99.0	100.5	100.0	100.1	101.3	103.2
Germany	96.0	94.7	91.5	94.8	94.7	90.6	91.7	93.4	99.2	101.1	100.0	100.0	101.4	102.8
Greece	104.8	103.1	101.3	98.2	98.6	92.1	93.0	94.7	99.3	100.9	100.0	100.0	101.4	103.7
Hungary	137.8	117.4	108.7	98.5	94.9	90.0	91.8	98.1	97.5	99.5	100.0	93.6	99.1	99.7
Iceland	90.1	89.6	91.6	94.1	95.6	96.6	82.3	84.9	88.9	89.9	100.0	89.5	90.5	66.1
Ireland	96.8	99.3	99.1	96.2	93.4	87.0	88.1	90.2	98.0	100.2	100.0	100.2	102.7	107.8
Italy	83.6	92.0	93.2	95.2	95.0	91.6	92.7	94.5	99.2	100.8	100.0	100.1	101.3	102.9
Japan	100.1	87.3	83.4	86.6	99.5	108.3	99.9	95.7	99.0	103.1	100.0	92.5	87.2	97.3
Korea	113.2	115.0	106.4	77.0	88.4	94.7	87.5	90.4	89.8	89.8	100.0	107.9	107.2	86.5
Luxembourg	100.1	99.0	96.8	97.8	97.5	94.8	95.2	96.2	99.5	100.6	100.0	100.0	101.1	101.9
Mexico	164.4	139.6	137.0	121.7	116.1	118.6	121.9	118.3	103.3	97.2	100.0	99.4	97.5	95.1
Netherlands	96.5	95.2	90.7	93.8	93.6	88.8	90.0	92.1	98.3	100.7	100.0	100.0	101.8	103.9
New Zealand	86.1	91.6	93.8	84.2	81.3	73.7	72.7	78.7	89.5	95.5	100.0	92.3	98.6	92.1
Norway	94.5	94.6	95.5	92.7	92.4	90.5	93.4	101.4	99.2	95.8	100.0	99.4	100.9	100.9
Poland	118.4	110.4	102.5	100.3	93.6	96.5	106.3	101.7	91.4	89.5	100.0	103.0	106.5	115.7
Portugal	100.0	99.6	98.2	98.2	97.6	95.3	96.2	97.2	99.8	100.5	100.0	100.0	100.7	101.9
Slovak Republic	91.2	92.0	96.2	96.1	89.3	90.8	88.6	89.0	94.1	98.1	100.0	103.0	113.5	121.6
Spain	99.2	100.1	96.1	97.3	96.4	93.5	94.5	95.9	99.4	100.5	100.0	100.1	101.0	102.7
Sweden	95.2	104.8	101.5	101.2	101.0	101.3	93.1	95.3	100.8	102.6	100.0	100.3	101.5	99.7
Switzerland	94.0	92.8	87.6	91.3	92.0	90.4	94.1	98.8	100.4	100.8	100.0	98.5	95.8	101.1
Turkey	2 625.3	1 539.7	915.3	550.5	363.4	265.0	149.1	110.7	97.5	95.0	100.0	93.1	95.0	91.2
United Kingdom	76.9	78.6	91.7	97.6	98.0	100.7	99.6	100.8	97.0	101.5	100.0	100.4	102.1	89.2
United States	84.7	89.5	95.8	105.8	105.4	108.0	113.7	114.2	107.5	102.7	100.0	98.3	93.9	91.0
Euro area	90.1	92.0	86.1	91.2	90.2	82.1	84.1	87.3	97.9	101.6	100.0	100.1	103.1	107.1
Brazil	223.5	208.7	207.4	202.1	130.4	134.8	109.0	96.7	83.2	83.4	100.0	111.0	119.6	125.0
China	86.0	89.7	95.5	103.5	103.0	104.7	109.9	109.7	104.2	100.3	100.0	102.4	104.7	112.1
India	115.8	109.5	116.1	111.0	109.4	110.7	110.3	105.4	101.3	98.7	100.0	96.0	99.6	92.1
Indonesia	366.7	374.6	344.3	106.1	129.5	123.7	108.1	118.1	120.4	110.2	100.0	104.3	100.0	90.6
Russian Federation	509.2	479.6	478.9	383.9	126.2	122.0	123.0	111.0	100.1	99.1	100.0	103.0	101.8	99.0

StatLink ᴍᴤᴾ http://dx.doi.org/10.1787/825033285632

Nominal effective exchange rates
Year 1995 = 100

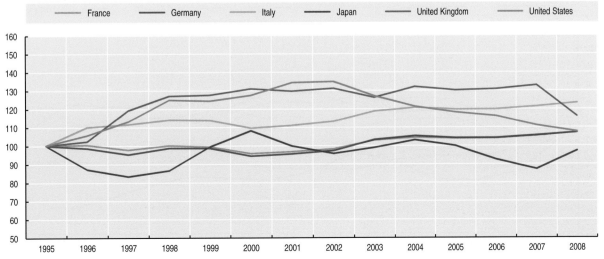

StatLink ᴍᴤᴾ http://dx.doi.org/10.1787/820024628626

EFFECTIVE EXCHANGE RATES

Real effective exchange rates based on consumer price indices
Year 2005 = 100

	1995	1996	1997	1998	1999	2000	2001	2002	2003	2004	2005	2006	2007	2008
Australia	82.0	89.7	88.8	81.2	81.7	78.1	75.1	79.4	89.7	97.1	100.0	99.9	106.0	104.0
Austria	105.7	103.3	99.6	99.8	98.7	96.3	96.5	96.9	99.6	100.5	100.0	99.4	99.7	99.9
Belgium	103.3	100.7	95.5	96.4	95.1	91.4	92.3	93.7	98.1	99.8	100.0	99.7	100.4	103.3
Canada	89.5	89.5	88.8	83.8	83.2	83.7	81.1	80.4	89.4	94.3	100.0	105.6	109.7	107.5
Czech Republic	67.7	72.1	73.3	80.3	79.2	80.8	86.2	95.8	93.7	94.3	100.0	105.5	108.3	123.9
Denmark	97.5	96.1	93.6	95.8	95.8	92.5	93.9	95.7	100.4	101.0	100.0	99.7	100.2	101.8
Finland	109.3	102.9	99.2	100.8	100.7	96.4	97.7	98.8	102.8	102.6	100.0	99.0	100.2	102.0
France	104.2	103.6	99.2	100.1	98.0	93.6	93.5	94.9	99.5	101.0	100.0	99.6	99.9	100.7
Germany	112.5	108.0	102.5	103.7	101.3	95.2	95.2	96.1	100.6	101.9	100.0	99.3	100.5	100.3
Greece	92.3	94.9	95.6	94.1	94.6	88.5	89.4	92.0	97.5	99.6	100.0	100.9	102.5	104.7
Hungary	67.1	67.8	72.0	72.4	74.5	75.6	81.8	90.1	92.0	98.0	100.0	95.3	106.2	108.8
Iceland	77.4	76.8	78.5	80.5	82.8	86.0	76.4	81.7	85.9	88.1	100.0	93.7	97.5	76.4
Ireland	87.9	89.3	88.5	86.5	83.8	80.7	83.9	88.5	97.6	100.0	100.0	101.8	106.9	112.8
Italy	84.8	93.8	94.1	95.5	94.7	91.1	92.3	94.4	99.5	101.1	100.0	99.9	100.4	101.3
Japan	130.9	109.4	102.9	103.6	116.3	123.1	110.2	103.4	104.6	106.2	100.0	90.5	83.0	89.6
Korea	95.4	98.8	92.7	70.4	80.3	86.5	81.9	86.3	87.6	89.0	100.0	108.2	107.4	87.1
Luxembourg	102.4	99.9	96.3	96.3	95.6	93.6	94.3	95.5	99.0	100.2	100.0	100.9	102.3	103.2
Mexico	67.8	75.7	87.5	88.4	96.7	105.1	112.1	112.5	100.4	96.4	100.0	100.0	99.1	97.5
Netherlands	98.1	95.4	90.1	92.8	92.2	87.3	89.9	93.4	99.9	101.4	100.0	99.0	99.8	100.2
New Zealand	86.4	91.7	93.2	83.1	79.1	71.8	71.0	77.8	88.4	94.6	100.0	93.2	99.7	93.2
Norway	94.1	93.0	94.0	91.7	92.2	91.1	94.7	102.1	100.5	96.0	100.0	99.9	99.7	99.7
Poland	74.6	80.1	82.8	88.2	85.7	94.5	106.6	101.8	90.3	89.4	100.0	102.5	105.6	115.2
Portugal	94.1	94.0	92.8	93.6	93.7	91.8	94.1	96.3	99.9	100.7	100.0	100.6	101.2	101.2
Slovak Republic	66.8	66.7	70.3	70.8	69.9	77.1	78.1	79.1	89.1	97.6	100.0	105.4	116.1	125.7
Spain	92.1	93.6	89.3	90.3	90.2	88.2	90.3	92.7	97.3	99.3	100.0	101.5	103.0	105.1
Sweden	108.6	116.9	111.0	108.1	106.1	104.6	96.0	98.5	104.1	104.3	100.0	99.5	100.5	98.1
Switzerland	110.6	106.6	98.2	100.5	99.3	96.5	98.8	102.6	102.8	101.9	100.0	97.4	93.2	97.2
Turkey	66.5	67.2	71.6	79.0	83.1	92.9	75.8	82.6	87.0	89.9	100.0	99.6	107.9	109.4
United Kingdom	84.5	85.9	98.9	104.5	104.1	104.9	102.3	102.8	98.0	101.7	100.0	100.6	102.1	89.0
United States	88.8	91.6	96.2	103.8	102.6	106.0	112.2	112.5	105.9	101.5	100.0	99.3	95.1	91.6
Euro area	104.0	102.6	93.4	95.8	92.5	83.4	85.0	88.3	98.7	102.1	100.0	99.6	101.8	103.8
Brazil	124.7	130.9	135.0	132.6	88.3	95.8	83.5	80.0	77.1	80.5	100.0	112.3	121.7	128.4
China	87.3	93.9	99.1	103.6	100.9	102.6	107.8	106.7	101.9	100.1	100.0	101.8	106.8	116.5
India	85.1	84.8	93.4	98.0	98.1	100.8	101.7	100.0	97.9	96.9	100.0	99.3	106.9	101.6
Indonesia	122.8	132.0	125.2	59.7	87.2	85.0	81.8	99.3	106.4	101.4	100.0	115.9	115.4	110.1
Russian Federation	74.1	98.2	107.0	94.4	61.0	69.0	81.7	83.2	83.5	89.7	100.0	110.7	116.2	123.9
South Africa	..	..	110.5	102.3	96.4	94.1	83.1	71.7	93.4	99.5	100.0	94.9	88.2	77.1

StatLink ⟨⟩ http://dx.doi.org/10.1787/825060786731

Real effective exchange rates based on consumer price indices
Year 1995 = 100

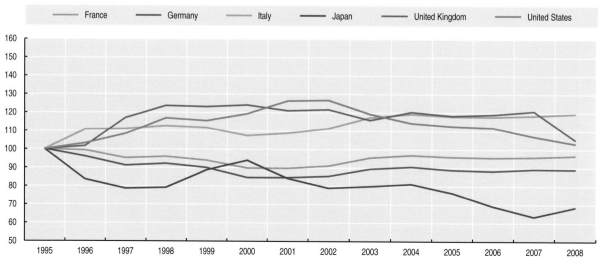

France — Germany — Italy — Japan — United Kingdom — United States

StatLink ⟨⟩ http://dx.doi.org/10.1787/820030485023

Real effective exchange rates based on unit labour costs in manufacturing

Year 2005 = 100

	1995	1996	1997	1998	1999	2000	2001	2002	2003	2004	2005	2006	2007	2008
Australia	72.1	80.1	80.9	74.1	78.3	73.3	67.7	71.2	81.9	92.0	100.0	101.1	108.6	107.3
Austria	107.8	102.4	99.6	101.2	100.1	94.7	94.2	95.0	98.6	100.0	100.0	97.9	97.6	96.9
Belgium	104.5	100.0	92.6	93.5	94.6	89.8	91.9	93.9	99.1	100.0	100.0	100.6	102.5	104.1
Canada	72.6	76.0	75.8	71.7	71.3	68.4	69.3	71.1	81.7	91.0	100.0	107.7	114.3	115.1
Czech Republic	67.8	73.8	74.5	83.5	76.8	75.5	85.4	96.8	100.9	98.5	100.0	101.3	101.9	113.7
Denmark	83.5	84.9	82.3	85.7	86.4	83.6	85.6	89.2	95.4	98.0	100.0	101.8	105.5	111.0
Finland	127.2	118.8	112.2	113.3	113.5	101.7	101.0	98.8	101.1	101.4	100.0	94.8	89.9	90.6
France	114.4	113.8	106.8	104.3	101.3	95.7	94.6	96.0	98.6	101.1	100.0	101.4	103.4	103.8
Germany	115.6	113.7	104.8	107.6	107.5	101.2	100.0	101.8	106.2	105.8	100.0	95.9	93.6	91.1
Greece	113.1	115.8	124.0	119.0	115.5	107.7	104.9	126.1	127.1	120.1	100.0	100.0	105.2	107.4
Hungary	94.6	87.4	86.1	80.1	77.3	79.9	86.4	92.8	90.2	96.9	100.0	92.3	98.0	102.4
Iceland	60.9	60.7	64.1	70.0	77.7	84.4	73.8	78.3	82.6	85.3	100.0	97.4	104.3	77.8
Ireland	122.6	122.1	116.1	105.1	97.5	89.8	87.0	82.1	90.7	94.4	100.0	97.7	94.4	100.0
Italy	69.1	78.4	81.2	82.1	83.3	79.2	80.6	84.3	93.7	98.4	100.0	101.1	103.7	108.9
Japan	151.0	123.7	117.8	121.5	138.8	143.5	130.1	121.5	114.2	111.0	100.0	87.8	78.9	84.6
Korea	114.7	124.2	109.7	76.2	80.0	85.2	80.1	84.7	84.0	87.0	100.0	104.5	101.4	75.9
Luxembourg	100.5	98.9	93.7	90.0	86.4	85.6	90.4	91.2	94.2	95.5	100.0	110.8	110.8	118.8
Mexico	55.7	59.0	70.1	72.0	82.3	95.4	106.2	111.6	99.9	96.5	100.0	100.5	98.7	94.5
Netherlands	97.5	94.3	91.5	95.1	94.7	88.2	89.9	93.5	101.3	102.8	100.0	99.0	100.4	103.0
New Zealand	71.8	78.3	81.2	73.5	70.5	62.2	63.8	69.5	80.6	89.1	100.0	96.1	105.1	99.7
Norway	76.4	75.8	80.1	79.7	86.4	88.4	91.4	101.8	96.7	93.3	100.0	108.8	115.1	116.0
Poland	111.2	118.4	122.2	129.4	123.5	126.7	131.2	115.3	94.2	88.8	100.0	97.2	96.7	102.1
Portugal	94.2	91.1	89.7	92.5	94.6	93.1	93.3	95.0	96.6	98.3	100.0	101.5	98.9	98.2
Slovak Republic	93.8	98.0	117.4	107.1	99.2	116.1	103.7	103.8	104.0	100.2	100.0	104.6	108.5	124.7
Spain	86.4	88.4	86.5	86.9	85.2	84.5	85.7	88.0	93.6	97.2	100.0	102.4	104.9	110.4
Sweden	124.6	141.0	131.7	124.2	115.2	115.9	111.5	107.8	110.1	105.9	100.0	94.6	99.0	100.0
Switzerland	91.2	87.8	82.7	85.4	86.8	86.4	91.9	97.8	99.4	98.7	100.0	99.6	98.4	103.6
Turkey	69.8	68.2	76.8	83.8	108.1	116.3	88.1	89.5	87.2	90.3	100.0	96.8	102.5	103.2
United Kingdom	70.3	70.6	84.5	96.1	97.7	100.3	98.0	101.4	97.7	102.7	100.0	103.0	107.4	93.9
United States	108.5	109.6	113.6	121.4	120.2	126.1	128.1	122.3	114.3	104.5	100.0	97.6	91.6	87.0
Euro area	105.3	106.0	95.7	97.2	95.6	84.8	84.4	88.8	100.0	103.7	100.0	98.5	99.4	102.1
Brazil	154.4	162.2	160.7	152.5	94.3	98.9	82.8	77.0	72.6	78.6	100.0	111.9	121.8	132.0
Indonesia	167.2	164.0	159.0	46.4	71.0	72.7	82.7	98.2	104.8	102.1	100.0	115.2	110.0	100.9
Russian Federation	71.8	103.6	113.8	101.8	44.0	57.5	78.2	83.3	83.7	93.3	100.0	116.0	134.1	151.8

StatLink ⬛ http://dx.doi.org/10.1787/825118704336

Real effective exchange rates based on unit labour costs in manufacturing

Year 1995 = 100

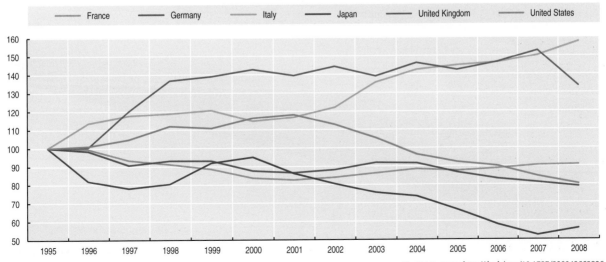

StatLink ⬛ http://dx.doi.org/10.1787/820042662806

ENERGY

ENERGY SUPPLY

An analysis of energy problems requires a comprehensive presentation of basic supply and demand data for all fuels in a manner which allows the easy comparison of the contribution that each fuel makes to the economy and their interrelationships through the conversion of one fuel into another. This type of presentation is suitable for the study of energy substitution, energy conservation and forecasting.

Definition

The table refers to total primary energy supply (TPES). TPES equals production plus imports minus exports minus international bunkers plus or minus stock changes. Note that starting this year, international aviation bunkers are subtracted out of supply in the same way as international marine bunkers. The IEA energy balance methodology is based on the calorific content of the energy commodities and a common unit of account. The unit of account adopted is the tonne of oil equivalent (toe) which is defined as 10^7 kilocalories (41.868 gigajoules). This quantity of energy is, within a few per cent, equal to the net heat content of one tonne of crude oil. The difference between the "net" and the "gross" calorific value for each fuel is the latent heat of vaporisation of the water produced during combustion of the fuel. For coal and oil, net calorific value is about 5% less than gross, for most forms of natural and manufactured gas the difference is 9-10%, while for electricity there is no

difference. The IEA balances are calculated using the physical energy content method to calculate the primary energy equivalent. The forecasts provided in the table refer to the Reference Scenario of the *World Energy Outlook*; this scenario projects supply and demand if present policies were to continue. The *World Energy Outlook* also presents a scenario for stabilising greenhouse gas concentrations at 450 parts per million (ppm) of CO_2-equivalent (which would limit the temperature increase to about 2°C).

Comparability

While every effort is made to ensure the accuracy of the data, quality is not homogeneous for all countries and regions. In some countries, data are based on secondary sources, and where incomplete or unavailable, the IEA has made estimates. In general, data are likely to be more accurate for production and trade than for international bunkers or stock changes. Moreover, statistics for combustible renewables and waste are less accurate than those for traditional commercial energy data in most countries.

Overview

Between 1971 and 2007, the world's total primary energy supply increased by 117%, reaching 12 029 Mtoe (million tonnes of oil equivalent). This equates to a compound growth rate of 2.2% per annum. By comparison, world population grew by 1.6% and gross domestic product by 3.5% per annum in real terms over the same period.

Energy supply growth was fairly constant over the period, except in 1974-1975 and in the early 1980s as a consequence of the first two oil shocks, and in the early 1990s following the dissolution of the Soviet Union. With the current economic crisis, early indicators suggest that growth in energy supply slowed in 2008 and may have declined in 2009.

The share of OECD in world primary energy supply decreased again in 2007. Strong economic development in Asia led to a large increase in the share of non-OECD Asia (including China) in world energy supply, from 13% in 1971 to 28% in 2007. By contrast, the combined share of the former USSR and non-OECD Europe decreased significantly in the late 1980s.

Sources
* IEA (2009), *Energy Balances of Non-OECD Countries*, IEA, Paris.
* IEA (2009), *Energy Balances of OECD Countries*, IEA, Paris.
* IEA (2009), *World Energy Outlook 2009*, IEA, Paris.

Further information
Analytical publications
* IEA (2008), *Energy Technology Perspectives: Scenarios and Strategies to 2050*, IEA, Paris.
* IEA (2009), *Energy Policies of IEA Countries*, series, IEA, Paris.
* IEA (2009), *Energy Technology Transitions for Industry: Strategies for the Next Industrial Revolution*, IEA, Paris.
* IEA (2009), *IEA Scoreboard 2009: 35 Key Energy Trends over 35 Years*, IEA, Paris.
* IEA (2009), *Sectoral Approaches in Electricity – Building Bridges to a Safe Climate*, IEA, Paris.

Online databases
* *World Energy Statistics and Balances.*

Web sites
* International Energy Agency, *www.iea.org*.

Total primary energy supply
Million tonnes of oil equivalent (Mtoe)

	1971	1990	1998	1999	2000	2001	2002	2003	2004	2005	2006	2007	2008	2030
Australia	51.6	86.2	104.0	106.2	108.9	107.2	110.7	111.6	112.1	120.8	122.6	124.1	129.0	..
Austria	18.8	24.8	28.7	28.7	28.5	30.2	31.0	32.7	33.0	33.7	34.2	33.2	32.3	..
Belgium	39.7	48.2	57.7	58.2	58.5	58.3	56.4	59.2	58.9	58.7	58.1	57.0	57.8	..
Canada	141.3	208.7	237.3	244.5	251.2	248.1	248.7	261.6	268.2	271.7	269.2	269.4	267.4	..
Czech Republic	45.4	48.8	41.0	38.3	40.3	41.3	41.8	44.4	45.5	44.9	45.9	45.8	45.4	..
Denmark	18.5	17.3	20.0	19.2	18.6	19.1	19.0	20.1	19.4	18.8	20.1	19.6	19.2	..
Finland	18.2	28.4	32.6	32.5	32.1	32.8	34.5	36.6	36.8	34.0	37.0	36.5	34.8	..
France	158.6	224.5	250.8	250.6	253.2	261.2	261.9	266.7	270.7	271.4	267.7	263.7	266.9	..
Germany	305.0	351.4	343.3	335.6	337.3	347.4	339.3	342.1	343.5	338.7	341.2	331.3	334.8	..
Greece	8.7	21.4	25.6	25.7	27.1	28.0	28.3	29.1	29.7	30.2	30.2	32.2	32.6	..
Hungary	19.0	28.7	25.7	25.5	25.0	25.6	25.6	26.1	26.2	27.6	27.3	26.7	26.6	..
Iceland	0.9	2.1	2.6	3.0	3.1	3.2	3.3	3.3	3.4	3.5	4.2	4.9	4.7	..
Ireland	6.7	10.0	12.8	13.1	13.6	14.5	14.7	14.2	14.3	14.4	14.7	15.1	15.1	..
Italy	105.4	146.7	165.5	167.5	170.7	171.3	171.6	178.5	180.6	182.9	181.1	178.2	174.5	..
Japan	267.5	438.1	499.8	507.5	517.7	509.5	509.0	504.8	520.9	518.9	518.3	513.5	491.1	488
Korea	17.0	93.1	159.5	176.1	188.9	191.4	201.8	205.7	211.2	210.4	213.8	222.2	227.2	..
Luxembourg	4.1	3.4	3.0	3.1	3.3	3.4	3.6	3.8	4.2	4.3	4.3	4.2	4.1	..
Mexico	43.0	121.2	143.9	146.9	147.4	149.4	153.8	158.4	163.3	175.2	175.1	184.3	186.3	..
Netherlands	50.9	65.7	71.9	71.0	73.1	75.3	75.8	78.1	79.2	78.8	76.6	80.4	79.6	..
New Zealand	6.9	13.3	16.3	17.1	16.8	16.9	17.1	16.5	16.7	16.4	16.6	16.8	17.2	..
Norway	13.3	21.0	25.1	26.3	25.4	26.1	24.7	26.9	27.9	28.2	29.1	26.9	31.0	..
Poland	86.1	103.1	95.5	93.0	89.1	89.7	88.9	91.1	91.4	92.4	97.3	97.1	98.4	..
Portugal	6.3	16.7	22.8	24.5	24.7	24.8	25.8	25.1	25.8	26.4	24.7	25.1	24.4	..
Slovak Republic	14.3	21.3	17.6	17.7	17.7	18.6	18.7	18.6	18.4	18.8	18.6	17.8	18.2	..
Spain	42.6	90.1	110.9	116.2	121.9	125.0	128.9	133.2	139.1	141.8	141.5	144.0	137.8	..
Sweden	36.0	47.2	51.1	50.1	47.6	50.5	51.8	50.6	52.6	51.6	50.2	50.4	49.7	..
Switzerland	16.4	23.8	24.9	24.8	24.5	26.0	25.3	25.5	25.9	25.8	27.0	25.7	26.7	..
Turkey	19.5	52.8	71.7	70.4	76.3	70.4	74.2	77.8	80.9	84.4	93.0	100.0	96.5	..
United Kingdom	208.7	207.2	222.2	222.7	224.0	224.9	219.2	223.2	222.7	222.7	219.4	211.3	207.4	..
United States	1 587.5	1 913.2	2 162.8	2 220.2	2 283.3	2 239.4	2 269.3	2 264.3	2 311.0	2 323.4	2 302.8	2 339.9	2 297.0	2 396
EU27 total	..	1 636.9	1 687.1	1 673.2	1 685.7	1 725.3	1 720.1	1 760.5	1 777.9	1 778.9	1 778.9	1 758.8	..	1 781
OECD total	3 357.9	4 478.2	5 046.5	5 136.2	5 249.7	5 229.6	5 274.6	5 330.0	5 433.2	5 470.7	5 461.8	5 497.1	5 433.7	5 811
Brazil	69.6	139.5	182.2	187.0	189.2	190.3	195.9	198.9	210.0	215.7	222.9	235.6	..	..
Chile	8.7	13.8	24.7	25.8	26.2	25.6	26.6	26.9	28.9	29.6	30.5	30.8	..	..
China	391.7	863.1	1 083.9	1 083.7	1 092.2	1 087.6	1 176.5	1 339.2	1 558.2	1 689.8	1 845.4	1 955.8	..	3 827
Estonia	..	9.6	4.9	4.6	4.5	4.7	4.5	5.0	5.1	5.2	5.0	5.6	..	..
India	156.2	318.2	423.0	448.4	457.4	463.9	476.2	488.7	516.6	534.1	561.0	594.9	..	1 287
Indonesia	36.1	102.5	132.3	147.6	150.9	157.9	161.1	164.1	171.2	175.2	180.6	190.6	..	..
Israel	5.7	11.6	17.4	17.0	18.4	19.4	19.3	20.0	19.9	20.5	21.2	22.0	..	..
Russian Federation	..	870.0	577.8	599.3	610.1	617.3	613.8	635.6	637.5	651.3	670.8	672.1	..	812
Slovenia	..	5.7	6.4	6.4	6.4	6.7	6.8	6.9	7.1	7.3	7.3	7.3	..	..
South Africa	45.1	90.9	108.1	108.2	110.3	108.3	104.3	117.1	128.6	126.8	129.2	134.3	..	..
World	5 533.2	8 761.7	9 614.7	9 805.8	10 018.7	10 050.8	10 271.5	10 628.1	11 122.7	11 425.5	11 720.1	12 029.3	..	16 790

StatLink http://dx.doi.org/10.1787/825128533540

Total primary energy supply by region
Million tonnes of oil equivalent (Mtoe)

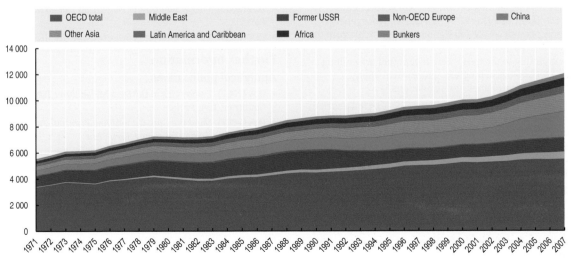

StatLink http://dx.doi.org/10.1787/820073558273

ENERGY INTENSITY

A common way to measure and compare the energy intensity of different countries, and how this changes over time, is to look at the ratio of energy supply to GDP. It should be noted that energy intensity is only a poor proxy of energy efficiency, as the latter depends on numerous elements (such as climate, output composition, outsourcing of goods produced by energy-intensive industries, etc.) that are not considered by the simple measure of energy supply to GDP shown here.

Definition

The table shows total primary energy supply (TPES) per thousand US dollars of GDP. The ratios are calculated by dividing each country's annual TPES by each country's annual GDP expressed in constant 2000 prices and converted to US dollars using purchasing power parities (PPPs) for the year 2000.

TPES consists of primary energy production adjusted for net trade, bunkers and stock changes. Production of secondary energy (e.g. oil/coal products, electricity from fossil fuels, etc.) is not included since the "energy equivalent" of the primary fuels used to create the secondary products or electric power has already been counted. TPES is expressed in tonnes of oil equivalent (see the IEA sources below for details on how TPES is calculated).

Comparability

Care should be taken when comparing energy intensities between countries and over time since different national circumstances (e.g. density of population, country size, average temperatures and economic structure) will affect the ratios. A decrease in the TPES/GDP ratio may reflect a restructuring of the economy and the transfer of energy-intensive industries such as iron and steel out of the country. The harmful effects of such outsourcing may increase the global damage to the environment if the producers abroad use less energy efficient techniques. Data for Latin America include the Caribbean islands.

Total primary energy supply per unit of GDP

Tonnes of oil equivalent (toe) per thousand 2000 US dollars of GDP calculated using PPPs, 2007

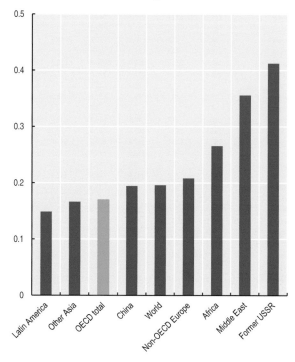

StatLink ⟨⟩ http://dx.doi.org/10.1787/820143523054

Overview

Sharp improvements in the efficiency of key end uses, shifts to electricity, and some changes in manufacturing output and consumer behaviour have occurred in many OECD countries since 1971. As a consequence, energy supply per unit of GDP fell significantly, particularly in the 1979-1990 period.

Contributing to the trend were higher fuel prices, long-term technological progress, government energy efficiency programmes and regulations.

The ratio of energy supply to GDP (TPES/GDP) fell less than the ratio of energy consumption to GDP (TFC/GDP, not shown here), because of increased use of electricity. The main reason for this divergence is that losses in electricity generation outweighed intensity improvements achieved in end uses such as household appliances.

Among OECD countries, the ratio of energy consumption to GDP varies considerably. Apart from energy prices, winter weather is a key element in these variations, as are raw materials processing techniques, the distance goods must be shipped, the size of dwellings, the use of private rather than public transport and other lifestyle factors.

Sources

- IEA (2009), *Energy Balances of Non-OECD Countries*, IEA, Paris.
- IEA (2009), *Energy Balances of OECD Countries*, IEA, Paris.

Further information

Analytical publications

- IEA (2007), *Energy Use in the New Millennium: Trends in IEA Countries*, IEA, Paris.
- IEA (2007), *Mind the Gap: Quantifying Principal-Agent Problems in Energy Efficiency*, IEA, Paris.
- IEA (2009), *Energy Policies of IEA Countries*, series, IEA, Paris.
- IEA (2009), *IEA Scoreboard 2009: 35 Key Energy Trends over 35 Years*, IEA, Paris.
- IEA (2009), *World Energy Outlook 2009*, IEA, Paris.

Online databases

- World Energy Statistics and Balances.

Web sites

- International Energy Agency, *www.iea.org*.

Total primary energy supply per unit of GDP

Tonnes of oil equivalent (toe) per thousand 2000 US dollars of GDP calculated using PPPs

	1971	1990	1997	1998	1999	2000	2001	2002	2003	2004	2005	2006	2007	2008
Australia	0.24	0.23	0.22	0.21	0.21	0.21	0.20	0.20	0.19	0.19	0.20	0.19	0.19	0.19
Austria	0.18	0.14	0.14	0.13	0.13	0.12	0.13	0.13	0.14	0.14	0.13	0.13	0.12	0.12
Belgium	0.28	0.21	0.22	0.22	0.21	0.21	0.21	0.20	0.20	0.20	0.19	0.18	0.18	0.18
Canada	0.41	0.32	0.32	0.30	0.29	0.29	0.28	0.27	0.28	0.28	0.27	0.26	0.26	0.25
Czech Republic	0.44	0.33	0.29	0.28	0.26	0.26	0.26	0.26	0.27	0.26	0.24	0.23	0.22	0.21
Denmark	0.23	0.15	0.14	0.14	0.13	0.12	0.12	0.12	0.13	0.12	0.11	0.12	0.11	0.11
Finland	0.31	0.26	0.28	0.27	0.26	0.24	0.24	0.25	0.26	0.25	0.23	0.23	0.22	0.21
France	0.22	0.18	0.18	0.18	0.17	0.17	0.17	0.17	0.17	0.17	0.16	0.16	0.15	0.15
Germany	0.29	0.20	0.17	0.17	0.16	0.16	0.16	0.16	0.16	0.16	0.15	0.15	0.14	0.14
Greece	0.08	0.13	0.14	0.14	0.13	0.13	0.13	0.13	0.13	0.12	0.12	0.12	0.12	0.12
Hungary	0.28	0.25	0.24	0.22	0.21	0.20	0.20	0.19	0.18	0.18	0.18	0.17	0.16	0.16
Iceland	0.31	0.33	0.35	0.35	0.38	0.38	0.38	0.39	0.38	0.36	0.35	0.40	0.45	0.42
Ireland	0.27	0.18	0.15	0.14	0.13	0.12	0.13	0.12	0.11	0.11	0.10	0.10	0.09	0.10
Italy	0.15	0.12	0.12	0.12	0.12	0.12	0.12	0.12	0.12	0.12	0.12	0.12	0.11	0.11
Japan	0.20	0.15	0.16	0.16	0.16	0.16	0.16	0.16	0.15	0.15	0.15	0.15	0.14	0.14
Korea	0.17	0.22	0.25	0.25	0.25	0.24	0.24	0.24	0.23	0.23	0.22	0.21	0.21	0.21
Luxembourg	0.58	0.24	0.17	0.15	0.14	0.14	0.14	0.14	0.15	0.16	0.15	0.15	0.14	0.13
Mexico	0.13	0.17	0.16	0.16	0.16	0.15	0.15	0.15	0.16	0.16	0.16	0.15	0.16	0.16
Netherlands	0.24	0.19	0.17	0.17	0.16	0.16	0.16	0.16	0.16	0.16	0.16	0.15	0.15	0.15
New Zealand	0.16	0.22	0.22	0.22	0.22	0.21	0.20	0.20	0.18	0.18	0.17	0.17	0.17	0.17
Norway	0.23	0.19	0.16	0.16	0.17	0.16	0.16	0.16	0.15	0.16	0.16	0.16	0.14	0.16
Poland	0.41	0.37	0.29	0.26	0.24	0.22	0.22	0.21	0.21	0.20	0.20	0.19	0.18	0.18
Portugal	0.10	0.13	0.14	0.14	0.15	0.14	0.14	0.14	0.14	0.14	0.15	0.13	0.13	0.13
Slovak Republic	0.38	0.39	0.32	0.30	0.30	0.30	0.30	0.29	0.28	0.26	0.25	0.23	0.20	0.19
Spain	0.12	0.14	0.14	0.14	0.14	0.14	0.14	0.14	0.14	0.14	0.14	0.14	0.13	0.13
Sweden	0.27	0.23	0.23	0.23	0.21	0.19	0.20	0.20	0.20	0.20	0.19	0.18	0.17	0.17
Switzerland	0.11	0.12	0.12	0.11	0.11	0.11	0.11	0.11	0.11	0.11	0.11	0.11	0.10	0.10
Turkey	0.11	0.13	0.13	0.13	0.13	0.13	0.13	0.13	0.13	0.12	0.11	0.12	0.12	0.11
United Kingdom	0.27	0.17	0.16	0.16	0.15	0.15	0.14	0.14	0.14	0.13	0.13	0.12	0.12	0.11
United States	0.41	0.27	0.25	0.24	0.24	0.23	0.23	0.23	0.22	0.22	0.21	0.20	0.20	0.20
EU27 total	..	0.19	0.17	0.17	0.16	0.16	0.16	0.16	0.16	0.16	0.15	0.15	0.14	..
OECD total	0.29	0.21	0.20	0.20	0.19	0.19	0.19	0.19	0.18	0.18	0.18	0.17	0.17	0.17
Brazil	0.17	0.14	0.15	0.15	0.16	0.15	0.15	0.15	0.15	0.15	0.15	0.15	0.15	..
Chile	0.20	0.18	0.18	0.18	0.19	0.19	0.18	0.18	0.17	0.18	0.17	0.17	0.16	..
China	0.88	0.47	0.27	0.25	0.24	0.22	0.20	0.20	0.21	0.22	0.21	0.21	0.20	..
Estonia	..	0.70	0.46	0.42	0.39	0.35	0.34	0.30	0.31	0.30	0.28	0.24	0.26	..
India	0.25	0.23	0.20	0.20	0.19	0.19	0.18	0.18	0.17	0.17	0.16	0.15	0.15	..
Indonesia	0.34	0.26	0.22	0.23	0.26	0.25	0.25	0.25	0.24	0.24	0.23	0.23	0.23	..
Israel	0.14	0.13	0.13	0.13	0.12	0.12	0.13	0.13	0.13	0.12	0.12	0.12	0.11	..
Russian Federation	..	0.57	0.64	0.66	0.64	0.59	0.57	0.54	0.52	0.49	0.47	0.45	0.42	..
Slovenia	..	0.20	0.22	0.21	0.19	0.19	0.19	0.19	0.18	0.18	0.18	0.17	0.16	..
South Africa	0.22	0.28	0.30	0.30	0.29	0.29	0.27	0.25	0.28	0.28	0.29	0.27	0.26	..
World	0.32	0.26	0.23	0.23	0.23	0.22	0.22	0.21	0.21	0.21	0.21	0.20	0.20	..

StatLink http://dx.doi.org/10.1787/825166083786

Total primary energy supply per unit of GDP

Tonnes of oil equivalent (toe) per thousand 2000 US dollars of GDP calculated using PPPs

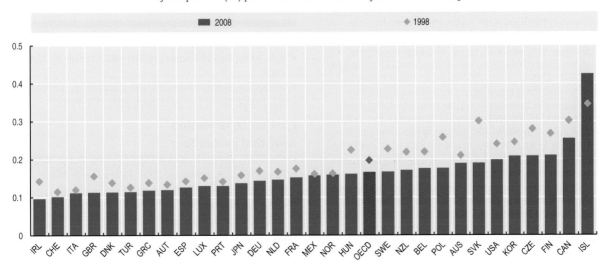

■ 2008   ◆ 1998

StatLink http://dx.doi.org/10.1787/820111418344

ENERGY SUPPLY PER CAPITA

Total primary energy supply per capita is a common, albeit imperfect, measure of energy efficiency in a country. For instance, neither the impact of climate on energy use (heating, cooling) nor the size of the country and the density of the population are taken into account when comparing countries. Energy analysts usually prefer to compare energy use per unit of output or per unit of GDP. However, energy supply per capita is presented here since its use is widespread.

Definition

The table refers to total primary energy supply (TPES) per head of population. The ratio is expressed in tonnes of oil equivalent (toe) per person (see the IEA sources below for details on how TPES is calculated). TPES consists of primary energy production adjusted for net trade, bunker use and stock changes. Production of secondary energy (e.g. oil/coal products, electricity from fossil fuels, etc.) is not included since the "energy equivalent" of the primary fuels used to create the secondary products or electric power has already been counted. The forecasts provided in the table refer to the Reference Scenario of the *World Energy Outlook*.

Overview

The level of energy supply on a per capita basis varied significantly across OECD countries. The countries with the highest ratios are those with the smallest populations. In 2008, the energy supply per capita for Iceland was 15.2 toe/capita, while that for Luxembourg was 8.5 toe/capita. The high ratio for Iceland is explained partly by the climate but also by the availability of cheap – and non-polluting – thermal energy from hot springs. In the case of Luxembourg, the high ratio is partly due to low sales taxes on petroleum products, which encourage motorists and other consumers from neighbouring countries – Belgium, France and Germany – to buy their supplies in Luxembourg.

The United States and Canada also have high energy supply per capita, with ratios of 7.5 and 8.1 toe/capita in 2008. At the other end of the scale, the countries with the lowest TPES/capita were Turkey (1.3 toe/capita) and Mexico (1.7 toe/capita).

Between 1971 and 2008, trends in energy supply per capita differ markedly across OECD countries. Compared to 1971, TPES/capita in 2008 was nine times higher in Korea and three times higher in Greece, Iceland and Portugal. On the other hand, the ratio decreased over this period in six OECD countries: Luxembourg (-29%), the United Kingdom (-9%), Denmark (-6%), the Czech Republic (-4%), Poland (-2%) and the United States (-1%).

In general, the TPES/capita ratios of non-OECD countries are lower than for OECD countries. In 2007, the ratios for China (1.5 toe/capita) and Indonesia (0.8 toe/capita) were three times greater than in 1971. Chile (1.9 toe/capita) and India (0.5 toe/capita) doubled over the period while Israel (3.1 toe/capita), South Africa (2.8 toe/capita) and Brazil (1.2 toe/capita) grew slightly more slowly.

Comparability

Care should be taken when comparing energy supply per capita between countries and over time. Different national circumstances (such as density of population, country size, temperatures, economic structure and domestic energy resources) affect the ratios. Data for Latin America include the Caribbean islands.

Total primary energy supply per capita
Tonnes of oil equivalent (toe) per capita, 2007

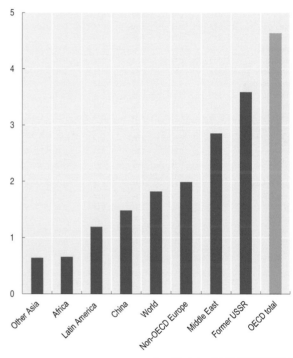

StatLink http://dx.doi.org/10.1787/820182563243

Sources
- IEA (2009), *Energy Balances of Non-OECD Countries*, IEA, Paris.
- IEA (2009), *Energy Balances of OECD Countries*, IEA, Paris.
- IEA (2009), *World Energy Outlook 2009*, IEA, Paris.

Further information
Analytical publications
- IEA (2009), *Energy Policies of IEA Countries*, series, IEA, Paris.
- IEA (2009), *IEA Scoreboard 2009: 35 Key Energy Trends over 35 Years*, IEA, Paris.

Online databases
- *World Energy Statistics and Balances.*

Web sites
- International Energy Agency, *www.iea.org*.

Total primary energy supply per capita
Tonnes of oil equivalent (toe) per capita

	1971	1990	1998	1999	2000	2001	2002	2003	2004	2005	2006	2007	2008	2030
Australia	3.91	5.02	5.53	5.58	5.65	5.49	5.60	5.58	5.54	5.88	5.89	5.87	6.11	..
Austria	2.51	3.23	3.60	3.59	3.56	3.76	3.83	4.03	4.04	4.10	4.12	3.99	3.90	..
Belgium	4.11	4.84	5.66	5.69	5.71	5.68	5.46	5.71	5.65	5.60	5.51	5.37	5.44	..
Canada	6.44	7.53	7.87	8.04	8.18	8.00	7.93	8.26	8.38	8.41	8.25	8.17	8.07	..
Czech Republic	4.62	4.70	3.98	3.73	3.92	4.03	4.10	4.35	4.46	4.39	4.47	4.43	4.42	..
Denmark	3.73	3.37	3.77	3.60	3.48	3.57	3.53	3.72	3.59	3.47	3.69	3.60	3.50	..
Finland	3.94	5.69	6.32	6.28	6.20	6.33	6.64	7.03	7.04	6.48	7.02	6.90	6.59	..
France	3.03	3.86	4.18	4.15	4.17	4.27	4.25	4.30	4.33	4.32	4.24	4.15	4.17	..
Germany	3.89	4.43	4.19	4.09	4.10	4.22	4.11	4.15	4.16	4.11	4.14	4.03	4.07	..
Greece	0.97	2.07	2.36	2.36	2.48	2.56	2.58	2.64	2.69	2.72	2.71	2.88	2.91	..
Hungary	1.84	2.76	2.50	2.49	2.45	2.51	2.52	2.58	2.59	2.73	2.71	2.66	2.65	..
Iceland	4.38	8.19	9.41	10.69	11.03	11.36	11.40	11.33	11.50	11.76	13.68	15.74	15.21	..
Ireland	2.26	2.84	3.45	3.50	3.58	3.74	3.74	3.55	3.53	3.46	3.45	3.46	3.41	..
Italy	1.95	2.59	2.91	2.94	3.00	3.01	3.00	3.10	3.10	3.12	3.07	3.00	2.96	..
Japan	2.55	3.55	3.95	4.01	4.08	4.01	3.99	3.95	4.08	4.06	4.06	4.02	3.85	4.14
Korea	0.52	2.17	3.45	3.78	4.02	4.04	4.24	4.30	4.40	4.37	4.43	4.59	4.68	..
Luxembourg	11.88	8.93	7.04	7.21	7.55	7.78	8.11	8.45	9.16	9.21	9.11	8.79	8.48	..
Mexico	0.86	1.49	1.51	1.52	1.50	1.50	1.53	1.55	1.59	1.69	1.67	1.74	1.75	..
Netherlands	3.86	4.39	4.58	4.49	4.59	4.70	4.69	4.82	4.86	4.83	4.69	4.91	4.82	..
New Zealand	2.41	3.96	4.26	4.45	4.36	4.36	4.34	4.11	4.12	4.00	4.01	4.01	4.08	..
Norway	3.41	4.95	5.66	5.90	5.64	5.77	5.44	5.90	6.08	6.11	6.23	5.71	6.60	..
Poland	2.63	2.71	2.49	2.43	2.33	2.35	2.32	2.39	2.39	2.42	2.55	2.55	2.59	..
Portugal	0.72	1.67	2.25	2.41	2.41	2.41	2.49	2.41	2.46	2.51	2.33	2.36	2.33	..
Slovak Republic	3.13	4.03	3.26	3.27	3.29	3.46	3.48	3.47	3.41	3.50	3.46	3.31	3.37	..
Spain	1.24	2.31	2.79	2.91	3.03	3.07	3.12	3.17	3.26	3.27	3.21	3.21	3.02	..
Sweden	4.45	5.51	5.78	5.66	5.36	5.68	5.80	5.65	5.85	5.71	5.53	5.51	5.40	..
Switzerland	2.58	3.50	3.50	3.48	3.41	3.61	3.49	3.49	3.51	3.48	3.62	3.42	3.55	..
Turkey	0.54	0.94	1.13	1.09	1.13	1.03	1.07	1.10	1.13	1.17	1.27	1.35	1.29	..
United Kingdom	3.73	3.62	3.80	3.79	3.80	3.80	3.69	3.75	3.72	3.70	3.62	3.48	3.40	..
United States	7.64	7.65	7.83	7.95	8.08	7.85	7.87	7.78	7.87	7.84	7.70	7.75	7.53	6.53
EU27 total	..	3.46	3.51	3.47	3.49	3.56	3.54	3.61	3.63	3.62	3.60	3.55	..	3.50
OECD total	3.81	4.29	4.54	4.59	4.65	4.59	4.60	4.62	4.67	4.68	4.64	4.64	4.56	4.44
Brazil	0.71	0.93	1.08	1.09	1.09	1.08	1.09	1.09	1.14	1.15	1.18	1.23	..	..
Chile	0.89	1.05	1.64	1.69	1.70	1.64	1.68	1.68	1.79	1.82	1.85	1.86	..	..
China	0.47	0.76	0.87	0.86	0.86	0.86	0.92	1.04	1.20	1.30	1.41	1.48	..	2.62
Estonia	..	6.10	3.56	3.35	3.29	3.43	3.32	3.67	3.80	3.85	3.74	4.20	..	..
India	0.28	0.37	0.43	0.45	0.45	0.45	0.45	0.46	0.48	0.49	0.51	0.53	..	0.90
Indonesia	0.30	0.57	0.66	0.73	0.73	0.76	0.76	0.76	0.79	0.79	0.81	0.84	..	..
Israel	1.87	2.49	2.92	2.77	2.93	3.01	2.94	2.99	2.92	2.96	3.00	3.06	..	..
Russian Federation	..	5.87	3.93	4.10	4.17	4.23	4.22	4.40	4.43	4.55	4.71	4.75	..	6.31
Slovenia	..	2.84	3.25	3.23	3.23	3.38	3.43	3.46	3.57	3.65	3.65	3.63	..	..
South Africa	2.00	2.58	2.58	2.52	2.51	2.42	2.31	2.56	2.78	2.70	2.73	2.82	..	..
World	1.47	1.67	1.63	1.64	1.65	1.63	1.65	1.69	1.74	1.77	1.79	1.82	..	2.04

StatLink ᑌᖴᎦᒪ http://dx.doi.org/10.1787/825224084556

Total primary energy supply per capita
Tonnes of oil equivalent (toe) per capita

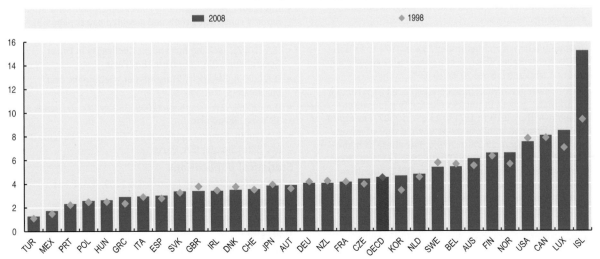

■ 2008   ◆ 1998

StatLink ᑌᖴᎦᒪ http://dx.doi.org/10.1787/820166684466

ELECTRICITY GENERATION

The amount of electricity generated by a country, and the breakdown of that production by type of fuel, reflects the natural resources, imported energy, national policies on security of energy supply, population size, electrification rate as well as the stage of development and rate of growth of the economy in each country.

Definition

The table shows data on electricity generation from fossil fuels, nuclear, hydro (excluding pumped storage), geothermal, solar, biomass, etc. It includes electricity produced in electricity-only plants and in combined heat and power plants. Both main activity producer and autoproducer plants are included, where data are available. Main activity producers generate electricity for sale to third parties as their primary activity. Autoproducers generate electricity wholly or partly for their own use as an activity which supports their primary activity. Both types of plants may be privately or publicly owned. The forecasts provided in the table refer to the Reference Scenario of the *World Energy Outlook*.

Electricity generation is measured in terawatt hours, which expresses the generation of 1 terawatt (10^{12} watts) of electricity for one hour.

Comparability

Some countries, both OECD member and non-member countries, have trouble reporting electricity generation from autoproducer plants. In some OECD non-member countries it is also difficult to obtain information on electricity generated by combustible renewables and waste; For example, electricity generated from waste biomass in sugar refining remains largely unreported in some of these countries.

Overview

World electricity generation rose at an average annual rate of 3.8% from 1971 to 2007, greater than the 2.2% growth in total primary energy supply. This increase was largely due to more electrical appliances, the development of electrical heating in several developed countries and of rural electrification programmes in developing countries.

The share of electricity production from fossil fuels has gradually fallen, from just under 75% in 1971 to 68% in 2007. This decrease was due to a progressive move away from oil, which fell from 20.9% to 5.6%.

Oil for power generation has been displaced in particular by dramatic growth in nuclear electricity generation, which rose from 2.1% in 1971 to 13.8% in 2007. The share of coal remained stable, at 40-41% while that of natural gas increased from 13.3% to 20.9%. The share of hydro-electricity decreased from 23.0% to 15.6%. Due to large development programmes in several OECD countries, the share of new and renewable energies, such as solar, wind, geothermal, biomass and waste increased. However, these energy forms remain of limited importance: in 2007, they accounted for only 2.6% of total electricity production for the world as a whole.

World electricity generation by source of energy

As a percentage of world electricity generation

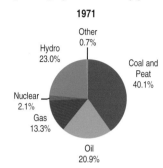

1971

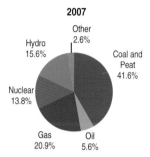

2007

StatLink 🔗 http://dx.doi.org/10.1787/820207287871

Sources

- IEA (2009), *Energy Balances of Non-OECD Countries*, IEA, Paris.
- IEA (2009), *Energy Balances of OECD Countries*, IEA, Paris.
- IEA (2009), *World Energy Outlook 2009*, IEA, Paris.

Further information

Analytical publications

- IEA (2007), *Fossil Fuel-Fired Power Generation: Case studies of recently constructed coal- and gas-fired power plants*, IEA, Paris.
- IEA (2007), *Tackling Investment Challenges in Power Generation in IEA Countries*, IEA, Paris.
- IEA (2009), *Electricity Transmission: Getting the Best Investments*, IEA, Paris.
- IEA (2009), *IEA Scoreboard 2009: 35 Key Energy Trends over 35 Years*, IEA, Paris.
- IEA (2009), *Sectoral Approaches in Electricity – Building Bridges to a Safe Climate*, IEA, Paris.

Statistical publications

- IEA (2009), *Electricity Information 2009*, IEA, Paris.

Online databases

- *World Energy Statistics and Balances*.

Web sites

- International Energy Agency, *www.iea.org*.

Electricity generation
Terawatt hours (TWh)

	1971	1990	1998	1999	2000	2001	2002	2003	2004	2005	2006	2007	2008	2030
Australia	53.0	154.3	195.6	203.0	207.4	216.5	226.2	227.9	234.3	245.1	251.3	254.6	265.3	..
Austria	28.2	49.3	55.9	59.7	59.9	60.7	60.3	57.7	61.6	63.0	60.8	60.9	64.1	..
Belgium	33.2	70.3	82.1	83.4	82.8	78.6	80.9	83.6	84.4	85.7	84.3	87.5	83.1	..
Canada	221.8	482.0	561.6	578.9	605.6	589.8	601.2	589.5	599.9	626.0	615.9	639.7	632.6	..
Czech Republic	36.4	62.3	64.6	64.2	72.9	74.2	76.0	82.8	83.8	81.9	83.7	87.8	83.2	..
Denmark	18.6	26.0	41.1	38.9	36.0	37.7	39.3	46.2	40.4	36.2	45.6	39.2	36.4	..
Finland	21.7	54.4	70.2	69.5	70.0	74.5	74.9	84.2	85.8	70.6	82.3	81.2	77.1	..
France	155.8	417.2	507.3	521.3	536.1	545.7	553.9	561.8	569.1	571.5	569.3	564.4	569.9	..
Germany	327.2	547.7	552.4	552.5	572.3	581.9	582.0	601.5	608.5	613.4	629.4	629.5	626.7	..
Greece	11.6	34.8	46.2	49.4	53.4	53.1	53.9	57.9	58.8	59.4	60.2	62.7	58.6	..
Hungary	15.0	28.4	37.2	37.8	35.2	36.4	36.2	34.1	33.7	35.8	35.9	40.0	40.0	..
Iceland	1.6	4.5	6.3	7.2	7.7	8.0	8.4	8.5	8.6	8.7	9.9	12.0	16.5	..
Ireland	6.3	14.2	20.9	21.8	23.7	24.6	24.8	24.9	25.2	25.6	27.1	27.9	28.5	..
Italy	123.9	213.1	253.7	259.3	269.9	271.9	277.5	286.3	295.8	296.8	307.7	308.2	312.4	..
Japan	382.9	835.5	1 010.0	1 027.9	1 048.6	1 029.8	1 048.4	1 037.5	1 067.2	1 088.4	1 093.0	1 123.5	1 078.1	1·302
Korea	10.5	105.4	216.1	235.6	288.5	309.1	329.8	343.2	366.6	387.9	402.3	425.9	440.5	..
Luxembourg	1.3	0.6	0.4	0.4	0.4	0.5	2.8	2.8	3.4	3.4	3.5	3.2	2.7	..
Mexico	31.0	124.1	181.2	189.9	203.6	209.1	214.6	217.8	224.1	242.0	249.6	257.5	258.3	..
Netherlands	44.9	71.9	91.2	86.9	89.7	93.8	96.1	96.8	100.8	100.2	98.4	103.2	107.7	..
New Zealand	15.5	32.3	36.3	38.2	39.2	39.4	41.1	41.2	42.9	43.1	43.5	43.8	43.8	..
Norway	63.5	121.6	116.1	122.3	139.6	119.2	130.3	106.8	110.2	137.2	121.2	136.4	141.7	..
Poland	69.5	134.4	140.8	140.0	143.2	143.7	142.5	150.0	152.6	155.4	160.8	158.8	154.0	..
Portugal	7.9	28.4	38.9	42.9	43.4	46.2	45.7	46.5	44.8	46.2	48.6	46.9	45.4	..
Slovak Republic	10.9	25.5	25.7	28.1	30.8	31.9	32.2	31.0	30.5	31.4	31.3	27.9	29.3	..
Spain	61.6	151.2	193.4	205.9	222.2	233.2	241.6	257.9	277.2	288.9	295.5	300.2	306.5	..
Sweden	66.5	146.0	158.8	154.8	145.2	161.6	146.7	135.4	151.7	158.4	143.3	148.8	149.5	..
Switzerland	31.2	55.0	62.3	68.7	66.1	71.1	65.5	65.4	63.9	57.8	62.1	66.5	67.2	..
Turkey	9.8	57.5	111.0	116.4	124.9	122.7	129.4	140.6	150.7	162.0	176.3	191.6	198.6	..
United Kingdom	255.8	317.8	361.1	365.3	374.4	382.4	384.6	395.5	391.2	395.4	394.0	392.3	386.2	..
United States	1 703.4	3 202.8	3 804.5	3 873.5	4 025.7	3 838.6	4 026.1	4 054.4	4 147.7	4 268.4	4 274.3	4 322.9	4 329.4	5 277
EU27 total	..	2 567.8	2 886.8	2 914.5	2 996.7	3 077.1	3 099.1	3 187.4	3 252.6	3 273.7	3 318.4	3 327.9	..	3 968
OECD total	3 820.7	7 568.5	9 042.9	9 243.6	9 618.5	9 486.0	9 772.8	9 869.7	10 115.1	10 385.7	10 460.9	10 645.0	10 633.2	13 215
Brazil	51.6	222.8	321.9	334.7	349.2	327.9	345.7	364.9	387.5	403.0	419.3	445.1	..	..
Chile	8.5	18.4	35.5	38.4	40.1	42.5	43.7	46.8	51.2	52.5	55.3	58.5	..	..
China	138.4	621.2	1 166.6	1 239.8	1 356.2	1 472.4	1 641.4	1 908.5	2 201.0	2 499.6	2 864.2	3 279.2	..	8 847
Estonia	..	17.4	8.9	8.3	8.5	8.5	8.6	10.2	10.3	10.2	9.7	12.2	..	..
India	66.4	289.4	496.9	537.4	562.2	581.0	598.4	635.2	667.6	699.1	753.0	803.4	..	2 737
Indonesia	2.4	33.3	77.3	84.3	92.6	101.6	108.2	112.9	120.2	127.4	133.1	142.2	..	..
Israel	7.6	20.9	38.0	39.2	42.7	44.0	45.5	47.0	47.2	48.6	50.6	53.8	..	..
Russian Federation	..	1 082.2	826.2	845.3	876.5	889.3	889.3	914.3	929.9	951.2	993.9	1 013.4	..	1 424
Slovenia	..	12.4	13.7	13.3	13.6	14.5	14.6	13.8	15.3	15.1	15.1	15.0	..	..
South Africa	54.6	165.4	203.0	200.4	207.8	208.2	215.7	231.2	240.9	242.1	250.9	260.5	..	..
World	5 245.7	11 813.7	14 282.9	14 685.0	15 378.0	15 477.2	16 085.1	16 678.7	17 446.6	18 226.0	18 934.5	19 771.1	..	34 292

StatLink ᴍ⬚◖ http://dx.doi.org/10.1787/825244047220

World electricity generation by source of energy
Terawatt hours (TWh)

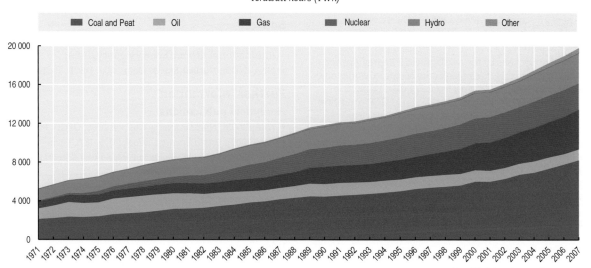

StatLink ᴍ⬚◖ http://dx.doi.org/10.1787/820187571144

NUCLEAR ENERGY

In 2008 nuclear energy provided over 21% of total electricity supply in OECD countries. However, the use of nuclear energy varies widely. In all, 17 of the 30 OECD countries use nuclear energy at present, with seven generating one-third or more of their power from this source. Collectively, OECD countries produce about 83% of the world's nuclear energy. The remainder is produced in 14 non-OECD economies.

Definition

The table gives the nuclear electricity generation in terawatt hours (TWh) in each of the OECD member countries and in selected non-OECD countries. The chart shows the percentage share of nuclear in total electricity generation, in each country and in the OECD as a whole.

The table also provides information on the number of nuclear power plants in operation and under construction as of 31 October 2009.

Comparability

Some generation data are provisional and may be subject to revision. Generation data for Japan are for the fiscal year. The number of plants connected to the grid includes two units in Canada and one in Japan that have been shut down for an extended period but are expected to return to operation.

Overview

After growing strongly in the 1970s and 1980s, nuclear energy has since stagnated. Only a few new nuclear power plants have been ordered in the last 20 years, with the Czech Republic, Japan and Korea being the only OECD countries where new nuclear plants have entered operation since 2000. However, Finland, France, Japan, Korea, the Slovak Republic and the United States all presently have one or more nuclear plants under construction.

The role of nuclear energy in reducing greenhouse gas emissions and in increasing energy diversification and security of supply has been increasingly recognised over the last few years. This has led to renewed interest in building new nuclear plants in several countries. As a result, nuclear capacity is now expected to grow more strongly over the next 10 to 20 years and beyond. Much of this growth is expected to be in non-OECD countries. China in particular has begun a rapid expansion of nuclear capacity, starting construction of 10 additional units during the last year. India and the Russian Federation also have several new plants under construction. Among OECD members, Canada, the Czech Republic, Finland, France, Japan, Korea, Turkey, the United Kingdom and the United States are actively planning to construct additional nuclear capacity, while several others (Hungary, Italy, Mexico, the Netherlands, Poland and Switzerland) have also begun considering new nuclear plants.

Recent projections by the OECD Nuclear Energy Agency (NEA) indicate that, in the high case scenario, worldwide nuclear capacity could grow from 372 GWe (gigawatts electrical) in 2007 (of which 310 GWe is in OECD countries) to about 470 GWe by 2020. In this scenario, nuclear capacity could reach around 600 GWe by 2030 and 1 400 GWe by 2050, potentially increasing the nuclear share of global electricity production from 14% at present to 22-25% by 2050. However, the NEA low case scenario projects only around 400 GWe by 2030 and 580 GWe by 2050. This reflects uncertainties about success with the construction and operation of the next generation of nuclear plants, public and political acceptance of nuclear energy, and the extent to which other low-carbon energy sources are successfully developed.

Sources
- Data for non-OECD countries provided by the International Atomic Energy Agency (IAEA).
- NEA (2009), *Nuclear Energy Data 2009*, OECD, Paris.

Further information
Analytical publications
- NEA (2008), *Nuclear Energy Outlook 2008*, OECD, Paris.
- IEA (2009), *World Energy Outlook 2009*, IEA, Paris.
- IEA (2008), *Energy Technology Perspectives: Scenarios and Strategies to 2050*, IEA, Paris.
- NEA and IAEA (2008), *Uranium 2007: Resources, Production and Demand*, OECD, Paris.
- NEA (2007), *Innovation in Nuclear Energy Technology*, OECD, Paris.

Web sites
- Nuclear Energy Agency, *www.nea.fr*.

Nuclear electricity generation and nuclear power plants

	Year 2008		Number, as at 31 October 2009	
	Terawatt hours	As a percentage of total electricity generation	Plants connected to the grid	Plants under construction
Australia	–	–	–	–
Austria	–	–	–	–
Belgium	43.4	53.8	7	–
Canada	87.9	14.5	20	–
Czech Republic	25.0	32.4	6	–
Denmark	–	–	–	–
Finland	22.1	29.9	4	1
France	418.3	76.2	59	1
Germany	140.9	23.4	17	–
Greece	–	–	–	–
Hungary	14.0	37.7	4	–
Iceland	–	–	–	–
Ireland	–	–	–	–
Italy	–	–	–	–
Japan	240.5	24.9	54	2
Korea	144.0	36.7	20	6
Luxembourg	–	–	–	–
Mexico	9.4	4.0	2	–
Netherlands	4.0	3.8	1	–
New Zealand	–	–	–	–
Norway	–	–	–	–
Poland	–	–	–	–
Portugal	–	–	–	–
Slovak Republic	15.4	57.0	4	2
Spain	56.4	18.3	8	–
Sweden	61.3	42.0	10	–
Switzerland	26.1	39.0	5	–
Turkey	–	–	–	–
United Kingdom	47.7	13.2	19	–
United States	806.2	19.6	104	1
EU27 total	888.7	27.9	145	6
OECD total	2 162.6	21.5	344	13
Brazil	14.0	3.1	2	–
Chile	–	–	–	–
China	65.3	2.1	11	16
Estonia	–	–	–	–
India	13.2	2.0	17	6
Indonesia	–	–	–	–
Israel	–	–	–	–
Russian Federation	152.1	16.9	31	9
Slovenia	6.0	41.7	1	–
South Africa	12.7	5.2	2	–

StatLink http://dx.doi.org/10.1787/825270840530

Nuclear electricity generation
As a percentage of total electricity generation, 2008

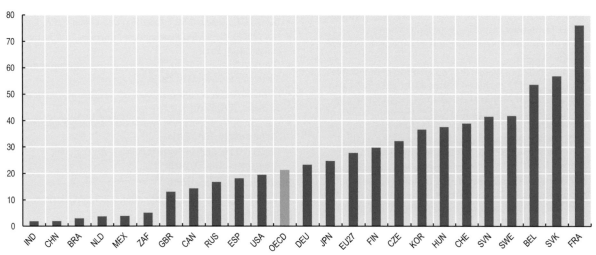

StatLink http://dx.doi.org/10.1787/820210813782

RENEWABLE ENERGY

More and more governments are recognising the importance of promoting sustainable development and combating climate change when setting out their energy policies. Higher energy use has contributed to higher greenhouse gas emissions and higher concentration of these gases in the atmosphere. One way to reduce greenhouse gas emissions is to replace energy from fossil fuels by energy from renewables.

Definition

The table refers to the contribution of renewables to total primary energy supply (TPES) in OECD countries. Renewables include the primary energy equivalent of hydro (excluding pumped storage), geothermal, solar, wind, tide and wave. It also includes energy derived from solid biomass, biogasoline, biodiesel, other liquid biofuels, biogas, industrial waste and municipal waste. Biomass is defined as any plant matter used directly as fuel or converted into fuels (*e.g.* charcoal) or electricity and/or heat. Included here are wood, vegetal waste (including wood waste and crops used for energy production), ethanol, animal materials/wastes and sulphite lyes. Municipal waste comprises wastes produced by the residential, commercial and public service sectors that are collected by local authorities for disposal in a central location for the production of heat and/or power. The forecasts provided in the table refer to the Reference Scenario of the *World Energy Outlook*.

Comparability

Biomass and waste data are often based on small sample surveys or other incomplete information. Thus, the data give only a broad impression of developments and are not strictly comparable between countries. In some cases, complete categories of vegetal fuel are omitted due to lack of information.

Overview

In OECD countries, total renewables supply grew by 2.4% per annum between 1971 and 2008 as compared to 1.3% per annum for total primary energy supply. Annual growth for hydro (1.1%) was lower than for other renewables such as geothermal (5.6%) and combustible renewables and waste (2.8%). Due to a very low base in 1971, solar and wind experienced the most rapid growth in OECD member countries, especially where government policies have stimulated expansion of these energy sources.

For the OECD as a whole, the contribution of renewables to energy supply increased from 4.8% in 1971 to 7.1% in 2008. The contribution of renewables varied greatly by country. On the high end, renewables represented 82% of energy supply in Iceland and 43% in Norway. On the low end, renewables contributed 3% or less of the energy supply for Japan, Korea, Luxembourg and the United Kingdom.

In general, the contribution of renewables to the energy supply in non-OECD countries is higher than in OECD countries. In 2007, renewables contributed 44% to the energy supply of Brazil, 31% in Indonesia, 29% in India, 12% in China, 10% in South Africa and 3% in the Russian Federation.

Sources

- IEA (2009), *Energy Balances of Non-OECD Countries*, IEA, Paris.
- IEA (2009), *Energy Balances of OECD Countries*, IEA, Paris.
- IEA (2009), *World Energy Outlook 2009*, IEA, Paris.

Further information

Analytical publications

- IEA (2007), *Renewables for Heating and Cooling*, IEA, Paris.
- IEA (2008), *Deploying Renewables: Principles for Effective Policies*, IEA, Paris.
- IEA (2008), *Energy Technology Perspectives: Scenarios and Strategies to 2050*, IEA, Paris.
- IEA (2009), *IEA Scoreboard 2009: 35 Key Energy Trends over 35 Years*, IEA, Paris.
- IEA (2009), *Transport Energy and CO$_2$: Moving towards Sustainability*, IEA, Paris.
- OECD (2008), *Biofuel Support Policies: An Economic Assessment*, OECD, Paris.

Statistical publications

- IEA (2009), *Renewables Information 2009*, IEA, Paris.

Online databases

- *World Energy Statistics and Balances*.

Web sites

- International Energy Agency, *www.iea.org*.

Contribution of renewables to energy supply
As a percentage of total primary energy supply

	1971	1990	1998	1999	2000	2001	2002	2003	2004	2005	2006	2007	2008	2030
Australia	8.8	6.1	6.1	6.1	6.0	6.2	6.2	6.0	6.0	5.5	5.3	5.6	5.3	..
Austria	10.9	21.0	21.6	23.9	24.0	23.3	23.3	20.9	22.2	22.4	23.9	25.6	25.8	..
Belgium	..	1.6	1.7	1.8	1.8	2.1	2.1	2.4	2.6	2.8	3.4	3.8	4.4	..
Canada	15.3	16.2	16.5	16.9	16.9	16.0	16.9	15.7	15.6	16.1	15.8	16.2	16.5	..
Czech Republic	0.2	0.2	1.7	2.4	2.0	2.1	2.5	3.7	4.1	4.3	4.6	5.0	5.1	..
Denmark	1.8	6.9	9.1	10.1	11.4	12.0	12.9	13.9	15.7	17.1	16.3	18.1	18.5	..
Finland	27.3	19.3	22.8	22.8	24.8	23.3	22.9	21.9	23.6	23.7	23.3	23.5	25.2	..
France	8.6	7.3	7.1	7.5	7.2	7.1	6.5	6.6	6.6	6.4	6.7	7.2	7.5	..
Germany	1.2	1.8	2.8	2.8	3.2	3.5	3.8	4.3	4.9	5.2	6.1	8.6	8.4	..
Greece	7.8	5.1	5.4	5.8	5.4	4.9	5.0	5.4	5.4	5.5	5.9	5.4	5.1	..
Hungary	2.9	2.7	3.4	3.5	3.5	3.6	3.6	3.5	3.7	4.5	4.8	5.4	6.1	..
Iceland	46.7	67.0	70.2	74.0	74.5	75.6	75.0	75.2	74.5	75.6	78.4	80.8	82.4	..
Ireland	0.6	1.7	1.8	1.7	1.7	1.6	1.8	1.6	2.0	2.5	2.9	3.1	3.7	..
Italy	5.6	4.5	5.6	6.0	6.1	6.2	6.0	6.3	7.1	6.7	7.3	7.2	8.2	..
Japan	2.7	3.5	3.5	3.4	3.3	3.3	3.3	3.6	3.5	3.3	3.5	3.4	3.2	6.8
Korea	0.6	1.4	0.9	0.9	0.9	1.0	0.9	1.1	1.1	1.2	1.3	1.4	1.5	..
Luxembourg	..	0.9	1.7	1.6	1.5	1.7	1.4	1.6	1.7	1.9	1.9	2.8	2.4	..
Mexico	16.8	11.4	10.6	10.7	10.8	10.3	9.6	9.6	9.8	9.7	9.5	9.3	9.6	..
Netherlands	..	1.5	2.3	2.4	2.5	2.6	2.8	2.7	3.0	3.6	3.8	3.9	4.5	..
New Zealand	32.0	35.8	32.0	32.2	29.8	27.8	29.7	29.7	31.6	32.1	31.7	32.6	33.9	..
Norway	40.9	54.5	44.7	45.5	52.5	45.0	50.9	38.8	38.2	46.1	40.1	48.3	43.4	..
Poland	1.6	2.3	4.6	4.5	4.8	5.1	5.2	5.1	5.3	5.4	5.7	5.7	6.0	..
Portugal	19.6	19.6	16.3	13.7	15.6	16.5	14.1	17.3	15.1	13.6	17.6	18.3	18.2	..
Slovak Republic	2.4	1.5	4.0	4.4	4.6	4.4	4.2	3.6	4.2	4.6	4.7	5.7	5.1	..
Spain	6.5	6.9	6.3	5.4	5.8	6.7	5.5	7.0	6.5	6.0	6.6	7.1	7.5	..
Sweden	20.4	24.9	27.9	27.2	31.7	28.8	26.0	25.3	25.8	29.7	29.7	31.1	32.6	..
Switzerland	15.5	14.9	17.0	19.1	18.6	19.3	17.6	18.0	18.4	18.5	18.0	20.7	20.4	..
Turkey	31.0	18.3	16.0	15.2	13.2	13.3	13.5	12.9	13.3	12.0	11.2	9.6	9.5	..
United Kingdom	0.1	0.5	1.0	1.0	1.1	1.3	1.5	1.6	1.7	2.0	2.1	2.4	2.8	..
United States	3.7	5.2	5.1	5.0	4.8	4.3	4.3	4.6	4.6	4.8	5.0	5.0	5.3	10.9
EU27 total	..	4.5	5.9	5.9	6.2	6.2	6.1	6.4	6.8	6.9	7.4	8.2	..	17.0
OECD total	4.8	6.0	6.2	6.2	6.2	5.9	5.9	6.1	6.2	6.3	6.6	6.9	7.1	12.9
Brazil	56.4	46.9	40.3	40.1	39.0	37.5	39.3	42.0	42.3	42.9	43.3	44.4	..	..
Chile	20.8	25.0	23.2	20.5	22.6	23.9	23.8	22.7	21.4	22.5	23.0	21.8	..	..
China	40.0	24.5	20.4	20.4	20.3	20.7	19.1	16.7	14.7	13.8	12.8	12.3	..	8.9
Estonia	..	2.0	10.3	11.3	11.3	11.5	12.2	11.7	11.7	11.2	10.6	10.7	..	..
India	62.9	43.9	35.8	34.3	34.0	33.9	33.3	33.0	31.8	31.4	30.4	29.2	..	17.2
Indonesia	76.0	45.4	35.2	36.5	36.4	35.9	35.4	34.9	33.7	33.0	32.6	31.2	..	..
Israel	..	3.1	3.2	3.2	3.3	3.3	3.5	3.5	3.7	3.6	3.5	3.5	..	..
Russian Federation	..	3.0	3.4	3.6	3.5	3.5	3.4	3.1	3.5	3.4	3.4	3.3	..	4.7
Slovenia	..	9.2	8.7	8.6	12.3	11.6	10.4	10.4	11.6	10.8	10.7	10.4	..	..
South Africa	10.4	11.6	11.3	11.4	11.5	12.0	12.7	11.3	10.4	10.7	10.7	10.3	..	..
World	13.2	12.8	13.2	13.2	13.1	13.0	12.9	12.8	12.6	12.6	12.6	12.6	..	14.1

StatLink http://dx.doi.org/10.1787/825324676083

OECD renewable energy supply
Million tonnes of oil equivalent (Mtoe)

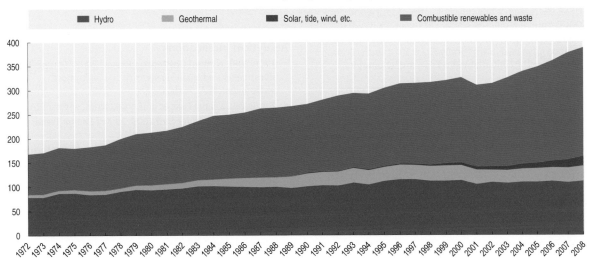

StatLink http://dx.doi.org/10.1787/820212576811

ENERGY PRODUCTION

Energy production is a function of the natural resources of each country and of the economic incentives to exploit those resources. Countries will also take into consideration energy security and environmental protection when making decisions on how much and what type of energy to produce.

Definition

Production refers to the quantities of fuels extracted from the ground after the removal of inert matter or impurities (*e.g.* sulphur from natural gas). For non-combusted energy such as nuclear, hydro and solar, the primary energy equivalent is calculated using the physical energy content method, which expresses the energy content of each source in million tonnes of oil equivalent (Mtoe) energy.

Comparability

In general, data on energy production are of high quality. In some instances, information is based on secondary sources or estimated by the International Energy Agency.

Total energy production by product
As a percentage of total energy production

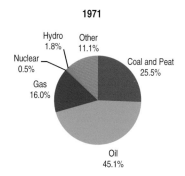

1971

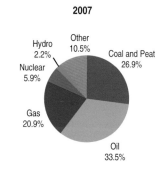

2007

StatLink http://dx.doi.org/10.1787/820216046881

Overview

World energy production increased by 2.1% per year between 1971 and 2007, reaching 11 940 million tonnes of oil equivalent (Mtoe). The OECD, with a 32% share of world production, was the main energy producing region in 2007. China accounted for 15% of world energy production, the United States for 14%, the Middle East region for 13% and the Russian Federation for 10%. Since 1971, the shares of the OECD, Middle East and Former USSR decreased, while those of Latin America and non-OECD Europe remained stable. On the other hand, the share of energy production in China (as well as the rest of Asia) increased dramatically since 1971, with China overtaking the United States as the largest energy producer in 2006.

The energy mix has changed significantly between 1971 and 2007. Nuclear energy, which experienced an annual average growth of 9.3% since 1971, increased its share of production from 0.5% to 5.9%. In absolute terms, renewable energy also experienced a high growth rate over the last 35 years, but its share of total production has remained low since it was starting from a very low base. The share of natural gas in total production increased from 16.0% in 1971 to 20.9% in 2007, while the share of oil fell from 45.1% to 33.5%. The share of coal and peat production increased slightly to 26.9%.

Sources

- IEA (2009), *Energy Balances of Non-OECD Countries*, IEA, Paris.
- IEA (2009), *Energy Balances of OECD Countries*, IEA, Paris.

Further information

Analytical publications

- IEA (2008), *Natural Gas Market Review 2008: Optimising investments and ensuring security in a high-priced environment*, IEA, Paris.
- IEA (2009), *Energy Policies of IEA Countries*, series, IEA, Paris.
- IEA (2009), *IEA Scoreboard 2009: 35 Key Energy Trends over 35 Years*, IEA, Paris.
- NEA (2006), *Forty Years of Uranium Resources, Production and Demand in Perspective: The Red Book Retrospective*, OECD, Paris.

Online databases

- *World Energy Statistics and Balances.*

Web sites

- International Energy Agency, *www.iea.org.*

Total production of energy
Million tonnes of oil equivalent (Mtoe)

	1971	1990	1997	1998	1999	2000	2001	2002	2003	2004	2005	2006	2007	2008
Australia	53.9	157.5	201.0	216.5	213.6	234.4	250.6	255.3	254.6	259.7	270.4	270.0	289.2	290.5
Austria	7.4	8.1	8.7	8.9	9.7	9.8	9.9	10.2	10.0	10.3	10.0	10.4	10.9	10.4
Belgium	6.8	13.1	13.4	13.1	13.9	13.7	13.3	13.5	13.7	13.7	13.9	13.8	14.4	14.3
Canada	155.8	273.8	365.0	365.6	364.6	372.6	377.0	384.0	386.0	397.6	401.0	410.5	413.2	404.5
Czech Republic	39.9	40.1	32.9	30.8	28.1	29.9	30.6	30.7	33.4	34.5	32.9	33.6	33.7	33.0
Denmark	0.3	10.1	20.2	20.4	23.8	27.7	27.1	28.6	28.5	31.1	31.3	29.6	27.0	26.6
Finland	5.0	12.1	15.0	13.6	15.4	15.1	15.0	16.0	15.9	15.7	16.5	18.0	15.9	16.1
France	47.6	112.5	129.5	126.5	128.4	132.2	133.0	135.0	136.8	138.0	137.8	137.7	135.4	136.2
Germany	175.2	186.2	143.6	136.0	137.2	135.3	134.7	134.5	135.9	138.0	135.3	136.4	137.0	133.2
Greece	2.1	9.2	9.6	9.8	9.5	10.0	10.0	10.2	9.9	10.3	10.3	10.1	12.1	12.0
Hungary	11.8	14.6	13.3	12.5	11.9	11.6	11.3	11.2	10.4	10.2	10.4	10.3	10.2	10.4
Iceland	0.4	1.4	1.7	1.8	2.2	2.3	2.5	2.5	2.5	2.5	2.6	3.3	4.0	3.8
Ireland	1.4	3.5	2.9	2.5	2.5	2.2	1.8	1.5	1.8	1.9	1.6	1.6	1.4	1.5
Italy	19.5	25.3	30.4	30.3	29.2	28.2	26.9	27.5	27.8	28.4	27.8	27.4	26.4	27.1
Japan	35.8	75.1	106.2	109.1	104.5	105.8	104.7	96.9	84.0	95.0	100.4	101.3	90.5	87.1
Korea	6.4	22.6	23.7	27.1	30.6	32.6	33.2	35.0	38.1	38.4	43.0	43.8	42.5	44.7
Luxembourg	..	..	..	0.1	-	0.1	0.1	0.1	0.1	0.1	0.1	0.1	0.1	0.1
Mexico	43.4	193.4	222.0	227.3	223.0	225.9	230.2	230.4	242.8	253.8	259.8	256.1	251.1	234.6
Netherlands	37.3	60.5	65.8	63.0	59.0	57.2	61.0	60.4	58.4	67.7	61.9	60.8	61.5	67.1
New Zealand	3.4	12.0	14.8	13.8	14.5	14.3	14.2	14.5	13.1	12.9	12.6	13.1	14.0	15.1
Norway	6.0	119.1	212.6	205.7	209.4	226.4	223.9	232.6	233.1	229.0	224.6	216.7	213.9	211.5
Poland	99.2	103.9	100.0	87.6	83.9	79.6	80.3	80.2	79.9	78.8	78.6	77.9	72.6	70.6
Portugal	1.4	3.4	3.7	3.7	3.4	3.8	4.1	3.6	4.3	3.9	3.6	4.3	4.6	4.4
Slovak Republic	2.7	5.3	4.9	5.0	5.5	6.3	6.7	6.8	6.6	6.5	6.6	6.6	6.0	6.5
Spain	10.4	34.6	31.7	32.3	30.7	31.7	33.5	31.8	33.0	32.6	30.1	31.3	30.3	29.7
Sweden	7.4	29.7	32.4	34.0	33.2	30.5	33.9	31.8	30.9	34.3	34.7	32.8	33.6	33.3
Switzerland	2.9	9.7	10.8	11.0	11.5	11.5	12.0	11.6	11.8	11.8	10.9	12.1	12.6	12.7
Turkey	13.8	25.8	28.0	29.1	27.5	25.9	24.4	24.1	23.6	24.1	23.9	26.3	27.3	27.3
United Kingdom	109.8	208.0	268.3	271.9	281.6	272.4	262.3	258.3	246.6	225.6	205.0	186.6	176.2	166.9
United States	1 436.4	1 649.4	1 683.7	1 696.9	1 678.5	1 675.3	1 697.3	1 664.6	1 633.4	1 644.4	1 629.9	1 653.5	1 665.2	1 716.1
EU27 total	..	944.7	980.3	953.4	955.0	946.3	946.0	944.7	937.2	934.0	900.2	881.0	860.6	..
OECD total	2 343.7	3 420.0	3 795.8	3 805.8	3 786.8	3 824.2	3 865.5	3 843.5	3 807.0	3 851.0	3 827.5	3 836.0	3 832.9	3 847.5
Brazil	49.0	103.7	126.1	133.3	141.7	148.4	152.4	167.7	178.4	183.1	195.3	206.8	215.6	..
Chile	5.3	7.4	8.4	8.1	7.5	8.2	8.7	8.7	8.3	8.1	8.9	9.1	8.5	..
China	394.1	886.3	1 094.3	1 083.5	1 059.6	1 061.0	1 089.7	1 166.2	1 311.2	1 486.5	1 615.6	1 718.4	1 814.0	..
Estonia	..	5.1	3.5	3.0	2.8	2.9	3.0	3.2	3.7	3.5	3.9	3.7	4.4	..
India	141.5	291.1	351.6	350.3	357.4	364.3	372.3	381.4	394.3	407.4	420.3	435.8	450.9	..
Indonesia	72.8	170.0	230.2	223.6	242.7	235.5	241.6	246.3	257.0	263.1	276.0	309.7	331.1	..
Israel	5.9	0.4	0.6	0.6	0.6	0.7	0.7	0.7	0.8	1.8	2.1	2.7	2.7	..
Russian Federation	..	1 280.3	921.6	928.4	950.5	966.5	996.1	1 034.5	1 106.9	1 158.4	1 197.1	1 220.0	1 230.6	..
Slovenia	..	3.1	3.0	3.1	2.9	3.1	3.2	3.3	3.3	3.5	3.5	3.4	3.5	..
South Africa	37.8	114.5	143.4	145.0	145.0	145.6	144.9	143.7	153.3	157.5	158.6	158.0	159.6	..
World	5 655.0	8 796.7	9 620.8	9 730.6	9 729.7	9 968.9	10 104.0	10 208.4	10 602.5	11 097.3	11 456.0	11 742.0	11 939.5	..

StatLink http://dx.doi.org/10.1787/825347546714

Total energy production by region
Million tonnes of oil equivalent (Mtoe)

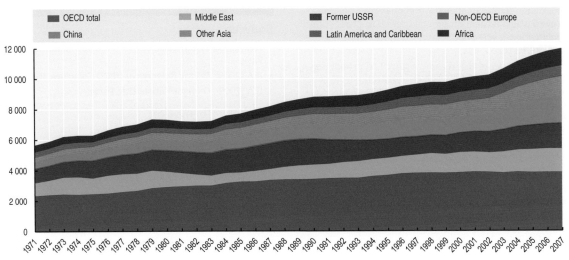

StatLink http://dx.doi.org/10.1787/820215663115

OIL PRODUCTION

The Middle East and North Africa are exceptionally well-endowed with energy resources, holding about 70% of the world's proven conventional oil reserves at the end of 2008. Current oil production is relatively low in comparison to these reserves and further development of them will be critical to meeting global energy needs in the coming decades. Unconventional oil (*e.g.* oil shale and sands, liquid supplies based on coal and biomass, and liquids arising for the chemical processing of natural gas) is also expected to play an increasing role in meeting world demand.

Definition

Crude oil production refers to the quantities of oil extracted from the ground after the removal of inert matter or impurities. It includes crude oil, natural gas liquids (NGLs) and additives. Crude oil is a mineral oil consisting of a mixture of hydrocarbons of natural origin, being yellow to black in colour, of variable density and viscosity. NGLs are the liquid or liquefied hydrocarbons produced in the manufacture, purification and stabilisation of natural gas. Additives are non-hydrocarbon substances added to or blended with a product to modify its properties, for example, to improve its combustion characteristics (*e.g.* MTBE and tetraethyl lead).

Refinery production refers to the output of secondary oil products from an oil refinery.

Comparability

In general, data on oil production are of high quality. In some instances, information has been based on secondary sources or estimated by the International Energy Agency.

Share of refinery production by product
As a percentage of refinery production

1971

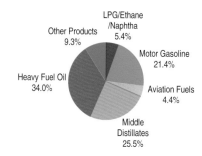

2007

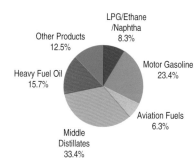

StatLink ⇗ http://dx.doi.org/10.1787/820305252613

Overview

World crude oil production increased by 57% over the 36 years from 1971 to 2007. In 2007, production reached 3 916 million tonnes or about 82 million barrels per day. Growth was not constant over the period as production declined in the aftermath of two oil shocks in the early and late 1970s.

In 2007, the Middle East region's share of oil production was 31% of the world total. However, both the level of production and its share in the world total varied significantly over the period, from 33% of the world total in 1971 to less than 19% in 1985. Increased production in the 1980s and 1990s put the OECD on par with the Middle East during that period, but by 2007, the share of OECD oil production had fallen to 23%.

Refinery production of secondary oil products changed significantly between 1971 and 2007. The share of heavy fuel oil in the refinery mix fell from 34% in 1971 to 16% in 2007 whereas the share of middle distillates increased from 25% to 33%.

Sources

- IEA (2009), *Energy Balances of Non-OECD Countries*, IEA, Paris.
- IEA (2009), *Energy Balances of OECD Countries*, IEA, Paris.
- IEA (2009), *Oil Information*, IEA, Paris.

Further information

Analytical publications

- IEA (2008), *Oil Supply Security: Emergency Response of IEA Countries 2007*, IEA, Paris.
- IEA (2009), *Energy Policies of IEA Countries*, series, IEA, Paris.

Online databases

- *World Energy Statistics and Balances*.

Web sites

- International Energy Agency, *www.iea.org*.

Production of crude oil

Million tonnes

	1971	1990	1997	1998	1999	2000	2001	2002	2003	2004	2005	2006	2007	2008
Australia	14.3	27.5	26.7	29.4	23.7	32.1	33.1	31.3	29.1	26.2	22.9	21.9	24.0	22.2
Austria	2.6	1.2	1.0	1.0	1.1	1.1	1.0	1.0	1.0	1.1	1.0	1.0	1.0	1.0
Canada	70.6	91.6	119.0	124.7	119.9	124.8	126.6	132.9	140.4	145.4	143.5	151.3	156.8	154.6
Czech Republic	..	0.2	0.4	0.4	0.4	0.4	0.4	0.4	0.5	0.6	0.6	0.4	0.4	0.4
Denmark	..	6.0	11.1	11.4	14.5	17.8	16.9	18.1	18.1	19.3	18.5	16.8	15.2	14.0
Finland	..	..	0.1	0.1	0.1	0.1	0.1	0.1	0.1	0.1	0.1	0.2	0.1	0.1
France	2.5	3.5	2.3	2.1	2.0	1.9	1.6	1.5	1.6	1.6	1.4	1.1	1.1	1.1
Germany	7.6	5.3	3.7	3.8	3.8	4.3	4.3	4.6	4.8	4.9	5.2	5.2	5.2	4.9
Greece	..	0.8	0.5	0.3	..	0.3	0.2	0.2	0.1	0.1	0.1	0.1	0.1	0.1
Hungary	2.0	2.3	2.0	1.8	1.8	1.7	1.5	1.6	1.6	1.6	1.4	1.3	1.2	1.2
Italy	1.3	4.7	6.1	5.8	5.2	4.8	4.2	5.8	5.9	5.7	6.4	6.3	6.6	6.3
Japan	0.8	0.5	0.7	0.6	0.6	0.6	0.6	0.6	0.6	0.7	0.7	0.7	0.7	0.7
Korea	..	..	0.5	0.4	0.4	0.7	0.6	0.5	0.5	0.4	0.5	0.6	0.6	0.5
Mexico	25.4	151.1	169.0	171.9	166.9	169.3	175.5	178.3	189.3	191.4	187.6	183.2	175.4	159.5
Netherlands	1.7	4.0	2.9	2.7	2.5	2.4	2.3	3.1	3.1	2.9	2.3	2.0	3.0	2.5
New Zealand	..	1.9	2.8	2.3	2.0	1.8	1.8	1.6	1.2	1.1	1.0	1.0	2.0	2.8
Norway	0.3	82.1	156.5	149.8	149.4	161.0	162.5	157.7	153.6	143.9	132.8	123.6	119.4	107.2
Poland	0.4	0.2	0.4	0.4	0.5	0.7	0.8	0.8	0.8	0.9	0.9	0.8	0.7	0.8
Slovak Republic	0.2	0.1	0.1	0.1	0.1	0.1	0.1	0.1	..	..	..	..	..	..
Spain	0.1	1.1	0.4	0.5	0.3	0.2	0.3	0.3	0.3	0.3	0.2	0.1	0.1	0.1
Turkey	3.5	3.7	3.4	3.2	2.9	2.8	2.5	2.4	2.4	2.3	2.3	2.2	2.1	2.2
United Kingdom	0.2	91.6	128.4	132.5	137.2	126.4	116.8	116.1	106.2	95.5	84.7	76.6	76.8	72.2
United States	527.7	413.3	380.9	369.8	354.2	353.0	349.9	348.1	338.4	325.9	310.0	304.4	304.0	300.5
EU27 total	..	129.0	166.4	170.1	176.2	168.7	157.3	161.5	151.7	140.7	129.0	118.0	116.8	..
OECD total	661.1	892.7	1 018.8	1 015.2	989.4	1 008.0	1 003.6	1 007.1	999.8	971.9	924.1	900.8	896.7	854.9
Brazil	8.4	32.4	43.7	50.6	57.2	64.3	67.4	75.6	77.9	77.6	85.7	90.8	92.4	..
Chile	1.7	1.1	0.4	0.4	0.4	0.4	0.4	0.4	0.4	0.4	0.3	0.3	0.5	..
China	39.4	138.3	160.7	161.2	160.2	163.1	164.1	167.1	169.7	175.9	181.4	184.9	186.4	..
India	7.3	34.6	37.4	36.4	36.4	36.4	36.2	37.4	37.7	38.3	36.3	38.1	38.2	..
Indonesia	44.1	73.2	78.9	75.5	74.7	69.9	68.3	62.8	59.4	54.9	51.4	48.2	45.3	..
Israel	5.7	..	..	..	..	..	..	..	..	..	..	..	..	..
Russian Federation	..	523.7	303.9	301.4	303.2	321.7	345.8	377.2	418.6	456.3	466.4	475.8	487.7	..
South Africa	..	..	0.8	0.9	0.8	1.0	0.8	1.0	0.7	1.7	1.7	1.5	1.2	..
World	2 487.1	3 159.4	3 479.1	3 552.1	3 478.9	3 605.1	3 616.7	3 599.2	3 723.4	3 857.7	3 914.3	3 926.0	3 915.4	..

StatLink ᴍᔕᒪ *http://dx.doi.org/10.1787/825357604764*

Production of crude oil by region

Million tonnes

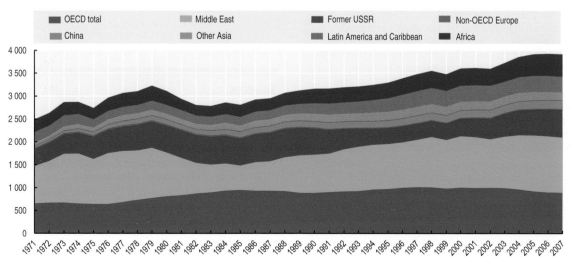

StatLink ᴍᔕᒪ *http://dx.doi.org/10.1787/820237786452*

OIL PRICES

The price of crude oil, from which petroleum products such as gasoline are derived, is influenced by a number of factors beyond the traditional movements of supply and demand, notably geopolitics. Some of the lowest cost reserves are located in sensitive areas of the world. There is not one price for crude oil but many. World crude oil prices are established in relation to three market traded benchmarks (West Texas Intermediate [WTI], Brent, Dubai), and are quoted at premiums or discounts to these prices.

Definition

Crude oil import prices come from the Crude Oil Import Register. Information is collected according to type of crude and average prices are obtained by dividing value by volume as recorded by customs administrations for each tariff position. Values are recorded at the time of import and include cost, insurance and freight (c.i.f.) but exclude import duties.

The nominal crude oil spot price from 1985 to 2008 is for Dubai and from 1970 to 1984 for Arabian Light. These nominal spot prices are expressed in US dollars per barrel of oil. The real price was calculated using the deflator for GDP at market prices and rebased with base year 1970 = 100.

Comparability

Average crude oil import prices are affected by the quality of the crude oil that is imported into a country. High quality crude oils such as UK Forties, Norwegian Oseberg and Venezuelan Light are more expensive than lower quality crude oils such as Canadian Heavy and Venezuelan Extra Heavy. For a given country, the mix of crude oils imported each month will affect the average monthly price.

Overview

The 1973 Arab oil embargo had a major price impact as Arabian Light prices surged from USD 1.84/barrel in 1972 to USD 10.77 in 1974. The next spike after 1973 came in 1981, in the wake of the Iranian revolution, when prices rose to a high of nearly USD 40. Prices declined gradually after this crisis. They dropped considerably in 1986 when Saudi Arabia increased its oil production substantially. The first Gulf crisis in 1990 brought a new peak. In 1997, crude oil prices started to decline due to the impact of the Asian financial crisis.

Prices started to increase again in 1999 with OPEC target reductions and tightening stocks. A dip occurred in 2001 and 2002, but the expectation of war in Iraq raised prices to over USD 30 in the first quarter of 2003. Prices remained high in the latter part of 2003 and in 2004. Crude oil prices increased dramatically in late August 2005 after Hurricane Katrina hit the eastern coast of the US Gulf of Mexico. Prices continued to increase throughout 2006 as the demand for oil in emerging economies, especially China, put pressure on the supply/demand balance, averaging 24 per cent higher than the previous year. In 2007, the increase continued with Dubai hitting USD 88.82/barrel at the beginning of November and WTI climbing to USD 96.50/barrel.

In early 2008, prices crossed the symbolic $100/barrel threshold and reached a new peak just under USD 150/barrel in July 2008; this brought the real price of oil in 2008 to an all time high. At the beginning of 2009, prices fell to USD 40/barrel as the impact of high prices and the onset of the global financial crisis sharply curbed oil demand. Later in the year, prices ranged between USD 70 and 80/barrel.

Sources
* IEA (2009), *Energy Prices and Taxes*, IEA, Paris.

Further information
Analytical publications
* IEA (2007), *Natural Gas Market Review 2007: Security in a Globalising Market to 2015*, IEA, Paris.
* IEA (2009), *Energy Policies of IEA Countries*, series, IEA, Paris.
* IEA (2009), *World Energy Outlook 2009*, IEA, Paris.

Online databases
* *Energy Prices and Taxes*.

Web sites
* International Energy Agency, *www.iea.org*.

Crude oil import prices

US dollars per barrel, average unit value, c.i.f.

	1976	1990	1997	1998	1999	2000	2001	2002	2003	2004	2005	2006	2007	2008
Australia	..	24.21	21.78	14.60	18.38	30.79	26.61	25.80	31.24	40.93	56.71	66.71	77.13	107.83
Austria	12.85	24.58	21.31	14.34	17.54	29.39	25.32	24.64	29.59	38.21	53.15	64.44	71.86	103.05
Belgium	12.64	21.11	18.65	11.97	17.33	27.87	24.20	24.35	27.72	35.35	50.06	61.06	70.35	96.01
Canada	..	24.15	20.59	13.15	17.85	29.10	24.87	24.97	29.53	38.13	52.37	64.33	70.04	101.41
Czech Republic	..	..	..	..	..	26.59	23.74	23.37	28.13	34.82	51.28	62.05	68.54	97.71
Denmark	12.98	23.18	20.15	13.49	17.71	29.66	24.82	24.88	29.68	38.78	54.40	66.92	74.94	96.48
Finland	..	..	19.44	12.80	18.31	28.13	23.49	24.51	27.72	36.09	51.12	63.37	70.48	94.79
France	..	..	18.99	12.43	17.45	28.18	24.13	24.63	28.87	37.61	52.74	63.69	72.22	97.63
Germany	13.27	23.17	19.01	12.48	17.51	28.09	24.15	24.40	28.44	36.65	52.30	63.29	71.60	96.70
Greece	12.13	22.42	18.45	11.66	16.64	26.95	23.22	24.08	27.17	34.53	50.33	60.97	69.93	93.60
Hungary	..	..	16.74	10.77	16.05	26.22	..	..	..	..	..	..	..	..
Ireland	..	25.55	19.99	13.55	17.14	29.88	25.31	25.52	29.66	39.24	55.24	66.38	74.16	100.39
Italy	12.41	23.23	18.88	12.21	17.10	27.77	23.87	24.34	28.58	36.60	51.33	62.50	70.20	96.67
Japan	12.59	22.64	20.55	13.68	17.38	28.72	25.01	24.96	29.26	36.59	51.57	62.82	70.09	100.98
Korea	..	..	20.34	13.72	16.91	28.22	24.87	24.12	28.80	36.15	50.19	62.82	70.01	98.11
Netherlands	13.06	21.83	18.37	11.98	16.97	27.59	23.48	23.99	27.67	35.02	50.00	61.47	68.74	97.89
New Zealand	..	21.97	21.65	14.63	18.16	29.95	26.14	25.89	31.00	41.71	56.07	67.36	73.84	105.80
Norway	..	18.46	16.71	12.23	17.46	28.91	23.43	24.46	30.41	39.20	53.08	58.83	70.16	80.22
Portugal	12.14	22.75	18.95	12.21	17.38	28.20	24.02	24.27	28.72	37.89	51.94	62.77	70.23	98.83
Spain	12.54	21.88	18.34	11.80	16.99	27.16	23.32	23.95	28.13	36.03	50.54	60.99	68.66	94.86
Sweden	13.22	23.02	18.90	12.61	17.68	28.13	24.03	23.86	28.60	36.47	51.78	62.50	70.13	95.09
Switzerland	13.87	24.23	20.50	13.38	18.35	29.53	25.04	25.34	30.26	38.73	55.81	66.76	74.92	101.03
Turkey	..	23.11	18.79	11.99	16.07	26.61	22.98	23.57	27.05	34.90	50.65	61.48	68.59	98.07
United Kingdom	12.57	22.92	19.32	12.64	18.01	28.45	24.45	24.58	29.13	37.75	53.79	65.00	73.80	99.34
United States	13.48	21.07	18.34	12.02	17.06	27.54	22.07	23.52	27.66	35.86	48.82	59.15	66.77	94.97

StatLink http://dx.doi.org/10.1787/825358536736

Crude oil spot prices

US dollars per barrel

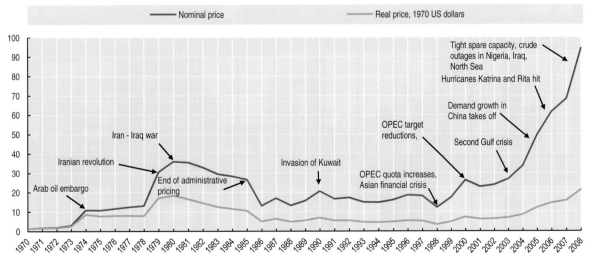

StatLink http://dx.doi.org/10.1787/820311462243

LABOUR

EMPLOYMENT RATES

Employment rates are a measure of the extent of utilisation of available labour resources. In the short term, these rates are sensitive to the economic cycle, but in the longer term they are significantly affected by government policies with regard to higher education and income support and by policies that facilitate employment of women.

Definition

Employment rates are calculated as the ratio of the employed to the working age population. Employment is generally measured through household labour force surveys. According to the ILO Guidelines, employed persons are defined as those aged 15 or over who report that they have worked in gainful employment for at least one hour in the previous week. Those not in employment consist of persons who are classified as either unemployed or inactive, in the sense that they are not included in the labour force for reasons of study, incapacity or the need to look after young children or elderly relatives.

The working age population refers to persons aged 15 to 64. Employment rates are here shown for both total employment and for men and women separately.

Comparability

All OECD countries use the ILO Guidelines for measuring employment. Operational definitions used in national labour force surveys may vary slightly from country to country. Employment levels are also likely to be affected by changes in the survey design and the survey conduct. Despite these changes, the employment rates shown here are fairly consistent over time.

Overview

Total employment rates over the three years to 2008 are, in most OECD countries, slightly above the levels achieved in the period 1995 to 1997. In Ireland and Spain the increase in employment rates exceed 10 points, while gains are more moderate for most other OECD countries. However, the Czech Republic, Poland, the Slovak Republic, Turkey and the United States recorded modest falls in employment rates over this period. By the end of the period, employment rates ranged between 45% in Turkey and 85% in Iceland. Among the non-OECD countries shown here, employment rates in Brazil, Estonia and Russia are slightly above OECD average, rising by 5 percentage points over the past years in Russia and Slovenia. By contrast, employment rates in Chile and Israel are below the OECD average, despite modest rises since the mid-1990s. All these developments have preceded those associated to the financial crisis of 2008-2009, whose employment impacts are described later in this volume.

Employment rates for men are higher than those for women in all OECD countries. While employment rates for men have remained fairly stable in most OECD countries, there are larger differences across countries in how those for women have evolved. In particular, in Italy, Luxembourg, Spain, Ireland and the Netherlands employment rates for women have increased by more than 10 percentage points in this period, contributing to much of the rise in the total employment. In non-OECD countries, employment rates of men are markedly higher than those of women, by more than 20 points in Brazil and Chile and by 5 to 10 points in Estonia, Israel, Russia and Slovenia. Brazil, Chile and Israel have below OECD-average employment rates for women despite increases since the mid-1990s in excess of those recorded for men. By contrast, Estonia, Russia and Slovenia have above OECD-average employment rates for women, rising at a somewhat quicker pace than those of men since the mid-1990s.

Sources

- OECD (2009), *OECD Employment Outlook*, OECD, Paris.

Further information

Analytical publications

- Jeaumotte, F. (2003), *Female Labour Force Participation*, OECD Economics Department Working Papers, No. 376, OECD, Paris.
- OECD (2002-2008), *Babies and Bosses – Reconciling Work and Family Life*, series, OECD, Paris.

Statistical publications

- OECD (2004), *Quarterly Labour Force Statistics*, OECD, Paris.
- OECD (2009), *Labour Force Statistics*, OECD, Paris.

Online databases

- *Employment Statistics*.

Web sites

- OECD Labour Statistics Database, *www.oecd.org/statistics/labour*.
- Putting More Women to Work: A Colloquium on Employment, Child Care and Taxes, *www.oecd.org/employment/colloquium/women*.

Employment rates: total

Share of persons of working age in employment

	1995	1996	1997	1998	1999	2000	2001	2002	2003	2004	2005	2006	2007	2008
Australia	67.7	67.6	67.4	67.9	68.4	69.3	69.0	69.4	70.0	70.3	71.5	72.2	72.8	73.2
Austria	68.7	67.8	67.8	67.8	68.4	68.3	68.2	68.8	68.9	67.8	68.6	70.2	71.4	72.1
Belgium	56.3	56.3	57.0	57.3	58.9	60.9	59.7	59.7	59.3	60.5	61.0	60.4	61.6	62.0
Canada	67.5	67.3	68.0	68.9	70.0	70.9	70.8	71.4	72.2	72.5	72.5	72.9	73.6	73.7
Czech Republic	69.4	69.3	68.7	67.5	65.9	65.2	65.3	65.7	64.9	64.2	64.8	65.3	66.1	66.6
Denmark	73.9	74.0	75.4	75.3	76.5	76.4	75.9	76.4	75.1	76.0	75.5	76.9	77.3	78.4
Finland	61.9	62.8	63.5	64.8	66.6	67.5	68.3	68.3	67.9	67.8	68.5	69.6	70.5	71.3
France	59.1	59.2	58.9	59.4	59.8	61.1	62.0	62.2	63.3	63.1	63.2	63.3	64.0	64.6
Germany	64.6	64.3	63.8	64.7	65.2	65.6	65.8	65.3	64.6	65.0	65.5	67.2	69.0	70.2
Greece	54.5	54.9	54.8	55.6	55.4	55.9	55.6	57.7	58.9	59.6	60.3	61.0	61.5	62.2
Hungary	52.9	52.7	52.7	53.6	55.4	56.0	56.2	56.2	57.0	56.8	56.9	57.3	57.3	56.7
Iceland	80.5	80.4	80.0	82.2	84.2	84.6	84.6	82.8	84.1	82.8	84.4	85.3	85.7	84.2
Ireland	54.1	55.0	56.3	59.6	62.5	64.5	65.0	65.0	64.9	65.4	67.1	68.2	69.0	68.1
Italy	51.2	51.4	51.6	52.2	52.9	53.9	54.9	55.6	56.2	57.4	57.5	58.4	58.7	58.7
Japan	69.2	69.5	70.0	69.5	68.9	68.9	68.8	68.2	68.4	68.7	69.3	70.0	70.7	70.7
Korea	63.5	63.7	63.7	59.2	59.6	61.5	62.1	63.3	63.0	63.6	63.7	63.8	63.9	63.8
Luxembourg	58.5	59.1	59.9	60.2	61.6	62.7	63.0	63.6	62.2	62.5	63.6	63.6	63.6	64.4
Mexico	57.2	58.1	60.3	60.4	60.4	60.1	59.4	59.3	58.8	59.9	59.6	61.0	61.1	61.3
Netherlands	65.1	66.0	67.9	69.5	70.8	72.1	73.1	73.2	72.6	71.8	71.9	73.2	74.8	76.1
New Zealand	70.1	71.1	70.6	69.6	70.1	70.7	71.8	72.4	72.5	73.5	74.6	75.2	75.4	74.9
Norway	73.5	75.3	77.0	78.3	78.0	77.9	77.5	77.1	75.8	75.6	75.2	75.5	76.9	78.1
Poland	58.1	58.4	58.8	58.9	57.5	55.0	53.5	51.7	51.4	51.9	53.0	54.5	57.0	59.2
Portugal	63.2	63.6	64.7	66.8	67.4	68.3	68.6	68.1	67.1	67.8	67.5	67.9	67.8	68.2
Slovak Republic	60.2	61.9	61.1	60.5	58.1	56.8	56.9	56.9	57.7	57.0	57.7	59.4	60.7	62.3
Spain	48.3	49.3	50.7	52.4	55.0	57.4	58.8	59.5	60.7	62.0	64.3	65.7	66.6	65.3
Sweden	72.2	71.6	70.7	71.5	72.9	74.2	75.2	74.9	74.3	73.5	73.9	74.5	75.7	75.7
Switzerland	76.4	77.0	76.9	78.0	78.4	78.4	79.2	78.9	77.9	77.4	77.2	77.9	78.6	79.5
Turkey	52.4	52.5	51.3	51.4	50.8	48.9	47.8	46.7	45.5	46.1	45.9	45.9	44.6	44.9
United Kingdom	69.2	69.7	70.6	71.0	71.5	72.2	72.5	72.3	72.6	72.7	72.6	72.5	72.3	72.7
United States	72.5	72.9	73.5	73.8	73.9	74.1	73.1	71.9	71.2	71.2	71.5	72.0	71.8	70.9
OECD total	64.2	64.5	65.0	65.1	65.3	65.6	65.4	65.1	64.9	65.2	65.5	66.2	66.6	66.7
Brazil	67.7	65.1	65.3	64.4	64.6	..	64.3	65.4	65.0	66.4	67.0	67.4	67.4	68.3
Chile	..	55.8	55.8	55.5	54.4	53.8	54.0	53.8	54.3	55.2	55.0	56.5	57.1	57.8
Estonia	65.5	64.9	65.2	64.5	61.6	60.7	61.1	61.7	62.6	62.6	64.0	67.7	69.1	69.5
Israel	56.5	56.4	55.7	55.2	55.5	56.1	55.6	54.8	55.0	55.7	56.7	57.6	58.9	59.8
Russian Federation	64.5	63.4	60.4	58.4	61.6	63.3	63.2	64.5	64.2	65.0	66.1	66.5	68.3	68.8
Slovenia	62.8	61.9	63.5	63.3	62.5	62.9	63.9	63.4	62.6	65.3	66.0	66.6	67.8	68.6

StatLink http://dx.doi.org/10.1787/825386018701

Employment rates: total

Share of persons of working age in employment

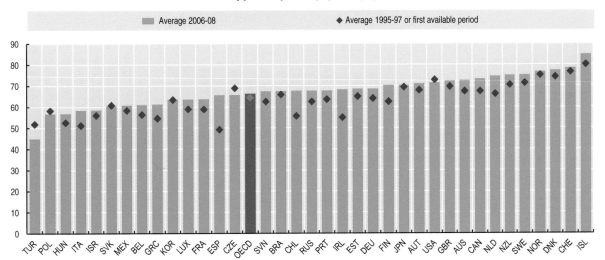

StatLink http://dx.doi.org/10.1787/820337340873

Employment rates: men

Share of men of working age in employment

	1995	1996	1997	1998	1999	2000	2001	2002	2003	2004	2005	2006	2007	2008
Australia	76.4	76.3	75.8	76.2	76.6	77.1	76.4	76.7	77.0	77.6	78.5	78.8	79.6	79.6
Austria	78.6	77.4	77.2	77.0	77.5	77.3	76.6	76.4	76.4	74.9	75.4	76.9	78.4	78.5
Belgium	66.9	66.8	67.1	67.0	67.5	69.8	68.5	68.1	67.1	67.9	67.7	67.0	68.2	68.3
Canada	73.4	73.2	73.8	74.3	75.4	76.2	75.7	75.9	76.4	76.7	76.7	76.8	77.2	77.2
Czech Republic	77.9	78.1	77.4	76.3	74.3	73.6	73.6	74.2	73.4	72.4	73.3	73.7	74.8	75.4
Denmark	80.7	80.5	81.3	80.2	81.2	80.7	80.2	80.2	79.7	79.9	80.1	80.6	81.3	82.4
Finland	64.8	66.0	66.6	68.2	69.6	70.5	71.2	70.4	70.1	70.0	70.5	71.8	72.4	73.4
France	66.7	66.8	66.3	66.6	66.8	68.1	69.0	68.6	69.1	68.7	68.6	68.4	68.6	69.2
Germany	73.7	72.8	72.1	72.9	72.8	72.9	72.8	71.7	70.4	70.8	71.4	72.8	74.7	75.9
Greece	72.2	72.6	71.9	71.6	70.9	71.3	70.9	72.5	73.5	74.0	74.5	74.6	74.9	75.4
Hungary	60.2	60.2	60.3	60.3	62.2	62.7	63.0	62.9	63.4	63.1	63.1	63.8	64.0	63.0
Iceland	84.0	84.3	84.2	86.0	88.2	88.2	88.0	85.7	86.8	86.2	87.4	88.7	89.5	87.8
Ireland	66.7	66.6	67.8	71.0	73.5	75.6	76.0	74.9	74.6	75.1	76.2	77.4	77.4	75.6
Italy	67.0	66.9	66.8	67.1	67.6	68.2	68.7	69.2	69.7	69.7	69.7	70.5	70.7	70.3
Japan	81.9	82.1	82.4	81.7	81.0	80.9	80.5	79.9	79.8	80.0	80.4	81.0	81.7	81.6
Korea	76.8	76.7	76.2	71.3	71.3	73.1	73.5	74.9	75.0	75.2	75.0	74.6	74.7	74.4
Luxembourg	74.3	74.4	74.3	74.6	74.4	75.0	74.9	75.5	73.3	72.8	73.3	72.6	72.8	72.8
Mexico	79.9	81.4	83.7	83.5	83.7	82.8	82.3	81.6	80.8	81.0	80.2	81.6	80.9	80.7
Netherlands	76.0	76.8	78.1	79.6	80.3	81.2	81.9	81.4	80.3	79.3	78.9	79.9	81.0	81.9
New Zealand	78.6	79.0	78.6	77.3	77.4	78.2	79.1	79.8	79.4	80.8	81.5	82.1	82.1	81.0
Norway	78.1	80.0	81.7	82.8	82.1	81.7	81.0	80.2	78.7	78.4	78.3	78.6	79.7	80.6
Poland	64.7	65.2	66.1	65.8	63.6	61.2	59.2	57.0	56.7	57.4	59.0	60.9	63.6	66.3
Portugal	72.1	72.0	72.5	75.6	75.6	76.3	76.5	75.7	73.9	74.1	73.4	73.9	73.9	74.0
Slovak Republic	67.6	69.2	68.4	67.8	64.3	62.2	62.1	62.5	63.4	63.2	64.6	67.0	68.4	70.0
Spain	64.0	64.7	66.1	68.3	70.8	72.7	73.8	73.9	74.5	74.9	76.4	77.3	77.4	74.6
Sweden	73.5	73.2	72.4	73.6	74.8	76.2	76.9	76.4	75.7	75.0	75.9	76.8	78.0	78.1
Switzerland	87.3	86.8	85.9	87.2	87.1	87.3	87.6	86.2	85.1	84.5	83.9	84.7	85.6	85.4
Turkey	74.6	74.9	74.8	74.3	72.7	71.7	69.3	66.9	65.9	67.9	68.2	68.0	66.8	66.6
United Kingdom	76.1	76.3	77.4	78.0	78.3	78.9	79.1	78.6	78.9	78.9	78.8	78.4	78.4	78.5
United States	79.5	79.7	80.1	80.5	80.5	80.6	79.4	78.0	76.9	77.2	77.6	78.1	77.8	76.4
OECD total	75.4	75.6	76.0	76.0	76.0	76.2	75.7	75.0	74.6	74.8	75.1	75.7	76.0	75.7
Brazil	83.1	80.8	80.7	79.5	78.8	..	78.2	78.7	77.9	79.3	79.4	79.6	79.7	80.6
Chile	..	76.7	76.7	74.4	73.0	72.1	72.3	71.8	71.7	71.9	71.6	72.6	72.6	72.5
Estonia	70.9	69.8	70.4	68.9	65.6	64.8	65.2	66.0	66.7	65.7	66.2	70.5	72.6	73.0
Israel	65.0	64.2	63.1	61.9	61.3	61.4	60.8	59.5	59.4	60.4	61.0	61.8	63.3	64.1
Russian Federation	69.9	68.6	65.3	63.1	65.9	67.6	67.4	68.3	67.9	68.6	69.6	69.7	71.8	73.0
Slovenia	67.7	66.2	67.9	67.7	66.9	67.2	68.7	68.2	67.4	70.0	70.4	71.1	72.7	72.7

StatLink http://dx.doi.org/10.1787/825405675131

Employment rates: men

Share of men of working age in employment

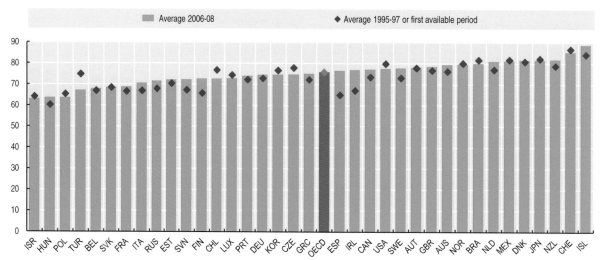

StatLink http://dx.doi.org/10.1787/820376622564

Employment rates: women
Share of women of working age in employment

	1995	1996	1997	1998	1999	2000	2001	2002	2003	2004	2005	2006	2007	2008
Australia	59.0	58.9	58.9	59.6	60.0	61.4	61.7	62.0	63.0	63.0	64.6	65.5	66.1	66.7
Austria	58.9	58.3	58.4	58.5	59.4	59.4	59.9	61.2	61.6	60.7	62.0	63.5	64.4	65.8
Belgium	45.4	45.6	46.7	47.5	50.2	51.9	50.7	51.1	51.4	53.0	54.1	53.6	54.9	55.7
Canada	61.6	61.5	62.1	63.5	64.6	65.6	65.9	67.0	67.9	68.4	68.3	69.0	70.1	70.1
Czech Republic	61.0	60.6	59.9	58.7	57.4	56.9	57.0	57.1	56.3	56.0	56.3	56.8	57.3	57.6
Denmark	67.0	67.4	69.4	70.3	71.6	72.1	71.4	72.6	70.5	72.0	70.8	73.2	73.3	74.4
Finland	59.0	59.5	60.4	61.3	63.6	64.5	65.4	66.1	65.7	65.5	66.5	67.3	68.5	69.0
France	51.6	51.8	51.7	52.4	53.0	54.3	55.2	55.8	57.6	57.7	58.0	58.2	59.4	60.1
Germany	55.3	55.5	55.3	56.3	57.4	58.1	58.7	58.8	58.7	59.2	59.6	61.4	63.2	64.3
Greece	38.0	38.5	39.1	40.3	40.7	41.3	41.2	43.1	44.5	45.5	46.2	47.5	48.1	49.0
Hungary	45.9	45.5	45.5	47.3	48.9	49.6	49.8	49.8	50.9	50.7	51.0	51.2	50.9	50.6
Iceland	76.8	76.5	75.6	78.3	80.2	81.0	81.1	79.8	81.2	79.4	81.2	81.6	81.7	80.3
Ireland	41.5	43.3	44.7	48.2	51.3	53.3	54.0	55.0	55.2	55.6	57.9	58.7	60.3	60.5
Italy	35.4	36.0	36.4	37.3	38.3	39.6	41.1	42.0	42.7	45.2	45.3	46.3	46.6	47.2
Japan	56.4	56.8	57.6	57.2	56.7	56.7	57.0	56.5	56.8	57.4	58.1	58.8	59.5	59.7
Korea	50.5	51.1	51.6	47.3	48.1	50.0	50.9	52.0	51.1	52.2	52.5	53.1	53.2	53.2
Luxembourg	42.2	43.6	45.4	45.6	48.5	50.0	50.8	51.5	50.9	51.9	53.7	54.6	54.5	55.8
Mexico	36.0	36.8	39.1	39.3	39.1	39.6	39.0	39.5	39.1	40.9	41.6	42.9	43.6	44.1
Netherlands	53.9	54.9	57.4	59.1	61.1	62.7	64.1	64.8	64.7	64.1	64.8	66.4	68.5	70.2
New Zealand	61.7	63.4	62.8	62.1	63.0	63.5	64.8	65.3	65.7	66.5	68.0	68.4	69.0	69.0
Norway	68.8	70.4	72.2	73.6	73.8	74.0	73.8	73.9	72.7	72.7	72.0	72.3	74.0	75.4
Poland	51.8	51.8	51.8	52.2	51.6	48.9	47.8	46.4	46.2	46.4	47.0	48.2	50.6	52.4
Portugal	54.8	55.6	57.2	58.3	59.5	60.5	61.0	60.8	60.6	61.7	61.7	62.0	61.9	62.5
Slovak Republic	53.0	54.6	54.0	53.5	52.1	51.5	51.8	51.4	52.2	50.9	50.9	51.9	53.0	54.6
Spain	32.5	33.8	35.2	36.5	39.1	42.0	43.8	44.9	46.8	49.0	51.9	54.0	55.5	55.7
Sweden	70.9	69.9	68.9	69.4	70.9	72.2	73.5	73.4	72.8	71.8	71.8	72.1	73.2	73.2
Switzerland	65.6	67.1	67.8	68.8	69.6	69.4	70.7	71.5	70.7	70.3	70.4	71.1	71.6	73.5
Turkey	30.2	30.3	28.0	28.5	28.9	26.2	26.3	26.6	25.2	24.3	23.7	23.8	22.8	23.5
United Kingdom	62.5	63.3	64.0	64.2	65.0	65.6	66.0	66.3	66.4	66.6	66.7	66.8	66.3	66.9
United States	65.8	66.3	67.1	67.4	67.6	67.8	67.1	66.1	65.7	65.4	65.6	66.1	65.9	65.5
OECD total	53.2	53.6	54.2	54.4	54.9	55.2	55.3	55.3	55.3	55.7	56.1	56.9	57.5	57.8
Brazil	53.1	50.3	50.7	50.1	51.3	..	51.3	52.9	52.9	54.3	55.3	55.9	55.8	56.8
Chile	..	35.5	35.5	36.9	36.3	35.7	35.8	35.8	37.1	38.8	38.7	40.5	41.6	43.2
Estonia	60.6	60.5	60.5	60.5	57.9	57.0	57.3	57.8	58.8	59.8	61.9	65.1	65.7	66.3
Israel	48.1	48.6	48.4	48.7	49.8	50.9	50.4	50.2	50.6	51.0	52.5	53.3	54.6	55.6
Russian Federation	59.4	58.5	55.8	54.0	57.5	59.3	59.3	61.0	60.8	61.7	62.8	63.6	65.1	64.9
Slovenia	57.9	57.7	59.0	58.8	57.9	58.5	58.9	58.6	57.6	60.5	61.3	61.8	62.6	64.2

StatLink http://dx.doi.org/10.1787/825430142350

Employment rates: women
Share of women of working age in employment

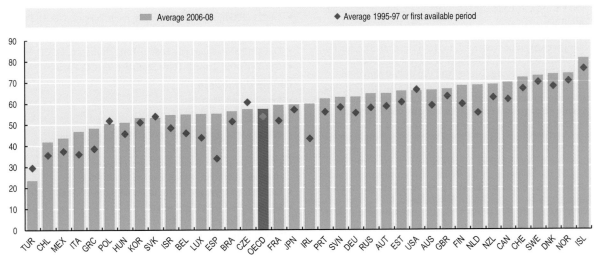

StatLink http://dx.doi.org/10.1787/820422085208

EMPLOYMENT RATES BY AGE GROUP

Labour markets differ in how they allocate employment opportunities among people of different ages. Employment rates for people of different ages are significantly affected by government policies with regard to higher education, pensions and retirement age.

Definition

The employment rate for a given age group is measured as the number of employed people of a given age as a ratio of the total number of people in that same age group.

Employment is generally measured through household labour force surveys. In accordance with the ILO Guidelines, employed persons are those aged 15 or over who report that they have worked in gainful employment for at least one hour in the previous week. Those not in employment consist of persons who are classified as either unemployed or inactive, in the sense that they are not included in the labour force for reasons of study, incapacity or the need to look after young children or elderly relatives.

Employment rates are shown for three age groups: persons aged 15 to 24 are those just entering the labour market following education; persons aged 25 to 54 are those in their prime working lives; persons aged 55 to 64 are those who are approaching retirement.

Comparability

All OECD countries use the ILO Guidelines for measuring employment. Operational definitions used in national labour force surveys may, however, vary slightly from country to country. Employment levels are also likely to be affected by changes in the survey design and the survey conduct. Despite these changes, the employment rates shown here are fairly consistent over time.

Overview

Employment rates for people aged 25 to 54 are relatively similar between OECD countries, with all countries except Turkey ranging between 70% and 90% in 2008. Cross-country differences are larger when looking at the youngest age group where, in 2008, employment rates ranged between less than 25% in Hungary, Korea, Greece and Italy and over 60% in Iceland, the Netherlands, Denmark, Australia, and Switzerland. Employment rates for the oldest age group also vary considerably, between 70% or more in Iceland, New Zealand and Sweden and less than 35% in Turkey, Hungary, Poland, Belgium, and Italy. In non-OECD countries, employment rates for youths are above OECD average only in Brazil, while those for people of prime working age exceed the OECD average by more than 5 points in Slovenia, Russia and Estonia, and those for older workers are above the OECD average in Estonia, Israel, Chile and Brazil.

Over the period from 1990 to 2008, employment rates for the youngest age group have declined by more than 5 points for the OECD as a whole, with large decreases in Sweden, Portugal, Luxembourg, Turkey and the United Kingdom. This partly reflects government policies to encourage young people to increase their educational qualifications and general employment conditions, but also the difficulties experienced by some youths to get a foothold in the labour market. For people in their prime working age employment rates have increased slightly for the OECD as a whole, with significant falls in Turkey, and Sweden, and large gains in Ireland, the Netherlands and Spain. The employment rates for older workers increased by 6 points on average, with the largest increases recorded in New Zealand, the Netherlands, the Slovak Republic, Germany, Ireland and Finland but declined in Turkey. Among the non-OECD countries included here, employment rates increased for all age groups.

Sources

- OECD (2009), *OECD Employment Outlook*, OECD, Paris.
- For Non-Member Countries: National Sources.

Further information

Analytical publications

- Burniaux, J.-M., R. Duval and F. Jaumotte (2004), *Coping with Ageing*, OECD Economics Department Working Papers, No. 371, OECD, Paris.
- OECD (2000), *From Initial Education to Working Life: Making Transitions Work*, OECD, Paris.
- OECD (2006), *Ageing and Employment Policies*, OECD, Paris.

Statistical publications

- OECD (2004), *Quarterly Labour Force Statistics*, OECD, Paris.
- OECD (2009), *Labour Force Statistics*, OECD, Paris.

Online databases

- *Employment Statistics*.

Web sites

- NERO Meeting on Labour Market Issues, Paris, 25 June 2004, *www.oecd.org/eco/nero*.
- OECD Ageing and Employment Policies, *www.oecd.org/els/employment/olderworkers*.
- OECD Employment Data, *www.oecd.org/els/employment/*.
- OECD Jobs for Youth Project, *www.oecd.org/employment/youth*.
- OECD Labour Statistics Database, *www.oecd.org/statistics/labour*.
- Youth Employment Summit, *www.yesweb.org*.

Employment rates by age group

As a percentage of population in that age group

	Persons 15-24 in employment				Persons 25-54 in employment				Persons 55-64 in employment			
	1990	2000	2005	2008	1990	2000	2005	2008	1990	2000	2005	2008
Australia	62.7	62.1	63.3	64.3	76.0	76.3	78.8	80.3	41.5	46.2	53.5	57.4
Austria	..	52.8	53.1	55.9	..	82.5	82.6	84.4	..	28.3	31.8	41.0
Belgium	30.4	30.3	26.6	26.9	71.7	77.9	78.3	80.5	21.4	25.0	32.1	32.8
Canada	61.3	56.3	57.8	59.6	78.1	79.9	81.3	82.3	46.2	48.1	54.8	57.5
Czech Republic	..	38.3	27.3	28.1	..	81.6	82.0	83.8	..	36.3	44.6	47.6
Denmark	65.0	67.1	62.0	68.5	84.0	84.3	83.9	87.9	53.6	54.6	59.8	57.7
Finland	55.2	42.9	42.1	46.4	87.9	80.9	81.7	84.3	42.8	42.3	52.6	56.4
France	29.5	23.2	29.3	30.7	77.4	78.3	80.7	83.2	35.6	34.3	38.7	38.2
Germany	56.4	47.2	42.6	47.2	73.6	79.3	77.4	81.0	36.8	37.6	45.5	53.8
Greece	30.3	26.9	25.3	24.0	68.5	70.2	74.3	76.6	40.8	39.0	41.6	42.9
Hungary	..	32.5	21.8	20.0	..	73.0	73.7	74.4	..	21.9	33.0	31.4
Iceland	..	68.2	71.6	72.1	..	90.6	88.2	88.1	..	84.2	84.8	83.3
Ireland	41.4	48.2	46.4	46.1	60.0	75.3	77.8	78.0	38.6	45.2	51.7	53.9
Italy	29.8	27.8	25.5	24.4	68.2	68.0	72.2	73.5	32.6	27.7	31.4	34.4
Japan	42.2	42.7	40.9	41.4	79.6	78.6	79.0	80.2	62.9	62.8	63.9	66.3
Korea	32.5	29.4	29.9	23.8	73.2	72.2	73.4	74.2	61.9	57.8	58.7	60.6
Luxembourg	43.3	31.8	24.9	26.2	71.8	78.2	80.7	80.2	28.2	27.2	31.7	38.3
Mexico	..	48.9	43.7	44.3	..	67.4	68.8	70.6	..	51.7	52.6	54.7
Netherlands	54.5	66.5	64.2	69.2	71.2	81.0	81.8	85.7	29.7	37.6	44.0	50.7
New Zealand	59.1	54.6	56.9	56.5	76.3	78.6	82.0	82.2	41.8	57.2	69.7	71.9
Norway	53.4	58.1	52.9	58.0	82.2	85.3	83.2	86.8	61.5	67.1	67.6	69.3
Poland	..	24.5	20.9	27.3	..	70.9	69.5	77.5	..	28.4	29.1	31.6
Portugal	54.8	42.0	36.1	34.7	78.4	81.8	80.8	81.6	47.0	50.8	50.5	50.8
Slovak Republic	..	29.0	25.6	26.2	..	74.7	75.3	80.1	..	21.3	30.4	39.3
Spain	38.3	36.3	41.9	39.5	61.4	68.4	74.4	75.3	36.9	37.0	43.1	45.6
Sweden	66.1	46.1	42.5	45.9	91.6	83.8	83.9	86.5	69.5	65.1	69.6	70.3
Switzerland	..	65.1	59.9	62.4	..	85.4	85.1	87.2	..	63.3	65.1	68.4
Turkey	45.9	37.0	31.2	30.3	61.6	56.7	54.1	53.5	42.7	36.4	30.8	27.4
United Kingdom	70.1	61.5	58.6	56.4	79.1	80.2	81.1	81.6	49.2	50.4	56.7	58.2
United States	59.8	59.7	53.9	51.2	79.7	81.5	79.3	79.1	54.0	57.8	60.8	62.1
OECD total	48.8	45.6	43.1	43.2	75.8	76.0	75.9	77.2	48.0	47.9	51.9	54.0
Brazil	..	51.7	52.7	53.4	..	73.2	75.9	77.0	..	52.2	54.1	55.1
Chile	..	26.3	25.7	27.5	..	65.9	68.2	71.1	..	47.8	51.7	56.6
Estonia	..	..	29.1	36.4	..	..	79.6	83.9	..	..	56.1	62.4
Israel	23.6	28.2	26.6	27.6	66.5	70.4	70.6	73.9	48.5	46.6	52.4	58.4
Russian Federation	..	34.6	32.9	37.0	..	80.2	82.9	84.2	..	34.8	44.6	50.7
Slovenia	..	..	34.1	38.4	..	..	83.8	86.8	..	..	30.7	32.8

StatLink ᘈ᠍᠍᠍ᘙᘊ http://dx.doi.org/10.1787/825481425236

Employment rates for age group 15-24

Persons in employment as a percentage of population in that age group

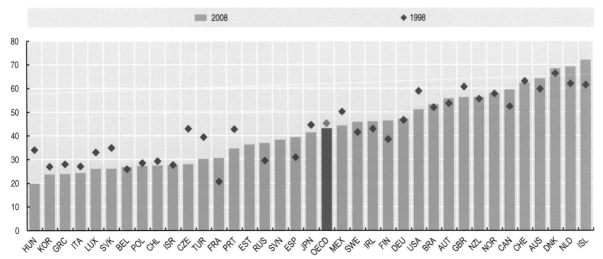

StatLink ᘈ᠍᠍᠍ᘙᘊ http://dx.doi.org/10.1787/820428223537

PART-TIME EMPLOYMENT

Opportunities for part-time work are especially important for people whose obligations prevent them from working full-time, such as women with young children and those caring for elderly relatives. Indeed, recent surveys in a large number of OECD countries show that most people who work part-time do so from choice. This suggests that countries with little part-time employment could foster increased employment by policies that promote the availability of part-time positions.

Definition

Part-time employment refers to persons who usually work less than 30 hours per week in their main job. This definition has the advantage of being comparable across countries as national definitions of part-time employment vary greatly from one country to another. Part-time workers include both employees and the self-employed.

Employment is generally measured through household labour force surveys. According to the ILO Guidelines, employed persons are those aged 15 or over who report that they have worked in gainful employment for at least one hour in the previous week. The rates shown here refer to the number of persons who usually work less than 30 hours per week as a percentage of the total number of those in employment.

Comparability

All OECD countries use the ILO Guidelines for measuring employment. Operational definitions used in national labour force surveys may, however, vary slightly across countries. Employment levels are also likely to be affected by changes in the survey design and the survey conduct. Despite these changes, the employment rates shown here are fairly consistent over time. Information on the number of hours usually worked is collected in household labour force surveys. The part-time rates shown here are considered to be of good comparability.

Overview

The incidence of part-time employment for the OECD area as a whole was 15.5% in 2008. But this incidence in 2008 differed significantly across countries. In the Netherlands and Switzerland over 25% of all those in employment were working part-time, while this share was under 10% in one third of OECD countries, as especially low in the Slovak Republic, Hungary and the Czech Republic, as well as in several non-member countries – Estonia, Slovenia, the Russian Federation and Chile.

In recent years, part-time work has accounted for a substantial share of overall employment growth in many OECD countries. For the OECD as a whole, the incidence of part-time employment rates increased by 3.6 percentage points between 1998 and 2008. Part-time employment rates grew by more than 5 percentage points in Austria, Germany, Italy and the Netherlands, while they fell by more than 1 percentage point in several countries including Iceland, Poland, Greece and France, as well as in the Russian Federation.

The growth of part-time employment has been especially important for groups that are often under-represented in the labour force such as women, youths and, to a lesser extent, older workers.

Sources
- OECD (2009), *OECD Employment Outlook*, OECD, Paris.
- For Non-Member Countries: National Sources.

Further information
Analytical publications
- OECD (1999), *Implementing the OECD Jobs Strategy: Assessing Performance and Policy*, OECD, Paris.
- OECD (2002-2008), *Babies and Bosses – Reconciling Work and Family Life*, series, OECD, Paris.
- OECD (2003), *The Sources of Economic Growth in OECD Countries*, OECD, Paris.

Statistical publications
- OECD (2009), *Labour Force Statistics*, OECD, Paris.

Online databases
- *Employment Statistics*.

Web sites
- OECD Employment Data, *www.oecd.org/els/employment/*.
- OECD Labour Statistics Database, *www.oecd.org/statistics/labour*.

Incidence of part-time employment

As a percentage of total employment

	1995	1996	1997	1998	1999	2000	2001	2002	2003	2004	2005	2006	2007	2008
Australia	..	..	..	..	..	..	24.1	24.0	24.3	23.8	24.0	23.9	23.7	23.8
Austria	11.1	10.9	10.8	11.5	12.3	12.2	12.4	13.6	13.5	15.4	16.0	17.3	17.2	17.6
Belgium	14.6	14.8	15.0	15.6	19.9	19.0	17.0	17.9	18.0	18.9	18.5	19.3	18.3	18.7
Canada	18.8	19.1	19.1	18.8	18.4	18.1	18.1	18.8	18.9	18.5	18.3	18.1	18.2	18.4
Czech Republic	3.4	3.4	3.4	3.3	3.4	3.2	3.2	2.9	3.2	3.1	3.3	3.3	3.5	3.5
Denmark	16.9	16.6	17.2	17.1	15.3	16.1	14.7	16.0	15.7	17.3	17.6	18.1	17.7	18.0
Finland	8.7	8.5	9.3	9.7	9.9	10.4	10.5	11.0	11.3	11.3	11.2	11.4	11.7	11.5
France	14.2	14.0	14.8	14.7	14.6	14.2	13.8	13.8	12.9	13.3	13.4	13.3	13.4	13.4
Germany	14.2	14.9	15.8	16.6	17.1	17.6	18.3	18.8	19.6	20.1	21.8	22.0	22.2	22.1
Greece	7.8	8.0	8.3	9.1	8.0	5.5	4.9	5.6	5.6	6.0	6.1	7.5	7.8	7.8
Hungary	2.8	2.7	2.9	3.2	3.2	2.9	2.5	2.6	3.2	3.3	3.2	2.7	2.8	3.1
Iceland	22.5	20.9	22.4	23.2	21.2	20.4	20.4	20.1	16.0	16.6	16.4	16.0	15.9	15.1
Ireland	14.3	14.2	15.0	17.6	17.9	18.1	17.9	18.6	19.3	19.3	19.6	19.9	20.3	21.0
Italy	10.5	10.5	11.3	11.2	11.8	12.2	12.2	11.9	12.0	14.8	14.6	14.9	15.1	16.3
Japan	..	..	..	..	..	..	..	17.7	18.2	18.1	18.3	18.0	18.9	19.6
Korea	4.3	4.3	5.0	6.7	7.7	7.0	7.3	7.6	7.7	8.4	9.0	8.8	8.9	9.3
Luxembourg	11.3	10.4	11.0	12.6	12.1	12.4	13.3	12.5	13.3	13.2	13.9	12.7	12.7	12.7
Mexico	16.6	14.9	15.5	15.0	13.7	13.5	13.7	13.5	13.4	15.1	..	..	..	..
Netherlands	29.4	29.3	29.1	30.0	30.4	32.1	33.0	33.9	34.6	35.0	35.7	35.5	36.1	36.1
New Zealand	20.9	21.9	22.3	22.7	23.0	22.2	22.4	22.6	22.3	22.0	21.7	21.3	22.0	22.4
Norway	21.4	21.6	21.0	20.8	20.7	20.2	20.1	20.6	21.0	21.1	20.8	21.1	20.4	20.3
Poland	..	..	11.9	11.8	14.0	12.8	11.6	11.7	11.5	12.0	11.7	10.8	10.1	9.3
Portugal	8.6	9.2	10.2	10.0	9.4	9.4	9.2	9.7	10.0	9.6	9.8	9.3	10.0	9.7
Slovak Republic	2.3	2.1	2.0	2.1	1.8	1.9	1.9	1.6	2.3	2.8	2.6	2.5	2.6	2.7
Spain	7.0	7.5	7.9	7.7	7.8	7.7	7.8	7.7	8.0	8.5	11.3	11.1	10.9	11.1
Sweden	15.1	14.8	14.2	13.5	14.5	14.0	13.9	13.8	14.1	14.4	13.5	13.4	14.4	14.4
Switzerland	22.9	23.7	24.0	24.2	24.8	24.4	24.8	24.8	25.1	24.9	25.1	25.5	25.4	25.9
Turkey	6.4	5.5	6.1	6.0	7.7	9.4	6.2	6.6	6.0	6.6	5.8	7.9	8.4	8.4
United Kingdom	22.3	22.9	22.9	23.0	22.9	23.0	22.7	23.3	23.7	24.0	23.4	23.3	23.0	22.9
United States	14.0	13.9	13.5	13.4	13.3	12.6	12.8	13.1	13.2	13.2	12.8	12.6	12.6	12.8
OECD total	11.6	11.5	11.8	11.9	12.1	11.9	12.1	14.6	14.7	15.1	15.2	15.2	15.3	15.5
Brazil	16.2	15.3	15.9	16.3	16.9	..	16.0	17.0	17.1	17.3	18.0	18.1	17.3	16.9
Chile	..	5.4	4.7	4.9	5.2	5.4	5.8	6.0	6.1	7.5	7.6	7.8	8.7	..
Estonia	..	..	..	..	..	..	..	6.9	7.5	6.8	6.7	6.7	6.8	6.2
Israel	15.2	15.1	14.2	15.4	15.9	15.6	16.3	16.5	16.6	16.8	16.9	16.6	16.1	..
Russian Federation	11.2	10.6	9.1	9.6	11.2	10.2	9.0	8.5	8.3	8.1	8.3	7.6	7.5	8.0
Slovenia	..	..	..	..	..	..	..	4.9	5.0	7.5	7.4	7.8	7.8	7.5

StatLink ᎏᎶᔍ http://dx.doi.org/10.1787/825487183524

Incidence of part-time employment

As a percentage of total employment

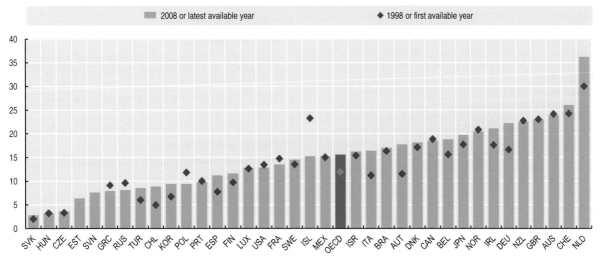

StatLink ᎏᎶᔍ http://dx.doi.org/10.1787/820431217732

SELF-EMPLOYMENT

Self-employment may be seen either as a survival strategy for those who cannot find any other means of earning an income or as evidence of entrepreneurial spirit and a desire to be one's own boss. The self-employment rates shown here reflect these various motives.

Definition

Employment is generally measured through household labour force surveys. According to the ILO Guidelines, employed persons are defined as those aged 15 or over who report that they have worked in gainful employment for at least one hour in the previous week.

Self-employed persons include employers, own-account workers, members of producers' co-operatives, and unpaid family workers. People in the last of these groups do not have a formal contract to receive a fixed amount of income at regular intervals, but they share in the income generated by the enterprise; unpaid family workers are particularly important in farming and retail trade. Note that all persons who work in corporate enterprises, including company directors, are considered to be employees.

The rates shown here are the percentages of the self-employed in total civilian employment i.e. total employment less military employees.

Comparability

All OECD countries use ILO Guidelines for measuring employment, although the operational definitions used in national labour force surveys may vary slightly across countries. Employment levels are also likely to be affected by changes in the survey design, questions sequencing and/or the ways in which surveys are conducted. Despite this, employment rates are likely to be fairly consistent over time.

Overview

In 2008, the share of self-employed workers in the total (men and women together) ranged from under 9% in Luxembourg, United States, the Russian Federation, Estonia, Norway, and Denmark to well over 30% in Korea, Brazil, Mexico, Greece, Turkey. In general, self-employment rates are highest in countries with low per capita income although Italy, with a self-employment rate of around 25.7%, is a striking exception. Ireland and Spain also combine high per capita incomes and high self-employment rates.

Close to 55% per cent of all self-employed workers are in the agricultural sector in Poland and Turkey, while this share amounts to 40% in Portugal, 30% in Greece, 24% in Mexico and 21% in Korea. The distribution of the self-employed among the categories of employers, own-account workers, members of producers' co-operatives, and unpaid family workers also varies considerably among countries. In particular, countries with relatively large numbers of small farms, such as Brazil, Mexico and Turkey, have relatively large numbers of unpaid family workers.

Over the period 1998-2008, self-employment rates have been falling in most countries although small increases were recorded in Germany, and larger ones in the Czech Republic, the Slovak Republic, and the Russian Federation albeit from low levels. Conversely, there have been sharp declines in self-employment rates in Turkey, Greece, Korea, Brazil, Mexico and Spain, starting from a higher level.

Levels and changes in total self-employment rates conceal significant differences between men and women. In 2008, in half of the countries, over 17% of all men in employment were self-employed; the corresponding figure for women was under 9%. Also, self-employment rates for men rose by more than one percentage point in the Slovak Republic, the Czech Republic, the Russian Federation, the Netherlands and Austria, while receding by more than one percentage point in close to two third of OECD countries, in particular in Turkey, Greece, Mexico, Brazil, Korea, Poland, Portugal and Spain. For women, self-employment grew significantly only in the Slovak Republic, the Russian Federation and the Czech Republic, while dropping by more than 10 percentage points in Turkey, Greece and Korea.

Sources
- OECD (2009), *Labour Force Statistics*, OECD, Paris.
- For Non-Member Countries: National Sources.

Further information

Analytical publications
- OECD (2000)," The Partial Renaissance of the Self-Employed", *OECD Employment Outlook*, Chapter 5, OECD, Paris, pp. 155-199.
- OECD (2005), *OECD SME and Entrepreneurship Outlook – 2005 Edition*, OECD, Paris.
- OECD (2009), *OECD Employment Outlook*, OECD, Paris.

Statistical publications
- OECD (2004), *Quarterly Labour Force Statistics*, OECD, Paris.

Online databases
- *Employment Statistics*.

Web sites
- OECD Directorate for Employment, Labour and Social Affairs, *www.oecd.org/els*.
- OECD Entrepreneurship at Local Level, *www.oecd.org/tds/leed/entrepreneurship*.

Self-employment rates
As a percentage of total employment by gender

	Total				Men				Women			
	1990	2000	2005	2008	1990	2000	2005	2008	1990	2000	2005	2008
Australia	15.1	14.0	12.9	11.7	17.2	16.7	15.5	14.1	12.1	10.7	9.7	8.9
Austria	14.2	13.1	13.3	13.8	..	13.9	15.3	15.7	..	12.2	10.9	11.5
Belgium	18.1	15.8	15.2	14.2	18.5	17.5	17.5	17.0	17.5	13.5	12.3	10.8
Canada	9.5	10.6	9.4	9.1	10.8	11.7	10.5	10.2	7.8	9.2	8.1	7.8
Czech Republic	..	15.2	16.1	16.2	..	19.1	20.4	20.3	..	10.2	10.4	10.6
Denmark	11.7	8.7	8.7	8.8	..	11.7	11.6	12.1	..	5.5	5.3	5.1
Finland	15.6	13.7	12.7	12.8	19.5	17.8	16.7	16.8	11.3	9.2	8.5	8.6
France	13.2	9.3	9.1	9.0	14.9	11.5	11.5	11.6	10.9	6.7	6.3	6.2
Germany	..	11.0	12.4	11.7	..	13.4	14.9	14.1	..	7.9	9.4	8.9
Greece	47.7	42.0	36.4	35.1	47.5	43.7	39.1	37.8	48.0	38.9	32.0	30.9
Hungary	..	15.2	13.8	12.3	..	19.1	17.3	15.5	..	10.5	9.9	8.6
Iceland	..	18.0	14.2	12.7	..	24.0	20.1	17.1	..	11.0	7.4	7.4
Ireland	24.9	18.9	17.3	17.3	32.3	25.8	24.7	24.9	10.9	9.0	7.4	7.5
Italy	28.7	28.5	27.0	25.7	31.1	32.3	31.2	30.1	24.1	22.0	20.6	19.3
Japan	22.3	16.6	14.7	13.0	18.9	15.5	14.5	13.4	27.4	18.3	14.9	12.4
Korea	39.5	36.8	33.6	31.3	36.9	35.7	34.0	31.9	43.2	38.4	32.9	30.4
Luxembourg	9.1	7.4	6.5	5.9	9.1	7.7	7.4	6.8	9.1	6.9	5.3	4.7
Mexico	31.9	36.0	35.5	33.9	35.5	36.4	35.7	33.5	20.4	35.2	35.3	34.7
Netherlands	11.6	11.2	12.4	13.2	..	12.6	14.6	15.8	..	9.4	9.7	10.1
New Zealand	19.7	20.8	18.5	17.3	24.6	25.8	23.0	21.4	13.3	14.7	13.4	12.7
Norway	11.3	7.4	7.4	7.8	14.6	9.8	10.2	10.9	7.4	4.8	4.4	4.5
Poland	27.2	27.4	25.8	22.9	..	29.5	27.9	25.0	..	24.8	23.1	20.4
Portugal	29.4	26.1	25.1	24.1	..	27.5	26.7	25.6	..	24.4	23.3	22.4
Slovak Republic	..	8.0	12.6	13.8	..	10.8	17.2	18.4	..	4.6	6.9	7.8
Spain	25.8	20.2	18.2	17.7	25.8	22.2	20.8	20.9	25.9	16.6	14.5	13.3
Sweden	9.2	10.3	9.8	10.4	12.9	14.5	14.0	14.5	5.2	5.7	5.3	5.9
Switzerland	..	13.2	11.2	11.1	..	13.9	11.6	11.6	..	12.3	10.6	10.4
Turkey	61.0	51.4	45.8	39.0	53.5	46.5	42.2	36.1	78.4	64.7	56.2	46.8
United Kingdom	15.1	12.8	12.9	13.4	19.9	16.7	17.4	17.8	8.9	8.3	7.7	8.2
United States	8.8	7.4	7.5	7.0	10.5	8.6	8.8	8.3	6.7	6.1	5.9	5.6
EU27 total	..	18.3	17.3	16.5	..	20.9	20.5	19.7	..	14.8	13.2	12.5
OECD total	..	17.6	16.8	15.8	..	19.5	19.1	18.0	..	15.0	13.9	13.0
Brazil	38.2	36.5	34.9	31.9	37.9	38.4	36.3	33.4	38.6	33.8	33.2	30.0
Chile	..	32.2	31.2	29.1	..	33.3	32.3	29.2	..	29.6	29.0	28.9
Estonia	3.2	9.0	8.1	7.7	3.2	11.6	11.2	10.5	3.1	6.4	5.1	4.9
Israel	..	14.2	13.1	12.7	..	18.3	17.3	16.5	..	9.3	8.2	8.2
Russian Federation	..	10.1	7.8	7.3	..	10.5	8.3	7.9	..	9.7	7.3	6.7
Slovenia	..	15.8	15.1	14.1	..	18.5	17.2	16.5	..	12.7	12.6	11.3

StatLink http://dx.doi.org/10.1787/825506483182

Self-employment rates: total
As a percentage of total employment

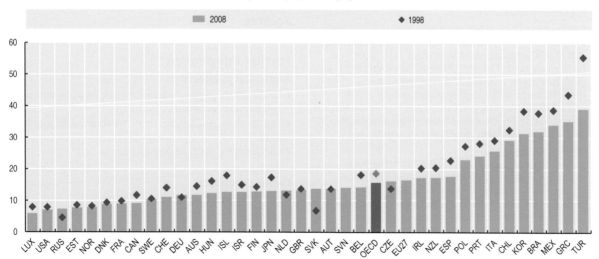

StatLink http://dx.doi.org/10.1787/820502247761

EMPLOYMENT BY REGION

Inequalities in economic performance across regions partly reflect the extent to which each region is able to utilise its available labour resources, and especially to increase job opportunities for under-represented groups.

Definition

Employed persons are all persons who during the reference week of the survey worked at least one hour for pay or profit, or were temporarily absent from such work. The employment rate is the number of employed persons as a percentage of the working age (25-64) population.

Comparability

As for the other regional statistics, comparability is affected by differences in the meaning of the word "region". The word "region" can mean very different things both within and among countries, with significant differences in terms of area and population. To address this issue, the OECD has classified regions within each country based on two levels:

territorial level 2 (TL2, large regions) and territorial level 3 (TL3, small regions). Labour market data for Australia and Canada refer to a different regional grouping, labelled non official grids (NOG) comparable to the small regions. For Brazil, Chile, China, India, Russian Federation and South Africa only large regions have been defined so far.

While employment and unemployment rates are available for small regions (territorial level 3, TL3), female employment rates are usually available only for large regions (territorial level 2, TL2).

Data on employment growth refer to small (TL3) regions for all countries except Mexico. Data refer to 1999-2008 for all countries except Germany, Italy, Japan, Ireland and Portugal (1996-2007), Iceland (1999-2005) and Mexico (2000-2007). Data on the employment rate of women refer to 2008 for all countries except Australia (2007), Iceland (2005), Korea (2006) and Switzerland (2007).

Overview

Differences in employment growth among regions within a country are often larger than across countries. During the period from 1999 to 2008, differences in employment growth across regions were above 7 percentage points in Poland, Denmark, Finland, Sweden and Mexico. Wide differences in employment growth across regions were experienced both in countries with high employment growth at the national level, such as Spain; and in countries where employment growth at the national level was low such as Poland.

Employment creation at the national level is largely due to a small number of dynamic regions. On average, the 10% of OECD regions with the stronger pace of job creation accounted for 46% of overall employment growth between 1999 and 2006. The regional contribution to national employment growth of the more dynamic regions was particularly high in Turkey, Greece, the United States and Sweden (where more than 60% of the employment growth at the national level was spurred by 10% of regions).

Even though the female employment rate has been rising in recent years, almost one-third of the OECD countries where regional data are available have a female employment rate at least 10 percentage points lower than the total employment rate. The largest regional differences in the female employment rates are observed in Turkey, the United States, Korea and Italy.

Sources

• OECD (2009), *OECD Regions at a Glance 2009*, OECD, Paris.

Further information
Analytical publications

• OECD (2009), *Regions Matter: Economic Recovery, Innovation and Sustainable Growth*, OECD, Paris.
• OECD (2009), *How Regions Grow: Trends and Analysis*, OECD, Paris.
• OECD (2007), *OECD Regions at a Glance: 2007 Edition*, OECD, Paris.

Online databases

• *OECD Regional Database*.

Web sites

• OECD eXplorer, *www.oecd.org/gov/regionaldevelopment*.
• Territorial grids, *www.oecd.org/gov/regional/statisticsindicators*.

Differences in annual employment growth across regions, small regions

Percentage, 1999-2008 or latest available period

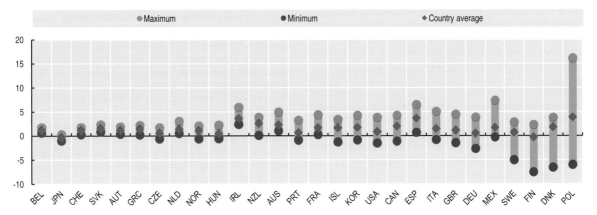

StatLink http://dx.doi.org/10.1787/820503806202

Share of national employment growth due to the ten per cent of most dynamic regions, small regions

Percentage, 1999-2008 or latest available period

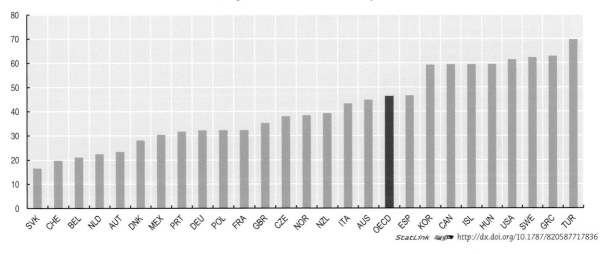

StatLink http://dx.doi.org/10.1787/820587717836

Regional differences in the employment rate of women, large regions

Percentage, 2008 or latest available year

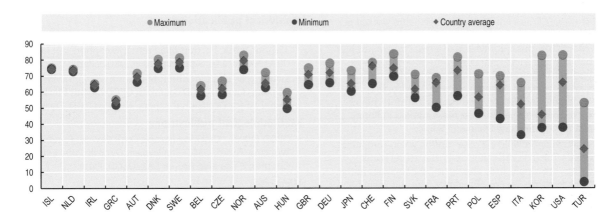

StatLink http://dx.doi.org/10.1787/820538020632

HOURS WORKED

Lower hours worked is one of the forms in which the benefits of productivity growth have been shared by people. In recent years, governments of several OECD countries have also pursued policies to make it easier for parents to reconcile work and family life, and some of these policies have tended to reduce working time.

Definition

The average number of hours worked per year is calculated as the total numbers of hours actually worked over the year divided by the average number of people in employment. The data cover employees and self-employed workers; they include both full-time and part-time employment.

Employment is generally measured through household labour force surveys. In accordance with the ILO Guidelines, employed persons are defined as those aged 15 years or over who report that they have worked in gainful employment for at least one hour in the previous week.

Estimates of the hours actually worked are also based on household labour force surveys in most countries, while others use establishment surveys, administrative records or a combination of sources. Actual hours worked include regular work hours of full-time and part-time workers, overtime (paid and unpaid), hours worked in additional jobs, and time not worked because of public holidays, annual paid leave, illness, maternity and parental leave, strikes and labour disputes, bad weather, economic conditions and several other minor reasons.

Comparability

National statisticians and the OECD work to ensure that hours worked data are as comparable as possible. These data are however based on a range of sources of varying reliability. For example, for a number of EU countries, data are OECD estimates based on results from the *Spring European Labour Force Survey*; these results reflect a single observation in the year, and have to be supplemented by information from other sources on hours not worked due to public holidays and annual paid leave. Annual working hours reported for the other countries are provided by national statistical offices and are estimated using the best available sources. These national data are intended for comparisons of trends in productivity and labour inputs and are not fully suitable for inter-country comparisons of the level of hours worked because of differences in their sources and other uncertainties about their international comparability.

Overview

In the large majority of OECD countries, average hours worked per employed person have fallen over the period from 1998 to 2008. However, this decline was rather small in most countries, as compared to the decline in earlier decades. Part of the observed decline in average hours worked between these two years may reflect business cycle effects.

For the OECD as a whole, the average hours worked per employed person fell from 1821 annual hours in 1998 to 1764 in 2008; this is equivalent to a reduction of just less than one and a half hours over a 40-hour work-week. Annual working hours fell in a majority of countries, increasing only in Denmark, Greece, Mexico, the Netherlands and Turkey. Reductions in annual hours worked over this period were most marked in Korea, Ireland, Luxembourg, Spain and France.

Although one should exercise caution when comparing levels across countries, it is clear that actual hours worked are significantly above the OECD average in the Czech Republic, Greece, Hungary, Korea and Poland and significantly below the OECD average in France, Germany, Luxembourg, the Netherlands and Norway.

Sources

• OECD (2009), *OECD Employment Outlook*, OECD, Paris.

Further information
Analytical publications

• Durand, M., J. Martin and A. Saint-Martin (2004), "The 35-hour week: Portrait of a French exception", *OECD Observer, No. 244, September 2004*, OECD, Paris.
• Evans, J., D. Lippoldt and P. Marianna (2001), *Trends in Working Hours in OECD Countries*, OECD Labour Market and Social Policy Occasional Papers, No. 45, OECD, Paris.

Methodological publications

• OECD (2004), "Clocking In (and Out): Several Facets of Working Time", *OECD Employment Outlook: 2004 Edition*, Chapter 1, see also Annex I.A1, OECD, Paris.

Web sites

• OECD Employment Data, *www.oecd.org/els/employment/*.
• OECD Labour Statistics Database, *www.oecd.org/statistics/labour*.

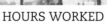

Average hours actually worked

Hours per year per person in employment

	1995	1996	1997	1998	1999	2000	2001	2002	2003	2004	2005	2006	2007	2008
Australia	1 793	1 792	1 784	1 778	1 763	1 783	1 756	1 734	1 737	1 735	1 730	1 728	1 730	1 732
Austria	1 654	1 659	1 667	1 668	1 656	1 658	1 657	1 652	1 658	1 663	1 652	1 642	1 635	1 626
Belgium	1 580	1 554	1 567	1 578	1 581	1 545	1 577	1 580	1 575	1 549	1 565	1 566	1 560	1 568
Canada	1 761	1 774	1 767	1 767	1 769	1 768	1 762	1 744	1 734	1 752	1 738	1 738	1 735	1 727
Czech Republic	2 064	2 066	2 067	2 075	2 088	2 092	2 000	1 980	1 972	1 986	2 002	1 997	1 985	1 992
Denmark	1 499	1 494	1 512	1 528	1 539	1 554	1 562	1 556	1 552	1 556	1 556	1 562	1 577	1 587
Finland	1 776	1 775	1 770	1 761	1 765	1 750	1 734	1 728	1 720	1 724	1 718	1 714	1 710	1 705
France	1 651	1 655	1 649	1 637	1 630	1 591	1 579	1 537	1 533	1 561	1 559	1 536	1 553	1 544
Germany	1 534	1 518	1 509	1 503	1 492	1 473	1 458	1 445	1 439	1 442	1 434	1 430	1 431	1 430
Greece	2 123	2 098	2 065	2 063	2 107	2 121	2 123	2 106	2 116	2 064	2 081	2 150	2 122	2 120
Hungary	2 039	2 035	2 059	2 052	2 067	2 061	2 019	2 027	1 998	1 998	1 997	1 993	1 988	1 988
Iceland	1 832	1 860	1 839	1 817	1 873	1 885	1 847	1 812	1 807	1 810	1 794	1 795	1 807	1 795
Ireland	1 875	1 882	1 832	1 754	1 725	1 719	1 713	1 698	1 671	1 668	1 654	1 642	1 631	1 601
Italy	1 859	1 873	1 863	1 880	1 876	1 861	1 843	1 831	1 826	1 826	1 819	1 815	1 817	1 802
Japan	1 884	1 892	1 865	1 842	1 810	1 821	1 809	1 798	1 799	1 787	1 775	1 784	1 785	1 772
Korea	2 658	2 648	2 592	2 496	2 502	2 520	2 506	2 465	2 434	2 404	2 364	2 357	2 316	2 256
Luxembourg	1 719	1 691	1 678	1 672	1 669	1 662	1 646	1 635	1 630	1 586	1 570	1 580	1 515	1 555
Mexico	1 857	1 902	1 927	1 878	1 922	1 888	1 864	1 888	1 857	1 849	1 909	1 883	1 871	1 893
Netherlands	1 394	1 421	1 414	1 380	1 361	1 374	1 373	1 348	1 363	1 362	1 375	1 389	1 390	1 389
New Zealand	1 842	1 833	1 821	1 824	1 838	1 830	1 817	1 817	1 813	1 827	1 810	1 787	1 771	1 753
Norway	1 488	1 483	1 478	1 476	1 473	1 455	1 429	1 414	1 399	1 417	1 420	1 414	1 417	1 422
Poland	..	..	..	..	..	1 988	1 974	1 979	1 984	1 983	1 994	1 985	1 976	1 969
Portugal	1 897	1 848	1 812	1 799	1 812	1 765	1 769	1 767	1 742	1 763	1 752	1 757	1 727	1 745
Slovak Republic	1 878	1 842	1 839	1 809	1 809	1 815	1 790	1 733	1 678	1 733	1 768	1 773	1 776	1 769
Spain	1 733	1 729	1 728	1 732	1 732	1 731	1 727	1 721	1 706	1 690	1 668	1 656	1 636	1 647
Sweden	1 640	1 653	1 658	1 656	1 665	1 642	1 618	1 595	1 582	1 605	1 605	1 599	1 615	1 625
Switzerland	1 704	1 678	1 665	1 672	1 694	1 688	1 650	1 630	1 643	1 673	1 667	1 652	1 643	1 642
Turkey	1 876	1 892	1 878	1 884	1 925	1 937	1 942	1 943	1 943	1 918		..	..	..	..
United Kingdom	1 743	1 742	1 741	1 735	1 723	1 712	1 715	1 696	1 677	1 672	1 676	1 671	1 673	1 653
United States	1 845	1 835	1 846	1 847	1 847	1 836	1 814	1 810	1 800	1 802	1 800	1 801	1 798	1 792
OECD total	1 838	1 840	1 835	1 821	1 820	1 811	1 796	1 788	1 778	1 777	1 777	1 774	1 769	1 764
Chile	..	2 312	2 256	2 300	2 277	2 263	2 241	2 250	2 234	2 232	2 157	2 165	2 128	2 095
Estonia	..	..	..	..	..	1 987	1 978	1 983	1 985	1 996	2 010	2 001	1 999	1 969
Israel	1 956	1 966	1 966	1 929	1 945	1 966	1 919	1 940	1 924	1 930	1 989	1 888	1 930	1 898
Slovenia	1 991	2 006	2 015	2 019	2 006	1 983	1 987	1 983	1 960	1 973	1 975	1 956	1 956	1 956

StatLink 🔗 http://dx.doi.org/10.1787/825563825252

Average hours actually worked

Hours per year per person in employment

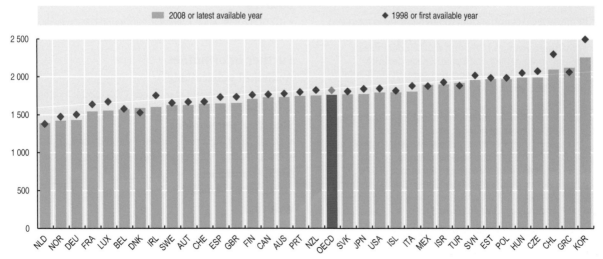

StatLink 🔗 http://dx.doi.org/10.1787/820606401832

UNEMPLOYMENT RATES

The unemployment rate is one measure of the extent of labour market slack, as well as being an important indicator of economic and social well-being. Breakdowns of unemployment by gender show how certain groups are faring compared to others and to the overall population.

Definition

Unemployed persons are defined as those who report that they are without work, that they are available for work and that they have taken active steps to find work in the last four weeks. The ILO Guidelines specify what actions count as active steps to find work; these include answering vacancy notices, visiting factories, construction sites and other places of work, and placing advertisements in the press as well as registering with labour offices.

The unemployment rate is defined as the number of unemployed persons as a percentage of the labour force, where the latter consists of the unemployed plus those in employment.

The unemployment rates shown here differ from rates derived from registered unemployed at labour offices which are often published in individual countries. Data on registered unemployment have limited international comparability, as the rules for registering at labour offices vary from country to country.

When unemployment is high, some persons become discouraged and stop looking for work; they are then excluded from the labour force. This implies that the unemployment rate may fall, or stop rising, even though there has been no underlying improvement in the labour market.

Comparability

All OECD countries use the ILO Guidelines for measuring unemployment. The operational definitions used in national labour force surveys may, however, vary slightly across countries. Unemployment levels are also likely to be affected by changes in the survey design and the survey conduct. Despite these limits the unemployment rates shown here are fairly consistent over time.

Overview

When looking at total unemployment rates averaged over the three years ending in 2008, countries can be divided into three groups: a low unemployment group with rates below 4.0% (Iceland, Norway, the Netherlands, Korea, Switzerland, Denmark, Mexico, and New Zealand); a middle group with unemployment rates between 4.0% and 8.5%; and a high unemployment group with unemployment rates of 8.5% and above (France, Germany, Poland, Slovak Republic, Spain, and Turkey).

In most OECD countries, unemployment rates averaged over the three years to 2008 were below those recorded in the three years to 1997, with marked declines in Finland, Ireland, Italy and Spain. These declines obviously preceded the global recession of 2008-2009, whose labour market impacts are described later in this volume.

There is no obvious pattern when looking at differences in unemployment rates for men and women. Unemployment rates for women are usually higher than for men, but the gap has narrowed more recently, with some countries either showing very little difference (Japan, Norway, Turkey and the United States) or having lower unemployment for women (the Slovak Republic, Spain, and Turkey) than for men. Part of the reason may be that, in these countries, women are more likely than men to withdraw from the labour force when unemployed.

Sources

- OECD (2010), *Main Economic Indicators*, OECD, Paris.
- For Non-Member Countries: National Sources.

Further information

Analytical publications

- OECD (2007), *Society at a Glance: OECD Social Indicators – 2006 Edition*, OECD, Paris.

Statistical publications

- OECD (2004), *Quarterly Labour Force Statistics*, OECD, Paris.
- OECD (2009), *OECD Employment Outlook*, OECD, Paris.

Online databases

- *Employment Statistics*.

Web sites

- OECD Employment Data, *www.oecd.org/els/employment/*.
- OECD Employment Policy, *www.oecd.org/els/employment*.
- OECD Labour Statistics Database, *www.oecd.org/statistics/labour*.

Unemployment rates: total

As a percentage of labour force

	1995	1996	1997	1998	1999	2000	2001	2002	2003	2004	2005	2006	2007	2008
Australia	8.2	8.2	8.3	7.7	6.9	6.3	6.8	6.4	5.9	5.4	5.0	4.8	4.4	4.2
Austria	3.9	4.3	4.4	4.5	3.9	3.6	3.6	4.2	4.3	4.9	5.2	4.8	4.4	3.9
Belgium	9.7	9.6	9.2	9.3	8.5	6.9	6.6	7.5	8.2	8.4	8.5	8.3	7.5	7.0
Canada	9.5	9.6	9.1	8.3	7.6	6.8	7.2	7.7	7.6	7.2	6.8	6.3	6.0	6.1
Czech Republic	4.1	3.9	4.8	6.4	8.6	8.7	8.0	7.3	7.8	8.3	7.9	7.1	5.3	4.4
Denmark	6.8	6.3	5.2	4.9	5.1	4.3	4.5	4.6	5.4	5.5	4.8	3.9	3.8	3.4
Finland	15.1	14.9	12.7	11.4	10.3	9.6	9.1	9.1	9.1	8.8	8.3	7.7	6.9	6.4
France	11.0	11.5	11.4	11.0	10.4	9.0	8.3	8.6	9.0	9.2	9.3	9.3	8.3	7.9
Germany	8.0	8.7	9.4	9.1	8.3	7.5	7.6	8.4	9.3	9.8	10.6	9.8	8.4	7.3
Greece	9.0	9.7	9.6	11.0	12.0	11.2	10.7	10.3	9.7	10.5	9.9	8.9	8.3	7.7
Hungary	10.4	9.6	9.0	8.4	6.9	6.4	5.7	5.8	5.9	6.1	7.2	7.4	7.4	7.8
Iceland	4.9	3.7	3.9	2.7	2.0	2.3	2.3	3.3	3.4	3.1	2.6	2.9	2.3	3.0
Ireland	12.3	11.7	9.9	7.6	5.7	4.4	3.9	4.5	4.8	4.5	4.4	4.5	4.6	6.0
Italy	11.2	11.2	11.3	11.4	11.0	10.2	9.1	8.6	8.5	8.0	7.7	6.8	6.1	6.8
Japan	3.1	3.4	3.4	4.1	4.7	4.7	5.0	5.4	5.3	4.7	4.4	4.1	3.9	4.0
Korea	2.1	2.0	2.6	7.0	6.6	4.4	4.0	3.3	3.6	3.7	3.7	3.5	3.2	3.2
Luxembourg	2.9	2.9	2.7	2.7	2.4	2.2	1.9	2.6	3.8	5.0	4.6	4.6	4.2	4.9
Mexico	6.2	5.5	3.7	3.2	2.5	2.5	2.8	3.0	3.4	3.9	3.6	3.6	3.7	4.0
Netherlands	6.6	6.0	4.9	3.8	3.2	2.8	2.2	2.8	3.7	4.6	4.7	3.9	3.2	2.8
New Zealand	6.5	6.3	6.8	7.7	7.0	6.1	5.4	5.3	4.8	4.0	3.8	3.8	3.7	4.2
Norway	5.5	4.8	3.9	3.1	3.0	3.2	3.4	3.7	4.2	4.3	4.5	3.4	2.6	2.5
Poland	13.3	12.4	10.9	10.2	13.4	16.2	18.3	20.0	19.7	19.0	17.8	13.8	9.6	7.2
Portugal	7.2	7.3	6.8	5.0	4.5	4.0	4.0	5.1	6.4	6.7	7.7	7.8	8.1	7.8
Slovak Republic	13.1	11.3	11.8	12.6	16.3	18.8	19.3	18.7	17.6	18.2	16.2	13.4	11.2	9.6
Spain	18.4	17.8	16.7	15.0	12.5	11.1	10.4	11.1	11.1	10.6	9.2	8.5	8.3	11.4
Sweden	8.8	9.5	9.8	8.1	6.7	5.6	5.9	6.1	6.8	7.6	7.7	7.0	6.1	6.2
Switzerland	3.5	3.9	4.2	3.5	3.0	2.6	2.6	3.2	4.3	4.4	4.4	4.0	3.6	3.5
Turkey	..	..	..	..	..	..	..	..	..	..	..	8.4	8.6	9.8
United Kingdom	8.5	7.9	6.8	6.1	5.9	5.4	5.0	5.1	5.0	4.7	4.8	5.4	5.3	5.6
United States	5.6	5.4	4.9	4.5	4.2	4.0	4.7	5.8	6.0	5.5	5.1	4.6	4.6	5.8
EU27 total	11.3	11.4	11.1	10.5	9.7	8.7	8.5	8.9	9.0	9.1	8.9	8.2	7.1	7.0
OECD total	7.3	7.2	6.9	6.8	6.7	6.2	6.5	7.1	7.3	7.1	6.8	6.2	5.7	6.1
Brazil	..	..	..	..	..	..	9.4	9.1	9.7	9.2	9.6	8.7	8.3	7.3
Chile	..	6.3	6.1	6.3	9.8	9.2	9.1	9.0	8.5	8.8	8.0	7.7	7.2	7.8
Estonia	..	..	9.7	9.2	11.4	12.8	12.3	10.3	10.0	9.6	7.9	5.9	4.7	5.6
Israel	6.9	6.7	7.7	8.5	8.9	8.8	9.4	10.3	10.7	10.4	9.0	8.4	7.3	6.1
Russian Federation	9.4	9.7	11.8	13.3	13.0	10.6	9.0	7.9	8.2	7.8	7.2	7.2	6.1	..
Slovenia	..	6.9	6.9	7.4	7.4	6.8	6.2	6.3	6.7	6.3	6.5	6.0	4.8	4.4

StatLink http://dx.doi.org/10.1787/825613006672

Unemployment rates: total

As a percentage of labour force

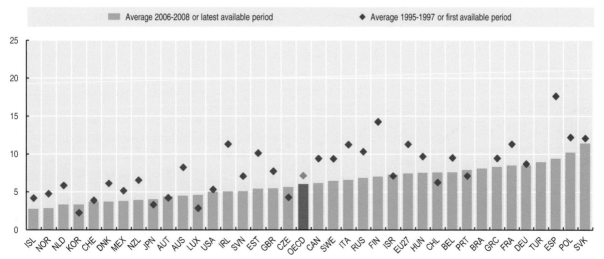

Legend: ▪ Average 2006-2008 or latest available period ◆ Average 1995-1997 or first available period

StatLink http://dx.doi.org/10.1787/820615781567

Unemployment rates: men

As a percentage of male labour force

	1995	1996	1997	1998	1999	2000	2001	2002	2003	2004	2005	2006	2007	2008
Australia	8.7	8.5	8.6	8.1	7.2	6.5	7.1	6.6	5.9	5.3	4.9	4.7	4.1	3.9
Austria	3.1	3.6	3.6	3.8	3.3	3.0	3.2	4.0	4.0	4.4	4.9	4.3	4.0	3.6
Belgium	7.6	7.4	7.3	7.6	7.2	5.6	5.9	6.6	7.7	7.5	7.6	7.4	6.7	6.5
Canada	9.8	9.9	9.3	8.5	7.8	6.9	7.5	8.1	7.9	7.5	7.0	6.5	6.4	6.6
Czech Republic	3.5	3.4	4.0	5.0	7.3	7.3	6.7	6.0	6.2	7.1	6.5	5.8	4.3	3.5
Denmark	5.7	5.3	4.5	3.9	4.5	3.9	4.1	4.3	4.9	5.1	4.4	3.4	3.4	3.1
Finland	15.2	15.0	12.3	10.9	9.7	8.7	8.7	9.1	9.3	8.8	8.1	7.4	6.6	6.2
France	9.3	10.0	10.0	9.4	8.9	7.5	7.0	7.7	8.1	8.4	8.4	8.5	7.8	7.4
Germany	7.2	8.2	9.0	8.8	8.1	7.5	7.8	8.8	9.9	10.3	11.2	10.2	8.5	7.4
Greece	6.2	6.0	6.3	7.3	7.9	7.4	7.2	6.8	6.2	6.6	6.1	5.6	5.2	5.1
Hungary	11.8	10.2	9.7	9.0	7.4	7.0	6.3	6.1	6.1	6.1	7.0	7.1	7.1	7.6
Iceland	4.8	3.4	3.3	2.2	1.4	1.8	2.1	3.6	3.6	3.2	2.6	2.7	2.3	3.3
Ireland	12.2	11.5	9.9	7.7	5.8	4.4	4.0	4.7	5.0	4.9	4.6	4.6	4.9	7.1
Italy	8.6	8.7	8.7	8.8	8.5	7.9	7.1	6.7	6.5	6.4	6.1	5.5	5.0	5.5
Japan	3.1	3.3	3.4	4.2	4.8	4.9	5.2	5.5	5.5	4.9	4.6	4.3	3.9	4.1
Korea	2.3	2.4	2.8	7.8	7.4	5.0	4.5	3.7	3.8	3.9	4.0	3.8	3.7	3.6
Luxembourg	2.0	2.2	2.0	1.9	1.8	1.8	1.6	2.0	3.0	3.6	3.6	3.6	3.4	4.1
Mexico	..	..	..	..	..	..	2.4	2.6	2.9	3.3	3.4	3.4	3.5	3.9
Netherlands	5.5	4.7	3.7	3.0	2.3	2.2	1.8	2.5	3.5	4.3	4.4	3.5	2.8	2.6
New Zealand	6.4	6.3	6.8	7.8	7.3	6.3	5.5	5.1	4.5	3.6	3.5	3.6	3.4	4.1
Norway	5.7	4.7	3.7	3.0	3.2	3.4	3.5	3.8	4.5	4.6	4.7	3.5	2.6	2.7
Poland	12.1	11.0	9.1	8.5	11.8	14.4	16.9	19.1	19.0	18.2	16.6	13.0	9.0	6.5
Portugal	6.4	6.4	6.0	4.0	3.9	3.2	3.2	4.2	5.5	5.9	6.8	6.6	6.7	6.6
Slovak Republic	12.6	10.2	11.1	12.2	16.3	18.9	19.8	18.6	17.4	17.4	15.5	12.3	10.0	8.4
Spain	14.8	14.3	13.1	11.2	9.0	7.9	7.5	8.1	8.2	8.0	7.1	6.3	6.4	10.1
Sweden	9.7	10.1	10.1	8.2	6.6	5.9	6.1	6.4	7.2	7.8	7.7	6.9	5.9	6.0
Switzerland	3.0	3.7	4.2	3.1	2.6	2.2	2.0	3.0	4.0	4.0	3.9	3.4	3.0	3.0
Turkey	..	..	..	..	..	..	..	..	..	..	..	8.4	8.6	9.7
United Kingdom	9.9	9.2	7.7	6.8	6.5	5.9	5.5	5.7	5.5	5.1	5.2	5.8	5.6	6.1
United States	5.6	5.4	4.9	4.4	4.1	3.9	4.8	5.9	6.3	5.6	5.1	4.6	4.7	6.1
EU27 total	10.3	10.5	10.2	9.5	8.7	7.8	7.8	8.3	8.4	8.5	8.3	7.6	6.6	6.6
OECD total	6.8	6.8	6.4	6.4	6.3	5.9	6.3	7.0	7.2	6.9	6.6	6.0	5.6	6.1
Brazil	..	..	..	..	..	..	7.5	7.2	7.8	7.0	7.3	6.6	6.2	5.3
Chile	..	5.6	5.4	5.7	9.4	8.7	8.9	8.6	7.9	7.9	7.0	6.7	6.3	9.5
Estonia	..	..	10.4	9.9	12.5	13.8	12.6	10.8	10.2	10.3	8.6	6.2	5.4	5.9
Israel	5.6	5.8	6.8	8.0	8.5	8.4	8.9	10.1	10.2	9.5	8.5	7.8	6.8	5.7
Russian Federation	9.7	10.0	12.1	13.5	13.2	10.8	9.3	8.1	8.5	8.0	7.3	7.5	6.4	..
Slovenia	..	7.1	6.8	7.3	7.2	6.5	5.7	5.9	6.4	5.9	6.1	4.9	4.0	4.0

StatLink http://dx.doi.org/10.1787/825616821748

Unemployment rates: men

As a percentage of male labour force

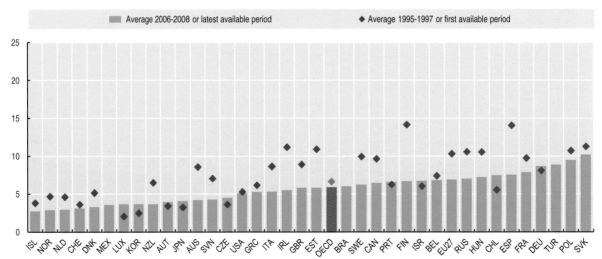

■ Average 2006-2008 or latest available period ♦ Average 1995-1997 or first available period

StatLink http://dx.doi.org/10.1787/820632115210

Unemployment rates: women
As a percentage of female labour force

	1995	1996	1997	1998	1999	2000	2001	2002	2003	2004	2005	2006	2007	2008
Australia	7.9	7.9	8.1	7.5	6.8	6.2	6.5	6.2	6.0	5.6	5.2	4.9	4.8	4.6
Austria	5.0	5.3	5.4	5.4	4.7	4.3	4.2	4.4	4.7	5.4	5.5	5.2	5.0	4.1
Belgium	12.7	12.5	11.9	11.6	10.3	8.5	7.5	8.7	8.9	9.6	9.5	9.3	8.5	7.6
Canada	9.1	9.3	8.9	8.0	7.3	6.7	6.9	7.1	7.2	6.9	6.5	6.1	5.6	5.7
Czech Republic	4.8	4.7	5.9	8.1	10.3	10.4	9.7	9.0	9.9	9.9	9.8	8.8	6.8	5.6
Denmark	8.1	7.5	6.2	6.0	5.7	4.8	5.0	5.0	6.1	6.0	5.3	4.5	4.1	3.7
Finland	15.0	14.8	13.0	11.9	10.8	10.5	9.7	9.1	8.9	9.0	8.6	8.1	7.2	6.7
France	13.0	13.3	13.2	12.8	12.1	10.8	9.9	9.8	10.0	10.2	10.3	10.1	8.9	8.4
Germany	9.0	9.2	9.8	9.3	8.5	7.5	7.4	7.9	8.7	9.1	10.0	9.4	8.3	7.2
Greece	13.8	15.4	14.8	17.0	18.2	17.1	16.1	15.7	15.0	16.2	15.3	13.6	12.8	11.4
Hungary	8.7	8.8	8.1	7.8	6.3	5.6	5.0	5.4	5.6	6.1	7.4	7.8	7.7	8.0
Iceland	4.9	4.1	4.5	3.2	2.6	2.9	2.5	2.9	3.1	2.9	2.6	3.1	2.3	2.6
Ireland	12.5	11.8	9.9	7.3	5.7	4.3	3.8	4.1	4.3	4.1	4.0	4.2	4.2	4.6
Italy	15.4	15.2	15.3	15.4	14.9	13.7	12.2	11.5	11.4	10.5	10.1	8.8	7.9	8.6
Japan	3.2	3.4	3.4	4.0	4.5	4.5	4.7	5.1	4.9	4.4	4.2	3.9	3.7	3.8
Korea	1.7	1.6	2.3	5.7	5.3	3.6	3.3	2.7	3.3	3.4	3.4	2.9	2.6	2.6
Luxembourg	4.3	4.2	3.9	4.0	3.3	2.9	2.4	3.5	4.9	6.8	6.0	6.0	5.2	5.8
Mexico	..	..	..	..	..	..	3.5	3.7	4.3	5.1	4.0	3.9	4.1	4.1
Netherlands	8.1	7.7	6.6	5.0	4.4	3.7	2.8	3.1	3.9	4.9	5.1	4.4	3.6	3.0
New Zealand	6.5	6.3	6.8	7.6	6.7	6.0	5.4	5.5	5.1	4.5	4.1	4.2	4.0	4.2
Norway	5.1	4.8	4.1	3.2	2.9	3.1	3.3	3.5	3.9	3.9	4.3	3.3	2.5	2.3
Poland	..	..	13.0	12.2	15.2	18.2	19.9	20.9	20.4	20.0	19.1	14.9	10.4	8.0
Portugal	8.1	8.2	7.6	6.2	5.1	5.0	5.1	6.1	7.3	7.7	8.7	9.2	9.6	9.1
Slovak Republic	13.8	12.7	12.8	13.2	16.4	18.6	18.7	18.7	17.8	19.2	17.2	14.7	12.7	11.0
Spain	24.7	23.7	22.6	21.2	18.1	16.1	14.8	15.7	15.3	14.3	12.2	11.6	10.9	13.1
Sweden	7.8	9.0	9.4	8.0	6.8	5.3	5.7	5.8	6.4	7.4	7.7	7.2	6.4	6.5
Switzerland	4.0	4.2	4.1	4.0	3.5	3.2	3.4	3.5	4.6	4.9	5.1	4.7	4.4	4.1
Turkey	..	..	..	..	..	..	..	..	..	..	..	8.4	8.6	10.0
United Kingdom	6.7	6.3	5.8	5.3	5.1	4.8	4.4	4.5	4.3	4.3	4.3	5.0	5.0	5.1
United States	5.6	5.4	5.0	4.6	4.3	4.1	4.7	5.6	5.7	5.4	5.1	4.6	4.5	5.4
EU27 total	12.5	12.5	12.4	11.8	10.9	9.8	9.4	9.7	9.7	9.8	9.6	8.9	7.8	7.5
OECD total	7.8	7.7	7.5	7.4	7.2	6.7	6.8	7.3	7.4	7.3	7.1	6.5	6.0	6.2
Brazil	..	..	..	..	..	..	11.9	11.6	12.4	11.9	12.5	11.3	11.1	9.8
Chile	..	7.9	7.7	7.6	10.7	10.0	9.7	9.6	9.7	10.5	9.8	9.5	8.8	6.8
Estonia	..	..	8.9	8.4	10.2	11.7	12.1	9.7	9.8	8.9	7.1	5.6	3.9	5.3
Israel	8.6	7.8	8.8	9.2	9.4	9.2	9.9	10.6	11.3	11.4	9.5	9.0	7.9	6.5
Russian Federation	9.2	9.3	11.5	13.0	12.9	10.4	8.6	7.6	8.0	7.5	7.0	6.8	5.8	..
Slovenia	..	6.7	7.1	7.5	7.6	7.0	6.8	6.8	7.1	6.9	7.1	7.2	5.9	4.8

StatLink http://dx.doi.org/10.1787/825622685822

Unemployment rates: women
As a percentage of female labour force

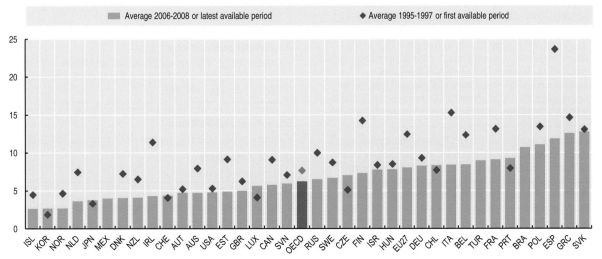

■ Average 2006-2008 or latest available period   ◆ Average 1995-1997 or first available period

StatLink http://dx.doi.org/10.1787/820722572804

LONG-TERM UNEMPLOYMENT

Long-term unemployment is of particular concern to the people affected and to policy makers. Quite apart from the mental stress caused to the unemployed and their families, high rates of long-term unemployment indicate that labour markets are operating inefficiently. In countries that pay generous unemployment benefits, the existence of long-term unemployment is also a significant burden on government finances.

Definition

Long-term unemployment is here defined as referring to people who have been unemployed for 12 months or more. The ratios calculated here show the proportion of these long-term unemployed among all unemployed, hereafter called long-term unemployment rates. Lower duration limits (*e.g.* six months or more) are sometimes considered in national statistics on the subject.

Unemployment is defined in most OECD countries in accordance with the ILO Guidelines. Unemployment is usually measured by household labour force surveys and the unemployed are defined as those persons who report that they have worked in gainful employment for less than one hour in the previous week, who are available for work and who have taken actions to seek employment in the previous four weeks. The ILO Guidelines specify the kinds of actions that count as seeking work.

Comparability

All OECD countries use the ILO Guidelines for measuring unemployment. Operational definitions used in national labour force surveys may vary slightly across countries. Unemployment levels may also be affected by changes in the survey design and the survey conduct. The long-term unemployment rates shown here are fairly consistent over time.

In comparing rates of long-term unemployment, it is important to bear in mind differences in institutional arrangements between countries. Rates of long-term unemployment will generally be higher in countries where unemployment benefits are relatively generous and are available for long periods of unemployment. In countries where the benefits are low and of limited duration, unemployed persons will more quickly lower their wage expectations or consider taking jobs that are in other ways less attractive than those which they formerly held.

Overview

Rates of long-term unemployment are generally lower in countries that have enjoyed high GDP growth rates in recent years. There appears to be a two-way causal relationship here; on the one hand, jobs are easier to find in a faster growing economy; on the other, in economies that grow faster, unemployment will become increasingly unattractive relative to having a paid job. Lower rates of long-term unemployment may also occur at the onset of an economic downturn due to rising inflow of newly unemployed persons. However, developments described here preceded those associated to the financial crisis of 2008-2009, whose impacts are described later in this volume.

In 2008, rates of long-term unemployment have varied from 10% or less in Canada, Iceland, Korea, Mexico, New Zealand and Norway, to 50% or more in Belgium, the Czech Republic, Germany and the Slovak Republic. In non-OECD counties, Estonia, Israel, the Russian Federation and Slovenia have experienced long-term unemployment rates above OECD-average, while Chile has recorded lower shares of long-term unemployment.

Over the period 1998-2008, long-term unemployment rates have receded for the OECD as a whole by more than 7 percentage points. Sharp rises, of 5 percentage points or more, were recorded in the Czech Republic, Japan, Luxembourg and the Slovak Republic, while sharp falls occurred in about two third of countries, with Ireland, Spain and Sweden recording the steepest fall. In non-OECD countries, long-term unemployment rates have almost doubled over the 10 years to 2008 in Israel, while they have receded markedly in Estonia and Slovenia.

Sources
- OECD (2009), *Labour Force Statistics*, OECD, Paris.
- For Non-Member Countries: National Sources.

Further information
Analytical publications
- OECD (2002), "The Ins and Outs of Long-term Unemployment", *OECD Employment Outlook*, Chapter 4, OECD, Paris, pp. 187-243.
- OECD (2009), *OECD Employment Outlook*, OECD, Paris.

Statistical publications
- OECD (2004), *Quarterly Labour Force Statistics*, OECD, Paris.

Online databases
- *Employment Statistics*.

Web sites
- OECD Employment Data, *www.oecd.org/els/employment/*.
- OECD Employment Outlook, *www.oecd.org/els/employmentoutlook*.
- OECD Labour Statistics Database, *www.oecd.org/statistics/labour*.

Long-term unemployment

Persons unemployed for 12 months or more as a percentage of total unemployed

	1995	1996	1997	1998	1999	2000	2001	2002	2003	2004	2005	2006	2007	2008
Australia	32.0	28.5	31.2	29.7	28.3	25.5	22.0	22.4	21.5	20.7	18.3	18.1	15.4	14.9
Austria	29.1	24.9	27.5	30.3	29.2	25.8	23.3	19.2	24.5	27.6	25.3	27.3	26.8	24.2
Belgium	62.4	61.3	60.5	61.7	60.5	56.3	51.7	49.6	46.3	49.6	51.6	55.6	50.0	52.6
Canada	16.8	16.8	16.1	13.8	11.7	11.2	9.5	9.6	10.0	9.5	9.6	8.7	7.5	7.1
Czech Republic	31.2	31.3	30.5	31.2	37.1	48.8	52.7	50.7	49.9	51.8	53.6	55.2	53.4	50.2
Denmark	27.9	26.5	27.2	26.9	20.5	20.0	22.2	19.7	19.9	22.6	25.9	20.4	18.2	16.1
Finland	37.6	34.5	29.8	27.5	29.6	29.0	26.2	24.4	24.7	23.4	24.9	24.8	23.0	18.2
France	42.5	39.6	41.4	44.2	40.4	42.6	37.6	33.8	41.0	40.9	41.4	42.2	40.4	37.9
Germany	48.7	47.8	50.1	52.6	51.7	51.5	50.4	47.9	50.0	51.8	54.1	57.3	56.6	53.4
Greece	51.4	56.7	55.7	54.9	55.3	56.4	52.8	52.7	56.3	54.8	53.7	55.6	50.3	49.6
Hungary	50.6	54.4	51.3	50.1	49.4	49.0	46.6	44.8	42.2	45.1	46.0	46.1	47.6	47.6
Iceland	16.8	19.8	16.3	16.1	11.7	11.8	12.5	11.1	8.1	11.2	13.3	7.3	8.0	4.1
Ireland	61.6	59.5	57.0	..	55.3	..	33.1	29.4	35.5	34.3	34.3	34.3	30.3	29.4
Italy	63.6	65.6	66.3	59.6	61.4	61.3	63.4	59.2	58.2	49.7	52.2	52.9	49.9	47.5
Japan	18.1	19.3	21.8	20.3	22.4	25.5	26.6	30.8	33.5	33.7	33.3	33.0	32.0	33.3
Korea	4.4	3.8	2.6	1.5	3.8	2.3	2.3	2.5	0.6	1.1	0.8	1.1	0.6	2.7
Luxembourg	23.2	27.6	34.6	31.3	32.3	22.4	28.4	27.4	24.7	21.0	26.4	29.5	34.5	38.6
Mexico	1.5	2.2	1.8	0.8	1.5	1.2	1.0	0.9	0.9	1.1	2.3	2.5	2.7	1.7
Netherlands	46.8	50.0	49.1	47.9	43.5	..	..	26.7	29.2	32.5	40.1	45.2	41.7	36.3
New Zealand	25.7	20.8	19.3	19.3	20.9	19.3	16.7	14.5	13.5	11.7	9.4	7.1	5.7	4.4
Norway	24.2	14.2	12.4	8.3	7.1	5.3	5.5	6.4	6.4	9.2	9.5	14.5	8.8	6.0
Poland	40.0	39.0	38.0	37.4	34.8	37.9	43.1	48.4	49.7	47.9	52.2	50.4	45.9	29.0
Portugal	50.9	53.1	55.6	44.7	41.2	42.9	38.1	35.5	32.8	43.2	48.6	51.8	47.3	48.3
Slovak Republic	54.1	52.6	51.6	51.3	47.7	54.6	53.7	59.8	61.1	60.6	68.1	73.1	70.8	66.1
Spain	57.1	55.9	55.7	54.3	51.2	47.6	44.0	40.2	39.8	37.7	32.6	29.5	27.6	23.8
Sweden	27.8	30.1	33.4	33.5	30.1	26.4	22.3	21.0	17.8	18.9	..	..	13.0	12.4
Switzerland	33.6	25.6	28.2	34.8	39.6	29.0	29.9	21.8	26.1	33.5	39.0	39.1	40.8	34.3
Turkey	36.4	44.3	41.6	40.3	28.2	21.1	21.3	29.4	24.4	39.2	39.6	35.8	30.3	26.9
United Kingdom	43.6	39.8	38.6	32.7	29.6	28.0	27.8	22.9	22.8	21.4	22.3	22.1	24.5	25.5
United States	9.7	9.5	8.7	8.0	6.8	6.0	6.1	8.5	11.8	12.7	11.8	10.0	10.0	10.6
OECD total	34.0	34.2	35.0	33.1	31.7	31.4	29.5	29.4	30.7	31.7	32.8	32.1	29.1	25.9
Chile	..	9.2	6.9	7.3	12.2	15.6	18.2	16.9	16.7	17.1	16.5	11.5	12.6	..
Estonia	31.7	55.3	45.7	47.0	45.8	45.4	48.3	52.8	45.9	52.2	53.4	48.1	49.4	30.9
Israel	16.2	14.3	14.2	15.6	18.9	18.8	17.0	19.2	25.0	32.6	32.5	32.6	30.9	..
Russian Federation	29.7	32.6	38.2	40.7	47.0	46.2	39.2	39.2	37.6	39.0	38.5	41.7	40.6	..
Slovenia	53.2	52.0	56.7	57.7	57.7	62.4	61.4	57.7	55.5	52.7	49.2	51.8	47.9	44.2

StatLink 🔢 http://dx.doi.org/10.1787/825635733410

Long-term unemployment

Persons unemployed for 12 months or more as a percentage of total unemployed

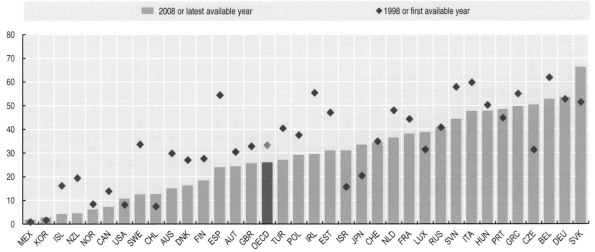

StatLink 🔢 http://dx.doi.org/10.1787/820736681663

UNEMPLOYMENT BY REGION

Unemployment rates vary significantly among countries but large international differences hide even larger differences among regions. In 2008, regional differences in unemployment rates were above 10 percentage points in one third of OECD countries. In some regions, unemployment also remained persistently high in the decade leading up to 2008, even before the impact of the economic crisis on the labour market.

Definition

Unemployed persons are defined as those who report that they are without work, that they are available for work and that they have taken active steps to find work in the last four weeks preceding the survey. The ILO Guidelines specify what actions count as active steps to find work and these include answering vacancy notices, visiting factories, construction sites and other places of work, and placing advertisements in the press as well as registering with labour offices.

The unemployment rate is defined as the number of unemployed persons as a percentage of the labour force, where the latter consists of unemployed and employed persons.

When unemployment is high, some persons become discouraged and stop looking for work. They are then excluded from the labour force so that the unemployment rate may fall, or stop rising, even though there has been no underlying improvement in the labour market.

The Gini index offers a picture of regional disparities. It looks not only at the regions with the highest and the lowest rates of unemployment but also at the differences among all regions. The index ranges between 0 and 1: the higher its value, the larger the regional disparities. Regional disparities tend to be underestimated when the size of regions is large.

The youth unemployment rate is defined as the ratio between the unemployed person aged between 15 and 24 and the labour force in the same age group.

Comparability

As for the other regional statistics, the comparability of unemployment rates is affected by differences in the meaning of the word region. The word "region" can mean very different things both within and among countries, with significant differences in terms of area and population. To address this issue, the OECD has classified regions within each country based on two levels: territorial level 2 (TL2, large regions) and territorial level 3 (TL3, small regions). Labour market data for Australia and Canada refer to a different regional grouping, labelled non official grids (NOG) comparable to the small regions. For Brazil, Chile, China, India, Russian Federation and South Africa only large regions have been defined so far.

Overview

In one third of the countries the difference between the regions with highest and lowest unemployment rate is higher than 10 percentage points. In 2008, the Russian Federation, Finland, Germany and Italy displayed regions with essentially no unemployment rate and regions where the unemployment rate was above 10%. After the Russian Federation, Iceland, Italy and Belgium were the countries with the largest disparities in unemployment rate according to the Gini index.

There are also significant differences in youth unemployment rates among regions within a country. The Slovak Republic, Belgium, Italy and Spain were the countries with the highest regional inequality in youth unemployment. In half of the countries considered, the regional variation in youth unemployment rate is higher than 10 per cent points.

Sources

- OECD (2009), *OECD Regions at a Glance 2009*, OECD, Paris.

Further information

Analytical publications

- OECD (2009), *Regions Matter: Economic Recovery, Innovation and Sustainable Growth*, OECD, Paris.
- OECD (2005), *Local Governance and the Drivers of Growth*, OECD, Paris.
- Oliveira Martins J., F. Gonand, P. Antolin, C. de la Maisonneuve and K.-Y. Yoo (2005), *The Impact of Ageing on Demand, Factor Markets and Growth*, OECD Economics Department Working Papers, No. 420, OECD, Paris.

Online databases

- *OECD Regional Database.*

Web sites

- OECD eXplorer, *www.oecd.org/gov/regionaldevelopment*.
- Territorial grids, *www.oecd.org/gov/regional/statisticsindicators*.

Range in regional unemployment rate, small regions
Percentage, 2008

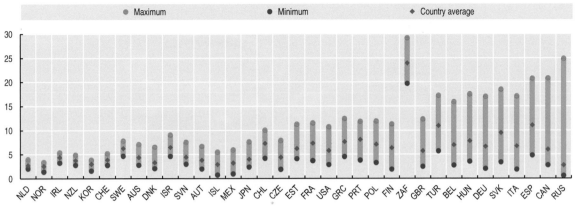

StatLink http://dx.doi.org/10.1787/820741213136

Gini index of regional unemployment rates, small regions
Year 2008

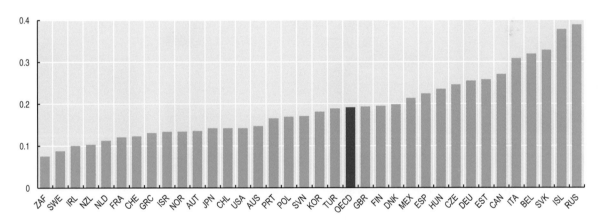

StatLink http://dx.doi.org/10.1787/820840076676

Regional variation of the youth unemployment rate, large regions
Percentage, 2008

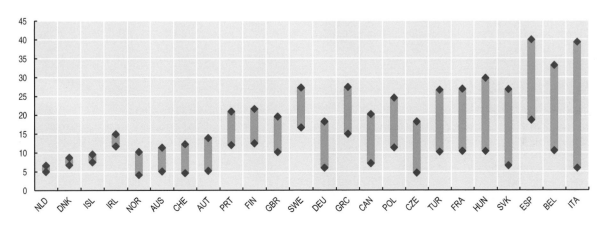

StatLink http://dx.doi.org/10.1787/820813366103

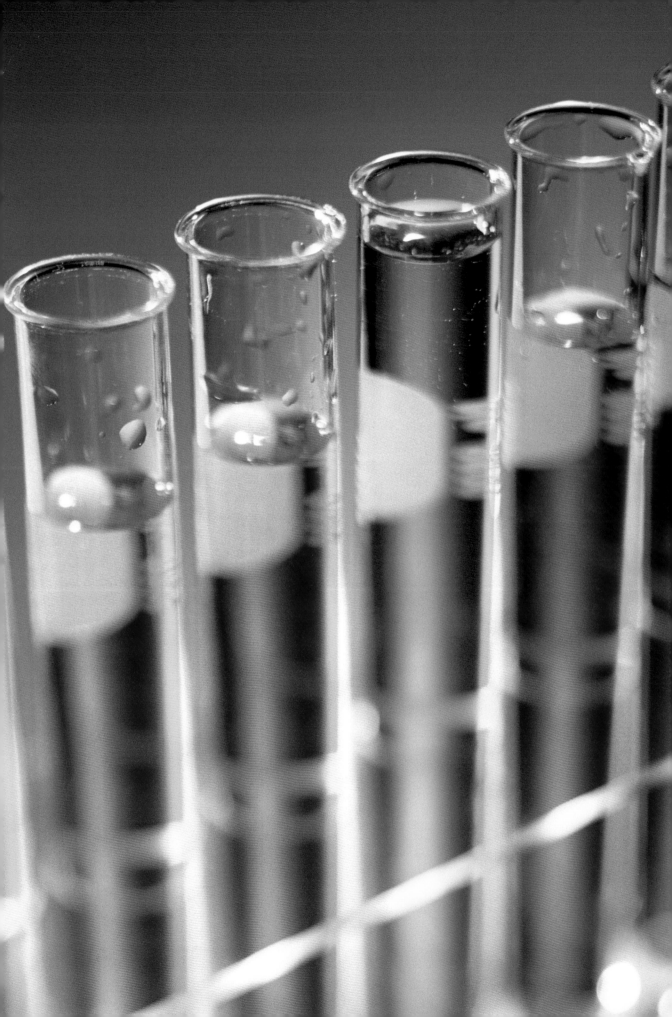

SCIENCE AND TECHNOLOGY

RESEARCH AND DEVELOPMENT

INFORMATION AND COMMUNICATIONS

EXPENDITURE ON R&D

Expenditure on research and development (R&D) is a key indicator of government and private sector efforts to obtain competitive advantage in science and technology.

Definition

Research and development (R&D) comprise creative work undertaken on a systematic basis in order to increase the stock of knowledge (including knowledge of man, culture and society) and the use of this knowledge to devise new applications. R&D covers three activities: basic research, applied research, and experimental development. Basic research is experimental or theoretical work undertaken primarily to acquire new knowledge of the underlying foundation of phenomena and observable facts, without any particular application or use in view. Applied research is also original investigation undertaken in order to acquire new knowledge; it is, however, directed primarily towards a specific practical aim or objective. Experimental development is systematic work, drawing on existing knowledge gained from research and/or practical experience, which is directed to producing new materials, products or devices, to installing new processes, systems and services, or to improving substantially those already produced or installed.

The main aggregate used for international comparisons is gross domestic expenditure on R&D (GERD). This consists of the total expenditure (current and capital) on R&D by all resident companies, research institutes, university and government laboratories, etc. It excludes R&D expenditures financed by domestic firms but performed abroad. GERD is here expressed as a share of GDP.

Comparability

The R&D data shown here have been compiled according to the guidelines of the *Frascati Manual*. It should, however, be noted that, over the period shown, several countries have improved the coverage of their surveys of R&D activities in the services sector (Japan, Netherlands, Norway and United States) and in higher education (Finland, Greece, Japan, Netherlands, Spain and the United States). Some of the changes shown in the table will hence reflect these methodological improvements as well as the underlying changes in R&D expenditures.

For Korea, prior to 2007, social sciences and the humanities are excluded from the R&D data. For the United States, capital expenditure is not covered.

Data for Brazil and India do not fully comply with the guidelines of the *Frascati Manual*, and were compiled from national sources. Data for Brazil and South Africa are likely to be underestimated as are the data for China before 2000.

Overview

In 2007, research and development amounted to 2.3% of GDP for the OECD as a whole. Finland, Japan, Korea and Sweden were the only OECD countries in which the R&D-to-GDP ratio exceeded 3%, well above the OECD average. Since 2000, R&D expenditure relative to GDP has increased significantly in Japan and only slightly in the United States, while it remained relatively stable (at 1.8% in 2007) in the EU. In China, R&D intensity increased from 0.9% in 2000 to 1.4% in 2007.

Since the mid-1990s, R&D expenditure in real terms has been growing the fastest (among OECD countries) in Turkey and Portugal, both with average annual growth rates above 10%. In China, growth in real R&D spending since 2000 has exceeded 20% per year.

Sources
- OECD (2009), *Main Science and Technology Indicators*, OECD, Paris.

Further information
Analytical publications
- OECD (2009), *OECD Science, Technology and Industry Scoreboard 2009*, OECD, Paris.
- OECD (2008), *OECD Science, Technology and Industry Outlook 2008*, OECD, Paris.

Statistical publications
- OECD (2009), *OECD Science, Technology and R&D Statistics on CD-ROM*, OECD, Paris.

Methodological publications
- OECD (2003), *Frascati Manual 2002: Proposed Standard Practice for Surveys on Research and Experimental Development*, OECD, Paris.

Web sites
- OECD Science, Technology and Industry, *www.oecd.org/sti*.

Gross domestic expenditure on R&D
As a percentage of GDP

	1995	1996	1997	1998	1999	2000	2001	2002	2003	2004	2005	2006	2007	2008
Australia	..	1.61	..	1.47	..	1.51	..	1.69	..	1.78	..	2.06	..	..
Austria	1.55	1.60	1.70	1.78	1.90	1.94	2.07	2.14	2.26	2.26	2.45	2.47	2.54	2.67
Belgium	1.67	1.77	1.83	1.86	1.94	1.97	2.07	1.94	1.88	1.86	1.83	1.86	1.90	1.92
Canada	1.70	1.65	1.66	1.76	1.80	1.91	2.09	2.04	2.04	2.07	2.05	1.97	1.90	1.84
Czech Republic	0.95	0.97	1.08	1.15	1.14	1.21	1.20	1.20	1.25	1.25	1.41	1.55	1.54	1.47
Denmark	1.82	1.84	1.92	2.04	2.18	..	2.39	2.51	2.58	2.48	2.46	2.48	2.55	2.72
Finland	2.26	2.52	2.70	2.87	3.16	3.35	3.30	3.36	3.43	3.45	3.48	3.45	3.47	3.49
France	2.29	2.27	2.19	2.14	2.16	2.15	2.20	2.23	2.17	2.15	2.10	2.10	2.04	2.02
Germany	2.19	2.19	2.24	2.27	2.40	2.45	2.46	2.49	2.52	2.49	2.49	2.53	2.53	..
Greece	0.43	..	0.45	..	0.60	..	0.58	..	0.57	0.55	0.59	0.58	0.58	..
Hungary	0.72	0.63	0.70	0.66	0.67	0.79	0.92	1.00	0.93	0.87	0.94	1.00	0.97	..
Iceland	1.53	..	1.83	2.00	2.30	2.67	2.95	2.95	2.82	..	2.77	2.99	2.70	2.65
Ireland	1.26	1.30	1.27	1.24	1.18	1.12	1.10	1.10	1.17	1.23	1.25	1.25	1.28	1.43
Italy	0.97	0.99	1.03	1.05	1.02	1.05	1.09	1.13	1.11	1.10	1.09	1.13	1.18	1.18
Japan	2.92	2.81	2.87	3.00	3.02	3.04	3.12	3.17	3.20	3.17	3.32	3.40	3.44	..
Korea	2.27	2.33	2.38	2.25	2.16	2.30	2.47	2.40	2.49	2.68	2.79	3.01	3.21	..
Luxembourg	..	..	..	..	..	1.65	..	1.65	1.63	1.56	1.65	1.57	1.62	
Mexico	0.28	0.28	0.31	0.34	0.39	0.34	0.36	0.40	0.40	0.40	0.41	0.39	0.37	..
Netherlands	1.97	1.98	1.99	1.90	1.96	1.82	1.80	1.72	1.76	1.81	1.79	1.78	1.71	..
New Zealand	0.95	..	1.09	..	1.00	..	1.14	..	1.19	..	1.16	..	1.21	..
Norway	1.69	..	1.63	..	1.64	..	1.59	1.66	1.71	1.59	1.52	1.52	1.64	1.62
Poland	0.63	0.65	0.65	0.67	0.69	0.64	0.62	0.56	0.54	0.56	0.57	0.56	0.57	0.61
Portugal	0.54	0.57	0.59	0.65	0.71	0.76	0.80	0.76	0.74	0.77	0.81	1.02	1.21	1.51
Slovak Republic	0.92	0.91	1.08	0.78	0.66	0.65	0.63	0.57	0.57	0.51	0.51	0.49	0.46	0.47
Spain	0.79	0.81	0.80	0.87	0.86	0.91	0.91	0.99	1.05	1.06	1.12	1.20	1.27	1.35
Sweden	3.26	..	3.48	..	3.61	..	4.17	..	3.85	3.62	3.60	3.74	3.61	3.75
Switzerland	..	2.65	..	..	..	2.53	..	..	..	2.90	..	..	..	..
Turkey	0.28	0.34	0.37	0.37	0.47	0.48	0.54	0.53	0.48	0.52	0.59	0.58	0.72	..
United Kingdom	1.91	1.83	1.77	1.76	1.82	1.81	1.79	1.79	1.75	1.69	1.73	1.76	1.82	1.88
United States	2.50	2.54	2.57	2.60	2.64	2.71	2.72	2.62	2.61	2.54	2.57	2.61	2.66	2.77
EU27 total	1.66	1.66	1.66	1.67	1.72	1.74	1.75	1.76	1.75	1.73	1.74	1.76	1.77	..
OECD total	2.05	2.08	2.10	2.12	2.16	2.19	2.23	2.20	2.20	2.17	2.21	2.24	2.28	..
Brazil	0.80	0.72	..	..	..	1.02	1.04	0.98	0.96	0.90	0.97	1.00	1.10	1.13
Chile	..	..	..	..	..	..	..	0.68	0.67	0.67	..	..	..	..
China	0.57	0.57	0.64	0.65	0.76	0.90	0.95	1.07	1.13	1.23	1.34	1.42	1.44	..
Estonia	..	..	..	0.57	0.68	0.60	0.70	0.72	0.77	0.85	0.93	1.14	1.11	1.27
India	..	0.69	0.71	0.76	0.77	0.81	0.84	0.81	0.80	0.79	0.84	0.88	0.87	0.88
Israel	2.57	2.74	3.00	3.14	3.58	4.32	4.60	4.59	4.32	4.26	4.37	4.40	4.76	4.86
Russian Federation	0.85	0.97	1.04	0.95	1.00	1.05	1.18	1.25	1.28	1.15	1.07	1.07	1.12	1.03
Slovenia	1.53	1.29	1.28	1.34	1.37	1.39	1.50	1.47	1.27	1.40	1.44	1.56	1.45	1.66
South Africa	..	..	0.60	..	..	..	0.73	..	0.80	0.86	0.92	0.95	..	..

StatLink ᵫᶳᵇ http://dx.doi.org/10.1787/825643730162

Gross domestic expenditure on R&D
As a percentage of GDP

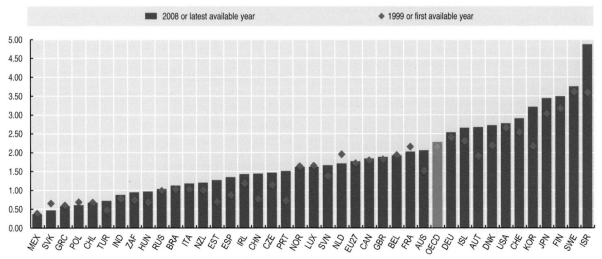

StatLink ᵫᶳᵇ http://dx.doi.org/10.1787/820860264335

RESEARCHERS

Researchers are the central element of the research and development system.

Definition

Researchers are professionals engaged in the conception and creation of new knowledge, products, processes, methods and systems, as well as those who are directly involved in the management of projects. They include researchers working in both civil and military research in government, universities and research institutes as well as in the business sector.

The number of researchers is measured in full-time equivalent (i.e. a person working half-time on R&D is counted as 0.5 person-year) and expressed per thousand people employed in each country. The number of researchers includes staff engaged in R&D during the course of one year.

Comparability

The data on researchers have been compiled on the basis of the methodology of the *Frascati Manual*. Comparability over time is affected to some extent by improvements in the coverage of national R&D surveys and by the efforts of countries to improve the international comparability of their data.

For the United States beginning 2000, the total numbers of researchers are OECD estimates. Also, data for the United States since 1985 exclude military personnel.

Data for Brazil and India do not fully comply with the guidelines of the *Frascati Manual*, and were compiled from national sources. Data for Brazil and South Africa are likely to be underestimated, as are the data for China before 2000.

Overview

In the OECD area, around 4 million persons were employed in research and development in 2006. Approximately two-thirds of these were engaged in the business sector.

In 2006, there were about 7.6 researchers per thousand of employed people in the OECD area, compared with 5.9 per thousand employed in 1995. This indicator has steadily increased over the last two decades.

Among the major OECD areas, Japan has the highest number of researchers relative to total employment, followed by the United States and the European Union.

Finland, Iceland, Japan, and New Zealand have the highest number of research workers per thousand persons employed. Rates are also high in Denmark, Sweden, Norway and the United States. Conversely, research workers per thousand of employed people are low in Mexico and Turkey.

Among the major non-member countries, growth in the number of researchers has been steady in China although the overall level, at 1.8 per thousand of people employed in 2007, still remains well below the OECD average. The number of researchers per thousand of people employed for the Russian Federation has been falling since 1994 but this level, at 6.4 researchers per thousand employed in 2008, is similar to that of EU countries.

Sources
- OECD (2009), *Main Science and Technology Indicators*, OECD, Paris.

Further information
Analytical publications
- OECD (2009), *OECD Science, Technology and Industry Scoreboard 2009*, OECD, Paris.
- OECD (2008), *OECD Science, Technology and Industry Outlook 2008*, OECD, Paris.

Statistical publications
- OECD (2009), *OECD Science, Technology and R&D Statistics on CD-ROM*, OECD, Paris.

Methodological publications
- OECD (2003), *Frascati Manual 2002: Proposed Standard Practice for Surveys on Research and Experimental Development*, OECD, Paris.

Web sites
- OECD Measuring Science and Technology, *www.oecd.org/sti/measuring-scitech*.
- OECD Science, Technology and Industry, *www.oecd.org/sti*.
- OECD Science, Technology and Industry Scoreboard, *www.sourceoecd.org/scoreboard*.

Researchers
Per thousand employed, full-time equivalent

	1995	1996	1997	1998	1999	2000	2001	2002	2003	2004	2005	2006	2007	2008
Australia	..	7.3	..	7.3	..	7.3	..	7.8	..	8.4	..	8.5	..	..
Austria	..	..	..	5.1	..	..	..	6.3	..	6.7	7.2	7.3	7.8	8.3
Belgium	6.0	6.5	6.7	6.9	7.4	7.4	7.7	7.4	7.4	7.7	7.8	8.1	8.3	8.2
Canada	6.4	6.5	6.6	6.6	6.7	7.2	7.5	7.4	7.7	8.1	8.3	8.3	..	..
Czech Republic	2.3	2.5	2.4	2.5	2.7	2.8	3.0	3.0	3.2	3.3	4.8	5.2	5.3	5.6
Denmark	6.1	6.3	6.5	..	6.9	..	7.0	9.2	9.0	9.6	10.2	10.2	10.4	10.6
Finland	8.2	..	12.3	13.9	14.5	15.2	15.8	16.4	17.7	17.3	16.5	16.6	15.6	16.1
France	6.7	6.8	6.8	6.7	6.8	7.1	7.2	7.5	7.7	8.1	8.1	8.3	8.4	..
Germany	6.1	6.1	6.3	6.3	6.6	6.6	6.7	6.8	6.9	6.9	7.0	7.2	7.3	..
Greece	2.3	..	2.7	..	3.5	..	3.4	..	3.5	..	4.3	4.3	4.4	..
Hungary	2.9	2.9	3.1	3.2	3.3	3.7	3.8	3.9	3.9	3.6	3.8	4.2	4.2	..
Iceland	7.6	..	9.4	9.6	10.3	..	11.7	..	12.2	..	13.4	14.2	12.5	12.9
Ireland	4.5	4.8	5.0	5.1	4.9	5.0	5.1	5.3	5.5	5.9	5.9	6.0	6.0	..
Italy	3.5	3.5	3.0	2.9	2.9	2.9	2.9	3.0	2.9	3.0	3.4	3.6	3.7	3.8
Japan	10.1	9.2	9.3	9.8	10.0	9.9	10.4	10.1	10.6	10.6	11.0	11.1	11.0	..
Korea	4.9	4.8	4.8	4.6	4.9	5.1	6.3	6.4	6.8	6.9	7.9	8.6	9.5	..
Luxembourg	..	..	..	..	..	6.2	..	..	6.7	6.8	7.2	6.4	6.6	6.5
Mexico	0.6	0.6	0.6	0.6	0.6	..	..	..	0.9	1.0	1.1	0.9	0.9	..
Netherlands	4.8	4.9	5.0	5.1	5.1	5.2	5.5	4.6	4.5	5.8	5.7	6.2	5.8	5.8
New Zealand	4.7	..	6.2	..	6.2	..	9.1	..	10.4	..	10.5	..	10.8	..
Norway	7.5	..	7.9	..	7.9	..	8.6	..	9.1	9.1	9.2	9.5	9.8	10.0
Poland	3.3	3.4	3.5	3.5	3.5	3.5	4.0	4.1	4.3	4.4	4.4	4.1	4.0	3.9
Portugal	2.6	2.7	2.9	3.0	3.2	3.3	3.5	3.7	4.0	4.0	4.1	4.8	5.5	..
Slovak Republic	4.6	4.7	4.7	4.8	4.5	4.9	4.7	4.5	4.7	5.2	5.2	5.5	5.7	5.6
Spain	3.5	3.7	3.8	4.0	3.9	4.7	4.7	4.8	5.2	5.5	5.7	5.8	5.9	6.4
Sweden	8.2	..	9.1	..	9.5	..	10.5	..	11.0	11.2	12.7	12.6	10.6	10.6
Switzerland	..	5.6	..	..	..	6.4	..	..	..	6.1	..	..	..	..
Turkey	0.8	0.9	0.9	0.9	0.9	1.1	1.1	1.1	1.5	1.6	1.8	1.9	2.4	..
United Kingdom	5.2	5.1	5.1	5.5	5.7	5.8	6.1	6.6	7.1	7.5	8.0	8.1	8.1	8.3
United States	8.1	..	8.8	..	9.3	9.3	9.5	9.7	10.2	9.8	9.6	9.7	..	..
EU27 total	4.8	4.9	4.9	5.0	5.1	5.2	5.4	5.6	5.8	6.0	6.3	6.4	6.4	..
OECD total	5.9	6.1	6.2	6.4	6.5	6.6	6.9	7.0	7.3	7.3	7.5	7.6	..	..
Brazil	..	..	..	..	..	1.6	1.5	1.5	1.7	1.7	2.0	2.1	2.2	..
Chile	..	..	..	..	..	..	..	..	2.2	2.3	..	..	..	..
China	0.8	0.8	0.8	0.7	0.7	1.0	1.0	1.1	1.2	1.2	1.5	1.6	1.8	..
Estonia	..	..	..	4.9	5.2	4.7	4.6	5.2	5.1	5.7	5.5	5.4	5.6	7.9
India	..	..	..	..	..	0.3	..	..	..	..	0.4	..	..	..
Russian Federation	9.2	8.5	8.2	7.7	7.8	7.8	7.8	7.5	7.4	7.1	6.8	6.7	6.7	6.4
Slovenia	5.6	5.2	4.5	4.8	5.0	4.8	4.9	5.1	4.2	4.3	5.5	6.1	6.3	7.1
South Africa	..	..	..	..	..	1.3	..	1.2	1.5	1.4	1.5	..	..	..

StatLink http://dx.doi.org/10.1787/825648663103

Researchers
Per thousand employed, full-time equivalent

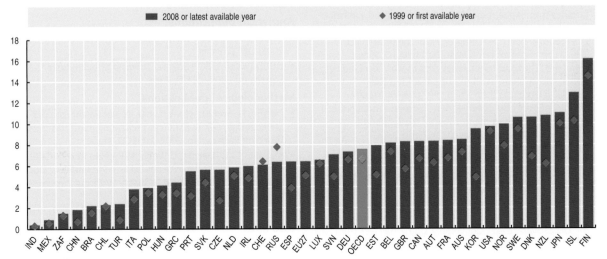

StatLink http://dx.doi.org/10.1787/820871730225

PATENTS

Patent-based indicators provide a measure of the output of a country's R&D, *i.e.* its inventions. The methodology used for counting patents can however influence the results, as simple counts of patents filed at a national patent office are affected by various kinds of limitations (such as weak international comparability) and highly heterogeneous patent values. To overcome these limits, the OECD has developed triadic patent families, which are designed to capture all important inventions and to be internationally comparable.

Definition

A patent family is defined as a set of patents registered in various countries (*i.e.* patent offices) to protect the same invention. Triadic patent families are a set of patents filed at three of these major patent offices: the European Patent Office (EPO), the Japan Patent Office (JPO) and the United States Patent and Trademark Office (USPTO).

Triadic patent family counts are attributed to the country of residence of the inventor and to the date when the patent was first registered.

Triadic patent families are expressed as numbers and per million inhabitants.

Overview

Growth in the number of triadic patent families during the second half of the 1990s was at a steady 5% a year. The beginning of the 21st century was marked by a slowdown, with patent families increasing by 1.6% a year on average. The United States, the European Union and Japan show a similar declining trend.

About 52 000 triadic patent families were filed in 2007, with a sharp increase from less than 41 000 registered in 1997. The United States accounts for 31% of patent families, a lower share compared to the one recorded in 1997 (33.4%). The share of triadic patent families originating from Europe has also tended to decrease, losing more than 3 percentage points between 1997 and 2007 (to 29% in 2007). Although the number of patent families from Japan remained stable since 2000, Japan's share in triadic patent families increased by 1 percentage point, reaching 28.2% of the total in 2007. The origin of patent families shifted towards Asian countries. The most spectacular growth was observed by Korea, whose share of all triadic patent families increased from less than 1% in 1997 to 4.4% in 2007. Strong rises are also observed for China and India, with an average growth in the number of triadic patents of more than 23% a year between 1997 and 2007.

When triadic patent families are expressed relative to the total population, Switzerland, Japan, Sweden and Germany are the four most inventive countries in 2007, with the highest values recorded in Switzerland (118) and Japan (115). Ratios for Austria, Denmark, Finland, Israel, Korea and the Netherlands are also above the OECD average (42). Conversely, China has less than 0.5 patent families per million population.

Comparability

The concept of triadic patent families has been developed in order to improve the international comparability and quality of patent-based indicators. Indeed, only patents registered in the same set of countries are included in the family: home advantage and influence of geographical location are therefore eliminated. Furthermore, patents included in the triadic family are typically of higher economic value: patentees only take on the additional costs and delays of extending the protection of their invention to other countries if they deem it worthwhile.

Share of countries in triadic patent families
Percentage, 2007

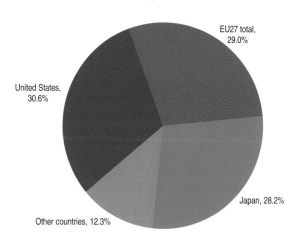

StatLink ⌨ http://dx.doi.org/10.1787/821012825718

Sources
- *OECD Patent Database.*

Further information
Analytical publications
- OECD (2008), *OECD Science, Technology and Industry Outlook 2008*, OECD, Paris.
- OECD (2009), *OECD Science, Technology and Industry Scoreboard 2009*, OECD, Paris.

Methodological publications
- Dernis, H. and M. Khan (2004), *Triadic Patent Families Methodology*, OECD Science, Technology and Industry Working Papers, No. 2004/2, OECD, Paris.
- Maraut, S., H. Dernis, C.Webb, V. Spiezia and D. Guellec (2008), *The OECD REGPAT database: a Presentation*, OECD Science, Technology and Industry Working Papers, No. 2008/2, OECD, Paris.
- OECD (2009), *OECD Patent Statistics Manual*, OECD, Paris.

Web sites
- OECD Intellectual Property Rights, *www.oecd.org/sti/ipr*.
- OECD Work on Patents, *www.oecd.org/sti/ipr-statistics*.

Triadic patent families
Number

	1994	1995	1996	1997	1998	1999	2000	2001	2002	2003	2004	2005	2006	2007
Australia	239	233	234	277	297	317	362	324	347	338	362	373	351	352
Austria	211	221	214	257	269	254	270	255	315	335	378	370	409	418
Belgium	354	373	362	432	396	397	361	336	343	327	415	415	414	425
Canada	370	386	426	531	531	544	535	535	589	576	652	761	740	719
Czech Republic	5	3	11	11	16	10	9	15	16	16	15	14	19	20
Denmark	185	188	227	217	270	233	239	227	233	249	301	314	300	328
Finland	354	317	357	449	443	454	372	348	274	300	338	329	330	321
France	1 924	1 970	2 155	2 209	2 269	2 309	2 278	2 198	2 224	2 276	2 421	2 437	2 460	2 462
Germany	4 424	4 873	5 511	5 680	6 133	5 948	6 079	5 683	5 533	5 747	6 069	6 270	6 224	6 283
Greece	5	2	13	10	12	10	7	6	8	13	9	15	14	13
Hungary	20	25	25	32	18	40	35	31	28	41	44	42	43	46
Iceland	3	6	7	4	6	7	11	4	8	4	2	5	6	5
Ireland	32	31	28	37	38	73	41	51	51	66	69	68	73	78
Italy	627	619	704	735	672	656	680	720	721	717	770	780	783	769
Japan	8 286	9 583	10 673	11 238	11 481	12 664	14 779	13 864	13 574	13 598	13 447	13 899	14 632	14 665
Korea	213	326	323	388	467	576	719	925	1 227	1 715	2 138	2 314	2 465	2 264
Luxembourg	8	14	16	16	22	22	20	24	13	20	24	20	25	20
Mexico	5	12	10	9	9	12	8	11	9	16	14	17	17	17
Netherlands	686	758	806	834	849	903	989	1 190	1 061	1 054	1 060	1 033	1 044	1 043
New Zealand	22	21	31	40	52	47	51	41	60	62	63	59	54	50
Norway	87	87	76	100	93	103	108	90	106	97	105	128	127	124
Poland	5	5	10	9	4	9	9	10	14	11	16	16	17	21
Portugal	2	3	4	8	5	5	4	6	6	7	7	12	11	11
Slovak Republic	1	2	1	5	3	2	2	2	3	5	3	4	5	4
Spain	88	82	92	108	126	124	151	160	163	167	218	201	227	236
Sweden	675	753	912	982	852	870	685	673	698	675	699	753	794	846
Switzerland	731	765	815	822	799	792	832	807	808	847	883	893	897	899
Turkey	2	2	4	3	7	3	4	9	7	7	8	12	20	24
United Kingdom	1 548	1 571	1 665	1 636	1 776	1 689	1 675	1 595	1 639	1 655	1 647	1 707	1 691	1 666
United States	11 260	12 241	13 012	13 919	14 458	14 686	14 348	13 592	14 446	15 239	15 941	16 002	16 047	15 883
EU27 total	11 163	11 820	13 128	13 680	14 191	14 023	13 921	13 548	13 366	13 725	14 531	14 842	14 928	15 062
OECD total	32 372	35 467	38 722	40 997	42 372	43 759	45 664	43 731	44 524	46 181	48 119	49 262	50 238	50 014
Brazil	15	16	19	29	29	29	32	46	43	48	48	51	56	65
Chile	2	2	3	-	2	2	2	5	4	2	5	5	5	6
China	19	21	22	44	47	58	66	103	152	216	244	373	489	587
Estonia	-	-	4	2	2	1	1	2	1	4	-	2	5	5
India	6	10	15	23	32	39	50	94	133	142	140	154	178	192
Indonesia	-	-	-	2	3	1	4	2	2	-	-	1	..	..
Israel	140	159	214	288	298	276	302	320	268	298	354	415	483	494
Russian Federation	53	62	57	70	95	61	69	55	50	52	60	71	67	66
Slovenia	4	7	5	5	12	4	7	6	14	14	12	17	17	18
South Africa	22	24	31	33	36	27	35	24	28	32	29	34	32	31
World	32 746	35 882	39 272	41 655	43 128	44 484	46 484	44 665	45 522	47 333	49 409	50 820	52 031	51 990

StatLink http://dx.doi.org/10.1787/825682522218

Triadic patent families
Number per million inhabitants, 2007

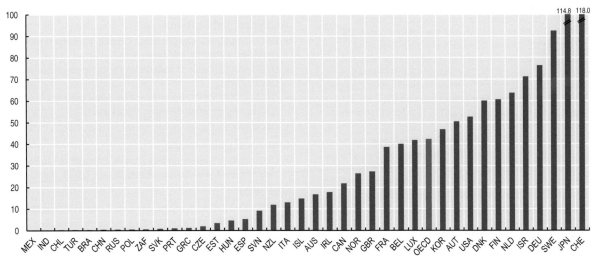

StatLink http://dx.doi.org/10.1787/820878701421

SIZE OF THE ICT SECTOR

Information and communication technologies (ICT) have been at the heart of economic changes for more than a decade. ICT-producing sectors and ICT employment contribute to technological progress and productivity growth.

Definition

The industry-based definition of the ICT sector is based on Revision 3 of the International Standard Industrial Classification (ISIC Rev. 3).

The principles underlying this definition are the following. For manufacturing industries, an ICT product must fulfil the function of information processing and communication, including transmission and display; and they must use electronic processing to detect, measure and/or record physical phenomena or control a physical process. For services industries, ICT products must enable information processing and communication by electronic means. These two measures of ICT production are expressed as a share of the total value added in the manufacturing and business services.

Two measures of ICT employment are shown here: a narrow measure, comprising ICT specialists whose job is directly focused on ICT such as software engineers; and a broader measure including jobs that regularly use ICT but are not focused on ICT per se (these occupations include scientists and engineers, as well as office workers, but exclude teachers and medical specialists for whom the use of ICT is not essential for their tasks). These two measures of ICT employment are expressed as a share of total employment.

Comparability

The existence of a widely accepted definition of the ICT sector is the first step towards making comparisons across time and countries possible. However, this definition is not yet consistently applied. Data provided by OECD countries have been combined with different data sources to estimate ICT aggregates compatible with national accounts totals. For this reason, statistics presented here may differ from figures contained in national reports and in previous OECD publications.

Data for EU countries are based on the International Standard Classification of Occupations (ISCO 88) while data for non-EU countries are based on national classification systems. The classification and the selection of occupations are not harmonised internationally. This implies that the level of the indicators is not directly comparable across countries. Furthermore, there may be differences in ICT usage in occupations, both within and between countries, even when they are based on the same classification.

Overview

In 2006, the ICT manufacturing sector represented between 2.3% and 21% of total manufacturing value added in OECD countries with available data. The average share for the 23 OECD countries for which data are available was 7.2%. The share of ICT services was generally smaller than for manufacturing, being largest in Greece, Hungary, Korea, Portugal and the Czech Republic, and smallest in Ireland, Sweden, France and Austria.

In 2007, the narrow definition of ICT employment (ICT specialists) accounted for between 3 and 4% of total employment in most OECD countries. This share has risen in recent years in most countries, despite the stagnation in the share of ICT sector employment in business sector employment. The broader grouping of ICT-using occupations (including specialists) accounts for over 20% of total employment in most countries.

Sources
- OECD (2009), *OECD Science, Technology and Industry Scoreboard 2009*, OECD, Paris.
- OECD (2008), *OECD Information Technology Outlook 2008*, OECD, Paris.

Further information
Analytical publications
- OECD (2003), *ICT and Economic Growth: Evidence from OECD countries, industries and firms*, OECD, Paris.
- OECD (2005), *Guide to Measuring the Information Society*, OECD, Paris.
- OECD (2006), *OECD Reviews of Risk Management Policies – Norway: Information Security*, OECD, Paris.
- OECD (2008), *OECD e-Government Studies*, OECD, Paris.

Statistical publications
- OECD (2004), *Understanding Economic Growth A Macro-level, Industry-level, and Firm-level Perspective*, OECD, Paris.

Web sites
- OECD Key ICT indicators, www.oecd.org/sti/ictindicators.
- OECD Science, Technology and Industry, www.oecd.org/sti.
- OECD Telecommunications and Internet Policy, www.oecd.org/sti/telecom.

Share of ICT in value added and in employment
Percentage

| | Share of ICT in value added | | | | Share of ICT-related occupations in total employment | | | |
| | ICT manufacturing As a percentage of total manufacturing value added | | ICT services As a percentage of total business services value added | | | ICT specialists As a percentage of total employment | | ICT specialists, advanced and basic users As a percentage of total employment | |
	2006	Percentage point change 1995-2006	Telecommunication services, 2006	Other ICT services, 2006	Percentage point change 1995-2006	2007	Percentage point change 1995-2007	2007	Percentage point change 1995-2007
Australia	2.8	−0.3	4.1	3.9	−1.0	3.6	0.3	20.8	−0.2
Austria	5.6	−1.6	2.9	4.4	0.4	3.0	0.4	20.5	5.5
Belgium	3.5	−0.6	4.0	5.0	2.3	2.9	0.8	21.7	3.0
Canada	4.6	−1.6	4.1	4.6	1.3	4.2	1.2	20.5	−0.1
Czech Republic	5.0	2.2	5.3	3.8	3.2	4.5	..	22.4	..
Denmark	4.8	0.4	2.9	6.0	1.5	4.0	1.1	27.2	6.8
Finland	20.1	11.4	5.0	6.8	4.1	4.4	1.7	24.9	4.9
France	5.2	−1.1	2.8	5.8	0.3	2.6	−0.3	20.1	1.4
Germany	5.6	1.0	3.0	4.5	−0.6	3.1	0.9	21.6	1.2
Greece	3.0	1.2	6.0	0.6	0.8	2.2	0.0	14.9	4.6
Hungary	12.6	7.8	5.8	4.3	2.8	2.7	..	22.6	..
Iceland	..	..	..	..	..	3.1	..	22.5	..
Ireland	11.5	−2.7	2.6	9.9	4.1	2.4	−0.3	20.9	6.4
Italy	4.2	–	3.5	5.2	2.2	2.8	0.4	22.2	1.3
Japan	12.8	0.2	3.3	2.4	1.1	..	..	..	..
Korea	21.1	5.1	5.6	2.7	1.6	..	..	..	..
Luxembourg	..	..	..	..	..	3.2	0.3	30.6	7.6
Mexico	5.6	0.4	3.6	1.2	0.7	..	..	..	..
Netherlands	3.8	−2.4	3.7	7.0	3.2	3.9	0.6	23.4	0.4
Norway	4.6	0.2	3.5	6.0	2.5	4.8	..	23.8	..
Poland	..	..	..	..	..	2.8	..	17.9	..
Portugal	2.8	−1.0	5.5	3.0	0.7	2.8	−0.1	14.3	−2.1
Slovak Republic	..	..	..	..	..	3.5	..	19.1	..
Spain	2.3	−1.5	4.3	4.0	1.1	2.9	0.7	18.6	2.8
Sweden	9.3	1.7	2.7	8.8	2.7	4.9	1.1	24.6	4.2
Switzerland	..	..	..	..	..	5.2	..	23.0	..
Turkey	..	..	..	..	..	1.7	..	11.8	..
United Kingdom	6.0	−2.3	3.9	7.9	2.1	3.2	0.2	28.0	0.3
United States	7.7	−2.6	4.7	4.2	0.3	3.7	0.4	20.2	−1.0
OECD average	7.2	0.3	4.0	4.9	1.6	..	..	..	..
Estonia	5.7	..	5.4	3.2	..	2.6	..	21.8	..
Israel	20.9	..	6.2	13.4	..	..	..	..	..
Slovenia	3.6	..	7.1	4.9	..	3.1	0.3	23.9	4.0

StatLink http://dx.doi.org/10.1787/825710055655

Share of ICT in value added
Share of ICT manufacturing and ICT services value added, 2006

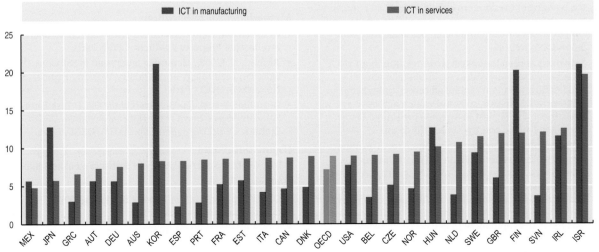

StatLink http://dx.doi.org/10.1787/821048646754

INVESTMENT IN ICT

Investment in information and communication technology (ICT) has been the most dynamic component of investment in late 1990s and early 2000s. This investment has enabled new technologies to enter the production process, to expand and renew the capital stock, and to sustain economic growth.

Definition

Investment is defined in accordance with the 1993 *System of National Accounts*. ICT investment covers the acquisition of equipment and computer software that is used in production for more than one year. ICT has three components: information technology equipment (computers and related hardware); communications equipment; and software. Software includes acquisition of pre-packaged software, customised software and software developed in-house.

The investment shares shown in the table and graph are percentages of each country's gross fixed capital formation, excluding residential construction.

Comparability

Data availability and measurement of ICT investment vary considerably across OECD countries, especially in terms of measurement of investment in software, deflators applied, breakdown by institutional sector and temporal coverage.

In the national accounts, expenditure on ICT is considered investment only if the products can be physically isolated (*i.e.* ICT embodied in equipment is considered not as investment but as intermediate consumption). This means that ICT investment may be underestimated, with the size of the underestimation differing depending on how intermediate consumption and investment are treated in each country's accounts. In particular, it is only recently that expenditure on software has started being treated as investment in the national accounts, and methodologies still vary across countries. The difficulties of measuring software investment are also linked to the ways in which software can be acquired, *e.g.* via rental and licences or embedded in hardware. Moreover, software is often developed on own account. To tackle the specific problems relating to software in the national accounts, a joint OECD-EU task force on the measurement of software has developed recommendations concerning the capitalisation of software. These are now being implemented by OECD member countries.

Note that ICT components that are incorporated in other products, such as motor vehicles or machine tools, are included in the value of those other products and excluded from ICT investment as defined here.

Sources

- *OECD Productivity Database.*

Further information

Analytical publications

- OECD (2003), *ICT and Economic Growth: Evidence from OECD countries, industries and firms*, OECD, Paris.
- OECD (2007), *OECD Communications Outlook 2007*, OECD, Paris.
- OECD (2007), *OECD Science, Technology and Industry Scoreboard 2007*, OECD, Paris.
- OECD (2008), *Broadband Growth and Policies in OECD Countries*, OECD, Paris.
- OECD (2008), *OECD Information Technology Outlook 2008*, OECD, Paris.

Statistical publications

- OECD (2010), *National Accounts of OECD Countries*, OECD, Paris.
- OECD (2008), *STAN Industry Structural Analysis Database on CD-Rom*, OECD, Paris.

Methodological publications

- OECD (2010), Handbook on Deriving Capital Measures of Intellectual Property Products, OECD, Paris.
- Ahmad, N. (2003), *Measuring Investment in Software*, OECD Science, Technology and Industry Working Papers, No. 2003/6, OECD, Paris.
- Lequillier, F. *et al.* (2003), *Report of the OECD Task Force on Software Measurement in the National Accounts*, OECD Statistics Working Papers, No. 2003/1, OECD, Paris.

Online databases

- *STAN: OECD Structural Analysis Statistics – online database.*

Web sites

- OECD Compendium of Patents Statistics 2007, *www.oecd.org/sti/ipr-statistics*.
- OECD Productivity Database, *www.oecd.org/statistics/productivity*.

Overview

ICT shares in total non-residential investment doubled, and in some cases, even quadrupled between 1980 and 2000. These shares then started to decrease, following the bursting of the dot-com bubble. In 2008, ICT shares were particularly high (at 24% or more of the total) in the United States, Sweden and Denmark, while they were below 6% in Ireland.

Software has been the fastest growing component of ICT investment. In many countries, its share in non-residential investment multiplied several times between 1980 and 2008. In 2008, software's share in total investment was highest in Sweden, the United States, Denmark, Finland and the United Kingdom.

In the recent years, software accounted for 50% or more of total ICT investment in France, Finland, Sweden, Japan, Korea, Denmark, the United Kingdom, the United States, Canada, Switzerland and Netherlands. Communication equipment was the major component of ICT investment in Portugal and Greece. IT equipment was the major component in Belgium and Ireland.

Shares of ICT investment in non-residential gross fixed capital formation

As a percentage of total non-residential gross fixed capital formation, total economy

	1995	1996	1997	1998	1999	2000	2001	2002	2003	2004	2005	2006	2007	2008
Australia	19.1	19.9	21.1	21.0	22.6	24.8	23.7	21.2	21.0	16.8	14.9	14.3	13.3	..
Austria	11.3	10.8	11.2	12.6	13.5	13.4	14.0	14.5	13.1	12.4	11.9	12.1	12.3	..
Belgium	18.0	18.4	19.4	21.5	21.7	24.2	23.3	20.3	19.9	20.1	..	..	..	..
Canada	16.8	18.0	17.5	18.8	19.9	20.6	20.2	19.2	18.8	18.5	17.6	17.0	16.5	16.2
Denmark	19.7	18.5	19.8	19.5	21.6	19.9	19.2	22.0	22.1	23.7	24.8	24.5	24.6	..
Finland	19.9	17.5	17.5	18.7	19.4	19.5	17.9	18.5	20.1	19.2	21.2	..	..	..
France	13.9	15.5	17.5	18.7	19.9	19.2	20.5	19.2	18.6	17.6	17.4	17.0	16.1	16.0
Germany	13.3	14.1	14.5	15.3	16.6	17.5	17.8	17.0	15.3	14.8	14.4	14.0	14.1	13.4
Greece	10.0	10.9	11.0	12.4	11.7	12.8	14.3	11.5	10.8	10.9	..	..	..	..
Ireland	10.4	11.4	9.6	11.0	10.1	10.1	9.9	8.2	7.9	7.9	6.2	6.8	5.6	..
Italy	13.0	13.6	14.8	14.1	13.8	14.6	13.6	12.3	11.6	11.4	11.6	10.9	10.6	10.7
Japan	10.8	12.6	12.1	12.0	13.0	15.0	15.1	14.8	14.8	14.6	14.3	13.4	13.2	..
Korea	9.0	10.6	11.8	13.3	14.9	17.0	15.1	13.9	11.8	11.8	12.2	..	..	..
Netherlands	15.7	16.4	17.9	18.9	19.1	19.9	19.9	19.1	20.0	21.3	22.0	22.3	19.5	..
New Zealand	18.9	18.9	20.6	24.4	23.3	26.2	22.4	21.1	21.8	21.6	21.6	22.3	22.3	23.6
Portugal	12.2	12.2	12.0	13.0	13.4	12.4	13.1	11.9	13.6	12.9	12.7	..	..	..
Spain	12.5	14.6	14.5	14.7	14.9	14.7	14.3	13.8	13.6	13.3	12.7	13.0	13.6	13.7
Sweden	24.1	23.3	24.8	27.1	28.7	31.3	28.7	26.3	24.7	24.3	25.6	25.0	..	..
Switzerland	15.7	16.2	17.9	18.0	19.1	18.9	19.3	20.7	20.7	21.9	21.0	20.3	..	..
United Kingdom	23.0	25.1	23.8	25.6	27.2	30.0	28.0	26.5	24.5	25.0	24.6	24.7	23.8	..
United States	27.2	27.8	28.9	29.1	30.6	32.0	30.3	29.1	28.9	28.1	26.5	25.6	26.0	26.3

StatLink http://dx.doi.org/10.1787/825718115232

Shares of ICT investment in non-residential gross fixed capital formation

As a percentage of total non-residential gross fixed capital formation, total economy, 2008 or latest available year

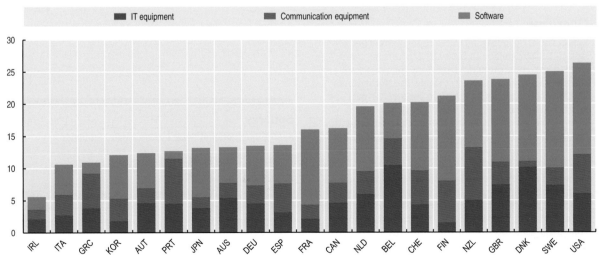

StatLink http://dx.doi.org/10.1787/821147776225

EXPORTS OF ICT EQUIPMENT

Information and communication (ICT) goods have been among the most dynamic components of international trade over the last decade.

Definition

The ICT commodities trade list is defined according to the OECD definition (OECD, 2009b) based on the 2002 version of the World Customs Organisation's Harmonized System (HS). Data in this section refer to the value of ICT exports in US dollars.

Comparability

The data for this table are taken from the statistics on international trade. These are compiled according to internationally agreed standards and are generally considered to assure good comparability.

It is however difficult to compare values of OECD ICT goods trade in 2007 with those for earlier years owing to the new HS classification adopted in 2007, which differs radically from earlier revisions. The OECD is developing a correspondence between the HS 2002 and the HS 2007 for ICT goods. Further efforts will be also required to quantify and adjust for the impact of Missing Trader Intra-Community (MTIC) VAT Fraud from the mid-2000s, which mainly affected the movements of ICT goods within the EU.

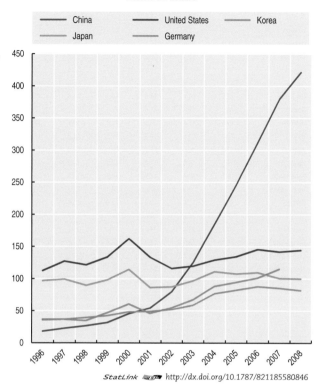

Exports of ICT equipment
Billion US dollars

StatLink ⬛⬛ http://dx.doi.org/10.1787/821185580846

Overview

Exports of ICT goods by all OECD countries reached a total of USD 815 billion in 2008. OECD countries can be divided into three groups; a first group includes the United States, Japan, Germany, Korea, the Netherlands and Mexico, countries with high exports of ICT goods; a second group includes the United Kingdom, France, Ireland, Hungary, Canada and the Czech Republic, with intermediate levels of their ICT exports; the last groups includes all other countries, which are characterised by low values of ICT exports.

Growth of ICT exports has been steady for almost all OECD countries. This growth has been particularly strong for countries that started with a low base in 1998, in particular the Slovak Republic, the Czech Republic, Poland and Hungary.

China has experienced a spectacular growth in exports of ICT goods. Between 1998 and 2008, the value of ICT exports from China has been growing at an average rate of 31% per year. By 2004, China's ICT exports surpassed those from the United States.

Sources
• *ITCS International Trade by Commodity Statistics.*

Further information
Analytical publications
• OECD (2008), *OECD Information Technology Outlook 2008*, OECD, Paris.
• OECD (2009), *OECD Communications Outlook 2009*, OECD, Paris.

Methodological publications
• Guide to Measuring the Information Society, OECD, Paris, *www.oecd.org/dataoecd/41/12/36177203.pdf.*

Web sites
• OECD Key ICT indicators, *www.oecd.org/sti/ictindicators.*

Exports of ICT equipment
Million US dollars

	1996	1997	1998	1999	2000	2001	2002	2003	2004	2005	2006	2007	2008
Australia	2 081	2 162	1 733	1 708	1 893	1 772	1 546	1 672	1 820	1 912	1 927	2 067	2 230
Austria	2 747	3 353	4 097	4 320	4 888	5 040	5 790	6 404	7 199	7 883	8 013	8 895	9 140
Belgium	..	..	..	9 253	11 147	11 885	10 137	12 051	13 029	13 908	12 739	12 201	12 954
Canada	13 043	13 927	13 663	15 015	22 425	14 071	10 693	10 557	12 387	14 581	15 409	15 577	14 813
Czech Republic	711	..	1 074	807	1 396	2 651	4 252	5 312	8 079	8 952	12 778	17 352	21 368
Denmark	2 618	..	3 319	3 536	3 739	3 623	4 878	4 443	4 826	6 019	5 493	5 040	4 393
Finland	5 281	6 213	7 888	8 541	10 783	8 591	8 965	10 082	10 465	13 293	13 310	14 060	14 471
France	23 209	25 344	29 264	29 368	32 673	27 089	24 574	24 344	27 977	28 420	32 678	27 493	26 677
Germany	35 374	36 250	38 905	41 942	48 027	48 794	51 777	58 715	76 444	82 070	87 620	85 045	81 490
Greece	154	195	249	309	476	366	341	425	558	522	668	611	721
Hungary	498	3 079	4 445	5 602	7 289	7 286	8 841	10 948	15 757	16 005	17 926	21 397	24 656
Iceland	..	..	1	1	2	2	2	3	2	4	6	8	10
Ireland	16 590	19 012	21 712	27 079	29 455	32 011	28 676	23 868	24 922	26 107	25 473	24 527	21 592
Italy	10 886	9 730	9 871	9 852	10 836	10 774	9 432	10 030	11 637	11 791	11 579	11 394	10 508
Japan	96 553	99 060	89 345	97 610	113 763	86 088	87 088	96 460	110 610	107 101	109 099	100 255	99 471
Korea	36 246	36 244	34 300	46 452	60 317	45 721	54 407	66 996	88 118	94 141	100 879	114 521	..
Luxembourg	..	..	..	985	1 015	1 467	1 248	1 068	1 167	1 303	1 000	1 099	784
Mexico	15 497	18 975	22 910	27 858	35 251	35 440	33 763	32 352	37 558	39 036	47 385	48 346	57 642
Netherlands	25 170	31 781	31 278	35 157	39 594	34 010	29 508	44 478	55 612	60 981	64 275	70 103	63 687
New Zealand	203	241	231	213	242	235	256	293	361	380	385	430	421
Norway	989	1 133	1 171	1 179	1 134	1 209	996	1 052	1 210	1 335	1 536	1 732	2 174
Poland	627	850	1 230	1 175	1 357	1 638	2 011	2 453	2 989	3 745	5 786	8 210	12 275
Portugal	1 145	1 098	1 166	1 494	1 527	1 746	1 736	2 391	2 578	2 993	3 699	4 073	3 867
Slovak Republic	..	234	327	358	395	496	503	861	1 708	3 024	5 259	8 478	11 869
Spain	4 326	4 521	5 042	5 481	5 457	5 433	5 234	6 757	7 228	7 411	7 516	6 861	..
Sweden	10 683	11 868	12 471	12 912	15 593	8 771	9 854	10 687	14 275	15 294	15 891	15 365	16 911
Switzerland	2 649	2 433	2 649	3 055	3 356	2 895	2 269	2 577	3 074	3 682	3 292	3 338	3 687
Turkey	447	588	976	870	1 029	1 071	1 623	2 016	2 956	3 248	3 202	2 907	2 433
United Kingdom	40 596	43 794	44 857	45 302	51 693	49 509	48 491	38 940	39 706	42 926	49 944	35 525	29 495
United States	112 123	126 869	121 198	133 271	161 976	133 096	115 633	119 332	128 915	133 928	145 195	141 610	144 033
OECD total	460 450	498 951	505 372	570 704	678 728	582 783	564 522	607 567	713 165	751 996	809 963	804 517	815 153
Brazil	..	1 035	1 014	1 269	2 253	2 349	2 197	2 130	2 042	3 735	4 004	2 676	3 168
Chile	..	42	45	52	47	60	60	41	43	53	57	82	92
China	17 854	22 357	26 356	31 354	45 317	54 144	79 637	125 015	185 002	245 943	311 858	379 690	421 052
Estonia	151	322	429	410	969	854	581	824	1 026	1 337	1 278	722	729
India	747	675	451	511	737	911	842	1 095	1 235	1 327	1 536	1 793	1 849
Indonesia	3 250	2 885	2 338	3 091	7 620	6 163	6 331	5 707	6 550	6 971	6 170	6 053	6 540
Israel	3 078	3 732	4 159	4 891	6 806	5 913	4 506	4 382	5 248	3 367	3 638	1 564	6 524
Russian Federation	..	677	370	538	521	436	403	421	548	516	888	916	1 098
Slovenia	193	172	175	135	174	212	232	273	292	249	308	411	644
South Africa	..	..	..	..	422	447	399	471	594	609	760	859	817

StatLink http://dx.doi.org/10.1787/825851135382

Exports of ICT equipment
Million US dollars, 2008 or latest available year

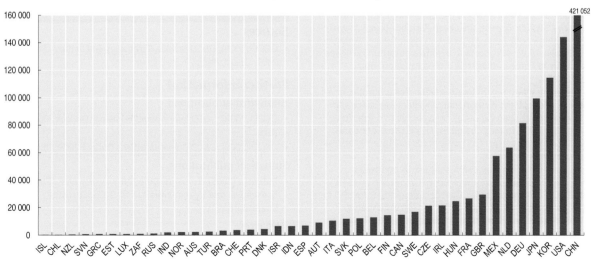

StatLink http://dx.doi.org/10.1787/821156650656

COMPUTER, INTERNET AND TELECOMMUNICATION

Communication access and computers are increasingly present in homes in OECD countries, both in countries that already have high penetration rates and in those where adoption has lagged.

Definition

For access to home computers, the table shows the number of households that reported having at least one personal computer in working order in their home. The second part of the table shows the percentage of households who reported that they had access to the Internet. In almost all cases this access is via a personal computer either using a dial-up, ADSL or cable broadband access.

The table also shows total communication access paths. For OECD countries and China, these refer to the total number of fixed lines (standard analogue access lines and ISDN lines), DSL, Cable modem subscribers and mobile telephone subscribers. For Brazil, India, the Russian Federation and South Africa, total communication access paths are the sum of main telephone lines in operation, ISDN lines, DSL and cable modem subscribers and cellular mobile telephone subscribers.

Comparability

The OECD has addressed issues of international comparability by developing a model survey on ICT use in households/by individuals. The model survey uses modules addressing different topics so that additional components can be added as technologies reflecting usage practices and policy interests change. The ICT access and use by households and individuals model survey is available on the OECD website.

Statistics on ICT use by households may run into problems of international comparability because of structural differences in the composition of households. On the other hand, statistics on ICT use by individuals may refer to people of different ages, and age is an important determinant of ICT use.

Household- and person-based measures yield different figures in terms of levels and growth rates of ICT use. Such differences complicate international comparisons and make benchmarking exercises based on a single indicator of Internet access or use misleading, since country rankings change according to the indicator used.

For telecommunications access, data for OECD countries are collected according to agreed definitions and are highly comparable. The data shown for the nine non-OECD countries were partly collected according to the OECD definitions and partly provided by the International Telecommunication Union (ITU). The definition used by ITU is slightly narrower than the one used by the OECD, although data reported for the two sets of countries can be regarded as broadly comparable.

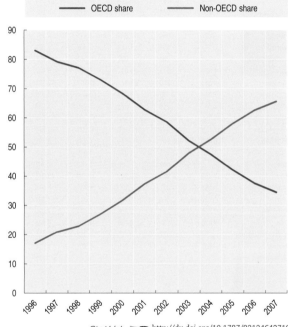

Mobile cellular subscribers
OECD and non-OECD share in the world total

StatLink http://dx.doi.org/10.1787/821246427106

Sources

- OECD (2009), *OECD Science, Technology and Industry Scoreboard 2009*, OECD, Paris.

Further information

Analytical publications

- OECD (2008), *OECD Information Technology Outlook 2008*, OECD, Paris.
- OECD (2009), *OECD Communications Outlook 2009*, OECD, Paris.

Statistical publications

- Eurostat (2005), *Eurostat community survey on ICT usage in households and by individuals*, May 2005, Eurostat, Luxemboug.

Web sites

- OECD Science, Technology and Industry, *www.oecd.org/sti*.
- OECD Telecommunications and Internet Policy, *www.oecd.org/sti/telecom*.

Overview

ICT penetration rates are highest in Iceland, the Netherlands, Japan, Denmark, Sweden, Norway and Korea, where 80% or more of households had access to a home computer by 2007. On the other hand, shares in Turkey, Mexico, Greece, the Czech Republic and Portugal were below 50%. Between 2001 and 2007, the percentages of households with access to a home computer increased sharply in France, Japan, the United Kingdom and Germany.

The picture with regard to Internet access is similar. In Korea, Iceland, the Netherlands, Sweden, Denmark and Norway, more than 75% of all households had Internet access in 2007. In Mexico and Brazil, on the other hand, less than one quarter of all households had Internet access in the same year.

Access to telecommunications networks continues to expand in all OECD countries. Access increased by 164% in the OECD area as a whole in last decade, going from 59.5 to 156.7 telecommunications paths per 100 inhabitants. Growth rates in telecommunication paths were ever higher in China (which experienced growth in access penetration of a 986% in the last decade), Mexico (654%), the Russian Federation (521 %) and Estonia (341%).

Households with access to home computers, Internet and telephone

	Percentage of households with access to a home computer				Percentage of households with access to the Internet				Number of telecommunication access paths per 100 inhabitants			
	2000	2005	2007	2008	2000	2005	2007	2008	1995	2000	2005	2007
Australia	53.0	70.0	75.0	..	32.0	60.0	67.0	..	62.3	96.1	147.8	167.3
Austria	34.0	63.1	70.7	75.9	19.0	46.7	59.6	68.9	51.6	120.2	152.2	170.4
Belgium	..	..	67.2	70.0	..	50.2	60.2	63.6	48.3	100.0	150.5	159.5
Canada	55.2	72.0	78.4	..	42.6	64.3	72.7	..	68.8	96.7	138.3	153.1
Czech Republic	..	30.0	43.4	52.4	..	19.1	35.1	45.9	23.7	80.3	147.5	161.1
Denmark	65.0	83.8	83.0	85.5	46.0	74.9	78.1	81.9	77.2	124.4	174.6	190.8
Finland	47.0	64.0	74.0	75.8	30.0	54.1	68.8	72.4	75.5	131.7	168.3	179.2
France	27.0	..	61.6	68.4	11.9	..	49.2	62.3	57.8	97.9	136.1	152.0
Germany	47.3	69.9	78.6	81.8	16.4	61.6	70.7	74.9	53.7	107.2	156.4	187.0
Greece	..	32.6	40.2	44.0	..	21.7	25.4	31.0	51.1	107.1	163.3	202.9
Hungary	..	42.3	53.5	58.8	..	22.1	38.4	48.4	24.1	65.3	128.3	154.8
Iceland	..	89.3	89.1	91.9	..	84.4	83.7	87.7	67.2	134.4	179.5	183.3
Ireland	32.4	54.9	65.5	70.3	20.4	47.2	57.3	63.0	40.1	96.3	148.7	172.7
Italy	29.4	45.7	53.4	56.0	18.8	38.6	43.4	46.9	50.7	117.5	174.6	203.5
Japan	50.5	80.5	85.0	85.9	..	57.0	62.1	63.9	58.5	102.0	134.8	137.1
Korea	71.0	78.9	80.5	80.9	49.8	92.7	94.1	94.3	45.6	113.1	143.4	155.0
Luxembourg	..	74.5	80.0	82.8	..	64.6	74.6	80.1	62.7	125.7	222.6	222.1
Mexico	..	18.3	22.0	26.1	..	8.8	11.9	13.7	10.4	26.9	66.0	88.2
Netherlands	..	77.9	86.3	87.7	41.0	78.3	82.9	86.1	55.5	122.1	161.5	174.1
New Zealand	..	..	..	..	..	..	..	..	56.7	102.2	138.0	162.7
Norway	..	74.2	82.4	85.8	..	64.0	77.6	84.0	78.6	125.8	164.7	170.6
Poland	..	40.1	53.7	58.9	..	30.4	41.0	47.6	15.2	46.2	107.3	141.9
Portugal	27.0	42.5	48.3	49.8	8.0	31.5	39.6	46.0	39.2	102.3	152.7	170.7
Slovak Republic	..	46.7	55.4	63.2	..	23.0	46.1	58.3	21.1	55.4	108.8	140.0
Spain	30.4	54.6	60.4	63.6	..	35.5	44.6	51.0	40.7	103.7	154.8	171.1
Sweden	59.9	79.7	82.9	87.1	48.2	72.5	78.5	84.4	91.0	139.0	176.8	190.2
Switzerland	57.7	76.5	..	..	..	..	73.9	..	70.2	122.9	165.7	181.1
Turkey	..	12.2	..	..	6.9	7.7	..	..	23.7	49.6	89.0	115.9
United Kingdom	38.0	70.0	75.4	78.0	19.0	60.2	66.7	71.1	58.4	114.2	175.4	195.3
United States	51.0	..	..	..	41.5	..	61.7	..	71.4	115.3	154.3	167.5
EU27 total	..	..	64.0	67.9	..	48.4	54.1	60.4	..	..	..	..
OECD average	..	..	..	..	..	..	..	..	51.7	96.1	139.1	156.7
Brazil	..	16.9	24.0	..	..	12.9	17.0	..	9.2	31.6	73.0	..
Chile	17.5	..	..	..	8.6	..	..	..	..	44.1	94.2	112.1
China	..	..	..	..	..	..	..	..	..	11.4	58.5	73.0
Estonia	..	43.0	57.0	..	..	39.0	53.0	..	..	79.3	145.9	191.0
India	..	..	..	..	..	..	..	..	1.3	3.6	12.9	..
Israel	47.1	62.4	68.9	71.0	19.8	48.9	59.3	61.8	..	116.8	165.8	181.3
Russian Federation	..	26.0	..	..	..	25.0	..	..	16.9	24.2	112.7	..
Slovenia	..	61.0	66.0	..	..	48.0	58.0	..	..	..	194.0	188.6
South Africa	..	..	..	..	..	..	..	..	11.1	29.6	82.2	..

StatLink ⟐⟐ http://dx.doi.org/10.1787/825881036804

Households with access to home computers
As a percentage of all households

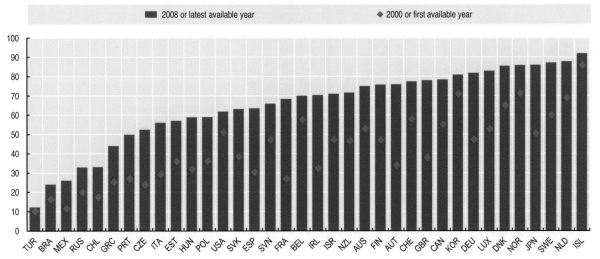

StatLink ⟐⟐ http://dx.doi.org/10.1787/821215531881

ENVIRONMENT

WATER AND NATURAL RESOURCES
WATER CONSUMPTION
FISHERIES

AIR AND LAND
EMISSIONS OF CARBON DIOXIDE
MUNICIPAL WASTE

WATER CONSUMPTION

Freshwater resources are of major environmental and economic importance. Their distribution varies widely among and within countries. In arid regions, freshwater resources may at times be limited to the extent that demand for water can be met only by going beyond sustainable use, leading to reductions in terms of freshwater quantities.

Freshwater abstractions, particularly for public water supplies, irrigation, industrial processes and cooling of electric power plants, exert a major pressure on water resources, with significant implications for their quantity and quality. Main concerns relate to the inefficient use of water and to its environmental and socio-economic consequences: low river flows, water shortages, salinisation of freshwater bodies in coastal areas, human health problems, loss of wetlands, desertification and reduced food production.

Definition

Water abstractions refer to freshwater taken from ground or surface water sources, either permanently or temporarily, and conveyed to the place of use. If the water is returned to a surface water source, abstraction of the same water by the downstream user is counted again in compiling total abstractions: this may lead to double counting.

Mine water and drainage water are included, while water used for hydroelectricity generation (which is considered an in situ use) is excluded.

Comparability

Definitions and estimation methods employed by countries to compile data on water abstractions and supply may vary considerably and may have changed over time. In general, data availability and quality are best for water abstractions for public supply, which represent about 15% of the total water abstracted in OECD countries.

Water abstractions in OECD countries
Year 1980 = 100

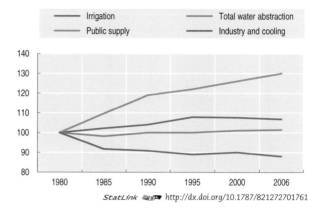

StatLink ᴹˢᴸ http://dx.doi.org/10.1787/821272701761

Sources

- OECD (2008), *OECD Environmental Data Compendium 2006-2008*, updates from the 2008 OECD/Eurostat Questionnaire on the State of the Environment., OECD, Paris.
- OECD (2006), *Environment at a Glance: OECD Environmental Indicators*, OECD, Paris.

Further information

Analytical publications

- OECD, WHO (2003), *Assessing Microbial Safety of Drinking Water: Improving Approaches and Methods*, OECD, Paris.
- OECD (2003), *Social Issues in the Provision and Pricing of Water Services*, OECD, Paris.
- OECD (2003), *OECD Environmental Performance Reviews, Water: Performance and Challenges in OECD Countries*, OECD, Paris.
- OECD (2003), *Improving Water Management: Recent OECD Experience*, OECD, Paris.
- OECD (2006), *China in the Global Economy – Environment, Water Resources and Agricultural Policies: Lessons from China and OECD Countries*, OECD, Paris.
- OECD (2006), *Environmental Performance Reviews – Water: the experience in OECD countries*, OECD, Paris.
- OECD (2006), *Financing Water and Environment Infrastructure: The Case of Eastern Europe, the Caucasus and Central Asia*, OECD, Paris.
- OECD (2006), *OECD Trade Policy Studies – Liberalisation and Universal Access to Basic Services: Telecommunications, Water and Sanitation, Financial Services, and Electricity*, OECD, Paris.
- OECD (2006), *Water and Agriculture: Sustainability, Markets and Policies*, OECD, Paris.
- OECD (2008), *OECD Environmental Outlook to 2030*, OECD, Paris.
- OECD (2008), *OECD Insights: Sustainable Development: Linking Economy, Society, Environment*, OECD, Paris.
- OECD (2009), *Managing Water for All: An OECD Perspective on Pricing and Financing*, OECD, Paris.

Web sites

- OECD Environmental Indicators, *www.oecd.org/env/indicators*.
- The Water Challenge: OECD's Response, *www.oecd.org/env/water*.

Overview

Most OECD countries increased their total water abstractions over the 1960s and 1970s in response to higher demand by the agricultural and energy sectors. However, since the 1980s, some countries have succeeded in stabilizing their total water abstractions through more efficient irrigation techniques, the decline of water-intensive industries (*e.g.* mining, steel), the increased use of cleaner production technologies and reduced losses in pipe networks. More recently, this stabilisation of water abstractions has partly reflected the consequences of droughts (with population growth continuing to drive increases in public supply).

At world level, it is estimated that, over the last century, the growth in water demand was more than double the rate of population growth, with agriculture being the largest user of water.

Water abstractions

	Total gross abstractions Million m³						Per capita abstractions m³/capita
	1980	1985	1990	1995	2000	2007 or latest available year	2007 or latest available year
Australia	10 900	14 600	..	24 070	21 705	18 765	930
Austria	3 340	3 580	3 805	3 450	3 670	3 815	470
Belgium	..	..	..	8 240	7 535	6 390	600
Canada	37 595	42 385	45 095	42 215	..	..	..
Czech Republic	3 255	3 335	3 305	2 495	1 920	1 705	170
Denmark	1 205	..	1 260	885	725	680	130
Finland	3 700	4 000	2 340	2 350	2 345	2 320	450
France	30 970	34 885	39 325	..	32 715	32 550	530
Germany	42 205	..	47 875	43 375	40 590	35 555	430
Greece	5 040	5 495	7 835	8 695	..	..	..
Hungary	4 805	6 265	6 295	..	6 620	5 820	580
Iceland	110	110	165	165	165	165	560
Ireland	1 070	..	..	1 175	..	..	..
Italy	..	..	..	..	41 980	..	..
Japan	85 990	87 210	88 905	88 880	86 970	83 415	650
Korea	17 510	18 580	20 570	23 670	26 020	29 165	610
Luxembourg	..	65	60	55	60	..	..
Mexico	56 005	..	..	73 670	..	78 900	750
Netherlands	9 200	9 350	7 985	6 505	8 915	9 780	600
New Zealand	..	..	..	..	2 510	3 925	940
Norway	..	2 025	..	2 420	2 350	2 475	540
Poland	15 130	16 410	15 165	12 925	11 995	12 025	320
Portugal	10 500	..	8 600	10 850	8 810	9 150	860
Slovak Republic	2 230	2 060	2 115	1 385	1 170	690	130
Spain	39 920	46 250	36 900	33 290	37 070	33 760	770
Sweden	4 105	2 970	2 970	2 725	2 690	2 630	290
Switzerland	2 590	2 645	2 665	2 570	2 565	2 660	360
Turkey	16 200	19 400	28 075	33 480	43 650	42 377	610
United Kingdom	13 515	11 535	12 050	9 550	11 200	9 270	170
United States	517 720	467 335	468 620	470 515	476 800	..	1 690
OECD total	991 400	972 400	986 700	994 100	1 005 300	998 900	860
China	..	..	..	..	..	563 300	432
Israel	..	..	..	..	..	2 199	305
Russian Federation	113 178	117 273	111 100	91 921	80 784	74 633	525
Slovenia	..	..	..	..	..	935	465
World	..	..	..	..	..	..	610

StatLink http://dx.doi.org/10.1887/825886642723

Water abstractions
m³/capita, 2007 or latest available year

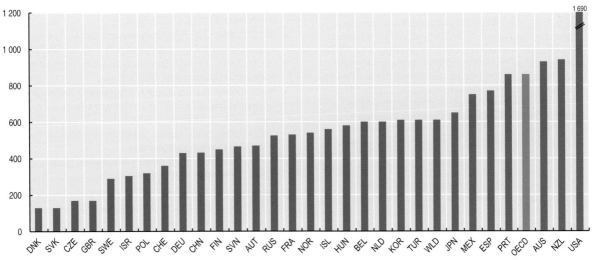

StatLink http://dx.doi.org/10.1787/821246523012

FISHERIES

Fisheries make an important contribution to sustainable incomes, employment opportunities and food protein intake. On the other hand, overfishing of some species in some areas is threatening stocks with depletion. In certain countries, including at least two OECD countries – Iceland and Japan – fish is the main source of protein intake for the local population.

Definition

The figures shown here refer to the tonnage of landed catches of marine fish, and to cultivated fish and crustaceans taken from inland waters and sea tanks. Landed catches of marine fish for each country cover landings in both foreign and domestic ports. The table distinguishes between marine capture fisheries and aquaculture because of their different production systems and growth rates.

Comparability

The time series presented are relatively comprehensive and consistent across the years. Some of the variation over time may however reflect changes in national reporting systems.

Fish landings in domestic and foreign ports
As a percentage of OECD total, 2007

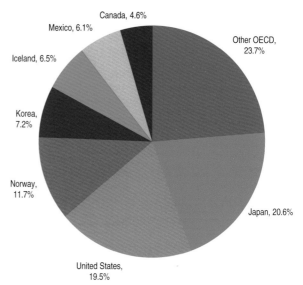

Canada, 4.6%
Mexico, 6.1%
Iceland, 6.5%
Korea, 7.2%
Norway, 11.7%
Other OECD, 23.7%
Japan, 20.6%
United States, 19.5%

StatLink ⬛🇬🇧 http://dx.doi.org/10.1787/821365470825

Overview

Japan, the United States, Norway and Korea are the largest marine capture fisheries producers, accounting for close to 60% of the total OECD production. Total OECD marine capture production in 2007 increased slightly, to more than 22 million tonnes; this represents a little less than a quarter of the global marine production. Overall, the OECD marine capture production decreased by 2.4% per year over the last decade. Denmark and Poland are the most affected by this decrease. Only Germany, Turkey and the Netherlands showed positive growth rates above 1%.

While global aquaculture production has kept increasing as a share of the global aquatic protein supply, total OECD aquaculture production remained relatively stable at 5 million tonnes. Korea is consolidating its position as the major producer, accounting for 27% of the total OECD aquaculture production.

Sources
• OECD (2009), *Review of Fisheries in OECD Countries: Policies and Summary Statistics 2008*, OECD, Paris.

Further information
Analytical publications
• OECD and FAO (2008), *Globalisation and Fisheries – Proceedings of an OECD-FAO Workshop*, OECD, Paris.
• OECD (2003), *Liberalising Fisheries Markets: Scope and Effects*, OECD, Paris.
• OECD (2003), *The Costs of Managing Fisheries*, OECD, Paris.
• OECD (2004), *Fish Piracy: Combating Illegal, Unreported and Unregulated Fishing*, OECD, Paris.
• OECD (2005), *Why Fish Piracy Persists: The Economics of Illegal, Unreported and Unregulated Fishing*, OECD, Paris.
• OECD (2006), *Financial Support to Fisheries: Implications for Sustainable Development*, OECD, Paris.
• OECD (2006), *The Development Dimension – Fishing for Coherence: Proceedings of the Workshop on Policy Coherence for Development in Fisheries*, OECD, Paris.
• OECD (2006), *Using Market Mechanisms to Manage Fisheries: Smoothing the Path*, OECD, Paris.
• OECD (2007), *Structural Change in Fisheries: Dealing with the Human Dimension*, OECD, Paris.

Statistical publications
• OECD (2009), *Reducing Fishing Capacity: Best Practices for Decommissioning Schemes*, OECD, Paris.

Web sites
• OECD Fisheries, *www.oecd.org/fisheries*.

Marine capture and aquaculture production
Thousand tonnes

	Fish landings in domestic and foreign ports							Aquaculture						
	1995	2000	2003	2004	2005	2006	2007	1995	2000	2003	2004	2005	2006	2007
Australia	201	185	215	231	237	192	186	24	37	44	51	48	54	60
Austria	..	..	..	..	..	..	..	4	..	..	..	..	..	..
Belgium	29	27	24	24	22	20	22	2	2	..	..	..	..	..
Canada	854	1 008	1 088	1 452	1 020	1 070	983	66	127	157	145	145	171	-
Czech Republic	..	..	..	..	..	..	..	19	19	20	19	20	20	20
Denmark	2 025	1 524	1 028	1 090	913	857	645	45	44	38	43	39	38	40
Finland	106	92	76	89	77	102	117	17	15	13	13	14	13	13
France	616	682	695	663	606	602	474	281	267	240	244	244	238	238
Germany	241	194	222	223	246	259	262	40	45	64	57	57	45	52
Greece	153	93	90	91	90	94	95	33	88	102	98	110	113	110
Hungary	..	..	..	..	..	..	..	9	..	..	..	..	..	..
Iceland	1 603	1 930	1 981	1 730	1 669	1 018	1 399	4	4	6	8	8	10	5
Ireland	379	291	195	306	282	282	219	27	41	63	59	61	87	48
Italy	301	387	312	288	268	286	267	225	228	192	233	234	242	247
Japan	7 450	5 092	4 743	4 515	4 466	4 511	4 417	1 390	1 292	1 306	1 261	1 257	1 224	1 279
Korea	2 322	2 090	1 831	1 752	1 829	1 311	1 550	1 017	667	844	938	1 057	1 280	1 408
Mexico	1 222	1 193	1 303	1 246	1 246	1 244	1 312	158	46	70	80	80	123	128
Netherlands	463	404	391	379	413	469	464	84	92	..	52	68	42	-
New Zealand	567	536	688	633	633	442	427	69	87	87	94	105	108	112
Norway	2 701	2 894	2 702	2 671	2 546	2 402	2 520	278	492	584	637	657	712	830
Poland	241	200	160	174	136	126	133	25	32	32	35	36	35	36
Portugal	242	172	182	163	157	181	196	5	8	8	7	7	8	-
Slovak Republic	..	..	..	..	..	..	..	..	1	1	1	1	2	1
Spain	1 075	1 002	774	687	717	677	752	224	312	313	362	273	273	285
Sweden	379	341	281	262	248	262	246	8	6	7	7	7	9	-
Switzerland	..	..	..	..	..	..	..	1	..	..	..	..	..	..
Turkey	577	461	463	505	380	489	589	22	79	79	94	118	129	140
United Kingdom	912	748	575	654	670	614	888	92	144	212	202	152	157	148
United States	4 783	4 245	4 402	4 492	3 641	4 374	4 188	413	373	420	408	408	360	-
OECD total	29 442	25 791	24 421	24 320	22 512	21 884	22 348	4 582	4 548	4 902	5 148	5 206	5 385	5 141
Chile	7 684	4 547	3 921	5 317	4 738	4 462	4 133	206	425	607	696	739	836	804
Estonia	129	110	79	75	96	90	98	-	-	-	-	1	1	1
Israel	5	6	4	3	4	4	3	14	20	21	22	22	22	21
Russian Federation	..	4 289	3 426	3 174	..	..	..	..	205	289	302	..	..	..
Slovenia	2	2	1	1	1	1	1	1	1	1	2	1	1	1

StatLink ⟋⟋⟍⟍ http://dx.doi.org/10.1787/826000788474

Fish landings in domestic and foreign ports
Average annual growth in percentage, 1997-2007 or latest available period

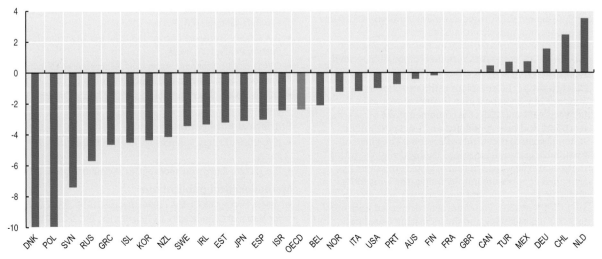

StatLink ⟋⟋⟍⟍ http://dx.doi.org/10.1787/821345622234

EMISSIONS OF CARBON DIOXIDE

Carbon dioxide (CO_2) makes up the largest share of greenhouse gases. The addition of man-made greenhouse gases to the atmosphere disturbs the earth's radiative balance (*i.e.* the balance between the solar energy that the earth absorbs and radiates back into space). This is leading to an increase in the earth's surface temperature and to related effects on climate, sea level and world agriculture.

Definition

The table refers to emissions of CO_2 from burning oil, coal and gas for energy use. Carbon dioxide also enters the atmosphere from burning wood and waste materials and from some industrial processes such as cement production. However, emissions of CO_2 from these other sources are a relatively small part of global emissions, and are not included in the statistics shown here. The *Revised 1996 IPCC Guidelines for National Greenhouse Gas Inventories* (see below) provide a fuller, technical definition of how CO_2 emissions have been estimated for this table. The forecasts provided in the table refer to the Reference Scenario of the *World Energy Outlook*.

Comparability

These emissions estimates are affected by the quality of the underlying energy data. For example, some countries, both OECD and non-OECD, have trouble reporting information on bunker fuels and incorrectly define bunkers as fuel used abroad by their own ships and planes. Since emissions from bunkers are excluded from the national totals, this affects the comparability of the estimates across countries. On the other hand, since these estimates have been made using the same method and emission factors for all countries, in general, the comparability across countries is quite good.

Overview

Global emissions of carbon dioxide have risen by 105%, or on average 2.0% per year, since 1971. They are projected to rise by another 39% by 2030, or by 1.4% per year. In 1971, the current OECD countries were responsible for 66% of the world CO_2 emissions. As a consequence of rapidly rising emissions in the developing world, the OECD contribution to the total fell to 45% in 2007, and is expected to fall further to 31% by 2030. By far, the largest increases in non-OECD countries occurred in Asia, where China's emissions of CO_2 from fuel combustion have risen by 5.8% per annum between 1971 and 2007. The use of coal in China increased the levels of CO_2 emissions by 5.2 billion tonnes over the 36 years to 2007.

Two significant downturns in OECD CO_2 emissions occurred following the oil shocks of the mid-1970s and early 1980s. Emissions from the economies in transition declined over the last decade, helping to offset the OECD increases between 1990 and the present. However, this decline did not stabilise global emissions as emissions in developing countries continued to grow. With the current economic crisis, early indicators suggest that growth in CO_2 emissions from fuel combustion slowed in 2008 and may have declined in 2009.

Disaggregating the emissions estimates shows substantial variations within individual sectors. Between 1971 and 2007, the combined share of electricity and heat generation and transport shifted from one-half to two-thirds of the total. The share of fossil fuels in overall emissions changed slightly during the period. The weight of coal in global emissions has remained at approximately 40% since the early 1970s, while the share of natural gas increased from 15% in 1971 to 20% in 2007. The share of oil decreased from 49% to 38%. Fuel switching and the increasing use of non-fossil energy sources reduced the CO_2/total primary energy supply (TPES) ratio by 5% over the past 36 years.

Sources

- IEA (2009), *CO_2 Emissions from Fuel Combustion: 2009 Edition*, IEA, Paris.
- IEA (2009), *World Energy Outlook 2009*, IEA, Paris.

Further information

Analytical publications

- ECMT (2007), *Cutting Transport CO_2 Emissions: What Progress?*, ECMT, Paris.
- IEA (2008), *CO_2 Capture and Storage: A Key Carbon Abatement Option 2008*, IEA, Paris.
- IEA (2008), *Energy Technology Perspectives: Scenarios and Strategies to 2050*, IEA, Paris.
- IEA (2009), *Energy Technology Transitions for Industry: Strategies for the Next Industrial Revolution*, IEA, Paris.
- IEA (2009), *IEA Scoreboard 2009: 35 Key Energy Trends over 35 Years*, IEA, Paris.
- IEA (2009), *Sectoral Approaches in Electricity – Building Bridges to a Safe Climate*, IEA, Paris.
- IEA (2009), *Transport Energy and CO_2: Moving towards Sustainability*, IEA, Paris.
- OECD (2008), *Economic Aspects of Adaptation to Climate Change: Costs, Benefits and Policy Instruments*, OECD, Paris.
- OECD (2008), *Space Technologies and Climate Change*, OECD, Paris.

Statistical publications

- IEA (2009), *Energy Balances of Non-OECD Countries*, IEA, Paris.
- IEA (2009), *Energy Balances of OECD Countries*, IEA, Paris.

Methodological publications

- WMO, UNEP, OECD, IEA (1996), *Revised 1996 IPCC Guidelines for National Greenhouse Gas Inventories*, IPCC/OECD/IEA, Paris.

Online databases

- *CO_2 Emissions from Fuel Combustion.*

CO_2 emissions from fuel combustion
Million tonnes

	1971	1990	1997	1998	1999	2000	2001	2002	2003	2004	2005	2006	2007	2030
Australia	144	260	303	323	332	339	351	359	360	368	386	391	396	..
Austria	49	56	62	63	61	61	65	68	73	74	74	74	70	..
Belgium	117	108	118	121	117	119	119	112	120	117	113	110	106	..
Canada	339	432	497	500	511	533	526	533	555	551	556	538	573	..
Czech Republic	151	155	124	118	111	122	122	117	121	122	120	121	122	..
Denmark	55	50	61	57	54	50	51	51	56	51	47	55	50	..
Finland	40	54	60	57	56	54	59	62	72	67	55	67	64	..
France	432	352	362	385	378	377	384	376	385	385	388	378	369	..
Germany	979	950	867	860	829	827	845	833	842	843	811	823	798	..
Greece	25	70	79	83	82	87	90	90	94	93	95	94	98	..
Hungary	62	67	57	57	57	54	56	55	57	56	56	56	54	..
Iceland	1	2	2	2	2	2	2	2	2	2	2	2	2	..
Ireland	22	31	35	38	39	41	43	43	42	42	44	45	44	..
Italy	293	398	410	421	422	424	426	433	449	450	454	455	438	..
Japan	759	1 065	1 157	1 126	1 166	1 181	1 167	1 203	1 210	1 211	1 218	1 202	1 236	984
Korea	52	229	418	361	395	431	449	457	459	479	469	477	489	..
Luxembourg	15	10	8	7	7	8	8	9	10	11	11	11	11	..
Mexico	97	293	329	349	342	357	356	364	373	376	404	418	438	..
Netherlands	130	157	173	174	169	173	179	179	184	185	183	178	182	..
New Zealand	14	21	29	29	31	32	34	35	36	36	36	37	35	..
Norway	24	28	35	37	38	34	33	33	35	37	35	36	37	..
Poland	287	344	336	313	304	292	290	280	291	295	294	306	305	..
Portugal	14	39	49	53	60	59	59	63	58	60	63	56	55	..
Slovak Republic	39	57	41	40	39	37	38	38	38	37	38	37	37	..
Spain	120	206	241	249	269	284	285	302	310	327	340	332	345	..
Sweden	82	53	57	58	57	53	52	54	55	54	50	48	46	..
Switzerland	39	41	41	43	43	42	43	41	43	44	44	44	42	..
Turkey	41	127	177	178	177	201	182	192	202	207	216	240	265	..
United Kingdom	623	553	516	520	517	526	539	524	536	536	534	536	523	..
United States	4 291	4 863	5 477	5 475	5 501	5 693	5 673	5 614	5 689	5 772	5 784	5 698	5 769	5 535
EU27 total	..	4 059	3 882	3 882	3 813	3 831	3 905	3 877	3 993	4 003	3 970	3 988	3 926	3 516
OECD total	9 337	11 073	12 122	12 097	12 169	12 492	12 527	12 520	12 755	12 887	12 922	12 866	13 001	12 494
Brazil	91	193	275	283	293	303	312	311	304	321	327	333	347	..
Chile	21	33	55	57	60	56	54	55	58	63	64	66	71	..
China	800	2 211	3 101	3 156	3 046	3 038	3 084	3 309	3 830	4 546	5 058	5 604	6 028	11 615
Estonia	..	36	17	16	15	14	15	14	16	17	16	15	18	..
India	199	589	869	878	942	976	985	1 015	1 041	1 112	1 154	1 244	1 324	3 362
Indonesia	25	140	235	232	253	265	282	291	299	316	331	344	377	..
Israel	14	34	51	50	51	56	57	60	62	61	61	63	66	..
Russian Federation	..	2 180	1 444	1 438	1 474	1 514	1 514	1 505	1 540	1 524	1 531	1 587	1 587	1 928
Slovenia	..	13	15	15	14	14	15	15	15	15	16	16	16	..
South Africa	174	255	299	310	291	299	284	295	321	338	331	332	346	..
World	14 095	20 981	22 684	22 813	22 954	23 497	23 664	24 067	25 110	26 336	27 147	28 028	28 962	40 226

StatLink http://dx.doi.org/10.1787/826007022078

World CO_2 emissions from fuel combustion, by region
Million tonnes

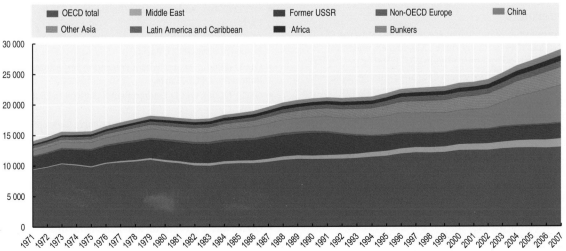

StatLink http://dx.doi.org/10.1787/821401265015

MUNICIPAL WASTE

The amount of municipal waste generated in a country is related to the rate of urbanisation, the types and patterns of consumption, household revenue and lifestyles. While municipal waste is only one part of total waste generated in each country, its management and treatment often absorbs more than one third of the public sector's financial efforts to abate and control pollution.

The main concerns raised by municipal waste are the potential impact from inappropriate waste management on human health and the environment (soil and water contamination, air quality, land use and landscape).

Definition

Municipal waste is waste collected and treated by or for municipalities. It covers waste from households, including bulky waste, similar waste from commerce and trade, office buildings, institutions and small businesses, yard and garden waste, street sweepings, the contents of litter containers, and market cleansing waste. The definition excludes waste from municipal sewage networks and treatment, as well as waste from construction and demolition activities.

The kilogrammes of municipal waste per capita produced each year – or "waste generation intensities" – provide one broad indicator of the potential environmental and health pressures from municipal waste. They should be complemented with information on waste management practices and costs, and on consumption levels and patterns.

Comparability

The definition of municipal waste and the surveying methods used to collect information vary from country to country.

The main problems in terms of data comparability relate to the coverage of household-like waste from commerce and trade, and of separate waste collections carried out by private companies.

Data for Canada and New Zealand refer to household waste only. Data for China do not cover waste produced in rural areas.

Time series data for the OECD total exclude the Czech Republic, Hungary, Korea, Poland and the Slovak Republic. The per capita values for the latest year available cover all OECD countries and are partly based on OECD estimates. EU27 total refers to data provided by Eurostat.

Sources

- OECD (2008), *OECD Environmental Data Compendium 2006-2008*, updates from the 2008 OECD/Eurostat Questionnaire on the State of the Environment, OECD, Paris.
- OECD (2006), *Environment at a Glance: OECD Environmental Indicators*, OECD, Paris.
- OECD (2008), *OECD Environmental Outlook to 2030*, OECD, Paris.

Further information

Analytical publications

- OECD (2004), *Addressing the Economics of Waste*, OECD, Paris.
- OECD (2004), *Economic Aspects of Extended Producer Responsibility*, OECD, Paris.
- OECD (2004), *Toward Waste Prevention Performance Indicators*, OECD, Paris.
- OECD (2008), *OECD Environmental Outlook to 2030*, OECD, Paris.
- OECD (2008), *OECD Insights: Sustainable Development: Linking Economy, Society, Environment*, OECD, Paris.
- OECD (2008), *OECD Sustainable Development Studies: Conducting Sustainability Assessments*, OECD, Paris.

Web sites

- OECD Environmental Indicators, *www.oecd.org/env/indicators*.
- OECD Waste Prevention and Management, *www.oecd.org/waste*.

Overview

The quantity of municipal waste generated in the OECD area has risen strongly since 1980, and exceeded an estimated 650 million tonnes in 2007 (5560 kg per capita).

In most countries for which data are available, increased affluence, associated with economic growth, and changes in consumption patterns tend to generate higher rates of waste per capita. Over the past twenty years, waste generation has however risen at a lower rate than private final consumption expenditure and GDP, with a slowdown in recent years.

The amount and composition of municipal waste going to final disposal depends on national waste management practices. Despite improvements in these practices, only a few countries have succeeded in reducing the quantity of solid waste to be disposed of.

Municipal waste generation

	Total amount generated Thousand tonnes						Generation intensities kg/capita
	1980	1985	1990	1995	2000	2007 or latest available year	2007 or latest available year
Australia	10 000	..	12 000	..	13 200	..	..
Austria	..	..	3 200	3 480	4 260	4 850	590
Belgium	2 760	3 055	3 440	4 585	4 860	5 210	490
Canada	..	..	8 925	7 030	11 280	12 980	400
Czech Republic	..	2 600	..	3 200	3 435	3 025	290
Denmark	2 045	2 430	..	2 960	3 545	4 365	800
Finland	..	..	..	2 110	2 600	2 675	510
France	..	..	26 220	28 250	31 230	34 310	540
Germany	..	..	49 860	50 895	52 810	47 890	580
Greece	2 500	3 000	3 000	3 200	4 450	5 000	450
Hungary	..	..	5 500	4 750	4 550	4 595	460
Iceland	..	..	..	115	130	175	560
Ireland	640	1 100	..	1 850	2 280	3 400	780
Italy	14 040	15 000	20 000	25 780	28 960	32 550	550
Japan	43 940	42 095	50 260	52 225	54 830	52 035	410
Korea	..	20 995	30 645	17 440	16 950	18 375	380
Luxembourg	130	130	225	240	285	330	690
Mexico	..	..	21 060	30 510	30 730	36 865	350
Netherlands	7 050	6 930	7 430	8 470	9 770	10 310	630
New Zealand	880	..	1 140	1 430	1 540	..	..
Norway	1 700	1 970	2 000	2 720	2 755	3 860	830
Poland	10 055	11 090	11 100	10 985	12 225	12 265	320
Portugal	1 980	2 350	3 000	3 855	4 530	5 005	470
Slovak Republic	..	1 900	1 600	1 620	1 710	1 580	290
Spain	..	..	..	18 730	24 730	26 154	580
Sweden	2 510	2 650	3 200	3 555	3 795	4 720	520
Switzerland	2 790	3 400	4 100	4 200	4 730	5 355	710
Turkey	12 000	18 000	22 315	27 235	30 620	30 000	430
United Kingdom	..	..	27 100	28 900	33 955	34 780	570
United States	137 570	149 190	186 170	193 870	216 865	230 555	760
EU27 total	..	..	..	226 530	252 480	258 200	520
OECD total	377 250	405 345	488 960	527 575	589 845	622 685	560
Brazil	..	..	..	..	58 000		
Chile	..	..	..	..	4 680	5 330	325
China	..	..	67 670	106 710	118 190	154 145	115
Estonia	..	..	..	535	600	600	450
India	..	..	..	..	108 000		..
Israel	..	..	..	..	3 970	4 325	600
Russian Federation	22 000	24 800	28 000	50 000	51 850	63 075	445
Slovenia	..	..	..	1 190	1 020	885	440
South Africa	..	..	..	..	..	20 000	420

StatLink 🌐 http://dx.doi.org/10.1787/826022128246

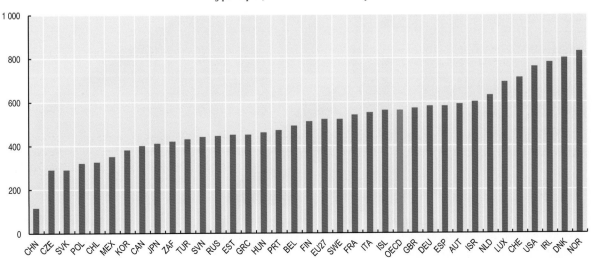

Municipal waste generation
kg per capita, 2007 or latest available year

StatLink 🌐 http://dx.doi.org/10.1787/821457711321

EDUCATION

INTERNATIONAL STUDENT ASSESSMENT

How effective are school systems at providing young people with a solid foundation of knowledge and skills that will equip them for life and learning beyond school? OECD's Programme for International Student Assessment (PISA) assesses student knowledge and skills at age 15, i.e. towards the end of compulsory education. PISA 2006 also assesses the attitudes that students have towards science and the environment, their interest in science, the extent to which they are aware of the life opportunities that science competencies may open, and the science learning opportunities and environment which their schools offer.

Definition

The PISA survey covers science, mathematics and reading. For the 2006 round of PISA, three and a half hours of testing time was in science, two hours for mathematics and one hour for reading. Each student spent two hours on the assessment items.

Scientific literacy is the capacity to use scientific knowledge, to identify questions, to acquire new knowledge, to explain scientific phenomena, and to draw evidence-based conclusions about science-related issues. Mathematical literacy is the capacity to identify and understand the role that mathematics plays in the world, to make well-founded judgments and to use and engage with mathematics in ways that meet the needs of that individual's life as a constructive, concerned and reflective citizen. Reading literacy is the capacity to understand, use and reflect on written texts in order to achieve one's goals, to develop one's knowledge and potential and to participate in society.

Comparability

Leading experts in countries participating in PISA advise on the scope and nature of the assessments, with final decisions taken by OECD governments. Substantial efforts and resources are devoted to achieving cultural and linguistic breadth and balance in the assessment materials. Stringent quality assurance mechanisms are applied in translation, sampling and data collection.

Over 400 000 15-year-old students in 57 participating countries were assessed for PISA 2006. Because the results are based on probability samples, standard errors are shown in the tables.

Overview

The graph shows the results for science in terms of differences from the OECD average score (500, on the left-hand axis). As in the 2003 PISA, Finland is the country topping the league. For Hungary, Sweden, Poland, Denmark and France the science scores are not significantly different from the OECD average. The graph also shows results for reading relative to the OECD average score (492). Cross-country correlations in scores across the two domains are high, but there are also countries displaying significant differences, as in the case of Korea (with better scores in reading than science) and Russia (where the opposite pattern prevails).

The table presents scores by gender. In the case of science, on average, boys are doing slightly better than girls, significantly so in Denmark, Luxembourg, Mexico, the Netherlands, Switzerland and United Kingdom. Girls achieve better results than boys in Greece and Turkey. In the case of mathematics, girls remain at a disadvantage in many countries, with on average gap of 11 score points relative to boys. Conversely, girls report higher reading scores than boys in all countries: on average, across OECD countries, girls are 38 score points ahead of their male counterparts.

Sources

- OECD (2001), *PISA Knowledge and Skills for Life – First Results from PISA 2000*, OECD, Paris.
- OECD (2004), *PISA Learning for Tomorrow's World: First Results from PISA 2003*, OECD, Paris.
- OECD (2007), *PISA 2006: Science Competencies for Tomorrow's World: Volume 1 Analysis*, OECD, Paris.

Further information
Analytical publications
- OECD (2009), *Top of the Class: High Performers in Science in PISA 2006*, OECD, Paris.
- OECD (2009), *Equally Prepared for Life?: How 15-Year-Old Boys and Girls Perform in School*, OECD, Paris.
- OECD (2009), *Green at Fifteen?: How 15-Year-Olds Perform in Environmental Science and Geoscience in PISA 2006*, OECD, Paris.

Methodological publications
- OECD (2006), *Assessing Scientific, Reading and Mathematical Literacy: A Framework for PISA 2006*, OECD, Paris.

Online databases
- *OECD PISA Database.*

Web sites
- PISA Web site, *www.pisa.oecd.org.*

Mean scores and gender differences in PISA 2006

	Science scale				Mathematics scale				Reading scale			
	Males		Females		Males		Females		Males		Females	
	Mean score	S.E.	Mean score	S.E.	Mean score	S.E.	Mean score	S.E.	Mean score	S.E.	Mean score	S.E.
Australia	527	3.2	527	2.7	527	3.2	513	2.4	495	3.0	532	2.2
Austria	515	4.2	507	4.9	517	4.4	494	4.1	468	4.9	513	5.5
Belgium	511	3.3	510	3.2	524	4.1	517	3.4	482	4.1	522	3.5
Canada	536	2.5	532	2.1	534	2.4	520	2.0	511	2.8	543	2.5
Czech Republic	515	4.2	510	4.8	514	4.2	504	4.8	463	5.0	509	5.4
Denmark	500	3.6	491	3.4	518	2.9	508	3.0	480	3.6	509	3.5
Finland	562	2.6	565	2.4	554	2.7	543	2.6	521	2.7	572	2.3
France	497	4.3	494	3.6	499	4.0	492	3.3	470	5.2	505	3.9
Germany	519	4.6	512	3.8	513	4.6	494	3.9	475	5.3	517	4.4
Greece	468	4.5	479	3.4	462	4.3	457	3.0	432	5.7	488	3.5
Hungary	507	3.3	501	3.5	496	3.5	486	3.7	463	3.7	503	3.9
Iceland	488	2.6	494	2.1	503	2.6	508	2.2	460	2.8	509	2.3
Ireland	508	4.3	509	3.3	507	3.7	496	3.2	500	4.5	534	3.8
Italy	477	2.8	474	2.5	470	2.9	453	2.7	448	3.4	489	2.8
Japan	533	4.9	530	5.1	533	4.8	513	4.9	483	5.4	513	5.2
Korea	521	4.8	523	3.9	552	5.3	543	4.5	539	4.6	574	4.5
Luxembourg	491	1.8	482	1.8	498	1.7	482	1.8	464	2.0	495	2.1
Mexico	413	3.2	406	2.6	410	3.4	401	3.1	393	3.5	427	3.0
Netherlands	528	3.2	521	3.1	537	3.1	524	2.8	495	3.7	519	3.0
New Zealand	528	3.9	532	3.6	527	3.1	517	3.6	502	3.6	539	3.6
Norway	484	3.8	489	3.2	493	3.3	487	2.8	462	3.8	508	3.3
Poland	500	2.7	496	2.6	500	2.8	491	2.7	487	3.4	528	2.8
Portugal	477	3.7	472	3.2	474	3.7	459	3.2	455	4.4	488	3.5
Slovak Republic	491	3.9	485	3.0	499	3.7	485	3.5	446	4.2	488	3.8
Spain	491	2.9	486	2.7	484	2.6	476	2.6	443	2.6	479	2.3
Sweden	504	2.7	503	2.9	505	2.7	500	3.0	488	4.0	528	3.5
Switzerland	514	3.3	509	3.6	536	3.3	523	3.6	484	3.2	515	3.3
Turkey	418	4.6	430	4.1	427	5.6	421	5.1	427	5.1	471	4.3
United Kingdom	520	3.0	510	2.8	504	2.6	487	2.6	480	3.0	510	2.6
United States	489	5.1	489	4.0	479	4.6	470	3.9	..	..	..	..
OECD average	501	0.7	499	0.6	503	0.7	492	0.6	473	0.7	511	0.7
Brazil	395	3.2	386	2.9	380	3.4	361	3.0	376	4.3	408	3.7
Chile	448	5.4	426	4.4	424	5.5	396	4.7	434	6.0	451	5.4
Estonia	530	3.1	533	2.9	515	3.3	514	3.0	478	3.2	524	3.1
Indonesia	399	8.2	387	3.7	399	8.3	382	4.0	384	8.7	402	4.2
Israel	456	5.6	452	4.2	448	6.6	436	4.3	417	6.5	460	4.6
Russian Federation	481	4.1	478	3.7	479	4.6	473	3.9	420	4.8	458	4.3
Slovenia	515	2.0	523	1.9	507	1.8	502	1.8	467	1.9	521	1.4

StatLink http://dx.doi.org/10.1787/826022780458

Performance on the science and reading scales in PISA 2006

Mean score

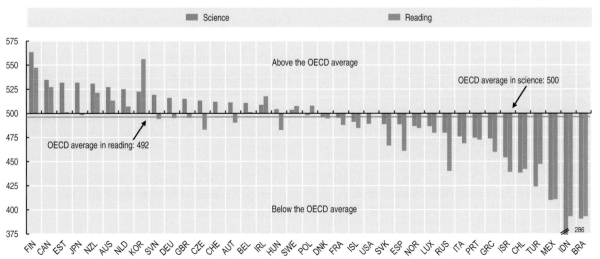

StatLink http://dx.doi.org/10.1787/821466523110

TOP PERFORMING STUDENTS

The rapidly growing demand for highly skilled workers has led to a global competition for talent. High-level skills are critical for the creation of new knowledge, technologies and innovation. They are therefore an important determinant of economic growth and social development. Drawing on data from the OECD's Programme for International Student Assessment (PISA), this entry looks at top-performing students in science.

Definition

Achievement scores are based on assessments administered as part of the OECD PISA programme, which were carried out in 2006 (with a special focus on students' abilities in science). "Students" refers here to 15-year-olds enrolled in secondary education. "Top performers" refers to students who attain Levels 5 and 6 on the PISA science scale,

Level 5 on the reading scale, and Levels 5 and 6 on the mathematics scale.

Comparability

Leading experts in countries participating in PISA advise on the scope and nature of the assessments, with final decisions on this taken by OECD governments. Substantial efforts and resources are devoted to achieving cultural and linguistic breadth and balance in the assessment materials. Stringent quality assurance mechanisms are applied in translation, sampling and data collection.

Over 400 000 15-year-old students in 57 participating countries were assessed for PISA 2006. Because the results are based on probability samples, the standard errors are shown in the tables.

Overview

The proportion of top performers in science varies widely across countries. Across countries, scientific excellence is only weakly related to average performance in the same field. While, across OECD countries, 9% of students reach PISA's Level 5 in science, and slightly more than 1% reach Level 6, these proportions vary substantially across countries. For example, seven OECD countries have at least 13% of the top performers in science, whereas this proportion is only 5% or less in six countries. On average, the proportions of top performers in reading and mathematics are respectively 9% and 13%. In reading, these proportions range from more than 13% in four OECD countries to less than 5% in six OECD countries. In mathematics, two OECD countries have less than 5% of top performers, while 13 OECD countries have more than 13% of top performers. Across OECD countries, 4% of students are top performers in all three subject areas (science, reading and mathematics), while 18% of students are top performers in at least one of these subject areas.

Girls are as likely to achieve top performance as boys. On average, 4.1% of girls and 3.9% of boys are top performers in all three subject areas and 17.3% of girls and 18.6% of boys are top performers in at least one subject area. While the gender gap among students who are top performers in science only is small, this gap is significantly higher among students who are top performers in reading only and in mathematics only. While there is no difference in the average performance in science of boys and girls, boys tend to show a marked advantage among the top performers. In eight of the 17 OECD countries with at least 3% of both boys and girls among the top performers in science, a significantly higher proportion of them are boys. On average, almost half of the top performers in science (44%) were also top performers in reading and mathematics, but this was the case for 50% of girls and for 37% of boys.

Sources

- OECD (2007), *PISA 2006: Science Competencies for Tomorrow's World: Volume 1 Analysis*, OECD, Paris.
- OECD (2009), *Top of the Class: High Performers in Science in PISA 2006*, OECD, Paris.

Further information

Analytical publications

- OECD (2009), *Equally Prepared For Life?: How 15-Year-Old Boys and Girls Perform in School*, OECD, Paris.
- OECD (2009), *Green at Fifteen?: How 15-Year-Olds Perform in Environmental Science and Geoscience in PISA 2006*, OECD, Paris.

Methodological publications

- OECD (2006), *Assessing Scientific, Reading and Mathematical Literacy: A Framework for PISA 2006*, OECD, Paris.

Online databases

- OECD PISA Database.

Web sites

- PISA Web site, *www.pisa.oecd.org*.

Percentage of top performers by domain in PISA 2006

	Science scale		Reading scale		Mathematics scale		Top performers in all three domains	
	Percentage	S.E.	Percentage	S.E.	Percentage	S.E.	Percentage	S.E.
Australia	14.6	0.7	10.6	0.6	16.4	0.8	6.6	0.4
Austria	10.0	0.8	9.0	0.7	15.8	1.0	4.4	0.4
Belgium	10.1	0.5	11.3	0.6	22.3	0.8	5.8	0.4
Canada	14.4	0.5	14.5	0.7	17.9	0.7	7.0	0.4
Czech Republic	11.6	0.9	9.2	0.8	18.3	1.2	5.5	0.6
Denmark	6.8	0.7	5.9	0.6	13.7	0.8	3.0	0.5
Finland	20.9	0.8	16.7	0.8	24.4	1.0	9.5	0.5
France	8.0	0.7	7.3	0.7	12.5	0.9	2.8	0.4
Germany	11.8	0.7	9.9	0.7	15.4	1.0	5.2	0.5
Greece	3.4	0.4	3.5	0.4	5.0	0.5	0.9	0.2
Hungary	6.9	0.6	4.7	0.6	10.3	0.9	2.4	0.4
Iceland	6.3	0.5	6.0	0.5	12.7	0.7	2.8	0.3
Ireland	9.4	0.7	11.7	0.8	10.2	0.8	4.8	0.5
Italy	4.6	0.3	5.2	0.4	6.2	0.5	1.3	0.2
Japan	15.1	0.8	9.4	0.7	18.3	1.0	5.5	0.5
Korea	10.3	1.1	21.7	1.4	27.1	1.5	7.8	0.8
Luxembourg	5.9	0.4	5.6	0.4	10.6	0.5	2.5	0.3
Mexico	0.3	0.1	0.6	0.1	0.8	0.2	0.0	0.0
Netherlands	13.1	0.9	9.1	0.6	21.1	1.1	5.8	0.5
New Zealand	17.6	0.8	15.9	0.8	18.9	0.9	8.9	0.6
Norway	6.1	0.5	7.7	0.6	10.4	0.7	2.7	0.3
Poland	6.8	0.5	11.6	0.8	10.6	0.8	3.7	0.4
Portugal	3.1	0.4	4.6	0.5	5.7	0.5	1.5	0.2
Slovak Republic	5.8	0.5	5.4	0.5	11.0	0.9	2.3	0.3
Spain	4.9	0.4	1.8	0.2	7.2	0.5	0.8	0.2
Sweden	7.9	0.5	10.6	0.8	12.6	0.7	4.1	0.3
Switzerland	10.5	0.8	7.7	0.7	22.6	1.2	5.0	0.5
Turkey	0.9	0.3	2.1	0.6	4.2	1.2	0.4	0.2
United Kingdom	13.7	0.6	9.0	0.6	11.1	0.6	4.9	0.3
United States	9.1	0.7	..	..	7.6	0.8	..	..
OECD average	9.0	0.1	8.6	0.1	13.4	0.2	4.1	0.1
Brazil	0.6	0.2	1.1	0.3	1.0	0.3	0.2	0.1
Chile	1.9	0.3	3.5	0.6	1.5	0.4	0.4	0.1
Estonia	11.5	0.8	6.0	0.6	12.5	0.8	3.9	0.5
Indonesia	..	..	0.1	0.0	0.4	0.2	..	..
Israel	5.2	0.6	5.0	0.5	6.1	0.6	1.7	0.2
Russian Federation	4.2	0.5	1.7	0.3	7.4	0.8	0.6	0.1
Slovenia	12.9	0.6	5.3	0.5	13.7	0.6	3.3	0.4

StatLink http://dx.doi.org/10.1787/826068484665

Top performing students in the three domains in PISA 2006

As a percentage of top performers in science

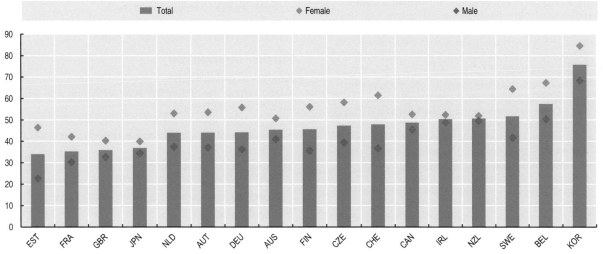

■ Total ◆ Female ◆ Male

StatLink http://dx.doi.org/10.1787/821471061130

EXPECTATIONS FOR SCIENCE-RELATED CAREERS BY GENDER

Gender patterns in education are important for identifying the sources of inequalities in learning, for increasing average performance and for improving understanding of how and why students learn. Gender differences in expectations for science-related careers can be described drawing on data from the OECD's Programme for International Student Assessment (PISA).

Definition

Achievement scores are based on assessments administered as part of the OECD PISA programme, which was carried out in 2006 (with a special focus on science). Students refer to 15-year-olds enrolled in secondary education. Science-related careers include those that involve a considerable amount of science, plus those careers that involve tertiary education in a scientific field as well as some specific careers such as engineer, weather forecaster, optician and medical doctor. Specifically, students were asked "What kind of job do you expect to have when you are about 30 years old?". Answers were then coded using ISCO codes.

Comparability

Leading experts in countries participating in PISA advise on the scope and nature of the assessments, and final decisions on this are taken by OECD governments. Substantial efforts and resources are devoted to achieving cultural and linguistic breadth and balance in the assessment materials. Stringent quality assurance mechanisms are applied in translation, sampling and data collection.

Over 400 000 15-year-old students in 57 participating countries were assessed for PISA 2006. Because the results are based on probability samples, standard errors are shown in the tables.

Overview

Males and females did not have significantly different attitudes to school science. However, when looking at their future aspirations, there are marked differences in their expectations for a science-related career at the age of 30.

On average, across OECD countries, 25% of students expected a science-related career at age 30, with only small differences between boys (24%) and girls (27%). However, when looking at the particular type of science job that students indicated, there are some large gender differences. Across the OECD, 17% of boys who expected a scientific career indicated computer sciences compared to 2% of girls, with no country showing a higher percentage for females. In some countries the difference is very large. In the Slovak Republic, for example, 44% of boys who expected a scientific career chose computer sciences compared to 2% of girls.

There were also large differences between boys and girls expecting to become engineers. Across OECD countries, an average of 30% of boys who anticipated a scientific career expected to be an engineer compared with 10% of girls. This gender difference prevails in all countries, and is especially marked in Ireland (with a difference of 36 percentage points) and Denmark (with a difference of 35 percentage points).

On the other hand there were also occupations which girls reported more frequently than boys. For example, 30% of girls who expressed an expectation for a science-related career named nursing, compared to only 4% of boys. In Belgium, the shares were 44% for females compared with 7% for males. A similar pattern holds for occupations relating to health sciences (including medical doctor, dentists, veterinarians and pharmacists). Across the OECD, 42% of girls who expressed an expectation for a science-related career reported health sciences compared with 20% of males. In France the equivalent figures were 58% for girls and 18% for boys.

Sources
- OECD (2007), *PISA 2006: Science Competencies for Tomorrow's World: Volume 1 Analysis*, OECD, Paris.
- OECD (2009), *Equally Prepared for Life?: How 15-Year-Old Boys and Girls Perform in School*, OECD, Paris.

Further information
Analytical publications
- OECD (2009), *Top of the Class: High Performers in Science in PISA 2006*, OECD, Paris.
- OECD (2009), *Green at Fifteen?: How 15-Year-Olds Perform in Environmental Science and Geoscience in PISA 2006*, OECD, Paris.

Methodological publications
- OECD (2006), *Assessing Scientific, Reading and Mathematical Literacy: A Framework for PISA 2006*, OECD, Paris.

Online databases
- *OECD PISA Database.*

Web sites
- PISA Web site, *www.pisa.oecd.org.*

EXPECTATIONS FOR SCIENCE-RELATED CAREERS BY GENDER

Students expecting a science-related career at age 30 by field of science in PISA 2006

	Share of all students aged 15				Share of students expecting a science-related career, by field:							
					Computer sciences and Engineering				Heath sciences and Nursing			
	Males		Females		Males		Females		Males		Females	
	Percentage	S.E.	Percentage	S.E.	Percentage	S.E.	Percentage	S.E.	Percentage	S.E.	Percentage	S.E.
Australia	27.0	0.7	28.7	0.8	46.3	1.7	8.1	0.5	26.2	1.4	64.9	1.2
Austria	17.8	1.6	22.3	1.2	32.8	3.1	9.9	1.5	18.3	2.4	75.6	2.5
Belgium	25.7	1.0	28.4	0.9	52.9	2.0	13.0	1.1	23.3	1.5	75.4	1.5
Canada	32.7	0.8	41.4	0.9	45.7	1.2	6.5	0.6	31.5	1.3	75.4	1.2
Czech Republic	17.0	1.0	18.0	1.3	57.1	2.7	18.5	4.1	11.7	1.7	64.4	4.1
Denmark	18.9	0.9	24.8	0.9	49.3	2.3	8.7	1.3	24.2	1.8	71.9	1.9
Finland	15.1	0.7	21.1	1.0	40.2	2.8	8.2	1.3	24.6	2.7	76.5	1.8
France	26.6	1.3	29.9	1.0	37.2	2.2	7.4	1.0	25.4	1.9	79.2	1.5
Germany	18.0	0.9	18.8	0.8	39.2	2.3	11.8	1.6	18.8	2.1	66.0	2.5
Greece	23.7	1.1	26.4	1.0	42.4	2.6	19.3	1.8	20.8	2.0	57.0	2.1
Hungary	17.3	1.2	16.2	1.1	66.6	2.8	15.2	2.2	17.8	2.2	68.5	2.7
Iceland	27.4	1.1	37.1	1.1	34.9	2.0	15.9	1.4	33.1	2.2	68.3	1.9
Ireland	28.3	1.2	30.2	0.9	51.4	2.2	9.2	1.4	27.9	2.1	77.5	1.8
Italy	32.3	1.1	31.0	1.0	49.7	2.8	13.2	1.4	25.3	2.6	73.2	1.7
Korea	20.4	0.8	16.6	0.9	44.7	2.7	13.4	1.8	25.6	1.7	72.5	2.9
Luxembourg	23.4	0.8	24.9	1.0	47.4	2.3	15.9	1.5	22.1	1.7	70.0	2.0
Mexico	35.6	1.3	33.6	1.0	52.6	1.4	17.0	1.2	25.4	1.3	60.9	1.8
Netherlands	15.9	0.8	30.0	1.1	39.1	3.1	7.0	1.0	33.7	3.1	83.6	1.3
New Zealand	20.5	1.0	27.6	1.0	41.5	2.3	10.3	1.1	34.3	2.4	70.3	1.5
Norway	20.8	0.9	29.3	1.0	63.8	2.2	18.5	1.8	18.2	1.8	70.4	1.9
Poland	33.9	1.1	28.7	1.0	44.8	1.9	19.2	1.5	14.9	1.2	70.5	1.5
Portugal	35.4	1.4	42.1	1.0	50.9	2.3	12.1	1.1	25.0	1.6	71.9	1.4
Slovak Republic	21.7	1.2	17.5	1.3	62.3	3.0	10.9	2.0	14.9	2.0	75.9	3.1
Spain	25.2	1.0	30.3	0.9	57.7	1.6	14.2	1.1	21.4	1.5	71.6	1.4
Sweden	20.3	1.0	24.6	1.0	37.4	2.4	12.3	1.6	19.1	2.0	65.3	2.2
Switzerland	20.7	0.6	23.2	0.8	49.9	2.3	10.3	1.3	12.7	1.2	67.8	1.9
Turkey	23.1	1.5	25.3	1.4	53.8	2.3	21.3	2.5	32.9	2.5	69.8	2.8
United Kingdom	22.5	0.9	26.6	0.8	45.4	1.8	6.4	0.8	31.9	1.7	75.1	1.5
United States	32.0	1.2	44.4	1.1	40.3	1.7	5.3	0.7	35.1	1.6	80.3	1.3
OECD average	23.5	0.2	27.0	0.2	47.5	0.4	12.4	0.3	24.0	0.4	71.4	0.4
Brazil	28.6	1.1	41.9	1.1	10.1	1.1	4.9	0.8	39.3	2.3	74.2	1.6
Chile	39.8	1.4	40.9	1.8	47.4	1.8	11.7	1.1	31.8	1.6	74.3	1.6
Estonia	21.4	0.9	20.2	1.0	67.7	2.2	29.0	2.0	8.5	1.1	51.2	2.6
Indonesia	17.7	1.3	28.3	1.3	22.9	7.2	13.3	2.9	50.4	9.9	68.4	3.7
Israel	37.5	1.7	40.8	1.2	35.0	3.1	11.5	1.4	38.2	3.0	73.3	1.8
Russian Federation	22.7	1.3	22.8	2.5	64.3	2.8	18.0	2.0	13.6	1.7	67.4	2.5
Slovenia	28.1	0.8	17.6	2.0	44.4	1.8	7.5	1.3	20.2	1.6	74.2	1.8

StatLink http://dx.doi.org/10.1787/826070053352

Ratio of students by science field in PISA 2006
As a percentage of students expecting a science-related career

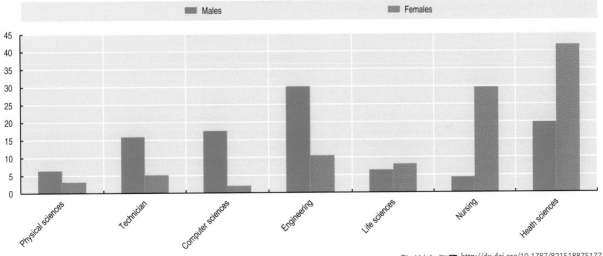

StatLink http://dx.doi.org/10.1787/821518875177

TERTIARY GRADUATION AND ENTRY RATES

Most students are today graduating from upper secondary programmes designed to provide access to tertiary education, leading to higher enrolments in tertiary programmes. Countries with high graduation rates at the tertiary level are also the ones most likely to be developing or maintaining a highly skilled labour force.

Definition

The tertiary graduation rate is the share of each age cohort that will complete tertiary-type A education based on current patterns of graduation; this indicator only includes first-time graduates, and provides a measure of the current output of the tertiary educational system. The tertiary entry rate is an estimate of the share of a youth cohort that will enter different types of tertiary education during their lifetime; it is computed as the sum of entry rates for students by single year of age. The two indicators inform about the rate at which countries produce advanced knowledge.

The data on tertiary education shown here refer to traditional university degrees, i.e. those associated with completion of "type A" tertiary courses. Excluded from these data are shorter and often vocationally oriented courses, which usually lead to direct labour market access (i.e. "type B" tertiary).

Comparability

Graduation is measured by the sum of net graduation rates. For countries that are unable to provide information on net graduation, the data refer to gross graduation rates, i.e. the number of graduates, regardless of their age, divided by the population at the typical graduation age. The graduation rates for countries with a high proportion of international students (e.g. Australia and New Zealand) may be artificially inflated, as all international graduates are considered as first-time graduates, regardless of their previous education in other countries.

Entry rates correspond to the sum of net entry rates for all ages. The net entry rate for a specific age is obtained by dividing the number of first-time entrants to each type of tertiary education by the total population in the corresponding age group. The sum of net entry rates is calculated by adding the rates for each year of age.

Data on graduation and entry rates at tertiary level for the years 1995, 2000-2004 are based on a special survey carried out in January 2007 in OECD countries and four partner economies. The data for the years 2005-2007 are based on the UNESCO/OECD/Eurostat data collection on education statistics.

Overview

Based on current patterns of graduation, 39% of an age cohort in 2007 is estimated to complete tertiary education among the 22 OECD countries with comparable data. This share ranged from less than 20% in Greece to 45% or more in Ireland, Denmark, New Zealand, Finland, Poland, Australia and Iceland. On average, across OECD countries, tertiary graduation rates increased by 18 percentage points over the last twelve years. In virtually every country for which comparable data are available, these rates increased between 1995 and 2007, often quite substantially.

It is estimated that 56% of young adults in OECD countries will enter tertiary programmes during their lifetime, assuming that current patterns of entry continue. In Australia, Poland, New Zealand, the Slovak Republic, Iceland, Sweden and Finland 70% or more of young adults enter tertiary programmes. On average, in all OECD countries with comparable data, the share of young adults who entered tertiary programmes in 2007 is 9 percentage points higher than in 2000, and 19 percentage points higher than in 1995. Entry rates in tertiary education increased by more than 15 percentage points between 2000 and 2007 in the Slovak Republic, the Czech Republic, Australia, Israel and Korea.

Sources
• OECD (2009), *Education at a Glance*, OECD, Paris.

Further information
Analytical publications
• OECD (2008), *Trends Shaping Education – 2008 Edition*, OECD, Paris.

Methodological publications
• OECD (2004), *OECD Handbook for Internationally Comparative Education Statistics: Concepts, Standards, Definitions and Classifications*, OECD, Paris.
• UIS, OECD and Eurostat (2009), *UOE Data Collection – 2009 Data Collection on Education Systems: Definitions, Explanations and Instructions*, OECD, Paris.

Web sites
• OECD Education at a Glance, *www.oecd.org/edu/eag2009*.

Tertiary graduation rates and tertiary entry rates (Tertiary type-A level)

| | Tertiary graduation rates | | | | | | | Tertiary entry rates | | | | | | |
	Sum of graduation rates for single year of age							Sum of net entry rates for single year of age						
	1995	2000	2003	2004	2005	2006	2007	1995	2000	2003	2004	2005	2006	2007
Australia	..	36	50	51	50	50	..	..	59	68	70	82	84	86
Austria	10	15	19	20	20	21	22	27	34	34	37	37	40	42
Belgium	..	..	..	..	..	..	..	..	..	33	34	33	29	30
Canada	27	27	28	29	35	31	..	..	..	..	..	..	..	..
Czech Republic	13	14	17	20	25	29	35	..	25	33	38	41	50	54
Denmark	25	37	43	44	46	45	47	40	52	57	55	57	59	57
Finland	20	41	48	47	48	48	48	39	71	73	73	73	76	71
Germany	14	18	18	19	20	21	23	26	30	36	37	36	35	34
Greece	14	15	20	24	25	20	18	15	30	35	35	43	49	43
Hungary	..	..	..	29	36	30	29	..	64	69	68	68	66	63
Iceland	..	33	45	51	56	63	63	..	66	83	79	74	78	73
Ireland	..	30	37	39	38	39	45	..	32	41	44	45	40	44
Italy	..	19	..	36	41	39	35	..	39	54	55	56	55	53
Japan	25	29	34	35	36	39	39	31	40	43	42	44	45	46
Korea	..	..	..	..	..	..	..	41	45	47	49	51	59	61
Mexico	..	..	..	..	..	..	..	..	27	29	30	30	31	32
Netherlands	29	35	38	40	42	43	43	44	53	52	56	59	58	60
New Zealand	33	50	49	50	51	52	48	83	95	107	86	79	72	76
Norway	26	37	39	45	41	43	43	59	67	75	72	76	67	66
Poland	..	34	44	45	45	47	49	36	65	70	71	76	78	78
Portugal	15	23	33	32	32	33	43	..	..	..	..	..	53	64
Slovak Republic	15	..	25	28	30	35	39	28	37	40	47	59	68	74
Spain	24	30	32	33	33	33	32	..	47	46	44	43	43	41
Sweden	24	28	35	37	38	41	40	57	67	80	79	76	76	73
Switzerland	9	12	22	26	27	30	31	17	29	38	38	37	38	39
Turkey	6	9	11	11	11	15	..	18	21	23	26	27	31	29
United Kingdom	..	37	38	39	39	39	39	..	47	48	52	51	57	55
United States	33	34	32	33	34	36	37	..	43	63	63	64	64	65
OECD average	20	28	33	35	36	37	39	37	47	53	53	55	56	56
Brazil	..	10	15	..	..	..	..	..	..	..	..	..	..	..
Chile	..	..	..	..	..	..	..	..	..	33	34	48	43	41
Estonia	..	..	..	..	..	..	..	..	..	..	..	55	41	39
Israel	..	..	31	32	35	36	37	..	32	41	44	55	56	57
Russian Federation	..	..	..	..	..	..	..	..	..	..	..	67	65	66
Slovenia	..	..	..	..	18	21	20	..	..	..	..	40	46	50

StatLink ⟨⟨ http://dx.doi.org/10.1787/826088613422

Tertiary-type A graduation rates

Percentage of tertiary-type A graduates to the population at the typical age of graduation

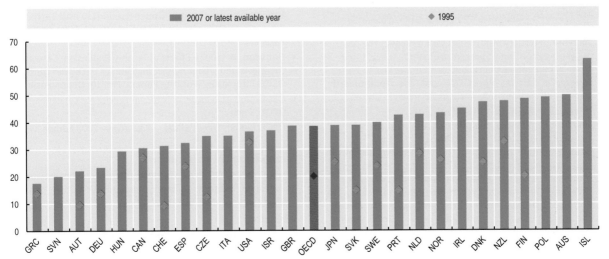

StatLink ⟨⟨ http://dx.doi.org/10.1787/821522348872

EDUCATION ATTAINMENT

A well-educated and well-trained population is essential for the social and economic well-being of countries. Education plays a key role in providing individuals with the knowledge, skills and competencies needed to participate effectively in society and in the economy. It also contributes to the expansion of scientific and cultural knowledge. Educational attainment is a commonly used proxy for the stock of "human capital", i.e. the skills available in the population and the labour force.

Definition

Educational attainment refers to the highest level of education completed by each person, shown as a percentage of all persons in that age group. Tertiary education includes both tertiary-type "A programmes", which are largely theoretically-based and designed to provide qualifications for entry to advanced research programmes and professions with high skill requirements; and tertiary-type "B programmes", which are more occupationally-oriented and lead to direct labour market access. Upper secondary education typically follows completion of lower secondary schooling. Lower secondary education completes provision of basic education, usually

in a more subject-oriented way and with more specialised teachers.

Comparability

The International Standard Classification of Education (ISCED-97) is used to define the levels of education in a comparable way across countries. See the OECD Handbook for Internationally Comparative Education Statistics for a description of ISCED-97 education programmes and attainment levels and their mappings for each country.

Overview

OECD countries have seen significant increases in the proportion of the adult population attaining tertiary education over the last decades. In 15 OECD countries the share of the population aged 25-64 having attained the tertiary level of education is 30% or more. In Canada, Japan, New Zealand and the United States, this share is significantly higher. Conversely, in the Czech Republic, Italy and Turkey the share of the population 25 to 64 with tertiary attainment is below 14%.

An indication of long term trends in educational attainment can be obtained by comparing the current attainment levels of younger and older age cohorts. For instance, comparing the tertiary attainment levels of 25-34 year olds with those of 55-64 year olds shows an increase in tertiary attainment for Korea over the past 30 years exceeding 40 percentage points; this is more than 30 percentage points higher than the OECD average. In contrast, other OECD countries over the same period experienced only marginal increases (United States) or even falls (Germany).

The overall growth in the number of individuals who have completed tertiary education provides a complementary indication of the increase in the stock of human capital available in each country. The number of individuals that have attained tertiary education has increased each year by 7% or more in Ireland, Poland, Portugal, Spain, and Turkey. In Ireland, Spain and Turkey, the overall population growth has put additional strains on the higher education system, whereas this has been of less concern in Germany and Japan.

Sources

• OECD (2009), *Education at a Glance*, OECD, Paris.

Further information

Analytical publications

• Blöndal S., S. Field and N. Girouard (2002), *Investment in Human Capital Through Post-Compulsory Education and Training: Selected Efficiency and Equity Aspects*, OECD Economics Department Working Papers, No. 333, OECD, Paris.
• Blöndal, S., S. Field and N. Girouard (2002), "Investment in Human Capital through Upper-Secondary and Tertiary Education", *OECD Economic Studies*, No. 34, 2002/I, OECD, Paris.
• Hansson, B. (2007), *Effects of Tertiary Expansion: Crowding-out effects and labour market matches for the higher educated*, OECD Education Working Papers, No. 10, OECD, Paris.
• OECD (2008), *Reviews of National Policies for Education*, OECD, Paris.
• OECD (2008), *Trends Shaping Education – 2008 Edition*, OECD, Paris.

Methodological publications

• OECD (2004), *OECD Handbook for Internationally Comparative Education Statistics: Concepts, Standards, Definitions and Classifications*, OECD, Paris.

Web sites

• OECD Centre for Educational Research and Innovation (CERI), *www.oecd.org/edu/ceri*.
• OECD Education at a Glance, *www.oecd.org/edu/eag2009*.

Education attainment
As a percentage of total population in that age group

	Population with tertiary education, 2007					Population aged 25-64								
						Below upper secondary			Upper secondary and post-secondary non-tertiary			Tertiary education		
	25-64	25-34	35-44	45-54	55-64	1997	1998	2007	1997	1998	2007	1997	1998	2007
Australia	33.7	40.7	33.9	32.2	26.6	46.7	44.0	31.8	29.0	30.6	34.4	24.3	25.4	33.7
Austria	17.6	18.9	19.1	17.5	13.9	26.4	25.8	19.9	63.0	60.5	62.6	10.6	13.7	17.6
Belgium	32.1	41.3	35.5	28.3	22.3	45.0	43.3	32.0	29.9	31.4	35.9	25.1	25.3	32.1
Canada	48.3	55.8	52.6	44.6	38.9	22.3	21.4	13.4	40.3	40.4	38.3	37.4	38.2	48.3
Czech Republic	13.7	15.5	14.3	14.2	10.7	15.0	14.7	9.5	74.3	74.9	76.8	10.6	10.4	13.7
Denmark	32.2	40.1	34.1	30.4	24.2	..	21.5	24.5	..	53.2	43.3	..	25.4	32.2
Finland	36.4	39.3	42.7	35.8	28.2	31.7	31.0	19.5	38.9	38.8	44.2	29.4	30.2	36.4
France	26.8	41.4	28.7	19.8	16.6	40.5	39.3	31.3	39.5	40.1	41.9	20.0	20.6	26.8
Germany	24.3	22.6	25.7	25.1	23.1	16.8	16.2	15.6	60.6	60.8	60.1	22.6	23.0	24.3
Greece	22.7	28.1	25.9	20.7	14.1	55.9	54.1	40.4	28.6	29.1	36.9	15.5	16.8	22.7
Hungary	17.7	22.0	17.4	15.8	15.7	37.0	36.7	20.8	50.8	50.1	61.2	12.2	13.2	18.0
Iceland	29.8	31.0	35.4	27.9	22.6	43.9	44.6	35.5	35.3	34.4	34.7	20.9	21.0	29.8
Ireland	32.2	43.9	34.3	25.2	17.5	50.4	48.7	32.4	26.8	30.2	35.4	22.8	21.1	32.2
Italy	13.6	18.9	14.0	11.3	9.0	..	59.3	47.7	..	32.1	38.7	..	8.6	13.6
Japan	41.0	53.7	46.2	41.4	23.9	20.3	20.0	..	49.1	49.4	59.0	30.6	30.6	41.0
Korea	34.6	55.5	40.0	21.0	10.9	37.9	33.6	22.1	42.3	43.9	43.3	19.8	22.5	34.6
Luxembourg	26.5	35.7	27.3	22.0	18.9	..	..	34.3	..	..	39.2	..	..	26.5
Mexico	15.9	19.5	15.9	14.9	9.0	72.2	72.0	66.7	15.8	15.8	18.4	12.0	12.2	14.9
Netherlands	30.8	36.7	30.8	30.2	25.8	..	35.7	26.8	..	40.1	42.4	..	24.2	30.8
New Zealand	41.0	47.3	41.4	39.4	34.7	39.0	38.0	28.4	33.5	33.9	30.6	27.5	28.1	41.0
Norway	34.2	42.7	36.2	30.8	26.5	17.0	15.4	21.1	57.2	57.2	44.7	25.8	27.4	34.2
Poland	18.7	30.0	17.7	12.8	12.3	23.0	21.7	13.7	66.8	67.4	67.6	10.2	10.9	18.7
Portugal	13.7	21.4	13.6	10.4	7.4	..	82.1	72.5	..	9.6	13.8	..	8.3	13.7
Slovak Republic	14.1	17.5	13.0	13.8	10.8	21.4	19.8	13.0	68.1	69.9	72.9	10.5	10.3	14.1
Spain	29.0	38.9	32.2	22.7	15.9	68.8	67.1	49.3	12.6	13.2	21.7	18.6	19.7	29.0
Sweden	31.3	40.0	31.0	28.9	25.9	24.7	23.9	15.4	47.8	48.1	53.3	27.5	28.0	31.3
Switzerland	31.3	35.0	33.8	30.0	25.6	18.7	16.4	14.6	59.1	61.4	55.5	22.2	22.2	29.9
Turkey	10.8	13.6	9.6	8.8	7.9	79.0	78.2	71.3	13.4	14.4	17.9	7.6	7.5	10.8
United Kingdom	31.8	37.1	32.3	30.5	25.1	40.9	39.9	31.7	36.5	36.3	36.5	22.6	23.8	31.8
United States	40.3	40.4	42.2	39.6	38.5	14.1	13.5	12.1	51.8	51.6	47.6	34.1	34.9	40.3
OECD average	27.5	34.2	29.2	24.9	20.1	37.0	37.8	29.8	42.6	41.8	43.2	20.4	20.5	27.4
Brazil	9.6	10.0	9.5	10.1	8.2	..	..	63.2	..	..	27.2	..	..	9.6
Chile	13.2	18.3	12.5	11.4	8.7	..	..	50.0	..	..	36.9	..	..	13.2
Estonia	33.3	34.6	33.7	35.5	28.4	..	..	10.9	..	..	55.8	..	..	33.6
Israel	43.6	41.5	45.8	44.1	43.5	..	..	19.6	..	..	36.8	..	..	43.6
Russian Federation	54.0	55.5	58.1	54.3	44.5	..	..	11.1	..	..	34.0	..	..	54.9
Slovenia	22.2	30.1	22.6	19.5	15.6	..	..	18.2	..	..	59.6	..	..	22.2

StatLink http://dx.doi.org/10.1787/826124112463

Population that has attained at least tertiary education
Percentage, 2007

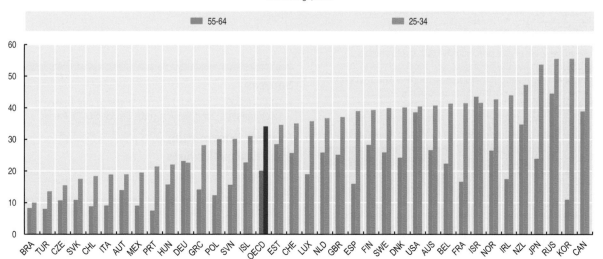

StatLink http://dx.doi.org/10.1787/821553547007

TEACHING AND LEARNING CONDITIONS

Most countries face major challenges in improving the conditions for teaching and learning. These include a shortage of well-trained teachers and a failure to provide teachers with sufficient opportunities for the professional development they need.

Definition

TALIS, the OECD's *Teaching and Learning International Survey*, provides the first internationally comparative perspective on conditions of teaching and learning in public and private schools at lower secondary education. The survey was implemented in 16 OECD and 7 partner countries, and provides information of teachers' professional development;

their beliefs, attitudes and practices; their appraisal and feedback; and their assessment of school leadership. The survey results give insights into some of the factors that lie behind the differences in students' learning outcomes (such as those revealed by the OECD's Programme for International Student Assessment, PISA) and help countries to review and develop policies to make the teaching profession more attractive and more effective.

Comparability

The survey design assures good comparability of results across countries. Around 200 schools were randomly selected in each country participating in the survey. In each school, one questionnaire was filled in by the school principal and another by 20 randomly selected teachers. Each questionnaire took about 45 minutes to complete and could be filled in either on paper or on-line. In total, TALIS sampled around 75 000 teachers representing more than 2 million teachers in 23 participating countries. TALIS was also conducted in the Netherlands, but the results for this country have been excluded because the required sampling standards were not met.

Data for Belgium refer to the Flemish regions.

Overview

In Austria, Ireland and Portugal, a third or more of teachers worked in schools whose school principal reported no school evaluations (either an external evaluation or a self-evaluation by the school principal) in the previous five years. This was also the case for around a quarter of teachers in Denmark and Spain, and for around a fifth in Brazil and Italy. By contrast, in 10 countries (Australia, Brazil, Hungary, Italy, Korea, Mexico, Poland, the Slovak Republic, Slovenia and Turkey), at least half of teachers worked in schools whose school principal reported at least an annual school evaluation.

Teachers' appraisal and feedback are rarely associated with material incentives, such as financial benefits or career advancement. Across all countries participating in the survey, just 9% of teachers reported that appraisal or feedback had a moderate or large impact upon their salary; fewer than 11% reported that appraisal or feedback had a moderate or large impact on a financial bonus or another kind of monetary reward.

Non-material incentives are also relatively infrequent. Slightly more than a third of all teachers said their appraisal and feedback had led to a moderate or large change in the recognition they received from their school principal and/or from other colleagues within the school; just under a quarter said it led to a moderate or a large change in their opportunities for professional development.

Teachers who did receive appraisal and feedback had a positive view of the process. Overall, such teachers considered that the appraisal and feedback they received represented a fair assessment of their work, and that it had a positive impact upon their job satisfaction.

While teachers may have found individual benefits from these systems of appraisal and feedback, they felt that, overall, such systems did not recognise their efforts and accomplishments, did not reward effective teachers and effective teaching practices, and did not provide adequate incentives to teachers. In most countries, a majority of teachers reported that sustained poor performance would not lead to dismissal, while more than three-quarters reported that their school principal did not take any step to alter the monetary rewards of a persistently underperforming teacher.

Sources
- OECD (2009), *Creating Effective Teaching and Learning Environments: First Results from TALIS*, OECD, Paris.

Further information
Analytical publications
- OECD (2009), *Education at a Glance 2009: OECD Indicators*, OECD, Paris.
- OECD (2009), *Highlights from Education at a Glance 2009*, OECD, Paris.

Web sites
- OECD TALIS, *www.oecd.org/edu/talis*.
- OECD Education at a Glance, *www.oecd.org/edu/eag2009*.

Teachers with no appraisal or feedback and no school evaluation

As a percentage of all teachers, 2007-08

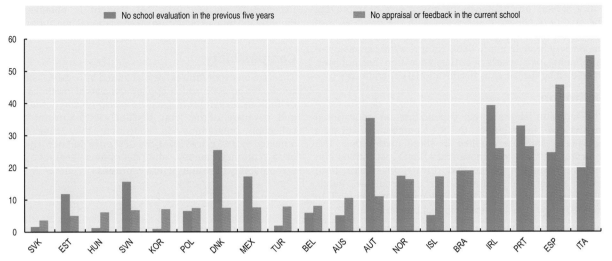

StatLink http://dx.doi.org/10.1787/821553842867

Perception of teachers of the appraisal and feedback and its impact in their school

Percentage, 2007-08

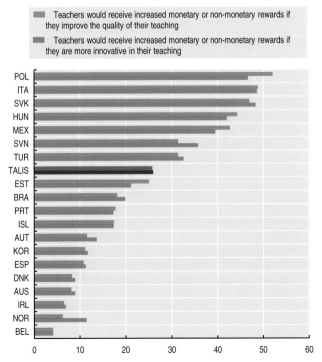

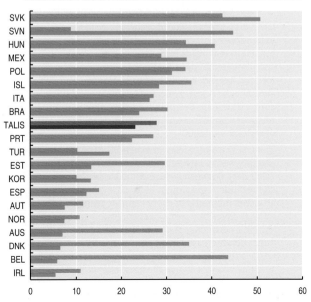

StatLink http://dx.doi.org/10.1787/821567602881

EDUCATIONAL EXPENDITURE PER STUDENT

Policy makers must balance the importance of improving the quality of educational services with the desirability of expanding access to educational opportunities, notably at the tertiary level. In many OECD countries the expansion of enrolments, particularly in tertiary education, has not been paralleled by similar rises in educational expenditures.

Definition

The indicator shows direct expenditure on educational institutions in relation to the number of full-time equivalent students enrolled in these institutions. The indicator includes only those educational institutions and programmes, both public and private, for which both enrolment and expenditure data are available. Public subsidies for students' living expenses are excluded to ensure international comparability of the data.

Educational expenditure in national currency for 2006 is expressed in US dollars at PPP exchange rates. PPP exchange rates are used because market exchange rates are affected by many factors (*e.g.* interest rates, trade policies, expectations of economic growth, etc.) that are unrelated to the purchasing power of currencies in different countries.

Expenditure on education per student is obtained by dividing the total expenditure on educational institutions by the number of full-time equivalents students.

Comparability

The data on expenditures were obtained by a special survey conducted in 2008 which applied consistent methods and definitions. Expenditure data are based on the definitions and coverage of the joint UNESCO-OECD-Eurostat data collection programme on education; they have been adjusted to 2006 prices using the GDP price deflator. The use of a common survey and definitions ensures good comparability of results across countries.

Overview

In 2006, the average level of expenditure per tertiary student, across OECD countries, was 12 336 USD. Spending per student at tertiary level student ranges between 4 063 USD in Estonia and more than 20 000 USD in Switzerland and the United States. OECD countries in which most R&D is performed by tertiary educational institutions tend to report higher tertiary expenditure per student than countries in which a large part of R&D is performed in other public institutions or by industry.

On average, for the countries where data are available, expenditure per student on tertiary education increased by 11% in real terms from 2000 to 2006. However, spending per student declined in Germany, Hungary, Iceland, Ireland, the Netherlands, Norway and Sweden, as well as in Brazil, Chile and Israel. In all of these countries except Germany, this decline was mainly the result of a rapid increase (by 10% or more) in the number of tertiary students.

The OECD average level of expenditure per student for primary, secondary and post-secondary education was 7 283 USD. Between 2000 and 2006, a period of relatively stable student enrolment at these levels, spending per students increased in every country, rising by 24% on average. Over this period, expenditure per student in primary, secondary and post-secondary non-tertiary education increased by at least 10% in 22 out of the 30 OECD and partner countries for which data are available. The rise exceeds 30% in the Czech Republic, Hungary, Iceland, Ireland, Korea, Poland, the Slovak Republic and the United Kingdom, as well as in Brazil and Estonia.

Sources

• OECD (2009), *Education at a Glance*, OECD, Paris.

Further information

Analytical publications

• OECD (2004), *Internationalisation and Trade in Higher Education: Opportunities and Challenges*, OECD, Paris.
• OECD (2004), *Quality and Recognition in Higher Education: The Cross-border Challenge*, OECD, Paris.
• OECD (2006), *Education Policy Analysis: Focus on Higher Education*, OECD, Paris.
• OECD (2008), *Higher Education Management and Policy*, OECD, Paris.
• OECD (2008), *Reviews of National Policies for Education*, OECD, Paris.
• OECD (2008), *Trends Shaping Education – 2008 Edition*, OECD, Paris.

Methodological publications

• OECD (2004), *OECD Handbook for Internationally Comparative Education Statistics: Concepts, Standards, Definitions and Classifications*, OECD, Paris.
• UIS, OECD and Eurostat (2009), *UOE Data Collection – 2009 Data Collection on Education Systems: Definitions, Explanations and Instructions*, OECD, Paris.

Web sites

• OECD Education at a Glance, *www.oecd.org/edu/eag2009*.

Expenditure on educational institutions per student and change in expenditure due to different factors

Year 2006

	Primary, secondary and post-secondary non-tertiary education				Tertiary education			
	Expenditure per student US dollars, 2006 constant prices and PPPs	Index of change, year 2000 = 100			Expenditure per student US dollars, 2006 constant prices and PPPs	Index of change, year 2000 = 100		
		Expenditure	Number of students	Expenditure per student		Expenditure	Number of students	Expenditure per student
Australia	7 459	116	105	111	15 016	130	111	117
Austria	9 910	106	97	109	15 148	139	100	139
Belgium	7 980	110	107	102	13 244	110	105	104
Canada	7 774	119	95	125	22 810	124	..	..
Czech Republic	4 532	137	91	152	7 989	189	145	130
Denmark	9 270	119	106	112	15 391	117	101	116
Finland	6 891	125	105	119	12 845	119	106	112
France	7 712	101	98	103	11 568	110	105	105
Germany	6 985	100	97	104	13 016	107	108	99
Hungary	4 188	151	91	167	6 367	133	152	88
Iceland	8 877	143	106	135	8 579	139	154	90
Ireland	7 318	165	104	159	11 832	110	121	91
Italy	8 204	112	102	110	8 725	116	112	104
Japan	7 661	101	91	112	13 418	114	102	112
Korea	6 089	155	98	159	8 564	144	107	134
Luxembourg	15 440	..	..	..	..	..	..	..
Mexico	2 072	125	107	117	6 462	137	124	111
Netherlands	8 109	121	104	116	15 196	117	120	98
New Zealand	5 589	106	..	..	9 288	131	..	..
Norway	10 448	110	107	103	16 235	111	115	97
Poland	3 568	118	84	141	5 224	157	124	127
Portugal	5 967	99	89	112	9 724	146	108	135
Slovak Republic	3 032	140	89	157	6 056	171	158	108
Spain	7 016	112	94	119	11 087	119	94	127
Sweden	8 123	114	101	114	16 991	118	118	100
Switzerland	11 129	109	102	106	22 230	135	132	102
Turkey	1 286	..	..	..	4 648	..	..	..
United Kingdom	8 306	134	89	150	15 447	149	107	139
United States	10 267	117	103	114	25 109	122	118	103
OECD average	7 283	121	98	124	12 336	130	118	111
Brazil	1 550	171	103	165	10 294	124	147	84
Chile	2 089	105	102	103	6 292	113	167	68
Estonia	4 147	140	83	170	4 063	121	117	104
Israel	5 322	113	108	105	11 132	113	126	89
Russian Federation	2 399	174	..	..	4 279	258	..	..
Slovenia	7 759	..	..	..	8 251	..	..	..

StatLink http://dx.doi.org/10.1787/826203021461

Changes in expenditure on educational institutions in tertiary education by factor

Changes in 2000-2006, year 2000 = 100

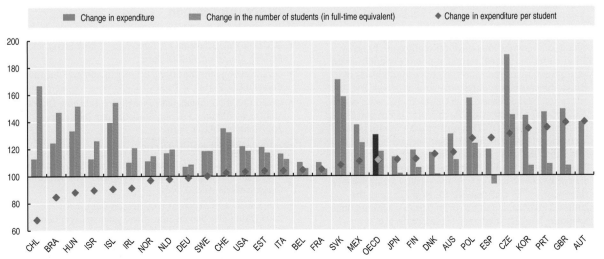

StatLink http://dx.doi.org/10.1787/821567825256

PUBLIC AND PRIVATE EXPENDITURE ON EDUCATION

Cost-sharing between participants in the education system, and in society as a whole, is an issue discussed in many countries. It is especially relevant for pre-primary and tertiary education, for which full or nearly full public funding is rare. As new client groups participate in a wider range of educational programmes from increasing numbers of providers, governments are forging new partnerships to mobilise the necessary resources and to share costs and benefits more equitably.

Definition

Governments can spend public funds directly on educational institutions or use them to provide subsidies to private entities for the purpose of education; both types of outlays are included in the data on public expenditure shown in this section. Private expenditure includes all direct expenditure on educational institutions, whether partially covered by public subsidies or not.

These expenditure data are limited to outlays by educational institutions. Excluded are the costs incurred by families to purchase textbooks and materials commercially, or to pay for private tutoring for their children provided outside educational institutions. Also excluded are students' living costs and foregone earnings, which can account for a significant proportion of the costs of education for students at the tertiary level.

Comparability

The broad definition of institutions outlined above ensures that expenditure on services, which are provided in some OECD countries by schools and universities and in others by agencies other than schools, are covered on a comparable basis. The data on expenditure were obtained by a special survey conducted in 2008 which applied consistent methods and definitions.

Overview

Around 85% of all funds for educational institutions in OECD countries come from public sources. At tertiary level, the share of public funding in 2006 represented 73% of the total, on average, across OECD countries. The proportion of expenditure on tertiary institutions covered by individuals, businesses and other private sources, including subsidised private payments, ranges from less than 5% in Denmark, Finland and Norway, to more than 40% in Australia, Canada, Japan, the United States and Israel, and to over 75% in Korea and Chile.

The share of public expenditure at the tertiary level has declined over time, falling from 78% in 2000 to 73% in 2006 on average. In nearly one-half of the countries with comparable data for 2000 and 2006, the private share increased by 3 percentage points or more. This increase exceeds 9 percentage points in Austria, Mexico, Portugal and the Slovak Republic. Only Ireland – and to a lesser extent in Poland and Spain – show a significant decrease in the share of private spending in the total allocated to tertiary educational institutions.

At the tertiary level, rises in private expenditure on educational institutions have generally gone hand in hand with rises (in real terms) in public expenditure on educational institutions, as they have for all levels of education combined. Public investment in tertiary education has increased in all OECD countries for which 2000 to 2006 data are available except in Japan and Chile. In six out of the 11 OECD countries with the highest increases in public expenditure on tertiary education (the Czech Republic, Hungary, Iceland, Poland, the Slovak Republic and Switzerland), tertiary institutions charge low or no tuition fees and tertiary attainment is relatively low. By contrast, Korea, New Zealand, the United Kingdom and in the United States, where public spending has also increased significantly, are characterised by a high reliance on private funding of tertiary education.

Sources
• OECD (2009), *Education at a Glance*, OECD, Paris.

Further information
Analytical publications
• OECD (2006), *Schooling for Tomorrow – Think Scenarios, Rethink Education*, OECD, Paris.
• OECD (2006), *Starting Strong II: Early Childhood Education and Care*, OECD, Paris.
• OECD (2008), *Students with Disabilities, Learning Difficulties and Disadvantages: Policies, Statistics and Indicators – 2007 Edition*, OECD, Paris.

Methodological publications
• OECD (2004), *OECD Handbook for Internationally Comparative Education Statistics: Concepts, Standards, Definitions and Classifications*, OECD, Paris.
• UIS, OECD and Eurostat (2009), *UOE Data Collection – 2009 Data Collection on Education Systems: Definitions, Explanations and Instructions*, OECD, Paris.

Web sites
• OECD Education at a Glance, *www.oecd.org/edu/eag2009*.

Share of private expenditure on educational institutions

Percentage of total expenditure on educational institutions

	Pre-primary education (for children 3 years and older)		Primary, secondary and post-secondary non-tertiary education		Tertiary education		Total all levels of education	
	2000	2006	2000	2006	2000	2006	2000	2006
Australia	33.8	36.9	15.6	17.2	49.0	52.4	24.7	27.6
Austria	22.8	36.6	4.2	5.7	3.7	15.5	6.0	10.8
Belgium	3.1	3.6	5.3	4.9	8.5	9.4	5.7	5.6
Canada	..	..	7.6	11.3	39.0	46.6	20.1	26.2
Czech Republic	12.3	9.3	8.3	9.2	14.6	17.9	10.1	11.6
Denmark	14.4	18.6	2.2	2.1	2.4	3.6	4.0	8.1
Finland	12.1	9.2	0.7	1.0	2.8	4.5	2.0	2.5
France	4.6	4.5	7.4	7.5	15.6	16.3	8.8	9.1
Germany	24.3	27.8	13.7	13.0	11.8	15.0	14.4	14.8
Greece	..	..	8.3	..	0.3	..	6.2	..
Hungary	12.1	6.2	7.3	5.3	23.3	22.1	11.7	9.5
Iceland	35.5	30.4	3.6	3.9	8.2	9.8	10.0	10.2
Ireland	5.8	..	4.0	3.1	20.8	14.9	9.5	6.0
Italy	..	6.5	2.2	2.8	22.5	27.0	5.7	7.7
Japan	47.7	56.6	10.2	10.1	61.5	67.8	29.0	33.3
Korea	..	53.7	19.2	22.4	76.7	76.9	40.8	41.2
Mexico	9.7	16.8	13.9	17.3	20.6	32.1	14.7	19.8
Netherlands	1.6	1.4	14.3	13.1	23.5	26.6	15.9	15.7
New Zealand	..	37.6	..	13.4	..	37.0	..	20.1
Norway	..	9.5	1.0	..	3.7	3.0	5.0	..
Poland	12.9	14.7	4.6	1.4	33.4	29.6	11.0	9.5
Portugal	..	..	0.1	0.1	7.5	33.3	1.4	8.0
Slovak Republic	..	20.8	2.4	13.2	8.8	17.9	3.6	14.8
Spain	18.5	14.3	7.0	6.3	25.6	21.8	12.6	11.1
Sweden	10.7	0.0	0.1	0.1	8.7	10.9	3.0	2.7
Switzerland	..	..	10.8	13.4	..	..	7.9	..
Turkey	..	..	..	..	4.6	..	1.4	..
United Kingdom	4.1	7.3	11.3	23.2	32.3	35.2	14.8	24.7
United States	25.1	22.4	8.4	8.5	68.9	66.0	32.7	32.0
OECD average	16.4	20.2	7.2	8.8	22.2	27.4	11.9	15.3
Chile	..	29.1	31.6	27.2	80.5	83.9	44.8	44.4
Estonia	..	1.2	..	1.5	..	26.9	..	7.0
Israel	33.1	22.4	5.9	7.8	43.5	49.9	20.0	23.2
Slovenia	..	18.3	..	9.2	..	23.1	..	13.0

StatLink 🔗 http://dx.doi.org/10.1787/826213234488

Share of private expenditure on educational institutions

Percentage of total expenditure on educational institutions

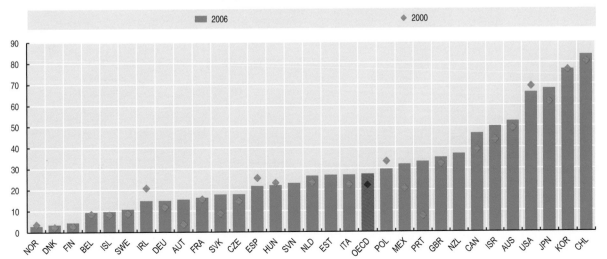

StatLink 🔗 http://dx.doi.org/10.1787/821575222084

PUBLIC FINANCE

GOVERNMENT EXPENDITURE, REVENUES AND DEFICITS

Government deficits or surpluses are sensitive to the economic cycle as well as to government taxation and spending policies. These deficits or surpluses affect economic activity, inflationary pressures and external imbalances.

Definition

The net borrowing or net lending of the general government is the balancing item of the non-financial account for this sector (according to the 1993 System of National Accounts). It is also equal to the difference between total revenue and total expenditure, including capital expenditure. The general government sector consists mainly of central, state and local government units together with social security funds controlled by those units. The main revenue of general government consists of taxes, social contributions, dividends and other property income. The main expenditure items consist of the compensation of civil servants, social benefits, interest on the public debt, subsidies and gross fixed capital formation. A negative figure indicates a deficit.

The data shown here are on a national accounts basis. These may differ from the numbers reported to the European Commission under the excessive deficit procedure (EDP) for some EU countries and for some years.

Overview

In the run-up to monetary union, EU countries that expected to adopt the Euro as their currency followed fiscal policies aimed at reducing government deficits. Deficit reduction policies were successfully implemented in several other countries, including New Zealand since 1994 and Australia, Denmark, Finland and Sweden since 1998. Korea is the only country which has recorded surpluses throughout the period, although Norway has had surpluses in most years since 1990.

For the OECD as a whole, deficits as a percentage of GDP reached a peak in 1993 but then fell over the next six years (with the exception of the large one-off rise which occurred in Japan in 1998) and turned into surpluses (net lending) at the peak of the economic cycle in 2000. In the period that followed, government deficits rose until 2003 in most countries, especially in France, Germany, Japan, the United Kingdom and the United States. During the period 2004-2006, the deficit to GDP ratios fell in most countries except Hungary, Italy, Portugal and the Slovak Republic. In 2007 most countries improved further their fiscal position, with the exception of Belgium, France, Greece, Japan, the United Kingdom and the United States, where deficits continued to increase.

Fiscal positions in 2008 deteriorated in all countries reported here, with the exception of Norway and Switzerland. The government deficit rose to 13.6% of GDP in Iceland, and to 7.8% in Greece, while in Ireland the small surplus of 2007 gave way to a deficit of 7.2% of GDP in 2008. The government deficit also increased to 6.5% of GDP in the United States and to 5.3% of GDP in the United Kingdom.

Comparability

Data are based on the 1993 System of National Accounts or on the 1995 European System of Accounts so that all countries are using a common set of definitions. In several OECD countries the accounts for 2000, 2001 or 2002 were affected by the sale of mobile telephone licenses, recorded in national accounts as a negative expenditure (the sale of an asset) thereby reducing the deficit. To ensure consistency with official national accounts data some very large one-offs transactions which had been excluded in the past have been reintegrated in the data (Germany and Netherlands in 1995, Japan in 1998). See the OECD Economic Outlook Sources and Methods (www.oecd.org/eco/sources-and-methods) for more details.

Data for Brazil are calculated as total claims on the general government from the monetary survey. Data for South Africa refer to fiscal years, running from 1 April to 31 March; data come from the National Treasury and differ from those reported by Statistics South Africa and the South African Reserve Bank.

Sources
- OECD (2009), OECD Economic Outlook, Nov. No. 86 – Vol 2009/2, OECD, Paris.

Further information
Analytical publications
- OECD (2008), OECD Economic Surveys, OECD, Paris.

Statistical publications
- OECD (2010), National Accounts of OECD Countries, OECD, Paris.

Methodological publications
- OECD (2008), OECD Glossary of Statistical Terms, OECD, Paris.

Online databases
- OECD National Accounts Statistics.
- OECD Economic Outlook Statistics.

Web sites
- OECD Economic Outlook – Sources and Methods, www.oecd.org/eco/sources-and-methods.

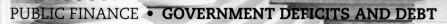

General government net borrowing or net lending
As a percentage of GDP

	1995	1996	1997	1998	1999	2000	2001	2002	2003	2004	2005	2006	2007	2008
Australia	-3.7	-2.4	-0.7	1.6	2.0	0.9	-0.1	1.3	1.8	1.2	1.7	1.9	1.8	1.0
Austria	-5.9	-4.1	-2.0	-2.5	-2.4	-1.9	-0.2	-0.9	-1.6	-4.5	-1.7	-1.7	-0.7	-0.5
Belgium	-4.5	-4.0	-2.3	-1.0	-0.7	-0.1	0.4	-0.2	-0.2	-0.4	-2.8	0.2	-0.2	-1.2
Canada	-5.3	-2.8	0.2	0.1	1.6	2.9	0.7	-0.1	-0.1	0.9	1.5	1.6	1.6	0.1
Czech Republic	-13.4	-3.3	-3.8	-5.0	-3.7	-3.7	-5.6	-6.8	-6.6	-2.9	-3.6	-2.6	-0.7	-2.0
Denmark	-2.9	-1.9	-0.5	-	1.4	2.3	1.2	0.2	-0.1	1.9	5.0	5.0	4.5	3.4
Finland	-6.2	-3.5	-1.3	1.6	1.6	6.9	5.0	4.1	2.4	2.2	2.6	3.9	5.2	4.4
France	-5.5	-4.0	-3.3	-2.6	-1.8	-1.5	-1.6	-3.2	-4.1	-3.6	-3.0	-2.3	-2.7	-3.4
Germany	-9.7	-3.3	-2.6	-2.2	-1.5	1.3	-2.8	-3.6	-4.0	-3.8	-3.3	-1.6	0.2	-
Greece	-9.1	-6.6	-5.9	-3.8	-3.1	-3.7	-4.4	-4.8	-5.7	-7.4	-5.3	-3.2	-4.0	-7.8
Hungary	-8.7	-4.6	-6.1	-7.9	-5.4	-3.0	-4.1	-8.9	-7.2	-6.4	-7.9	-9.4	-5.0	-3.7
Iceland	-3.0	-1.6	-	-0.4	1.1	1.7	-0.7	-2.6	-2.8	-	4.9	6.3	5.4	-13.6
Ireland	-2.0	-0.1	1.4	2.3	2.6	4.8	0.9	-0.3	0.4	1.4	1.7	3.0	0.2	-7.2
Italy	-7.4	-7.0	-2.7	-3.1	-1.8	-0.9	-3.1	-3.0	-3.5	-3.6	-4.4	-3.3	-1.5	-2.7
Japan	-4.7	-5.1	-4.0	-11.2	-7.4	-7.6	-6.3	-8.0	-7.9	-6.2	-6.7	-1.6	-2.5	-2.7
Korea	3.8	3.4	3.3	1.6	2.7	5.4	4.3	5.1	0.5	2.7	3.4	3.9	4.7	3.3
Luxembourg	2.4	1.2	3.7	3.4	3.4	6.0	6.1	2.1	0.5	-1.1	-	1.3	3.7	2.5
Netherlands	-9.2	-1.9	-1.2	-0.9	0.4	2.0	-0.3	-2.1	-3.2	-1.8	-0.3	0.5	0.2	0.7
New Zealand	2.8	2.8	1.4	0.4	-	1.9	1.8	3.8	4.0	4.1	5.2	5.9	5.0	3.1
Norway	3.2	6.3	7.6	3.3	6.0	15.4	13.3	9.2	7.3	11.1	15.1	18.5	17.7	18.8
Poland	-4.4	-4.9	-4.6	-4.3	-2.3	-3.0	-5.1	-5.0	-6.3	-5.7	-4.1	-3.6	-1.9	-3.7
Portugal	-5.0	-4.5	-3.5	-3.4	-2.8	-3.0	-4.3	-2.9	-3.0	-3.4	-6.1	-3.9	-2.7	-2.8
Slovak Republic	-3.4	-9.9	-6.3	-5.3	-7.4	-12.3	-6.5	-8.2	-2.8	-2.4	-2.8	-3.5	-1.9	-2.3
Spain	-6.5	-4.9	-3.4	-3.2	-1.4	-1.0	-0.7	-0.5	-0.2	-0.4	1.0	2.0	1.9	-4.1
Sweden	-7.3	-3.3	-1.6	1.2	1.2	3.7	1.7	-1.4	-1.2	0.6	2.0	2.4	3.8	2.5
Switzerland	-2.0	-1.8	-2.8	-1.9	-0.5	0.1	-0.1	-1.2	-1.7	-1.8	-0.7	0.8	1.6	1.6
United Kingdom	-5.8	-4.2	-2.2	-0.1	0.9	3.7	0.6	-2.0	-3.7	-3.6	-3.3	-2.7	-2.7	-5.3
United States	-3.3	-2.3	-0.9	0.3	0.7	1.5	-0.6	-4.0	-5.0	-4.4	-3.3	-2.2	-2.8	-6.5
OECD total	-4.8	-3.1	-1.7	-1.9	-0.8	0.2	-1.3	-3.3	-4.1	-3.4	-2.7	-1.3	-1.3	-3.5
Brazil	-5.3	-4.8	-5.1	-6.5	-5.3	-3.4	-3.3	-4.4	-5.1	-2.8	-3.4	-3.5	-2.8	-2.0
Chile	3.1	2.2	2.0	0.4	-2.1	-0.7	-0.5	-1.2	-0.5	2.1	4.6	7.7	8.8	5.3
India	-6.7	-6.3	-6.3	-9.5	-9.5	-8.9	-10.3	-9.3	-9.4	-7.5	-7.1	-5.6	-4.4	-7.3
Indonesia	..	..	..	..	..	..	..	..	..	..	..	-1.0	-1.2	-0.1
Israel	-4.9	-6.4	-4.8	-4.7	-3.6	-1.5	-4.0	-5.3	-6.2	-4.1	-2.2	-0.7	-0.2	-2.4
Slovenia	-8.4	-1.1	-2.4	-2.4	-3.0	-3.7	-4.0	-2.5	-2.7	-2.2	-1.4	-1.3	-	-1.8
South Africa	..	..	..	..	..	..	..	..	..	..	0.3	1.4	1.8	-1.0

StatLink http://dx.doi.org/10.1787/826240080468

General government net borrowing or net lending
As a percentage of GDP

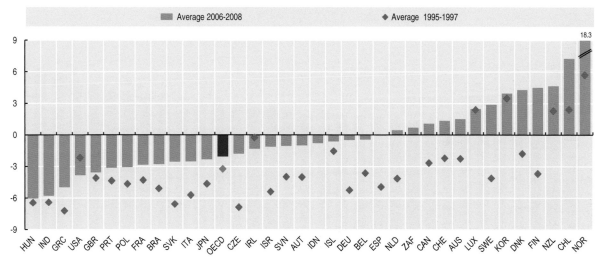

StatLink http://dx.doi.org/10.1787/821602618102

GOVERNMENT EXPENDITURE, REVENUES AND DEFICITS

General government revenues

As a percentage of GDP

	1995	1996	1997	1998	1999	2000	2001	2002	2003	2004	2005	2006	2007	2008
Australia	34.5	34.9	35.6	36.8	36.9	36.1	35.8	36.7	36.4	36.3	36.5	36.4	36.0	35.3
Austria	50.4	51.9	51.7	51.5	51.3	50.3	51.4	50.1	50.0	49.6	48.4	47.9	48.2	48.4
Belgium	47.6	48.5	49.0	49.4	49.5	49.1	49.5	49.7	50.9	49.1	49.3	48.7	48.2	48.9
Canada	43.2	43.8	44.5	44.9	44.3	44.1	42.6	41.1	41.1	40.7	40.8	41.0	40.7	39.8
Czech Republic	40.5	39.1	39.4	38.1	38.5	37.9	38.5	39.4	40.5	41.9	41.1	40.5	41.1	40.0
Denmark	56.2	56.7	55.9	56.0	56.5	55.5	55.0	54.5	54.6	56.1	57.5	56.3	55.1	55.0
Finland	55.2	56.3	55.0	54.2	53.2	55.2	52.9	53.1	52.6	52.4	52.9	52.5	52.6	53.4
France	48.9	50.4	50.8	50.1	50.8	50.1	50.0	49.4	49.1	49.6	50.5	50.3	49.6	49.3
Germany	45.1	46.0	45.7	45.9	46.7	46.4	44.7	44.4	44.4	43.5	43.6	43.7	43.8	43.8
Greece	36.7	37.4	39.1	40.6	41.3	43.0	40.9	40.3	39.0	38.0	38.5	39.7	40.4	40.6
Hungary	46.6	45.8	43.4	42.6	43.3	43.9	43.1	42.2	42.2	42.2	42.2	42.6	44.8	45.5
Iceland	39.8	40.6	40.7	40.9	43.2	43.6	41.9	41.7	42.8	44.1	47.1	48.0	47.9	44.3
Ireland	39.1	39.0	38.1	36.8	36.7	36.1	34.2	33.2	33.6	34.9	35.4	37.2	36.5	34.9
Italy	45.1	45.5	47.6	46.2	46.5	45.3	44.9	44.4	44.7	44.2	43.8	45.3	46.4	46.0
Japan	31.2	31.6	31.7	31.3	31.2	31.4	32.2	30.8	30.5	30.9	31.7	34.5	33.5	34.4
Korea	23.6	24.0	24.5	25.2	25.4	27.9	28.3	28.7	29.4	28.8	30.0	31.7	33.3	33.3
Luxembourg	42.1	42.3	44.3	44.4	42.6	43.6	44.2	43.6	42.2	41.5	41.5	39.7	39.9	40.2
Netherlands	47.2	47.5	46.3	45.8	46.4	46.1	45.1	44.1	43.9	44.3	44.5	46.1	45.7	46.6
New Zealand	45.0	43.9	43.2	41.9	41.2	41.1	40.4	41.4	42.5	42.1	44.2	46.1	45.2	44.2
Norway	54.2	54.8	54.5	52.5	53.7	57.7	57.5	56.3	55.5	56.7	57.3	59.1	58.7	58.8
Poland	43.3	46.1	41.8	40.1	40.4	38.1	38.6	39.2	38.4	36.9	39.4	40.2	40.3	39.6
Portugal	38.4	39.7	39.7	39.4	40.5	40.2	40.1	41.4	42.5	43.1	41.6	42.3	43.2	43.2
Slovak Republic	45.2	43.8	42.6	40.5	40.7	39.9	38.0	36.8	37.4	35.3	35.2	33.4	32.5	32.4
Spain	38.0	38.4	38.2	37.8	38.4	38.1	38.0	38.4	38.2	38.5	39.4	40.4	41.1	37.0
Sweden	58.0	59.6	59.0	59.7	61.4	60.7	62.9	54.3	54.8	55.0	56.0	55.3	55.1	54.3
Switzerland	33.0	33.5	32.7	33.8	33.8	35.2	34.7	35.0	34.6	34.2	34.6	34.3	33.9	33.6
United Kingdom	38.2	38.0	38.4	39.4	39.8	40.3	40.6	39.0	38.7	39.6	40.8	41.4	41.4	42.2
United States	33.8	34.3	34.6	34.9	34.9	35.4	34.4	31.9	31.3	31.6	33.0	33.8	34.0	32.3
OECD total	37.9	38.5	38.6	38.7	38.8	39.0	38.4	37.0	36.8	36.8	37.7	38.6	38.6	37.9
Brazil	27.3	26.7	26.9	27.8	29.1	30.4	31.3	31.9	31.4	32.2	33.4	33.5	34.8	35.9
Chile	21.7	21.8	21.6	21.1	20.4	21.6	21.7	21.1	20.7	22.0	23.8	25.9	27.5	26.5
Slovenia	44.3	43.3	42.5	43.3	43.4	43.0	43.6	43.9	43.7	43.6	43.8	43.2	42.4	42.4

StatLink ᵐˢ⁴ http://dx.doi.org/10.1787/826245431564

General government revenues

As a percentage of GDP

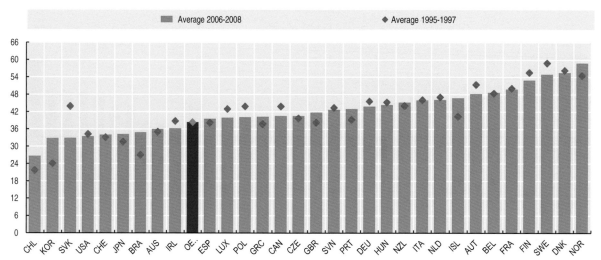

■ Average 2006-2008   ◆ Average 1995-1997

StatLink ᵐˢ⁴ http://dx.doi.org/10.1787/821625868348

General government expenditures
As a percentage of GDP

	1995	1996	1997	1998	1999	2000	2001	2002	2003	2004	2005	2006	2007	2008
Australia	38.2	37.2	36.3	35.2	34.8	35.2	35.9	35.4	34.6	35.1	34.8	34.5	34.2	34.3
Austria	56.2	56.1	53.7	54.0	53.7	52.2	51.6	51.0	51.5	54.1	50.1	49.7	48.8	48.9
Belgium	52.1	52.6	51.2	50.4	50.2	49.2	49.2	49.8	51.1	49.5	52.2	48.5	48.4	50.1
Canada	48.5	46.6	44.3	44.8	42.7	41.1	42.0	41.2	41.2	39.9	39.3	39.4	39.1	39.7
Czech Republic	54.0	42.4	43.2	43.1	42.3	41.6	44.1	46.2	47.1	44.8	44.7	43.1	41.7	42.1
Denmark	59.1	58.7	56.4	56.0	55.1	53.3	53.9	54.2	54.7	54.3	52.5	51.3	50.7	51.5
Finland	61.4	59.8	56.3	52.6	51.6	48.3	47.9	49.0	50.1	50.2	50.3	48.6	47.4	49.0
France	54.4	54.5	54.1	52.7	52.6	51.6	51.6	52.6	53.2	53.3	53.4	52.7	52.3	52.7
Germany	54.8	49.3	48.3	48.1	48.2	45.1	47.5	48.0	48.4	47.3	46.9	45.3	43.6	43.8
Greece	45.7	44.1	45.0	44.4	44.4	46.7	45.3	45.1	44.7	45.4	43.8	42.9	44.4	48.3
Hungary	55.3	50.4	49.4	50.5	48.7	46.9	47.2	51.1	49.4	48.6	50.1	52.0	49.8	49.2
Iceland	42.7	42.2	40.7	41.3	42.0	41.9	42.6	44.3	45.6	44.1	42.2	41.7	42.5	57.8
Ireland	41.1	39.1	36.7	34.5	34.1	31.3	33.2	33.5	33.2	33.5	33.7	34.2	36.2	42.0
Italy	52.5	52.5	50.2	49.3	48.2	46.1	48.0	47.4	48.3	47.8	48.1	48.7	47.9	48.7
Japan	36.0	36.7	35.7	42.5	38.6	39.0	38.6	38.8	38.4	37.0	38.4	36.2	36.0	37.1
Korea	19.8	20.6	21.3	23.5	22.7	22.4	23.9	23.6	28.9	26.1	26.6	27.7	28.7	30.0
Luxembourg	39.7	41.1	40.7	41.0	39.2	37.6	38.1	41.5	41.8	42.5	41.5	38.3	36.2	37.7
Netherlands	56.4	49.4	47.5	46.7	46.0	44.2	45.4	46.2	47.1	46.1	44.8	45.5	45.5	45.9
New Zealand	42.2	41.1	41.7	41.5	41.2	39.2	38.6	37.6	38.5	38.0	39.1	40.1	40.2	41.1
Norway	50.9	48.5	46.9	49.2	47.7	42.3	44.2	47.1	48.3	45.6	42.3	40.6	41.0	40.0
Poland	47.7	51.0	46.4	44.3	42.7	41.1	43.8	44.2	44.6	42.6	43.4	43.9	42.2	43.3
Portugal	43.4	44.1	43.2	42.8	43.2	43.1	44.4	44.3	45.5	46.5	47.6	46.3	45.8	46.0
Slovak Republic	48.6	53.7	49.0	45.8	48.1	52.2	44.5	45.0	40.1	37.6	38.0	36.9	34.4	34.7
Spain	44.4	43.2	41.6	41.1	39.9	39.1	38.6	38.9	38.4	38.9	38.4	38.4	39.2	41.1
Sweden	65.3	62.9	60.7	58.5	60.2	57.0	61.2	55.8	56.0	54.4	54.0	52.9	51.3	51.8
Switzerland	35.0	35.3	35.5	35.8	34.3	35.1	34.8	36.2	36.4	35.9	35.3	33.5	32.2	32.0
United Kingdom	44.1	42.2	40.6	39.5	38.8	36.6	39.9	40.9	42.4	43.1	44.1	44.1	44.1	47.5
United States	37.1	36.6	35.4	34.6	34.2	33.9	35.0	35.9	36.3	36.0	36.2	36.0	36.8	38.8
OECD total	42.7	41.6	40.4	40.6	39.7	38.7	39.8	40.3	40.8	40.2	40.5	39.9	39.9	41.4
Brazil	32.6	31.5	32.0	34.3	34.4	34.4	35.0	35.7	36.7	35.3	37.0	37.3	37.5	37.9
Chile	18.6	19.6	19.6	20.7	22.5	22.3	22.2	22.3	21.2	19.9	19.3	18.2	18.7	21.2
Slovenia	52.6	44.5	44.8	45.7	46.5	46.7	47.6	46.3	46.4	45.8	45.2	44.5	42.4	44.2

StatLink http://dx.doi.org/10.1787/826282384058

General government expenditures
As a percentage of GDP

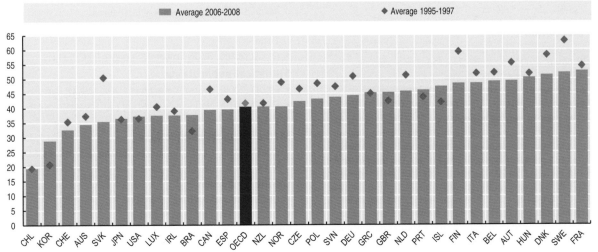

StatLink http://dx.doi.org/10.1787/821627002788

GOVERNMENT DEBT

The accumulation of government debt is a key factor for the sustainability of public finances. Changes in government debt over time reflect the effects of both government deficits and of financial transactions that fall outside the boundaries of the government appropriation account.

Definition

Government debt can be measured in terms of either the government's gross financial liabilities or its net financial liabilities, i.e. gross financial liabilities less financial assets. The data shown here refer to gross financial liabilities as a percentage of GDP. For most countries, gross financial liabilities refer to the liabilities (short and long-term) of all the institutions in the general government sector, as defined in the 1993 *System of National Accounts* (SNA) or in the 1995 European System of Accounts (ESA).

This definition differs from the definition of debt applied under the Maastricht Treaty. First, gross debt according to the Maastricht definition excludes trade credits and advances, as well as shares and insurance technical reserves. Second, government bonds according to the Maastricht definition are valued at nominal rather than market value (or issue price plus accrued interest) as required by the SNA rules. The United States and Canada also value government bonds at their nominal value.

The general government sector consists mainly of central, state and local government units together with social security funds controlled by those units. In principle, debts within and between different levels of government are consolidated. In other terms, a loan from one level of government to another represents both an asset for the first level and a liability for the second, and they cancel out (i.e. it is "consolidated") for the general government sector as a whole. See the OECD Economic Outlook Sources and Methods (*www.oecd.org/eco/sources-and-methods*) for more details.

Comparability

The comparability of data on government debt can be affected both across countries, through national differences in implementing SNA/ESA definitions, and within a country, due to and by changes in how SNA/ESA definitions are implemented over time.

For Brazil, the debt statistics exclude government securities held by the central bank and include repurchase agreements issued by the Central Bank.

Overview

In 2008, government debt as a share of GDP was highest in Japan, at 172.1%, with Greece and Italy also showing debt ratios above 100%. Australia, Korea, Luxembourg and New Zealand were the only countries to boast government debt to GDP ratios below 30% in 2008.

Government debt as a percentage of GDP increased in most countries from 1990 to 1996, while it declined in several countries during the period 1997 to 2007 (with the exceptions of Japan, Korea, France, Germany, Greece and Portugal). In 2008, government debt as a percentage of GDP increased in the majority of OECD countries due to the financial crisis. The most significant increases were those recorded in Iceland (from 53.6% of GDP in 2007 to 96.3% of GDP in 2008) and Ireland (rising from 28.3% of GDP in 2007 to 48.5% of GDP in 2008).

Sources
- OECD (2008), *OECD Economic Outlook, Nov. No. 84 – Vol 2008/2*, OECD, Paris.

Further information

Analytical publications
- OECD (2002), *Debt Management and Government Securities Markets in the 21st Century*, OECD, Paris.
- OECD (2006), *Credit Risk and Credit Access in Asia*, OECD, Paris.
- OECD (2008), *OECD Economic Surveys*, OECD, Paris.

Statistical publications
- OECD (2008), *Central Government Debt*, OECD, Paris.
- OECD (2010), *National Accounts of OECD Countries*, OECD, Paris.

Methodological publications
- OECD (2008), *OECD Glossary of Statistical Terms*, OECD, Paris.

Online databases
- *OECD National Accounts Statistics.*
- *OECD Economic Outlook Statistics.*

Web sites
- OECD Economic Outlook – Sources and Methods, *www.oecd.org/eco/sources-and-methods.*

General government gross financial liabilities

As a percentage of GDP

	1995	1996	1997	1998	1999	2000	2001	2002	2003	2004	2005	2006	2007	2008
Australia	42.5	39.6	37.9	32.7	28.4	25.4	22.5	20.5	19.0	17.2	16.9	16.2	15.3	14.3
Austria	69.5	70.3	66.7	68.5	71.2	71.1	72.1	73.2	71.3	70.8	70.8	66.4	62.2	66.2
Belgium	135.4	133.4	128.0	123.2	119.6	113.8	112.0	108.4	103.4	98.5	95.9	91.6	88.1	93.5
Canada	101.6	101.7	96.3	95.2	91.4	82.1	82.7	80.6	76.6	72.6	71.6	69.5	65.0	69.7
Czech Republic	..	..	..	..	..	..	..	33.1	34.9	34.8	34.9	34.6	38.0	40.7
Denmark	79.3	76.6	72.1	69.7	64.1	57.1	55.0	55.4	53.6	50.1	42.4	38.3	31.6	39.8
Finland	65.2	66.0	64.6	60.9	54.7	52.3	49.9	49.5	51.4	51.5	48.5	45.2	41.5	40.7
France	62.7	66.3	68.8	70.3	66.8	65.6	64.3	67.3	71.4	73.9	75.7	70.9	69.9	75.7
Germany	55.7	58.8	60.3	62.2	61.5	60.4	59.7	61.1	65.3	68.7	71.1	69.2	65.3	68.8
Greece	101.1	103.1	100.0	97.7	101.1	114.9	117.7	117.2	112.0	114.2	114.5	107.9	103.9	102.6
Hungary	88.6	75.8	66.4	64.4	66.5	60.9	59.7	60.7	61.7	65.0	68.8	72.1	72.2	77.0
Iceland	..	..	..	77.3	73.6	72.9	75.0	72.0	71.0	64.5	52.6	57.5	53.6	96.3
Ireland	..	..	..	62.2	51.3	40.2	37.4	35.2	34.1	32.7	32.7	28.8	28.3	48.5
Italy	122.5	128.9	130.3	132.0	125.8	121.0	120.2	119.4	116.8	117.3	119.9	117.1	112.5	114.4
Japan	86.2	93.8	100.5	113.2	127.0	135.4	143.7	152.3	158.0	165.5	175.3	172.1	167.1	172.1
Korea	5.2	5.6	7.2	12.6	15.0	15.7	16.6	15.8	17.4	21.3	23.1	26.1	25.7	26.8
Luxembourg	9.5	10.1	10.2	11.2	10.0	9.2	8.2	8.4	7.9	8.6	7.6	11.3	10.9	16.3
Netherlands	89.6	88.1	82.2	80.8	71.6	63.9	59.4	60.3	61.9	62.2	61.1	54.9	52.1	65.8
New Zealand	51.3	44.9	42.3	42.2	39.6	37.4	35.4	33.5	31.4	28.6	27.4	27.0	26.2	25.3
Norway	40.9	36.6	32.1	30.3	31.0	34.2	33.0	40.6	50.2	52.7	49.1	60.5	58.4	56.0
Poland	51.6	51.4	48.3	43.8	46.6	45.4	43.8	55.0	55.3	54.6	54.7	55.1	51.7	54.0
Portugal	68.8	68.4	67.4	65.2	62.1	62.0	63.3	66.5	68.0	70.6	74.0	73.1	71.1	75.2
Slovak Republic	38.2	37.7	39.0	41.1	53.5	57.5	57.0	50.1	48.2	46.9	38.4	33.8	32.2	30.8
Spain	69.3	76.0	75.0	75.3	69.4	66.5	61.9	60.3	55.3	53.4	50.6	46.2	42.1	47.0
Sweden	81.0	84.4	83.2	82.5	73.7	64.7	63.3	60.8	60.0	60.1	60.7	53.6	47.9	47.1
Switzerland	47.7	50.1	52.1	54.9	51.9	52.5	51.3	57.2	57.0	57.9	56.4	50.3	47.2	44.0
United Kingdom	51.6	51.2	52.0	52.5	47.4	45.1	40.4	40.8	41.2	43.5	46.1	45.9	46.9	56.8
United States	70.6	69.8	67.3	64.1	60.4	54.4	54.4	56.7	60.1	61.1	61.3	60.8	61.8	70.0
OECD total	69.6	71.5	71.6	72.0	71.2	68.3	68.5	70.5	72.6	74.3	75.9	74.6	73.1	78.4
Chile	17.8	15.1	13.2	12.7	13.9	13.8	15.1	15.7	13.0	10.7	7.3	5.3	4.1	5.2
Israel	102.4	100.6	99.9	101.3	95.3	85.1	89.9	97.6	99.9	98.2	94.2	85.7	79.4	78.0
Slovenia	..	..	..	..	..	..	33.7	34.8	34.2	35.0	33.9	33.8	30.0	29.8

StatLink ⟐⟐ http://dx.doi.org/10.1787/826288620551

General government gross financial liabilities

As a percentage of GDP

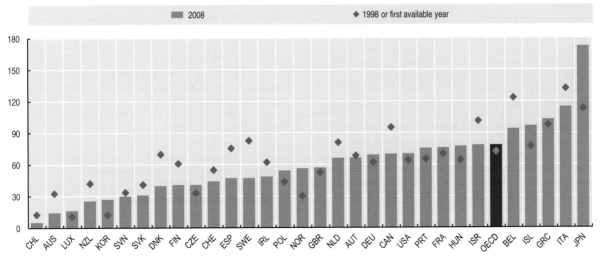

StatLink ⟐⟐ http://dx.doi.org/10.1787/821711743838

SOCIAL EXPENDITURE

Social expenditures are a measure of the extent to which countries assume responsibility for supporting the standard of living of disadvantaged or vulnerable groups.

Definition

Social expenditure comprises cash benefits, direct "in-kind" provision of goods and services, and tax breaks with social purposes. Benefits may be targeted at low-income households, the elderly, disabled, sick, unemployed, or young persons. To be considered "social" programmes have to involve either redistribution of resources across households, or compulsory participation. Social benefits are classified as public when general government (that is central, state, and local governments, including social security funds) controls the relevant financial flows. All social benefits not provided by general government are considered "private". Private transfers between households are not considered as "social" and not included here.

Comparability

For cross-country comparisons, the most commonly used indicator of social support is gross (before tax) public social expenditure relative to GDP. Measurement problems do exist, particularly with regard to spending by lower tiers of government, which may be underestimated in some countries. Data on private social spending are often of lesser quality than for public spending.

No data for private expenditure are currently collected for countries ranked separately on the left-hand side of the chart.

Overview

In 2005, on average, public social expenditure amounted to 21% of GDP. In Sweden and France, public social spending is about 29% of GDP while it is 7% in Mexico and Korea.

Gross public social expenditure increased from about 16% in 1980 to 18% in 1990 and to 21% of GDP in 2005 across OECD countries. On average, public social spending-to-GDP ratios increased the most in the early 1980s, early 1990s and in the beginning of this millennium . In between these decennial turning points spending-to-GDP ratios changed little; during the 1980s the average OECD public social spending to GDP ratio oscillated just below 20% of GDP while during the 1990s it trended downwards after the economic downturn in the early 1990s, fluctuating around 20% of GDP.

The three biggest categories of social transfers are pensions (on average 7% of GDP), health (6%) and income transfers to the working-age population (4%). Public spending on other social services exceeds 5% of GDP only in the Nordic countries, where the public role in providing services to the elderly, the disabled and families is the most extensive.

There are also considerable differences across countries in the extent to which social protection systems rely on private provision. In 2005, gross private social spending was highest (at just over 10% of GDP) in the United States and lowest (at less than 1% of GDP) in the Czech Republic, Hungary, Luxembourg, Mexico, Poland, New Zealand, Spain and Turkey. In some OECD countries, the role of private social benefits has increased in recent years, especially in Canada, the Netherlands and the United States. Reductions in the generosity of public employment-related social benefits (sickness and incapacity related income support) since the 1980s have encouraged the growth of private benefits to top-up public programmes. In Denmark, the Netherlands and Sweden, governments have legislated increased employer's responsibility for the provision of sickness benefits during the first part of the 1990s.

Sources

- *Social Expenditure Database*, (See *www.oecd.org/els/social/expenditure*).

Further information

Analytical publications

- Adema, W. and M. Ladaique (2009), *How Expensive is the Welfare State? Gross and Net Indicators in the OECD Social Expenditure Database (SOCX)*, OECD Social Employment and Migration Working Papers, No. 92, OECD, Paris.
- OECD (2002-2008), *Babies and Bosses – Reconciling Work and Family Life*, (See *www.oecd.org/els/social/expenditure*), OECD, Paris, (See *www.oecd.org/els/social/family*).
- OECD (2009), *Society at a Glance: OECD Social Indicators – 2009 Edition*, OECD, Paris, (See *www.oecd.org/els/social/indicators/SAG*).
- OECD (2009), *Doing Better for Children*, OECD, Paris, (See *www.oecd.org/els/social/childwellbeing*).
- OECD (2009), *Sickness, Disability and Work*, OECD, Paris, (See *www.oecd.org/els/disability*).

Web sites

- OECD Social and Welfare Statistics, *www.oecd.org/statistics/social*.

Public and private social expenditure
As a percentage of GDP

	Public expenditure						Private expenditure					
	1990	1995	2000	2003	2004	2005	1990	1995	2000	2003	2004	2005
Australia	13.6	16.6	17.8	17.8	17.7	17.1	..	4.5	5.4	4.5	3.6	3.7
Austria	23.9	26.5	26.4	27.5	27.3	27.2	2.2	2.1	2.0	2.0	1.9	1.9
Belgium	24.9	26.2	25.3	26.5	26.6	26.4	1.6	2.1	2.4	4.1	4.2	4.5
Canada	18.1	18.9	16.5	17.2	16.6	16.5	3.3	4.4	5.0	5.4	5.5	5.5
Czech Republic	16.0	18.2	19.8	20.7	19.7	19.5	0.0	0.1	0.4	0.4	0.3	0.4
Denmark	25.1	28.9	25.8	27.8	27.7	27.1	2.1	2.4	2.4	2.5	2.6	2.6
Finland	24.2	30.9	24.3	25.8	26.0	26.1	1.1	1.3	1.2	1.2	1.2	1.1
France	25.1	28.6	27.9	29.0	29.1	29.2	1.9	2.0	2.4	2.8	2.9	3.0
Germany	22.3	26.5	26.2	27.3	26.7	26.7	3.1	3.1	3.1	3.1	3.0	3.0
Greece	16.5	17.3	19.2	19.9	19.9	20.5	2.1	1.9	2.3	2.1	1.8	1.7
Hungary	..	..	20.0	22.2	21.7	22.5			0.0	0.1	0.1	0.1
Iceland	13.7	15.2	15.3	18.2	17.9	16.9	3.0	3.5	4.2	5.0	4.9	4.9
Ireland	14.9	15.7	13.6	15.8	16.2	16.7	1.4	1.7	1.3	1.3	1.3	1.3
Italy	19.9	19.9	23.3	24.4	24.7	25.0	4.0	4.2	2.2	2.2	2.1	2.1
Japan	11.4	14.3	16.5	18.1	18.2	18.6	..	..	3.7	3.6	3.6	3.8
Korea	2.9	3.3	5.0	5.6	6.3	6.9	0.4	2.3	2.9	2.9	2.3	2.5
Luxembourg	19.1	20.8	19.7	23.4	23.9	23.2	0.0	0.0	0.1	1.1	1.2	1.1
Mexico	3.6	4.7	5.8	7.3	7.2	7.4	0.1	0.1	0.1	0.2	0.2	0.2
Netherlands	25.6	23.8	19.8	21.2	21.1	20.9	6.1	6.7	7.3	7.9	8.2	8.3
New Zealand	21.8	18.9	19.4	18.2	18.0	18.5	0.2	0.5	0.5	0.5	0.4	0.4
Norway	22.3	23.3	21.3	24.5	23.2	21.6	1.9	1.7	2.0	2.6	2.3	2.1
Poland	14.9	22.6	20.5	22.3	21.4	21.0	0.0	0.0	0.0	0.0	0.0	0.0
Portugal	12.9	17.0	19.6	22.9	23.1	23.1	0.9	1.2	1.6	0.8	1.9	1.9
Slovak Republic	..	18.6	17.9	17.1	16.5	16.6	0.0	0.7	0.8	1.2	1.3	1.0
Spain	19.9	21.4	20.3	21.0	21.2	21.2	0.2	0.3	0.3	0.5	0.5	0.5
Sweden	30.2	32.1	28.5	30.4	29.9	29.4	1.2	2.4	2.7	3.0	2.9	2.8
Switzerland	13.4	17.5	17.9	20.3	20.3	20.3	5.3	7.6	8.3	8.2	8.6	8.4
Turkey	7.6	7.5	13.3	13.5	13.6	13.7	0.0	0.0	0.0	0.0	0.0	0.0
United Kingdom	17.0	20.2	19.2	20.5	21.1	21.3	5.1	6.7	7.8	6.7	6.7	7.1
United States	13.4	15.3	14.5	16.2	16.1	15.9	7.6	8.3	9.2	10.1	10.1	10.1
OECD total	18.1	19.9	19.3	20.8	20.6	20.6	2.1	2.5	2.7	2.9	2.8	2.9
Chile	..	..	10.7	10.3	9.4	9.2	..	..	..	..	..	..
Estonia	..	..	13.9	12.5	13.0	12.6	..	..	..	..	..	..
Israel	..	16.6	17.2	18.3	17.2	16.5	..	..	..	..	..	..
Slovenia	..		24.2	23.7	23.4	23.0	..	..	..	..	..	..

StatLink ᵐˢᵖ http://dx.doi.org/10.1787/826301580471

Public and private social expenditure
As a percentage of GDP, 2005

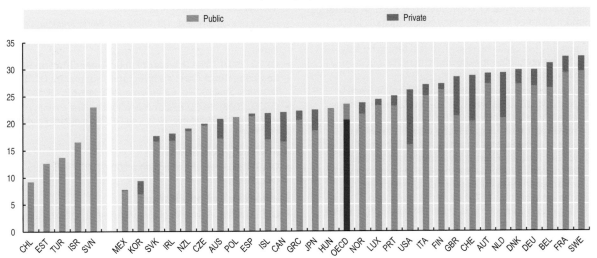

StatLink ᵐˢᵖ http://dx.doi.org/10.1787/821714230340

HEALTH EXPENDITURE

In most OECD countries, spending on health is a large and growing share of both public and private expenditure. Health spending as a share of GDP varies widely across countries, reflecting market and social factors as well as the diverse financing and organisational structures of the health system in each country.

Definition

Total expenditure on health care measures the final consumption of health goods and services plus capital investment in health care infrastructure. It includes spending by both public and private sources (including households) on medical goods and services, on public health and prevention programmes and on administration.

Comparability

OECD countries are at varying stages of reporting health-care expenditure data according to the definition proposed in the OECD manual A *System of Health Accounts* (SHA). While the comparability of health expenditure data has improved recently, some limitations do remain, *e.g.* on the measurement of long-term care.

The size of a country's GDP, and hence its ratio of total health expenditure to GDP, can also be affected by the size of retained earnings of foreign companies operating in the country (see the section on Size of GDP).

No data for private expenditure are currently collected for countries ranked separately on the left-hand side of the chart.

Overview

In 2007, OECD countries devoted 8.9% of their GDP to health spending. The share of health spending to GDP ranged from less than 6% in Turkey and Mexico to 16% in the United States. Following the United States were France (11.0%), Switzerland (10.8%), and Germany (10.4%). The share of public expenditure on health to GDP also varied across countries, from a high of 8.7% of GDP in France to lows of 3.7% and 2.7% of GDP, respectively, in Korea and Mexico.

There is a positive association between GDP per capita and health expenditure per capita across OECD countries. While countries with higher GDP spend a greater amount on health, there is also wide variation across countries. For example, despite having a similar GDP per capita, the health spending per capita of Japan is less than 75% of the level of Germany.

Across the OECD area, per capita health spending increased in real terms by 4.1% annually from 1997 to 2007. In many countries, this growth rate peaked around 2001-02 and then declined. In general, countries that experienced the highest growth over this period are those with lower levels at the beginning of the period (*e.g.* Korea and Turkey). Other countries, such as Ireland and the United Kingdom, pursued specific policies to increase public spending on health. In Germany, health spending per capita increased, in real terms, by only 1.7% per year, following the implementation of cost-containment policies.

Trends in the ratio of health spending to GDP are the result of changes in both GDP and health expenditures. Generally, health spending grew more quickly than GDP over the last ten years, resulting in an increase in the share of GDP allocated to health. This share may increase further following the recession of 2008 and 2009. There is little evidence that GDP changes impact on health spending in the short term, although the experience of some OECD countries that faced substantial recessions in the past 20 years is that health expenditures may be reduced in the aftermath of the recession.

Sources

- OECD (2009), *OECD Health Data 2009*, OECD, Paris.

Further information

Analytical publications

- OECD (2004), *The OECD Health Project: Private Health Insurance in OECD Countries*, OECD, Paris.
- OECD (2004), *The OECD Health Project: Towards High-Performing Health Systems*, OECD, Paris.
- OECD (2005), *The OECD Health Project: Health Technologies and Decision Making*, OECD, Paris.
- OECD (2006), *Sickness, Disability and Work: Breaking the Barriers (Vol. 1): Norway, Poland and Switzerland*, OECD, Paris.
- OECD (2007), "The Drivers of Public Expenditure on Health and Long-Term Care: an Integrated Approach", *OECD Economic Studies*, No. 43 Volume 2006 Issue 2, OECD, Paris.
- OECD (2008), *OECD Health Policy Studies: The Looming Crisis in the Health Workforce: How Can OECD Countries Respond?*, OECD, Paris.

Statistical publications

- OECD (2009), *Health at a Glance 2009: OECD Indicators*, OECD, Paris.

Methodological publications

- OECD (2000), *A System of Health Accounts*, OECD, Paris.

Online databases

- *OECD Health Data*.

Public and private expenditure on health

As a percentage of GDP

	Public expenditure										Private expenditure
	1980	1990	2000	2001	2002	2003	2004	2005	2006	2007	2007
Australia	3.9	4.6	5.5	5.6	5.8	5.6	5.9	5.8	5.9	6.0	2.9
Austria	5.1	6.1	7.6	7.7	7.7	7.8	7.9	7.9	7.8	7.7	2.4
Belgium	..	5.7	6.1	6.3	6.3	7.2	7.5	7.4	7.2	7.4	2.4
Canada	5.3	6.6	6.2	6.5	6.7	6.9	6.9	7.0	7.0	7.1	3.0
Czech Republic	..	4.6	5.9	6.0	6.4	6.7	6.5	6.3	6.1	5.8	1.0
Denmark	7.9	6.9	6.8	7.1	7.3	7.8	7.9	7.9	8.1	8.2	1.5
Finland	5.0	6.2	5.1	5.3	5.6	5.9	6.0	6.2	6.2	6.1	2.1
France	5.6	6.4	8.0	8.1	8.4	8.6	8.7	8.8	8.7	8.7	2.3
Germany	6.6	6.3	8.2	8.3	8.4	8.5	8.1	8.2	8.1	8.0	2.4
Greece	3.3	3.5	4.7	5.3	5.3	5.4	5.1	5.7	5.9	5.8	3.8
Hungary	..	6.3	4.9	4.9	5.3	6.0	5.8	6.0	5.9	5.2	2.2
Iceland	5.5	6.8	7.7	7.6	8.3	8.5	8.0	7.7	7.5	7.7	1.6
Ireland	6.8	4.4	4.6	5.1	5.4	5.7	5.9	5.6	5.5	6.1	1.5
Italy	..	6.1	5.8	6.1	6.2	6.2	6.6	6.8	6.9	6.7	2.0
Japan	4.7	4.6	6.2	6.5	6.5	6.6	6.6	6.7	6.6	6.6	1.5
Korea	0.8	1.6	2.1	2.7	2.6	2.6	2.7	3.0	3.3	3.5	2.8
Luxembourg	4.8	5.0	5.2	5.6	6.1	6.8	7.3	6.9	6.6	6.6	0.7
Mexico	..	1.8	2.4	2.4	2.5	2.6	2.7	2.7	2.6	2.7	3.2
Netherlands	5.1	5.4	5	5.2	5.5	6.0	6.0	5.9	7.4	7.3	1.7
New Zealand	5.2	5.7	6.0	6.0	6.4	6.2	6.5	6.7	7.2	7.1	1.9
Norway	5.9	6.3	6.9	7.4	8.2	8.4	8.1	7.6	7.2	7.5	1.4
Poland	..	4.4	3.9	4.2	4.5	4.4	4.3	4.3	4.3	4.6	1.9
Portugal	3.4	3.8	6.4	6.3	6.5	7.1	7.2	7.3	7.1	7.1	2.8
Slovak Republic	..	..	4.9	4.9	5.0	5.1	5.3	5.2	5.0	5.2	2.6
Spain	4.2	5.1	5.2	5.2	5.2	5.7	5.8	5.8	6.0	6.1	2.4
Sweden	8.2	7.4	7.0	7.3	7.6	7.8	7.5	7.5	7.4	7.4	1.7
Switzerland	..	4.3	5.6	6.0	6.3	6.6	6.6	6.7	6.4	6.4	4.4
Turkey	0.7	1.6	3.1	3.8	4.1	4.3	4.3	4.1	4.1	4.1	1.6
United Kingdom	5.0	4.9	5.6	5.8	6.1	6.2	6.6	6.7	6.9	6.9	1.5
United States	3.7	4.8	5.9	6.3	6.6	6.8	6.9	7.0	7.1	7.3	8.7
OECD average	4.9	5.1	5.6	5.9	6.1	6.3	6.4	6.4	6.4	6.4	2.4
Chile	..	..	2.8	3.0	3.0	3.0	2.8	2.8	2.8	3.0	..
Estonia	..	..	..	..	..	..	..	..	..	4.0	1.3
Israel	..	..	4.7	4.8	4.9	4.8	4.6	4.5	4.3	4.3	..
Slovenia	..	..	..	..	..	..	..	..	..	5.6	2.2

StatLink http://dx.doi.org/10.1787/826302287457

Public and private expenditure on health

As a percentage of GDP, 2007 or latest available year

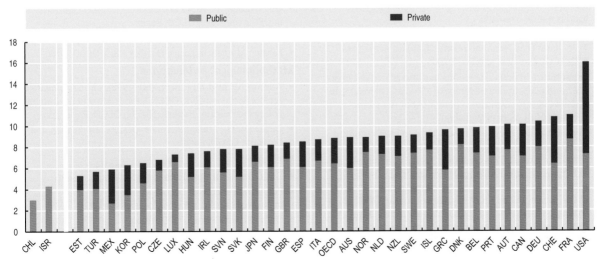

StatLink http://dx.doi.org/10.1787/821724862007

PUBLIC AND PRIVATE PENSION EXPENDITURE

Pension systems vary across countries and no single model fits all. Generally, there is a mix of public and private provision. Public pensions are statutory, most often financed on a pay-as-you-go (PAYG) basis – where current contributions pay for current benefits – and managed by public institutions. Private pensions are in some cases mandatory but more usually voluntary, funded, employment-based (occupational) pension plans or individual retirement savings plans (personal pensions).

Definition

Old-age pension benefits are treated as public when relevant financial flows are controlled by general government (i.e. central and local governments or social security funds). Pension benefits provided by governments to their own employees and paid directly out of the government's current budget are also considered to be public. Public pensions are generally financed on a PAYG basis, but also include some funded arrangements. All pension benefits not provided by general government are within the private domain.

Private expenditures on pensions include payments made to private pension plan members (or dependants) after retirement. All types of plans are included (occupational and personal, mandatory and voluntary, funded and book reserved), covering persons working in both the public and private sectors.

Outlays on public and private pension benefits are expressed as a percentage of GDP. The data are shown for old-age benefits only (i.e. they do not include survivors' benefits).

Comparability

Public pension expenditures come from the OECD Social Expenditure (SOCX) database while pension expenditures for private pension arrangements come from the OECD Global Pension Statistics (GPS) database. The GPS database provides information on funded pension arrangements, which includes both private and public pension plans that are funded. However, only private expenditures are considered for this indicator. At the time of writing, only data up until 2005 were available in the SOCX database.

The GPS database does not cover all types of private pension arrangements for all countries: the private pension data for Austria, Canada, Germany, Luxembourg and the United States include only autonomous pension funds. The break in series for Mexico reflects the inclusion of occupational pension plans registered by CONSAR since 2005.

No data for private expenditure are currently collected for countries ranked separately on the left-hand side of the chart.

Overview

Public spending on old-age benefits averaged 6.5% of GDP in 2005, compared with private pension benefits of an average of 1.5% of GDP in the same year (in the countries for which data are available). Public spending on old-age pensions is highest – greater than 10% of GDP – in Austria, France, Germany, Greece, Italy and Poland. By contrast, Australia, Iceland, Ireland, Korea and Mexico spend 3.5% of GDP or less on public old-age pensions.

Private expenditure on old-age benefits is the highest in Australia, Denmark, Iceland, the Netherlands and Switzerland, where it exceeds 3.5% of GDP. However, private benefit spending is negligible in around a third of OECD countries.

The share of private pensions in total expenditures on old-age benefits exceeds 50% in just Australia and Iceland. The average share of private pensions in the total is a little over 20%.

Over time, public pension expenditures have grown a little faster than national income: from an average of 5.6% of GDP in 1990 to 6.5% in 2005.

Expenditure in private pensions has also grown between 2001 and 2005, from an average of 1.8% of GDP in 2001 to 2.1% in 2008 (in countries where most of the trend between both years is available).

In recent years, there has been a shift towards funding and private sector management within statutory pension systems. This trend has been especially strong in Latin America and Central and Eastern Europe. Although negligible now, private pension expenditures in the future will be much higher in Hungary, Mexico, Poland and the Slovak Republic, for example. Other OECD countries with mandatory private pensions include Australia, Iceland, Norway, Sweden and Switzerland.

Sources

- Social Expenditure Database,
  (See www.oecd.org/els/social/expenditure).
- OECD Pension Statistics.

Further information

Analytical publications

- OECD (2008), Complementary and Private Pensions throughout the World 2008, OECD, Paris.
- OECD (2008), OECD Private Pensions Outlook, OECD, Paris.
- OECD (2009), Pensions at a Glance: Retirement-Income Systems in OECD countries, OECD, Paris.
- OECD (2009), Pensions at a Glance: Asia/Pacific, OECD, Paris.
- Pension Markets in Focus, October 2009, OECD Paris.

Methodological publications

- Adema, W. and M. Einerhand (1998), The Growing Role of Private Social Benefits, OECD Labour Market and Social Policy Occasional Papers, No. 32, OECD, Paris.
- OECD (2005), Private Pensions: OECD Classification and Glossary, OECD, Paris.

Web sites

- OECD work on pensions, www.oecd.org/pensions.
- Pension Markets in Focus,
  www.oecd.org/daf/pensions/pensionmarkets.
- OECD Private Pensions Outlook,
  www.oecd.ord/daf/pensions/outlook.
- OECD Pensions at a Glance,
  www.oecd.ord/cls/social/pensions/PAG.

Public and private expenditure on pension

As a percentage of GDP

	Public expenditure							Private expenditure						
	1990	1995	2000	2002	2003	2004	2005	2002	2003	2004	2005	2006	2007	2008
Australia	2.8	3.4	3.6	3.2	3.2	3.4	3.2	4.4	4.3	3.6	3.7	3.9	3.4	3.9
Austria	11.1	12.1	11.9	12.3	12.4	12.2	12.2	0.2	0.2	0.2	0.2	0.2	0.3	0.2
Belgium	6.5	6.9	6.8	6.9	7.0	7.0	7.0	1.4	1.4	1.4	1.3	1.3	2.8	2.6
Canada	3.8	4.2	3.9	3.9	3.9	3.8	3.7	2.1	2.1	2.2	2.0	2.2	2.2	2.4
Czech Republic	5.2	6.0	7.3	7.4	7.3	7.0	7.2	0.2	0.2	0.2	..	..	0.3	0.3
Denmark	5.1	6.2	5.3	5.3	5.4	5.3	5.4	3.1	3.2	3.2	3.4	3.8	3.3	4.1
Finland	6.3	7.7	6.7	7.1	7.4	7.4	7.5	..	..	..	..	0.5	0.5	0.5
France	9.0	10.4	10.3	10.2	10.3	10.4	10.6	..	..	..	..	..	..	..
Germany	9.4	10.0	10.5	10.9	11.0	11.0	11.0	0.1	0.1	0.1	0.1	0.1	0.1	0.1
Greece	9.3	9.1	10.0	10.4	10.3	10.3	10.7	..	..	..	..	..	0.0	0.0
Hungary	..	..	7.1	7.8	7.7	7.8	8.3	0.1	0.1	0.1	0.2	0.1	0.2	0.2
Iceland	2.2	2.3	2.1	2.1	2.3	2.1	2.0	3.2	3.4	3.4	3.4	3.5	3.7	3.8
Ireland	2.9	2.6	2.3	2.5	2.5	2.6	2.6	..	..	..	..	..	..	..
Italy	8.2	9.3	11.1	11.2	11.3	11.4	11.5	..	..	..	0.2	0.2	0.2	0.3
Japan	4.0	5.1	6.2	6.9	7.1	7.2	7.4	..	..	..	..	..	..	..
Korea	0.6	1.1	1.2	1.0	1.1	1.2	1.3	1.0	1.0	0.6	0.8	0.9	1.0	0.8
Luxembourg	7.4	8.1	6.9	5.1	5.2	5.2	5.2	..	..	..	0.1	0.1	0.1	0.1
Mexico	0.4	0.6	0.6	0.8	1.0	0.9	1.0	0.0	0.1	0.1	0.1	0.2	0.3	0.2
Netherlands	5.8	5.0	4.6	4.6	4.7	4.7	4.7	3.1	3.2	3.4	3.5	3.6	3.6	3.7
New Zealand	7.2	5.6	4.9	4.5	4.4	4.2	4.2	2.0	1.8	1.4	1.3	1.5	1.3	1.4
Norway	5.2	5.1	4.5	4.9	5.0	4.8	4.6	..	..	..	1.4	1.4	2.0	..
Poland	4.1	7.6	9.6	10.8	11.0	10.8	10.4	..	..	..	0.0	0.0	0.0	0.0
Portugal	4.1	6.2	6.9	7.6	8.1	8.6	..	1.0	0.9	0.9	0.9	1.0	1.0	1.4
Slovak Republic	..	6.1	6.2	6.3	6.1	6.1	6.0	..	..	..	..	..	..	..
Spain	7.1	8.1	8.0	7.8	7.6	7.6	7.5	0.6	0.4	0.5	0.5	0.6	0.5	0.6
Sweden	7.0	7.4	6.7	6.7	7.2	7.2	7.0	..	..	..	1.0	1.1	1.3	1.2
Switzerland	5.2	6.2	6.2	6.3	6.5	6.4	6.4	4.8	5.1	5.3	5.3	5.3	5.4	5.3
Turkey	2.2	2.9	..	..	..	..	6.3	..	..	0.0	0.0	0.0	0.0	0.1
United Kingdom	4.6	5.1	5.2	5.3	5.3	5.4	5.5	3.0	2.9	2.8	3.0	3.1	2.8	2.9
United States	5.1	5.3	5.1	5.3	5.3	5.3	5.3	3.0	2.8	2.9	2.9	3.1	3.3	..
OECD average	5.6	6.1	6.2	6.4	6.4	6.4	6.5	1.9	1.8	1.8	1.8	1.9	2.0	2.1

StatLink http://dx.doi.org/10.1787/826342882165

Public and private pension expenditure

As a percentage of GDP, 2005

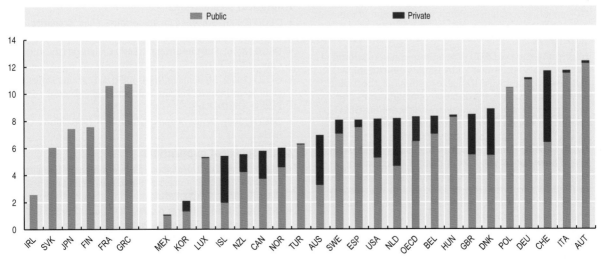

StatLink http://dx.doi.org/10.1787/821740343242

EDUCATION EXPENDITURE

Expenditure on education is an investment that can foster economic growth, enhance productivity, contribute to personal and social development, and reduce social inequality. The proportion of total financial resources devoted to education is one of the key choices made by governments, enterprises, students and their families.

Definition

This indicator covers expenditure on schools, universities and other public and private institutions delivering or supporting educational services. Expenditure on institutions is not limited to expenditure on instruction services but includes public and private expenditure on ancillary services for students and their families, where these services are provided through educational institutions. At the tertiary level, spending on research and development can also be significant and is included in this indicator, to the extent that the research is performed by educational institutions.

In principle, public expenditure includes both direct expenditure on educational institutions and educational-related public subsidies to households administered by educational institutions. Private expenditure is recorded net of these public subsidies attributable to educational institutions; it also excludes expenditures made outside educational institutions (such as textbooks purchased by families, private tutoring for students and student living costs).

Comparability

The broad definition of educational institutions used here ensures that expenditures on services are covered on a comparable basis, whether they are provided by schools and universities (as it occurs in many OECD countries) or by agencies other than schools (as it happens in other countries).

The data on expenditure were obtained by a special survey conducted in 2008 which applied consistent methods and definitions.

No data for private expenditure are currently collected for countries ranked separately on the left-hand side of the chart.

Overview

Expenditure on educational institutions represent a financial burden for society as a whole. This burden, however, does not fall on public funding alone. In 2006, taking into account both public and private sources, OECD countries as a whole spent 6.1% of their GDP on educational institutions at the pre-primary, primary, secondary and tertiary levels. More than three-quarters of this amount comes from public sources. The highest spending on educational institutions is in Denmark, Iceland, Korea, the United States as well as in Israel, with at least 7% of GDP accounted for by public and private spending on educational institutions. Ten out of 34 countries for which data are available spend 5% or less of GDP on educational institutions; in Turkey and in the Russian Federation, these shares are 2.7 and 3.9%, respectively.

Nearly one-third of OECD expenditures on educational institutions is accounted for by tertiary education. At this level, the pathways available to students, the tuition fees paid by student, the duration of programmes and the organisation of teaching vary greatly among OECD countries, resulting in significant differences in the expenditure allocated to tertiary education. On the one hand, Canada, Korea, the United States as well as Israel spend between 1.8 and 2.9% of their GDP on tertiary institutions; these countries are also among those with the highest proportion of private expenditure on tertiary education. On the other hand, Belgium, France, Iceland, Mexico and the United Kingdom spend on tertiary institutions a share of GDP that is below the OECD average; these countries, however, are among those with a higher share of GDP spent for primary, secondary and post-secondary non-tertiary education.

Sources
- OECD (2009), *Education at a Glance*, OECD, Paris.

Further information
Analytical publications
- OECD (2006), *Schooling for Tomorrow – Think Scenarios, Rethink Education*, OECD, Paris.
- OECD (2006), *Starting Strong II: Early Childhood Education and Care*, OECD, Paris.
- OECD (2008), *Students with Disabilities, Learning Difficulties and Disadvantages: Policies, Statistics and Indicators – 2007 Edition*, OECD, Paris.
- OECD (2008), *Trends Shaping Education – 2008 Edition*, OECD, Paris.

Methodological publications
- OECD (2004), *OECD Handbook for Internationally Comparative Education Statistics: Concepts, Standards, Definitions and Classifications*, OECD, Paris.
- UIS, OECD and Eurostat (2009), *UOE Data Collection – 2009 Data Collection on Education Systems: Definitions, Explanations and Instructions*, OECD, Paris.

Web sites
- OECD Education at a Glance, *www.oecd.org/edu/eag2009*.

Public and private expenditure on education

Year 2006

	As a percentage of GDP						Index of change, year 2000 = 100					
	Primary, secondary and post-secondary non-tertiary education		Tertiary education		All levels of education		Primary, secondary and post-secondary non-tertiary education		Tertiary education		All levels of education	
	Public	Private	Public	Private	Public	Private	Public	Private	Public	Private	Public	Private
Australia	3.3	0.7	0.8	0.8	4.1	1.6	114	128	122	139	115	134
Austria	3.5	0.2	1.2	0.1	5.2	0.4	104	144	122	580	106	202
Belgium	3.9	0.2	1.2	0.1	5.9	0.2	110	102	109	122	112	109
Canada	3.3	0.4	1.5	1.3	4.8	1.7	114	176	108	148	108	152
Czech Republic	2.7	0.3	1.0	0.2	4.2	0.6	136	153	183	233	145	170
Denmark	4.3	0.1	1.6	0.1	6.7	0.6	119	115	116	174	115	242
Finland	3.7	..	1.6	0.1	5.7	0.1	125	185	116	195	122	153
France	3.7	0.2	1.1	0.2	5.5	0.4	101	102	109	114	103	107
Germany	2.7	0.4	0.9	0.2	4.1	0.7	101	96	102	135	103	107
Hungary	3.2	0.2	0.9	0.3	5.1	0.5	155	110	135	127	152	121
Iceland	5.1	0.2	1.0	0.1	7.2	0.8	142	152	137	165	144	147
Ireland	3.4	0.1	1.0	0.2	4.4	0.3	167	128	119	79	151	92
Italy	3.4	0.1	0.7	0.2	4.6	0.3	115	148	108	138	111	141
Japan	2.6	0.3	0.5	1.0	3.3	1.7	101	101	95	125	101	123
Korea	3.4	0.9	0.6	1.9	4.5	2.9	149	181	143	144	151	153
Luxembourg	3.3	..	..	..	..	..	..	..	..	..	..	..
Mexico	3.2	0.6	0.8	0.4	4.6	1.1	120	156	118	214	123	176
Netherlands	3.3	0.4	1.1	0.4	4.8	0.8	123	110	111	131	120	118
New Zealand	3.8	0.6	0.9	0.5	5.0	1.3	106	..	131	..	111	..
Norway	3.7	..	1.2	..	5.4	..	110	..	111	..	120	..
Poland	3.7	..	0.9	0.4	5.2	0.5	122	35	166	139	128	109
Portugal	3.6	..	0.9	0.4	5.1	0.4	99	93	102	624	101	608
Slovak Republic	2.4	0.4	0.8	0.2	3.6	0.6	124	776	152	345	127	585
Spain	2.7	0.2	0.9	0.2	4.2	0.5	113	100	125	102	121	105
Sweden	4.1	..	1.4	0.2	6.2	0.2	114	95	114	146	118	106
Switzerland	3.7	0.5	1.4	..	5.4	..	109	138	135	..	112	138
Turkey	1.9	..	0.8	..	2.7	..	144	..	137	..	..	..
United Kingdom	3.9	0.3	0.9	0.4	5.2	0.7	115	273	138	157	117	220
United States	3.7	0.3	1.0	1.9	5.0	2.4	117	118	133	117	120	116
OECD average	3.4	0.3	1.0	0.5	4.9	0.8	120	157	125	187	121	177
OECD total	3.4	0.3	0.9	1.1	4.7	1.5	..	..	..	..	..	..
Brazil	3.8	..	0.8	..	4.9	..	171	..	124	..	157	..
Chile	2.5	0.9	0.3	1.4	3.1	2.5	112	91	93	117	114	112
Estonia	3.4	0.1	0.9	0.2	4.6	0.3	140	..	121	..	..	..
Israel	4.1	0.3	1.0	0.8	6.2	1.6	111	148	100	129	110	133
Russian Federation	2.0	..	0.8	..	3.9	..	174	..	258	..	190	..
Slovenia	3.8	0.4	1.0	0.3	5.3	0.8	..	..	..	..	..	..

StatLink http://dx.doi.org/10.1787/826362456147

Public and private expenditure on education for all level of education

As a percentage of GDP, 2006

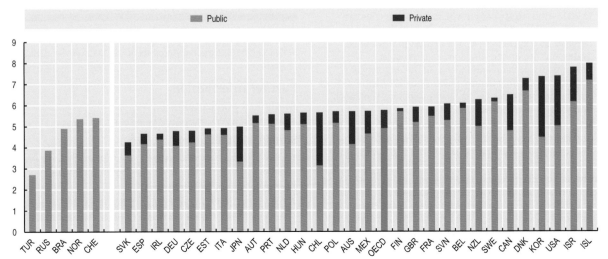

StatLink http://dx.doi.org/10.1787/821750634772

LAW, ORDER AND DEFENCE EXPENDITURE

Two essential tasks of every government are to protect its citizens from external aggression and maintain law and public order within its frontiers.

Definition

Data on public expenditures on law, order and defence are taken from national accounts sources, compiled according to the Classification of the Functions of Government (COFOG). These data cover all expenditures, whether current or capital, undertaken by general government.

Law and order covers expenditure for police forces, intelligence services, prisons and other correctional facilities, the judicial system, and ministries of internal affairs. Defence expenditures are those related to military and civil defence, military aid in the form of grants (in cash or in kind), loans (including equipment) and contributions to international peacekeeping forces, and research and development expenditures related to defence.

Comparability

National accounts data conform to the definitions of the 1993 *System of National Accounts* and are broadly comparable.

In the case of Japan, expenditure data on law, order and defence refer to fiscal years whereas GDP refers to calendar year. Data for New Zealand refer to fiscal years.

Public expenditure on law, order and defence
As a percentage of GDP

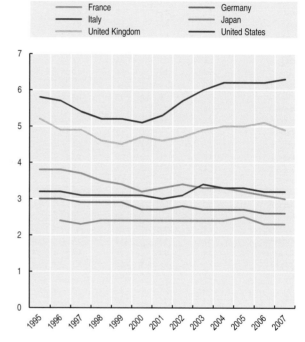

StatLink ⎘ http://dx.doi.org/10.1787/821874301585

Overview

In 2007 – the latest year for which most countries can supply data – public expenditure on law, order and defence, as a share of GDP, was highest in the United States and the United Kingdom and lowest in Luxembourg, Iceland and Ireland. In the majority of countries these shares have fallen since 1997 with particularly large falls in the Slovak Republic, the Czech Republic, Norway, Sweden and France.

Within the total, the shares of law and order, on one side, and defence, on the other, vary considerably among countries, with high shares for defence expenditures in the United States, Greece and Korea, and high shares for law and order in Iceland, Luxembourg, and Ireland. For most countries shown in the table, expenditures on law and order at the end of the period were larger than expenditures on defence. The ratio between the two has grown in most countries since the beginning of the period.

Sources
- OECD (2010), *National Accounts of OECD Countries*, OECD, Paris.

Further information
Analytical publications
- OECD (2004), *The Security Economy*, OECD, Paris.

Statistical publications
- OECD (2009), *National Accounts at a Glance 2009*, OECD, Paris.

Methodological publications
- UN, OECD, IMF, Eurostat (eds.) (1993), *System of National Accounts 1993*, United Nations, Geneva, Paragraph XVIII.9, http://unstats.un.org/unsd/sna1993.

Online databases
- *OECD National Accounts Statistics*.

Public expenditure on law, order and defence

As a percentage of GDP

	1995	1996	1997	1998	1999	2000	2001	2002	2003	2004	2005	2006	2007	2008
Austria	2.6	2.5	2.6	2.5	2.5	2.5	2.4	2.4	2.4	2.4	2.4	2.3	2.3	2.5
Belgium	2.9	2.9	2.8	2.8	2.8	2.7	2.8	2.9	2.9	2.8	2.8	2.7	2.7	..
Canada	3.3	3.2	2.9	3.0	2.9	2.7	2.8	2.7	2.7	2.6	2.6	2.6	..	..
Czech Republic	4.5	4.1	4.1	3.7	4.0	4.1	3.8	3.7	4.2	3.5	3.9	3.4	3.3	..
Denmark	2.8	2.7	2.7	2.7	2.6	2.5	2.6	2.6	2.6	2.6	2.5	2.6	2.6	2.6
Finland	3.3	3.4	3.2	3.0	2.9	2.8	2.7	2.6	2.8	2.9	2.9	2.7	2.6	..
France	3.8	3.8	3.7	3.5	3.4	3.2	3.3	3.4	3.3	3.3	3.2	3.1	3.0	..
Germany	3.0	3.0	2.9	2.9	2.9	2.7	2.7	2.8	2.7	2.7	2.7	2.6	2.6	..
Greece	..	..	..	..	..	4.7	4.5	4.7	4.2	4.0	3.7	3.3	3.6	..
Hungary	..	..	..	..	..	..	3.2	3.7	3.5	3.4	3.4	3.6	3.2	..
Iceland	..	..	1.6	1.5	1.5	1.5	1.5	1.5	1.6	1.5	1.5	1.5	1.5	..
Ireland	2.7	2.6	2.5	2.5	2.2	2.1	2.2	2.0	1.9	1.9	1.8	1.9	2.0	..
Italy	3.2	3.2	3.1	3.1	3.1	3.1	3.0	3.1	3.4	3.3	3.3	3.2	3.2	..
Japan	..	2.4	2.3	2.4	2.4	2.4	2.4	2.4	2.4	2.4	2.5	2.3	2.3	..
Korea	..	..	..	..	..	4.0	3.7	3.5	3.7	3.5	3.7	3.8	3.8	..
Luxembourg	1.3	1.3	1.4	1.3	1.1	1.1	1.2	1.3	1.3	1.3	1.3	1.1	1.1	1.2
Netherlands	3.3	3.3	3.1	3.0	3.1	3.0	3.1	3.2	3.3	3.2	3.2	3.2	3.2	3.2
New Zealand	..	..	..	..	..	..	..	..	2.9	2.7	2.9	..	..	..
Norway	..	3.4	3.3	3.4	3.3	2.9	2.9	3.2	3.1	2.9	2.5	2.5	2.5	..
Poland	..	..	..	..	..	..	..	2.8	2.9	2.6	2.8	3.0	3.2	..
Portugal	3.3	3.4	3.3	3.3	3.2	3.3	3.2	3.3	3.4	3.4	3.4	3.2	2.7	..
Slovak Republic	5.6	5.8	5.7	5.5	4.8	4.9	5.0	4.8	3.7	4.2	3.7	3.8	3.5	..
Spain	3.4	3.2	3.1	3.0	3.0	2.9	3.0	3.0	2.9	2.9	2.9	2.9	2.9	..
Sweden	3.8	3.9	3.7	3.7	3.8	3.6	3.5	3.5	3.4	3.2	3.1	3.1	2.9	..
United Kingdom	5.2	4.9	4.9	4.6	4.5	4.7	4.6	4.7	4.9	5.0	5.0	5.1	4.9	..
United States	5.8	5.7	5.4	5.2	5.2	5.1	5.3	5.7	6.0	6.2	6.2	6.2	6.3	..
Estonia	4.3	4.1	3.9	4.0	4.1	4.1	3.8	3.9	4.1	3.5	3.5	3.4	3.5	..
Israel	10.4	10.6	10.4	10.2	10.2	9.8	10.2	11.3	10.7	9.8	9.6	9.7	9.3	..
Slovenia	..	..	..	..	..	2.8	3.1	3.0	3.1	3.1	3.0	3.1	..	..

StatLink ⟶ http://dx.doi.org/10.1787/826376433538

Public expenditure on law, order and defence

As a percentage of GDP

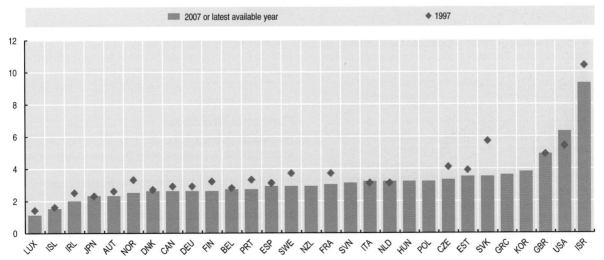

StatLink ⟶ http://dx.doi.org/10.1787/821831416880

GOVERNMENT SUPPORT FOR AGRICULTURE

Governments provide support to agriculture through a variety of means, ranging from budgetary transfers financed by taxpayers to policies such as border protection and administered pricing that, by raising farm prices above the levels that would otherwise prevail, are equivalent to an implicit tax on consumers. While some of these measures may pursue commendable goals such as sustaining rural communities and encouraging more environmentally-friendly agricultural practices, they may also lead to trade distortions, over-production and environmental damage.

Definition

The OECD PSE is an indicator of the annual monetary value of gross transfers from consumers and taxpayers to agricultural producers, measured at the farmgate level, arising from policy measures that support agriculture, regardless of their nature, objectives or impacts on farm production or income. It can be expressed as a total monetary amount, but is more usually quoted as a percentage of gross farm receipts (%PSE). This is the measure used here.

The measure is agreed by OECD member countries and is widely recognised as the only reliable indicator for comparing support across countries and over time. The producer support estimate (PSE) indicator that is available on a timely and comprehensive basis for all 30 of the OECD's countries (the European Union is treated as a single entity) and selected non-members.

Comparability

Continuous efforts are made to ensure consistency in the treatment and completeness of coverage of policies in all

OECD countries through the annual preparation of the Monitoring and Evaluation report. Each year, PSE provisional estimates are reviewed and approved by representatives of OECD's member countries, as are all methodological developments.

In the table, data are not shown for individual EU member countries. Austria, Finland and Sweden are included in EU15 since 1995. The Czech Republic, Hungary, Poland and the Slovak Republic, together with the EU members which are not members of the OECD, are included in EU25 from 2004 to 2006 and EU27 from 2007. The OECD total includes the Czech Republic, Hungary, Poland and the Slovak Republic for the entire period but excludes the EU countries not members of the OECD.

Agricultural producer support estimate for selected countries
As a percentage of gross farm receipts

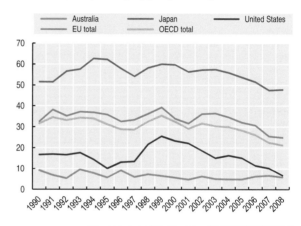

StatLink ⬛⬛ http://dx.doi.org/10.1787/822042462767

Overview

There are large differences in the levels of agricultural support among OECD countries. Producer support estimates as a percentage of gross farm receipts currently range from almost zero to 62%. These differences reflect among other things, variations in policy objectives, different historical uses of policy instruments, and the varying pace and degrees of progress in agricultural policy reform. Over the longer term, the level of producer support has fallen in most OECD countries. The average support as a share of gross farm receipt in 2006-08 at 23% is lower than the 1986-88 average of 37% and has fallen in most countries. There has also been some change in the way support is delivered to the sector. Support known to be the most distorting in terms of production and trade is also less dominant today (56% of total support during the 2006-2008 period) than in the past (over 86% in 1986-1988).

For the emerging economies covered here the %PSE has been significantly lower than the OECD average, ranging from 4% for Chile to 16% for Israel in 2005-07. Trends in the level of producer support vary between economies. While in Chile, Israel, the Russian Federation and South Africa the level of producer support has fallen, in Brazil and China it has increased since the mid-1990s.

Sources

- OECD (2009), *Agricultural Policies in OECD Countries 2009: Monitoring and Evaluation*, OECD, Paris.
- OECD (2009), *Agricultural Policies in Emerging Economies 2009: Monitoring and Evaluation*, OECD, Paris.
- OECD (2010), *OECD Review of Agricultural Policies: Israel 2010*, OECD, Paris.

Further information
Analytical publications
- OECD (2008), *Agricultural Policy Design and Implementation: A synthesis*, OECD, Paris.
- OECD, FAO (2008), *OECD-FAO Agricultural Outlook 2008-2017*, OECD, Paris.

Methodological publications
- OECD (2009), *OECD's Producer Support Estimate and Related Indicators of Agricultural Support: Concepts, Calculations, Interpretation and Use (The PSE Manual)*, OECD, Paris.

Agricultural producer support estimate by country

As a percentage of gross farm receipts

	1995	1996	1997	1998	1999	2000	2001	2002	2003	2004	2005	2006	2007	2008
Australia	5.8	9.1	6.0	7.3	6.5	5.7	4.8	6.3	5.1	4.9	4.9	6.3	6.7	5.9
Canada	19.5	16.1	14.4	17.0	18.0	20.0	15.8	21.5	25.4	20.9	21.9	21.7	19.4	13.0
Iceland	59.6	58.7	59.8	71.3	72.0	67.2	63.4	67.5	66.4	66.0	67.1	65.3	56.8	51.0
Japan	62.2	57.9	54.2	58.2	60.0	59.7	56.3	57.2	57.5	55.9	53.7	51.5	47.5	47.8
Korea	72.0	64.2	63.0	56.2	64.7	66.0	60.3	63.8	60.6	65.8	65.6	65.3	65.1	51.7
Mexico	-4.2	5.0	14.5	17.5	17.3	23.4	18.2	26.9	19.2	11.5	12.8	13.8	13.6	13.1
New Zealand	1.5	1.0	1.1	1.0	0.9	0.5	0.7	0.4	0.9	0.9	1.5	1.0	1.0	0.8
Norway	65.0	66.8	69.0	71.2	71.9	67.0	66.2	74.7	72.0	67.4	66.9	65.3	58.7	61.9
Switzerland	64.8	69.1	69.7	71.8	75.9	70.4	67.9	71.3	70.0	69.9	66.9	66.4	55.0	58.1
Turkey	13.0	16.0	24.9	26.4	22.3	20.8	3.9	20.9	28.3	26.2	25.1	19.9	18.9	24.5
United States	10.1	13.1	13.5	21.6	25.5	23.3	22.1	18.6	15.1	16.3	15.1	11.5	10.2	6.8
EU total	35.8	32.5	33.4	36.2	39.3	33.9	31.6	36.1	36.4	34.6	32.1	30.7	25.5	24.9
OECD total	31.2	28.9	28.7	32.5	35.4	32.5	29.2	31.7	30.4	30.0	28.3	26.2	22.5	21.3
Brazil	-7.7	-0.1	-1.8	6.8	1.3	5.8	4.2	5.7	5.9	4.6	6.3	6.1	5.0	..
Chile	8.5	7.1	7.8	10.6	10.5	9.9	6.2	10.8	5.3	4.9	4.9	4.3	3.9	..
China	6.2	1.8	1.8	1.5	-2.4	3.4	5.9	8.8	10.1	7.2	7.8	11.0	8.6	..
Israel	24.2	24.5	23.1	23.8	25.1	28.9	26.3	26.6	22.0	20.7	17.5	17.6	11.8	20.9
Russian Federation	13.2	17.7	26.4	18.6	-0.7	4.6	9.2	14.6	20.9	21.9	13.3	17.5	10.8	..
South Africa	14.7	7.6	10.8	10.7	8.2	5.2	3.9	11.0	7.1	7.7	6.5	7.5	3.3	..

StatLink http://dx.doi.org/10.1787/826383215346

Agricultural producer support estimate by country

As a percentage of gross farm receipts

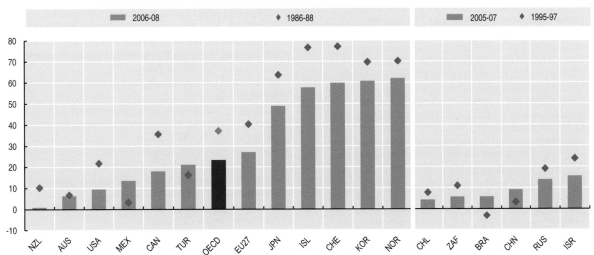

StatLink http://dx.doi.org/10.1787/822022843872

GOVERNMENT SUPPORT FOR FISHING

OECD governments provide financial support to the fishing industry, typically for the purposes of management, including surveillance and research. This financial support is important to ensure a sustainable and responsible fisheries sector.

Definition

The indicator on "Government financial transfers (GFTs)" provides a measure of the financial support provided by governments to the fisheries sector. GFT consists of direct revenue enhancing transfers (direct payments), i.e. transfers that reduce the operating costs and the costs of general services provided to the fishing industry. These general services consist mainly of fishery protection services and fisheries management; in some cases they also include the costs of local area weather forecasting and the costs of navigation and satellite surveillance systems designed to assist fishing fleets.

Comparability

The data are relatively comprehensive and consistent across the years. However, some year-to-year variations may reflect changes in national statistical systems. General services provided by governments may also include large and irregular capital investments. It should also be noted that some types of GFT (e.g. at maritime surveillance) may be provided by another agency than fisheries agencies (e.g. in some countries maritime surveillance is carried out by the navy); some of these data may not be available. Also, some figures, in particular for later years, are still preliminary.

GFT to fishing for selected countries
Million US dollars

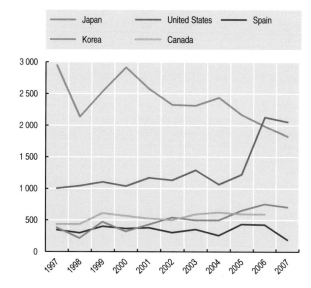

StatLink http://dx.doi.org/10.1787/822130571445

Sources

- OECD (2007), *Review of Fisheries in OECD Countries: Vol. 2 – Country Statistics, 2002-2004, 2006 Edition*, OECD, Paris.
- OECD (2009), *Review of Fisheries in OECD Countries: Policies and Summary Statistics 2008*, OECD, Paris.
- OECD (2010), (Forthcoming), *Review of Fisheries in OECD Countries 2009: Policies and Summary Statistics*, OECD, Paris.

Further information

Analytical publications

- Cox, A. (2003), *OECD Work on Defining and Measuring Subsidies in Fisheries*, OECD, Paris.
- Cox, A. (2004), *Subsidies and Deep-Sea Fisheries Management: Policy Issues and Challenges*, OECD, Paris.
- Cox, A. and C. Schmidt (2003), *Subsidies in the OECD Fisheries Sector: A Review of Recent Analysis and Future Directions*, background paper for the FAO Expert Consultation on Identifying, Assessing and Reporting on Subsidies in the Fishing Industry, Rome, 3-6 December 2002.
- OECD (2000), *Transition to Responsible Fisheries: Economic and Policy Implications*, OECD, Paris.
- OECD (2005), *Environmentally Harmful Subsidies: Challenges for Reform*, OECD, Paris.
- OECD (2006), *OECD Sustainable Development Studies – Subsidy Reform and Sustainable Development: Economic, Environmental and Social Aspects*, OECD, Paris.
- OECD and FAO (2008), *Globalisation and Fisheries – Proceedings of an OECD-FAO Workshop*, OECD, Paris.
- OECD (2006), *Financial Support to Fisheries: Implications for Sustainable Development*, OECD, Paris.
- OECD (2007), *Structural Change in Fisheries: Dealing with the Human Dimension*, OECD, Paris.
- OECD (2009), *Reducing Fishing Capacity: Best Practices for Decommissioning Schemes*, OECD, Paris.

Web sites

- OECD Fisheries, *www.oecd.org/fisheries*.

Overview

Total government support for fishing peaked at USD 6.6 billion in 2006. Overall, transfers to the fishing industry in OECD countries have been fluctuating at around USD 6 billion over the last decade. The majority of GFTs are categorized as general services, accounting for 75% of the total GFTs in 2006. OECD governments spent USD 1.6 billion for management and enforcement, and USD 736 million to conduct fisheries research. Other types of general services covered by GFTs include harbor construction and maintenance, as well as stock enhancement and habitat conservation. A large part of GFTs for general services (USD 2.1 billion out of 5.3 billion) are included in the "not specified" category, as several countries have not reported sufficient details.

Direct payments represent 19% of total GFTs. In 2006, USD 250 million were dedicated to decommissioning schemes, while USD 32 million were used to construct or modernize fishing vessels. Other direct payments included unemployment insurance (USD 223 million) and disaster relief (USD 188 million). The third category of GFTs, cost reducing transfers, accounted for 6% of the total GFTs.

Government financial transfers to fishing
Thousand US dollars

	1997	1998	1999	2000	2001	2002	2003	2004	2005	2006	2007
Australia	41 230	..	..	82 272	75 902	78 038	95 558	95 560	46 299	52 080	60 355
Belgium	4 949	..	4 473	6 849	2 830	1 607	1 668	6 328	8 613	7 103	3 140
Canada	433 309	..	606 443	564 497	521 355	497 771	589 975	618 787	591 000	596 195	..
Denmark	82 030	90 507	27 765	16 316	..	68 769	37 659	28 505	58 108	90 036	62 105
Finland	26 198	26 888	19 236	13 908	16 510	16 025	20 231	19 397	24 817	17 496	20 892
France	140 807	..	71 665	166 147	141 786	155 283	179 740	236 811	126 194	36 535	35 229
Germany	63 215	16 488	31 276	29 834	28 988	28 208	33 890	18 326	30 928	4 878	6 819
Greece	46 958	26 908	43 030	87 315	86 957	88 334	119 045	35 500	61 013	58 276	35 267
Iceland	38 678	36 954	39 763	41 978	28 310	28 955	48 348	55 705	64 326	52 000	68 000
Ireland	98 880	..	143 184	..	..	63 632	64 960	21 448	22 144	19 743	6 167
Italy	91 811	..	200 470	217 679	231 680	159 630	149 270	170 055	119 239	165 161	..
Japan	2 945 785	2 135 946	2 537 536	2 913 149	2 574 086	2 323 601	2 310 744	2 437 934	2 165 198	1 950 000	1 824 000
Korea	378 994	211 927	471 556	320 449	428 313	538 695	495 280	495 280	649 387	644 000	703 000
Mexico	16 808	..	..	..	..	..	177 000	114 000	84 973	88 760	85 267
Netherlands	35 849	..	..	1 389	12 779	12 443	6 569	5 218	13 685	18 425	5 638
New Zealand	40 397	29 412	29 630	27 273	15 126	18 981	38 325	50 134	32 197	37 966	40 574
Norway	163 437	153 046	180 962	104 564	99 465	156 340	139 200	142 315	149 521	143 498	169 367
Poland	7 927	..	..	..	..	..	..	..	50 523	33 659	20 477
Portugal	65 077	..	28 674	25 578	25 066	24 899	26 930	26 930	32 769	29 219	30 896
Spain	344 581	296 642	399 604	364 096	376 614	301 926	353 290	256 569	433 786	246 625	188 207
Sweden	53 452	26 960	31 053	25 186	22 505	24 753	30 650	34 422	36 603	34 785	45 652
Turkey	15 114	..	1 277	26 372	17 721	16 167	16 300	59 500	98 072	136 182	144 739
United Kingdom	128 066	90 833	75 968	81 394	73 738	..	82 691	87 487	103 150	103 994	..
United States	1 002 580	1 041 000	1 103 100	1 037 710	1 169 590	1 130 810	1 290 440	1 064 400	..	2 043 425	2 053 142
OECD total	6 258 205	4 183 511	6 046 665	6 153 955	5 949 321	5 734 867	6 307 763	6 080 611	6 174 521	6 610 041	5 608 933
India	341	397	410	331	346	314	..	..	..	..	..
Slovenia	520	581	484	723	581	687	680	566	1 085	1 346	3 787

StatLink http://dx.doi.org/10.1787/826416450536

Government financial transfers to fishing
Average annual growth in percentage, 1997-2007 or latest available period

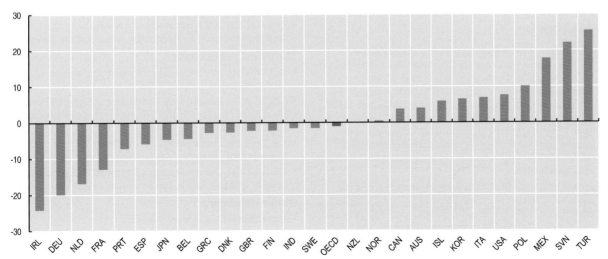

StatLink http://dx.doi.org/10.1787/822116435128

OFFICIAL DEVELOPMENT ASSISTANCE

Promoting economic and social development in non-member countries has been a principal objective of the OECD since its foundation. The share of national income devoted to official development assistance (ODA) is a test of a country's commitment to international development. A long-standing United Nations target is that developed countries should devote 0.7% of their gross national income (GNI) to ODA.

Definition

This section shows total net ODA as shares of GNI as well as the geographical distribution of bilateral ODA.

ODA is defined as government aid designed to promote the economic development and welfare of developing countries. Loans and credits for military purposes are excluded. Aid may be provided bilaterally, from donor to recipient, or channelled through a multilateral development agency such as the United Nations or the World Bank. Aid includes grants, "soft" loans and the provision of technical assistance. Soft loans are those where the grant element is at least 25% of the total.

The OECD maintains a list of developing countries and territories; only aid to these countries counts as ODA. The list is periodically updated and currently contains over 150 countries or territories with per capita incomes below USD 11 456 in 2007. Data refer to ODA provided by 22 OECD countries that are members of the Development Assistance Committee (DAC).

Data on the geographical distribution of aid are presented in this section on a gross basis (i.e. without any deductions for loan repayments) to show the level of new aid provided during the period.

Comparability

Statistics on ODA are compiled according to directives drawn up by the DAC. Each country's statistics are subject to regular peer reviews by other DAC members.

Sources
- *Development Assistance Committee Aid Statistics.*

Further information
Analytical publications
- OECD (2010), *OECD Journal on Development: Development Co-operation – 2010 Report – Efforts and Policies of the Members of the Development Assistance Committee Volume 10 Issue 1*, OECD, Paris.
- OECD (2008), *OECD Journal on Development Volume 9 Issue 2: Measuring Human Rights and Democratic Governance: Experiences and Lessons from Metagora*, OECD, Paris.
- OECD (2009), *Natural Resources and Pro-Poor Growth: The Economics and Politics, DAC Guidelines and Reference Series*, OECD, Paris.
- OECD (2008), *Governance, Taxation and Accountability: Issues and Practice, DAC Guidelines and Reference Series*, OECD, Paris.
- OECD (2008), *2008 Survey on Monitoring the Paris Declaration: Making Aid More Effective by 2010, Better Aid*, OECD, Paris.
- OECD (2009), *Aid Effectiveness: A Progress Report on Implementing the Paris Declaration, Better Aid*, OECD, Paris.

Statistical publications
- OECD (2010), *International Development Statistics on CD-Rom*, OECD, Paris.
- OECD (2010), *Geographical Distribution of Financial Flows to Developing Countries 2010: Disbursements, Commitments, Country Indicators*, OECD, Paris.
- OECD (2009), *Development Aid at a Glance 2008: Statistics by Region*, OECD, Paris.
- OECD (2008), *Creditor Reporting System 2008: Aid Activities in Support of Water Supply and Sanitation*, OECD, Paris.

Online databases
- *International Development Statistics.*

Web sites
- Development Assistance Committee Aid Statistics, *www.oecd.org/dac/stats.*
- OECD, Calculation of the Grant Element of Loans, *www.oecd.org/dataoecd/15/0/31738575.pdf.*

Overview

The weighted average of total ODA provided by DAC members, as a percentage of their total GNI, amounted to 0.31% in 2008; the unweighted average, measuring "average country effort", was 0.48%. The decline in both the weighted and unweighted averages recorded since 1990 was halted in 1999 and then reversed as DAC members took steps to meet the commitments they made at the Monterrey 2002 Financing for Development Conference and at the Gleneagles G8 and UN Millennium +5 summits in 2005.

In 2008, total net ODA from DAC members reached the highest value ever recorded (USD 121.5 billion), with an increase of 11.7% in real terms compared to 2007. The volume of bilateral ODA development projects and programmes has been on a rising trend in recent years and increased significantly between 2007 and 2008, indicating that donors are considerably scaling up their core aid programmes.

Net official development assistance

As a percentage of gross national income

	1995	1996	1997	1998	1999	2000	2001	2002	2003	2004	2005	2006	2007	2008
Australia	0.34	0.27	0.27	0.27	0.26	0.27	0.25	0.26	0.25	0.25	0.25	0.30	0.32	0.32
Austria	0.27	0.23	0.24	0.22	0.24	0.23	0.34	0.26	0.20	0.23	0.52	0.47	0.50	0.43
Belgium	0.38	0.34	0.31	0.35	0.30	0.36	0.37	0.43	0.60	0.41	0.53	0.50	0.43	0.48
Canada	0.38	0.32	0.34	0.30	0.28	0.25	0.22	0.28	0.24	0.27	0.34	0.29	0.29	0.32
Denmark	0.96	1.04	0.97	0.99	1.01	1.06	1.03	0.96	0.84	0.85	0.81	0.80	0.81	0.82
Finland	0.31	0.33	0.32	0.31	0.33	0.31	0.32	0.35	0.35	0.37	0.46	0.40	0.39	0.44
France	0.55	0.48	0.44	0.38	0.38	0.30	0.31	0.37	0.40	0.41	0.47	0.47	0.38	0.39
Germany	0.31	0.32	0.28	0.26	0.26	0.27	0.27	0.27	0.28	0.28	0.36	0.36	0.37	0.38
Greece	..	0.15	0.14	0.15	0.15	0.20	0.17	0.21	0.21	0.16	0.17	0.17	0.16	0.21
Ireland	0.29	0.31	0.31	0.30	0.31	0.29	0.33	0.40	0.39	0.39	0.42	0.54	0.55	0.59
Italy	0.15	0.20	0.11	0.20	0.15	0.13	0.15	0.20	0.17	0.15	0.29	0.20	0.19	0.22
Japan	0.27	0.20	0.21	0.27	0.27	0.28	0.23	0.23	0.20	0.19	0.28	0.25	0.17	0.19
Luxembourg	0.36	0.44	0.55	0.65	0.66	0.70	0.77	0.78	0.86	0.79	0.79	0.89	0.92	0.97
Netherlands	0.81	0.81	0.81	0.80	0.79	0.84	0.82	0.81	0.80	0.73	0.82	0.81	0.81	0.80
New Zealand	0.23	0.21	0.26	0.27	0.27	0.25	0.25	0.22	0.23	0.23	0.27	0.27	0.27	0.30
Norway	0.86	0.83	0.84	0.89	0.88	0.76	0.80	0.89	0.92	0.87	0.94	0.89	0.95	0.88
Portugal	0.25	0.21	0.25	0.24	0.26	0.26	0.25	0.27	0.22	0.63	0.21	0.21	0.22	0.27
Spain	0.24	0.22	0.24	0.24	0.23	0.22	0.30	0.26	0.23	0.24	0.27	0.32	0.37	0.45
Sweden	0.77	0.84	0.79	0.72	0.70	0.80	0.77	0.84	0.79	0.78	0.94	1.02	0.93	0.98
Switzerland	0.34	0.34	0.34	0.32	0.35	0.34	0.34	0.33	0.37	0.40	0.43	0.39	0.38	0.42
United Kingdom	0.29	0.27	0.26	0.27	0.24	0.32	0.32	0.31	0.34	0.36	0.47	0.51	0.35	0.43
United States	0.10	0.12	0.09	0.10	0.10	0.10	0.11	0.13	0.15	0.17	0.23	0.18	0.16	0.19
DAC total	0.26	0.25	0.22	0.23	0.22	0.22	0.22	0.23	0.25	0.26	0.33	0.31	0.28	0.31
of which: EU members	0.37	0.37	0.33	0.33	0.31	0.32	0.33	0.35	0.35	0.35	0.44	0.43	0.39	0.43

StatLink http://dx.doi.org/10.1787/826454736750

Net official development assistance

As a percentage of gross national income

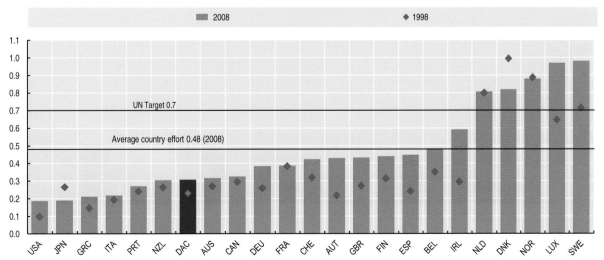

StatLink http://dx.doi.org/10.1787/822143200636

Distribution of gross bilateral ODA from DAC countries by income group and by region
Million US dollars, 2-year averages

	1987-88	1997-98	2007-08
Distribution of bilateral ODA by income group			
Least Developed Countries	8 604	8 197	22 819
Other Low-Income Countries	2 607	3 407	7 140
Lower Middle-Income Countries	11 408	15 596	32 291
Upper Middle-Income Countries	2 515	3 114	6 217
More Advanced Developing Countries and Territories	2 675	1 107	8
Unallocated	5 714	9 211	24 366
Distribution of bilateral ODA by region			
Sub-Saharan Africa	9 237	9 545	24 384
Middle East and North Africa	4 648	3 908	15 848
South and Central Asia	4 250	4 326	11 478
Other Asia and Oceania	6 465	8 902	11 818
Europe	763	1 445	3 056
Latin America and Caribbean	3 641	5 004	7 317
Unspecified	4 518	7 502	18 940
Bilateral ODA	33 522	40 632	92 841
Multilateral ODA	13 410	16 560	33 014
Total ODA	46 932	57 193	125 855

StatLink http://dx.doi.org/10.1787/826501547436

Distribution of gross bilateral ODA from DAC countries by region
Million US dollars

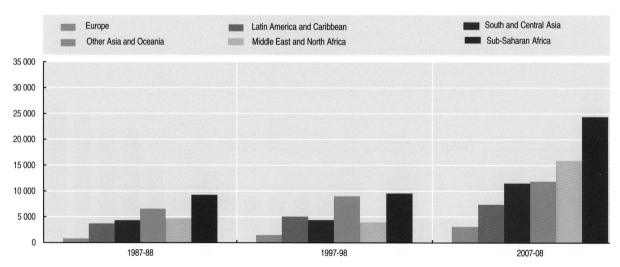

StatLink http://dx.doi.org/10.1787/822155163426

Major recipients of total gross bilateral ODA from DAC countries

2-year averages

	1987-88			1997-98			2007-08	
	Million US dollars	As a percentage of total ODA		Million US dollars	As a percentage of total ODA		Million US dollars	As a percentage of total ODA
Indonesia	1 764	3.8	China	1 863	3.3	Iraq	9 462	7.5
Egypt	1 615	3.4	Indonesia	1 711	3.0	Afghanistan	3 475	2.8
India	1 359	2.9	Egypt	1 613	2.8	China	2 601	2.1
Israel	1 349	2.9	India	1 556	2.7	Indonesia	2 543	2.0
China	1 088	2.3	Philippines	935	1.6	India	2 263	1.8
Bangladesh	961	2.0	Thailand	861	1.5	Vietnam	1 745	1.4
Pakistan	889	1.9	Bangladesh	758	1.3	Sudan	1 743	1.4
Philippines	836	1.8	Vietnam	714	1.2	Tanzania	1 603	1.3
Tanzania	765	1.6	Mozambique	694	1.2	Ethiopia	1 551	1.2
Mozambique	651	1.4	Tanzania	687	1.2	Cameroon	1 396	1.1
Kenya	566	1.2	Pakistan	622	1.1	Egypt	1 389	1.1
Thailand	562	1.2	Bosnia-Herzegovina	560	1.0	Bangladesh	1 310	1.0
Turkey	544	1.2	Cote d'Ivoire	506	0.9	Mozambique	1 222	1.0
Sudan	475	1.0	Madagascar	479	0.8	Nigeria	1 121	0.9
Ethiopia	445	0.9	Peru	464	0.8	Palestinian Administered Areas	1 108	0.9
Bilateral ODA	33 522	71.4	Bilateral ODA	40 632	71.0	Bilateral ODA	92 841	73.8
Multilateral ODA	13 410	28.6	Multilateral ODA	16 560	29.0	Multilateral ODA	33 014	26.2
Total ODA	46 932	100.0	Total ODA	57 193	100.0	Total ODA	125 855	100.0

StatLink http://dx.doi.org/10.1787/826508213458

Distribution of gross bilateral ODA from DAC countries by income group

Million US dollars

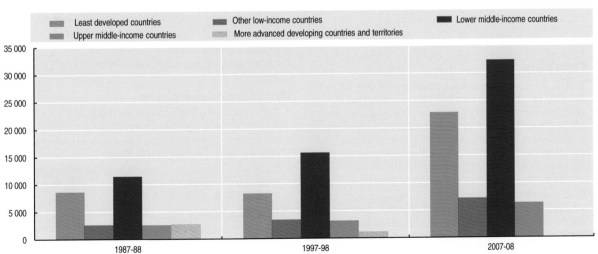

StatLink http://dx.doi.org/10.1787/822167225743

TOTAL TAX REVENUE

Total tax revenue as a percentage of GDP indicates the share of a country's output that is collected by the government through taxes. It can thus be regarded as one measure of the degree to which the government controls the economy's resources.

Definition

Taxes are defined as compulsory, unrequited payments to general government. They are unrequited in the sense that benefits provided by government to taxpayers are not normally in proportion to their payments. The data on total tax revenue shown here refer to the revenues collected from taxes on income and profits, social security contributions, taxes levied on goods and services, payroll taxes, taxes on the ownership and transfer of property and other taxes.

Taxes on incomes and profits cover taxes levied on the net income or profits (gross income minus allowable tax reliefs) of individuals and enterprises. They also cover taxes levied on the capital gains of individuals and enterprises, and gains from gambling.

Taxes on goods and services cover all taxes levied on the production, extraction, sale, transfer, leasing or delivery of goods, and the rendering of services, or on the use of goods or permission to use goods or to perform activities. They consist mainly of value added and sales taxes.

Note that the sum of taxes on goods and services and taxes on income and profits is less than the figure for total tax revenues.

Overview

In 2008, total tax revenues as a percentage of GDP fell in 17 OECD countries and rose in 9. This suggests that the OECD average of total revenues had fallen by about 0.5% of GDP from the level of 35.8% reached in 2007. The slow upward trend in this ratio recorded in almost all OECD countries during the 1990s stopped in 2000. Since 2001, the total tax revenue as a percentage of GDP for all OECD countries has fallen slightly.

Revenue collected from taxes on income and profit accounted for 13.2% of GDP on average in 2007. This ratio showed an upward trend in the second half of the 1990s reaching a peak in 2000. After declining slightly in the following years, the average ratio in 2007 rose above the 2000 peak.

The OECD average for tax revenues on goods and services has been remarkably stable since 1994 at a level of around 11% of GDP.

Comparability

The tax revenue data are collected in a way that makes them as internationally comparable as possible. Country representatives have agreed on the definitions of each type of tax and how they should be measured in all OECD countries, and they are then responsible for submitting data to the OECD that conform to these rules. The rules are set out in "The OECD Interpretative Guide" shown at the end of each edition of *Revenue Statistics*.

Sources
- OECD (2009), *Revenue Statistics 1965-2008 – Edition 2009*, OECD, Paris.

Further information

Analytical publications
- OECD (2004), *Recent Tax Policy Trends and Reforms in OECD Countries*, OECD Tax Policy Studies, No. 9, OECD, Paris.
- OECD (2005), *Consumption Tax Trends: VAT/GST and Excise rates, Trends and Administration Issues, 2005 Edition*, OECD, Paris.
- OECD (2006), *OECD Tax Policy Studies – N.15 Encouraging Savings through Tax-Preferred Accounts*, OECD, Paris.
- OECD (2006), *The Political Economy of Environmentally Related Taxes*, OECD, Paris.
- OECD (2008), *Consumption Tax Trends: VAT/GST and Excise Rates, Trends and Administration Issues, 2008*, OECD, Paris.
- OECD (2008), *Tax Co-operation 2008: Towards a Level Playing Field: Assessment by the Global Forum on Taxation*, OECD, Paris.

Statistical publications
- OECD (2009), *Taxing Wages 2007-2008, 2008 Edition*, OECD, Paris.

Methodological publications
- Electronic Model Tax Convention (eMTC), *www.sourceoecd.org/reference/modeltax*.
- OECD (1992-2008), *Model Tax Convention on Income and on Capital*, yearly updates, OECD, Paris.
- OECD (2005), *Model Tax Convention on Income and on Capital Model Tax Convention on Income and on Capital*, condensed version, OECD, Paris.

Online databases
- *Revenue Statistics of OECD Member Countries*.
- *Taxing Wages Statistics*.

Web sites
- OECD Centre for Tax Policy and Administration, *www.oecd.org/ctp*.
- Tax Administration in OECD Countries: Comparative Information Series (2004), *www.oecd.org/ctp/ta*.

Total tax revenue
As a percentage of GDP

	1995	1996	1997	1998	1999	2000	2001	2002	2003	2004	2005	2006	2007	2008
Australia	28.8	29.4	29.2	30.0	30.5	31.1	29.6	30.5	30.6	31.1	30.8	30.6	30.8	..
Austria	41.4	42.9	44.4	44.4	44.0	43.2	45.3	44.0	43.8	43.4	42.3	41.8	42.3	42.9
Belgium	43.6	44.0	44.5	45.2	45.2	44.9	44.9	45.0	44.6	44.8	44.7	44.4	43.9	44.3
Canada	35.6	35.9	36.7	36.7	36.4	35.6	34.8	33.7	33.7	33.6	33.4	33.5	33.3	32.2
Czech Republic	37.5	36.0	36.3	34.9	35.8	35.3	35.6	36.3	37.3	37.8	37.6	37.1	37.4	36.6
Denmark	48.8	49.2	48.9	49.3	50.1	49.4	48.4	47.8	48.0	49.0	50.8	49.6	48.7	48.3
Finland	45.7	47.0	46.3	46.1	45.8	47.2	44.6	44.6	44.0	43.5	44.0	43.5	43.0	42.8
France	42.9	44.1	44.4	44.2	45.1	44.4	44.0	43.4	43.2	43.5	43.9	44.0	43.5	43.1
Germany	37.2	36.5	36.2	36.4	37.1	37.2	36.1	35.4	35.5	34.8	34.8	35.6	36.2	36.4
Greece	28.9	35.9	30.3	32.0	32.9	34.0	32.9	33.6	32.2	31.1	31.4	31.2	32.0	31.3
Hungary	41.3	39.7	38.1	37.8	38.1	38.0	38.1	37.9	37.6	37.6	37.3	37.1	39.5	40.1
Iceland	31.2	32.3	32.2	34.5	36.9	37.2	35.4	35.3	36.7	38.0	40.6	41.5	40.9	36.0
Ireland	32.5	32.5	31.8	31.3	31.5	31.3	29.1	28.0	28.5	29.9	30.4	31.7	30.8	28.3
Italy	40.1	41.8	43.2	41.7	42.5	42.3	42.0	41.4	41.8	41.0	40.8	42.3	43.5	43.2
Japan	26.8	26.8	27.2	26.8	26.3	27.0	27.3	26.2	25.7	26.3	27.4	28.0	28.3	..
Korea	18.6	19.2	20.1	20.2	20.6	22.6	23.0	23.2	23.9	23.2	23.9	25.0	26.5	26.6
Luxembourg	37.1	37.6	39.3	39.4	38.3	39.1	39.7	39.3	38.1	37.2	37.6	35.8	36.5	38.3
Mexico	15.2	15.3	15.9	15.1	15.8	16.9	17.1	16.5	17.4	17.1	18.1	18.3	18.0	21.1
Netherlands	41.5	40.9	40.9	39.1	40.1	39.7	38.2	37.5	36.9	37.3	38.5	38.9	37.5	..
New Zealand	36.6	34.8	35.0	33.4	33.4	33.6	33.0	34.4	34.2	35.3	37.4	36.6	35.7	34.5
Norway	40.9	40.8	41.5	42.4	42.7	42.6	42.9	43.1	42.3	43.3	43.5	44.0	43.6	42.1
Poland	36.2	37.4	36.6	35.6	35.1	32.8	32.6	33.1	32.6	31.7	33.0	34.0	34.9	..
Portugal	32.1	32.7	32.8	33.0	33.9	34.1	33.8	34.5	34.7	33.9	34.7	35.5	36.4	36.5
Slovak Republic	..	..	..	36.7	35.4	34.1	33.2	33.2	33.1	31.6	31.4	29.4	29.4	29.3
Spain	32.1	31.9	32.9	33.2	34.1	34.2	33.8	34.2	34.2	34.6	35.7	36.7	37.2	33.0
Sweden	47.5	49.4	50.6	51.0	51.4	51.8	49.8	47.9	48.3	48.7	49.5	49.0	48.3	47.1
Switzerland	27.7	28.1	27.6	28.5	28.7	30.0	29.5	29.9	29.2	28.8	29.2	29.3	28.9	29.4
Turkey	16.8	18.9	20.7	21.1	23.1	24.2	26.1	24.6	25.9	24.1	24.3	24.5	23.7	23.5
United Kingdom	34.0	33.8	34.3	35.5	35.7	36.4	36.1	34.6	34.3	34.9	35.8	36.6	36.1	35.7
United States	27.9	28.3	28.7	29.3	29.4	29.9	28.8	26.5	25.9	26.1	27.5	28.2	28.3	26.9
OECD average	34.7	35.3	35.4	35.5	35.9	36.0	35.5	35.2	35.1	35.1	35.7	35.8	35.8	..
Slovenia	39.2	38.1	37.0	37.8	38.2	37.5	37.7	38.0	38.2	38.3	38.6	38.3	37.8	37.1

StatLink http://dx.doi.org/10.1787/826510051556

Total tax revenue
As a percentage of GDP

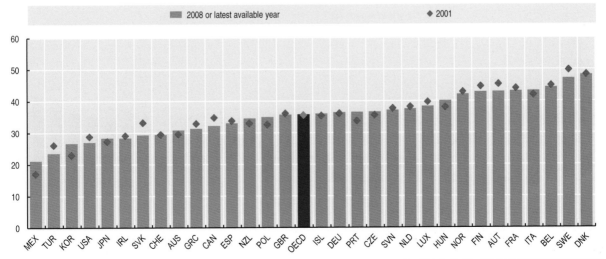

StatLink http://dx.doi.org/10.1787/822256363522

Taxes on income and profits
As a percentage of GDP

	1995	1996	1997	1998	1999	2000	2001	2002	2003	2004	2005	2006	2007	2008
Australia	15.9	16.6	16.5	17.7	18.3	18.1	16.7	17.2	17.3	18.2	18.2	18.1	18.4	..
Austria	10.9	11.9	12.7	12.9	12.5	12.3	14.1	13.0	12.8	12.6	12.0	12.1	12.7	13.2
Belgium	16.6	16.6	17.0	17.5	17.1	17.3	17.5	17.3	16.9	16.9	17.1	16.7	16.5	16.7
Canada	16.5	16.9	17.9	17.7	18.1	17.8	16.7	15.4	15.4	15.7	15.8	16.4	16.6	15.9
Czech Republic	9.4	8.1	8.7	8.1	8.3	8.0	8.6	9.0	9.5	9.5	9.1	9.1	9.4	8.5
Denmark	30.2	30.2	29.9	29.5	29.6	29.8	28.8	28.6	28.8	29.7	31.2	29.9	29.0	29.3
Finland	16.5	18.2	17.7	18.1	17.8	20.4	18.2	18.1	17.0	16.8	16.8	16.6	16.9	16.7
France	7.0	7.4	8.1	10.2	10.8	11.0	11.2	10.4	10.0	10.2	10.3	10.7	10.4	10.4
Germany	11.3	10.5	10.2	10.7	11.1	11.2	10.4	9.9	9.7	9.5	9.8	10.8	11.3	11.6
Greece	6.4	6.4	6.8	8.1	8.4	9.3	8.0	8.1	7.4	7.5	8.0	7.4	7.5	7.3
Hungary	8.7	8.7	8.3	8.4	8.9	9.2	9.8	10.0	9.3	8.9	8.8	9.1	10.0	10.4
Iceland	10.6	11.3	11.5	13.0	14.2	14.8	15.3	15.3	16.0	16.1	17.5	18.3	18.5	17.8
Ireland	12.7	13.2	13.1	12.9	13.2	13.2	12.2	11.1	11.3	11.8	11.7	12.5	12.1	10.6
Italy	14.2	14.5	15.3	13.6	14.4	14.0	14.3	13.4	12.9	12.9	12.9	13.9	14.7	14.9
Japan	10.3	10.2	10.1	9.0	8.4	9.4	9.1	8.0	7.9	8.4	9.3	9.9	10.3	9.7
Korea	5.9	5.8	5.3	6.1	5.1	6.5	6.1	5.9	6.7	6.5	7.0	7.4	8.4	8.2
Luxembourg	14.6	14.9	15.6	15.1	13.9	14.1	14.3	14.4	13.9	12.3	12.9	12.5	12.8	13.7
Mexico	3.8	3.7	4.2	4.3	4.6	4.6	4.8	4.8	4.6	4.2	4.4	4.6	5.0	5.2
Netherlands	10.9	11.1	10.7	10.3	10.2	10.0	10.1	10.2	9.4	9.2	10.7	10.6	10.9	..
New Zealand	22.4	20.7	20.9	19.4	19.4	20.2	19.5	20.5	20.4	21.6	23.6	22.7	22.5	20.6
Norway	14.3	14.8	15.7	15.7	16.0	19.2	19.3	18.8	18.5	20.1	21.4	22.0	21.0	21.2
Poland	11.1	10.7	10.4	10.3	7.4	6.8	6.4	6.3	6.0	5.9	6.4	7.0	8.0	..
Portugal	7.9	8.6	8.7	8.5	9.1	9.6	9.1	8.9	8.4	8.3	8.2	8.5	9.4	9.6
Slovak Republic	..	..	..	8.6	8.6	7.0	7.1	6.6	6.7	5.7	5.6	5.7	5.8	6.1
Spain	9.4	9.2	9.8	9.4	9.6	9.7	9.5	9.9	9.6	9.7	10.4	11.1	12.3	10.1
Sweden	18.6	19.3	19.9	19.9	20.8	21.2	18.9	17.1	17.8	18.6	19.4	19.3	18.7	17.1
Switzerland	11.9	12.3	11.9	12.5	12.0	13.2	12.4	12.9	12.5	12.5	13.0	13.4	13.2	13.9
Turkey	4.8	5.0	5.7	7.0	7.3	7.1	7.5	6.1	6.1	5.3	5.3	5.3	5.6	5.7
United Kingdom	12.6	12.4	12.7	13.8	13.8	14.2	14.3	13.2	12.6	12.8	13.7	14.5	14.3	14.2
United States	12.8	13.5	14.0	14.4	14.6	15.1	14.1	11.7	11.2	11.4	12.9	13.6	13.9	12.6
OECD average	12.4	12.5	12.7	12.8	12.8	13.1	12.8	12.4	12.2	12.3	12.8	13.0	13.2	..
Slovenia	6.5	7.0	7.1	6.9	6.9	6.9	7.1	7.4	7.6	7.8	8.3	8.7	8.8	8.4

StatLink http://dx.doi.org/10.1787/826542162885

Taxes on income and profits
As a percentage of GDP

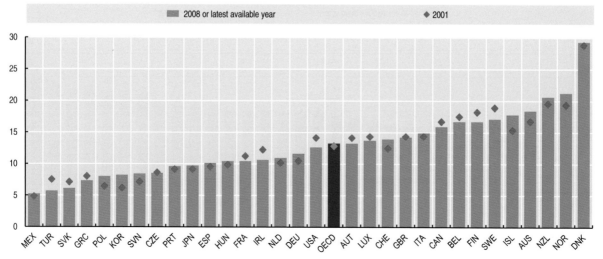

StatLink http://dx.doi.org/10.1787/822256756643

Taxes on goods and services
As a percentage of GDP

	1995	1996	1997	1998	1999	2000	2001	2002	2003	2004	2005	2006	2007	2008
Australia	8.4	8.2	8.0	8.2	8.0	8.9	8.9	9.2	9.1	8.9	8.6	8.3	8.2	..
Austria	11.9	12.3	12.8	12.5	12.6	12.3	12.4	12.6	12.5	12.4	12.1	11.7	11.7	11.6
Belgium	11.2	11.5	11.7	11.1	11.5	11.4	11.0	11.1	11.0	11.2	11.3	11.3	11.0	-
Canada	9.0	9.0	9.0	9.1	8.8	8.6	8.8	8.9	8.9	8.7	8.5	8.1	7.9	7.5
Czech Republic	12.1	11.8	11.3	10.8	11.5	11.2	10.8	10.8	11.1	11.8	11.8	11.2	11.1	11.4
Denmark	15.6	16.0	16.1	16.4	16.5	15.8	15.8	16.0	15.8	16.0	16.2	16.4	16.3	15.6
Finland	14.0	14.1	14.6	14.1	14.2	13.7	13.2	13.5	14.1	13.8	13.8	13.5	12.9	12.9
France	11.8	12.3	12.2	11.9	12.0	11.4	11.1	11.1	11.0	11.1	11.1	10.8	10.7	10.5
Germany	10.4	10.3	10.1	10.0	10.4	10.5	10.4	10.3	10.4	10.1	10.1	10.1	10.6	10.5
Greece	11.9	12.2	12.3	12.0	12.2	12.0	12.5	12.3	11.4	11.0	10.9	11.3	11.4	11.5
Hungary	16.8	16.2	15.0	14.7	15.4	15.4	14.7	14.2	14.8	15.4	14.8	14.3	14.9	14.9
Iceland	15.2	15.6	15.3	15.9	17.0	16.4	14.3	14.4	15.1	16.0	17.1	17.6	16.5	12.9
Ireland	13.2	13.0	12.6	12.2	12.1	11.7	10.6	10.9	10.8	11.2	11.4	11.4	11.1	10.5
Italy	10.9	10.8	11.2	11.5	11.7	11.8	11.2	11.2	10.7	10.8	10.8	11.1	11.0	10.5
Japan	4.2	4.3	4.7	5.3	5.4	5.2	5.3	5.3	5.2	5.3	5.3	5.2	5.1	5.1
Korea	8.0	8.5	8.6	7.7	8.3	8.7	9.1	9.0	8.9	8.4	8.2	8.1	8.3	8.4
Luxembourg	10.0	9.9	10.6	10.5	10.4	10.6	10.5	10.6	10.5	11.2	10.9	10.0	9.9	10.9
Mexico	8.2	8.5	8.6	7.5	7.9	8.9	8.8	8.1	9.1	9.5	10.3	10.3	9.5	12.4
Netherlands	11.3	11.6	11.3	11.3	11.7	11.5	11.8	11.6	11.7	11.9	12.2	11.9	11.2	..
New Zealand	12.2	12.2	12.2	12.1	12.1	11.7	11.8	12.1	12.1	11.9	12.0	11.9	11.3	11.8
Norway	15.8	15.5	15.4	15.8	15.6	13.5	13.3	13.3	12.9	12.7	12.1	12.0	12.4	10.8
Poland	12.8	13.7	13.1	12.3	12.8	11.8	11.4	12.1	12.2	11.9	12.7	13.3	13.3	..
Portugal	13.0	13.2	12.9	13.0	13.2	12.7	12.8	13.1	13.2	13.2	13.8	14.1	13.7	13.3
Slovak Republic	..	..	..	12.7	12.2	12.3	11.2	11.4	12.0	12.3	12.6	11.4	11.3	10.7
Spain	9.2	9.3	9.5	9.8	10.2	10.1	9.7	9.7	9.7	9.8	9.9	9.9	9.5	8.3
Sweden	13.4	12.9	13.0	12.7	12.6	12.8	12.7	12.9	12.9	12.7	12.9	12.8	12.9	13.1
Switzerland	6.1	6.0	6.0	6.2	6.6	6.7	6.8	6.8	6.8	6.8	6.9	6.8	6.5	6.5
Turkey	6.3	7.2	7.7	7.6	8.3	10.1	10.5	11.5	12.8	11.5	12.0	11.9	11.3	10.8
United Kingdom	12.0	12.0	11.9	11.7	11.8	11.6	11.3	11.2	11.2	11.1	10.8	10.6	10.5	10.3
United States	5.0	4.9	4.9	4.9	4.8	4.8	4.7	4.7	4.7	4.8	4.8	4.8	4.7	4.6
OECD average	11.0	11.1	11.1	11.0	11.3	11.1	10.9	11.0	11.1	11.1	11.2	11.1	10.9	..
Slovenia	15.2	14.9	13.9	14.5	15.0	14.1	13.7	13.9	14.0	13.8	13.6	13.3	13.2	13.2

StatLink http://dx.doi.org/10.1787/826555254320

Taxes on goods and services
As a percentage of GDP

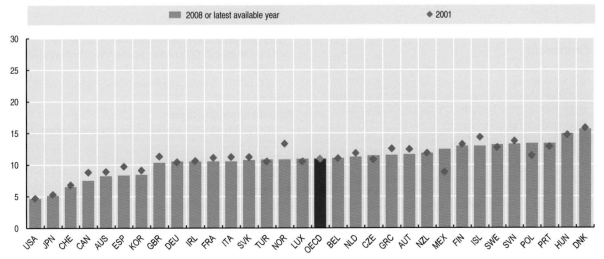

StatLink http://dx.doi.org/10.1787/822257310272

TAXES ON THE AVERAGE WORKER

Taxes on the average worker measures the ratio between the amount of taxes paid by an average single worker without children and the corresponding total labour cost for the employer. This tax wedge therefore measures the extent to which the tax system on labour income discourages employment.

Definition

The taxes included in the measure are personal income taxes, employees' social security contributions and employers' social security contributions. For the few countries that have them, it also includes payroll taxes. The amount of these taxes paid in relation to the employment of one average worker is expressed as a percentage of their labour cost (gross wage plus employers' social security contributions and payroll tax).

An average worker is defined as somebody who earns the average income of full-time workers of the country concerned in sectors C-K of the International Standard Industrial Classification (ISIC rev. 3). The average worker is single, meaning that he or she does not receive any tax relief in respect of a spouse, unmarried partner or child.

Comparability

The types of taxes included in the measure are fully comparable across countries. They are based on common definitions agreed by all OECD countries and published in OECD *Revenue Statistics*.

While the income levels of workers in sectors C-K differ across countries, they can be regarded as corresponding to comparable types of work in each country.

The information on the average worker's income level is supplied by the Ministries of Finance in all OECD countries and is based on national statistical surveys. The amount of taxes paid by the single worker is calculated by applying the tax laws in each country. These tax wedge measures are therefore derived from a modelling exercise rather than from the direct observation of taxes actually paid by workers and their employers.

Sources
- OECD (2009), *Taxing Wages 2007-2008, 2008 Edition*, OECD, Paris.

Further information
Analytical publications
- Immervoll, H. (2004), *Average and Marginal Effective Tax Rates Facing Workers in the EU: A Micro-Level Analysis of Levels, Distributions and Driving Factors*, OECD Social Employment and Migration Working Papers, No. 19, OECD, Paris.
- OECD (2006), *OECD Tax Policy Studies – N.15 Encouraging Savings through Tax-Preferred Accounts*, OECD, Paris.
- OECD (2006), *OECD Tax Policy Studies: No. 11: The Taxation of Employee Stock Options*, OECD, Paris.
- OECD (2007), *Benefits and Wages: OECD Indicators*, OECD, Paris.

Statistical publications
- OECD (2008), *OECD Latin American Economic Outlook 2009*, OECD, Paris.
- OECD (2009), *Revenue Statistics 1965-2008 – Edition 2009*, OECD, Paris.

Web sites
- OECD Benefits and Wages, *www.oecd.org/els/social/workincentives*.
- OECD Centre for Tax Policy and Administration, *www.oecd.org/ctp*.
- OECD Tax Policy Analysis, *www.oecd.org/ctp/tpa*.

Overview

In 2008, taxes on an average worker represented around 38% of their total labour costs, on average, across OECD countries. This tax wedge ranged between 15% in Mexico and 50% or more in Belgium, Hungary and Germany.

On average, taxes on an average worker have decreased very slightly since 2000 for the OECD as a whole. However, there are important differences between countries. 11 of the 30 OECD member countries experienced an overall increase in the taxes on an average worker since 2000. The countries with the largest increases were Greece, Japan, Korea and the Netherlands. Of the 19 countries that have experienced an overall decline, the largest decreases were for Finland, Ireland and Sweden.

Taxes on the average worker

As a percentage of labour cost

	2000	2001	2002	2003	2004	2005	2006	2007	2008
Australia	30.6	27.3	27.7	28.0	28.0	28.3	28.3	27.7	26.9
Austria	47.3	46.9	47.1	47.4	48.1	48.0	48.3	48.6	48.8
Belgium	57.1	56.7	56.3	55.7	55.4	55.5	55.5	55.8	56.0
Canada	33.2	32.0	32.1	32.0	32.0	31.9	31.9	31.2	31.3
Czech Republic	42.7	42.6	42.9	43.2	43.5	43.8	42.6	42.9	43.4
Denmark	44.3	43.6	42.6	42.6	41.3	41.1	41.3	41.4	41.2
Finland	47.8	46.4	45.9	45.0	44.5	44.6	44.0	43.6	43.5
France	49.6	49.8	49.8	49.8	49.9	50.0	50.1	49.2	49.3
Germany	54.0	53.0	53.5	54.2	53.2	53.1	53.3	52.6	52.0
Greece	38.5	38.2	39.0	37.9	40.0	40.5	41.9	42.3	42.4
Hungary	54.6	55.8	53.7	50.8	51.8	51.1	52.0	54.5	54.1
Iceland	26.2	26.9	28.5	29.3	29.8	29.7	29.5	28.1	28.3
Ireland	28.9	25.8	24.5	24.2	24.0	23.5	23.0	22.7	22.9
Italy	46.9	46.4	46.4	45.7	46.0	45.7	45.9	46.2	46.5
Japan	24.8	24.9	30.5	27.4	27.3	27.7	28.8	29.3	29.5
Korea	16.3	16.4	16.1	16.3	17.0	17.3	18.1	19.7	20.3
Luxembourg	37.5	35.8	32.9	33.5	33.9	34.7	35.3	36.3	35.9
Mexico	12.6	13.2	15.8	16.8	15.3	14.7	15.0	15.9	15.1
Netherlands	39.7	37.2	37.4	37.1	38.8	38.9	44.6	44.3	45.0
New Zealand	19.4	19.4	19.5	19.7	20.0	20.4	21.1	21.5	21.2
Norway	38.6	39.2	38.6	38.1	38.1	37.2	37.4	37.5	37.7
Poland	43.1	42.8	42.7	43.0	43.2	43.4	43.7	42.9	39.7
Portugal	37.3	36.4	36.6	36.8	37.8	37.3	37.4	37.7	37.6
Slovak Republic	41.7	42.7	42.5	42.9	42.5	38.3	38.5	38.6	38.9
Spain	38.6	38.8	39.1	38.5	38.7	38.9	39.1	38.9	37.8
Sweden	50.1	49.1	47.8	48.2	48.4	48.1	47.8	45.3	44.6
Switzerland	30.0	30.1	30.1	29.7	29.4	29.5	29.5	29.7	29.5
Turkey	40.4	43.6	42.5	42.2	42.8	42.8	42.7	42.7	39.7
United Kingdom	32.6	32.2	32.3	33.8	33.9	33.9	34.0	34.0	32.8
United States	30.4	30.3	30.1	29.9	29.8	29.7	29.9	29.7	30.1
OECD average	37.8	37.5	37.5	37.3	37.5	37.3	37.7	37.7	37.4
Israel	29.0	29.5	30.0	27.1	25.3	24.9	23.5	24.1	21.7
Slovenia	46.3	46.2	46.1	46.2	46.3	45.6	45.3	43.3	42.9

StatLink ⬛⬛ http://dx.doi.org/10.1787/826577603862

Taxes on the average worker

As a percentage of labour cost

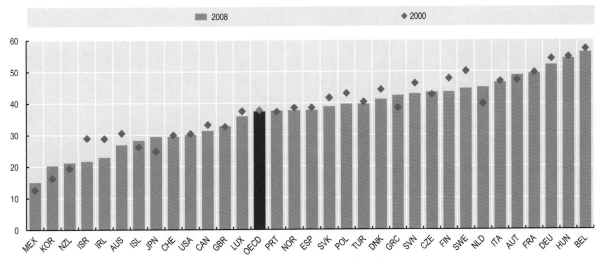

StatLink ⬛⬛ http://dx.doi.org/10.1787/822301233411

QUALITY OF LIFE

HEALTH
LIFE EXPECTANCY
INFANT MORTALITY
OBESITY

INCOME INEQUALITY AND POVERTY
INCOME INEQUALITY
POVERTY RATES AND GAPS

SOCIETY
SUICIDES
SUBJECTIVE WELL-BEING
SOCIAL BENEFITS OF EDUCATION
YOUTH INACTIVITY
TOURISM: HOTEL NIGHTS

SECURITY
PRISON POPULATION
ROAD FATALITIES

LIFE EXPECTANCY

Life expectancy at birth remains one of the most frequently quoted indicators of health status. Gains in life expectancy at birth in OECD countries in recent decades can be attributed to a number of factors, including rising living standards, improved lifestyle and better education, as well as greater access to quality health services. Other factors, such as better nutrition, sanitation and housing also played a role, particularly in developing countries.

Definition

Life expectancy at birth measures how long on average a person may expect to live based on the age-specific death rates prevailing in a country at the time of his or her birth. It should be noted that the actual age-specific death rates of any particular birth cohort cannot be known in advance; this implies that, if age-specific death rates are falling (as has been the case over the past few decades in all OECD countries), the actual life span of a person will be higher than the life expectancy calculated based on current death rates.

Comparability

Each country calculates life expectancy at birth according to methodologies that can vary somewhat from country to country. These differences in methodology can affect the comparability of reported life expectancy estimates, as different methods can change a country's estimates by a fraction of a year.

Overview

On average across OECD countries, life expectancy at birth for the whole population reached 79.1 years in 2007, more than ten years greater than in 1960. In almost half of OECD countries, life expectancy at birth exceeded 80 years in 2007. The country with the highest life expectancy was Japan, with a life expectancy of 82.6 years. At the other end of the scale, life expectancy in OECD countries was the lowest in Turkey, followed by Hungary. However, while life expectancy in Hungary has increased only modestly since 1960, it has increased sharply in Turkey, rapidly catching up with the OECD average. OECD countries with higher GDP per capita generally experience higher life expectancy at birth, although the relationship is less pronounced at higher income levels.

The gender gap in life expectancy stood at 5.6 years on average across OECD countries in 2007, with life expectancy reaching 76.3 years among men and 81.9 years among women. This gender gap increased by half-a-year on average across countries between 1960 and 2007. But this result hides different trends between earlier and later decades. While the gender gap in life expectancy increased substantially in many countries during the 1960s and the 1970s, it narrowed during the past 25 years, reflecting stronger gains in life expectancy among men than among women in most OECD countries. The narrowing of the gender gap in life expectancy over the past 25 years can been partly attributed to the narrowing of gap in risk-behaviours such as smoking between men and women, and to sharp reductions in mortality rates from cardio-vascular diseases among men.

Sources
* OECD (2009), *OECD Health Data 2009*, OECD, Paris.

Further information
Analytical publications
* OECD (2004), *The OECD Health Project: Towards High-Performing Health Systems*, OECD, Paris.
* OECD (2009), *Achieving Better Value for Money in Health Care*, OECD, Paris.

Statistical publications
* OECD (2009), *Health at a Glance 2009: OECD Indicators*, OECD, Paris.
* OECD (2009), *Society at a Glance 2009: OECD Social Indicators*, OECD, Paris.

Online databases
* *OECD Health Data.*

Web sites
* OECD Health Data, *www.oecd.org/health/healthdata.*
* OECD Health at a Glance, *www.oecd.org/health/healthataglance.*

Life expectancy at birth: total
Number of years

	1960	1970	1980	1990	1995	2000	2001	2002	2003	2004	2005	2006	2007
Australia	70.9	70.8	74.6	77.0	77.9	79.3	79.7	80.0	80.3	80.6	80.9	81.1	81.4
Austria	68.7	70.0	72.6	75.5	76.6	78.1	78.6	78.8	78.8	79.3	79.5	79.9	80.1
Belgium	69.8	71.1	73.3	76.1	76.9	77.8	78.1	78.1	78.2	78.9	79.0	79.5	79.8
Canada	..	..	75.3	77.6	78.1	79.3	79.6	79.7	79.9	80.2	80.4	80.7	..
Czech Republic	70.6	69.6	70.4	71.5	73.3	75.1	75.3	75.4	75.3	75.9	76.1	76.7	77.0
Denmark	72.4	73.3	74.3	74.9	75.3	76.8	77.0	77.1	77.4	77.8	78.2	78.4	78.4
Finland	69.0	70.8	73.6	75.0	76.6	77.7	78.1	78.3	78.5	78.9	79.1	79.5	79.5
France	70.3	72.2	74.3	76.9	77.9	79.1	79.2	79.4	79.4	80.3	80.2	80.7	81.0
Germany	69.1	70.6	72.9	75.3	76.6	78.2	78.5	78.5	78.6	79.2	79.4	79.8	80.0
Greece	69.9	72.0	74.5	77.1	77.7	78.0	78.5	78.7	78.9	79.1	79.3	79.6	79.5
Hungary	68.0	69.2	69.1	69.4	69.9	71.7	72.3	72.6	72.6	72.8	72.8	73.2	73.3
Iceland	72.9	74.3	76.7	78.0	78.0	80.1	80.2	80.6	81.2	81.0	81.2	81.2	81.2
Ireland	70.0	71.2	72.9	74.9	75.5	76.6	77.2	77.9	78.3	78.9	79.5	79.8	79.7
Italy	..	..	74.0	77.1	78.3	79.8	80.1	80.3	79.9	80.9	80.8	81.4	..
Japan	67.8	72.0	76.1	78.9	79.6	81.2	81.5	81.8	81.8	82.1	82.0	82.4	82.6
Korea	52.4	62.2	65.9	71.4	73.5	76.0	76.4	77.0	77.4	78.0	78.5	79.1	79.4
Luxembourg	69.4	..	72.8	75.5	76.8	78.0	77.9	78.1	77.8	79.2	79.5	79.4	79.4
Mexico	57.5	60.9	67.2	70.6	72.5	73.9	74.2	74.3	74.5	74.6	74.7	74.8	75.0
Netherlands	73.5	73.7	75.9	77.0	77.5	78.0	78.3	78.4	78.6	79.2	79.4	79.8	80.2
New Zealand	..	71.5	73.2	75.5	76.8	78.4	78.7	79.0	79.3	79.5	79.8	80.1	80.2
Norway	73.8	74.4	75.9	76.7	77.9	78.8	78.9	79.0	79.6	80.1	80.3	80.5	80.6
Poland	67.8	70.0	70.2	70.7	72.0	73.9	74.3	74.6	74.7	75.0	75.1	75.3	75.4
Portugal	63.9	66.7	71.4	74.1	75.4	76.7	77.0	77.2	77.4	78.3	78.1	78.9	79.1
Slovak Republic	70.6	69.8	70.6	71.0	72.4	73.3	73.6	73.8	73.9	74.1	74.0	74.3	74.3
Spain	69.8	72.0	75.4	77.0	78.1	79.4	79.7	79.8	79.7	80.3	80.3	81.1	81.0
Sweden	73.1	74.7	75.8	77.6	78.8	79.7	79.9	79.9	80.2	80.6	80.6	80.8	81.0
Switzerland	71.4	73.1	75.6	77.5	78.6	79.9	80.3	80.5	80.6	81.2	81.4	81.7	81.9
Turkey	48.3	54.2	58.1	67.5	69.3	71.1	71.5	71.9	72.2	72.6	73.0	73.2	73.4
United Kingdom	70.8	71.9	73.2	75.7	76.6	77.9	78.2	78.3	78.3	78.9	79.1	79.5	..
United States	69.9	70.9	73.7	75.3	75.7	76.8	77.1	77.2	77.5	77.8	77.8	78.1	..
OECD average	68.5	70.3	72.6	74.9	76.0	77.4	77.7	77.9	78.0	78.5	78.7	79.0	79.1
Brazil	..	..	62.7	66.6	68.6	70.5	70.8	71.1	71.4	71.7	72.0	72.3	..
Chile	..	..	68.6	73.3	74.9	76.5	76.9	77.3	77.7	77.9	78.0	78.2	78.3
China	..	..	..	68.6		71.4	..	..	..	..	73.0	..	..
Estonia	..	..	69.4	69.7	67.6	70.6	70.4	71.0	71.6	72.0	72.8	73.0	73.0
India	..	..	..	..	60.3	61.9	62.5	62.5	62.7	62.9	63.6	63.4	..
Indonesia	..	..	..	..	..	..	..	..	..	..	70.0	..	..
Israel	..	..	73.9	76.8	77.4	78.8	79.3	79.5	79.8	80.3	80.3	80.7	80.7
Russian Federation	..	68.8	67.5	69.2	64.5	65.3	65.2	65.0	64.9	65.3	65.3	66.6	67.5
Slovenia	..	..	71.2	73.3	74.0	75.6	75.9	76.1	77.1	77.4	77.8	78.5	78.3

StatLink ᕄᔕᕓ http://dx.doi.org/10.1787/826605861805

Life expectancy at birth: total
Number of years

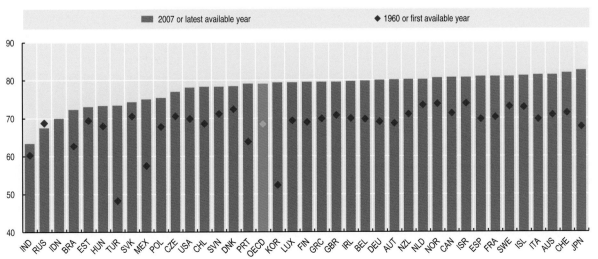

StatLink ᕄᔕᕓ http://dx.doi.org/10.1787/822308540314

Life expectancy at birth: men
Number of years

	1960	1970	1980	1990	1995	2000	2001	2002	2003	2004	2005	2006	2007
Australia	67.9	67.4	71.0	73.9	75.0	76.6	77.0	77.4	77.8	78.1	78.5	78.7	79.0
Austria	65.4	66.5	69.0	72.2	73.3	75.1	75.6	75.8	75.9	76.4	76.7	77.1	77.3
Belgium	66.8	67.9	69.9	72.7	73.5	74.6	75.0	75.1	75.3	76.0	76.2	76.6	77.1
Canada	..	..	71.7	74.4	75.1	76.7	77.0	77.2	77.4	77.8	78.0	78.4	..
Czech Republic	67.8	66.1	66.9	67.6	69.7	71.7	72.1	72.1	72.0	72.6	72.9	73.5	73.8
Denmark	70.4	70.7	71.2	72.0	72.7	74.5	74.7	74.8	75.0	75.4	76.0	76.1	76.2
Finland	65.5	66.5	69.3	71.0	72.9	74.2	74.6	74.9	75.2	75.4	75.6	75.9	76.0
France	67.0	68.4	70.2	72.8	73.8	75.3	75.4	75.7	75.8	76.7	76.7	77.2	77.5
Germany	66.5	67.5	69.6	72.0	73.3	75.1	75.6	75.7	75.8	76.5	76.7	77.2	77.4
Greece	67.3	70.1	72.2	74.6	75.0	75.5	75.9	76.2	76.5	76.6	76.8	77.1	77.0
Hungary	65.9	66.3	65.5	65.1	65.3	67.4	68.1	68.4	68.4	68.6	68.6	69.0	69.2
Iceland	70.7	71.2	73.7	75.4	75.9	78.4	78.1	78.7	79.7	79.2	79.2	79.4	79.4
Ireland	68.1	68.8	70.1	72.1	72.8	74.0	74.5	75.2	75.9	76.5	77.3	77.4	77.4
Italy	..	..	70.6	73.8	75.0	76.9	77.1	77.4	77.1	77.9	78.0	78.5	..
Japan	65.3	69.3	73.4	75.9	76.4	77.7	78.1	78.3	78.4	78.6	78.6	79.0	79.2
Korea	51.1	58.7	61.8	67.3	69.6	72.3	72.8	73.4	73.9	74.5	75.1	75.7	76.1
Luxembourg	66.5	..	70.0	72.4	73.0	74.6	75.1	74.7	74.8	76.0	76.7	76.8	76.7
Mexico	55.8	58.5	64.1	67.7	69.7	71.3	71.6	71.8	72.0	72.1	72.2	72.4	72.6
Netherlands	71.5	70.8	72.5	73.8	74.6	75.5	75.8	76.0	76.2	76.9	77.2	77.6	78.0
New Zealand	..	68.4	70.1	72.4	74.1	75.9	76.3	76.6	77.0	77.3	77.7	78.0	78.2
Norway	71.6	71.2	72.4	73.5	74.8	76.0	76.2	76.4	77.1	77.6	77.8	78.2	78.3
Poland	64.9	66.6	66.0	66.2	67.6	69.7	70.2	70.4	70.5	70.7	70.8	70.9	71.0
Portugal	61.1	63.7	67.9	70.6	71.7	73.2	73.5	73.8	74.2	75.0	74.9	75.5	75.9
Slovak Republic	68.4	66.7	66.8	66.6	68.4	69.1	69.5	69.8	69.9	70.3	70.1	70.4	70.5
Spain	67.4	69.2	72.3	73.4	74.4	75.8	76.2	76.3	76.3	76.9	77.0	77.7	77.8
Sweden	71.2	72.2	72.8	74.8	76.2	77.4	77.6	77.7	77.9	78.4	78.4	78.7	78.9
Switzerland	68.7	70.0	72.3	74.0	75.4	77.0	77.5	77.9	78.0	78.6	78.7	79.2	79.5
Turkey	46.3	52.0	55.8	65.4	67.2	69.0	69.4	69.8	70.1	70.5	70.9	71.1	71.1
United Kingdom	67.9	68.7	70.2	72.9	74.0	75.5	75.8	76.0	76.2	76.8	77.1	77.3	..
United States	66.6	67.1	70.0	71.8	72.5	74.1	74.4	74.5	74.8	75.2	75.2	75.4	..
OECD average	65.9	67.2	69.3	71.6	72.8	74.3	74.7	74.9	75.2	75.6	75.9	76.2	76.3
Brazil	..	..	59.6	62.8	64.8	66.7	67.0	67.3	67.6	67.9	68.1	68.4	..
Chile	..	..	65.3	70.3	72.0	73.6	74.0	74.4	74.8	74.9	75.1	75.2	75.4
Estonia	..	..	64.2	64.5	61.3	65.1	64.6	65.1	66.0	66.3	67.3	67.4	67.1
India	..	..	..	..	59.7	61.0	61.3	61.6	61.8	62.1	63.3	62.6	..
Indonesia	..	..	..	..	..	..	..	..	..	..	68.1		
Israel	..	..	72.1	74.9	75.5	76.7	77.3	77.5	77.6	78.0	78.2	78.7	78.7
Russian Federation	..	63.2	61.5	63.7	58.1	59.0	58.9	58.7	58.6	58.9	58.9	60.4	61.4
Slovenia	..	65.0	67.3	69.4	70.3	71.9	72.1	72.3	73.2	73.5	74.1	74.8	74.6

StatLink ⎙ http://dx.doi.org/10.1787/826617177173

Life expectancy at birth: men
Number of years

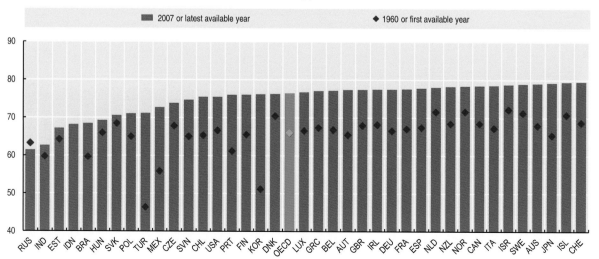

■ 2007 or latest available year   ◆ 1960 or first available year

StatLink ⎙ http://dx.doi.org/10.1787/822315487443

Life expectancy at birth: women

Number of years

	1960	1970	1980	1990	1995	2000	2001	2002	2003	2004	2005	2006	2007
Australia	73.9	74.2	78.1	80.1	80.8	82.0	82.4	82.6	82.8	83.0	83.3	83.5	83.7
Austria	71.9	73.4	76.1	78.8	79.9	81.1	81.5	81.7	81.6	82.1	82.2	82.7	82.9
Belgium	72.8	74.3	76.7	79.5	80.4	81.0	81.2	81.2	81.1	81.8	81.9	82.3	82.6
Canada	..	..	78.9	80.8	81.1	81.9	82.1	82.1	82.4	82.6	82.7	83.0	..
Czech Republic	73.5	73.1	74.0	75.5	76.8	78.5	78.6	78.7	78.6	79.2	79.3	79.9	80.2
Denmark	74.4	75.9	77.3	77.8	77.9	79.2	79.3	79.4	79.8	80.2	80.5	80.7	80.6
Finland	72.5	75.0	78.0	79.0	80.4	81.2	81.7	81.6	81.9	82.5	82.5	83.1	83.1
France	73.6	75.9	78.4	80.9	81.9	82.8	82.9	83.0	82.9	83.8	83.7	84.1	84.4
Germany	71.7	73.6	76.2	78.5	79.9	81.2	81.5	81.3	81.3	81.9	82.0	82.4	82.7
Greece	72.4	73.8	76.8	79.5	80.3	80.5	81.0	81.1	81.3	81.5	81.7	82.0	82.0
Hungary	70.1	72.1	72.7	73.7	74.5	75.9	76.4	76.7	76.7	76.9	76.9	77.4	77.3
Iceland	75.0	77.3	79.7	80.5	80.0	81.8	82.2	82.5	82.7	82.7	83.1	83.0	82.9
Ireland	71.9	73.5	75.6	77.7	78.3	79.2	79.9	80.5	80.8	81.4	81.8	82.2	82.1
Italy	..	..	77.4	80.3	81.5	82.8	83.1	83.2	82.8	83.8	83.6	84.2	..
Japan	70.2	74.7	78.8	81.9	82.9	84.6	84.9	85.2	85.3	85.6	85.5	85.8	86.0
Korea	53.7	65.6	70.0	75.5	77.4	79.6	80.0	80.5	80.8	81.4	81.9	82.4	82.7
Luxembourg	72.2	..	75.6	78.7	80.6	81.3	80.7	81.5	80.9	82.4	82.3	81.9	82.2
Mexico	59.2	63.2	70.2	73.5	75.2	76.5	76.7	76.8	77.0	77.0	77.1	77.2	77.4
Netherlands	75.4	76.5	79.2	80.1	80.4	80.5	80.7	80.7	80.9	81.4	81.6	81.9	82.3
New Zealand	..	74.5	76.2	78.4	79.5	80.8	81.1	81.3	81.5	81.8	82.0	82.2	82.2
Norway	76.0	77.5	79.3	79.9	80.9	81.5	81.7	81.6	82.1	82.6	82.7	82.9	82.9
Poland	70.6	73.3	74.4	75.2	76.4	78.0	78.3	78.7	78.8	79.2	79.4	79.6	79.7
Portugal	66.7	69.7	74.9	77.5	79.0	80.2	80.5	80.6	80.6	81.5	81.3	82.3	82.2
Slovak Republic	72.7	72.9	74.3	75.4	76.3	77.4	77.7	77.7	77.8	77.8	77.9	78.2	78.1
Spain	72.2	74.8	78.5	80.6	81.8	82.9	83.2	83.2	83.0	83.7	83.7	84.4	84.3
Sweden	74.9	77.1	78.8	80.4	81.4	82.0	82.1	82.1	82.5	82.7	82.8	82.9	83.0
Switzerland	74.1	76.2	79.0	80.9	81.9	82.8	83.2	83.2	83.2	83.8	84.0	84.2	84.4
Turkey	50.3	56.3	60.3	69.5	71.3	73.1	73.5	73.9	74.3	74.6	75.0	75.3	75.6
United Kingdom	73.7	75.0	76.2	78.5	79.3	80.3	80.5	80.6	80.5	81.0	81.2	81.7	..
United States	73.1	74.7	77.4	78.8	78.9	79.5	79.8	79.9	80.1	80.4	80.4	80.7	..
OECD average	71.0	73.3	76.0	78.3	79.2	80.3	80.6	80.8	80.9	81.3	81.5	81.8	81.9
Brazil	..	..	65.7	70.4	72.3	74.3	74.6	74.9	75.2	75.5	75.8	76.1	..
Chile	..	..	72.0	76.5	77.9	79.6	80.0	80.4	80.8	81.0	81.1	81.3	81.4
Estonia	..	..	74.2	74.7	74.1	76.0	76.2	77.0	76.9	77.8	78.1	78.5	78.7
India	..	..	..	..	60.9	62.7	63.6	63.3	63.5	63.7	63.9	64.2	..
Indonesia	..	..	..	..	..	..	..	..	..	..	72.0	..	..
Israel	..	..	75.7	78.4	79.5	80.9	81.2	81.5	81.8	82.4	82.2	82.5	82.4
Russian Federation	..	73.4	73.0	74.3	71.6	72.3	72.2	71.9	71.8	72.3	72.4	73.2	73.9
Slovenia	..	72.4	75.1	77.2	77.8	79.1	79.6	79.9	80.7	81.1	81.3	81.9	81.8

StatLink http://dx.doi.org/10.1787/826637385273

Life expectancy at birth: women

Number of years

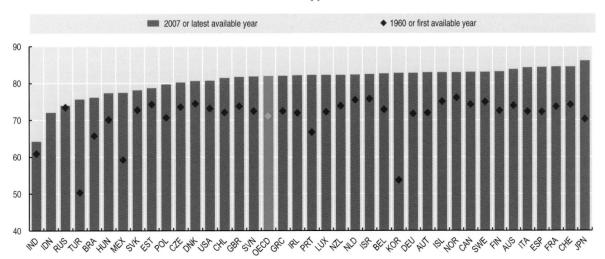

StatLink http://dx.doi.org/10.1787/822345280677

INFANT MORTALITY

Infant mortality is a key health outcome for people in their early years of life. Numerous studies have examined the effect of a variety of medical and non-medical determinants of infant mortality. These include the economic and social conditions of mothers and newborns, the social environment, individual lifestyles and attitudes as well as the characteristics of health systems. Some countries combine low levels of infant mortality with low levels of health expenditures, suggesting that higher spending is not necessarily a precondition to improve outcomes in this area.

Definition

The infant mortality rate is the number of deaths of children under one year of age, expressed per 1 000 live births. Neonatal mortality refers to the death of children during the first four weeks of life. Post neonatal mortality refers to deaths occurring between the second and the twelfth months of life.

Comparability

Some of the international variation in infant and neonatal mortality rates may be due to variations among countries in registering practices for premature infants. Most countries have no gestational age or weight limits for mortality registration. Limits exist for Norway (where the gestational age required to be counted as a death following a live birth must exceed 12 weeks) and in the Czech Republic, France, the Netherlands and Poland (which apply a minimum gestational age of 22 weeks and/or a weight threshold of 500 g).

Overview

All OECD countries have achieved remarkable progress in reducing infant mortality rates. In 1970, the average infant mortality rate for OECD countries approached 30 deaths per 1 000 live births; by 2007, this rate stood at 4.9 deaths per 1 000 live births, implying a reduction of over 80%. Portugal has reduced its infant mortality rate by over 90% since 1970, i.e. from the European country with the highest infant mortality rate in 1970 to one of the OECD countries with the lowest rate in 2007. The infant mortality rate recorded large reductions in Korea and smaller ones in the United States.

Around two-thirds of the deaths that occur during the first year of life are neonatal deaths, i.e. deaths that occur during the first four weeks of life; congenital malformations, prematurity and other conditions arising during pregnancy are the principal factors contributing to neonatal mortality in developed countries. For post neonatal mortality, i.e. deaths that occur beyond the first month of life, a greater range of causes comes into play – the most common being SIDS (Sudden Infant Death Syndrome), birth defects, infections and accidents.

With the increasing number of women deferring childbearing and the rise in multiple births linked with fertility treatments, the number of pre-term births has tended to increase. In several OECD countries, this has contributed to a leveling-off of the downward trend in infant mortality rates over the past few years.

Sources
• OECD (2009), OECD Health Data 2009, OECD, Paris.

Further information
Analytical publications
• OECD (2004), The OECD Health Project: Towards High-Performing Health Systems, OECD, Paris.
• OECD (2004), The OECD Health Project: Towards High-Performing Health Systems – Policy Studies, OECD, Paris.
• OECD (2008), OECD Health Policy Studies: The Looming Crisis in the Health Workforce: How Can OECD Countries Respond?, OECD, Paris.

Statistical publications
• OECD (2006), Economic Valuation of Environmental Health Risks to Children, OECD, Paris.
• OECD (2009), Health at a Glance 2009: OECD Indicators, OECD, Paris.

Online databases
• OECD Health Data.

Web sites
• OECD Health Data, www.oecd.org/health/healthdata.

Infant mortality

Deaths per 1 000 live births

	1970	1980	1990	1995	2000	2001	2002	2003	2004	2005	2006	2007
Australia	17.9	10.7	8.2	5.7	5.2	5.3	5.0	4.8	4.7	5.0	4.7	4.2
Austria	25.9	14.3	7.8	5.4	4.8	4.8	4.1	4.5	4.5	4.2	3.6	3.7
Belgium	21.1	12.1	8.0	6.0	4.8	4.5	4.4	4.1	3.8	3.7	4.0	4.0
Canada	18.8	10.4	6.8	6.1	5.3	5.2	5.4	5.3	5.3	5.4	5.0	..
Czech Republic	20.2	16.9	10.8	7.7	4.1	4.0	4.1	3.9	3.7	3.4	3.3	3.1
Denmark	14.2	8.4	7.5	5.1	5.3	4.9	4.4	4.4	4.4	4.4	3.8	4.0
Finland	13.2	7.6	5.6	3.9	3.8	3.2	3.0	3.1	3.3	3.0	2.8	2.7
France	18.2	10.0	7.3	5.0	4.5	4.6	4.2	4.2	4.0	3.8	3.8	..
Germany	22.5	12.4	7.0	5.3	4.4	4.3	4.2	4.2	4.1	3.9	3.8	3.9
Greece	29.6	17.9	9.7	8.1	5.4	5.1	5.1	4.0	4.1	3.8	3.7	3.6
Hungary	35.9	23.2	14.8	10.7	9.2	8.1	7.2	7.3	6.6	6.2	5.7	5.9
Iceland	13.3	7.8	5.8	6.0	3.0	2.7	2.3	2.4	2.8	2.3	1.4	2.0
Ireland	19.5	11.1	8.2	6.4	6.2	5.7	5.0	5.3	4.6	4.0	3.7	3.1
Italy	29.0	14.6	8.2	6.2	4.5	4.6	4.3	3.9	3.9	3.8	3.7	3.7
Japan	13.1	7.5	4.6	4.3	3.2	3.1	3.0	3.0	2.8	2.8	2.6	2.6
Korea	45.0	..	..	..	..	..	5.3	..	..	4.7	4.1	..
Luxembourg	24.9	11.5	7.3	5.5	5.1	5.9	5.1	4.9	3.9	2.6	2.5	1.8
Mexico	79.4	51.0	39.2	27.7	19.4	18.3	18.1	17.3	17.6	16.8	16.2	15.7
Netherlands	12.7	8.6	7.1	5.5	5.1	5.4	5.0	4.8	4.4	4.9	4.4	4.1
New Zealand	16.7	13.0	8.4	6.7	6.3	5.6	6.2	5.4	5.9	5.0	5.2	4.8
Norway	12.7	8.1	6.9	4.0	3.8	3.9	3.5	3.4	3.2	3.1	3.2	3.1
Poland	36.7	25.5	19.3	13.6	8.1	7.7	7.5	7.0	6.8	6.4	6.0	6.0
Portugal	55.5	24.2	11.0	7.5	5.5	5.0	5.0	4.1	3.8	3.5	3.3	3.4
Slovak Republic	25.7	20.9	12.0	11.0	8.6	6.2	7.6	7.9	6.8	7.2	6.6	6.1
Spain	28.1	12.3	7.6	5.5	4.4	4.1	4.1	3.9	4.0	3.8	3.8	3.7
Sweden	11.0	6.9	6.0	4.1	3.4	3.7	3.3	3.1	3.1	2.4	2.8	2.5
Switzerland	15.1	9.1	6.8	5.0	4.9	5.0	5.0	4.3	4.2	4.2	4.4	3.9
Turkey	145.0	117.5	55.4	43.0	28.9	27.8	26.7	28.7	24.6	23.6	22.3	20.7
United Kingdom	18.5	12.1	7.9	6.2	5.6	5.5	5.2	5.2	5.1	5.1	5.0	4.8
United States	20.0	12.6	9.2	7.6	6.9	6.9	7.0	6.8	6.8	6.9	6.7	..
OECD average	28.1	17.9	11.2	8.4	6.5	6.2	6.0	5.9	5.6	5.4	5.1	4.9
Brazil	..	69.1	47.0	37.9	30.1	29.2	28.4	27.5	26.6	25.8	25.0	..
Chile	82.2	31.1	15.9	11.3	9.3	8.7	8.1	8.2	8.7	8.2	7.9	8.3
China	..	..	32.9	..	28.4	..	..	..	..	24.3	..	..
Estonia	..	17.1	12.3	14.9	8.4	8.8	5.7	7.0	6.4	5.4	4.4	5.0
India	..	..	..	74.0	68.0	66.0	63.0	60.0	58.0	58.0	57.0	55.0
Indonesia	..	..	..	..	..	..	..	..	..	28.9	..	..
Israel	..	15.6	9.9	6.8	5.5	5.1	5.4	4.9	4.6	4.4	4.0	3.9
Russian Federation	23.0	22.1	17.4	18.1	15.3	14.6	13.3	12.4	11.6	11.0	10.2	9.4
Slovenia	24.5	15.3	8.4	5.5	4.9	4.2	3.8	4.0	3.7	4.1	3.4	2.8

StatLink http://dx.doi.org/10.1787/826718006252

Infant mortality

Deaths per 1 000 live births

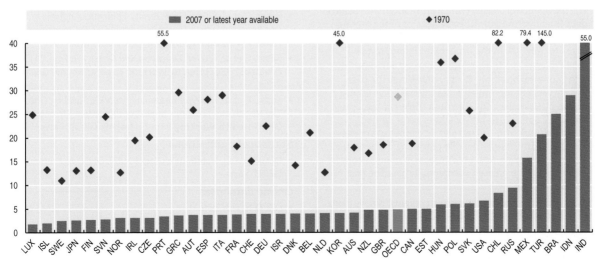

StatLink http://dx.doi.org/10.1787/822350026628

OBESITY

Obesity is a known risk factor for numerous health problems, including hypertension, high cholesterol, diabetes, cardiovascular diseases, respiratory problems (asthma), musculoskeletal diseases (arthritis) and some forms of cancer. At an individual level, several factors can lead to obesity, including excessive calorie consumption, lack of physical activity, genetic predisposition and disorders of the endocrine system. Because obesity is associated with higher risks of chronic illnesses, it is linked to significant additional health care costs.

Definition

The most frequently used measure of overweight and obesity is based on the body mass index (BMI), which is a single number that evaluates an individual's weight status in relation to his or her height (weight/height^2, with weight in kilograms and height in meters). Based on the WHO current classification, adults with a BMI between 25 and 30 are defined as overweight, and those with a BMI over 30 as obese.

Comparability

The BMI classification may not be suitable for all ethnic groups, who may be exposed to different levels of health risk for the same level of BMI. The thresholds for adults are also not suitable to measure overweight and obesity among children.

For most countries, data on obesity are self-reported through population-based health interviews. The exceptions are Australia, the Czech Republic (2005), Japan, Luxembourg, New Zealand, the Slovak Republic (2007), the United Kingdom and the United States; in these countries, data are derived from health examinations whereby actual measures are taken of people's height and weight. These differences in data collection methodologies seriously limit comparability of estimates across countries. Estimates of obesity based on health examinations are generally higher and more reliable than those coming from health interviews.

Overview

Half or more of the adult population is now defined as being either overweight or obese in 13 OECD countries: Mexico, the United States, the United Kingdom, Australia, Greece, New Zealand, Luxembourg, Hungary, the Czech Republic, Portugal, Ireland, Spain and Iceland. By comparison, overweight and obesity rates are much lower in Japan and Korea and in some European countries (France and Switzerland), although overweight and obesity rates are also increasing in these countries. The prevalence of obesity (which presents greater health risks than overweight) varies by a factor of ten among OECD countries, ranging from a low of 3% in Japan and Korea to over 30% in the United States and Mexico.

Based on consistent measures of obesity over time, the rate of obesity has more than doubled over the past twenty years in the United States, while it has almost tripled in Australia and more than tripled in the United Kingdom. Some 20 to 24% of adults in the United Kingdom, Australia, Iceland and Luxembourg are obese, about the same rate as the one prevailing in the United States in the early 1990s. Obesity rates in many European countries have increased substantially over the past decade.

In all countries, more men are overweight than women. However, in almost half of all OECD countries, more women are obese than men. Taking overweight and obesity together, the prevalence for women exceeds that for men only in Mexico and Turkey.

Sources
• OECD (2009), *OECD Health Data 2009*, OECD, Paris.

Further information
Analytical publications
• Sassi, F. et al. (2009), *The Obesity Epidemic: Analysis of Past and Projected Future Trends in Selected OECD Countries*, OECD Health Working Papers, No. 45, OECD, Paris.
• Sassi, F. et al. (2009), *Education and Obesity in Four OECD Countries*, OECD Health Working Papers, No. 46, OECD, Paris.
• Sassi, F. et al. (2009), *Improving Lifestyles, Tackling Obesity: The Health and Economic Impact of Prevention Strategies*, OECD Health Working Papers, No. 48, OECD, Paris.

Statistical publications
• OECD (2009), *Health at a Glance 2009: OECD Indicators*, OECD, Paris.

Online databases
• *OECD Health Data*.

Web sites
• OECD Health Data, *www.oecd.org/health/healthdata*.
• OECD Health at a Glance, *www.oecd.org/health/healthataglance*.

Overweight and obese population aged 15 and above

As a percentage of population aged 15 and above, 2007 or latest available year

	Females			Males			Total		
	Overweight	Obese	Overweight and obese	Overweight	Obese	Overweight and obese	Overweight	Obese	Overweight and obese
Australia	28.2	21.4	49.6	45.3	21.9	67.2	36.7	21.7	58.4
Austria	29.9	12.7	42.6	44.9	12.0	56.9	35.3	12.4	47.7
Belgium	24.4	13.4	37.8	38.7	11.9	50.6	31.4	12.7	44.1
Canada	24.9	14.3	39.2	38.0	16.5	54.5	31.4	15.4	46.8
Czech Republic	29.0	17.0	46.0	42.0	18.0	60.0	35.0	17.0	52.0
Denmark	26.4	11.8	38.2	40.9	11.0	51.9	33.2	11.4	44.6
Finland	28.8	14.0	42.8	40.7	16.0	56.7	34.0	14.9	48.9
France	21.2	10.4	31.6	32.0	10.5	42.5	26.5	10.5	37.0
Germany	28.7	12.8	41.5	43.5	14.4	57.9	36.0	13.6	49.6
Greece	34.9	18.3	53.2	48.1	14.3	62.4	41.3	16.4	57.7
Hungary	29.8	18.0	47.8	38.7	19.6	58.3	34.0	18.8	52.8
Iceland	32.2	21.3	53.5	47.7	18.9	66.6	40.1	20.1	60.2
Ireland	28.0	13.0	41.0	43.0	16.0	59.0	36.0	15.0	51.0
Italy	27.6	9.2	36.8	44.3	10.6	54.9	35.6	9.9	45.5
Japan	18.1	3.3	21.4	26.3	3.4	29.7	21.8	3.4	25.1
Korea	23.7	3.3	27.0	30.3	3.7	34.0	27.0	3.5	30.5
Luxembourg	25.6	18.8	44.3	41.5	20.9	62.4	34.7	20.0	54.8
Mexico	37.4	34.5	71.9	42.5	24.2	66.7	39.5	30.0	69.5
Netherlands	27.7	12.2	39.9	40.9	10.2	51.1	34.3	11.2	45.5
New Zealand	30.6	27.0	57.6	41.7	26.0	67.7	36.2	26.5	62.6
Norway	26.0	8.0	34.0	43.0	9.0	52.0	34.0	9.0	43.0
Poland	26.6	12.5	39.1	39.5	12.6	52.1	32.8	12.5	45.3
Portugal	31.4	16.1	47.5	41.4	14.6	56.0	36.2	15.4	51.6
Slovak Republic	24.4	15.9	40.3	39.5	18.1	57.6	29.5	16.7	46.2
Spain	28.6	14.7	43.4	43.6	15.1	58.6	36.2	14.9	51.1
Sweden	26.2	10.1	36.3	41.6	10.3	51.9	33.8	10.2	44.0
Switzerland	20.9	7.7	28.6	37.8	8.6	46.3	29.2	8.1	37.3
Turkey	28.9	14.5	43.4	33.6	9.7	43.3	31.6	12.0	43.4
United Kingdom	32.0	24.4	56.4	41.4	23.6	65.1	36.7	24.0	61.0
United States	26.2	35.3	61.5	40.0	33.3	73.3	33.0	34.3	67.3

StatLink ᗶ᠍᠍᠍ http://dx.doi.org/10.1787/826752626708

Obese population aged 15 and above

As a percentage of population aged 15 and above, 2007 or latest available year

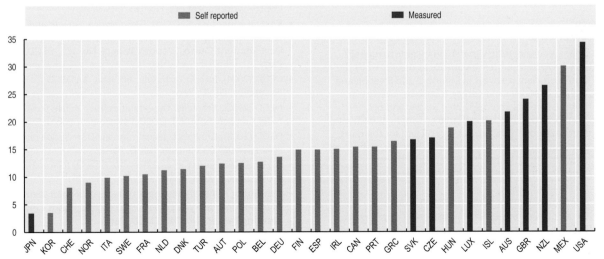

StatLink ᗶ᠍᠍᠍ http://dx.doi.org/10.1787/822414327028

INCOME INEQUALITY

Income inequalities are one of the most visible manifestations of differences in living standards within each country. High income inequalities typically imply a waste of human resources, in the form of a large share of the population out of work or trapped in low-paid and low-skilled jobs.

Definition

Income is defined as household disposable income in a particular year. It consists of earnings, self-employment and capital income and public cash transfers; income taxes and social security contributions paid by households are deducted. The income of the household is attributed to each of its members, with an adjustment to reflect differences in needs for households of different sizes (i.e. the needs of a household composed of four people are assumed to be twice as large as those of a person living alone).

Income inequality among individuals is measured here by five indicators. The Gini coefficient is based on the comparison of cumulative proportions of the population against cumulative proportions of income they receive, and it ranges between 0 in the case of perfect equality and 1 in the case of perfect inequality. The mean log deviation is the average value of the logarithm of the ratio of mean income to the income of each decile. The squared coefficient of variation is the variance of average income of each decile, divided by the square of the average income of the entire population. The P90/P10 ratio is the ratio of the upper bound value of the ninth decile (i.e. the 10% of people with highest income) to that of the first. The P50/P10 ratio is the ratio of median income to the upper bound value of the first decile. The mean log deviation and inter-decile ratios have a lower value of 1 and no upper bound, while the squared coefficient of variation has a lower bound of 0 and upper bound of infinity.

Comparability

Data used here were provided by national experts applying common methodologies and standardised definitions. In many cases, experts have made several adjustments to their source data to conform to standardized definitions. While this approach improves comparability, full standardisation cannot be achieved. Also, small differences between periods and across countries are usually not significant.

Results refer to different years. "Mid-2000s" data refer to the income earned in 2004 in all countries except Australia and New Zealand (2003/04); Hungary and the United Kingdom (2004/05); Switzerland (2004/05); Canada, Denmark, Netherlands and the United States (2005); and Korea (2006). "Mid-1990s" data refer to the income earned in 1995 in all countries except Austria and Italy (1993); Australia (1994/95); Denmark, France, Greece, Ireland, Japan, Mexico and Turkey (1994); and the Czech Republic, Luxembourg and New Zealand (1996). "Mid-1980s" data refer to the income earned in 1985 in all countries except Austria, Belgium, Denmark and Sweden (1983); France, Italy, Mexico, Turkey and the United States (1984); Finland, Luxembourg, New Zealand and Norway (1986); Ireland (1987); and Greece (1988). "Mid-1980s to Mid-1990s" data refer to changes from around 1990 to the mid-1990s for the Czech Republic, Hungary and Portugal and to the western Länder of Germany. "Mid-1990s to Mid-2000s" data refer to changes from the mid-1990s to around 2000 for Austria, Belgium, the Czech Republic, Ireland, Portugal and Spain (where 2005 data, based on EU-SILC, are not deemed to be comparable with those for earlier years), and to changes from 2000 to 2005 for Switzerland.

Sources

- OECD (2008), *Growing Unequal?: Income Distribution and Poverty in OECD Countries*, OECD, Paris.

Further information

Analytical publications

- Jomo, K. S. (2001), *Globalisation, Liberalisation, Poverty and Income Inequality in Southeast Asia*, OECD Development Centre Working Papers, No. 185, OECD, Paris.
- Kayizzi-Mugerwa, S. (2001), *Globalisation, Growth and Income Inequality: The African Experience*, OECD Development Centre Working Papers, No. 186, OECD, Paris.
- OECD (2004), *Income Disparities in China: An OECD Perspective*, OECD, Paris.
- OECD (2005), *Extending Opportunities: How Active Social Policy Can Benefit Us All*, OECD, Paris.
- OECD (2008), *Growing Unequal?: Income Distribution and Poverty in OECD Countries*, OECD, Paris.
- OECD (2009), *Society at a Glance: OECD Social Indicators – 2009 Edition*, OECD, Paris.
- Uchimura, H. (2005), *Impact of Changes in Social Institutions on Income Inequality in China*, OECD Development Centre Working Papers, No. 243, OECD, Paris.

Web sites

- OECD Social and Welfare Statistics, *www.oecd.org/statistics/social*.
- OECD work on income distribution and poverty, *www.oecd.org/els/social/inequality*.

Overview

There is considerable variation in income inequality across OECD countries. Inequality as measured by the Gini coefficient is lowest in Denmark and Sweden and highest in Mexico and Turkey. It is above-average in Poland, Portugal and the United States, and below-average in the remaining Nordic and many Continental European countries. The Gini coefficient for the most unequal country (Mexico) is double the value of the most equal country (Denmark). Overall, the different measures of income inequalities provide similar ranking across countries.

From the mid-1980s to the mid-2000s, inequality rose in 19 out of 24 countries. The increase was strongest in Finland, New Zealand and Portugal. Declines occurred in France, Greece, and Turkey, as well as Ireland and Spain (where trend data are limited to 2000). Income inequality generally rose faster from the mid-1980s to the mid-1990s than in the following decade.

Income inequality

Different summary measures, mid-2000s

	Gini coefficient		Mean Log Deviation		Standard Coefficient of Variation		Interdecile ratio P90/P10		Interdecile ratio P50/P10	
	Level	Rank	Level	Rank	Level	Rank	Level	Rank	Level	Rank
Australia	0.30	16	0.17	15	0.39	9	3.95	15	2.09	18
Austria	0.27	4	0.13	8	0.33	3	3.27	10	1.82	7
Belgium	0.27	9	0.13	6	0.30	1	3.43	14	1.97	14
Canada	0.32	18	0.18	17	0.59	17	4.12	17	2.14	20
Czech Republic	0.27	5	0.12	4	0.38	8	3.20	5	1.74	2
Denmark	0.23	1	0.10	2	0.60	18	2.72	1	1.75	3
Finland	0.27	7	0.13	7	0.81	24	3.21	6	1.86	11
France	0.28	13	0.14	9	0.37	7	3.39	13	1.82	8
Germany	0.30	15	0.16	14	0.45	13	3.98	16	2.08	17
Greece	0.32	21	0.18	16	0.43	12	4.39	21	2.18	21
Hungary	0.29	14	0.14	10	0.48	15	3.36	12	1.78	6
Iceland	0.28	12	0.16	13	0.54	16	3.10	4	1.76	4
Ireland	0.33	22	0.19	18	0.79	22	4.41	22	2.29	22
Italy	0.35	25	0.24	23	1.10	25	4.31	20	2.11	19
Japan	0.32	20	0.20	20	0.41	11	4.77	25	2.43	26
Korea	0.31	17	0.20	22	0.35	5	4.73	24	2.50	27
Luxembourg	0.26	3	0.12	3	0.30	2	3.25	8	1.86	10
Mexico	0.47	30	0.41	28	2.70	28	8.53	30	2.86	30
Netherlands	0.27	8	..	..	..	..	3.23	7	1.86	12
New Zealand	0.34	23	..	..	..	..	4.27	19	2.06	16
Norway	0.28	11	0.16	12	0.46	14	2.83	3	1.77	5
Poland	0.37	26	0.26	24	0.71	20	5.63	26	2.42	25
Portugal	0.42	28	0.31	26	1.13	26	6.05	28	2.35	24
Slovak Republic	0.27	5	0.13	5	0.37	6	3.26	9	1.86	13
Spain	0.32	19	0.20	21	0.41	10	4.59	23	2.32	23
Sweden	0.23	2	0.10	1	0.65	19	2.79	2	1.72	1
Switzerland	0.28	10	0.15	11	0.34	4	3.29	11	1.83	9
Turkey	0.43	29	0.32	27	1.45	27	6.49	29	2.67	28
United Kingdom	0.34	23	0.20	19	0.71	21	4.21	18	1.99	15
United States	0.38	27	0.29	25	0.81	23	5.91	27	2.69	29
OECD average	0.31	..	0.19	..	0.66	..	4.16	..	2.09	..

StatLink ᵍᵍᵏ http://dx.doi.org/10.1787/826773162617

Trends in income inequality

Percentage point changes in the Gini coefficient

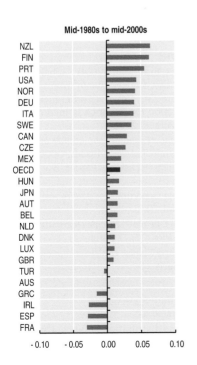

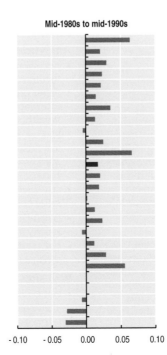

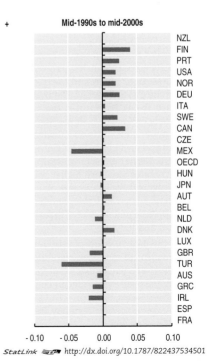

StatLink ᵍᵍᵏ http://dx.doi.org/10.1787/822437534501

POVERTY RATES AND GAPS

Avoiding economic hardship is a primary objective of social policy. As perceptions of "a decent standard of living" vary across countries and over time, no commonly agreed measure of "absolute" poverty across OECD countries exists. A starting point for measuring poverty is therefore to look at "relative" poverty, whose measure is based on the income that is most typical in each country in each year.

Definition

Relative income poverty is measured here by the poverty rate and the poverty gap. The poverty rate is the ratio of the number of people who fall below the poverty line and the total population; the poverty line is here taken as half the median household income. However, two countries with the same poverty rates may differ in terms of the income-level of the poor. To measure this dimension of poverty, the poverty gap, i.e. the percentage by which the mean income of the poor falls below the poverty line, is also presented.

Income is defined as household disposable income in a particular year. It consists of earnings, self-employment and capital income and public cash transfers; income taxes and social security contributions paid by households are deducted. The income of the household is attributed to each of its members, with an adjustment to reflect differences in needs for households of different sizes (i.e. the needs of a household composed of four people are assumed to be twice as large as those of a person living alone).

Comparability

Data used here were provided by national experts applying common methodologies and standardised definitions. In many cases, experts have made several adjustments to their source data to conform to standardized definitions. While this approach improves comparability, full standardisation cannot be achieved. Also, small differences between periods and across countries are usually not significant.

Measurement problems are especially severe at the bottom end of the income scale. Further, as large proportions of the population are clustered around the poverty line used here, small changes in their income can lead to large swings in poverty measures. Small differences between periods and across countries are usually not significant. Exact years for each country are provided under the section on "Measures of income inequality".

Overview

Across OECD countries, the average poverty rate was about 11% in the mid-2000s. There is considerable diversity across countries: poverty rates are 17% or more in the Mexico, Turkey and the United States, but below 6% in the Czech Republic, Denmark and Sweden. On average, in OECD countries, the mean income of poor people is 29% lower than median income (poverty gap), with larger gaps in Mexico, Switzerland and the United States and lower ones in Belgium, Luxembourg, Finland and the Netherlands. In general, countries with higher poverty rates also have higher poverty gaps but this is not universal (for example, Iceland and Switzerland combine low poverty rates and high poverty gaps, while the opposite pattern occurs in Australia, Canada, Greece, Ireland and Italy).

Over the past 20 years, poverty rates fell for 8 countries and rose for 16 countries, resulting in an overall increase of little over 1 percentage point for the OECD as a whole. Larger falls were registered in Belgium and Mexico, and the largest rises, between 4 and 5 percentage points, were experienced by Germany, Ireland, the Netherlands and New Zealand.

Sources
- OECD (2008), *Growing Unequal?: Income Distribution and Poverty in OECD Countries*, OECD, Paris.

Further information
Analytical publications
- Atkinson, A. B., and A. Brandolini (2004), Global World Income Inequality: Absolute, Relative or Intermediate?, Paper presented at the 28th General Conference of the International Association for Research in Income and Wealth, Cork, 22-28 August 2004.
- Förster, M. (1994), *Measurement of Low Incomes and Poverty in a Perspective of International Comparisons*, OECD Labour Market and Social Policy Occasional Papers, No. 14, OECD, Paris.
- OECD (2005), *Extending Opportunities: How Active Social Policy Can Benefit Us All*, OECD, Paris.
- OECD (2008), *Growing Unequal?: Income Distribution and Poverty in OECD Countries*, OECD, Paris.
- OECD (2009), *Society at a Glance: OECD Social Indicators – 2009 Edition*, OECD, Paris.

Web sites
- OECD Social and Welfare Statistics, *www.oecd.org/statistics/social*.
- OECD work on income distribution and poverty, *www.oecd.org/els/social/inequality*.

Poverty rates and poverty gaps
Mid-2000s

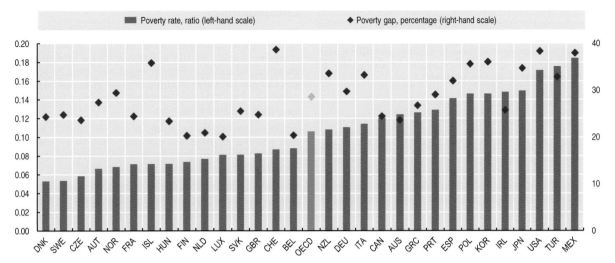

StatLink ⟨⟩ http://dx.doi.org/10.1787/822560430054

Trends in poverty rates
Percentage point changes in income poverty rate at 50% median level

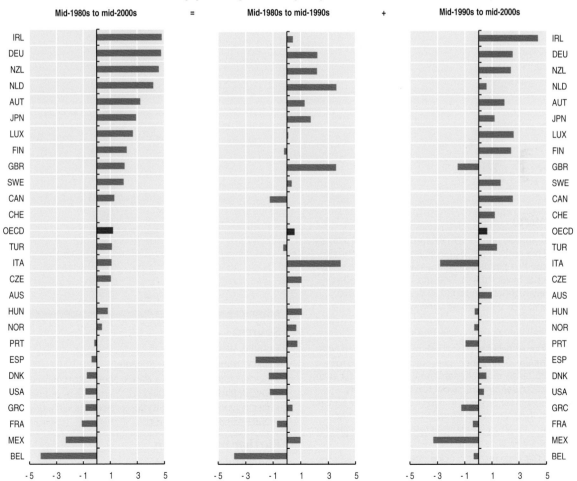

StatLink ⟨⟩ http://dx.doi.org/10.1787/822576570877

SUICIDES

Suicide is often considered as an extreme manifestation of depression and of poor quality of life. Because of its extreme nature, suicide can be viewed as the tip of an iceberg, with inter-temporal changes in rates of suicide, and differences between countries, giving an indication of the extent of broader problems of depressive illness.

Definition

Data on suicide rates are based on official registers on causes of death based on international conventions surrounding the International Statistical Classification of Diseases and Related Health Problems (ICD). The rates shown here are standardised using the OECD population structure of 1980, so as to allow controlling for differences in the age structure of the population across countries and over time.

Suicide rates are expressed as deaths per 100 000 individuals.

Comparability

Despite the ICD, there are comparability problems with suicide data. Countries have different procedures for recording suicide as the underlying cause of death, and these procedures may have changed over time. In addition suicide may be under-reported because of a societal stigma attached to it. This socio-cultural norm may vary across countries and over time.

Studies assessing the reliability of suicide statistics suggest that sources of error are random. Thus they have little impact on comparing rates between countries, between demographic groups or over time.

The data on life satisfaction are based on the *Gallup World Survey*. Regarding the comparability of these data, please see "Subjective Well-being".

Overview

Overall, suicide rates increased in the 1970s and peaked during the early 1980s. However, Japan and Ireland do not share this pattern. In Japan, suicide rates are today somewhat lower than in 1960, but have remained at relatively high levels (around 20 deaths per 100 000 persons) since 1997. Ireland shows a strong and continuous increase of suicide rates until 2000, followed by a small but continuous decline since then.

Suicide rates have fallen for both men and women, with little change in the gender gap. Suicide continues to be a predominantly male phenomenon. On average, for each female suicide there are about three male deaths. Gender gaps are larger in Mexico, Poland and the Slovak Republic and smaller in Korea, the Netherlands and Norway. Gender gaps in suicide rates are also smaller for younger cohorts.

Across OECD countries, suicide rates show no systematic relation with GDP per capita, while there is a weak negative correlation between suicide rates and subjective life-evaluations.

Sources
- *Gallup World Poll*.
- *OECD National Accounts Statistics*.
- OECD (2009), *Health at a Glance 2009: OECD Indicators*, OECD, Paris.
- OECD (2009), *Society at a Glance: OECD Social Indicators – 2009 Edition*, OECD, Paris.

Further information
Analytical publications
- Sainsbury P. and J.S. Jenkins (1982), "The accuracy of officially reported suicide statistics for purposes of epidemiological research", Journal of Epidemiology and Community Health, 36: 43-48.

Suicide rates
Per 100 000 persons

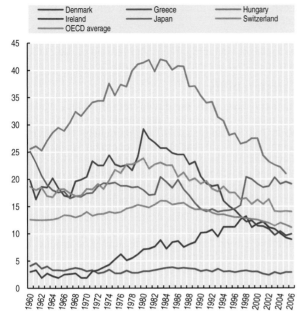

StatLink http://dx.doi.org/10.1787/822601475116

Suicide rates by gender
Per 100 000 persons, 2006 or latest available year

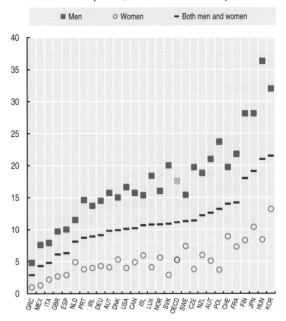

StatLink http://dx.doi.org/10.1787/822648661667

Suicide rates and per capita GDP
USD PPP, 2006 or latest available year

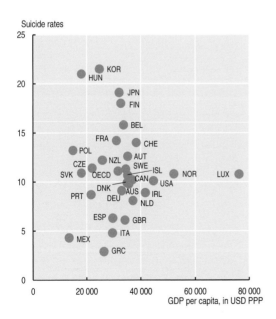

StatLink http://dx.doi.org/10.1787/822652086787

Suicide rates and subjective life satisfaction
Suicides rates (2006 or latest available year) and life satisfaction (2008 or latest available year)

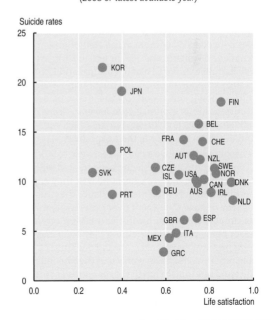

StatLink http://dx.doi.org/10.1787/822654326584

SUBJECTIVE WELL-BEING

Subjective well-being consists of life satisfaction the presence of positive experiences and feelings, and the absence of negative experiences and feelings. Each of these three dimensions matter for people's life, and is subject to a different range of determinants.

Definition

Measures of life satisfaction reflect the cognitive evaluation of life as a whole, now and five years from now, made by each person. The measures shown here are based on ladder-of-life questions, which ask respondents to rate their life from the worst (0) to the best (10) level, and refer to the share of people who rate their life (either today or in the future) at step 7 or higher.

Measures of positive and negative experiences and feelings refer to people who declared having experienced six different forms of negative and positive experiences during the previous day. Also shown are two composite indexes of positive and negative experiences, calculated at the individual record level. For each person, the 6 items are recoded so that positive answers are scored as 1 and negative answers (including "don't know" and "refused to answer") as 0; an individual record has an index calculated if it has at least 5 out of 6 valid scores. Each person's composite index is the mean of valid items multiplied by 100, and the country level score shown in the table is the mean of all individual records for which an index was calculated.

Population shares are calculated as a percentage of all respondents excluding those who refused or did not know how to answer the various survey questions.

Comparability

The data shown here are drawn from the *Gallup World Poll*, and refer to 2009 or the latest available year. The *Gallup World Poll* is conducted in approximately 140 countries around the world based on a common questionnaire, translated into the predominant languages of each country. With few exceptions, all samples are probability based and nationally representative of the resident population aged 15 and over in the entire country (including rural areas).

While this assures a high degree of comparability across countries, results may be affected by sampling and non-sampling errors. Sample sizes are limited to around 1 000 persons in each country.

Overview

On average, around 63% of people in OECD countries reported a high satisfaction with their life, with a higher share (71%) providing a positive evaluation of their life five years from now. Among OECD countries, the share of people reporting high life satisfaction at present ranges between 85% or more in the Netherlands, Denmark and Finland, and 36% or less in Hungary, the Slovak Republic, Turkey, Poland, Portugal and Korea. With the exception of Brazil, the major non-OECD countries shown here report low levels of satisfaction with current life (at around 25% or lower in China, India, Estonia, Indonesia and Russia) but are much more optimistic about their life in the near future.

When looking at positive experiences, close to 90% of the OECD population declare having been treated with respect, and more than 70% declared that they enjoyed something they did on the previous day or that they have autonomy on how they spent their time, while much lower proportions report having learned something (54%), or being proud of something they did (62%). Among negative experiences, around one third of OECD people report having been worried in the previous day and around one fourth that they experienced some form of pain, while around 10% reported feeling depressed.

Among OECD countries, the composite "positive experience" index is highest in Iceland and lowest in Turkey, while the "negative experience" index is highest in Spain and lowest in Denmark. Across these countries, high values of the positive experience index tend to be associated with high values for life evaluations, while there is a only a weak negative correlation between the positive and negative experience indices.

Sources

- *Gallup World Poll*.

Further information

Analytical publications

- Deaton A. (2008), "Income. Health and Well-Being Around the World: Evidence from the Gallup World Poll", *Journal of Economic Perspectives*, Vol. 22, No. 2, Spring.

People reporting various positive and negative experiences
2009 or latest available year

| | Positive experiences | | | | | | | Negative experiences | | | | | | |
| | As a percentage of respondents | | | | | | Positive Experience Index | As a percentage of respondents | | | | | | Negative Experience Index |
	Well rested	Treated with respect	Choose how time was spent	Proud of something you did	Learnt or did something interesting	Enjoyment		Pain	Worry	Sadness	Boredom	Depression	Anger	
Australia	65.8	90.6	70.7	73.7	58.9	83.2	74.3	23.0	30.6	17.3	20.3	8.2	17.6	22.1
Austria	73.5	93.8	78.3	63.8	52.7	84.4	75.1	21.2	23.5	16.5	11.6	5.8	12.3	18.2
Belgium	70.6	92.5	82.9	60.6	50.1	79.1	73.7	28.1	33.3	18.6	11.5	8.6	20.7	23.8
Canada	70.0	93.3	75.8	78.6	67.9	87.0	79.8	24.6	37.3	20.7	22.4	9.3	16.2	24.8
Czech Republic	59.8	74.0	54.6	52.2	50.8	77.9	62.2	20.9	33.9	18.8	14.9	13.0	30.9	22.8
Denmark	66.3	96.0	71.9	62.6	61.4	88.8	76.8	21.0	23.7	12.2	12.3	2.9	13.3	15.1
Finland	69.8	93.2	74.0	61.8	57.6	73.2	72.8	17.7	29.1	9.9	18.1	6.5	4.4	15.3
France	64.1	93.2	78.5	49.9	56.0	74.5	72.7	36.0	38.0	22.4	16.0	7.9	30.6	28.5
Germany	66.5	92.9	61.7	56.2	54.7	74.4	73.2	21.8	27.6	18.1	13.7	5.2	16.6	22.0
Greece	57.7	92.0	63.0	45.0	39.5	74.1	66.6	28.5	42.4	18.8	29.1	6.9	15.1	22.9
Hungary	65.2	88.4	..	..	35.8	74.2	64.8	27.6	35.5	23.3	..	26.8	9.2	26.4
Iceland	66.4	97.3	..	..	82.4	86.9	83.3	25.8	24.8	10.9	..	4.7	10.2	17.2
Ireland	70.4	93.6	80.6	75.2	56.2	83.8	77.0	18.8	28.5	22.5	21.6	8.8	19.4	23.0
Italy	64.5	93.5	79.7	63.0	54.4	75.2	73.2	26.3	43.9	25.8	23.7	11.3	13.9	27.2
Japan	76.8	61.2	85.3	46.9	54.7	74.0	69.7	20.5	29.9	12.7	21.8	20.6	14.7	20.7
Korea	75.3	68.9	78.8	62.3	37.9	64.4	61.9	23.9	32.4	14.4	29.7	18.7	15.9	22.8
Luxembourg	63.7	95.5	..	..	56.0	78.8	73.9	26.6	25.3	19.0	..	4.9	27.0	24.0
Mexico	74.3	92.9	76.9	70.0	58.8	85.6	78.0	22.3	33.0	15.6	30.8	12.1	10.3	20.4
Netherlands	67.1	94.3	67.6	65.1	46.6	80.0	72.2	16.3	31.5	13.8	9.5	4.3	9.4	15.8
New Zealand	66.3	91.1	70.5	76.4	70.9	84.6	77.8	23.5	31.4	18.0	24.0	8.8	20.2	23.6
Norway	66.1	91.8	66.8	58.6	63.4	86.1	75.5	16.5	20.5	13.2	22.2	8.1	12.9	16.1
Poland	66.5	94.2	70.6	63.1	43.6	74.0	67.7	17.3	33.5	20.8	22.3	6.2	19.0	19.9
Portugal	71.4	93.2	75.5	57.2	59.4	62.2	72.5	26.0	48.7	33.3	16.2	16.8	11.1	28.4
Slovak Republic	59.2	82.3	60.2	54.6	38.6	74.9	61.1	24.1	39.3	22.9	16.8	12.6	30.8	26.9
Spain	73.3	97.7	84.7	69.5	51.8	59.1	72.0	31.3	51.7	26.1	20.8	12.6	23.0	28.8
Sweden	64.1	94.1	70.0	66.5	61.6	86.8	76.4	22.9	15.9	12.0	19.0	4.4	12.4	15.8
Switzerland	69.8	94.4	70.1	60.3	57.5	86.1	76.4	26.2	32.1	17.9	14.2	4.2	13.8	20.7
Turkey	67.8	68.2	..	..	32.7	47.5	56.5	17.8	31.2	30.6	..	14.4	37.5	28.1
United Kingdom	66.9	91.3	75.6	59.1	54.7	84.3	75.5	24.1	32.5	20.0	27.1	9.0	16.9	23.7
United States	67.5	89.4	71.4	74.2	61.5	84.0	76.3	29.8	38.4	20.9	29.8	13.8	19.3	28.1
OECD average	67.6	89.5	72.9	62.6	54.3	77.6	72.3	23.7	32.6	18.9	20.0	9.9	17.5	22.4
Brazil	68.6	94.3	73.9	75.3	59.6	81.1	76.6	25.9	43.8	20.5	13.9	8.0	17.9	23.9
Chile	70.4	94.5	74.1	68.4	60.7	81.2	77.1	33.1	46.8	23.6	30.6	14.4	21.3	27.4
China	80.7	90.6	82.9	35.5	37.0	83.7	72.8	11.8	25.7	6.8	21.4	7.7	16.3	17.3
Estonia	59.4	88.8	60.4	51.9	45.9	70.1	60.0	20.6	34.6	24.8	17.6	11.8	14.1	20.3
India	66.4	80.7	53.6	33.0	36.6	79.3	67.1	29.6	35.6	25.4	21.5	23.0	29.4	27.8
Indonesia	87.6	94.3	69.9	69.8	55.0	87.3	81.0	16.6	25.2	15.4	31.8	1.2	17.3	13.3
Israel	58.6	75.8	56.2	58.0	49.6	72.2	63.1	38.4	43.2	24.3	31.3	15.0	30.7	31.1
Russian Federation	60.7	90.3	63.6	46.2	36.5	63.2	58.8	22.8	22.8	18.7	18.7	12.1	9.0	15.5
Slovenia	68.2	92.6	66.6	70.4	57.1	58.5	66.2	30.5	51.7	21.2	12.8	7.3	19.0	25.5
South Africa	76.5	82.6	70.6	56.0	48.9	73.5	71.1	25.6	31.0	18.8	22.0	13.5	19.5	23.3

StatLink http://dx.doi.org/10.1787/826807282861

People reporting high evaluation of their life as a whole
As a percentage of respondents, 2009 or latest available year

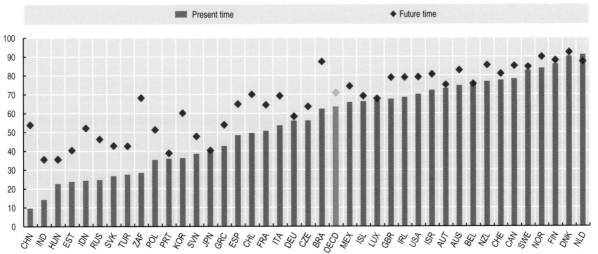

StatLink http://dx.doi.org/10.1787/822657515827

SOCIAL BENEFITS OF EDUCATION

This indicator examines the relationships between educational attainment and three outcomes that reflect the health and cohesiveness of the society: health, political interest and interpersonal trust.

Definition

Estimates of the marginal effects of education in each of the three domains capture the increase in the probability of individuals exhibiting positive social outcomes when moving from one level of educational attainment to the next higher level. It can also be interpreted as the difference in the share of individuals exhibiting positive outcomes across levels of education. Calculations are based on country-specific regression models that predict each dichotomous outcome variable (*e.g.* high versus low interest in politics) from individuals' educational attainment level.

Health is measured by the share of adults who rate their health as at least "good." Political interest is measured by the share of adults who say they are at least "fairly interested" in politics. Interpersonal trust is measured by the share of adults who believe that most people try to be fair.

Overview

Education affects people's lives in ways that go beyond economic outcomes such as labour market earnings. These effects include a variety of social outcomes such as health, political interest and interpersonal trust. Education can have an impact on individuals' health by helping them choose healthier lifestyles, better manage their illness and avoid conditions detrimental to their health, such as dangerous jobs and the stress of poverty. Education can raise political interest by providing relevant information and experience, by developing competencies, values, attitudes and beliefs that trigger interest in politics. Education can also affect interpersonal trust by helping individuals to better understand and embrace the values of social cohesion and diversity, or because people with higher education are more likely to live and work in environments in which crime and anti-social behaviour tend to be lower.

Educational attainment is positively associated with self-reported health, political interest and interpersonal trust. Adults who have higher levels of educational attainment are generally more likely than those with lower levels of attainment to report that their health is at least good, are at least fairly interested in politics, and believe that most people try to be fair. For self-reported health, an increase in educational attainment from below-upper secondary to upper-secondary level is associated with a stronger and more consistent increase in outcomes, compared to the increase associated to a move from upper-secondary to tertiary education in all surveyed countries except Poland. In the case of political interest and interpersonal trust, an increase in educational attainment from upper secondary to tertiary level is broadly associated with stronger and more consistent increases in social outcomes, compared to an increase in educational attainment from lower to upper secondary education.

Comparability

Calculations are based on micro-data for adults aged 25 to 64 from a range of surveys including the *European Social Survey* (ESS) of 2004 and 2006; the *Adult Literacy and Lifeskills Survey* (ALL) of 2003; the *World Values Survey* (WVS) of 2005; and the *International Social Survey Programme* (ISSP) of 2004 and 2006. These surveys are selected based on the availability of at least 1 000 observations and because of comparability of questions on self-reported health, political interest and interpersonal trust. The analysis has been limited to micro-data for which the distribution of educational attainment is within 10 percentage points from those published for comparable years in Education at a Glance. A few exceptions were made following the recommendations of the representatives from Canada, Finland, Korea and Norway in the INES (Indicators of Education Systems) Network.

In each chart, countries are grouped by data sources. For the chart on the effects of education on self-reported health, data in the first panel are based on ALL 2003 and WVS 2005, those in the second panel on ESS 2004, and those in the third panel on ESS 2006. For the chart on the effects of education on political interest, data in the first panel are based on ISSP 2004/06 and WVS 2005, those in the second panel on ESS 2004 while those in the third panel on ESS 2006. For the chart on the effects of education on interpersonal trust, data in the first panel are based on ISSP 2004 and WVS 2005, those in the second panel on ESS 2004 and those in the third panel on ESS 2006.

Sources
- OECD (2009), *Education at a Glance*, OECD, Paris.

Further information
Analytical publications
- OECD (2007), *Understanding the Social Outcomes of Learning*, OECD, Paris.

Web sites
- OECD Education at a Glance, *www.oecd.org/edu/eag2009*.

Marginal effects of education on self-reported health

Increase in the probability in percentage, 2006 or latest available year

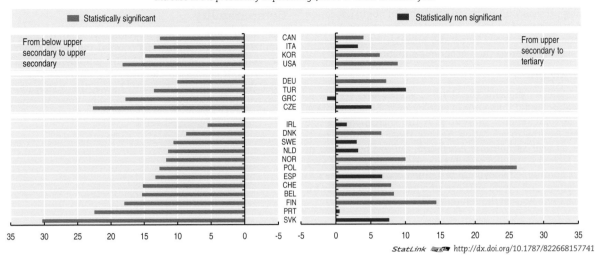

StatLink ⟨≡⟩ http://dx.doi.org/10.1787/822668157741

Marginal effects of education on political interest

Increase in the probability in percentage, 2006 or latest available year

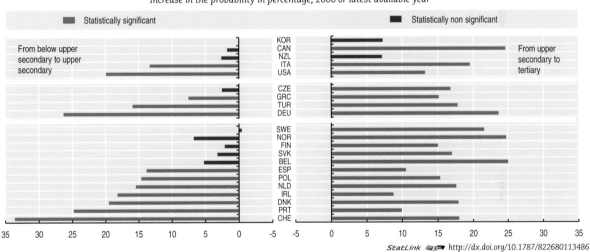

StatLink ⟨≡⟩ http://dx.doi.org/10.1787/822680113486

Marginal effects of education on interpersonal trust

Increase in the probability in percentage, 2006 or latest available year

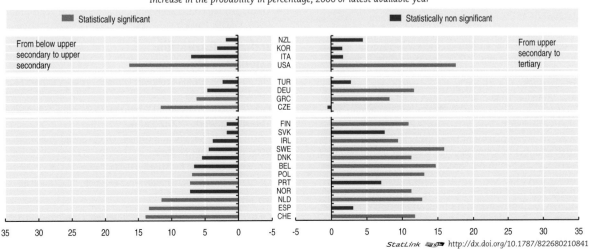

StatLink ⟨≡⟩ http://dx.doi.org/10.1787/822680210841

YOUTH INACTIVITY

Young persons who are not in employment nor in education and training are at risk of becoming socially excluded – persons with incomes below the poverty-line and lacking the skills to improve their economic situation.

Definition

The indicator presents the share of youths who are not in education and training nor in employment, as a percentage of the total number of youths in the corresponding age group. Youths in education include those attending part-time as well as full-time education, but exclude those in non-formal education and in educational activities of very short duration. Employment is defined according to the ILO Guidelines and covers all those who have worked for pay for at least one hour in the reference week of the survey.

Comparability

The main problem of comparability is that, in some countries, youths performing compulsory military service are considered as being not in employment nor in education. However, the duration of military services is in most countries generally short; hence, the reallocation of military conscripts to the employment/education category would not change the figures shown here by much.

Overview

On average, 15% of the 20-to-24-year-olds were neither in school nor at work in 2007. Differences across countries are large: in Denmark, Iceland, Japan, the Netherlands and Norway less than 9 % of youth were in this situation. The ratio is substantially higher in Italy, Poland, Slovak Republic, and the United Kingdom, where this share exceeded 18%, and in Turkey, where the share exceeded 40%. For the OECD as a whole, the share of youths aged 20-to-24-year-old who are not in employment nor in education has declined over time, mainly reflecting the fact that young people, and particularly females, spend more time in education than they did a decade ago. The share of youths who are not in education nor in employment was twice as high for youths aged 20 to 24 (14.9%) than for those aged 15 to 19 (7.2%). This share is even higher among people aged 25 to 29 (17% in 2007).

In most countries, a smooth transition from school to work is highly dependent on the business cycle and on economic conditions. When these conditions worsen, youths making their transition from school to work are the first affected. This is because, when employers are shedding workers, it is often impossible for young individuals to get a foothold in the labour market, as they compete for jobs with more experienced workers. Also, when employment rates drop, people's incentives to stay longer in school become stronger, as the potential earnings that students forego while studying will in many cases be close to zero. In this context, it is important for education systems to ease conditions of access to education and training and to make additional resources available to educational institutions.

Sources

- OECD (2009), *Education at a Glance*, OECD, Paris.
- OECD (2009), *OECD Economic Outlook, Interim Report March 2009*, OECD, Paris.

Further information

Analytical publications

- OECD (2009), *OECD Economic Outlook, Interim Report March 2009*, OECD, Paris.
- OECD (2000), *From Initial Education to Working Life: Making Transitions Work*, OECD, Paris.
- OECD (2007), *Society at a Glance: OECD Social Indicators – 2006 Edition*, OECD, Paris.
- OECD (2008), *Jobs for Youth*, OECD, Paris.
- OECD (2009), *OECD Employment Outlook*, OECD, Paris.

Web sites

- OECD Education at a Glance, *www.oecd.org/edu/eag2007*.
- Youth Employment Summit, *www.yesweb.org*.

Youths who are not in education nor in employment
As a percentage of persons in that age group

	Youths aged between 20 and 24							Youths aged between 15 and 19						
	1997	2000	2003	2004	2005	2006	2007	1997	2000	2003	2004	2005	2006	2007
Australia	17.5	13.3	13.3	12.3	11.6	11.5	10.7	8.1	6.8	6.8	7.5	7.4	7.1	6.5
Austria	..	..	10.4 |	12.9	12.4	12.5	11.0	..	..	5.6 |	7.3	6.9	6.6	5.3
Belgium	18.3	16.0	17.1	16.9	18.3	16.9	15.4	9.0	6.5	7.1	4.9	6.2	7.1	5.2
Canada	17.9	15.7	14.3	14.2	14.4	13.0	13.7	6.5	8.2	8.1	8.8	7.0	7.3	6.4
Czech Republic	18.2	20.3	18.0	18.5	16.6	14.1	11.0	5.0	7.9	5.8	5.7	5.3	4.5	2.9
Denmark	6.5	6.6	11.8	11.3	8.3	5.9	8.2	1.4	2.7	2.5	2.1	4.3	4.4	3.9
Finland	..	..	14.4	15.4	13.0	13.3	13.3	..	..	6.2	5.9	5.2	3.6	3.5
France	18.0	14.1	.. |	16.1	15.8	16.6	15.1	2.9	3.3	.. |	5.2	6.0	6.4	5.8
Germany	18.4	16.9	15.6	17.5	18.7	16.7	15.2	5.0	5.7	4.7	3.6	4.4	4.2	4.2
Greece	27.5	24.9	21.7	21.8	20.1	17.4	17.7	9.6	9.0	9.5	10.0	9.8	8.8	8.5
Hungary	29.2	22.0	19.9	18.6	18.9	18.5	16.9	8.9	8.6	6.8	6.2	6.4	6.0	5.0
Iceland	6.6	..	7.8	6.4	10.0	..	6.4	..	..	..	..	..	..	..
Ireland	..	9.7	11.5	11.6	12.3	11.8	12.1	..	4.4	5.3	4.9	4.5	5.0	5.1
Italy	..	27.5	21.7	23.6	24.1	22.8	22.6	..	13.1	9.3	11.0	11.2	11.8	10.2
Japan	7.7	8.8	9.8	9.2	8.8	9.1	7.6	..	..	..	..	..	..	..
Luxembourg	10.3	8.2	8.1	10.1	9.3	10.3	9.2	5.6	..	2.1	3.2	2.2	4.1	2.9
Mexico	28.7	27.1	27.6	27.4	..	..	..	19.0	18.3	17.8	17.0	..	..	..
Netherlands	7.1	8.2	9.4	9.3	9.1	7.3	6.9	2.8	3.7	4.3	3.3	3.9	3.0	3.6
New Zealand	..	..	..	..	13.7	13.0	13.7	..	..	..	..	7.2	8.3	9.3
Norway	11.7	8.0	10.6	9.8	9.6	9.1	8.8	..	..	2.7	2.8	2.5	3.4	3.7
Poland	25.3	30.8	25.5	24.1	20.1	20.7	18.3	5.3	4.5	3.3	2.6	1.7	3.8	2.5
Portugal	14.2	11.0	12.3	13.5	14.1	13.3	15.2	9.8	7.7	8.8	9.8	8.4	7.8	8.6
Slovak Republic	25.5	33.1	29.6	27.8	25.2	22.8	19.9	16.7	26.3	12.6	7.9	6.3	6.7	5.4
Spain	22.1	15.0	14.8	15.6	19.4	16.9	17.2	10.9	8.0	7.3	7.6	10.8	10.1	10.9
Sweden	16.3	10.7	11.8	13.6	13.4	15.2	13.1	4.6	3.6	4.2	4.8	4.7	5.3	5.4
Switzerland	10.3	5.9	12.7	11.0	11.0	10.8	10.4	7.4	7.9	7.8	7.2	7.5	7.6	8.2
Turkey	48.4	44.2	47.8	47.8	47.1	46.3	45.7	30.2	31.2	32.8	35.3	37.7	34.3	36.1
United Kingdom	..	15.4	15.3	14.8	16.8	18.2	18.1	..	8.0	9.4	9.0	9.3	10.9	10.7
United States	15.1	14.4	..	16.9	15.5	15.6	16.2	7.1	7.0	..	6.9	6.1	6.3	6.3
OECD average	18.8	17.5	16.9	17.0	16.3	15.8	14.9	8.8	9.3	8.0	7.7	7.4	7.5	7.2
Brazil	..	..	..	..	..	..	23.4	..	..	..	..	..	..	14.7
Estonia	..	..	18.0	19.5	16.3	15.4	15.3	..	..	3.3	7.6	5.2	3.7	5.7
Israel	..	..	44.2	40.9	40.3	40.6	39.6	..	..	25.2	25.6	24.7	24.3	25.7
Slovenia	..	..	13.0	11.2	13.0	13.7	10.4	..	..	4.8	4.3	4.9	4.2	4.3

StatLink http://dx.doi.org/10.1787/826876888878

Youths aged between 20 and 24 who are not in education nor in employment
As a percentage of persons in that age group

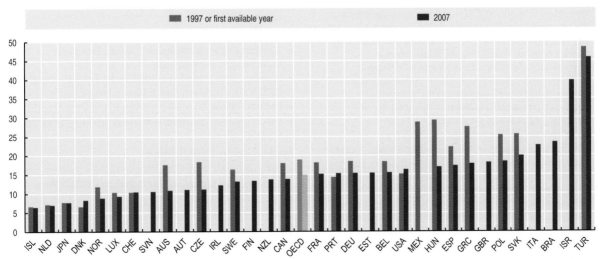

StatLink http://dx.doi.org/10.1787/822682373852

TOURISM: HOTEL NIGHTS

Arrivals of non-resident tourists in accommodation (hotel or similar establishments) is one of the standard measures of international tourism activity. It excludes domestic tourism.

Definition

This statistic refers to the number of non-residents who arrive in a hotel or similar establishment such as apartment-hotels, motels, roadside inns, beach hotels, residential clubs, boarding houses, and similar accommodation providing limited hotel services. Note that arrivals of non-resident tourists do not show the number of travellers. When a person visits the same country several times a year, each visit is counted as a separate arrival and if a person visits several countries during the course of a single trip, his/her arrival in each country is recorded as a separate arrival. Same day visitors and tourists who stay with friends or relatives are excluded.

Comparability

Several OECD countries cannot provide statistics on "arrivals of non-resident tourists in hotels or similar establishments". For those countries, the statistical profile presents "arrivals of non-residents at national borders". Canada, China, India, Ireland and the United States report the number of non-resident tourist arrivals at their national borders; a tourist is a visitor who intends to stay for at least one night. The figures for Japan, Korea and New Zealand include the number of non-resident visitor arrivals at their national borders; visitors include overnight (tourists) and same day visitors. For Australia (1990-97, 2007 visitors and 1998-2006 tourists) and South Africa (1990-94 visitors and 1995-2007 tourists) time series present mixed indicators.

Overview

According to *Tourism in OECD Countries 2008: Trends and Policies* (OECD, 2008), OECD member countries represent about 60% of international arrivals. Eight out of ten of the main tourism destinations in the world are OECD member countries. Tourism in OECD member countries accounts for between 2 and 12 per cent of GDP, between 3 and 11 per cent of employment, and on average about 30% of service exports. Tourism is also a key driver of globalisation. Its relevance to countries' economic, services industry and employment performance is widely recognised. Governments are also giving increased policy consideration to this industry at national, regional and local levels.

UNWTO's Tourism 2020 Vision forecasts that international arrivals will reach over 1.56 billion by the year 2020. East Asia and the Pacific, South Asia, the Middle East, and Africa are expected to record growth at rates of over 5% per year, compared with the world average of 4.1%. The more mature tourism regions, Europe and the Americas, are expected to show lower than average growth rates. Europe will maintain the highest share of world arrivals, although there will be a decline from 60% in 1995 to 46% in 2020.

Sources

- *The Statistical Office of the European Communities (Eurostat).*
- *World Tourism Organisation (UNWTO).*

Further information

Analytical publications

- OECD (2006), *Innovation and Growth in Tourism*, OECD, Paris.
- OECD (2008), *The Impact of Culture on Tourism*, OECD, Paris.
- OECD (2008), *Tourism in OECD Countries 2008: Trends and Policies*, OECD, Paris.

Statistical publications

- Eurostat (2007), *Panorama on Tourism*, European Commission, Luxembourg.
- Eurostat (2007), *Tourism statistics – Pocketbook – Data 2000-2005*, European Commission, Luxembourg.
- UNWTO (2003), *Tourism 2020 Vision*, UNWTO, Madrid.
- UNWTO (2008), *Yearbook of Tourism Statistics*, UNWTO, Madrid.

Methodological publications

- UN, Eurostat, OECD, WTO (2001), *Tourism Satellite Account: Recommended Methodological Framework*, OECD, Paris.
- UN, UNWTO (1994), *Recommendations on Tourism Statistics*, United Nations, New York.

Web sites

- Eurostat, *http://europa.eu.int/comm/eurostat/*.
- OECD tourism activities, *www.oecd.org/cfe/tourism*.
- World Tourism Organisation, *www.world-tourism.org*.

Arrivals of non-resident tourists in hotels and similar establishments or at borders
Thousands

	1994	1995	1996	1997	1998	1999	2000	2001	2002	2003	2004	2005	2006	2007
Australia	3 362	3 726	4 165	4 318	3 825	4 109	4 530	4 435	4 420	4 354	4 774	5 020	5 064	5 644
Austria	12 878	12 464	12 533	12 329	12 803	12 755	13 240	13 279	13 487	13 748	14 075	14 542	14 947	15 344
Belgium	3 947	4 138	4 469	4 710	4 859	4 983	5 163	5 117	5 323	5 261	5 385	5 409	5 665	5 713
Canada	15 972	16 932	17 286	17 669	18 870	19 411	19 627	19 679	20 057	17 534	19 145	18 770	18 265	17 931
Czech Republic	2 448	2 891	3 696	4 013	4 067	4 141	3 863	4 439	4 314	4 485	5 346	5 686	5 781	6 098
Denmark	..	..	1 307	1 317	1 305	1 268	1 347	1 310	1 284	1 294	1 363	1 350	1 357	1 308
Finland	1 633	1 587	1 537	1 618	1 655	1 613	1 751	1 774	1 796	1 800	1 825	1 828	2 045	2 188
France	27 121	27 018	27 096	29 625	32 339	34 267	36 474	35 097	36 093	32 520	33 988	35 033	32 506	33 463
Germany	12 269	12 683	13 042	13 745	14 457	14 965	16 719	15 754	15 672	15 979	17 620	18 761	20 630	21 449
Greece	6 659	6 250	5 973	6 785	7 276	7 229	7 767	6 997	6 654	6 574	6 313	7 143	7 548	8 746
Hungary	2 122	2 116	2 202	2 188	2 472	2 401	2 604	2 669	2 659	2 599	2 951	3 140	3 009	3 131
Iceland	..	..	311	354	400	431	451	465	513	569	615	643	714	782
Ireland	4 309	4 818	5 289	5 587	6 064	6 403	6 646	6 353	6 476	6 764	6 953	7 333	8 001	8 332
Italy	21 074	23 467	24 929	25 133	25 927	26 530	28 797	29 138	29 340	28 174	29 916	30 870	33 513	34 757
Japan	3 468	3 345	3 837	4 218	4 106	4 438	4 757	4 772	5 239	5 212	6 138	6 728	7 334	8 347
Korea	3 580	3 753	3 684	3 908	4 250	4 660	5 322	5 147	5 347	4 753	5 818	6 023	6 155	6 448
Luxembourg	492	496	461	508	525	580	589	577	599	581	613	667	673	706
Mexico	5 159	6 718	7 491	8 155	8 157	9 501	9 867	9 410	7 869	8 556	9 972	10 691	9 689	13 250
Netherlands	4 456	4 797	4 999	6 163	7 432	7 550	7 738	7 445	7 433	6 930	7 601	8 081	8 567	8 713
New Zealand	1 323	1 409	1 529	1 497	1 485	1 607	1 787	1 909	2 045	2 104	2 334	2 366	2 409	2 455
Norway	2 830	2 880	2 746	2 702	2 829	2 857	2 787	2 686	2 561	2 439	2 556	2 656	2 841	..
Poland	2 540	2 792	3 020	2 919	2 695	1 982	2 505	2 488	2 536	2 701	3 385	3 723	3 738	3 833
Portugal	3 809	4 000	4 069	4 314	4 974	4 911	5 119	4 934	5 060	4 906	5 201	5 355	5 883	7 045
Slovak Republic	680	735	758	660	701	767	836	927	1 041	1 043	1 094	1 203	1 292	1 350
Spain	15 310	16 286	17 008	18 250	20 199	26 799	27 150	27 012	26 611	27 249	27 620	29 029	34 412	35 844
Sweden	1 830	1 995	2 091	2 143	2 304	2 320	2 465	2 586	2 577	2 552	2 610	2 736	2 867	2 993
Switzerland	7 358	6 946	6 730	7 039	7 185	7 154	7 821	7 455	6 868	6 530	..	7 229	7 863	8 448
Turkey	3 716	4 617	6 440	9 382	7 539	4 805	6 789	8 769	9 859	8 983	10 962	12 937	11 883	14 788
United Kingdom	14 927	17 118	16 890	17 110	16 304	17 019	17 019	17 019	14 176	14 397	13 172	17 009	18 711	18 671
United States	44 753	43 490	46 636	47 875	46 377	48 510	51 237	46 927	43 581	41 218	46 086	49 206	50 978	55 986
Brazil	1 529	1 709	2 266	2 419	3 854	3 754	3 868	3 331	3 536	2 633	3 068	3 215	..	..
Chile	1 634	1 540	1 450	1 644	1 759	1 632	1 742	1 723	1 412	1 614	1 785	2 027	2 253	2 507
China	21 070	20 034	22 765	23 770	25 073	27 047	31 229	33 167	36 803	32 970	41 761	46 809	49 913	54 720
Estonia	..	331	403	504	602	..	..	848	937	1 009	1 300	1 358	1 330	1 286
India	1 886	2 124	2 288	2 374	2 359	2 482	2 649	2 537	2 384	2 726	3 457	3 919	4 447	5 082
Israel	2 595	2 978	2 765	2 461	2 283	2 895	3 165	1 077	694	900	1 374	2 005	2 131	2 748
Russian Federation	..	5 311	5 496	..	..	..	..	3 215	3 231	3 101	3 275	3 438	4 416	..
Slovenia	648	641	714	803	799	740	884	933	1 006	1 053	1 125	1 192	1 247	1 354
South Africa	3 897	4 488	4 915	4 976	5 732	5 890	5 872	5 787	6 430	6 505	6 678	7 369	8 396	9 091

StatLink 🔗 http://dx.doi.org/10.1787/826886665341

Arrivals of non-resident tourists in hotels and similar establishments or at borders
Average annual growth in percentage, 1997-2007 or latest available period

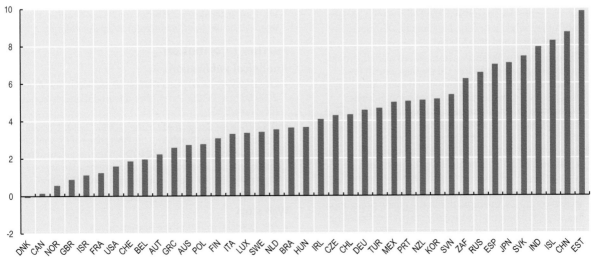

StatLink 🔗 http://dx.doi.org/10.1787/822707613066

PRISON POPULATION

Crime causes great suffering to victims and their families, but the costs associated with imprisonment can also be considerable. These costs are normally justified by the need to inflict retribution to offenders; to deter others from behaving in a similar way; and to prevent re-offending. The size of the prison population depends on the level of crime, the legislative measures and the efficiency of the enforcement measures.

Definition

The indicator shown here considers the total prison population, including pre-trial detainees and remand prisoners, per 100 000 of national population. This information has been collected by the *International Centre for Prison Studies* since 1992, every 3 years or so. It should be noted that not everyone in prison has been found guilty of a crime, due to the inclusion of those awaiting trial or adjudication.

Comparability

Imprisonment rates may vary by country according to the extent to which they apply home detention or residential rehabilitation as judicial sanctions. These latter applications of the justice system have some prison-like features, but they do not constitute incarceration in an official institution. Additional comparative information is available from the above source: this includes information on shares (in the total prison population) of pre-trial detainees/remand prisoners, female prisoners, young prisoners, foreign prisoners, and occupancy levels (in percentage) relative to official prison capacity.

Overview

Over the last fifteen years, most OECD countries have experienced a continuous rise in their prison population rates. On average, across the 30 OECD countries, this rate has increased from a level of 100 persons per 100 000 unit of the total population in the early 1990s to 140 persons in the late 2000s. The prison population rate is highest in the United-States, where 760 per 100 000 population were in prison in 2008: such level is three to four times higher than the second highest OECD country (Poland), and has increased rapidly.

The increase in the prison population extends to most other OECD countries. Since 1992, the prison population rate has more than doubled in the Netherlands, Mexico, and Turkey, while it declined in Canada, Denmark, Hungary, Korea and Switzerland.

There are large differences across countries in the make-up of the prison population. On average, one in four prisoners is a pre-trial detainee or a remand prisoner, but these two categories account for a much higher share of the prison population in Italy, Luxembourg and Turkey. Women and youths (aged below 18) account, on average, for 5% and 2% of the prison population respectively. A much larger share of prisoners is accounted for by foreigners (22% of all prisoners, on average), with this share exceeding 40% in Luxembourg, Switzerland, as well as Austria, Belgium and Greece. In several countries, the rapid rise in the prison population has stretched beyond the receptive capacity of existing institutions; occupancy levels are above 100% in more than half of OECD countries, and above 125% in Greece, Mexico and Spain.

Sources

- Walmsley, R. (2009), World Prison Population List (eighth edition), International Center for Prison Studies, London., *www.kcl.ac.uk/depsta/law/research/icps/worldbrief/*.

Further information
Analytical publications

- OECD (2009), *Society at a Glance: OECD Social Indicators – 2009 Edition*, OECD, Paris, (See *www.oecd.org/els/social/indicators/SAG*).
- UN Office on Drugs and Crime (2009), *United Nations Surveys on Crime Trends and the Operations of Criminal Justice Systems (eleventh survey)*, UNODC, Vienna, *www.unodc.org/unodc/en/data-and-analysis/United-Nations-Surveys-on-Crime-Trends-and-the-Operations-of-Criminal-Justice-Systems.html*.

Web sites

- OECD Social and Welfare Statistics, *www.oecd.org/statistics/social*.
- United Nations Office on Drugs and Crime, *www.unodc.org*.

Prison population rate
Number per 100 000 inhabitants

	1992	1995	1998	2001	2004	2009
Australia	89	96	107	116	120	129
Austria	87	78	87	86	110	99
Belgium	71	75	81	85	88	93
Canada	123	131	126	117	108	116
Czech Republic	123	181	209	210	169	209
Denmark	66	66	64	59	70	63
Finland	65	59	50	59	66	67
France	84	89	86	75	92	96
Germany	71	81	96	98	98	90
Greece	61	56	68	79	82	109
Hungary	153	121	140	170	164	152
Iceland	39	44	38	39	39	44
Ireland	61	57	71	78	76	85
Italy	81	87	85	95	96	97
Japan	36	38	42	51	60	63
Korea	126	133	147	132	119	97
Luxembourg	89	114	92	80	121	155
Mexico	98	102	133	164	183	208
Netherlands	49	66	85	95	123	100
New Zealand	119	128	143	152	160	195
Norway	58	55	57	59	65	70
Poland	160	158	141	208	211	225
Portugal	93	124	144	128	125	104
Slovak Republic	124	147	123	138	175	151
Spain	90	102	114	117	138	164
Sweden	63	65	60	68	81	74
Switzerland	79	80	85	71	81	76
Turkey	54	82	102	89	100	155
United Kingdom	91	100	125	126	140	153
United States	505	600	669	685	723	760
OECD average	100	111	119	124	133	140
Brazil	74	92	102	133	183	242
Chile	155	155	181	225	238	317
China	..	101	115	111	118	119
Estonia	306	295	330	351	339	273
India	..	..	28	30	30	33
Indonesia	21	21	26	31	44	58
Israel	201	189	147	153	209	325
Russian Federation	487	622	688	638	587	624
Slovenia	42	41	38	58	54	65
South Africa	280	280	387	409	333	329

StatLink ⧉ http://dx.doi.org/10.1787/827065685670

Prison population rate
Number per 100 000 inhabitants, 2009 or latest available year

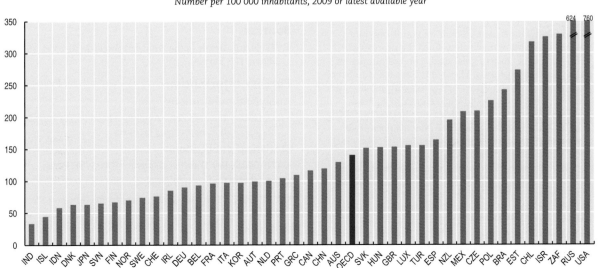

StatLink ⧉ http://dx.doi.org/10.1787/822712761682

ROAD FATALITIES

The number of road motor vehicles is high and rising among OECD countries, and reducing road accidents is a concern in all countries.

Definition

The table in this section shows the numbers of road fatalities per million inhabitants. The chart shows the number of road fatalities per million inhabitants and per million vehicles.

A road motor vehicle is a vehicle running on wheels and intended for use on roads with an engine providing its sole means of propulsion. They are normally used for carrying persons or goods or for drawing, on the road, vehicles used for the carriage of persons or goods. They include buses, coaches, freight vehicles, motor cycles and passenger motor cars. Motor vehicles running on rails are excluded.

Road fatality means any person killed immediately or dying within 30 days as a result of a road accident.

Comparability

Road motor vehicles are attributed to the countries where they are registered while deaths are attributed to the countries in which they occur. As a result, ratios of fatalities to million inhabitants and of fatalities to million vehicles cannot strictly be interpreted as indicating the proportion of a country's population that is at risk of suffering a fatal road accident or the likelihood of a vehicle registered in a given country being involved in a fatal accident. In practice, however, this is not a serious problem because discrepancies between the numerators and denominators tend to cancel out.

The numbers of vehicles entering the existing stock is usually accurate but information on the numbers of vehicles withdrawn from use is less certain.

Road fatalities
Per million inhabitants

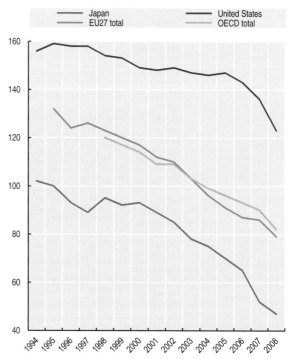

StatLink ⌗ http://dx.doi.org/10.1787/822772237260

Overview

In 2008, road fatalities per million inhabitants ranged from over 211 per million inhabitants in Russian Federation to 38 in Iceland. Over the period shown in the table, road fatalities rates have decreased in all countries except in India, with particularly sharp falls in Portugal, Luxembourg and Germany.

Road fatality rates per million inhabitants are only a partial indicator of road safety since the number of accidents depends to a great extent on the number of vehicles in each country. The chart shows the number of fatalities per million vehicles together with fatalities per million inhabitants. Both ratios refer to 2008. Road fatality rates per million vehicles are affected by driving habits, traffic legislation and the effectiveness of its enforcement, road design and other factors over which governments may exercise control. In 2008, fatality rates per million vehicles were less than 70 in Iceland and Switzerland, but exceeded 400 in Turkey and Russian Federation. Note that low fatality rates per million inhabitants may be associated with very high fatality rates per million vehicles. For example, a country with a small vehicle population (e.g. Turkey) may show a low fatality rate per million inhabitants but a high fatality rate per million vehicles.

Sources
- ITF (2010), *Trends in the Transport Sector 1970-2008*, 2010 Edition, ITF, Paris.

Further information
Analytical publications
- ITF (2008), *Towards Zero: Ambitious Road Safety Targets and the Safe System Approach*, ITF, Paris.

Statistical publications
- ITF (2008), *Key Transport Statistics 2008,*, ITF, Paris.

Methodological publications
- UNECE, ITF, Eurostat (2009), *Glossary for Transport Statistics, 4th Edition*, ITF, Paris.

Web sites
- International Transport Forum, *www.internationaltransportforum.org/*.

Road fatalities
Per million inhabitants

	1995	1996	1997	1998	1999	2000	2001	2002	2003	2004	2005	2006	2007	2008
Australia	111	108	95	94	93	95	90	87	82	79	81	78	77	68
Austria	150	127	137	121	135	122	119	118	114	108	94	89	83	81
Belgium	148	134	134	147	136	143	144	131	117	112	104	102	100	100
Canada	113	103	101	97	98	95	90	93	87	85	91	89	83	82
Czech Republic	154	152	155	132	141	145	130	140	142	136	126	104	118	103
Denmark	111	98	93	94	97	93	80	86	80	68	61	56	74	74
Finland	86	79	85	78	83	76	83	80	73	72	72	64	72	65
France	144	138	136	143	136	129	130	121	96	87	88	77	75	69
Germany	116	107	104	95	95	91	85	83	80	71	65	62	60	55
Greece	195	206	201	207	201	193	178	159	145	151	150	149	141	138
Hungary	155	135	137	136	130	118	122	141	131	129	127	130	123	99
Iceland	90	37	55	98	75	113	84	101	80	79	64	104	48	38
Ireland	122	125	129	124	110	110	107	96	84	94	84	87	77	63
Italy	122	115	116	118	116	115	117	117	105	98	94	89	86	79
Japan	100	93	89	95	92	93	89	85	78	75	70	65	52	47
Korea	..	..	..	226	232	218	171	152	151	136	132	131	127	121
Luxembourg	169	170	142	134	133	172	159	140	118	109	101	78	90	72
Mexico	51	52	53	53	53	53	52	49	46	45	46	47	51	51
Netherlands	86	76	74	73	75	73	67	66	67	54	50	50	48	46
New Zealand	162	141	144	132	134	121	118	103	115	107	99	95	100	86
Norway	70	58	69	79	68	76	61	68	61	56	49	52	49	53
Poland	179	165	189	183	174	163	143	152	148	150	143	138	147	143
Portugal	242	241	222	213	200	186	161	165	148	124	118	104	81	83
Slovak Republic	130	119	154	160	125	120	116	116	121	113	111	113	122	112
Spain	147	139	142	150	144	143	135	129	128	115	89	94	85	68
Sweden	65	61	61	60	65	67	65	63	59	53	49	49	51	43
Switzerland	98	87	83	84	81	82	75	70	74	69	55	50	51	47
Turkey	97	86	81	76	69	58	45	62	56	62	62	62	68	57
United Kingdom	66	65	65	62	62	62	63	63	62	57	55	55	50	43
United States	159	158	158	154	153	149	148	149	147	146	147	143	136	123
EU27 total	132	124	126	123	120	117	112	110	103	96	91	87	86	79
OECD total	..	..	..	120	117	114	109	109	103	99	96	93	90	82
Chile	131	132	127	131	109	110	100	98	107	109	100	101	99	106
Estonia	251	233	151	200	206	169	149	146	164	121	126	126	146	98
India	68	70	74	77	81	80	80	82	84	91	98	106	115	..
Israel	99	91	91	92	78	73	84	80	67	69	63	57	53	56
Russian Federation	221	199	188	198	203	203	213	228	248	241	237	230	235	211
Slovenia	209	195	180	156	168	157	140	134	121	137	129	130	145	105
South Africa	252	243	235	216	247	196	253	270	268	274	301	325	312	287

StatLink http://dx.doi.org/10.1787/827083480353

Road fatalities
2008 or latest available year

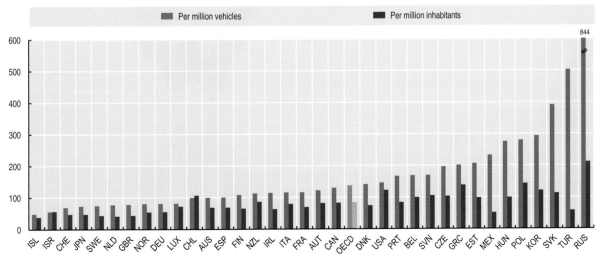

StatLink http://dx.doi.org/10.1787/822748755243

SPECIAL FOCUS

INTRODUCTION

"Financial genius is before the fall"
John Kenneth Galbraith, "A Short History of Financial Euphoria"

The world economy has gone through its worst crisis since World War II, and is today on the path of a slow recovery. Even if the crisis did not lead – to paraphrase a pop hit of a few years ago – to the "end of the world as we know it", there is at least agreement that it was more than just one of those turbulences that economies occasionally experience – and is often compared in its severity to the 1929 crisis that led to the Great Depression. The crisis followed a period of good economic performance and sound fundamentals, at least when judged by the standards used by most economists (solid GDP growth, low inflation and low unemployment). However, this environment, in conjunction with a rather lax regulatory framework, also led to a large expansion of credit and to the development of new financial products and financing vehicles. The full nature of some of the recent financial innovations may not have been clear even to many regulators and financial market experts, except some insiders. But this did not seem to matter too much as long as these innovations continued to generate huge profits for financial intermediaries and for investors at large. The warnings of risk managers and whistleblowers about the build-up of risks were too often ignored, and words of caution that were periodically voiced by some institutions and individual commentators were quickly dismissed after yet another market rally.

And then the crisis came, expanding from the 2007 subprime turmoil to a global crisis. The ensuing fall in GDP was the strongest on record since the establishment of the OECD, but the consequences of the crisis go well beyond lower economic activity. Financial institutions and investors suffered huge capital losses. Many people lost their jobs, houses and pensions, while others have lost their trust in the capacity of institutions to regulate markets for the public good. The rescue packages directed towards distressed financial institutions put in place by governments around the world may have returned financial markets to a state of normal functioning, but at the price of increases in public debt that many countries had never experienced in periods of peace and of higher taxes and lower public spending in the years to come. The implications of the crisis are also reaching beyond the regulatory framework for financial institutions, raising questions about the balance between public and private responsibilities more generally, and between economic performance and other dimensions by which to assess the performance of individual countries. Finally, the crisis questions the capacity of economists to understand the functioning of complex economic systems, the relevance of some theoretical models as well as the adequacy of some existing statistical tools to identify structural weaknesses, to value assets, and to monitor performance.

A fully-shared diagnosis of the nature of the crisis is not yet available. Yet, at least two facts are uncontroversial. The first is that the crisis started at the very centre of the developed world, the United States, rather than at its periphery, as had been the case of previous crises (Mexico in the early 1980s, Sweden and Japan in the early 1990s, South-East Asia and Russia in the later 1990s and Argentina in the early 2000s). From the United States, financial contagion spread rapidly to other parts of the world and to the real economy, underscoring that, beyond its benefits, globalisation also implies vulnerabilities that national policies are ill-equipped to address. The second is that the crisis had the financial sector as its focal point. This applies in particular to that "shadow" banking sector whose importance had grown exponentially since the late 1990s, beyond the reaches of the regulations and protections that apply to commercial banks. These institutions supported much of their long-term lending by issuing short-term paper, leading to large mismatches in the maturity composition of their assets and liabilities, and by increasing debt relative to own resources. Contagion then followed as credit institutions had created large scale securities based on loans that were then sold to other financial intermediaries.

There are more controversies about the "root causes" that led to the crisis. One of the factors often mentioned is the large imbalance in current accounts between countries, which contributed to large capital inflows towards the US financial markets, fuelling debt expansion and asset price inflation. Other factors relate to the policy environment, in particular in the United States, where low interest rates sustained credit demand. Yet other factors relate to the conditions of households, which – in many parts of the world – accumulated large amounts of debt, especially mortgages, based on expectations of ever-increasing housing prices; this debt was also used to sustain private consumption in a context characterised by stagnant income for most families and by gains concentrated at the top of the income distribution. While it is difficult to assess the relative role of each of these factors, they are likely to have interacted with each other in amplifying the extent of the crisis.

This special chapter of the 2010 Factbook does not aim to provide a full fledged description of the crisis. More modestly, it brings together a range of statistics relevant for the analysis of the crisis, of its build-up and, where data are available, of its aftermath. It provides evidence on some of the causes of the crisis, such as the correction in asset prices, the accumulation of debt and the spread of securitisation, or global imbalances in current account; on some of its consequences for economic activity, foreign trade, labour markets, confidence and household income; and on some of the main policy responses to the crisis, in the forms of liquidity injections and expansionary fiscal policies. In doing so, this chapter brings together a range of statistics produced by various parts of the Organisation, some of which have been previously disseminated through other reports, with others prepared specifically for this one. The goal of the chapter is to provide a concise but comprehensive assessment of the crisis and of its consequences. Achieving this goal has required the use of high-frequency data, thereby departing from the annual data used in other chapters of this report and in previous issues of the *OECD Factbook*.

While this chapter hopefully provides some additional insights, data availability has limited the amount of information provided. Thus the crisis is also an opportunity to assess the adequacy of our statistical infrastructure to monitor relevant developments. In this respect, it should be stressed that our statistical systems continue to have important gaps in terms of *coverage* (*e.g.* in terms of balance sheets and asset prices); *timeliness* (*e.g.* lags in financial statistics often exceed two years, and are even longer for other domains) and *access to micro-data* (critical to assess the concentration of specific risks in parts of system and to manage the consequences of the crisis as it unfolds). These limits have implications for policy, as they can lead to a biased assessment. This is especially evident in the current juncture, as swings in financial conditions (where information is available in almost real time) get much more attention than developments in living conditions for ordinary people (where information is available only with long delays). This asymmetry in statistical information may lead politicians to believe that the crisis is over at the very time where its social consequences are more intense.

GROSS DOMESTIC PRODUCT

For most OECD countries, the recent financial crisis led to the sharpest fall in economic activity (GDP) since the Great Depression.

Definition

GDP is the standard measure of the value of goods and services produced by a country during a period. It can be decomposed into five key aggregates of final demand. Private final consumption expenditure includes households' final consumption – the expenditure incurred by resident households on individual consumption goods and services, including any goods that households produce and consume themselves and imputed rent – and the consumption of non-profit institutions serving households. Government final consumption consists of expenditure incurred by general government to provide consumption goods and services to individual households and to the community as a whole. Gross capital formation (investment) is the value of a producer's acquisitions (less disposals) of fixed assets and valuables during the year, plus changes in inventories. Exports consist of goods and services obtained by non-residents from residents and imports consist of goods and services obtained by residents from non-residents.

The data shown here refer to quarterly national accounts aggregates at constant prices, as collected through the OECD Quarterly National Accounts database. For each country, the figure compares developments in real GDP during the recent recession and those experienced in the three previous decades. Data are indexed to the level achieved in the quarter preceding each recession, with quarters elapsed since then shown on the horizontal axis. The table shows the cumulated change of real seasonally adjusted GDP and its components between the first quarter of 2008 and the second quarter of 2009, for selected countries and regions.

Comparability

Data on quarterly GDP and demand components are based on the 1993 *System of National Accounts* (SNA). This assures good comparability across countries. But there are some deviations in some areas, for example the treatment of financial intermediation services indirectly measured and the production of software for own-use. The United States for example includes expenditures on military products that have no dual civilian role, as investment rather than as government final consumption, Compared to other OECD countries, government final consumption (and GDP) in the United States includes consumption of fixed capital related to the depreciation of military products.

Overview

The cumulative fall in real GDP experienced during the recession of 2008 and 2009 is unprecedented in recent history as demonstrated in the figures shown here. The contraction in GDP was sharper, more prolonged and more synchronised than in previous crises (starting everywhere in the first or second quarter of 2008). The cumulative fall in GDP reached 8 points in Japan, was around 6 points in the United Kingdom, Germany and Italy, and exceeded 3 points in France and the United States. By the third quarter of 2009, GDP had rebounded in all the countries shown with the exception of the United Kingdom.

The fall in real GDP for the OECD area (4.7 points between the first quarter of 2008 and the second quarter of 2009) mainly reflected the sharp decline in investment and exports, which more than offset the decline in import volumes. Government consumption significantly supported economic activity, although this support was more moderate in Japan. Real private consumption added to the decline in economic activity in the OECD area as a whole (especially in the United Kingdom) while it supported economic activity in France and Germany. Investment and international trade are significantly lower than pre-crisis levels for all selected countries. The crisis has not just affected OECD countries – as evidenced by a slowdown in GDP growth in China and by a much larger decline in GDP levels in the Russian Federation, mainly reflecting lower investment and private consumption.

Sources

• OECD (2009), *Quarterly National Accounts*, OECD, Paris.

Further information

Analytical publications

• OECD (2009), *OECD Economic Outlook: June. No. 85 – Volume 2009 issue 1*, OECD, Paris.

Statistical publications

• OECD (2009), *Quarterly National Accounts*, OECD, Paris.

Methodological publications

• OECD (2000), *OECD Glossaries, System of National Accounts, 1993 – Glossary*, OECD, Paris.

Web sites

• OECD National Accounts, *www.oecd.org/std/national-accounts*.

Changes in real GDP in recent crises

Peak quarter = 100, seasonally adjusted

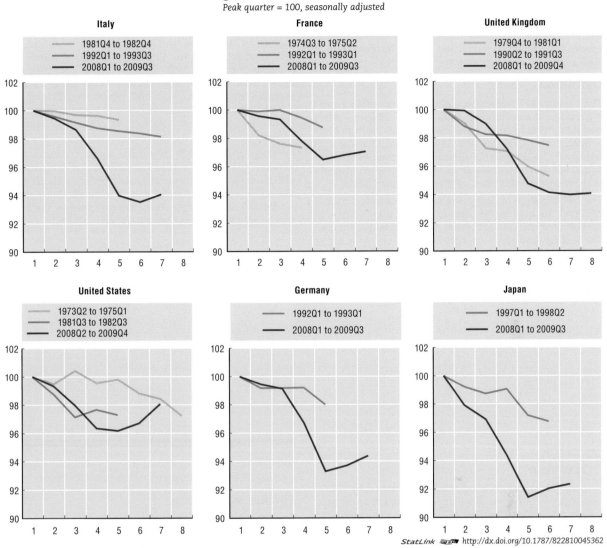

StatLink http://dx.doi.org/10.1787/822810045362

Changes in real GDP and demand components in the 2008-09 recession

Percentage, cumulative change between 2008Q1 and 2009Q2

	Gross domestic product	Private final consumption expenditure	Government final consumption expenditure	Gross capital formation	Exports of goods and services	Imports of goods and services
Canada	−3.1	−0.3	3.1	−11.1	−19.2	−19.0
France	−3.2	0.9	1.8	−8.4	−15.0	−12.5
Germany	−6.3	0.8	3.2	−10.6	−18.2	−12.9
Italy	−6.5	−2.6	2.2	−15.8	−23.9	−19.0
Japan	−8.0	−2.7	0.7	−16.7	−32.1	−20.5
United Kingdom	−5.9	−4.0	3.1	−18.0	−13.3	−16.7
United States	−3.5	−1.7	2.9	−16.7	−12.6	−19.5
Euro area	−5.1	−1.3	3.2	−12.4	−17.8	−15.3
OECD total	−4.7	−2.1	3.0	−13.9	−15.7	−17.4
Russian Federation	−9.7	−3.2	2.2	−21.0	−12.9	−35.1

StatLink http://dx.doi.org/10.1787/827110638046

INDUSTRIAL PRODUCTION AND RETAIL SALES

During the crisis, industrial production plunged in all OECD countries, while retail trade decreased significantly less. A rebound in industrial production started in the spring of 2009 and continued thereafter.

Definition

The industrial production index covers mining and quarrying, manufacturing and public utilities, while excluding construction. The classification of economic activities is based on the International Standard of Industrial Classification of all Economic Activities Revision 3 (ISIC Rev 3). The index of retail trade is based on turnover in the retail sector deflated by changes in retail prices.

The OECD system of Composite Leading Indicators (CLI) is designed to give early signals of turning points in economic activity, as measured by industrial production. The CLI for any given country is composed of a set of economic indicators. Turning points in the CLI tend to lead those in (de-trended) industrial production by between 6 to 9 months.

Comparability

Indices of industrial production generally follow the principles set out in the United Nations *Index Numbers of Industrial Production, 2009*. Data for some countries may depart from these principles because of the use of different classification systems (*e.g.* ISIC, NACE, NAICS etc) and different statistical units than the ones recommended. The industrial production index for Mexico includes construction.

Coverage of retail trade may differ across countries for a variety of reasons (*e.g.* administrative constraints, differences in the coverage of production units classified in the retail sector). For Japan and the United States (since April 2007) national data have been adjusted by the OECD for changes in consumer price inflation.

Overview

In the year to April 2009, industrial production fell by 30% in Japan, by more than 20% in the Euro area and by more than 12% in the United States. The decline in industrial production exceeds that of GDP due to its greater cyclical sensitivity. Since April 2009, industrial production has recovered in all countries considered except Ireland, with a strong rebound (exceeding 10%) in Brazil, India, Japan, Korea, Luxembourg and Slovak Republic. The rebound for the OECD area is limited to 4.3%, *i.e.* around one fourth of the decline recorded in the year to April 2009.

The decline in retail trade is generally less than that recorded for industrial production, reflecting the greater resilience of private consumption during the crisis. In Brazil and some European countries, retail trade continued to increase in the year to April 2009. Since then, retail trade has recovered in around half of the countries considered (as well as for the OECD average), while falling further in several European countries.

The OECD CLIs for the OECD area and for the five major countries in Asia (China, India, Indonesia, Japan and Korea) have shown strong signals of a recovery since early 2009. This should translate into a recovery of industrial production in the second half of 2009, possibly pushing it above its long-term trend in 2010. There are however large uncertainties in the estimates of this long-term trend when economic activity falls sharply.

Sources

- OECD (2010), *Main Economic Indicators*, OECD, Paris.

Further information

Analytical publications

- Nilsson, R. and E. Guidetti (2007), *Current Period Performance of OECD Composite Leading Indicators (CLIs)*, OECD Statistics Working Papers, No. 2007/1, OECD, Paris.
- Nilsson, R. (2006), *Composite Leading Indicators and Growth Cycles in Major OECD Non-Member Economies and Recently New OECD Member Countries*, OECD Statistics Working Papers, No. 2006/5, OECD, Paris.
- Nilsson, R. and O. Brunet (2006), *Composite Leading Indicators For Major OECD Non-Member Economies: Brazil, China, India, Indonesia, Russian Federation, South Africa*, OECD Statistics Working Papers, No. 2006/1, OECD, Paris.

Online databases

- *Main Economic Indicators*.

Methodological publications

- United Nations (2009), *International Recommendations for the Index of Industrial Production*, United Nation, New York.
- OECD (2002), *Main Economic Indicators: Comparative Methodological Analysis: Industry, Retail and Construction Indicators Volume 2002 Supplement 1*, OECD, Paris.
- *OECD System of Composite Leading Indicators*.

Web sites

- OECD Main Economic Indicators, *www.oecd.org/std/mei*.
- OECD Composite Leading Indicators, *www.oecd.org/std/cli*.

Industrial production index
Cumulative change in percentage, seasonally adjusted

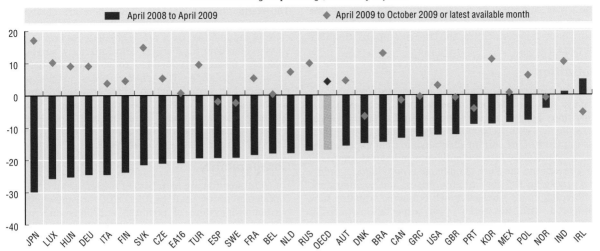

StatLink 🔗 http://dx.doi.org/10.1787/822823146248

Retail trade volume
Cumulative change in percentage, seasonally adjusted

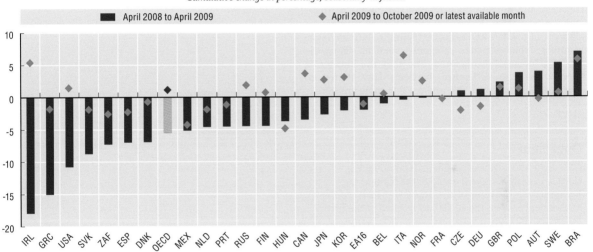

StatLink 🔗 http://dx.doi.org/10.1787/822823268034

Composite Leading Indicator
Amplitude adjusted, long-term trend = 100

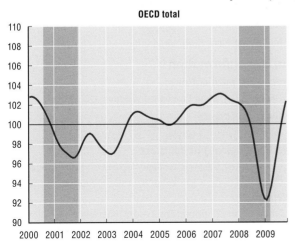

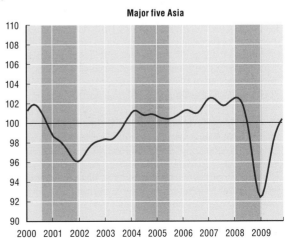

StatLink 🔗 http://dx.doi.org/10.1787/823002426041

BUSINESS AND CONSUMER CONFIDENCE

The crisis impacted in a disproportionate way on the confidence of business and consumers, while low confidence contributed to the freezing-up of financial markets.

Definition

Data on consumer and business confidence are based on surveys that provide qualitative information on economic conditions. Surveys are based on a sample of enterprises or households, with respondents questioned about their assessments of the current situation and their expectations for the immediate future. Confidence indicators are based on a composite measure of opinions on production, orders and stocks, in the case of enterprises; and to intentions concerning major purchases, own economic situation now compared with the recent past, expectations for the immediate future in the case of consumers.

These surveys usually probe respondents on the direction of change, or about how the current situation compares to a "normal" state. Answers are generally in the format "up/about the same/down" or "above normal/normal/below normal" in business surveys; and of the type "increase sharply/ increase slightly/remain the same/fall slightly/fall sharply" in consumer surveys. Responses are generally reported as "balances" of positive and negative replies in various fields; this implies that response categories such as about the "same" or "normal" are ignored, and that the balance is computed as the difference between the shares of respondents giving favourable and unfavourable answers.

The standardised indicators shown here are obtained by recalculation of national balances after smoothing to a scale centred around 100. Data are generally based on monthly surveys; for countries where only quarterly surveys are available, these are converted to monthly frequency by linear interpolation. The shaded areas in the graphs correspond to various period of cyclical slowdowns: the second oil crisis in 1978-79; the first Gulf war in 1991; the European exchange rate crisis of 1992; the emerging markets crisis in 1998; the Dot-Com crash of 2001; and the financial crisis that started in late-2008.

Comparability

For countries that are members of the European Union, the confidence series used by the OECD are drawn from a harmonised system of business and consumer surveys managed by the European Commission; hence data comparability is high. For other countries, the OECD has selected the series that best correspond to a "standard" wording; these series may not be fully comparable.

Overview

Consumer and business confidence started falling sharply in early 2008, well ahead of the burst of the financial crisis in the fall of the same year. The low point in confidence across the OECD was reached in the first quarter of 2009, when both business and consumer confidence reached historically low levels compared to previous periods of cyclical slowdown.

Since then, both series have shown signs of improvement. Business and consumers' confidence for the OECD total have now increased for eight consecutive months, following 20 months of decline. The rebound started earlier and was stronger in the United States (especially for businesses) and the United Kingdom (for both businesses and consumers); more recent but fairly strong in Japan; and it was recent and less pronounced for Germany. Confidence still remains below its long term level (100) in all countries except the United States (business) and the United Kingdom (consumers).

It is too early to say whether this recovery indicates a durable change in business and consumers' confidence, rather than a sober assessment of the crisis and a realisation that some of the doomsday scenarios now seem unlikely to materialise. Further, business and consumer confidence may stabilise at historically low levels rather than return to positive territory. In many ways, however, business and consumer confidence indicators are beginning to echo the positive messages conveyed by production measures in other areas.

Sources
• *Main Economic Indicators*.

Further information
Statistical publications
• OECD (2009), *Main Economic Indicators*, OECD, Paris.

Online databases
• *Main Economic Indicators*.

Methodological publications
• OECD (2003), *Business Tendency Surveys: A Handbook*, OECD, Paris.

Web sites
• OECD Main Economic Indicators, *www.oecd.org/std/mei*.
• OECD Leading Indicators and Tendency Surveys, *www.oecd.org/std/cli-ts* .

Business and consumer confidence

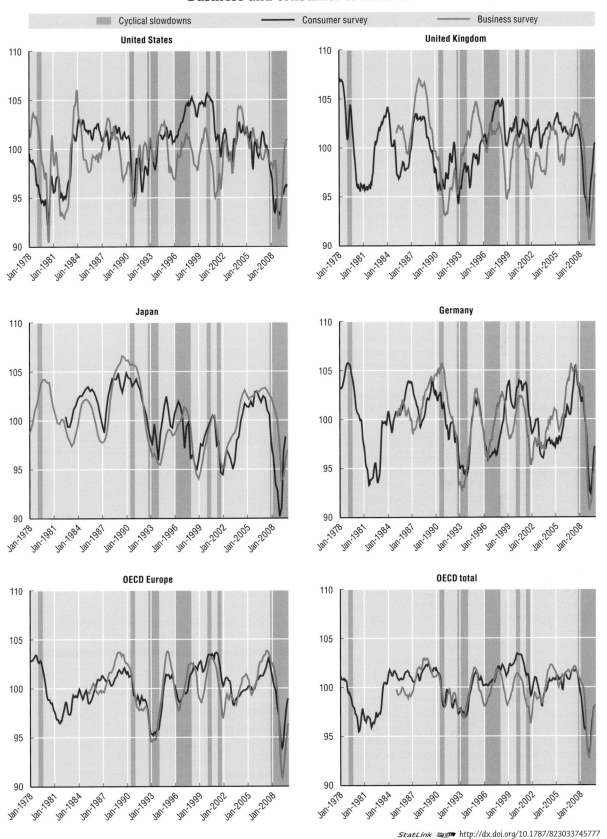

ASSET PRICES

The boom and bust in asset prices triggered the crisis, leading to lower net wealth of households and financial institutions. Among the types of assets most affected by these swings were residential housing and shares of quoted enterprises.

Definition

Share price indices refer to quoted prices and exclude dividend payments. Data refer to the Dow Jones EURO STOXX Index for the Euro area; to the Euronext Paris SBF 250 index for France; to the DB CDAX index for Germany; to the NYSE Composite index for the United States; to the BOVESPA index for Brazil; to the SSE composite index for China; to the TSE TOPIX index for Japan; and to the MICEX index for Russia. Monthly indices are generally computed as averages of daily closing quotes.

House prices indices shown here are representative of the prices of residential housing sales in various countries. Data refer to the S&P/Case-Shiller Home Price Indices (referring to the residential real estate market in 20 metropolitan regions) for the United States; to the quarterly Destatis House price index for new buildings for Germany; to the Nationwide House price benchmarks for the United Kingdom; to the price index of established houses (weighted average of 8 Capital cities) for Australia; to the INSEE real estate price index for single houses and apartments for France; to the index for selling prices of new houses constructed by residential general contractors for Canada; and to the general index of housing prices for Spain.

Overview

Share price indices started to decline in the fall of 2007, i.e. one year before the apex of the financial crisis (fourth quarter of 2008). For the United States, Germany, France and the Euro area, the fall of share prices started in the second half of 2007 and continued until March 2009 (totalling around 50%) before starting to recover. While changes in share prices across European countries and the United States exhibited a significant synchronisation, this is less the case for share prices in Brazil, China, Russian Federation and Japan. Whereas share prices have been declining in Japan since 2007, they increased five-fold in the two years to October 2007 in China, before falling by 70%. The rebound in share prices since the end of 2008 was especially sharp for Brazil, Russian Federation and China.

Prices of residential housing in the United States started falling in the first quarter of 2006, well ahead of other OECD countries, reaching a low point by the first quarter of 2009, with a cumulative decline of around 30%. In the United Kingdom, house prices peaked in the first quarter of 2007 before falling by 18% until the first quarter of 2009, with a rebound since then. House prices peaked later in 2008 for France and Spain, which experienced falls of lower intensity (compared with other countries) until the second quarter of 2009. Conversely, in Germany, house prices steadily increased until the fourth quarter of 2007 (the latest available data). In Australia, house prices in the third quarter of 2009 were still above their pre-crisis level, while for Canada, the decline was limited to 4%.

Prices are in nominal terms (i.e. they are not adjusted for overall inflation) and expressed as indices with the year 2005 equal to 100.

Comparability

For share prices, comparability is good, as national indexes generally refer to all shares (or to broad groups of shares) traded on the stock exchange market.

For house prices, comparability is much more limited due to differences in coverage, timeliness and methodology. The house price indices shown here are national averages for most countries, but they are limited to metropolitan areas or capital cities in other countries. These indexes may also refer to special types of dwellings, or be limited to some types of contractors. While the indexes shown are taken as representative of the conditions prevailing in the housing markets of individual countries, the extent to which they are fully representatives is an open question.

Sources
- For House price indices: National sources.

Further information
Analytical publications
- OECD (2009), *OECD Economic Outlook: Nov. No. 86 – Vol. 2009/2*, OECD, Paris.

Online databases
- *Main Economic Indicators.*
- *Genesis*, Destatis.
- *CANSIM*, Statistics Canada.

Web sites
- OECD Main Economic Indicators, *www.oecd.org/std/mei.*

Share price indices
Year 2005=100

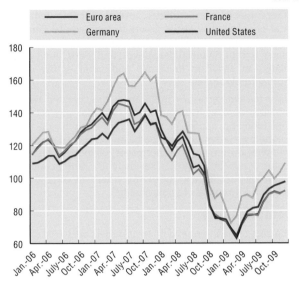

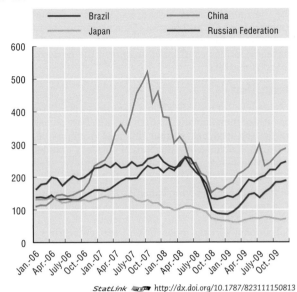

StatLink http://dx.doi.org/10.1787/823111150813

Housing price indices
Year 2005=100

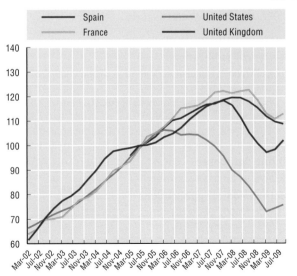

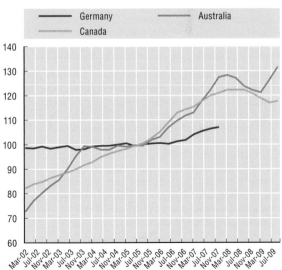

StatLink http://dx.doi.org/10.1787/823148755274

DEBT AND SECURITISATION

The decline in asset prices had a huge impact on households and firms because of the accumulation of debt, especially by financial institutions. The growth of asset-backed securities contributed to spread the crisis through financial markets.

Definition

Indebtedness of households and enterprises is measured by the ratio of their liabilities to their income. Data on liabilities are derived from the annual Financial Accounts of OECD countries. Liabilities are the sum of currency and deposits, securities, loans, shares and other equity, insurance technical reserves and other accounts payable.

For the households sector, liabilities are essentially made up of loans, and are expressed as a ratio of household gross disposable income; the data include the non-profit institutions serving households. For enterprises (both financial and non-financial), total liabilities are expressed as a ratio of gross operating surplus, which is a National Accounting measure of the surplus accruing to firms from production after deducting wages and salaries but before taking account of interest, rent or similar charges paid or received. The graph on leverage refers to the banking sector (Central banks and other depository corporations) including other financial intermediaries. Leverage is computed as the ratio of selected financial assets to total equity. Financial assets include currency and deposits; securities other than shares except financial derivatives; and loans. Total equity related to liabilities in shares and other equity except mutual funds shares.

Asset-backed securities (ABS) are bonds, created through securitisation, whose coupon or principal payments are dependent on a pool of assets, either purchased in the secondary market or from the balance sheet of an original collateral owner, such as mortgages, credit card loans and motor vehicle loans. Residential mortgage-backed securities (RMBS) are a type of ABS, where the collaterals are long-term mortgages to households.

Comparability

The data on liabilities and financial assets are based on non-consolidated accounts reflecting intra-sectoral assets and liabilities. Cross-country comparability in financial accounts is good, but there are issues in terms of coverage of specific instruments and financial sectors.

Overview

By 2008, household liabilities exceeded 120% of disposable income in the United Kingdom, Canada, the United States and Japan, while they were significantly lower in continental Europe. Over the past decade, this ratio increased significantly in most countries. Indebtedness is much higher for firms, and increased in all major OECD countries except Germany and Japan. In the United Kingdom and the United States, much of this rise in indebtedness reflected trends in the financial sector, whose liabilities increased since 1995 at a rate almost double that recorded by the non-financial sector.

In the financial sector, the increase in liabilities in the build-up to the crisis occurred alongside a change in their composition. At the height of the crisis, the leverage of the banking sector, i.e. the ratio between banks' financial assets and their own resources, had increased in most major OECD countries, partly due to the fact that banks repatriated their off-balance sheet exposures and deducted losses from shareholders value. In the aftermath of the crisis, leverage ratios are expected to come down again as deleveraging takes place throughout the economy.

Contagion between financial markets resulted from the financial institutions' strategy of creating large scale securities based on loans and holding different rights that were sold to other investors. The stock of ABS securities issued in the United States increased by five-times in the ten years to mid-2007, before falling by around 10% in the following months. The share of mortgage debt securitised out of total ABS issues increased from 40% in 1998 to around two-thirds in mid-2007.

Sources
• *OECD National Accounts Statistics.*

Further information
Statistical publications
• OECD (2009), *National Accounts at a Glance 2009*, OECD, Paris.
• OECD (2010), *National Accounts of OECD Countries*, OECD, Paris.
• OECD (2009), *National Accounts of OECD Countries 2008, Volume IIIb, Financial Balance Sheets: Stocks*, OECD, Paris.

Online databases
• *Thomson Reuters Datastream.*

Methodological publications
• OECD (2000), *OECD Glossaries, System of National Accounts, 1993 – Glossary*, OECD, Paris.
• IMF (2009), *Handbook on Securities Statistics, second draft, Part 1*, IMF, Washington, DC.
• OECD (2008), *System of National Accounts 2008*, OECD, Paris.

Web sites
• OECD (2008), Financial Market Trends, OECD, Paris, *www.sourceOECD.org/periodical/fmt.*
• OECD National Accounts, *www.oecd.org/std/national-accounts.*
• OECD (2009), OECD Financial Accounts, OECD, Paris, *www.sourceoecd.org/9789264082403.*

Indebtness of households
As a ratio of gross disposable income

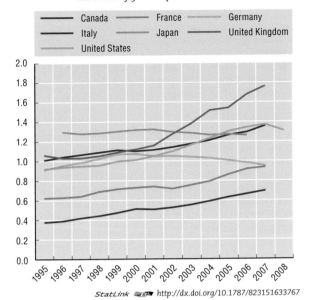

StatLink http://dx.doi.org/10.1787/823151633767

Indebtness of enterprises
As a ratio of gross operating surplus

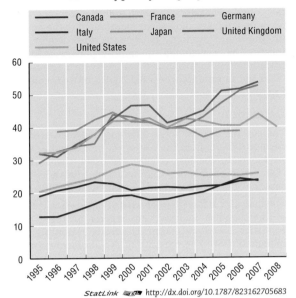

StatLink http://dx.doi.org/10.1787/823162705683

Leverage
of the banking sector
As a ratio of total equity

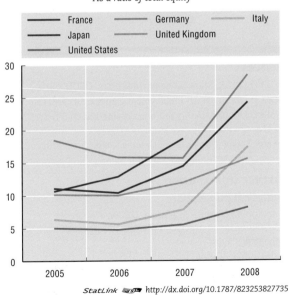

StatLink http://dx.doi.org/10.1787/823253827735

Asset-backed securities issued
in the United States
Billion US dollars

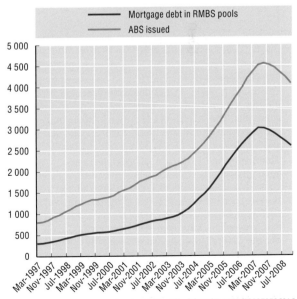

StatLink http://dx.doi.org/10.1787/823272536016

INTERNATIONAL TRADE

Large trade imbalances among countries running current account surpluses and deficits contributed to the crisis that hit the world economy in 2008, as they led to capital inflows that contributed to credit-expansion and asset-price inflation in the United States. In turn, the financial crisis led to an unprecedented, synchronised, collapse of international trade.

Definition

The current account is the difference between a country's current receipts from the rest of the world and its current payments to the rest of the world (see the section on "Balance of payments"). Current account balances refer to seasonally-adjusted quarterly data in billions USD.

The indicator of foreign trade used in this section is the sum of merchandise imports and exports of the 30 OECD countries, based on (seasonally-adjusted) monthly data in billions of USD. The measure of synchronisation of trade flows shown here is the share of OECD countries recording a year-on-year decline in the monthly value of their merchandise exports in excess of 10%.

Short-term trade finance is proxied by data on exposures of short-tem insured export credits with terms up to and including 12 months. Data refer to commitments contracted by private or public reinsurers (excluding interest). The indicator presented is the percentage change of end-of-quarter stocks for OECD economies, converted to USD using end-period exchange rates.

Comparability

Quarterly current account balances are compiled according to the International Monetary Fund (IMF) Balance of Payment Manual, fifth edition 1993, which assures good comparability. Data on current account balances for China are available on a half-yearly basis. Monthly data of merchandise trade conform to the United Nations guidelines and are further standardised by OECD, assuring a good degree of comparability.

Overview

The period that preceded the financial crisis of 2008 was characterised by large trade imbalances. China ran current account surpluses approaching 250 billions of USD in 2008 which, together with the surpluses recorded by Germany, Japan and oil-exporting countries, offset large current account deficits in the United States. While these trade imbalances have narrowed since the second half of 2008, there are uncertainties as to whether this movement will continue in the future.

The global crisis had a major impact on foreign trade. The monthly value of OECD merchandise trade fell by around one-third between early 2008 and the end of the same year. The collapse of OECD merchandise trade was accompanied by a smaller decline in the value of OECD services trade.

This decline in OECD trade reflected the high synchronisation of this fall between countries. By end-2008 more than 90% of OECD countries exhibited a (year-on-year) decline exceeding 10% in the monthly value of their merchandise exports; no previous periods ever exhibited such a large degree of synchronised trade decline. The fall in trade also reflected the collapse in confidence across the financial system and its impact on trade finance. Short-term trade lending to OECD countries started dropping in the third quarter of 2008, and even earlier in some countries. The drop in trade finance peaked in early 2009, easing thereafter. While the measure of trade finance shown here is only indicative of the factors at work, most analysts agree that the decline in trade finance exceeded that expected based on trade flows.

Sources
- OECD (2010), *Main Economic Indicators*, OECD, Paris.
- OECD (2009), *OECD Employment Outlook*, OECD, Paris.
- OECD (2009), *Monthly Statistics of International Trade*, OECD, Paris.
- *Berne Union (International Union of Credit & Investment Insurers).*

Further information
Analytical publications
- Araújo S., Oliveira Martins J. (2009), *The Great Synchronisation: tracking the trade collapse with high-frequency data.*

Online databases
- *Monthly International Trade.*
- *Main Economic Indicators.*

Methodological publications
- United Nations (1998), *International Merchandise Trade Statistics: Compilers' Manual*, United Nations, New York.
- Lindner, A., et al. (2001), *"Trade in Goods and Services: Statistical Trends and Measurement Challenges, OECD Statistics Brief, No. 1, October"*, OECD, Paris.

Current account balance in major economies

Billion US dollars, quarterly data, seasonally adjusted

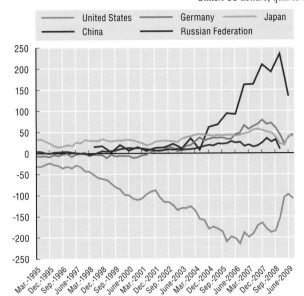

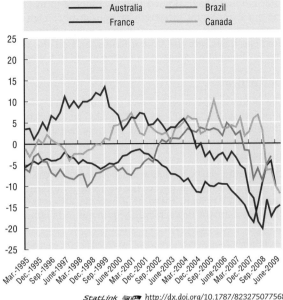

StatLink http://dx.doi.org/10.1787/823275077568

Merchandise trade and syncronisation of export values for OECD total

Billion US dollars, seasonally adjusted

OECD total (left scale)
% of OECD countries with trade growth less than -10% (right scale)

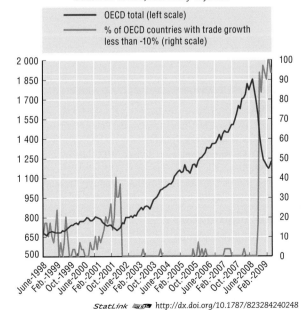

StatLink http://dx.doi.org/10.1787/823284240248

Short-term trade finance in the OECD area

Quarter-on-quarter percentage change

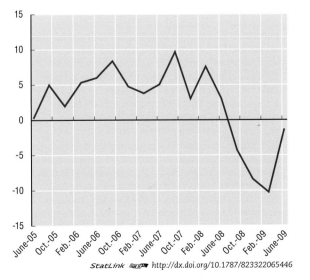

StatLink http://dx.doi.org/10.1787/823322065446

INTERNATIONAL FINANCIAL FLOWS

International financial flows take a variety of forms, one of the most important categories being that of foreign direct investment. This section also presents information on total financial flows into the United States, and on the reserve assets of monetary authorities for the world as a whole.

Definition

The definition of foreign direct investment (FDI) flows is provided under "FDI Flows and Stocks" in the Economic Globalisation section. Quarterly data are in billions of US dollars, and are expressed as an average of the last four quarters.

Cross-border portfolio flows and positions for the United States are collected as part of the US Treasury International Capital (TIC) system; these data exclude all cross-border direct investment flows. Monthly data are in billions of US dollars, and expressed as averages of the previous 12 months.

Reserve assets consist of those external assets that are readily available to, and controlled by, monetary authorities of individual countries for the financing of payments imbalances. These reserve assets comprise foreign exchange assets (currency and deposits, as well as securities), other claims, Special Drawing Rights and reserve position at the International Monetary Fund (IMF); they exclude central banks' holdings of gold. Data are expressed in billions of US dollars.

Comparability

Limits in the comparability of FDI data are discussed under "FDI Flows and Stocks" in the Economic Globalisation section.

US Treasury International Capital (TIC) data cover most types of international financial flows, while excluding data on direct investment flows, which are collected by the US Department of Commerce's Bureau of Economic Analysis. The TIC reporting system collects data on cross-border portfolio investment flows and positions between U.S. residents (including US-based branches of firms headquartered abroad) and foreign residents (including offshore branches of US firms).

Overview

The global financial crisis impacted drastically on FDI flows, which contracted by over 50% for the OECD area as a whole between the first quarter of 2008 and the first quarter of 2009. Within the OECD areas, the decline of FDI inflows was larger for the euro area (with a fall of 77%) but was limited to 14% in the United States. Inflows of FDI into emerging economies such as India and the Russian Federation also decreased by much less than for OECD countries, with cumulative declines of 20% for the Russian Federation and of 18% for India. FDI inflows into Brazil were relatively unaffected by the crisis.

Beyond FDI, the large global imbalances between countries running current account surpluses and those recording current account deficits had a counterpart in international financial flows. The Unites States, in particular, experienced huge inflows of financial capital, which fuelled asset price inflation and debt accumulation in the US. The size of these inflows contracted significantly since mid-2007 for private inflows, and since early 2008 for official flows. Following a rebound since May 2008, private inflows turned negative in the second half of 2009, leading to a significant depreciation of the US dollar.

Net official financial inflows into the US reflected the desire of central banks to accumulate large foreign reserves, which are mainly denominated in US dollars. Total reserve assets of China, other emerging and developing economies, and oil exporting countries increased hugely between 1990 and 2008, accelerating after the Asian crisis. During this period, the share of world official reserves held by China and Japan increased from 14% to 44% cent of the total reserves, while that of oil exporters doubled from 7% to 14%. The huge increase of total reserves of emerging Asian and oil exporting countries aimed at sustaining the pegging of their currencies to the US dollar.

Sources
- Visco, I. (2009), *The Global Crisis – the Role of Policies and the International Monetary System.*
- IMF (2009), *World Economic Outlook (WEO)*, IMF, Washington, DC.
- United States Department of the Treasury, *Treasury International Capital System.*

Further information
Analytical publications
- Johnson, K. H. (2009), *Gross or Net International Financial Flows, Understanding the Financial Crisis*, Council on Foreign Relations, Center for Geoeconomic Studies.

Online databases
- *Main Economic Indicators.*
- IMF, *International Financial Statistics.*

Web sites
- OECD Main Economic Indicators, *www.oecd.org/std/mei.*

Inflows of foreign direct investment in major economies
Billion US dollars, 4-quarter average

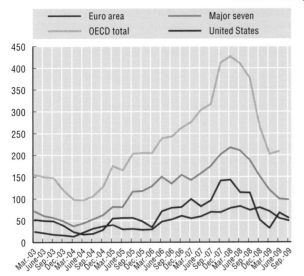

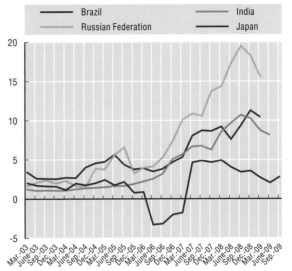

StatLink http://dx.doi.org/10.1787/823327284351

Net financial flows to the United States
Billion US dollars, 12 months through

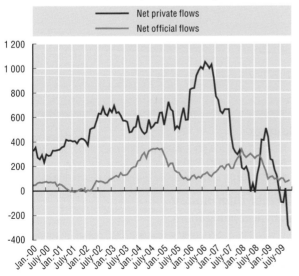

StatLink http://dx.doi.org/10.1787/823331821801

Reserves assets
Billion US dollars

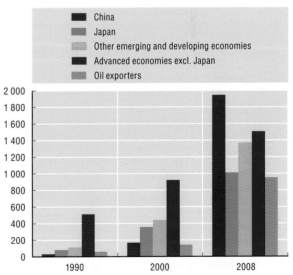

StatLink http://dx.doi.org/10.1787/823422237056

LABOUR MARKET CONSEQUENCES

The crisis has led to worsening labour market conditions in most OECD countries. Even though the recovery has begun, joblessness is likely to rise further during 2010. Further, even after reaching its peak, it will take time before the unemployment rate returns to pre-crisis levels, and there is the risk that some of the cyclical rise in unemployment becomes structural, as many unemployed drift into long-term joblessness or drop out of the labour force.

Definition

The definitions of employment and unemployment are those given in the "Labour" section of this publication. The indicator used here to compare the labour market consequences of the current crisis with the previous ones, is an index measuring the relative increase in the unemployment rate since the third quarter of 2007 through the end of 2011, with quarters elapsed since the first observation shown on the horizontal axis. Unemployment rates and projections are from *OECD Employment Outlook* 2009.

Overview

The rise in unemployment experienced since the onset of the crisis is the most severe in recent decades for the OECD area as a whole. The OECD unemployment rate is expected to increase by nearly 80% between its previous trough and the twelfth quarter of the downturn, whereas the corresponding increases ranged between 20% and 50% in the previous recessions. In the United States, the impact of this downturn on unemployment would be the worst of any recession since 1970 by a considerable margin. By contrast, the rise in unemployment for France, Germany, Italy and the United Kingdom is expected to be comparable with that experienced in both the 1970s and 1980s recessions, but larger than that associated with the two most recent ones. In Japan, the unemployment rate began to rise sharply only in the fourth quarter of the current downturn, and the ultimate impact will be to rise by approximately one-half; even though this increase in the unemployment rate would not be unprecedented, the level projected for the end of 2011 would represent a post-war high.

There is considerable variation across countries in how labour markets have developed during the current recession, with employment recording a cumulative fall since early-2008 of 12% in Ireland and small rises in Australia, Korea, Mexico, Poland and Switzerland. These differences reflect both the differences in the severity of the economic crisis and differences in how labour markets have adjusted to the crisis. In most economies, average hours worked per week have declined, limiting the loss of employment that followed the fall in GDP. This effect was particularly strong in Germany, where total employment has not fallen despite a sharp fall in output, but much weaker in the United States, where the fall in economic activity has translated into job suppressions to an unusual degree. These different profiles are set to shape job trends in the upturn, with job growth resuming earlier and at a more rapid pace in countries where hours worked have declined the least during the recession.

Data on the cumulative changes in employment since the first quarter of 2008 up to the second quarter of 2009, and the corresponding change in GDP, refer to seasonally adjusted data as available in the OECD Main Economic Indicators.

Comparability

Data on employment and unemployment are based on *Labour Force Surveys* in most countries but on the most commonly used source in a few others. This may limit comparability of levels of the various indicators, but it is less of a problem for comparing changes and trajectories.

Sources
- OECD (2009), *OECD Employment Outlook 2009: Tackling the Jobs Crisis*, OECD, Paris.
- OECD (2010), *Main Economic Indicators*, OECD, Paris.

Further information
Analytical publications
- OECD (2007), *Society at a Glance: OECD Social Indicators – 2006 Edition*, OECD, Paris.

Online databases
- *Main Economic Indicators*.
- *OECD Employment Outlook*.

Statistical publications
- *OECD Labour Statistics Database*.
- *OECD Employment Policy*.
- *OECD Employment Data*.
- *OECD Main Economic Indicators*.

Trends in unemployment rates in recent crises
Index base = quarterly unemployment rate at the preceding business cycle peak

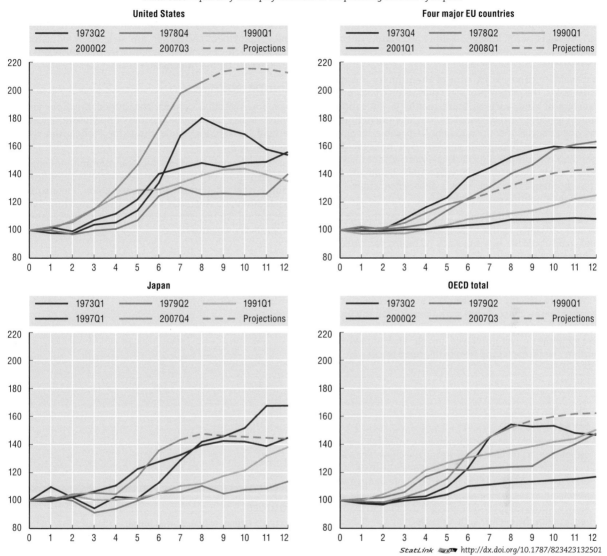

StatLink ⬛ http://dx.doi.org/10.1787/823423132501

Trends in employment and gross domestic product
Cumulated percentage change from 2008Q1 to 2009Q3, seasonally adjusted

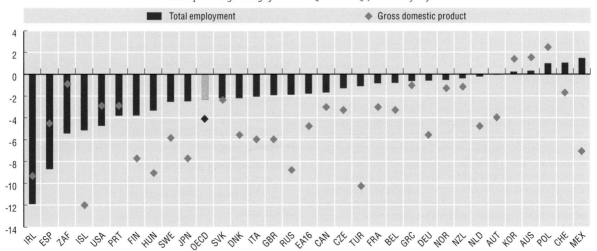

StatLink ⬛ http://dx.doi.org/10.1787/823428802057

HOUSEHOLD INCOME

The impacts of the crisis on household income have been muted so far due to higher net transfers from governments and the lag between lower GDP and lower employment.

Definition

Disposable income is the sum of the primary incomes of households, the current transfers they receive (except social transfers in kind, such as those related to education and health) less the current transfers they pay (including taxes and social security contributions). Disposable income can be seen as the maximum amount that households can spend on consumption goods or services without having to reduce their assets or to increase their liabilities, if one ignores changes in net worth that arise from capital transfers or holding gains.

Compensation of employees, according to the *System of National Accounts*, is the total remuneration, in cash or in kind, paid by firms to employees in return for work done during the accounting period.

Persons in employment are those above a specified age who, in a given period, worked for at least one hour or were temporarily absent from work. They include not only employees (the concept that would best match the national accounting concept of compensation of employees), but also employers, self-employed people and unpaid family workers, while excluding people in armed forces.

The figure displays, for each country, the evolution of real household disposable income, compensation of employees and employment. All series are seasonally adjusted and indexed to the level in the first quarter of 2008 (taken as the peak in GDP before the crisis).

Comparability

Data for Australia, Canada, the United Kingdom and the United States include the income of non-profit institutions serving households, while those for France and Sweden exclude them.

For France and Sweden, data on nominal income and compensation of employees were adjusted for inflation using the deflator for households' consumption expenditure; for Australia, Canada, the United Kingdom and the United States, the deflator for private consumption expenditure was used.

Overview

Real household disposable income continued to rise, although at a subdued pace, during the crisis. The cumulative increase ranged from between 2% in Canada, France and the United States, to 4% or more in Australia, Sweden and the United Kingdom. For all the countries shown, compensation of employees declined in real terms, with the decline sometimes lagging the start of the recession. Only in France did real compensation of employees increase slightly between the first quarter of 2008 and the second quarter of 2009.

Trends in real compensation of employees tracked closely those for employment in the United Sates, while declining at a higher pace in Sweden and the United Kingdom, and at a somewhat lower pace in Canada and France. Beyond the effect of differences in the pace of GDP falls, differences in employment performance during the crisis reflected the implementation of partial unemployment measures and the cushion provided by lower working hours in some countries.

For all the countries shown, real household disposable income increased despite stable or falling compensation of employees. The cumulative difference between trends in household disposable income and in compensation of employees, which exceeded 6 points in all countries except Australia, Canada and France, mainly reflected the impact of higher public transfers to households, and lower tax payments by them. The large and rising share of household income that is independent of employment prevented an even larger decline in GDP.

Sources

- OECD (2009), *National Accounts at a Glance 2009*, OECD, Paris.
- OECD (2009), *Quarterly National Accounts*, OECD, Paris.
- OECD (2010), *Main Economic Indicators*, OECD, Paris.

Further information

Analytical publications

- OECD (2009), *OECD Economic Outlook: June No. 85 – Volume 2009 Issue 1*, OECD, Paris.

Statistical publications

- OECD (2009), *Quarterly National Accounts*, OECD, Paris.
- OECD (2010), *Main Economic Indicators*, OECD, Paris.

Online databases

- *OECD Quarterly National Accounts.*
- *Main Economic Indicators.*

Methodological publications

- OECD (2000), *OECD Glossaries, System of National Accounts, 1993 – Glossary*, OECD, Paris.

Web sites

- OECD National Accounts, *www.oecd.org/std/national-accounts.*
- OECD Main Economic Indicators, *www.oecd.org/std/mei.*

Real gross disposable income, real compensation of employees and employment

2008Q1 = 100, seasonally adjusted

— Real gross disposable income   — Real compensation of employees   — Employment

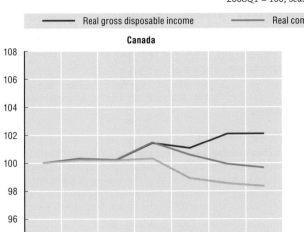

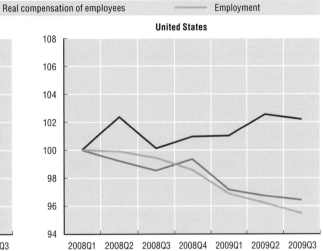

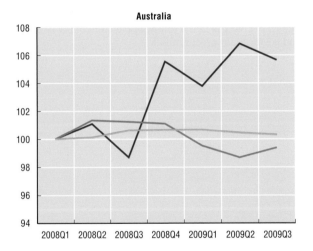

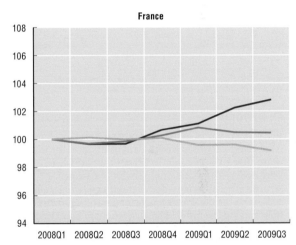

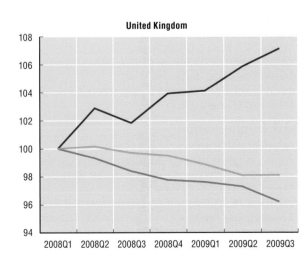

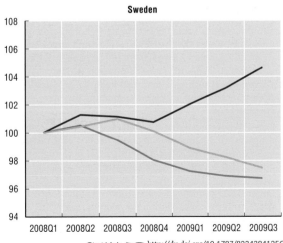

StatLink http://dx.doi.org/10.1787/823438412563

FISCAL POLICY

Fiscal policy can provide a very important cushion for economic activity during a downturn, through the workings of automatic stabilisers and discretionary fiscal easing. The result of the crisis has been a dramatic run-up in government deficits and debt in most OECD countries.

Definition

The negative effect of the crisis on fiscal positions can be analysed by looking at changes in general government balances (*i.e.* changes in the difference between general government receipts and spending). Cumulative changes in government balances over the period 2009-2011 are expressed here relative to the GDP of 2008. The decomposition of the cumulative changes into cyclical effects (*i.e.* the effect of the recession in lowering government tax receipts and in raising government outlays) and structural effects (capturing discretionary fiscal policy measures as well as the disappearance of exceptional revenue buoyancy prior to the crisis) is based on the OECD's assessment of the various factors at work. Data on the composition of initial plans for (discretionary) fiscal packages in response to the crisis are based on information collected by the OECD up to early June 2009.

Changes in general government debt (measured by gross financial liabilities) reflect both annual government deficits and financial operations (*e.g.* rescue packages for financial institutions) that are not recorded as part of government expenditure.

The "general government" sector comprises the central government, local authorities and the social security system).

Comparability

All fiscal measures are recorded on an accrual basis (*i.e.* the basis used for national accounting). This implies that measures based on changing the timing of payments, such as bringing forward government payments or postponing tax receipts, will not affect the data referring to a given year.

In the table, the total columns differ from the sum of components shown as some components either have not been clearly specified or are not classified in this breakdown. The column on net effect includes only discretionary fiscal measures in response to the financial crisis. It excludes the potential impact of recapitalisation, guarantees or other financial operations as well as the impact of changes in the timing of payment of tax liabilities and government procurement.

Overview

All OECD countries except Iceland and Hungary show large deteriorations in government balances in the three years after 2008. Also, all OECD countries are recording large cyclical deteriorations in their fiscal stance. Structural balances have deteriorated significantly since 2008, with the notable exception of Iceland, Hungary, Italy and the Czech Republic. Discretionary fiscal easing is supporting economic activity in almost all countries.

Fiscal packages differ across countries not just in size, but also in their composition. Most countries have adopted broad ranging stimulus programmes, adjusting various taxes and spending programmes simultaneously. Large tax cuts have been implemented in Finland, Korea and the United States, and large boosts in spending (above 2.5% of 2008 GDP) have been planned in Australia, Denmark, Japan, Korea and Turkey. Conversely, Hungary, Iceland and Ireland introduced fiscal consolidation packages, combining tax hikes and spending cuts.

The deterioration in fiscal deficits is expected to lead to a significant deterioration of public debt by 2011 relative to 2008 levels. This reflects the impact of both higher cumulative deficits (in most countries) and, to a lesser extent, other financial operations. Meanwhile most larger OECD countries have announced some form of medium-term consolidation programme, with the Japanese authorities envisaging publication of a medium-term fiscal plan in early 2010. However, the programmes of the major seven countries provide little information yet on the timing and the instruments of future fiscal consolidation.

Sources

- OECD (2009), *OECD Economic Outlook: June No. 85 – Volume 2009 Issue 1*, OECD, Paris.
- OECD (2009), *OECD Economic Outlook, Interim Report March 2009*, OECD, Paris.
- OECD (2009), *OECD Economic Outlook: November No. 86 – Volume 2009 Issue 2*, OECD, Paris.

Further information

Analytical publications

- Furceri, D. (2009), *Fiscal Convergence, Business Cycle Volatility and Growth*, OECD Economics Department Working Papers, No. 674, OECD, Paris.
- Afonso, A., L. Agnello and D. Furceri (2008), *Fiscal Policy Responsiveness, Persistence, and Discretion*, OECD Economics Department Working Papers, No. 659, OECD, Paris.

Web sites

- OECD Economic Outlook Statistics, *www.sourceOECD.org/database/oecdeconomicoutlook*.
- OECD Economic Outlook, *www.oecd.org/OECDEconomicOutlook*.

Cumulative changes in government balance 2009-11
As a percentage of 2008 GDP

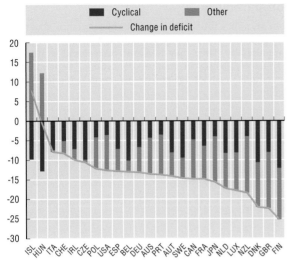

StatLink ⇢ http://dx.doi.org/10.1787/823445563033

Gross government debt
As a percentage of 2008 GDP, 2011 forecasts

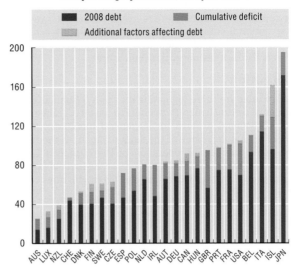

StatLink ⇢ http://dx.doi.org/10.1787/823474056333

Composition of fiscal packages
Total over 2008-2010 period, as a percentage of GDP in 2008

	Net effect	Tax measures					Spending measures					
		Total	Households	Businesses	Consumption	Social contributions	Total	Final consumption	Investment	Transfers to households	Transfers to businesses	Transfers to sub-national government
Australia	−5.4	−1.3	−1.1	−0.2	0.0	0.0	4.1	0.0	3.0	1.1	0.0	0.0
Austria	−1.2	−0.8	−0.8	−0.1	0.0	0.0	0.4	0.0	0.1	0.2	0.0	0.1
Belgium	−1.4	−0.3	0.0	−0.1	−0.1	0.0	1.1	0.0	0.1	0.5	0.5	0.0
Canada	−4.1	−2.4	−0.8	−0.3	−1.1	−0.1	1.7	0.1	1.3	0.3	0.1	..
Czech Republic	−2.8	−2.5	0.0	−0.7	−0.4	−1.4	0.3	−0.1	0.2	0.0	0.2	0.0
Denmark	−3.3	−0.7	0.0	0.0	0.0	0.0	2.6	0.9	0.8	0.1	0.0	0.0
Finland	−3.2	−2.7	−1.9	0.0	−0.3	−0.4	0.5	0.0	0.3	0.1	0.0	0.0
France	−0.7	−0.2	−0.1	−0.1	0.0	0.0	0.6	0.0	0.2	0.3	0.0	0.0
Germany	−3.2	−1.6	−0.6	−0.3	0.0	−0.7	1.6	0.0	0.8	0.3	0.3	0.0
Greece	0.8	0.8	0.8	0.0	0.0	0.0	0.0	−0.4	0.1	0.4	0.1	0.0
Hungary	7.7	0.2	−0.6	−0.1	2.3	−1.5	−7.5	−3.2	0.0	−3.4	−0.4	−0.5
Iceland	7.3	5.7	1.0	..	..	..	−1.6	..	..	..	..	..
Ireland	8.3	6.0	4.5	−0.2	0.5	1.2	−2.2	−1.8	−0.2	−0.1	0.0	0.0
Italy	0.0	0.3	0.0	0.0	0.1	0.0	0.3	0.3	0.0	0.2	0.1	0.0
Japan	−4.7	−0.5	−0.1	−0.1	−0.1	−0.2	4.2	0.2	1.2	0.6	1.5	0.6
Korea	−6.1	−2.8	−1.4	−1.1	−0.2	0.0	3.2	0.0	1.2	0.7	1.0	0.3
Luxembourg	−3.9	−2.3	−1.5	−0.8	0.0	0.0	1.6	0.0	0.4	1.0	0.2	0.0
Mexico	−1.7	−0.4	0.0	0.0	−0.4	0.0	1.2	0.1	0.7	0.1	0.0	0.0
Netherlands	−2.5	−1.6	−0.2	−0.5	−0.1	−0.8	0.9	0.0	0.5	0.1	0.0	0.0
New Zealand	−3.7	−4.1	−4.0	0.0	0.0	0.0	−0.3	0.1	0.6	−0.6	0.0	0.0
Norway·	−1.2	−0.3	0.0	−0.3	0.0	0.0	0.9	0.0	0.4	0.0	0.0	0.3
Poland	−1.2	−0.4	0.0	−0.1	−0.2	0.0	0.8	0.0	1.3	0.2	0.1	0.0
Portugal	−0.8	..	..	..	..	..	..	0.0	0.4	0.0	0.4	0.0
Slovak Republic	−1.3	−0.7	−0.5	−0.1	0.0	−0.1	0.7	0.0	0.0	0.1	0.6	0.0
Spain	−3.9	−1.7	−1.6	0.0	0.0	0.0	2.2	0.3	0.7	0.5	0.7	0.0
Sweden	−3.3	−1.7	−1.3	−0.2	0.0	−0.2	1.7	1.1	0.3	0.1	0.0	0.2
Switzerland	−0.5	−0.2	−0.2	0.0	0.0	0.0	0.3	0.3	0.0	0.0	0.0	0.0
Turkey	−4.4	−1.5	−0.2	−1.1	−0.2	0.0	2.9	0.6	1.2	0.0	0.3	0.6
United Kingdom	−1.9	−1.5	−0.5	−0.2	−0.6	0.0	0.4	0.0	0.4	0.2	0.0	0.0
United States	−5.6	−3.2	−2.4	−0.8	0.0	0.0	2.4	0.7	0.3	0.5	0.0	0.9

StatLink ⇢ http://dx.doi.org/10.1787/827168846578

MONETARY POLICY

Central banks across the OECD area have responded to the crisis in an unprecedented way, both by ways of conventional cuts in the policy rates regulating access to central banks' credit, and by expanding their balances sheets through unconventional measures.

Definition

Policy rates are those regulating the main refinancing operations of central banks. Data refers to the target range set by the US Federal Reserve for its federal fund rates; to the short-term policy rates of the Bank of Japan; to the rate on the main refinancing operation of the European Central Bank; and to the official interest rate of the Bank of England. Also shown in the figures are the overnight rates on the money market.

Overview

Most countries have used monetary policy in the aftermath of the crisis to stimulate aggregate demand. The stimulus from monetary policy has taken two main forms.

First, central banks have reduced rapidly their policy rates since the onset of the recession. The US Federal Reserve has established a target range for its Federal Reserve rate of 0% to 0.25% since December 2008, communicating its intention to keep rates exceptionally low for an extended period. The Bank of Japan used its (already limited) room for manoeuvre to cut policy rates to 0.1%, while the Bank of England lowered its policy rates to 0.5%. The European Central bank cut its main policy rate less aggressively, lowering its rate on the main refinancing operation to 1%. Other OECD and non-OECD countries have also substantially eased their policy rates. These reductions in policy rates have translated in similar reductions in governing rates on money markets, which reached negative levels in real terms.

Second, as most major central banks exhausted the room for further reduction in policy rates, the focus of monetary policy has shifted to more unconventional measures to support the functioning of financial markets. These unconventional measures to expand the supply of credit have generally taken the form of provision to banks of greater access to liquidity than would normally be required to keep market short-term rates in line with policy targets; of expanding money supply through quantitative easing and the creation of excess reserves; and of direct interventions in broader segments of credit markets (beyond the traditional counterparty of banks) aimed at easing overall credit conditions in the economy.

All these unconventional measures resulted in a significant expansion of central banks' balance sheets, particularly in the United States and the United Kingdom.

Monetary conditions are expected to remain loose until firm evidence of a recovery in economic activity takes hold. A few countries, such as Australia, Norway and Israel took steps to raise their policy rates in the second half of 2009.

Data on central banks' balance sheets are expressed in national currency and are drawn from Datastream, as available on 11, June 2009.

Comparability

Data on policy rates and central banks' balance sheets are drawn from official sources and have a high degree of comparability. They may however correspond to different degrees of easing in market conditions, depending on regulations restricting access to central banks' credit facilities.

.

Sources

- OECD (2009), *OECD Economic Outlook: June No. 85 – Volume 2009 Issue 1*, OECD, Paris.
- *Thomson Reuters Datastream*.

Further information

Analytical publications

- Minegishi, M., B. Cournède (2009), *The role of transparency in the conduct of monetary policy*, OECD Economics Department Working Papers, No. 724, OECD, Paris.

Statistical publications

- OECD (2010), *Main Economic Indicators*, OECD, Paris.

Online databases

- *Main Economic Indicators*.

Web sites

- OECD Economic Outlook, *www.oecd.org/OECDEconomicOutlook*.
- OECD Main Economic Indicators, *www.oecd.org/std/mei*.

Policy interest rates in major OECD economies
Percentage

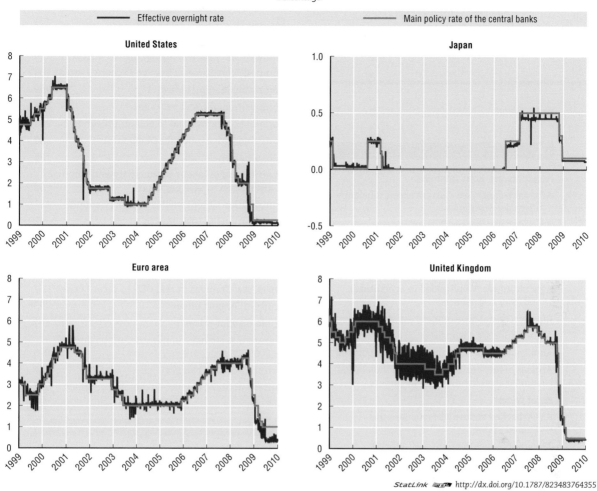

StatLink ᵐˢᵖ http://dx.doi.org/10.1787/823483764355

Expansion of central banks' balance sheets
National currencies

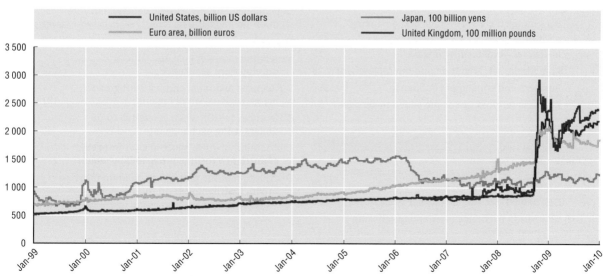

StatLink ᵐˢᵖ http://dx.doi.org/10.1787/823485026712

Analytical index

T

U

OECD PUBLICATIONS, 2, rue André-Pascal, 75775 PARIS CEDEX 16
PRINTED IN FRANCE
(30 2010 06 1 P) ISBN 978-92-64-08356-1 – No. 57293 2010